The Law of Sex Discrimination

SECOND EDITION

The Law of Sex Discrimination

SECOND EDITION

J. RALPH LINDGREN
Professor of Philosophy
Lehigh University
Bethlehem, Pennsylvania

NADINE TAUB
Professor of Law
Rutgers University School of Law
Newark, New Jersey

WEST PUBLISHING COMPANY

Minneapolis/St. Paul ■ New York ■ Los Angeles ■ San Francisco

WEST'S COMMITMENT TO THE ENVIRONMENT

In 1906, West Publishing Company began recycling materials left over from the production of books. This began a tradition of efficient and responsible use of resources. Today, up to 95 percent of our legal books and 70 percent of our college and school texts are printed on recycled, acid-free stock. West also recycles nearly 22 million pounds of scrap paper annually — the equivalent of 181,717 trees. Since the 1960s, West has devised ways to capture and recycle waste inks, solvents, oils, and vapors created in the printing process. We also recycle plastics of all kinds, wood, glass, corrugated cardboard, and batteries, and have eliminated the use of styrofoam book packaging. We at West are proud of the longevity and the scope of our commitment to the environment.

Production, Prepress, Printing and Binding by West Publishing Company.

 PRINTED ON 10% POST CONSUMER RECYCLED PAPER

Composition: Carlisle Communications
Copyeditor: Marilynn Taylor
Cover and Text Design: Lois Stanfield, LightSource Images
Cover Design: K. M. Weber

Lindgren, J. Ralph
    The law of sex discrimination / J. Ralph Lindgren, Nadine Taub. —
2nd ed.
        p.   cm.
    Includes index.
    ISBN 0-314-02708-4 (soft)
    1. Sex discrimination against women—Law and legislation—United
States—Cases.   2. Sex discrimination in employment—Law and
legislation—United States—Cases.   3. Women—Legal status, laws,
etc.—United States—Cases.   I. Taub, Nadine.   II. Title.
KF4758.A7L56   1994
342.73'0878—dc20
[347.302878]   93-25946
                                                        CIP

Contents

Table of Cases

Principal cases are in italic type. Cases cited or discussed are in roman type. References are to pages.

Preface

This book is designed to serve as a text for undergraduate courses concerned with sex discrimination law in the United States. Sex discrimination is neither a new nor an especially Western phenomenon. People have treated one another differently because of their sex throughout history. Legal codes as old as the Code of Hammurabi and the Mosaic Law have assigned different burdens and opportunities to people on the basis of their sex. From ancient times, law has reflected and reinforced the myriad social and institutional arrangements that have channeled women and men into different roles and allocated power between them.

The use of law to combat and dismantle pervasive sex discrimination is a relatively recent phenomenon in Western societies. This development in the law is fascinating in its own right and as an event within various larger settings. It may be studied, for example, as an occasion for ideological disputes; as a reflection of contemporary policy debates over future directions of society; as a part of the historical development of the feminist movement or as a response to that movement; or as a means for raising feminist consciousness.

In this volume, we attempt to present legal materials in a form that affords flexibility of approach. We seek to anticipate the needs of those who have had no formal legal training and who have little experience in working with court opinions. Legal technicalities are avoided wherever possible, and cases are abridged to retain the human drama, focus attention on key rulings, and emphasize crucial factors motivating the decisions. The book contains a variety of pedagogical elements. These features provide necessary background information as well as insight into the larger significance of legal events: a connecting narrative highlights the relationships between cases and identifies central themes, while study questions accompany both cases and readings. Other study aids are collected together at the end of the book. These include a list of suggested further readings, appendixes dealing with the court system, selected amendments to the U.S. Constitution, and a brief discussion on how to outline cases, as well as a glossary of legal and technical terms, a table of abbreviations, and an index.

Changes to the Second Edition

This edition encompasses revisions based on comments from instructors and students and developments in the field. Principal changes include the following:
- ☐ The second edition is accompanied by an Instructor's Manual, which contains teaching suggestions and a test bank.

☐ The connecting narrative is expanded in each chapter to help students to better grasp the issues developed in accompanying cases and materials as well as appreciate their place in the pattern of developments under discussion.

☐ Cases and materials are updated to reflect the current state of the law and of legal issues.

☐ In Chapter 1, selections from historical documents as well as materials relating to the first wave of feminism are expanded. The treatment of constitutional developments in the early twentieth century is more tightly focused.

☐ Chapter 2 sharpens the discussion of equal protection analysis. Constitutional cases are chosen more selectively, and ERA materials are integrated into the chapter.

☐ Chapter 3 is an entirely new chapter that identifies a core controversy in feminist legal thought—the meaning of equality—and the debates it has generated. Drawing particularly on the example of pregnancy in the workplace, the chapter explores the consequences of these ongoing debates and foreshadows their applications throughout the remainder of the book.

☐ Chapter 4 is redesigned as a self-contained introduction to Title VII. The sections are reordered to introduce the two concepts of discrimination before turning to the BFOQ exception, and BFOQ issues are focused more sharply. Finally, a shortened treatment of Title VII remedies is integrated into the chapter.

☐ In Chapter 5, the section on sexual harassment is thoroughly revised. In addition, the materials on the wage gap and workforce segregation are updated and graphically presented. Finally, a thoroughly reworked set of cases and materials on affirmative action is integrated into the chapter.

☐ Chapter 6 revises the order of the discussion to focus more clearly on Title IX. New materials are introduced to draw attention to issues and changes in women's athletics.

☐ Chapter 7 expands the coverage of divorce and custody matters and supplements it with new materials. Data on the status of women, recent tax and other legal developments, and decisions concerning sex relationships bring the chapter up to date.

☐ Chapter 8 is revised considerably in the light of recent developments. It reviews the nature of the reproductive rights as established historically and acknowledged today. New materials permit analysis of the right's application to contemporary problems ranging from the use of new reproductive technologies to the distribution of contraceptives.

☐ In Chapter 9, the discussion of rape is expanded considerably to include cases and materials on legal standards and date rape. Likewise, the latest materials are added to the discussion of pornography.

Acknowledgments

This book is the combined effort of the authors. They are jointly responsible for Chapters 1 through 3. Ralph Lindgren is primarily responsible for Chapters 4, 5, and 6; Nadine Taub for Chapters 7, 8, and 9. Both deeply appreciate the helpful comments and useful suggestions received from thoughtful colleagues, students, and the following reviewers:

Agnes Baro
Grand Valley State University

Carol Bohmer
Cornell University

Dianne L. Brooks
University of Massachusettes at Amherst

Doris-Jean Burton
Indiana University

Leigh Anne Chavez
University of New Mexico

Dayna F. Deck
Washington University

James C. Foster
Oregon State University

Pearl Jacobs
Sacred Heart University

Helen Jones
University of Nevada, Reno

Elizabeth Purdy
University of South Carolina at Aiken

David Schultz
Trinity University

Deborah Stone
Brandeis University

Susan Vance
St. Mary's College

Kathryn A. Winz
University of Wisconsin–Platteville

The Law of
Sex Discrimination

SECOND EDITION

1 The Historical Context

The ways that people are treated by the law have often been determined by certain immutable characteristics, such as race, place of birth, age, and sex. In choosing to give significance to these characteristics, and not to others, such as eye color or foot size, the law reflects, protects, and gives legitimacy to selected social customs and justifies those choices by doctrines, ideologies, or patterns of thinking about the world that represent those customs as right, correct, and/or beneficial. A person's sex has long been an important factor in determining legal rights, duties, powers, privileges, and immunities. Important changes made in recent years have altered the legal significance of one's sex. These developments are the subject of this volume.

The aim of this book is to help the student understand and evaluate the changing patterns of sex-based laws in the United States in terms of the preferences they reflect and the rationales used to justify them. A related objective is to provide the reader with a basis for evaluating future changes: Is society best served by a legal system that attempts to treat women and men as individuals or by a legal system that acknowledges differences, while seeking to eliminate hierarchical distinctions based upon them? Is it even possible to construct a legal system that meets the needs of both sexes in equal measure?

This chapter provides a background for appreciating the changes that have taken place in the legal significance assigned to sex in recent years. The court decisions and other materials in this chapter mark relevant moments in our cultural and legal heritage and provide the immediate historical context for recent legal developments. The decisions reached by the Supreme Court and other federal courts in constitutional cases are important for their concrete outcomes and their expression of contemporary norms governing gender and sex roles. However, these decisions must be placed in a historical context. Prior to the ratification of the Fourteenth Amendment in 1868, the United States Constitution offered little basis for challenging laws assigning rights, duties, and privileges on the basis of sex. To set the stage for the initial constitutional challenges to sex-based laws, we begin with historical readings that briefly sketch the nature of gender constraints in the early years of the country.

I. THE PATRIARCHAL TRADITION

Social systems that treat people differently because of their sex are of ancient origin. Although evidence exists of even earlier matriarchal practices, patriarchal patterns have dominated Western cultures for several millennia. Historian Gerda Lerner dates the rise of patriarchy as the period between 3100 to 600 B.C.E. She identifies the central features of this tradition as follows:

> Patriarchy . . . means the manifestation and institutionalization of male dominance over women and children in the family and the extension of male dominance over women in society in general. It implies that men hold power in all the important institutions of society and that women are deprived of access to such power. It does *not* imply that women are either totally powerless or totally deprived of rights, influence, and resources. *Gerda Lerner,* The Creation of Patriarchy. *New York: Oxford University Press, 1986. P. 239.*

Patriarchal patterns have been expressed, enforced, legitimated, and perpetuated in a variety of ways over the ages. One vehicle for instilling and preserving these practices and traditions is religion. Consider the relationships between males and females that are expressed and legitimated in the following legend.

The Eden Story

Genesis 2:5 - 3:24.
New Revised Standard Version.

In the day that the LORD God made the earth and the heavens, when no plant of the field was yet in the earth and no herb of the field had yet sprung up—for the LORD God had not caused it to rain upon the earth, and there was no one to till the ground; but a stream would rise from the earth, and water the whole face of the ground— then the LORD God formed man from the dust of the ground, and breathed into his nostrils the breath of life; and the man became a living be- ing. And the LORD God planted a garden in Eden, in the east; and there he put the man whom he had formed. Out of the ground the LORD God made to grow every tree that is pleasant to the sight and good for food, the tree of life also in the midst of the garden, and the tree of the knowledge of good and evil. . . .

The LORD God took the man and put him in the garden of Eden to till it and keep it. And the LORD God commanded the man, "You may freely eat of every tree of the garden; but of the tree of the knowledge of good and evil you shall not eat, for in the day that you eat of it you shall die."

Then the LORD God said, "It is not good that the man should be alone; I will make him a helper as his partner." So out of the ground the LORD God formed every animal of the field and every bird of the air, and brought them to the man to see what he would call them; and whatever the man called every living creature, that was its name. The man gave names to all cattle, and to the birds of the air, and to every animal of the field; but for the man there was not found a helper as his partner. So the LORD God caused a deep sleep to fall upon the man, and he slept; then he took one of his ribs and closed up its place with flesh. And the rib that the LORD God had taken from the man he made into a woman and brought her to the man. Then the man said,

> "This at last is bone of my bones,
> and flesh of my flesh;
> this one shall be called Woman,
> for out of Man this one was
> taken."

Therefore a man leaves his father and his mother and clings to his wife, and they become one flesh. And the man and his wife were both naked, and were not ashamed.

Now the serpent was more crafty than any other wild animal that the LORD God had made. He said to the woman, "Did God say, 'You shall not eat from any tree in the garden'?" The woman said to the serpent, "We may eat of the fruit of the trees in the garden; but God said, 'You shall not eat of the fruit of the tree that is in the middle of the garden, nor shall you touch it, or you shall die.'" But the serpent said to the woman, "You will not die; for God knows that when you eat of it your eyes will be opened, and you will be like God, knowing good and evil." So when the woman saw that the tree was good for food, and that it was a delight to the eyes, and that the tree was to be desired to make one wise, she took of its fruit and ate; and she also gave some to her husband, who was with her, and he ate. Then the eyes of both were opened, and they knew that they were naked; and they sewed fig leaves together and made loincloths for themselves.

They heard the sound of the LORD God walking in the garden at the time of the evening breeze, and the man and his wife hid themselves from the presence of the LORD God among the trees of the garden. But the LORD God called to the man, and said to him, "Where are you?" He said, "I heard the sound of you in the garden, and I was afraid, because I was naked; and I hid myself." He said, "Who told you that you were naked? Have you eaten from the tree of which I commanded you not to eat?" The man said, "The woman whom you gave to be with me, she gave me fruit from the tree, and I ate." Then the LORD God said to the woman, "What is this that you have done?" The woman said, "The serpent tricked me, and I ate." The LORD God said to the serpent,

"Because you have done this,
cursed are you among all animals
and among all wild creatures;
upon your belly you shall go,
and dust you shall eat
all the days of your life.
I will put enmity between you and
the woman,
and between your offspring and
hers;
he will strike your head,
and you will strike his heel."
To the woman he said,
"I will greatly increase your pangs in
childbearing;
in pain you shall bring forth
children,
yet your desire shall be for your
husband,
and he shall rule over you."
And to the man he said,
"Because you have listened to the
voice of your wife,
and have eaten of the tree
about which I commanded you,
'You shall not eat of it,'
cursed is the ground because of you;
in toil you shall eat of it all the
days of your life;
thorns and thistles it shall bring forth
for you;
and you shall eat the plants of the
field.
By the sweat of your face
you shall eat bread
until you return to the ground,
for out of it you were taken;
you are dust,
and to dust you shall return."

The man named his wife Eve, because she was the mother of all living. And the LORD God made garments of skins for the man and for his wife, and clothed them.

Then the LORD God said, "See, the man has become like one of us, knowing good and evil; and now, he might reach out his hand and take also from the tree of life, and eat, and live forever"—therefore the LORD God sent him forth from the garden of Eden, to till the ground from which he was taken. He drove out the man; and at the east of the garden of Eden he placed the cherubim, and a sword flaming and turning to guard the way to the tree of life.

STUDY QUESTIONS

1. According to Genesis, what role was the man assigned? What role was the woman assigned?
2. What significance is there in the point that the woman was derived from the man? That the man named her?
3. Why was the serpent able to persuade the woman, but presumably not the man, to taste the forbidden fruit? Why was the woman, but presumably not the serpent, able to persuade the man to eat the fruit?
4. What burdens placed on the woman are considered penalties for the transgression? Which burdens are placed on the man?

The Navajo Creation Story, as it survives in the oral tradition of our own day, provides an interesting contrast to the Eden Story. While both stories recognize differences in the roles of men and women, they portray the male-female relationship quite differently: One imposes a superior-subordinate relationship as a punishment for disloyalty; the other creates a partnership originating from a fair agreement.

A Harmonizing of Interests

Paul G. Zolbrod.
Dine Bahane: The Navajo Creation Story
Albuquerque: University of New Mexico Press, 1984. Pp. 272–75.

It is also said that four more days passed, and that four more nights went by. Four times the sun rose and set, and four times the moon passed overhead.

And on the morning of the fifth day *Asdzą́ą́ nádleehé* the Changing Woman made her way to the summit of *Ch'óol'į́į́* the Giant Spruce Mountain and sat down on a rock.

She recognized that spot well. It was where she had lain when she was all alone and wished for a consort. It was where she had first felt the warmth of the sun deep within her body.

And as she sat there recollecting, *Jóhonaa'éí* the Sun arrived and placed himself beside her.

He sought to embrace her.

But she struggled to free herself.

As she did so she said these words to him:

"What do you mean by molesting me so?" she said to him.

"I want no part of you!"

To which he gave her this reply:

"I mean simply that I want you for my own," he replied.

"I mean that I want you to come to the west and make a home for me there."

"But I wish to do no such thing," replied she.

"By what right do you make such a request of me?"

Said he then:

"Did I not give your sons the weapons they needed to slay Naayéé' the Alien Monsters? Have I not done a great deal for you and your people, in truth? In truth, shouldn't you reward me for what I have done?

Answered she then:

"But I was not the one who asked for those weapons. It was not I who asked for your help. What you gave you gave of your own free will. I owe you no reward."

Following her words there was a distance of silence.

Then he tried to embrace her again, offering yet another reason for allowing himself to do so:

"When our son *Naayéé' neizghání* the Monster Slayer last visited me, he promised you to me."

And again she struggled to free herself, offering yet another objection:

"What do I care for promises made by someone else in my behalf? I make my own promises or else there are no promises to be made. I speak for myself or else I am not spoken for. I alone decide what I shall do or else I do nothing."

Hearing which words he sighed, stood up, took four paces apart from her, and then turned suddenly to face her.

And this is what he said to her:

"Please!" he said to her.

"Come with me to the west and make a home for me.

"I am lonely.

"Each day I labor long and hard alone in the sky. I have no one to talk with. I have no companion for my nights.

"What good is all that I do if I must endure my days and nights all alone? What use is male without female? What use is female without male? What use are we two without one another?"

That is what *Jóhonaa'éí* the Sun said to *Asdzą́ą́ nádleehé* the Changing Woman.

She did not answer him at once, leaving another space of silence between his words and her reply.

Then at last she spoke. And this is what she said to him at last:

"You have a beautiful house in the east I am told," she said to him.

"I want just such a house in the west.

"I want it built floating on the shimmering water, away from the shore, so that when the Earth-Surface people multiply they will not bother me with their quarrels.

"And I want all sorts of gems.

"I want white shell. I want blue shell. I want turquoise. I want haliotis. I want soapstone, agate, redstone, jet.

"Such things I want planted around my house so that I may enjoy their beauty.

"Since I wish to live there without my sister and without our sons, I will be lonely while you are gone each day. So I will want animals to keep me company.

Give me elk. Give me buffalo. Give me deer. Give me long-tails. Give me mountain sheep, jackrabbits, prairie dogs, muskrats

"Provide me with those things and I shall go with you to the west."

That is what *Asdzáá nádleehé* the Changing Woman said to *Jóhonaa'éí* the Sun. And this is how he replied:

"What do you mean by making such demands of me?" he replied.

"Why should I provide you with all of those things?"

This time she answered him quickly. And this is what she said to him:

"I will tell you why," she said to him.

"You are male and I am female.

"You are of the sky and I am of the earth.

"You are constant in your brightness, but I must change with the seasons.

"You move constantly at the very edge of heaven, while I must remain fixed in one place.

"Remember that I willingly let you send your rays into my body. Remember that I gave birth to your son, enduring pain to bring him into the world. Remember that I gave that child growth and protected him from harm. Remember that I taught him to serve his people

unselfishly so that he would willingly fight the Alien Monsters.

"Remember, as different as we are, you and I, we are of one spirit. As dissimilar as we are, you and I, we are of equal worth. As unlike as you and I are, there must always be solidarity between the two of us. Unlike each other as you and I are, there can be no harmony in the universe as long as there is no harmony between us.

"If there is to be such harmony, my requests must matter to you. My needs are as important to me as yours are to you. My whims count as much as yours do. My fidelity to you is measured by your loyalty to me. My response to your needs is to reflect the way you respond to mine. There is to be nothing more coming from me to you than there is from you to me. There is to be nothing less."

That is what *Asdzáá nádleehé* the Changing Woman said to *Jóhonnaa'éí* the Sun there on the summit of *Ch'óol'íí* the Giant Spruce Mountain.

At first he gave no reply. He took time to weigh carefully all things that she had said.

Then, slowly, though[t]fully, he drew close to her.

Slowly and thoughtfully he placed his arm around her.

And this time she allowed him to do so.

Whereupon he promised her that all the things she wished for she would have. She would have a house in the west on the shimmering water. She would have gems whose beauty she could enjoy. She would have animals to keep her company. All that she wanted she would have.

So it is that she agreed; they would go to a place in the west where they would dwell together in the solid harmony of kinship.

STUDY QUESTIONS

1. In what ways are the man and the woman dissimilar? In what ways are they similar? Why did the woman require that she be recognized as being of equal value?
2. Why did the man accept those terms? Why did the woman?
3. Are the terms of the relationship that was agreed to really equal in your view?

The relationship between women and men expressed in the Eden Story has been reiterated down the centuries in a variety of ways. Paul described the ideal relationship of spouses in the Christian culture in his letter to the Ephesians: "Wives be subject to your husbands as you are to the Lord." *Ephesians,* 5:22-24. (New Revised Standard Version.)

Like religion, the law is an important cultural vehicle for sex-based customs. Just before the American Revolution, William Blackstone produced a recapitulation of the common law of England. This proved to be an especially influential treatise among American jurists of the day because of its portability. As it could be transported easily, Blackstone's *Commentaries* was relied upon even longer in America than in Blackstone's native England.

The legal arrangements that the colonists brought to the New World both reflected and reinforced the division of labor in society along gender lines and the subordination of women found in Europe. Life in colonial America was organized around a preindustrial, agricultural, family-based economy. Women made crucial economic contributions usually through the household production necessary to meet their family needs. Yet these contributions rarely allowed women to participate significantly in economic decision making, religious matters, or community affairs.

Although legal practices varied somewhat from colony to colony and were probably less rigid than their British counterparts, the principles and doctrines followed by the English courts of the day constituted the common point of departure. To the extent that the colonists followed the English law, they greatly restricted opportunities open to married women. Under the doctrine of coverture, developed in the English common law during the late Middle Ages, the husband was considered the lord of the manor. The husband and the wife were viewed legally as one person, and that "one person," as Justice Black pointed out in the 1960s, was the husband. William Blackstone summarized the principal features of the doctrine of coverture as it survived into the mid-eighteenth century.

Blackstone on Coverture

William Blackstone.
1765-69. *Commentaries on the Laws of England*. 4 vols. Book I, Chapter 15.

By marriage, the husband and wife are one person in law: that is, the very being or legal existence of the woman is suspended during the marriage, or at least is incorporated and consolidated into that of the husband: under whose wing, protection, and *cover,* she performs every thing; and is therefore called in our law-french a *feme-covert*; is said to be *covert-baron,* or under the protection and influence of her husband, her *baron,* or lord; and her condition during her marriage is called her *coverture*. Upon this principle, of an union of person in husband and wife, depend almost all the legal rights, duties, and disabilities, that either of them acquire by the marriage. I speak not at present of the rights of property, but of such as are merely *personal*. For this reason, a man cannot grant any thing to his wife, or enter into covenant with her: for the grant would be to suppose her separate existence; and to covenant with her, would be only to covenant with himself: and therefore it is also generally true, that all compacts made between husband and wife, when single, are voided by the intermarriage. A woman indeed may be attorney for her husband; for that implies no separation from, but is rather a representation of, her lord. And a husband may also bequeath any thing to his wife by will; for that cannot take effect till the coverture is determined by his death. The husband is bound to provide his wife with necessaries by law, as much as himself; and if she contracts debts for them, he is obliged to pay them: but for any thing besides necessaries, he is not chargeable. Also if a wife elopes, and lives with another man, the husband is not chargeable even for necessaries; at least if the person, who furnishes them, is sufficiently apprized of her elopement. If the wife be indebted before marriage, the husband is bound afterwards to pay the debt; for he has adopted her and her circumstances together. If the wife be injured in her person or her property, she can bring no action for redress without her husband's concurrence, and in his name, as well as her own: neither can she be sued, without making the husband a defendant. There is indeed one case where the wife shall sue and be sued as a feme sole, viz. where the husband has abjured the realm, or is banished: for then he is dead in law; and, the husband being thus disabled to sue for or defend the wife, it would be most unreasonable if she had no remedy, or could make no defence at all. In criminal prosecutions, it is true, the wife may be indicted and punished separately; for the union is only a civil union. But, in trials of any sort, they are not allowed to be evidence for, or against, each other: partly because it is impossible their testimony should be indifferent; but principally because of the union of person: and therefore, if they were admitted to be witnesses *for* each other, they would contradict one maxim of law, *"nemo in propria causa testis esse debet"* [one ought not be a witness in his own cause]; and if *against* each other, they would contradict another maxim, *"nemo tenetur seipsum accusare."* [no one is bound to accuse himself] But where the offence is directly against the person of the wife, this rule has been usually dispensed with: and therefore, by statute 3 Hen.VII. c. 2. in case a woman be forcibly taken away, and married, she may be a witness against such her husband, in order to convict him of felony. For in this case she can with no propriety be reckoned his wife; because a main ingredient, her consent, was wanting to the contract: and also there is another maxim of law, that no man shall take advantage of his own wrong; which the ravisher here would do, if by forcibly marrying a woman, he

could prevent her from being a witness, who is perhaps the only witness, to that very fact. . . .

But, though our law in general considers man and wife as one person, yet there are some instances in which she is separately considered; as inferior to him, and acting by his compulsion. And therefore all deeds executed, and acts done, by her, during her coverture, are void, or at least voidable; except it be a fine, or the like matter of record, in which case she must be solely and secretly examined, to learn if her act be voluntary. She cannot by will devise lands to her husband, unless under special circumstances; for at the time of making it she is supposed to be under his coercion. And in some felonies, and other inferior crimes, committed by her, through constraint of her husband, the law excuses her: but this extends not to treason or murder.

The husband also (by the old law) might give his wife moderate correction. For, as he is to answer for her misbehaviour, the law thought it reasonable to intrust him with this power of restraining her, by domestic chastisement, in the same moderation that a man is allowed to correct his servants or children; for whom the master or parent is also liable in some cases to answer. But this power of correction was confined within reasonable bounds; and the husband was prohibited to use any violence to his wife, *aliter quam ad virum, ex causa regiminis et castigationis uxoris suae, licite et rationabiliter pertinet* [other than what is reasonably necessary to the discipline and correction of the wife]. The civil law gave the husband the same, or a larger, authority over his wife; allowing him, for some misdemesnors, *flagellis et fustibus acriter verberare uxorem* [to wound his wife severely with whips and fists]; for others, only *modicam castigationem adhibere* [to apply modest corrective punishment]. But, with us, in the politer reign of Charles the second, this power of correction began to be doubted: and a wife may now have security of the peace against her husband; or, in return, a husband against his wife. Yet the lower rank of people, who were always fond of the old common law, still claim and exert their antient privilege: and the courts of law will still permit a husband to restrain a wife of her liberty, in case of any gross misbehaviour.

These are the chief legal effects of marriage during the coverture; upon which we may observe, that even the disabilities, which the wife lies under, are for the most part intended for her protection and benefit. So great a favourite is the female sex of the laws of England.

STUDY QUESTIONS

1. What were the legal consequences of marriage for the woman? For the man? Does that arrangement seem fair to the woman? To the man?

2. What are your reactions to Blackstone's discussion of "domestic chastisement"?

3. Were women legally better off if they did not marry? Why do you suppose they continued to marry?

The legal and cultural norms brought by the settlers, including the gender-based division of labor and the subordinate position of women, formed the dominant tradition shaping this country's legal, political, economic, and social institutions. This tradition reflects only part of this country's cultural heritage. Its nature may be better understood by contrasting it with other aspects of our heritage. Mary Ryan, an American historian, has pointed out, for example, that in encountering the Iroquois people, colonists discovered a culture that afforded women much more influence in the affairs of their communities.

> . . . [T]he gender system of the Iroquois, as described by French missionaries in the eighteenth century, seemed to have been remarkably generous to women. Although by no means a matriarchy, the Iroquois social system came perhaps as close as any known civilization to the standard of sexual equality. Iroquois matrons chose the chieftains and delegates to tribal councils, where they also had a vote on issues of war and peace. Women were even more influential in the everyday activities of their villages. They were responsible for distributing surplus produce and supervised the selection of marriage partners for their children. Half the positions of religious authority were also held by women who participated in organizing the major festivals and rituals of the tribe. Consequently, Iroquois culture treated women with relative dignity and respect. This was not a case of female domination; males alone, for example, were invested with the direct political authority of chiefs. Yet this native American tribe granted women a degree of political, economic, and cultural power that impresses anthropologists and historians alike.
> *Mary Ryan.* Womenhood in America. *2d ed. New York: New Viewpoints, 1979. Pp. xii–xiii.*

The legal status of married women continued to be governed by the law of coverture following the Revolutionary War. One direct result of strict adherence to the principles of coverture was that when women married, control of their property and their earnings passed to their husbands. A secondary consequence of this restriction was to reinforce the restriction on women's participation in political affairs. During the Revolutionary period, fundamental questions were being asked about citizens' right to participate in their own governance. Yet these rights pertained only to men. Abigail Adams asked that the interests of women be considered in these deliberations, but her husband, who was busy with the Second Continental Congress charting the course of the colonies after the British occupation of Boston, found that proposal amusing.

Remember the Ladies

Letters between Abigail and John Adams.
Charles Francis Adams.
*Familiar Letters of John Adams and
His Wife Abigail Adams, During the
Revolution.*
New York: Hurd and Houghton, 1876.
Pp. 149–150, 155, 169.

Abigail Adams to John Adams

Braintree, 31 March, 1776.

. . . I long to hear that you have declared an
independency. And, by the way, in the new
code of laws which I suppose it will be necessary for you to make, I desire you would
remember the ladies and be more generous and
favorable to them than your ancestors. Do not
put such unlimited power into the hands of the
husbands. Remember, all men would be tyrants
if they could. If particular care and attention is
not paid to the ladies, we are determined to
foment a rebellion, and will not hold ourselves
bound by any laws in which we have no voice
or representation.

That your sex are naturally tyrannical is a
truth so thoroughly established as to admit of
no dispute; but such of you as wish to be
happy willingly give up the harsh title of master
for the more tender and endearing one of
friend. Why, then, not put it out of the power
of the vicious and the lawless to use us with
cruelty and indignity with impunity? Men of
sense in all ages abhor those customs which
treat us only as the vassals of your sex; regard
us then as beings placed by Providence under
your protection, and in imitation of the Supreme Being make use of that power only for
our happiness.

John Adams to Abigail Adams

14 April (1776)

. . . As to declarations of independency, be
patient. Read our privateering laws, and our
commercial laws? What signifies a Word?

As to your extraordinary code of laws, I cannot
but laugh. We have been told that our struggle
has loosened the bonds of government everywhere; that children and apprentices were
disobedient; that schools and colleges were
grown turbulent; that Indians slighted their
guardians, and negroes grew insolent to their
masters. But your letter was the first intimation
that another tribe, more numerous and power-
full than all the rest, were grown discontented.
This is rather too coarse a compliment, but you
are so saucy, I won't blot it out. Depend upon it,
we know better than to repeal our masculine
systems. Although they are in full force, you
know they are little more than theory. We dare
not exert our power in its full latitude. We are
obliged to go fair and softly, and, in practice, you
know we are the subjects. We have only the
name of masters, and rather than give up this,
which would completely subject us to the despotism of the petticoat, I hope General Washington and all our brave heroes would fight; I am
sure every good politician would plot, as long as
he would against despotism, empire, monarchy,
aristocracy, oligarchy, or ochlocracy. . . .

Abigail Adams to John Adams

Braintree, 7 May, 1776

. . . I cannot say that I think you are very generous to the ladies; for, whilst you are proclaim-
ing peace and good-will to men, emancipating
all nations, you insist upon retaining an absolute
power over wives. But you must remember that
arbitrary power is like most other things which
are very hard, very liable to be broken; and,
notwithstanding all your wise laws and maxims,
we have it in our power, not only to free ourselves, but to subdue our masters, and, without
violence, throw both your natural and legal authority at our feet;—

"Charm by accepting, by submitting sway,
Yet have our humor most when we obey." . . .

STUDY QUESTIONS

1. Abigail argued that legal enforcement of
subservience makes women vulnerable to
"the power of the vicious and lawless to use

us with cruelty and indignity with impunity." To what abuses do you think she was alluding?

2. What seemed laughable about that argument for John? What considerations did he suggest temper the fear of abuse by one's spouse?

3. In her response, Abigail spoke of a power that, even in their subordinate position, women had to free themselves and subdue their masters. What is your interpretation of that passage?

As the Adams' correspondence suggests, the ways that women are treated depend on the way they are perceived. Perceptions of appropriate sex roles, however, change with changing circumstances. During the years that intervened between the Revolutionary and Civil Wars, the sexual division of labor in most American families further intensified. With the advent of industrialization, production increasingly moved out of the home. As Americans adapted to this trend, the population experienced a heightening of sex segregation. Increasingly, men went out of the home to work and women shouldered the responsibilities for managing the household and raising the children. As the following selection shows, advice about how women should adjust to these new realities was forthcoming from the media as well as the pulpit. Both endorsed a set of values and relationships that were variously referred to at the time and since as "the cult of domesticity" and "the cult of true womanhood."

The Cult of True Womanhood—1820–1860

Barbara Welter.
18 *American Quarterly* 151-74 (1966).

American Quarterly *Vol. 18 (1966). Reprinted by permission of The Johns Hopkins University Press.*

. . . Woman, in the cult of True Womanhood presented by the women's magazines, gift annuals and religious literature of the nineteenth century, was the hostage in the home. In a society where values changed frequently, where fortunes rose and fell with frightening rapidity, where social and economic mobility provided instability as well as hope, one thing at least remained the same—a true woman was a true woman, wherever she was found. If anyone, male or female, dared to tamper with the complex of virtues which made up True Womanhood, he was damned immediately as an enemy of God, of civilization and of the Republic. . . .

The attributes of True Womanhood, by which a woman judged herself and was judged by her husband, her neighbors and society, could be divided into four cardinal virtues—piety, purity, submissiveness and domesticity. Put them all together and they spelled mother, daughter, sister, wife—woman. Without them, no matter whether there was fame, achievement or wealth, all was ashes. With them she was promised happiness and power.

Religion or piety was the core of woman's virtue, the source of her strength. Young men looking for a mate were cautioned to search first for piety, for if that were there, all else would follow. Religion belonged to woman by divine right, a gift of God and nature. This "peculiar susceptibility" to religion was given her for a reason: "the vestal flame of piety, lighted up by Heaven in the breast of woman" would throw its beams into the naughty world of men. So far would its candle power reach that the "Universe might be Enlightened, Improved, and Harmonized by WOMAN!!" . . .

One reason religion was valued was that it did not take a woman away from her "proper sphere," her home. Unlike participation in other societies or movements, church work would not make her less domestic or submissive, less a True Woman. In religious vineyards, said the *Young Ladies' Literary and Missionary Report,* "you may labor without the apprehension of detracting from the charms of feminine delicacy." . . .

If religion was so vital to a woman, irreligion was almost too awful to contemplate. Women were warned not to let their literary or intellectual pursuits take them away from God. Sarah Josepha Hale spoke darkly of those who, like Margaret Fuller, threw away the "One True Book" for others, [that are] open to error. . . .

Purity was as essential as piety to a young woman, its absence as unnatural and unfeminine. Without it she was, in fact, no woman at all, but a member of some lower order. A "fallen woman" was a "fallen angel," unworthy of the celestial company of her sex. To contemplate the loss of purity brought tears; to be guilty of such a crime, in the women's magazines at least, brought madness or death. Even the language of the flowers had bitter words for it: a dried white rose symbolized "Death Preferable to Loss of Innocence." The marriage night was the single great event of a woman's life, when she bestowed her great treasure upon her husband, and from that time on was completely dependent upon him, an empty vessel, without legal or emotional existence of her own.

Therefore all True Women were urged, in the strongest possible terms, to maintain their virtue, although men, being by nature more sensual than they, would try to assault it. Thomas Branagan admitted in *The Excellency of the Female Character Vindicated* that his sex would sin and sin again, they could not help it, but woman, stronger and purer, must not give in and let man "take liberties incompatible with her delicacy." "If you do," Branagan addressed his gentle reader, "you will be left in silent sadness to bewail your credulity, imbecility, duplicity, and premature prostitution." . . .

If, however, a woman managed to withstand man's assaults on her virtue, she demonstrated her superiority and her power over him. Eliza Farnham, trying to prove this female superiority, concluded smugly that "the purity of women is the everlasting barrier against which the tides of man's sensual nature surge." . . .

Submission was perhaps the most feminine virtue expected of women. Men were supposed to be religious, although they rarely had time for it, and supposed to be pure, although it came awfully hard to them, but men were the movers, the doers, the actors. Women were the passive, submissive responders. The order of dialogue was, of course, fixed in Heaven. Man was "woman's superior by God's appointment, if not in intellectual dowry, at least in official decree." Therefore, as Charles Elliott argued in *The Ladies' Repository,* she should submit to him "for the sake of good order at least." In *The Ladies Companion* a young wife was quoted approvingly as saying that she did not think woman should "feel and act for herself" because "When, next to God, her husband is not the tribunal to which her heart and intellectual appeals—the golden bowl of affection is broken." Women were warned that if they tampered with this quality they tampered with the order of the Universe. . . .

Caroline Gilman's advice to the bride aimed at establishing this proper order from the beginning of a marriage: "Oh, young and lovely bride, watch well the first moments when your will conflicts with his to whom God and society have given the control. Reverence his *wishes* even when you do not his *opinions.*"

Mrs. Gilman's perfect wife in *Recollections of a Southern Matron* realizes that "the three golden treads with which domestic happiness is woven" are "to repress a harsh answer, to confess a fault, and to stop (right or wrong) in the midst of self-defense, in gentle submission." Woman could do this, hard though it was, because in her heart she knew she was right and so could afford to be forgiving, even a trifle condescending. "Men are not unreasonable," averred Mrs. Gilman. "Their difficulties lie in not understanding the moral and physical nature of our sex. They often would wound through ignorance, and are surprised at having offended." Wives were advised to do their best to reform men, but if they couldn't, to give up gracefully. "If any habit of his annoyed me, I spoke of it once or twice, calmly, then bore it quietly." . . .

The true woman's place was unquestionably by her own fireside—as daughter, sister, but most of all as wife and mother. Therefore domesticity was among the virtues most prized by the women's magazines. "As society is constituted," wrote Mrs. S. E. Farley, on the "Domestic and Social Claims of Woman," "the true dignity and beauty of the female character seem to consist in a right understanding and faithful and cheerful performance of social and family duties." Sacred Scripture re-enforced social pressure: "St. Paul knew what was best for women when he advised them to be domestic," said Mrs. Sanford. "There is composure at home; there is something sedative in the duties which home involves. It affords security not only from the world, but from delusions and errors of every kind."

From her home woman performed her great task of bringing men back to God. *The Young Ladies' Class Book* was sure that "the domestic fireside is the great guardian of society against the excesses of human passion." . . .

Home was supposed to be a cheerful place, so that brothers, husbands and sons would not go elsewhere in search of a good time. Woman was expected to dispense comfort and cheer. . . .

One of the most important functions of woman as comforter was her role as nurse. Her own health was probably, although regrettably, delicate. Many homes had "little sufferers," those pale children who wasted away to saintly deaths. And there were enough other illnesses of youth and age, major and minor, to give the nineteenth-century American woman nursing experience. The sickroom called for the exercise of her higher qualities of patience, mercy and gentleness as well as for her housewifely arts. She could thus fulfill her dual feminine function—beauty and usefulness. . . .

Most of this advice was directed to woman as wife. Marriage was the proper state for the exercise of the domestic virtues. . . . But although marriage was best, it was not absolutely necessary. The women's magazines tried to remove the stigma from being an "Old Maid." They advised no marriage at all rather than an unhappy one contracted out of selfish motives. Their stories showed maiden ladies as unselfish ministers to the sick, teachers of the young, or moral preceptors with their pens, beloved of the entire village. Usually the life of single blessedness resulted from the premature death of a fiance, or was chosen through fidelity to some high mission. . . . Very rarely, a "woman of genius" was absolved from the necessity of marriage, being so extraordinary that she did not need the security or status of being a wife. Most often, however, if girls proved "difficult," marriage and a family were regarded as a cure. The "sedative quality" of a home could be counted on to subdue even the most restless spirits. . . .

If any woman asked from greater scope for her gifts the magazines were sharply critical. Such women were tampering with society, undermining civilization. Mary Wollstonecraft, Frances Wright and Harriet Martineau were condemned in the strongest possible language— they were read out of the sex. "They are only semi-women, mental hermaphrodites." The Rev. Harrington knew the women of America could not possibly approve of such perversions and went to some wives and mothers to ask if they did not want a "wider sphere of interest" as these nonwomen claimed. The answer was reassuring. " 'No!' they cried simultaneously, 'Let the men take care of politics, *we take care of the children!* "

STUDY QUESTIONS

1. What virtues were recommended to women by the authors reviewed in this piece? Were they also commended to men? According to these authors, who stood to benefit from women who possessed them?

2. What devices were used to urge women to accept these teachings? How were women pictured who fell short of these ideals? In what ways were "true women" said to exercise power over men?

3. In what ways do these images of true womanhood survive in our own day? How are they perpetuated? How can they be challenged?

In the nineteenth century, ideology assumed even greater importance in shaping opportunities for women and men. During that period, the view that women and men had very different natures and occupied entirely different worlds became dominant. The "separate spheres" ideology was used in legal decisions to justify limiting the rights of women. Remnants of this view are with us today.

Separate Spheres

Nadine Taub and Elizabeth M. Schneider. "Perspectives on Women's Subordination and the Law." In *The Politics of Law,* edited by D. Kairys. New York: Pantheon, 1982. Pp. 125-26.

. . . Although women were in no way the equals of men during the colonial and Revolutionary periods, the nature of their subordination, particularly in the middle classes, changed dramatically between the end of the eighteenth century and the middle of the nineteenth century. The early stages of industrial capitalism involved increasing specialization and the movement of production out of the home, which resulted in heightened sex segregation. Men went out of the house to work; and women's work, influence, and consciousness remained focused at home. Although women continued to be dependent on and subservient to men, women were no longer placed at the bottom of a hierarchy dominated by men. Rather, they came to occupy women's "separate sphere," a qualitatively different world centered on home and family. Women's role was by definition incompatible with full participation in society.

"Separate-sphere" ideology clearly delineated the activities open to women. Women's role within the home was glorified, and women's limited participation in paid labor outside the home was most often in work that could be considered an extension of their work within the home. For example, native-born mill girls in

the 1820s and 1830s, and immigrant women in the 1840s and 1850s, worked in largely sex-segregated factories manufacturing textiles, clothing, and shoes. Likewise, after a period of time, teaching became a woman's occupation. Unpaid charitable and welfare activities, however, were encouraged as consistent with women's domestic responsibilities.

Although ultimately quite constraining, the development of women's separate sphere had some important benefits. While the emphasis on women's moral purity and the cult of domesticity tended to mask women's inferior position, it also allowed women a certain degree of autonomy. It gave them the opportunity to organize extensively into religious and secular welfare associations, afforded access to education, and provided them with a basis for uniting with other women. Evaluations of the cult of domesticity and women's separate sphere by feminist historians have consequently ranged from the view that women were victims of this ideology to the recognition that women found a source of strength and identity in their separate world.

The development of separate-sphere ideology appears in large measure to have been a consequence of changes in the conditions of production. Behavior was then further channeled by a vast cultural transformation promoted through books and magazines. The law does not seem to have played an overt role in the initial articulation of the separate-sphere ideology; but to the extent that the ideological transformation that occurred in the early part of the nineteenth century was a reaction to a strict hierarchy imposed by the previous legal order, the legal system may well have played an important part at the outset.

In any event, the law appears to have contributed significantly to the perpetuation of this ideology.

STUDY QUESTIONS

1. Describe the ways that sex roles and attitudes appear to have changed between colonial times and the nineteenth century.
2. How important do rules governing legal status appear to be in determining sex roles? How important do prevailing sex roles appear to be in determining the rules governing legal status?
3. To what extent was the differentiation of sex roles due to the way goods and services were produced? To what extent did it seem to work the other way around?
4. In what ways are the ideologies described in this and earlier readings relevant today?

The features described by Welter and by Taub and Schneider were not widely contested during the early decades of the nineteenth century. Indeed, reform-minded women of the day often appealed to the cult of true womanhood and the ideology of separate spheres to justify projects designed to enhance opportunities available to women. Catharine Beecher campaigned for improved education of girls and women on the grounds that it was necessary preparation for efficient domestic management and especially for the nurture of children. In doing so, she acknowledged that women had "duties of subordination."

The Peculiar Responsibilities of American Women

Catharine E. Beecher.
Treatise on Domestic Economy.
Rev. 3d ed. New York: Harper and Bros., 1847. Pp. 25–37.

There are some reasons, why American women should feel an interest in the support of the democratic institutions of their Country, which it is important that they should consider. The great maxim, which is the basis of all our civil and political institutions, is, that "all men are created equal," and that they are equally entitled to "life, liberty, and the pursuit of happiness." . . .

But, in order that each individual may pursue and secure the highest degree of happiness within his reach, unimpeded by the selfish interests of others, a system of laws must be established, which sustain certain relations and dependencies in social and civil life. What these

relations and their attending obligations shall be, are to be determined, not with reference to the wishes and interests of a few, but solely with reference to the general good of all; so that each individual shall have his own interest, as well as the public benefit, secured by them.

For this purpose, it is needful that certain relations be sustained, which involve the duties of subordination. There must be the magistrate and the subject, one of whom is the superior, and the other the inferior. There must be the relations of husband and wife, parent and child, teacher and pupil, employer and employed, each involving the relative duties of subordination. The superior, in certain particulars, is to direct, and the inferior is to yield obedience. Society could never go forward, harmoniously, nor could any craft or profession be successfully pursued, unless these superior and subordinate relations be instituted and sustained. . . .

The tendencies of democratic institutions, in reference to the rights and interests of the female sex, have been fully developed in the United States; and it is in this aspect, that the subject is one of peculiar interest to American women.

In this Country, it is established, both by opinion and by practice, that woman has an equal interest in all social and civil concerns; and that no domestic, civil, or political, institution, is right, which sacrifices her interest to promote that of the other sex. But in order to secure her the more firmly in all these privileges, it is decided, that, in the domestic relation, she take a subordinate station, and that, in civil and political concerns, her interests be intrusted to the other sex, without her taking any part in voting, or in making and administering laws. . . .

It appears, then, that it is in America, alone, that women are raised to an equality with the other sex; and that, both in theory and practice, their interests are regarded as of equal value. They are made subordinate in station, only where a regard to their best interests demands it, while, as if in compensation for this, by custom and courtesy, they are always treated as superiors. Universally, in this Country, through every class of society, precedence is given to woman, in all the comforts, conveniences, and courtesies, of life.

In civil and political affairs, American women take no interest or concern, except so far as they sympathize with their family and personal friends; but in all cases, in which they do feel a concern, their opinions and feelings have a consideration, equal, or even superior, to that of the other sex.

In matters pertaining to the education of their children, in the selection and support of a clergyman, in all benevolent enterprises, and in all questions relating to morals or manners, they have a superior influence. In such concerns, it would be impossible to carry a point, contrary to their judgement and feelings; while an enterprise, sustained by them, will seldom fail of success.

If those who are bewailing themselves over the fancied wrongs and injuries of women in this Nation, could only see things as they are, they would know, that, whatever remnants of a barbarous or aristocratic age may remain in our civil institutions, in reference to the interests of women, it is only because they are ignorant of them, or do not use their influence to have them rectified; for it is very certain that there is nothing

reasonable, which American women would unite in asking, that would not readily be bestowed.

The preceding remarks, then, illustrate the position, that the democratic institutions of this Country . . . tend to place woman in her true position in society, as having equal rights with the other sex; and that, in fact, they have secured to American women a lofty and fortunate position, which, as yet, has been attained by the women of no other nation. . . .

The success of democratic institutions, as is conceded by all, depends upon the intellectual and moral character of the mass of the people. If they are intelligent and virtuous, democracy is a blessing; but if they are ignorant and wicked, it is only a curse, and as much more dreadful than any other form of civil government, as a thousand tyrants are more to be dreaded than one. It is equally conceded, that the formation of the moral and intellectual character of the young is committed mainly to the female hand. The mother forms the character of the future man; the sister bends the fibres that are hereafter to be the forest tree; the wife sways the heart, whose energies may turn for good or for evil the destinies of a nation. Let the women of a country be made virtuous and intelligent, and the men will certainly be the same. The proper education of a man decides the welfare of an individual; but educate a woman, and the interests of a whole family are secured. . . .

No American woman, then, has any occasion for feeling that hers is an humble or insignificant lot. . . .

STUDY QUESTIONS

1. What justification does Beecher propose for women's "duties of subordination" to men in domestic relations? For the exclusion of women from civil and political responsibilities? How does that square with her view that in America, women and men enjoy equal status?

2. In what matters are women said to have superior influence to that of men? How do you suppose the education of women is related to those matters?

The cult of true womanhood and the ideology of separate spheres primarily reflected the experience of privileged white women. They did not accurately portray the lives of women of other races and classes. The contrast between the ideology's meaning for white women and for black women is particularly striking. Although there were parallels between the legal status of slaves and free women, as slaves, many black women were subjected to a particular mode of life.

Slavery in the United States was a political and economic system supported and reinforced by the law. It enabled white slave owners to extract as much labor as possible from their slaves by means of force and threat of force. Until the Emancipation Proclamation of 1862, slaves were reduced to chattels, owned for life. They were not citizens according to the Supreme Court in the infamous *Dred Scott* decision of 1857 because they were considered an inferior kind of being. As a result, they could not vote, own property, testify, sue, or be sued. Whites were rarely sanctioned for assaulting or even murdering blacks, while numerous crimes committed by blacks merited the death penalty. Barred by law from acquiring literacy skills, they were also legally incapable of marriage, and so their families were subject to separation at the master's will. On the plantation, slave women were assigned demanding physical labor in the fields along with the men. Slave women did not, however, learn skilled trades as did some male slaves. Along with children, they were at times assigned to domestic work in "the big house."

The following oral history was recorded in the early 1930s as part of the Federal Writers' Project. It gives a rare firsthand glimpse of an all-too-common experience among American slave women.

Rose Williams's Forced Marriage in Texas

Mary Beth Norton, ed.
Major Problems in American Women's History. New York: D.C. Heath & Co, 1989. Pp. 150–52.

What I say am the facts. If I's one day old, I's way over ninety, and I's born in Bell County, right here in Texas, and am owned by Massa William Black. He owns Mammy and Pappy, too. Massa Black has a big plantation, but he has more niggers than he need for work on that place, 'cause he am a nigger trader. He trade and buy and sell all the time.

Massa Black am awful cruel, and he whip the colored folks and works 'em hard and feed 'em poorly. We-uns have for rations the corn meal and milk and 'lasses and some beans and peas and meat once a week. We-uns have to work in the field every day from daylight 'til dark, and on Sunday we-uns do us washing. Church? Shucks, we-uns don't know what that mean.

I has the correct memorandum of when the war start. Massa Black sold we-uns right then. Mammy and Pappy powerful glad to git sold, and they and I is put on the block with 'bout ten other niggers. When we-uns gits to the trading block, there lots of white folks there what come to look us over. One man shows the interest in Pappy. Him named Hawkins. He talk to Pappy, and Pappy talk to him and say, "Them my woman and childs. Please buy all of us and have mercy on we-uns." Massa Hawkins say, "That gal am a likely-looking nigger; she am portly and strong. But three am more than I wants, I guesses."

The sale start, and 'fore long Pappy am put on the block. Massa Hawkins wins the bid for Pappy, and when Mammy am put on the block, he wins the bid for her. Then there am three or four other niggers sold before my time comes. Then Massa Black calls me to the block, and the auction man say, "What am I offer for this portly, strong young wench. She's never been 'bused and will make the good breeder."

I wants to hear Massa Hawkins bid, but him say nothing. Two other men am bidding 'gainst each other, and I sure has the worriment. There am tears coming down my cheeks 'cause I's being sold to some man that would make separation from my mammy. One man bids $500, and the auction man ask, "Do I hear more? She am gwine at $500." Then someone say, "$525," and the auction man say, "She am sold for $525 to Massa Hawkins." Am I glad and 'cited! Why, I's quivering all over.

Massa Hawkins takes we-uns to his place, and it am a nice plantation. Lots better than Massa Black's. There is 'bout fifty niggers what is growed and lots of children. The first thing Massa do when we-uns gits home am give we-uns rations and a cabin. You must believe this nigger when I says them rations a feast for us. There plenty meat and tea and coffee and white flour. I's never tasted white flour and coffee, and Mammy fix some biscuits and coffee. Well, the biscuits was yum, yum, yum to me, but the coffee I doesn't like.

The quarters am pretty good. There am twelve cabins all made from logs and a table and some benches and bunks for sleeping and a fireplace for cooking and the heat. There am no floor, just the ground.

Massa Hawkins am good to he niggers and not force 'em work too hard. There am as much difference 'tween him and Old Massa Black in the way of treatment as 'twixt the Lord and the devil. Massa Hawkins 'lows he niggers have reasonable parties and go fishing, but we-uns am never tooken to church and has no books for larning. There am no education for the niggers.

There am one thing Massa Hawkins does to me what I can't shunt from my mind. I knows he don't do it for meanness, but I always holds it 'gainst him. What he done am force me to live with that nigger, Rufus, 'gainst my wants.

After I been at he place 'bout a year, the massa come to me and say, "You gwine live with Rufus in that cabin over yonder. Go fix it for living." I's 'bout sixteen year old and has no larning, and I's just ignomus child. I's thought that him mean for me to tend the cabin for Rufus and some other niggers. Well, that am start the prestigation for me.

I's took charge of the cabin after work am done and fixes supper. Now, I don't like that Rufus, 'cause he a bully. He am big and 'cause he so, he think everybody do what him say. We-uns has supper, then I goes here and there talking, till I's ready for sleep, and then I gits in the bunk. After I's in, that nigger come and crawl in the bunk with me 'fore I knows it. I says, "What you means, you fool nigger?" He say for me to hush the mouth. "This am my bunk, too," he say.

"You's teched in the head. Git out, I's told him, and I puts the feet 'gainst him and give him a shove, and out he go on the floor 'fore he know what I's doing. That nigger jump up and he mad. He look like the wild bear. He starts for the bunk, and I jumps quick for the poker. It am 'bout three feet long, and when he comes at me I lets him have it over the head. Did that nigger stop in he tracks? I's say he did. He looks at me steady for a minute, and you could tell he thinking hard. Then he go and set on the bench and say, "Just wait. You thinks it am smart, but you am foolish in the head. They's gwine larn you something."

"Hush your big mouth and stay 'way from this nigger, that all I wants," I say, and just sets and hold that poker in the hand. He just sets, looking like the bull. There we-uns sets and sets for 'bout an hour, and then he go out, and I bars the door.

The next day I goes to the missy and tells her what Rufus wants, and Missy say that am the massa's wishes. She say, "You am the portly gal, and Rufus am the portly man. The massa wants you-uns for to bring forth portly children."

I's thinking 'bout what the missy say, but say to myself, "I's not gwine live with that Rufus." That night when him come in the cabin, I grabs the poker and sits on the bench and says, "Git 'way from me, nigger, 'fore I bust your brains out and stomp on them." He say nothing and git out.

The next day the massa call me and tell me, "Woman, I's pay big money for you, and I's done that for the cause I wants you to raise me childrens. I's put you to live with Rufus for that purpose. Now, if you doesn't want whipping at the stake, you do what I wants."

I thinks 'bout Massa buying me offen the block and saving me from being separated from my folks and 'bout being whipped at the stake.

There it am. What am I's to do? So I 'cides to do as the massa wish, and so I yields. . . .

I never marries, 'cause one 'sperience am 'nough for this nigger. After what I does for the massa, I's never wants no truck with any man. The Lord forgive this colored woman, but he have to 'scuse me and look for some others for to 'plenish the earth.

STUDY QUESTIONS

1. To what forms of abuse and exploitation was Rose Williams subjected because she was a slave? To what forms because she was a female slave?

2. What forms of harm did Rose Williams continue to suffer seventy years later?

3. Is there any indication in Williams's story that those to whom she was subordinated placed her on the pedestal of which Beecher spoke?

Slave owners exploited the sexuality of slave women in two ways. As we saw in Rose Williams's account, slave women increased their masters' workforce and enhanced their property. Slave women were also compelled to serve their masters sexually. As a consequence of these sexual functions, slave women were represented as being lascivious and immoral. This in turn served to rationalize their treatment. Given these circumstances, it is no surprise that the dominant Victorian ideology would have a very different impact on Southern white and slave women. The following selection explores that dual impact.

Casting of the Die

Paula Giddings.
When and Where I Enter. New York: William Morrow & Co., 1984.
Pp. 42–43.

The Victorian family ideal also carried a specific consequence for women. White southern women found themselves enmeshed in an interracial web in which wives, children, and slaves were *all* expected to obey the patriarchal head of the household, as historian Anne Firor Scott observed. The compliance of White women became inextricably linked to that of the slaves. For, it was believed, "any tendency of one member of the system to assert themselves against the master threatened the whole." As it was often asserted by slavery apologists, any change in the role of women *or* Blacks would contribute to the downfall not only of slavery, but of the family and society as well. Little wonder that the English-born feminist Margaret Fuller held that "There exists in the mind of men a tone of feeling toward women as toward slaves." Little wonder that the earliest White American feminists, Angelina and Sarah Grimké, had been reared in a wealthy slaveholding family. And little wonder, too, that southern women, as a group, were the most reluctant to assert a feminist sensibility.

The Victorian "extended" family also put the "moral" categories of women into sharp relief. The White wife was hoisted on a pedestal so high that she was beyond the sensual reach of her own husband. Black women were consigned to the other end of the scale, as mistresses, whores, or breeders. Thus, in the nineteenth century, Black women's resistance to slavery took on an added dimension. With the diminution of overt rebellion, their resistance became more covert or internalized. The focus of the struggle was no longer against the notion that they were less human, . . . but that they were different kinds of humans. For women this meant spurning their morally inferior roles of mistress, whore, and breeder—though under the "new" slavery they were "rewarded" for acquiescing in them. It was the factor of reward that made this resistance a fundamentally feminist one, for at its base was a rejection of the notion that they were the master's property. So Black women had a double chal-lenge under the new slavery: They had to resist the property relation (which was different in form, if not in nature, to that of White women) and they had to inculcate the same values into succeeding generations.

STUDY QUESTIONS

1. What parallels existed between the legal status of slaves and free women?
2. What consequences did the nineteenth-century ideology concerning sex roles have for the relations between African-American and white women?
3. What special burdens do you think African-American women bear today?

The dominant Victorian ideology prescribing separate spheres for women and men also had a special meaning for working class women. While women (along with children) had been encouraged to work at textile mills and other manufacturing operations being established in the early years of the nineteenth century, their par-ticipation in the paid labor force was later discouraged by the cult of domesticity. By 1860, the census estimated that only 15 percent of American women were engaged in paid labor at any one time. Although many women supplemented their family income by taking in boarders, doing laundry for others, and performing other work at home, approximately half of the female population would never work outside the home, and for two-thirds of the remaining half, wage work stopped at marriage. Only those compelled by economic necessity engaged in paid labor outside the home.

Female participation in the paid labor force increased substantially following the Civil War. The separate spheres ideology persisted nonetheless. At the end of the nineteenth century, working class women lived their lives, as had their mid-century sisters, at odds with prevailing notions of appropriate female behavior.

Victorian Ideology and Working Women

Sarah Eisenstein.
Give Us Bread But Give Us Roses.
London: Rotledge, Chapman and Hall, Inc., 1983. Pp. 50-55, 111-45.

The ideas with which women had to confront and interpret their increasing involvement in work outside the home at the turn of the century were rooted in basic Victorian not-ions about woman's place and woman's nature. . . . The basic themes of this ideology were the assumption that woman's place was in the home as wife and mother, and the image of the lady as the model for all women. . . .

This elevation of the standards and experi-ence of a class very different from their own into general principles for all women had very important consequences for working-class women, and particularly for those who worked outside their homes. In practice, they were excluded from the only socially accepted definitions of respectable womanhood. The conditions of their lives, their appearance, the forms of their social intercourse, the character

Reprinted from Give Us Bread But Give Us Roses, *by Sarah Eisenstein (1983), by permission of the publisher, Routledge, Chapman and Hall, Inc.*

of their relations with men, undermined their claim to respectability and to femininity itself. . . .

Working outside the home meant that a woman was unprotected, subject to close social and even physical contact with strange men, and to the orders of men who were not her father or husband. Service work in a store or restaurant left her open to improper advances, and put her in the position of serving the personal needs of men with whom she did not have properly sanctioned relationships. The rough physical nature of factory work was antithetical to notions of female delicacy. The conditions under which working women lived and worked made it difficult for them to achieve the dress, carriage, speech, and manners required for the appearance of gentility. . . .

By the 1880s and 1890s, however, various social changes, including the early victories of the feminists, had begun to weaken its hold and point up its inconsistencies. Women were going to college in increasing numbers, and entering the labor force in the professions as well as at wage labor. Even upper-class women were increasingly involved outside their homes, whether in pursuing very conspicuous consumptions, which would earlier have seemed (at best) unladylike, or in philanthropic work which took them into a wider range of social situations. The image of the lady loosened a bit, and began to include subtypes of a more active character: the college girl, the chum, even the career girl. . . .

There was also an increased awareness of the numbers of women going to work to support themselves. Shortly after the Civil War, commentators began to complain about the 'New Departure,' as they called the large increase in women working outside the home, brought on in part by the war itself, in part by the industrial use of the recently invented sewing machine. . . .

. . . [H]owever, the basic content of the ideology remained the same. In 1875, the Supreme Court of the State of Wisconsin ruled that "The law of nature destines and qualifies the female sex for the bearing and nurture of the children of our race and for the custody of the homes of the world in love and honor." The assumption that

woman's natural place was in the home as wife and mother, and the image, of the lady's gentility and respectability, albeit somewhat loosened now, as the definition of femininity formed the core of contemporary ideas about what women should be. They were the basic notions with which women had to confront their increasing involvement in work outside the home. . . .

Despite significant changes around the turn of the century in Victorian attitudes about women in general and their involvement in the labor force in particular, contemporary ideas about women and work remained exclusive of the reality of a large section, even a majority, of the working-class women of the period. . . .

Although there was a stronger sense of the emergence of working women as a definite social group, expecting as a matter of course that they would work at some point in their lives, there was still a strong reluctance to recognize the characteristic working woman in industries like garment or textiles, as a representative type. There was perhaps an uneasy recognition of the existence of such women, for whom work under deplorable conditions was a basic and determining factor, but no acceptance of their representativeness. . . .

Working women were, then, excluded from the acceptable image of womanhood and respectability shaped by the dominant values of the period. The question becomes, what was the impact of this situation on working women themselves? . . .

The majority of working women were young and lived at home, accepting family authority, and acceding to the demands of family loyalty and the requirements of their particular roles in family relationships. . . . Those women who could not live at home tried to approximate the family situation as closely as possible, paying tribute in their own ways not only to the practical advantages of family living, but to its psychic and imaginative importance to them. Lastly, even the relatively small group of women who seemed somewhat aware that their situations did not, and would not, approach family living, reflected the continuing importance of the idea of the 'home' in their sense of themselves as women. . . .

Contemporary observers consistently note the eagerness with which young working girls looked forward to marriage, and envisioned it as the crowning point of their lives. Indeed, they were often concerned that this absorption undermined women's commitment to their immediate work. . . .

The tendency to see marriage as an escape from the shop or factory was engendered by the conditions under which women worked, and the lack of opportunity to improve their situation as workers. But the importance of marriage in women's view of their lives must not be seen simply as a result of the work experience. Disappointment in the reality encountered at work may have reinforced women's desire to marry, but it did not create it. Women's attitudes about marriage were independent of their work, and indeed shaped their work experience.

In fact, women's prior commitment to marriage was often seen as a contributing factor to the difficult conditions under which they labored. Some commentators argued that women got lower wages and confronted worse conditions than men because, expecting to marry, they did not invest time or energy in training and preparation for skilled work. Women who tried to organize their co-workers into unions often cited the difficulties presented by women's commitment to eventual marriage. . . .

STUDY QUESTIONS

1. How do you imagine Victorian ideology might be used to justify laws restricting women's employment opportunities?
2. How do you suppose attitudes concerning women's destiny affected working conditions for women?

II. THE EARLY FEMINIST CHALLENGE

Among the earliest American writers to call for sexual equality were the Grimké sisters. Sarah and Angelina Grimké were daughters of a well-established, upper-class, slave-holding family in Charleston, South Carolina. During the late 1830s, while still in their twenties, they joined the Society of Friends, colloquially known as the Quaker religion, moved to Philadelphia, and took active parts in the abolitionist movement. It was their work in that movement that helped them recognize that women too were oppressed by existing social arrangements. The following selection illustrates the themes that Angelina Grimké stressed in her public addresses and writings.

Human Rights Not Founded on Sex

Angelina E. Grimké.
Letters to Catharine E. Beecher.
Boston: Isaac Knapp, 1838. Pp. 114-21.

East Boylston, Mass. *10th mo. 2d,* 1837.
Dear Friend:

The investigation of the rights of the slave has led me to a better understanding of my own. I have found the Anti-Slavery cause to be the high school of morals in our land—the school in which *human rights* are more fully investigated, and better understood and taught, than in any other. Here a great fundamental principle is uplifted and illuminated, and from this central light, rays innumerable stream all around. Human beings have *rights,* because they are *moral* beings: the rights of *all* men grow out of their moral nature; and as all men have the same moral nature, they have essentially the same rights. These rights may be wrested from the slave, but they cannot be alienated: his title to himself is as perfect *now,* as is that of Lyman Beecher: it is stamped on his moral being, and is, like it, imperishable. Now if rights are founded in the nature of our moral being, then the *mere circumstance of sex* does not give to man higher rights and responsibilities, than to woman. To suppose that it does, would be to deny the self-evident truth, that the 'physical constitution is the mere instrument of the moral nature.' To suppose that it does, would be to break up utterly the relations, of the two natures, and to reverse their functions, exalting the animal nature into a monarch, and humbling the moral into a slave; making the former a proprietor, and the latter its property. When human beings are regarded as *moral* beings, *sex,* instead of being enthroned upon the summit, administering upon rights and responsibilities, sinks into insignificance and nothingness. My doctrine then is, that whatever it is morally right for man to do, it is morally right for woman to do. Our duties originate, not from difference of sex, but from the diversity of our relations in life, the various gifts and talents committed to our care, and the different eras in which we live.

This regulation of duty by the mere circumstance of sex, rather than by the fundamental principle of moral being, has led to all that multifarious train of evils flowing out of the anti-christian doctrine of masculine and feminine virtues. By this doctrine, man has been converted into the warrior, and clothed with sternness, and those other kindred qualities, which in common estimation belong to his character as a *man;* whilst woman has been taught to lean upon an arm of flesh, to sit as a doll arrayed in 'gold, and pearls, and costly array,' to be admired for her personal charms, and caressed and humored like a spoiled child, or converted into a mere drudge to suit the convenience of her lord and master. Thus have all the diversified relations of life been filled with 'confusion and every evil work.' This principle has given to man a charter for the exercise of tyranny and selfishness, pride and arrogance, lust and brutal violence. It has robbed woman of essential rights, the right to think and speak and act on all great moral questions, just as men think and speak and act; the right to share their responsibilities, perils and toils; the right to fulfil the great end of her being, as a moral, intellectual and immortal creature, and of glorifying God in her body and her spirit which are His. Hitherto, instead of being a help mate to man, in the highest, noblest sense of the term, as a companion, a co-worker, an equal; she has been a mere appendage of his being, an instrument of his convenience and pleasure, the pretty toy with which he wiled away his leisure moments, or the pet animal whom he humored into playfulness and submission. Woman, instead of being regarded as the equal of man, has uniformly been looked down upon as his inferior, a mere gift to fill up the measure of his happiness. In 'the poetry of romantic gallantry,' it is true, she has been called 'the last *best* gift of God to man;' but I believe I speak forth the words of truth and soberness when I affirm, that woman never was given to man. . . .

Dost thou ask me, if I would wish to see woman engaged in the contention and strife of sectarian controversy, or in the intrigues of political partizans? I say no! never—never. I rejoice that she does not stand on the same platform which man now occupies in these respects; but I mourn, also, that he should thus prostitute his higher nature, and vilely cast away his birthright. I prize the purity of *his* character as highly as I do that of hers. As a moral being, *whatever it is morally wrong for her to do, it is morally wrong for him to do.* The fallacious doctrine of male and female virtues has well nigh ruined all that is morally great and lovely in his character: he has been quite as deep a sufferer by it as woman, though mostly in different respects and by other processes. . . .

That thou and all my country-women may better understand the true dignity of woman, is the sincere desire of

Thy Friend,

A. E. GRIMKÉ.

STUDY QUESTIONS

1. What grounds were advanced to support the claim that women and men have equal rights? Is this a claim that advocates of the cult of true womanhood and the separate spheres ideology would accept?

2. What are some of the evils Grimké saw as flowing from the view that masculine and feminine virtues are distinct? In her view, how are women diminished by that doctrine? How are men? Do you agree?

Before the Grimké sisters, women who sought to improve the condition of women generally worked within the traditional relationship of subordination. Catharine Beecher, for example, urged that societal interests are best served through a system of domestic and political subordination. What is distinctive about the contribution of the Grimké sisters is that they confronted the system of subordination directly. Whereas others had been willing to work within the confines of second-class citizenship and the domestic sphere, they were not. In their view, one's moral status or standing is a matter of yes or no, not a matter of more and less. Those who have moral standing and are treated in abusive ways have been denied what they have a right to demand. As African slaves have moral standing, treating them as though they were but domestic animals is morally outrageous. It was this step that enabled the Grimké sisters to recognize that the systematic subordination of women is also morally outrageous and for the same reason. Women have moral standing, just as do men, and so they should have the same political and legal rights as men.

Only a decade later, this same argument prevailed at the first women's rights convention, although on the basis of a different analogy. Organized by Elizabeth Cady Stanton and Lucretia Mott and attended by approximately three hundred women and men, including Frederick Douglass, the convention endorsed an argument based on a parallel with the Declaration of Independence in which American men asserted their legal rights on the basis of their moral standing. The convention produced what is widely regarded as the most famous document in the history of feminism.

Declaration of Sentiments

Seneca Falls, New York.
July 19–20, 1848.
In *The Concise History of Woman Suffrage,* edited by Mari Jo and Paul Buhle.
Urbana, Ill.: University of Illinois Press, 1978. Pp. 94–95.

When, in the course of human events, it becomes necessary for one portion of the family of man to assume among the people of the earth a position different from that which they have hitherto occupied, but one to which the laws of nature and of nature's God entitle them, a decent respect to the opinions of mankind requires that they should declare the causes that impel them to such a course.

We hold these truths to be self-evident: that all men and women are created equal; that they are endowed by their Creator with certain inalienable rights, that among these are life, liberty, and the pursuit of happiness; that to secure these rights governments are instituted, deriving their just powers from the consent of the governed. Whenever any form of government becomes destructive of these ends, it is the right of those who suffer from it to refuse allegiance to it, and to insist upon the institution of a new government, laying its foundation on such principles, and organizing its powers in such form as to them shall seem most likely to effect their safety and happiness.

Prudence, indeed, will dictate that governments long established should should not be changed for light and transient causes; and accordingly, all experience hath shown that mankind are more disposed to suffer, while evils are sufferable, than to right themselves by abolishing the forms to which they were accustomed. But when a long train of abuses and usurpations, pursuing invariably the same object evinces a design to reduce them under absolute despotism, it is their duty to throw off such government, and to provide new guards for their future security. Such has been the patient sufferance of the women under this government, and such is now the necessity which constrains them to demand the equal station to which they are entitled.

The history of mankind is a history of repeated injuries and usurpations on the part of man toward woman, having in direct object the establishment of an absolute tyranny over her. To prove this, let facts be submitted to a candid world.

He has never permitted her to exercise her inalienable right to the elective franchise.

He has compelled her to submit to laws, in the formation of which she had no voice.

He has withheld from her rights which are given to the most ignorant and degraded men—both natives and foreigners.

Having deprived her of this first right of a citizen, the elective franchise, thereby leaving her without representation in the halls of legislation, he has oppressed her on all sides.

He has made her, if married, in the eye of the law, civilly dead.

He has taken from her all right in property, even to the wages she earns.

He has made her, morally, an irresponsible being, as she can commit many crimes with impunity, provided they be done in the presence of her husband. In the covenant of marriage, she is compelled to promise obedience to her husband, he becoming, to all intents and purposes, her master—the law giving him power to deprive her of her liberty, and to administer chastisement.

He has so framed the laws of divorce, as to what shall be the proper causes of divorce; in case of separation, to whom the guardianship

of the children shall be given; as to be wholly regardless of the happiness of women—the law, in all cases, going upon a false supposition of the supremacy of man, and giving all power into his hands.

After depriving her of all rights as a married woman, if single and the owner of property, he has taxed her to support a government which recognizes her only when her property can be made profitable to it.

He has monopolized nearly all the profitable employments, and from those she is permitted to follow, she receives but a scanty remuneration.

He closes against her all the avenues to wealth and distinction, which he considers most honorable to himself. As a teacher of theology, medicine, or law, she is not known.

He has denied her the facilities for obtaining a thorough education—all colleges being closed against her.

He allows her in Church, as well as State, but a subordinate position, claiming Apostolic authority for her exclusion from the ministry, and, with some exceptions, from any public participation in the affairs of the Church.

He has created a false public sentiment, by giving to the world a different code of morals for men and women, by which moral delinquencies which exclude women from society, are not only tolerated but deemed of little account in man.

He has usurped the prerogative of Jehovah himself, claiming it as his right to assign for her a sphere of action, when that belongs to her conscience and to her God.

He has endeavored, in every way that he could, to destroy her confidence in her own powers, to lessen her self-respect, and to make her willing to lead a dependent and abject life.

Now, in view of this entire disfranchisement of one-half the people of this country, their social and religious degradation,—in view of the unjust laws above mentioned, and because women do feel themselves aggrieved, oppressed, and fraudulently deprived of their most sacred rights, we insist that they have immediate admission to all the rights and privileges which belong to them as citizens of the United States.

In entering upon the great work before us, we anticipate no small amount of misconception, misrepresentation, and ridicule; but we shall use every instrumentality within our power to effect our object. We shall employ agents, circulate tracts, petition the state and national legisla- tures, and endeavor to enlist the pulpit and the press in our behalf. We hope this Convention will be followed by a series of Conventions, embracing every part of the country.

STUDY QUESTIONS

1. Upon what document was the Declaration modeled?
2. What complaints against current legal arrangements were listed?
3. To what program of reform did the convention commit itself? Did nineteenth-century feminists call for a radical redistribution of roles within the family?
4. Seen in the context of that program, was the aspiration of suffrage likely to provoke ridicule?

During the Civil War years, feminists threw their support behind the abolitionists, temporarily suspending their push for equality of the sexes. The emergence of black suffrage as a central issue following the Civil War helped focus feminist demands on the vote. Political activity shifted from state legislatures to Congress, where feminists sought the inclusion of specific protections for women in the Fourteenth and Fifteenth Amendments. As adopted, however, the Fourteenth Amendment deliberately excluded women from its provisions by specifying that only "male" citizens would count in calculating congressional representation. The Republican Congress also refused to add "sex" to "race, color, or previous condition of servitude" in the wording of the Fifteenth Amendment listing the prohibited bases for denying the right to vote. It did so on the ground that "this is the Negro's hour." These defeats caused some feminists to collaborate with racists in opposing the adoption of the two amendments. That in turn led to long-lasting splits among feminists and between feminists and abolitionists. Stanton and others were deeply disheartened by this. As they saw it, the feminists had sacrificed for the benefit of the abolitionist cause, only to be abandoned in its moment of triumph.

True to their resolve at Seneca Falls, feminists did launch an impressive campaign for women's rights. One of its objects was the reform of the common law rules of coverture that severely limited married women's ability to own property and to sue and be sued in their own names. This feminist activity was one factor, though certainly not the only factor, leading states during the nineteenth century to adopt legislation known collectively as Married Women's Property Acts.

The Married Women's Property Acts, 1839–1865: Reform, Reaction, or Revolution?

Linda E. Speth.
In *Women and the Law: A Social*

Historical Perspective, edited by D. Kelly Weisberg. Vol. 2. Cambridge, Mass.: Schenkman, 1982. Pp. 69-85.

Prior to the enactment of the married women's property legislation, marriage for all practical purposes ensured a woman's "civil death." A wife could neither sue nor be sued. She could not execute a will or enter into a contract. The wife's civil disabilities and limitations were mirrored by a loss of economic autonomy. Her personal property became her husband's at the moment of marriage. He owned her jewels, furniture, or goods, whether she brought them with her to the marriage or thereafter acquired them, and he could sell or give away even the clothes on her back. In addition, any wages she received for work performed outside the home belonged to her husband. Though he could not sell her real estate without her permission, he acquired rights to control and manage her land. Any proceeds derived from improving the property, harvesting and selling crops, or leasing her land belonged to the husband alone. The common law also recognized the husband's total authority within the confines of the family. He could legally chastise his wife and had the sole right to appoint guardians of the children even while the mother was alive. . . .

During the second quarter of the nineteenth century, state legislatures and constitutional conventions began to make inroads on the common-law fiction of marital unity by enacting married women's property acts. Mississippi became the first state to enact such legislation in 1839, followed by Maryland in 1843. Later, states as geographically and economically diverse as Maine, Massachusetts, Iowa, and New York followed suit. By the end of the Civil War, a total of twenty-nine states had passed married women's property acts that seemed, at first glance, to herald a revolution in the legal and economic relationship between husband and wife. . . .

Despite these early objections to common-law inequities associated with coverture, the first married women's property acts in the nation had little to do with either feminist agitation or concern for female equality. Instead, initial legislative inroads on the common-law fiction of marital unity stemmed from many factors and were often supported by conservative groups.

In the winter of 1839, Mississippi led the way by enacting the nation's first married women's property act. The legislation was limited, however, and referred mainly to the wife's property rights in slaves. In fact, the act was passed not so much to improve women's rights but rather to protect family property, particularly slaves, from attachment by creditors. . . .

. . . Although the Mississippi act altered the traditional common-law relationship between husband and wife by creating a wife's separate estate, it accomplished little else. The husband still retained the sole right to manage and control the slaves and to enjoy any profits from their labor.

On March 10, 1843, another southern state whose planters were burdened by debts and economic difficulties passed a married women's property act. Maryland's legislation was similar to that of Mississippi in dealing primarily with the wife's property in slaves, and appears to have been passed for much the same reason. Overall, both the Mississippi and the Maryland acts, and later the Arkansas act of 1846, were limited in scope and represented a conservative effort to safeguard family property rather than an attempt to expand women's rights. . . .

The conservative efforts to protect family property and safeguard the wife's original economic assets from the husband's creditors were apparent in other jurisdictions as well. In 1844 Michigan passed an act stipulating that any personal or real property a woman received either before or after her marriage remained her separate estate. Within the next two years, Ohio, Indiana, and Iowa passed more limited legislation declaring that a wife's real estate could not be seized for her husband's debts. . . .

States along the eastern seaboard began altering the common-law fiction of marital unity during the same period. New England legislatures moved hesitantly to give law courts the power to enforce equity principles. As in the South, much of this legislation attempted to mitigate indebtedness. . . .

In the North, however, other factors along with creditor-debtor relations were at work in securing the passage of the married women's property acts, the codification movement and growing demands for female equality chief among them. . . .

The complex interplay of factors which led to the implementation of the nation's first married women's property acts can best be illustrated by examining one jurisdiction in some detail. . . .

In New York the codification movement led "inexorably" to the early married women's property act. Following the Revolution, many citizens of the new republic began to object to the legal heritage derived from England. The English common law was regarded as a feudal, anachronistic system that had little applicability to an egalitarian society. Both the common law and, at times, equity were perceived as judge-made rules that subverted the will of the people. It was argued that law should be known and rational, approved by the people via state legislatures and available to all by codification. During the 1820s proponents of codification turned to the works of Jeremy Bentham, the English utilitarian philosopher, who argued that codified law would ensure the greatest good of the greatest number. Besides attacking the common law, other codifiers also objected to trusts and uses as the trappings of and for an aristocratic elite. During the 1820s and 1830s New York began a conscious effort to "defeudalize" its law of real property and weaken equity as a separate system of law, available primarily to the wealthy. . . .

Ernestine Rose, a twenty-six-year-old Polish immigrant who had been involved in at least two legal cases in Europe that centered on a woman's property rights, believed that the economic dominance afforded the husband by law was nothing short of criminal. In 1836 she began a long battle to educate the public and convince the New York State Legislature to remedy the proprietary disabilities of the married woman. She lectured and traveled throughout the state in an effort to stir public consciousness but was able to obtain only six women's signatures (including her own) for a petition she drafted demanding equal property rights for wives. Initially, Rose's effort met with indifference or ridicule from both men and women, but she stubbornly persisted in attacking the legal disabilities of wives. By 1840 she was joined by other feminists such as Paulina Wright Davis and Elizabeth Cady Stanton. At this time, however, Rose's work probably constituted the most important feminist agitation for the legislation. Between 1837 and 1848 when New York passed its married women's property act, Rose drafted several more petitions and helped keep the issue of equal property rights before the politicians. . . .

Despite the intent or impact of the legislation, women did have some effect. Liberal feminist reform impulses became increasingly important in the twelve years before the Civil War. The limitations in the early legislation as well as the overall disabilities suffered by married women in other jurisdictions came under increasing attack by the fledgling women's rights movement. . . .

During the 1850s New York feminists mounted intensive lobbying and organizational drives to obtain a wife's rights to her own wages, a right that Rose had indicted the American legal system for systematically denying her. Two other women played critical roles as well in achieving some redress for married women in New York—Susan B. Anthony and Elizabeth Cady Stanton. . . .

By 1860, the groundwork laid by Anthony, Rose, and Stanton began to show results. . . . In March 1860 Stanton addressed a joint session of the legislature, and the following day the Married Women's Earning Act became law. In addition, New York wives gained greater rights and received equal power and authority with their husbands in guardianship matters.

Limitations in the first married women's property acts spurred feminists to action in other states as well. . . .

By the outbreak of the Civil War, the American woman's legal status and her corresponding proprietary disabilities differed in each jurisdiction. While generalizations need to be tested by systematic studies of each state, overall, northern wives had obtained more redress in their traditional legal disabilities than had southern wives. This rough geographical breakdown reinforces the supposition that the early women's rights movement had some connection with the most liberal legislation. At this time, the women's rights movement was primarily a northern phenomenon. Certainly feminist efforts were important in changing the original and tentative acts in the North. . . .

After the Civil War, feminists continued to fight for additional legislation for equality, although as in the earlier period, legislation was not passed solely in response to feminism. . . .

Despite such efforts, the battle for female legal and economic equality was far from won and seemed in abeyance, especially after the 1870s as the women's rights movement increasingly emphasized suffrage as the panacea for sex-based inequality. Ironically, the married women's property acts helped fuel and intensify the drive for the vote, often at the cost of obtaining other reforms for women. . . .

STUDY QUESTIONS

1. What aspects of the doctrine of coverture were modified by the different statutes? What aspects were not modified?
2. What motivated the states to adopt these changes? What role did feminists play?

One of the initiatives that feminists pressed after the Civil War was the elimination of restrictions on women's access to the professions. Myra Bradwell pressed this point in the form of a constitutional challenge before the U.S. Supreme Court. Bradwell, a feminist active in women's suffrage organizations, was the founder and editor of an important legal publication, the *Chicago Legal News*. Herself the beneficiary of special legislation chartering the paper and permitting her to contract, she was instrumental in obtaining legislation eliminating women's disabilities. She passed the Illinois bar exam in 1869 only to be denied admission to the practice of law by the Supreme Court of Illinois on the grounds that, under the law of that state, females were not eligible to practice law. Bradwell appealed that decision to the U.S. Supreme Court, arguing that the state of Illinois had violated her rights under the Fourteenth Amendment by denying one of her privileges of citizenship, viz., the privilege of practicing law. Writing for the Court, Justice Miller rejected her claim and held that the practice of law is not a privilege of citizenship protected by the Fourteenth Amendment. Justice Bradley concurred in the result but for different reasons. Justice Bradley's concurring opinion in *Bradwell* is a classic statement of the separate spheres ideology that had long been used to legitimate the exclusion of women from opportunities outside the home.

Bradwell v. Illinois
Supreme Court of the United States, 1873.
83 U.S. 130, 21 L.Ed. 442.

Mr. Justice MILLER delivered the opinion of the court.

The fourteenth amendment declares that citizens of the United States are citizens of the State within which they reside; therefore the plaintiff was, at the time of making her application, a citizen of the United States and a citizen of the State of Illinois.

In regard to that amendment counsel for the plaintiff in this court truly says that there are certain privileges and immunities which belong to a citizen of the United States as such; otherwise it would be nonsense for the fourteenth amendment to prohibit a State from abridging them, and he proceeds to argue that admission to the bar of a State of a person who possesses the requisite learning and character is one of those which a State may not deny.

In this latter proposition we are not able to concur with counsel. We agree with him that there are privileges and immunities belonging to citizens of the United States, in that relation and character, and that it is these and these alone which a State is forbidden to abridge. But the right to admission to practice in the courts of a State is not one of them. This right in no sense depends on citizenship of the United States. It has not, as far as we know, ever been made in any State, or in any case, to depend on citizenship at all. Certainly many prominent and distinguished lawyers have been admitted to practice, both in the State and Federal courts, who were not citizens of the United States or of any State. But, on whatever basis this right may be placed, so far as it can have any relation to citizenship at all, it would seem that, as to the courts of a State, it would relate to citizenship of the State, and as to Federal courts, it would relate to citizenship of the United States.

The opinion just delivered in the *Slaughter-House Cases* renders elaborate argument in the present case unnecessary; for, unless we are wholly and radically mistaken in the principles on which those cases are decided, the right to control and regulate the granting of license to practice law in the courts of a State is one of those powers which are not transferred for its protection to the Federal government, and its exercise is in no manner governed or controlled by citizenship of the United States in the party seeking such license.

Judgment affirmed.

Mr. Justice BRADLEY:

I concur in the judgment of the court in this case, by which the judgment of the Supreme Court of Illinois is affirmed, but not for the reasons specified in the opinion just read. . . .

The claim that, under the fourteenth amendment of the Constitution, which declares that no State shall make or enforce any law which shall abridge the privileges and immunities of citizens of the United States, the statute law of Illinois, or the common law prevailing in that State, can no longer be set up as a barrier against the right of females to pursue any lawful employment for a livelihood (the practice of law included), assumes that it is one of the privileges and immunities of women as citizens to engage in any and every profession, occupation, or employment in civil life.

It certainly cannot be affirmed, as an historical fact, that this has ever been established as one of the fundamental privileges and immunities of the sex. On the contrary, the civil law, as well as nature herself, has always recognized a wide difference in the respective spheres and destinies of man and woman. Man is, or should

be, woman's protector and defender. The natural and proper timidity and delicacy which belongs to the female sex evidently unfits it for many of the occupations of civil life. The constitution of the family organization, which is founded in the divine ordinance, as well as in the nature of things, indicates the domestic sphere as that which properly belongs to the domain and functions of womanhood. The harmony, not to say identity, of interests and views which belong, or should belong, to the family institution is repugnant to the idea of a woman adopting a distinct and independent career from that of her husband. So firmly fixed was this sentiment in the founders of the common law that it became a maxim of that system of jurisprudence that a woman had no legal existence separate from her husband, who was regarded as her head and representative in the social state; and, notwithstanding some recent modifications of this civil status, many of the special rules of law flowing from and dependent upon this cardinal principle still exist in full force in most States. One of these is, that a married woman is incapable, without her husband's consent, of making contracts which shall be binding on her or him. This very incapacity was one circumstance which the Supreme Court of Illinois deemed important in rendering a married woman incompetent fully to perform the duties and trusts that belong to the office of an attorney and counsellor.

It is true that many women are unmarried and not affected by any of the duties, complications, and incapacities arising out of the married state, but these are exceptions to the general rule. The paramount destiny and mission of woman are to fulfil the noble and benign offices of wife and mother. This is the law of the Creator. And the rules of civil society must be adapted to the general constitution of things, and cannot be based upon exceptional cases.

The humane movements of modern society, which have for their object the multiplication of avenues for woman's advancement, and of occupations adapted to her condition and sex, have my heartiest concurrence. But I am not prepared to say that it is one of her fundamental rights and privileges to be admitted into every office and position, including those which require highly special qualifications and demanding special responsibilities. In the nature of things it is not every citizen of every age, sex, and condition that is qualified for every calling and position. It is the prerogative of the legislator to prescribe regulations founded on nature, reason, and experience for the due admission of qualified persons to professions and callings demanding special skill and confidence. This fairly belongs to the police power of the State; and, in my opinion, in view of the peculiar characteristics, destiny, and mission of woman, it is within the province of the legislature to ordain what offices, positions, and callings shall be filled and discharged by men, and shall receive the benefit of those energies and responsibilities, and that decision and firmness which are presumed to predominate in the sterner sex.

For these reasons I think that the laws of Illinois now complained of are not obnoxious to the charge of abridging any of the privileges and immunities of citizens of the United States.

STUDY QUESTIONS

1. What assumption did Justice Bradley detect behind Bradwell's Fourteenth Amendment claim? Why might that have seemed preposterous at the time?
2. What reasons were given by Justice Bradley for rejecting that assumption? What kinds of differences did he identify between the sexes? Were they physical, social, or legal? Why did he consider these differences relevant in evaluating the assumption in question? Why did he accept the view that men and women belong to different spheres and have different destinies?
3. Which of these lines of reasoning seem most appropriate for a court to rely upon? Least appropriate? Which, if any, actually applied to Myra Bradwell?

A third feminist campaign was for suffrage. This objective eventually was achieved but at great cost. Having failed to gain explicit protections for women in the Fourteenth and Fifteenth Amendments, the more militant National Women's Suffrage Association (NWSA) pursued the legal argument that women were nevertheless enfranchised by those amendments. The argument's dramatic introduction by feminist and radical Victoria Woodhull at a congressional hearing in 1871 sparked a NWSA campaign for its recognition by congressional act or judicial decision. As part of that campaign, Susan B. Anthony and thirteen other women voted in Rochester, New York, on November 5, 1872. They were arrested and charged with the violation of a federal statute making it a crime for anyone to vote "without the lawful right to vote." At her trial, Anthony argued that by restricting the right to vote to male citizens, the state of New York had violated her rights as guaranteed by the Fourteenth Amendment. The court found her guilty on the ground that "[t]he Fourteenth Amendment gives no right to a woman to vote. . . ." *U.S. v. Anthony,* 24 Fed. Cas. 829, 831 (1873). The verdict could not be appealed because the judge declined to enforce his order that Anthony pay a fine of one hundred dollars.

Virginia Minor, who ironically had sought to interest the NWSA in the constitutional argument in 1869, carried the issue to the U.S. Supreme Court after she was barred from voting in the fall election of 1872. She argued that the state of Missouri had violated her rights under the Fourteenth Amendment as a person born or naturalized in the United States and therefore entitled to the privileges and immunities of national citizenship. The right to vote, she argued, is a privilege of citizenship. The Court, in rejecting her claim, admitted that women are citizens but insisted that not all citizens have the right to vote. In doing so, the Court asserted in effect that women enjoy a special class of citizenship—a second class.

Minor v. Happersett

Supreme Court of the United States, 1875.
88 U.S. 162, 22 L.Ed. 627.

The Chief Justice delivered the opinion of the court.

The question is presented in this case, whether, since the adoption of the fourteenth amendment, a woman, who is a citizen of the United States and of the State of Missouri, is a voter in that State, notwithstanding the provision of the constitution and laws of the State, which confine the right of suffrage to men alone.

It is contended that the provisions of the constitution and laws of the State of Missouri which confine the right of suffrage and registration therefore to men, are in violation of the Constitution of the United States, and therefore void. The argument is, that as a woman, born or naturalized in the United States and subject to the jurisdiction thereof, is a citizen of the United States and of the State in which she resides, she has the right of suffrage as one of the privileges and immunities of her citizenship, which the State cannot by its laws or constitution abridge.

There is no doubt that women may be citizens. They are persons, and by the fourteenth amendment "all persons born or naturalized in the United States and subject to the jurisdiction thereof" are expressly declared to be "citizens of the United States and of the State wherein they reside." But, in our opinion, it did not need this amendment to give them that position.

If the right of suffrage is one of the necessary privileges of a citizen of the United States, then the constitution and laws of Missouri confining it to men are in violation of the Constitution of the United States, as amended, and consequently void. The direct question is, therefore, presented whether all citizens are necessarily voters.

The Constitution does not define the privileges and immunities of citizens. For that definition we must look elsewhere. In this case we need not determine what they are, but only whether suffrage is necessarily one of them.

It certainly is nowhere made so in express terms. [The Court then outlined the voting restrictions in effect at the time that the Fourteenth Amendment was adopted.] . . .

The amendment did not add to the privileges and immunities of a citizen. It simply furnished an additional guaranty for the protection of such as he already had. No new voters were necessarily made by it. . . .

In this condition of the law in respect to suffrage in the several States it cannot for a moment be doubted that if it had been intended to make all citizens of the United States voters, the framers of the Constitution would not have left it to implication. So important a change in the condition of citizenship as it actually existed, if intended, would have been expressly declared. . . .

But we have already sufficiently considered the proof found upon the inside of the Constitution. That upon the outside is equally effective.

The Constitution was submitted to the States for adoption in 1787, and was ratified by nine States in 1788, and finally by the thirteen original States in 1790. Vermont was the first new State admitted to the Union, and it came in under a constitution which conferred the right of suffrage only upon men of the full age of twenty-one years, having resided in the State for the space of one whole year next before the election, and who were of quiet and peaceable behavior. This was in 1791. The next year, 1792, Kentucky followed with a constitution confining the right of suffrage to free male citizens of the age of twenty-one years who had resided in the State two years or in the county in which they offered to vote one year next before the election. Then followed Tennessee, in 1796, with voters of freemen of the age of twenty-one years and upwards, possessing a freehold in the county wherein they may vote, and being inhabitants of the State or freemen being inhabitants of any one county in the State six months immediately preceding the day of election. But we need not particularize further. No new State has ever been admitted to the Union which has conferred the right of suffrage upon women, and this has never been considered a valid objection to her admission. On the contrary, as is claimed in the argument, the right of suffrage was withdrawn from women as early as 1807 in the State of New Jersey, without any attempt to obtain the interference of the United States to prevent it. Since then the governments of the insurgent States have been reorganized under a requirement that before their representatives could be admitted to seats in Congress they must have adopted new constitutions, republican in form. In no one of these constitutions was suffrage conferred upon women, and yet the States have all been restored to their original position as States in the Union. . . .

Certainly, if the courts can consider any question settled, this is one. For nearly ninety years the people have acted upon the idea that the Constitution, when it conferred citizenship, did not necessarily confer the right of suffrage. If uniform practice long continued can settle the construction of so important an instrument as the Constitution of the United States confessedly is, most certainly it has been done here. Our province is to decide what the law is, not to declare what it should be.

We have given this case the careful consideration its importance demands. If the law is wrong, it ought to be changed; but the power for that is not with us. The arguments addressed to us bearing upon such a view of the subject may perhaps be sufficient to induce those having the power, to make the alteration, but they ought not to be permitted to influence our judgment in determining the present rights of the parties now litigating before us. No argument as to woman's need of suffrage can be considered. We can only act upon her rights as they exist. It is not for us to look at the hardship of withholding. Our duty is at an end if we find it is within the power of a State to withhold.

Being unanimously of the opinion that the Constitution of the United States does not confer the right of suffrage upon any one, and that the constitutions and laws of the several States which commit that important trust to men alone are not necessarily void, we

Affirm the judgment.

STUDY QUESTIONS

1. What reasons did the Court cite in support of its ruling that the right to vote is not a right of citizenship? That women do not have a right to vote? Do these reasons appear sufficient to justify the Court's decision?
2. Was the Chief Justice correct in saying that the duty of the Court is at an end when it finds what the law is? What are the alternatives, particularly where it seems clear that the provision in question was not originally intended to give the relief sought?
3. The Court handed down its decision in *Bradwell* two years before *Minor*. What effect do you suppose the feminists' failure to have specific guarantees for women included in the Civil War Amendments had on the justices' decision making process in these cases?

The Court's emphasis in *Minor* on the parallel between state and federal constitutional experience may have been overdrawn. While it was true in 1875 that no "new" states had ever extended the franchise to women, the same was not true of the original states. In the colonial period, unmarried women with enough property had the legal right to vote on local issues. All of the original states, except New Jersey, disenfranchised women when they drafted their first state constitutions. New Jersey did so, as the Court noted, in 1807. It is also worth noting that two new states admitted after the decision in *Minor* but before the adoption of the Nineteenth Amendment extended the franchise to women from their inception—Wyoming (1890) and Utah (1896).

The women's rights movement in the late nineteenth century was split into two camps. The more militant National Women's Suffrage Association, led by Elizabeth

Cady Stanton, predominated until the turn of the century. It was convinced that a complete transformation of the patriarchy that placed women in a separate sphere subordinate to men, indeed incorporated them into their husbands, had to take place if women were ever to be emancipated. To this end, it argued that women are the same as men in all relevant respects, and therefore no basis exists for treating women as separate and inferior. To the NWSA, the franchise was an incidental ingredient in the larger revolutionary package. The strategy and rhetoric of the NWSA so provoked the political mainstream that the women's rights program was perceived as radical. As such, it became political suicide for a public figure to be associated with the movement.

The feminist agenda began to unravel in the final decades of the century. The union, in 1890, of the NWSA with the more conservative American Women's Suffrage Association to form the National American Women's Suffrage Association (NAWSA) was a key moment for two developments within the movement. Unable to achieve consensus among themselves on the broader agenda of reform, feminists increasingly narrowed their objectives to the one thing that all agreed upon, viz., the vote. They came increasingly to substitute considerations of expediency for the appeal for equal treatment that had informed feminist aspirations since the Grimké sisters and the Declaration of Sentiments in mid-century. This second development continues to be a source of grave disappointment, as the following selection indicates.

The Rising Influence of Racism

Angela Y. Davis. *Women, Race & Class.* New York: Random House, 1983. Pp. 111-19.

Susan B. Anthony was never lacking in praises for Frederick Douglass, consistently reminding people that he was the first man to publicly advocate the enfranchisement of women. She considered him a lifetime honorary member of her suffrage organization. Yet, as Anthony explained [in conversation with Ida B.] Wells, she pushed Douglass aside for the sake of recruiting white Southern women into the movement for woman suffrage.

> In our conventions . . . he was the honored guest who sat on our platform and spoke at our gatherings. But when the . . . Suffrage Association went to Atlanta, Georgia, knowing the feeling of the South with regard to Negro participation on

> equality with whites, I myself asked Mr. Douglass not to come. I did not want to subject him to humiliation, and *I did not want anything to get in the way of bringing the southern white women into our suffrage association.* [Davis's emphasis]

In this particular conversation with Ida B. Wells, Anthony went on to explain that she had also refused to support the efforts of several Black women who wanted to form a branch of the suffrage association. She did not want to awaken the anti-Black hostility of her white Southern members, who might withdraw from the organization if Black women were admitted.

> "And you think I was wrong in so doing?" she asked. I answered uncompromisingly yes, for I felt that although she may have made gains for suffrage, she had also confirmed white women in their attitude of segregation.

This conversation between Ida B. Wells and Susan B. Anthony took place in 1894. Anthony's self-avowed capitulation to racism "on the ground of expediency" characterized her public stance on this issue until she resigned in 1900 from the presidency of the National American Woman Suffrage Association. When Wells admonished Anthony for legitimizing the Southern white women's commitment to segregation, the underlying question was far more consequential than Anthony's individual attitude. Racism was objectively on the rise during this period and the rights and lives of Black people were at stake. By 1894 the disfranchisement of Black people in the South, the legal system of segregation and the reign of lynch law were already well established. More than at any other time since the Civil War, this was an era demanding consistent and principled protests against racism. The increasingly influential "expediency" argument proposed by Anthony and her colleagues was a feeble justification for the suffragists' indifference to the pressing requirements of the times.

[Although other feminists had taken the expediency course during the years since the Civil War,] it was not until the last decade of the nineteenth century that the woman suffrage campaign began to definitively accept the fatal embrace of white supremacy. . . . In 1892 Elizabeth Cady Stanton had grown disillusioned about the ballot's potential power to liberate women and ceded the presidency of the National American Woman Suffrage Association to her colleague Susan B. Anthony. During the second year of Anthony's term the NAWSA passed [the following resolution].

> *Resolved*. That without expressing any opinion on the proper qualifications for voting, we call attention to the significant facts that in every State there are more women who can read and write than the whole number of illiterate male voters; more white women who can read and write than all negro voters; more American women who can read and write than all foreign voters; so that the enfranchisement of such women would settle the vexed question of rule by illiteracy, whether of home-grown or foreign-born production. . . .

In passing the 1893 resolution, the suffragists might as well have announced that if they, as white women of the middle classes and bourgeoisie, were given the power of the vote, they would rapidly subdue the three main elements of the U.S. working class: Black people, immigrants and the uneducated native white workers. . . .

During this 1899 convention of the NAWSA a revealing contradiction emerged. . . . [A] Black woman's appeal for a resolution against Jim Crow went entirely unheeded. The Black suffragist—Lottie Wilson Jackson—was admitted to the convention because the host state was Michigan, one of the few chapters welcoming Black women into the suffrage association. During her train trip to the convention Lottie Jackson had suffered the indignities of the railroads' segregationist policies. Her resolution was very simple: "That colored women ought not to be compelled to ride in smoking cars, and that suitable accommodations should be provided for them."

As the convention's presiding officer, Susan B. Anthony brought the discussion on the Black woman's resolution to a close. Her comments assured the overwhelming defeat of the resolution:

> We women are a helpless disfranchised class. Our hands are tied. While we are in this condition, it is not for us to go passing resolutions against railroad corporations or anybody else.

The meaning of this incident was far deeper than the issue of whether or not to send an official letter protesting a railroad company's racist policies. In refusing to defend their Black sister, the NAWSA symbolically abandoned the entire Black people at the moment of their most intense suffering since emancipation. This gesture definitively established the suffrage association as a potentially reactionary political force which would cater to the demands of white supremacy. . . .

Susan B. Anthony should not, of course, be held personally responsible for the suffrage movement's racist errors. But she was the movement's most outstanding leader at the turn of the century—and her presumably "neutral" public posture toward the fight for Black equality did indeed bolster the influence of racism within the NAWSA. Had Anthony seriously reflected on the findings of her friend Ida B. Wells, she might have realized that a noncommittal stand on racism implied that lynchings and mass murders by the thousands could be considered a neutral issue. . . .

STUDY QUESTIONS

1. What explanations did Stanton and Anthony give for adopting a "neutral public posture" on racial issues? Did Davis reject their reasons as incorrect or irrelevant? Did, indeed could, Stanton and Anthony deny Ida Wells's criticism?

2. What alternatives were available at the time? Did the abandonment of the equal treatment argument in favor of an appeal to expediency itself abandon a fundamental feature of feminism as we understand it?

By the turn of the century, after most members of the earlier feminist generation had died or become less active, the NAWSA focused on suffrage as the key to achieving complete emancipation and was committed to a strategy of reform rather than confrontation. Under the leadership of Carrie Chapman Catt and Jane Addams, the NAWSA argued for the extension of the franchise to women not because women are essentially the same but because women are essentially different from men. The special influence of sensitive, nurturing, spiritual creatures is needed in governmental matters just as it is needed in the home. They showed that the vote was compatible with, indeed a natural extension of the role of women in the home. The strategy and rhetoric of the women's rights movement under the leadership of Catt and Addams persuaded the public that the suffrage movement was middle-of-the-road and, therefore, politically congenial.

Catt designed a grassroots campaign for achieving the franchise. The campaign was well organized, timed, and executed. Beginning with Washington in 1910, six states amended their constitutions to extend the franchise to women. By 1919, twenty-six states had petitioned Congress to enact a similar amendment to the federal constitution. Congress passed the Nineteenth Amendment that same year by a wide margin. It was ratified within fourteen months with a minimum of controversy.

From the turn of the century, the movement concentrated its efforts on obtaining the vote as the key to making progress on the remaining issues identified in the Seneca Falls Declaration. It soon became apparent that this was not to be. By the mid-1920s, it was clear that women were not voting in a block. Indeed, there was little or no difference between the voting patterns of women and men.

It was also clear by the mid-1920s that after suffrage was obtained, the coalition that had fought so long and hard to achieve it had collapsed. The demise of the first feminist movement is still the subject of scholarly debate. Some argue that it expired because of the absence of an overarching agenda on which feminists could agree. Florence Kelley continued to emphasize the need for protective legislation; the National Women's Party espoused the Equal Rights Amendment, and African-American feminists emphasized the struggle against racial discrimination. Others argue that the first feminist movement collapsed long before the mid-1920s. In this view, it had passed from the scene when a disheartened leadership stopped arguing for a single moral standing for men and women and settled for arguments from expediency. This abandoned both the principles articulated by the Grimkés and the Seneca Falls Convention and solidarity with working-class women, women of color, and men who shared their convictions.

III. JUSTIFYING DIFFERENTIAL TREATMENT

During the late nineteenth century, in the *Bradwell* and *Minor* decisions, the Supreme Court approved limitations on women's employment opportunities and on their full participation in the responsibilities of citizenship. During the first six decades of the twentieth century, the federal courts continued along these same lines, although they tended to state more specific reasons. Two types of argument generally were used to justify sex-based laws during that period. First, restrictions on employment opportunities were frequently approved because they were thought necessary to protect women from workplace hazards that only men were believed capable of managing safely. Second, limitations on women's responsibilities as citizens were often approved as compensating for the fact that women bear special burdens not shared by men. Both rationales had been used over the ages to justify confining women to subordinate and dependent positions.

The protectionist rationale was developed first. At the turn of the century, the working conditions of most American workers were widely regarded as wretched. The grueling hours spent in filthy and dangerous workplaces by men, women, and children had sparked a drive for legislation at the state level that would shield workers from such gross exploitation by their employers. This drive was blocked by a Supreme Court decision that declared that states may not regulate working conditions in the interest of the general welfare, for that would be "an illegal interference with the rights of individuals to make contracts." This 1905 decision, *Lochner v. New York,* 198 U.S. 45, struck down a New York law limiting the hours of bakers to sixty per week or ten per day. The Court reasoned that the state's limitation of the hours of work denied workers the opportunity to contract for more hours if it suited their needs and therefore denied them of liberty without due process of law in violation of the Fourteenth Amendment.

The decision in *Lochner* did not stop the drive for state regulation of working conditions but only caused it to veer from its more extensive objective of securing safer working conditions for workers generally. It turned to gaining protection, if not for all workers, then at least for the women workers. Within three years of the *Lochner* decision, nineteen states had enacted laws setting maximum hours and/or prohibiting night work for women. The challenge to these laws came before the Supreme Court in the case of *Muller v. Oregon.* Carl Muller, the operator of a laundry that required a female employee to work more than the state-mandated maximum of ten hours in any one day, was tried, found guilty, and fined ten dollars by an Oregon court. He appealed, arguing that *Lochner* denied the state authority to interfere with his liberty of contract and that of his employee.

The state's argument in defense of the statute was supported by an *amicus curiae* (friend of the court) brief prepared by Louis Brandeis, Josephine and Pauline Gold-mark, and Florence Kelley on behalf of the National Consumer League (NCL), a middle- and upper-class organization that actively fought for sex-based protective legislation. The brief argued that the Oregon statute was well within the state's legitimate police powers because there existed reasonable grounds to believe that women's health in particular was severely jeopardized by long work days. The evidence offered in support of this contention consisted of a 113-page collection of short quotations that stressed women's special vulnerabilities and the implications of these for the well-being of family life. Although described in the brief as "facts of common knowledge," the passages were mainly anecdotal reports interwoven with expert opinion. The following selections illustrate the flavor of this famous document.

The Brandeis Brief

Louis D. Brandeis and
Josephine Goldmark.
Women in Industry. New York: Arno
& The New York Times, 1969.
Pp. 22-3, 45-6, 50-1.

*HYGIENE OF OCCUPATION IN REFER-
ENCE HANDBOOK OF THE MEDICAL
SCIENCES. GEORGE M. PRICE, M.D.,
MEDICAL SANITARY INSPECTOR,
HEALTH DEPARTMENT OF THE CITY
OF NEW YORK. VOL. VI.*

In many industries . . . female labor is very largely
employed; and the effect of work on them is very
detrimental to health. The injurious influences of
female labor are due to the following factors:
(1) The comparative physical weakness of the female organism; (2) The greater predisposition to
harmful and poisonous elements in the trades;
(3) The periodical semi-pathological state of
health of women; (4) The effect of labor on the
reproductive organs; and (5) The effects on the
offspring. As the muscular organism of woman is
less developed than that of man, it is evident that
those industrial occupations which require intense, constant, and prolonged muscular efforts
must become highly detrimental to their health.
This is shown in the general debility, anæmia,
chlorosis, and lack of tone in most women who
are compelled to work in factories and in shops
for long periods.

The increased susceptibility of women to industrial poisons and to diseases has been demonstrated by a great number of observers. The
female organism, especially when young, offers
very little resistance to the inroads of disease and
to the various dangerous elements of certain
trades. Hirt says, "It must be conceded that certain
trades affect women a great deal more injuriously
than men;" and he mentions, among others, the
effects of lead, mercury, phosphorus, and other
poisons. Even where there are no special noxious
elements, work may produce, as already mentioned, harmful effects on the health of women;
but when to the general effects of industrial oc-

cupation are added the dangers of dust, fumes,
and gases, we find that the female organism suc-
cumbs very readily, as compared with that of the
male. . . .

It has been estimated that out of every one
hundred days women are in a semi-pathological
state of health for from fourteen to sixteen days.
The natural congestion of the pelvic organs during menstruation is augmented and favored by
work on sewing-machines and other industrial
occupations necessitating the constant use of the
lower part of the body. Work during these periods
tends to induce chronic congestion of the uterus
and appendages, and dysmenorrhœa and flexion
of the uterus are well known affections of working girls. (Page 321).

*THE CASE FOR THE FACTORY ACTS.
EDITED BY MRS. SIDNEY WEBB. LON-
DON, 1901.*

If working long and irregular hours, accepting a
bare subsistence wage and enduring insanitary
conditions tended to increase women's physical
strength and industrial skill—if these conditions
of unregulated industry even left unimpaired
the woman's natural stock of strength and
skill—we might regard factory legislation as
irrelevant. But as a matter of fact a whole
century of evidence proves exactly the contrary.
To leave women's labor unregulated by law
means inevitably to leave it exposed to terribly
deteriorating influences. The woman's lack of
skill and lack of strength is made worse by lack
of regulation. And there is still a further deterioration. Any one who has read the evidence
given in the various inquiries into the Sweating
System will have been struck by the invariable
coincidence of a low standard of regularity,
sobriety, and morality, with the conditions to
which women, under free competition, are exposed. (Page 209.)

*LABOR LAWS FOR WOMEN IN GERMANY.
DR. ALICE SALOMON. PUBLISHED BY
THE WOMEN'S INDUSTRIAL COUNCIL.
LONDON, 1907.*

A study of the laws relating to female labor
reveals that it has been the special aim of the

legislators to protect and preserve the health of the women in their character as wives and as the mothers of future generations. On the one hand, the regulations are intended to prevent injury to health through over-long hours, or the resumption of work too soon after confinement, often the cause of serious illness which may render the patient incapable of bearing healthy offspring. . . . But if work in the factory be a necessity for women—even for married ones—it is all the more desirable that protective legislation should be so extended and worked out in such detail as to ensure the fullest attainment of its object, viz.: protection for the health of the female working population, as well as for the family and the home. (Page 5.)

STUDY QUESTIONS

1. What reasons are given for believing that long, hard hours have a greater impact on women workers than upon men workers in the same circumstances? Do these statements appear to rely on well-researched, factual information about women?
2. What consequences, beside those on women's health, are of concern to these authorities?
3. In *Lochner,* the Court was content to allow workers to look after their own health and safety interests when bargaining for their labor. Does the demand for special protection of women workers imply less confidence in women's ability to look after their own well-being?

Muller v. Oregon

Supreme Court of the United States, 1908.
208 U.S. 412, 28 S.Ct. 324, 52 L.Ed. 551.

Mr. Justice BREWER delivered the opinion of the court.

On February 19, 1903, the legislature of the state of Oregon passed an act (Session Laws 1903, p. 148) the first section of which is in these words:

"Sec. 1. That no female (shall) be employed in any mechanical establishment, or factory, or laundry in this state more than ten hours during any one day. The hours of work may be so arranged as to permit the employment of females at any time so that they shall not work more than ten hours during the twenty-four hours of any one day."

Sec. 3 made a violation of the provisions of the prior sections a misdemeanor subject to a fine of not less than $10 nor more than $25.

On September 18, 1905, an information was filed in the circuit court of the state for the county of Multnomah, charging that the defendant "on the 4th day of September, A.D. 1905, in the county of Multnomah and state of Oregon, then and there being the owner of a laundry, known as the Grand Laundry, in the city of Portland, and the employer of females therein, did then and there unlawfully permit and suffer one Joe Haselbock, he, the said Joe Haselbock, then and there being an overseer, superintendent, and agent of said Curt Muller, in the said Grand Laundry, to require a female, to wit, one Mrs. E. Gotcher, to work more than ten hours in said laundry on said 4th day of September, A.D. 1905, contrary to the statutes in such cases made and provided, and against the peace and dignity of the state of Oregon."

A trial resulted in a verdict against the defendant, who was sentenced to pay a fine of $10. The supreme court of the state affirmed the conviction, whereupon the case was brought here on writ of error.

The single question is the constitutionality of the statute under which the defendant was convicted, so far as it affects the work of a female in a laundry. . . .

We held in *Lochner v. New York* that a law providing that no laborer shall be required or permitted to work in bakeries more than sixty hours in a week or ten hours in a day was not as to men a legitimate exercise of the police power of the state, but an unreasonable, unnecessary, and arbitrary interference with the right and liberty of the individual to contract in relation to his labor, and as such was in conflict with, and void under, the Federal Constitution. That decision is invoked by plaintiff in error as decisive of the question before us. But this assumes that the difference between the sexes does not justify a different rule respecting a restriction of the hours of labor.

In patent cases counsel are apt to open the argument with a discussion of the state of the art. It may not be amiss, in the present case, before examining the constitutional question, to notice the course of legislation, as well as expressions of opinion from other than judicial sources. In the brief filed by Mr. Louis D. Brandeis for the defendant in error is a very copious collection of all these matters. . . .

The legislation and opinions referred to in the margin . . . are significant of a widespread belief that woman's physical structure, and the functions she performs in consequence thereof, justify special legislation restricting or qualifying the conditions under which she should be permitted to toil. Constitutional questions, it is true, are not settled by even a consensus of present public opinion, for it is the peculiar value of a written constitution that it places in unchanging form limitations upon legislative action, and thus gives a permanence and stability to popular government which otherwise would be lacking. At the same time, when a question of fact is debated and debatable, and the extent to which a special constitutional limitation goes is affected by the truth in respect to that fact, a widespread and long-continued belief concerning it is worthy of consideration. We take judicial cognizance of all matters of general knowledge. . . .

That woman's physical structure and the performance of maternal functions place her at a disadvantage in the struggle for subsistence is obvious. This is especially true when the burdens of motherhood are upon her. Even when they are not, by abundant testimony of the medical fraternity continuance for a long time on her feet at work, repeating this from day to day, tends to in-

jurious effects upon the body, and, as healthy mothers are essential to vigorous offspring, the physical well-being of woman becomes an object of public interest and care in order to preserve the strength and vigor of the race.

Still again, history discloses the fact that woman has always been dependent upon man. He established his control at the outset by superior physical strength, and this control in various forms, with diminishing intensity, has continued to the present. As minors, though not to the same extent, she has been looked upon in the courts as needing especial care that her rights may be preserved. Education was long denied her, and while now the doors of the schoolroom are opened and her opportunities for acquiring knowledge are great, yet even with that and the consequent increase of capacity for business affairs it is still true that in the struggle for subsistence she is not an equal competitor with her brother. Though limitations upon personal and contractual rights may be removed by legislation, there is that in her disposition and habits of life which will operate against a full assertion of those rights. She will still be where some legislation to protect her seems necessary to secure a real equality of right. Doubtless there are individual exceptions, and there are many respects in which she has an advantage over him; but looking at it from the viewpoint of the effort to maintain an independent position in life, she is not upon an equality. Differentiated by these matters from the other sex, she is properly placed in a class by herself, and legislation designed for her protection may be sustained, even when like legislation is not necessary for men, and could not be sustained. It is impossible to close one's eyes to the fact that she still looks to her brother and depends upon him. Even though all restrictions on political, personal, and contractual rights were taken away, and she stood, so far as statutes are concerned, upon an absolutely equal plane with him, it would still be true that she is so constituted that she will rest upon and look to him for protection: that her physical structure and a proper discharge of her maternal functions—having in view not merely her own health, but the well-being of the race—justify legislation to protect her from the greed as well as the passion of man. The limitations which this statute places upon her contractual powers, upon her right to agree with her employer as to the time she shall labor, are not imposed solely for her benefit, but also largely for the benefit of all. Many words cannot make this plainer. The two sexes differ in structure of body, in the functions to be performed by each, in the amount of physical strength, in the capacity for long continued labor, particularly when done standing, the influence of vigorous health upon the future well-being of the race, the self-reliance which enables one to assert full rights, and in the capacity to maintain the struggle for subsistence. This difference justifies a difference in legislation, and upholds that which is designed to compensate for some of the burdens which rest upon her. . . .

For these reasons, and without questioning in any respect the decision in *Lochner v. New York,* we are of the opinion that it cannot be adjudged that the act in question is in conflict with the Federal Constitution, so far as it respects the work of a female in a laundry, and

the judgment of the Supreme Court of Oregon is affirmed.

STUDY QUESTIONS

1. What differences between the sexes did the Court indicate are relevant in deciding whether a state may interfere with a woman's, but not a man's, liberty of contract? Are they physical, social, or legal differences? Compare these differences with those identified by Justice Bradley in *Bradwell.*
2. To what extent did the Court recognize that not all women share the characteristics that it attributes to them?
3. What interest did the Court assert a state has in protecting women from the hazards of long hours of arduous labor in an employment setting? Would that same argument be relevant to the long and arduous hours of labor that women perform in the home?
4. Does the distinctive reproductive function of men warrant different treatment?

In the wake of the *Muller* decision, states enacted legislation that limited women's employment opportunities in a variety of ways. Within the next nine years, for example, nineteen states passed laws restricting women's working day. As historian Alice Kessler-Harris points out, these restrictions contain many an irony.

> Regulations differed not only from state to state but from industry to industry within each state. Manufacturing and mercantile enterprises were the first statutory targets, with laundries and telegraph and telephone companies running a close second. Hotels, restaurants, and cabarets often escaped regulation entirely. Domestic service and agriculture, still the two leading female occupations and the most arduous, remained untouched.
>
> *Alice Kessler-Harris,* Out to Work: A History of Wage-Earning Women in the United States. *New York: Oxford University Press, 1982. Pp. 197-8.*

Another common technique for limiting the employment opportunities of women was to ban them from working nights in selected occupations. One such statute, a New York law prohibiting women from working in restaurants in cities between 10 P.M. and 6 A.M., was approved by the Supreme Court because "night work of the kind prohibited so injuriously affects the physical condition of women, and so threatens to impair their peculiar and natural functions, and so exposes them to the dangers and menaces incident to night life in large cities. . ." *Radice v. New York,* 264 U.S. 292 (1924). This language is clearly reminiscent of *Muller's* discussion of women's "physical structure," her "maternal functions," and her vulnerability to the "greed as well as the passion of man."

As is well recognized today, these "protective" regulations had two distinctive effects. On the one hand, they resulted in an immediate decrease in the weekly income of women who worked full-time outside the home. With fewer hours of work turned in at the same hourly wage rate, the result was less in the pay envelope. For women whose income was low to begin with, that decrease had to be offset by finding second jobs, such as doing the laundry for other families. On the other hand, women applicants for jobs became less attractive to prospective employers, because the law permitted men to be worked for more hours than women. By limiting the workdays and workweeks of women but not men, men's privileged situation in the American workplace became even more pronounced.

The strategy adopted by the NCL, Florence Kelley, Jane Addams, and other feminists who advocated "protective" legislation may have seemed worthwhile for the first nine years after the *Muller* decision. But then, in 1917, the Court approved maximum-hours laws for men (*Bunting v. Oregon,* 243 U.S. 426). The Court reached that decision based on arguments listing the hazards of long, arduous working hours for men without mentioning *Lochner. Bunting,* unlike *Muller,* however, was not followed by a flood of maximum-hour laws for men. Labor unions preferred organization as a strategy to protect their mainly male members and therefore did not press for further protective legislation.

Limiting the hours a person may work results in low take-home pay unless a minimum wage is established. Soon after *Muller,* Congress and the states began to enact minimum wage laws. They were immediately confronted by a Supreme Court that saw minimum wage laws as overt attempts to fix the price of labor. In 1923, the Court struck down a statute affecting the District of Columbia that fixed minimum wages for women and children (*Adkins v. Children's Hospital,* 261 U.S. 525). In distinguishing *Muller* and finding that woman's liberty of contract was now as great as man's, the Court emphasized recent legal developments concerning women's status. "In view of the great—not to say revolutionary—changes which have taken place since [*Muller*] in the contractual, political and civil status of women, culminating in the Nineteenth Amendment, it is not unreasonable to say that these differences [of physical structure, especially in respect of the maternal functions] have now come almost, if not quite, to the vanishing point."

Reasoning that there was no direct relationship between women's physical frailty and low wages, the Court declared the statute challenged in *Adkins* unconstitutional. This insensitivity to the actual circumstances of women workers combined with the Court's general willingness to invalidate state statutes regulating economic and social relations suggest that it might be well to take the Court's feminism with several grains of salt. Consider, for example, whether the Court could have upheld the statute in *Adkins* and extended its protection to men.

Beginning in 1934, after President Franklin Roosevelt's threat to expand the Court and fill it with more liberal justices, the Supreme Court granted greater deference to the judgment of legislatures. This change of posture showed itself in 1937 when, by a 5–4 decision, the Court overruled *Adkins* and approved a Washington state statute establishing a minimum wage for women and children. The case, *West Coast Hotel v. Parrish,* 300 U.S. 379, revived a principle announced in 1898 that a state may act to equalize inequalities of bargaining power between workers and employers. The majority went on to find, citing *Muller,* "that this established principle is peculiarly applicable in relation to the employment of women in whose protection the State has a special interest."

Statutes that excluded women altogether from certain occupations were commonplace until such practices were made unlawful by the Civil Rights Act of 1964.

The functions served by such restrictions were many: they reinforced the conventional view that a woman's place is in the home; they reduced the competition men faced in obtaining and holding jobs in affected professions; and they reduced the incidence of assaults on women by minimizing the occasions for women to work with men. The following decision, later disapproved in *Craig v. Boren* (see Chapter 2), illustrates these themes, as well as judicial attitudes at mid-century.

Goesaert v. Cleary

Supreme Court of the United States, 1948.
335 U.S. 464, 69 S.Ct. 198, 93 L.Ed. 163.

Mr. Justice FRANKFURTER delivered the opinion of the Court.

As part of the Michigan system for controlling the sale of liquor, bartenders are required to be licensed in all cities having a population of 50,000 or more, but no female may be so licensed unless she be "the wife or daughter of the male owner" of a licensed liquor establishment. The case is here on direct appeal from an order of the District Court of three judges . . . denying an injunction to restrain the enforcement of the Michigan law. The claim . . . is that Michigan cannot forbid females generally from being barmaids and at the same time make an exception in favor of the wives and daughters of the owners of liquor establishments. Beguiling as the subject is, it need not detain us long. To ask whether or not the Equal Protection of the Laws Clause of the Fourteenth Amendment barred Michigan from making the classification the State has made between wives and daughters of owners of liquor places and wives and daughters of nonowners, is one of those rare instances where to state the question is in effect to answer it.

We are, to be sure, dealing with a historic calling. We meet the ale-wife, sprightly and ribald, in Shakespeare, but centuries before him she played a role in the social life of England. The Fourteenth Amendment did not tear history up by the roots, and the regulation of the liquor traffic is one of the oldest and most untrammeled of legislative powers. Michigan could, beyond

question, forbid all women from working behind a bar. This is so despite the vast changes in the social and legal position of women. The fact that women may now have achieved the virtues that men have long claimed as their prerogatives and now indulge in vices that men have long practiced, does not preclude the States from drawing a sharp line between the sexes, certainly in such matters as the regulation of the liquor traffic. The Constitution does not require sociological insight, or shifting social standards, any more than it requires them to keep abreast of the latest scientific standards.

While Michigan may deny to all women opportunities for bartending, Michigan cannot play favorites among women without rhyme or reason. The Constitution in enjoining the equal protection of the laws upon States precludes irrational discrimination as between persons or groups of persons in the incidence of a law. But the Constitution does not require situations "which are different in fact or opinion to be treated in law as though they were the same." Since bartending by women may, in the allowable legislative judgment, give rise to moral and social problems against which it may devise preventive measures, the legislature need not go to the full length of prohibition if it believes that as to a defined group of females other factors are operating which either eliminate or reduce the moral and social problems otherwise calling for prohibition. Michigan evidently believes that the oversight assured through ownership of a bar by a barmaid's husband or father minimizes hazards that may confront a barmaid without such protecting oversight. This Court is certainly not in a position to gainsay such belief by the Michigan legislature. If it is entertainable, as we think it is, Michigan has not violated its duty to afford equal protection of its laws. We cannot cross-examine either actually or argumentatively the mind of Michigan legislators nor question their motives. Since the line they have drawn is not without a basis in reason, we cannot give ear to the suggestion that the real impulse behind this legislation was an unchivalrous desire of male bartenders to try to monopolize the calling.

It would be an idle parade of familiar learning to review the multitudinous cases in which the constitutional assurance of the equal protection of the laws has been applied. The generalities on this subject are not in dispute; their application turns peculiarly on the particular circumstances of a case. . . .Suffice it to say that "A statute is not invalid under the Constitution because it might have gone farther than it did, or because it may not succeed in bringing about the result that it tends to produce."

Nor is it unconstitutional for Michigan to withdraw from women the occupation of bartending because it allows women to serve as waitresses where liquor is dispensed. The District Court has sufficiently indicated the reasons that may have influenced the legislature in allowing women to be waitresses in a liquor establishment over which a man's ownership provides control. Nothing need be added to what was said below as to the other grounds on which the Michigan law was assailed.

Judgment affirmed.

Mr. Justice RUTLEDGE, with whom Mr. Justice DOUGLAS and Mr. Justice MURPHY join, dissenting.

While the equal protection clause does not require a legislature to achieve "abstract symmetry" or to classify with "mathematical nicety," that clause does require lawmakers to refrain from invidious distinctions of the sort drawn by the statute challenged in this case.

The statute arbitrarily discriminates between male and female owners of liquor establishments. A male owner, although he himself is always absent from his bar, may employ his wife and daughter as barmaids. A female owner may neither work as a barmaid herself nor employ her daughter in that position, even if a man is always present in the establishment to keep order. This inevitable result of the classification belies the assumption that the statute was motivated by a legislative solicitude for the moral and physical well-being of women who, but for the law, would be employed as barmaids. Since there could be no other conceivable justification for such discrimination against women owners of liquor establishments, the statute should be held invalid as a denial of equal protection.

STUDY QUESTIONS

1. To what "moral and social problems" was the Court referring? Who pays the cost of reducing the incidence of those problems? Did the Michigan statute "punish the victims"?
2. The Court refused even to consider that the statute was motivated by the desire to establish a male monopoly over the trade of bartending. Does that interpretation of the statutory objective seem more plausible than the one the Court adopted? Why did the Court refuse to even consider the alternative interpretation?

The dominant theme running through justifications given for differential treatment of women and men during the first half of the twentieth century was that of protection. Women were denied employment opportunities because they were believed to be too vulnerable to handle them safely and their "maternal function" was seen as too important to the survival of the species to leave such matters to individual choice. The foregoing cases illustrate that theme. A secondary justifying theme was that of compensation. Women were relieved of certain burdens of citizenship in order to compensate for or offset the heavier burdens they carry because of their "maternal functions."

The first decision to explicitly rely on the compensatory rationale came in 1937 in a case challenging a Georgia statute that exempted women from the payment of a poll tax. This type of tax, made unconstitutional by the Twenty-fourth Amendment that was ratified in 1964, was a device that served to deter poor people from voting. In upholding the statute, the Court declared that states may discriminate in favor of women by granting them special considerations that they deserve because of the special burdens associated with their reproductive role.

> The tax being upon persons, women may be exempted on the basis of special considerations to which they are naturally entitled. In view of burdens necessarily borne by them for the preservation of the race, the state reasonably may exempt them from poll taxes. The laws of Georgia declare the husband to be the head of the family and the wife to be subject to him. To subject her to the levy would be to add to his burden. *Breedlove v. Suttles*, 302 U.S. 277, 282 (1937).

The outcome in *Breedlove* does not seem, at first glance at least, to be lamentable. Who wouldn't welcome being excused from having to pay a tax? On the other hand, in *Breedlove*, as in *Minor*, the Court permitted a state to exclude women from one of the responsibilities of full citizenship. In the one case, the responsibility was paying a tax, in the other, voting. In this way, both decisions affirmed that women are second-class citizens. Seen in this light, *Breedlove* takes on a considerably more sinister coloration.

That interpretation is further bolstered when we notice the way that the Court, in *Breedlove*, saw the tax exemption as linked to the doctrine of coverture. According to that doctrine, the husband, as head of the family, is responsible in the eyes of the law for the obligations of the wife. By excusing women from this burden, the Court consciously acted to protect the doctrine of coverture. The decision that appeared to be a welcome courtesy to women in acknowledgement of their special needs turns out to be, on more thorough consideration, both one more nail in the coffin of second-class citizenship and part of the price that is paid for perpetuating the very system that creates the special needs that in turn warrant the special considerations.

As we have said, this way of justifying sex-based laws might be called a "compensatory" argument because such laws are represented as making up for the special burdens that women must bear "for the preservation of the race." By emphasizing that, as a result of their role in the bearing and raising of children, women assume special responsibilities not shared by men and by allowing women to be relieved of responsibilities relating to the conduct of public affairs in lieu of their duties in the home, the Court continued to give effect to the sexual division of labor in society.

Two decisions handed down during the 1960s, one by the Supreme Court, the other by a federal district court, illustrate both how attractive these "special considerations" can seem and how insidious they turn out to be. Both relate to excusing women from other burdens of full citizenship.

The right of a person charged in a criminal proceeding to a trial by an impartial jury is a cornerstone of American jurisprudence. Indeed, that right is guaranteed by the Sixth Amendment to the U.S. Constitution. Corresponding to that right is the duty of citizens to be available to serve on juries. Until the enactment of the Civil Rights Act of 1957, the inclusion or exclusion of women on federal juries depended upon whether they were eligible for jury service under the law of the state where the federal court sat. That act made women eligible for federal jury service even though ineligible under state law. States, however, were still permitted to exempt women from jury service. The following case, overturned in effect by *Taylor v. Louisiana*, 419 U.S. 522(1975), and *Duren v. Missouri*, 439 U.S. 357(1979), shows the rationale for this exemption.

Hoyt v. Florida

Supreme Court of the United States,
1961.
368 U.S. 57, 82 S.Ct. 159, 7 L.Ed.2d 118.

Mr. Justice HARLAN delivered the opinion of the Court.

Appellant, a woman, has been convicted in Hillsborough County, Florida, of second degree murder of her husband. On this appeal . . . from the Florida Supreme Court's affirmance of the judgment of conviction we noted probable jurisdiction to consider appellant's claim that her trial before an all-male jury violated rights assured by the Fourteenth Amendment. The claim is that such jury was the product of a state jury statute which works an unconstitutional exclusion of women from jury service

The jury law primarily in question is Fla Stat, 1959, § 40.01(1). This Act, which requires that grand and petit jurors be taken from "male and female" citizens of the State possessed of certain qualifications, contains the following proviso: "provided, however, that the name of no female person shall be taken for jury service unless said person has registered with the clerk of the circuit court her desire to be placed on the jury list."

Showing that since the enactment of the statute only a minimal number of women have so registered, appellant challenges the constitutionality of the statute both on its face and as applied in this case. For reasons now to follow we decide that both contentions must be rejected.

At the core of appellant's argument is the claim that the nature of the crime of which she was convicted peculiarly demanded the inclusion of persons of her own sex on the jury. She was charged with killing her husband by assaulting him with a baseball bat. An information was filed against her under Fla Stat, 1959, § 782.04, which punishes

as murder in the second degree "any act imminently dangerous to another, and evincing a depraved mind regardless of human life, although without any premeditated design to effect the death of any particular individual. . . ." As described by the Florida Supreme Court, the affair occurred in the context of a marital upheaval involving, among other things, the suspected infidelity of appellant's husband, and culminating in the husband's final rejection of his wife's efforts at reconciliation. It is claimed, in substance, that women jurors would have been more understanding or compassionate than men in assessing the quality of appellant's act and her defense of "temporary insanity."

Of course, these premises misconceive the scope of the right to an impartially selected jury assured by the Fourteenth Amendment. That right does not entitle one accused of crime to a jury tailored to the circumstances of the particular case, whether relating to the sex or other condition of the defendant, or to the nature of the charges to be tried. It requires only that the jury be indiscriminately drawn from among those eligible in the community for jury service, untrammeled by any arbitrary and systematic exclusions. The result of this appeal must therefore depend on whether such an exclusion of women from jury service has been shown.

In the selection of jurors Florida has differentiated between men and women in two respects. It has given women an absolute exemption from jury duty based solely on their sex, no similar exemption obtaining as to men. And it has provided for its effectuation in a manner less onerous than that governing exemptions exercisable by men: women are not to be put on the jury list unless they have voluntarily registered for such service; men, on the other hand, even if entitled to an exemption, are to be included on the list unless they have filed a written claim of exemption as provided by law.

In neither respect can we conclude that Florida's statute is not "based on some reasonable classification," and that it is thus infected with unconstitutionality. Despite the enlightened emancipation of women from the restrictions and protections of bygone years, and their entry into many parts of community life formerly considered to be reserved to men, woman is still regarded as the center of home and family life. We cannot say that it is constitutionally impermissible for a State, acting in pursuit of the general welfare, to conclude that a woman should be relieved from the civic duty of jury service unless she herself determines that such service is consistent with her own special responsibilities.

Likewise we cannot say that Florida could not reasonably conclude that full effectuation of this exemption made it desirable to relieve women of the necessity of affirmatively claiming it, while at the same time requiring of men an assertion of the exemptions available to them. Moreover, from the standpoint of its own administrative concerns the State might well consider that it was "impractical to compel large numbers of women, who have an absolute exemption, to come to the clerk's office for examination since they so generally assert their exemption."

Appellant argues that whatever may have been the design of this Florida enactment, the statute in practical operation results in an exclusion of women from jury service, because women, like men, can be expected to be available for jury service only under compulsion. In this connection she points out that by 1957, when this trial took place, only some 220 women out of approximately 46,000 registered female voters in Hillsborough County—constituting about 40 per cent of the total voting population of that county—had volunteered for jury duty since the limitation of jury service to males. . . .

We cannot hold this statute as written offensive to the Fourteenth Amendment.

Affirmed.

STUDY QUESTIONS

1. What "special responsibilities" do women bear that men do not? Are these the result of differences in their physical makeup, their social roles, or their legal status? Do all women have these responsibilities?

2. If being permitted, unlike men, to decide when they will serve on juries is another type of "special consideration to which they are naturally entitled," to use the language of *Breedlove*, should Florida women have a complaint of unjust treatment if this statute were overturned? Does this type of special consideration set that complaint to rest or only insulate the sexual division of labor from effective criticism?

One of the most conspicuous compensatory measures taken in behalf of women but not men has been the exemption from the military draft. The following decision by a lower federal court deals with a direct challenge to that exemption during the Vietnam War era. That exemption was also challenged indirectly in the U.S. Supreme Court in 1981 in the case of *Rostker v. Goldberg* (see Chapter 2). Both challenges were unsuccessful.

U.S. v. St. Clair

United States District Court, Southern District of New York, 1968.
291 F. Supp. 122.

BONSAL, District Judge.

On March 28, 1968, defendant James St. Clair was charged in a three-count Grand Jury indictment with violating the Military Selective Service Act of 1967. . . . The three counts of the indictment charge that defendant failed and refused (1) to submit to registration, (2) to have his Registration Certificate in his possession at all times, and (3) to complete the questionnaire which had been mailed to him by his Selective Service Local Board.

Defendant moves . . . for a jury hearing on the facts necessary to show that the draft system established under the Act is unnecessary and therefore unconstitutional. Defendant further moves to dismiss the indictment on the grounds that:

1) the Act is unconstitutional in that it subjects defendant to involuntary servitude in violation of his rights under the Thirteenth Amendment;

2) the Act is unconstitutional in that it makes an invidious discrimination on the basis of sex in violation of the defendant's right under the Fifth Amendment to due process of law; and

3) United States participation in the war in Vietnam violates international and domestic law. . . .

Defendant contends that the Act makes an invidious discrimination based upon sex in violation of his right to due process of law under the Fifth Amendment. Defendant argues that men are denied equal protection of the laws in being compelled to serve in the Armed Forces when women are not so compelled. Defendant points out that Congress has established women's corps in the various branches of the Armed Forces and therefore urges that Congress has treated the sexes equally with respect to their ability to serve in the Armed Forces.

In the Act and its predecessors, Congress made a legislative judgment that men should be subject to involuntary induction but that women, presumably because they are "still regarded as the center of home and family life" (Hoyt v. State of Florida) . . . should not.

In providing for involuntary service for men and voluntary service for women, Congress followed the teachings of history that if a nation is to survive, men must provide the first line of defense while women keep the home fires burning. Moreover, Congress recognized that in modern times there are certain duties in the Armed Forces which may be performed by women volunteers. For these reasons, the distinction between men and women with respect to service in the Armed Forces is not arbitrary, unreasonable or capricious.

Defendant's motion for a jury hearing and to dismiss the indictment is denied.

It is so ordered.

STUDY QUESTIONS

1. How did the court justify the different treatment of women and men under the draft law? What earlier cases, in addition to *Hoyt*, does the court's rationale bring to mind?
2. Is the ineligibility of women for the military draft and combat service likely to diminish the perceived value of their views on public affairs, especially when the nation is preoccupied with war and threats of war?
3. What is implied by the court's line of reasoning about women who volunteer to serve in the armed forces?

IV. THE TURN OF THE TIDE

From earliest colonial times, life choices, especially those of women, have been severely restricted by laws that treat people differently because of their sex. During the past century, courts have approved statutes diminishing the status of women as citizens by finding that they did not have the right to vote in federal elections (*Minor*); that they were not required to fulfill the duties of full citizenship, such as jury service (*Hoyt*); and that they were exempted from compulsory military service (*St. Clair*). During that same period, the courts approved statutes restricting women's employment opportunities by barring them entirely from certain occupations (*Bradwell*), limiting their access to others (*Goesaert*), imposing maximum working hours (*Muller*), and prohibiting night work (*Radice*). The cumulative effect of these and like measures was to inhibit the participation of women in the public life of the community and to confine them, for the most part, to a dependent role in the family.

The basic principle used to justify permitting these sex-based laws was most clearly expressed by Justice Holmes in *Quong Wing v. Kirkendall:* "... The 14th Amendment does not interfere [with state legislation] by erecting a fictitious equality where there is a real difference" (223 U.S. 59, 63 (1912)). During the nineteenth and early twentieth centuries, courts regularly found a variety of "real differences" between the sexes sufficient to make sex-based laws constitutionally acceptable. These ranged from physical differences, especially those associated with "maternal functions" (*Muller* and *Radice*); to social differences, especially those stereotypes representing woman as the center of family life and maintaining her vulnerability to harassment by men (*Goesaert, Hoyt,* and *St. Clair*); and to legal differences, especially those deriving from the medieval doctrine of coverture (*Bradwell* and *Breedlove*). By stressing these differences, the courts were able to deny constitutional remedies for legally enforced sex discrimination.

The ideological bases for considering these differences "real" have varied over the past century. The separate spheres ideology of the nineteenth century portrayed men and women as having different natures and different responsibilities (*Bradwell*). The justification of sex-based laws in the twentieth century retains many of the elements of the separate spheres ideology, but the coloration has changed. Court decisions in this century tend to highlight two justifying themes: viz., protection of women from the burdens perceived as more than they can safely or conveniently manage (*Muller, Radice,* and *Goesaert*) and compensation that, for one of several reasons, they are thought to be owed (*Breedlove, Hoyt,* and *St. Clair*). Until the early 1960s, these notions constituted the prevailing ideology of the country.

In certain key respects, the legal status of women had changed between colonial times and the 1960s. For example, by the 1960s, women could hold property, they could vote, and they could become lawyers. However, in many respects, their legal status was only marginally different from that of earlier days. The cult of domesticity and separate spheres ideology continued to shape their lives. But a second wave of feminism was on the way.

The second wave had many strands and involved many significant events. Particularly worth mention is the 1963 publication of Betty Friedan's best-seller *The Feminine Mystique*. A central thesis of her book struck a responsive chord with thousands of white, educated, middle-class housewives. Friedan called it "The Problem That Has No Name."

> The problem lay buried, unspoken, for many years in the minds of American women. It was a strange stirring, a sense of dissatisfaction, a yearning that women suffered in the middle of the twentieth century in the United States. Each suburban wife struggled with it alone. As she made the beds, shopped for groceries, matched slipcover material, ate peanut butter sandwiches with her children, chauffeured Cub Scouts and Brownies, lay beside her husband at night—she was afraid to ask even of herself the silent question—"Is this all?"
>
> *Betty Friedan*, The Feminine Mystique. *New York: Norton & Co., 1963. P. 11.*

Not all the expert advice nor all the cultural propaganda that daily taught the middle-class housewife how pleased she should be with herself for having attained the most desired status possible for women could allay the deep stirring of fundamental discontent. As the "problem that has no name" was discussed, it became increasingly clear that it was rooted, as was the discontent of the Grimké sisters, in outrage over the sex-based stratification that deprived women, and men as well, of their dignity as human beings.

Another important step forward occurred when Catharine East, senior staff aide to the various presidential commissions on the status of women between 1962 and 1967, persuaded Friedan to start an organization to lobby for the enforcement of the Civil Rights Act of 1964. When East arranged for Friedan to attend a 1966 conference of state commissions on the status of women, the National Organization for Women (NOW) was born. Within a few years, women and men by the thousands, sharing that perspective, joined NOW. The founding statement declared the purpose of NOW to be "to take action to bring women into full participation in the mainstream of American society now, exercising all the privileges and responsibilities thereof in truly equal partnership with men." In that statement, NOW acknowledged that "human rights are indivisible" and so pledged to work rather than compete with others who suffer discrimination. It rejected the tactics of both "pleas for special privilege [and] enmity toward men, who are also victims of the current, half-equality between the sexes," instead affirming the aspiration of an "active, self-respecting partnership with men." It pledged, finally, "to break through the silken curtains of prejudice and discrimination" that prevent women from taking full part in American life. With the dawning of the second feminist movement, hopes ran high that the mistakes of the first would not be repeated.

Complementing this relatively mainstream liberal effort was a more radical feminist movement. With roots in the civil rights movement of the 1960s, this movement congealed in the late 1960s. Terming its goal as "genuine self-determination" and not merely formal equality, the movement sought to reach beyond equal opportunity and to achieve basic changes in personal consciousness and in the distribution of power. The movement's prime organizing tool was its militant campaign for the repeal of the criminal abortion laws, both through legislation and litigation. Though short-lived, the movement made lasting contributions, not the least of which was the term "sexist" and its insights into the interrelations between sex and the family.

Between the late 1950s and the early 1970s, all three branches of the federal government endorsed basic departures from the traditional patriarchal approach to sex-based laws. Congress was the first to break ranks with the passages of the Civil Rights Act of 1957, the Equal Pay Act of 1963, and Title VII of the Civil Rights Act of 1964. The first permitted women to serve on federal juries, the second required that all workers—women as well as men—be paid on an "equal pay for equal work" basis (see Chapter 5), and the third became the bulwark of the fight against sex discrimination in employment (see Chapters 4 and 5). Congress also enacted Title IX of the Educational Amendments Act of 1972 prohibiting sex discrimination in education (see Chapter 6), amended Title VII to include governmental employers, and passed the Equal Rights Amendment (see Chapter 2).

The executive branch was the next to follow. In 1967, President Lyndon Johnson amended Executive Order 11246, thereby requiring federal contractors to accept a contractual obligation to avoid sex discrimination in their employment practices and to undertake affirmative action to insure equal employment opportunity for men and women. The Supreme Court broke new constitutional ground in 1971 when it unanimously struck down an Idaho statute that discriminated on the basis of sex (see Chapter 2).

Toward the end of the 1960s and the beginning of the 1970s, state supreme courts began to rethink the legal principles underlying the place of gender in the law.

These courts pointed the way later followed by the U.S. Supreme Court. The Supreme Court of California, in an influential decision handed down in 1971, struck down a provision of that state's Business and Professional Code that prohibited the hiring of women as bartenders. The court found the provision to be in violation of the California Constitution and of the Equal Protection Clause of the Fourteenth Amendment to the federal constitution. When discussing the equal protection grounds for its decision, the court declared sex and race discrimination to be analogous and helped disseminate a central image of the second wave of feminism—the pedestal as cage.

> Laws which disable women from full participation in the political, business and economic arenas are often characterized as "protective" and beneficial. Those same laws applied to racial or ethnic minorities would readily be recognized as invidious and impermissible. The pedestal upon which women have been placed has all too often, upon closer inspection, been revealed as a cage.
>
> Sail'er Inn, Inc. v. Kirby, *485 P.2d 529, 541 (Supreme Court of California, 1971).*

2 Constitutional Protection for Equality

The sex of individuals has determined their legal status since colonial times. The last chapter sketched the nature and justifications of gender constraints through the 1960s. Constitutional challenges decided during that period provide the immediate context for the recent changes in constitutional doctrine relating to sex-based laws discussed in this chapter.

Since 1971, the U.S. Supreme Court has reexamined and reconsidered the ideologies used to justify sex-based laws. This chapter reviews the key moments in that reconsideration. The Court continues to grapple with these vexing questions and has yet to develop a fully coherent constitutional doctrine for equal protection challenges to laws that treat people differently on the basis of their sex.

I. AN INTRODUCTION TO EQUAL PROTECTION ANALYSIS

The equal protection doctrine was developed primarily under the Fourteenth Amendment to the federal constitution. Similar analysis is now used when interpreting the Fifth Amendment and various state constitutional provisions. The Equal Protection Clause of the Fourteenth Amendment reads as follows: "... [N]or shall any state ... deny to any people in its jurisdiction the equal protection of the laws."

That guarantee was part of a package of post–Civil War provisions designed to eliminate the badges of slavery and to insure full rights for blacks. From 1868, when the Fourteenth Amendment was ratified, to 1954, when it was used in *Brown v. Board of Education,* 347 U.S. 483, to bar racial segregation in the public schools, equal protection analysis played a relatively modest role in Supreme Court decision making. Since the *Brown* decision, however, the doctrine has become extremely important. During the 1960s, a number of conceptual tools were developed by the Court under Chief Justice Earl Warren. Beginning in 1971, while Warren Burger was chief justice, these tools were applied in Supreme Court challenges to sex-based laws and government practices. This section reviews those key conceptual tools.

State Action and Formal Justice

Two general points are crucial to an understanding of equal protection guarantees. The first involves what is called *state action*. The Equal Protection Clause, like most provisions of the federal constitution, addresses government conduct. Private parties, be they individuals, groups, or corporations, cannot violate the Equal Protection Clause. Only governments can violate the command of that clause.

The state action requirement, however, has been construed rather broadly. It includes the actions of state, county, and local governments, as well as such state-operated entities as public schools and state universities. The federal government and its instrumentalities are also required to comply with the equal protection guarantee as a result of the Court's decision in *Bolling v. Sharpe,* 347 U.S. 497 (1954). That decision interprets the Due Process Clause of the Fifth Amendment to include the equal protection analysis developed under the Fourteenth Amendment. You will notice in this chapter that the equal protection challenges directed against the federal government are brought under the Due Process Clause of the Fifth Amendment. The first example of this is *Frontiero v. Richardson.*

The second general point is the meaning of "equality" under the Equal Protection Clause. The Equal Protection Clause does not require that people who are in fact different be treated in the same way by the law. What it actually requires is the subject of controversy among legal scholars. At times, the Court has appeared to be concerned with ensuring that people be placed in more equal positions. Since the early 1970s, a different and much less ambitious interpretation of the equal protection guarantee has been in evidence. The interpretation currently favored by the Court can be stated with deceptive simplicity by a term borrowed from the vocabulary of philosophy. It requires *formal justice,* i.e., that like cases be treated alike.

We noted that the definition of formal justice is deceptive in its simplicity. It is clear what the concept means, but it is not clear how to use it. If there were any cases that are exactly alike, we could easily arrange to treat them in identical ways. Since no two cases are ever exactly alike, equal protection analysis must be enriched beyond the mere definition of formal justice. Otherwise, the guarantee extended to citizens would be empty.

Statutory Objective and Statutory Classification

In everyday life, we tend to classify people and situations on the basis of similarities, even though each is unique. This is done by means of the criteria of relevance that enable us to decide which similarities are important or relevant for a given decision. Thus, agility is relevant when choosing members of a basketball team; race is not.

In law generally, and equal protection analysis in particular, the criterion of relevance used to identify similarly situated people is the aim or objective of the law in question. (For the sake of simplicity, such laws will be referred to as statutes. The same points apply, however, to ordinances, regulations, and government practices.) This is called the legislative or statutory objective of that law. A *statutory objective* can be defined as the result that courts understand the statute to be aimed at promoting. Of course, not every statutory objective is permitted under equal protection analysis, e.g., racially segregated schools.

Once the statutory objective is specified, the next steps are to identify the characteristics of people relevant to the advancement of that objective and to classify those possessing these characteristics. For the sake of clarity, the class of people and/or objects that possess *any* characteristic relevant to the advancement of the statutory objective can be called the *relevant population.*

Imagine that a town council wishes to improve pedestrian safety in the town's public park. Its first task is to identify factors that might pose a hazard for pedestrians in its park. If the council decides to act on that statutory objective, it must decide which hazards it will try to lessen and how to go about doing that. Suppose that it resolves to do so by means of an ordinance that provides for the imposition of a fine of fifteen dollars on anyone who operates a vehicle in the public park. In doing so, the council has used a statutory classification. A *statutory classification* may be defined as those characteristics used to identify people who will be treated alike under the statute. Here the statutory classification is "anyone who operates a vehicle in the public park," and the like treatment is the fine of fifteen dollars. Again, for the sake of clarity, call the class of people who possess the characteristics mentioned in the statutory classification the *targeted population*. Neither relevant nor targeted population are legal concepts, but they will help clarify the legal concepts that follow.

The Rational Basis and Strict Scrutiny Standards

If the elegance of law were the same as the elegance of logic or mathematics, equal protection analysis would require no futher development. In that case, all that would be needed to ensure compliance with the equal protection guarantee would be to see to it that for every governmental action, the targeted population is co-extensive with the relevant population. The requirement does not seem, on the face of it, to be an especially difficult one to understand. The fact is, however, that it is not just a tall order; it's an impossible one! Scarce resources, such as funds, personnel, time, organization, reliable information, and political will, always prevent governments from tackling all dimensions of any problem. Like all of us, governments too must attack problems piecemeal.

The Equal Protection Clause does not require that our laws fully satisfy the requirements of formal justice. It does, however, require that they be approximated. During the last half of this century, the courts developed a set of standards that are used in deciding whether particular statutes approximate the requirements of formal justice well enough to satisfy the equal protection guarantee. By the early 1970s, the Supreme Court had developed two contrasting equal protection standards. These can be understood as lying along a continuum ranging from lenient to stern. At the lenient end is the rational basis standard that is used when reviewing the great majority of laws and regulations. At the stern end is the strict scrutiny standard that is used when the statute is suspected of being used as an instrument for discrimination against a traditionally disadvantaged group.

These standards differ in three ways. The rational basis standard (1) places the burden of proof on those who challenge a law to show that either (2) the statutory objective is not legitimate or (3) the statutory classification is not rationally related to the advancement of its objective. Suppose that someone were to challenge the ordinance in our park example on equal protection grounds. To prevail under the rational basis standard, she would need to show that either the town council lacks the authority to attempt improving pedestrian safety in the public park or the ban on vehicular traffic from the park has no reasonable chance of making the park safer for pedestrians. Until 1971, sex-based laws were reviewed under this lenient standard. As the cases discussed in Chapter 1 show, challengers seldom prevail when the courts invoke that equal protection standard.

When the courts believe that a law or government practice is being used invidiously to discriminate against traditionally disadvantaged groups, matters are quite different. Then the courts (1) place the burden of proof on the government to show that (2) the statutory objective is of compelling importance *and* (3) the use of the statutory classification is necessary to the advancement of that objective. For example, in *McLaughlin v. Florida,* 379 U.S. 184 (1964), the Supreme Court struck down laws that prohibited interracial cohabitation because these were seen as designed to maintain white supremacy. Although race is the clearest case of a suspect classification, the Court also regards national origin and alien status as suspect classifications because these too involve a long history of unfair treatment. Ironically, the first case in which the Court declared that "legal restrictions which curtail the civil rights of a single racial group are immediately suspect" (*Korematsu v. U.S.,* 323 U.S. 214, 216 (1944)) was the infamous decision that approved the internment of Japanese-Americans living on the West Coast following Japan's attack on Pearl Harbor at the beginning of World War II. For practical purposes, however, the strict scrutiny standard is barely distinguishable from an absolute bar, so rarely do statutes survive review under this standard.

Table 2.1 summarizes the contrast between the two equal protection standards that had been developed prior to 1971.

II. A NEW BEGINNING

During the 1960s and the early 1970s, feminists argued that government-sanctioned discrimination against people on the basis of sex is analogous to race discrimination. Sex discrimination also relegates an entire group of people, viz., women, to an inferior status on the basis of a highly visible, immutable characteristic. For that reason it too should be recognized as a suspect classification that requires strict judicial scrutiny.

In November 1971, for the first time in its history, the Supreme Court overturned a state statute on the grounds of sex discrimination. The statute was quite ordinary by mid-twentieth century standards. Under the Idaho law before the Court, men were to be preferred to equally qualified women as administrators of estates. The statutory objective undoubtedly had been based on familiar assumptions. One constitutional scholar speculated that two were involved: "wives are more likely than husbands to be dependent, and men are more apt than women to be more experienced in managing money." Harry Wellington, *Interpreting the Constitution* (New Haven: Yale University Press, 1990, p. 17). As we saw in Chapter 1, statutes such as these had been routinely approved without a second glance throughout the Court's history. On this day, however, a unanimous court asserted that the equal protection guarantee requires that sex-based laws meet a somewhat more demanding standard. In doing so, the Court signaled the beginning of a new judicial era. Governmental bodies can no longer confidently assume that sex-based laws will be routinely approved by the courts. The case that set the courts on this new heading, however, raised more questions than it answered.

TABLE 2.1 Pre-1971 Equal Protection Standards

Constitutional Standard	Burden of Proof	Objective Must Be:	Classification Must Be:
Rational Basis	Challenger	Legitimate	Rationally Related
Strict Scrutiny	Government	Compelling	Necessary

Reed v. Reed

Supreme Court of the
United States, 1971.
404 U.S. 71, 92 S.Ct. 251, 30 L.Ed.2d
225.

Mr. Chief Justice BURGER delivered the opinion
of the Court.

Richard Lynn Reed, a minor, died intestate in
Ada County, Idaho, on March 29, 1967. His
adoptive parents, who had separated sometime
prior to his death, are the parties to this appeal.
Approximately seven months after Richard's
death, his mother, appellant Sally Reed, filed a
petition in the Probate Court of Ada County,
seeking appointment as administratrix of her
son's estate. Prior to the date set for a hearing on
the mother's petition, appellee Cecil Reed, the
father of the decedent, filed a competing petition seeking to have himself appointed administrator of the son's estate. The probate court held
a joint hearing on the two petitions and
thereafter ordered that letters of administration
be issued to appellee Cecil Reed upon his taking
the oath and filing the bond required by law.
The court treated §§ 15–312 and 15–314 of the
Idaho Code as the controlling statutes and read
those sections as compelling a preference for
Cecil Reed because he was a male.

Section 15–312 designates the persons who
are entitled to administer the estate of one who
dies intestate. In making these designations,
that section lists 11 classes of persons who are
so entitled and provides, in substance, that the
order in which those classes are listed in the
section shall be determinative of the relative
rights of competing applicants for letters of
administration. One of the 11 classes so enu-
merated is "[t]he father or mother" of the person dying intestate. Under this section, then,
appellant and appellee, being members of the
same entitlement class, would seem to have
been equally entitled to administer their son's
estate. Section 15–314 provides, however, that
"[o]f several persons claiming and equally entitled [under § 15–312] to administer, males must

be preferred to females, and relatives of the
whole to those of the half blood."

In issuing its order, the probate court implicitly recognized the equality of entitlement of
the two applicants under § 15–312 and noted
that neither of the applicants was under any
legal disability; the court ruled, however, that
appellee, being a male, was to be preferred to
the female appellant "by reason of Section
15–314 of the Idaho Code." In stating this
conclusion, the probate judge gave no indication that he had attempted to determine the
relative capabilities of the competing applicants
to perform the functions incident to the administration of an estate. It seems clear the probate
judge considered himself bound by statute to
give preference to the male candidate over the
female, each being otherwise "equally entitled."

Sally Reed appealed from the probate court
order, and her appeal was treated by the District
Court of the Fourth Judicial District of Idaho as
a constitutional attack on § 15–314. In dealing
with the attack, that court held that the challenged section violated the Equal Protection
Clause of the Fourteenth Amendment and was,
therefore, void; the matter was ordered "returned to the Probate Court for its determination of which of the two parties" was better
qualified to administer the estate.

This order was never carried out, however,
for Cecil Reed took a further appeal to the
Idaho Supreme Court, which reversed the District Court and reinstated the original order
naming the father administrator of the estate. In
reaching this result, the Idaho Supreme Court
first dealt with the governing statutory law and
held that under § 15–312 "a father and mother
are 'equally entitled' to letters of administration," but the preference given to males by §
15–314 is "mandatory" and leaves no room for
the exercise of a probate court's discretion in
the appointment of administrators. . . .

Sally Reed thereupon appealed for review by
this Court. . . . Idaho does not, of course, deny
letters of administration to women altogether.
. . . Section 15–314 is restricted in its operation
to those situations where competing applications for letters of administration have been
filed by both male and female members of the

same entitlement class established by § 15–312. In such situations, § 15–314 provides that different treatment be accorded to the applicants on the basis of their sex; it thus establishes a classification subject to scrutiny under the Equal Protection Clause.

In applying that clause, this Court has consistently recognized that the Fourteenth Amendment does not deny to States the power to treat different classes of persons in different ways. The Equal Protection Clause of that amendment does, however, deny to States the power to legislate that different treatment be accorded to persons placed by a statute into different classes on the basis of criteria wholly unrelated to the objective of that statute. A classification "must be reasonable, not arbitrary, and must rest upon some ground of difference having a fair and substantial relation to the object of the legislation, so that all persons similarly circumstanced shall be treated alike." *Royster Guano Co. v. Virginia,* 253 US 412, 415 (1920). The question presented by this case, then, is whether a difference in the sex of competing applicants for letters of administration bears a rational relationship to a state objective that is sought to be advanced by the operation of §§ 15–312 and 15–314.

In upholding the latter section, the Idaho Supreme Court concluded that its objective was to eliminate one area of controversy when two or more persons, equally entitled under § 15–312, seek letters of administration and thereby present the probate court "with the issue of which one should be named." The court also concluded that where such persons are not of the same sex, the elimination of females from consideration "is neither an illogical nor arbitrary method devised by the legislature to resolve an issue that would otherwise require a hearing as to the relative merits . . . of the two or more petitioning relatives. . . ."

Clearly the objective of reducing the workload on probate courts by eliminating one class of contests is not without some legitimacy. The crucial question, however, is whether § 15–314 advances that objective in a manner consistent with the command of the Equal Protection Clause. We hold that it does not. To give a mandatory preference to members of either sex over members of the other, merely to accomplish the elimination of hearings on the merits, is to make the very kind of arbitrary legislative choice forbidden by the Equal Protection Clause of the Fourteenth Amendment; and whatever may be said as to the positive values of avoiding intrafamily controversy, the choice in this context may not lawfully be mandated solely on the basis of sex.

The judgment of the Idaho Supreme Court is reversed and the case remanded for further proceedings not inconsistent with this opinion.

Reversed and remanded.

STUDY QUESTIONS

1. What was the statutory classification here? The statutory objective? The relevant population? The targeted population?
2. The Court spoke of the need to show that sex bears a "rational relationship" to the objective of the legislation. Did the Court actually employ the rational basis test here? What language in the opinion sets forth the test the Court used? Who had the burden of proof?
3. Might an opposite decision have been justified by reference to protective and compensatory themes in much the same way as had been done, for example, in *Goesaert* and *Hoyt?* Does this case indicate that the Court no longer sees these as valid justifications of differential treatment?

Although *Reed* was not the legal equivalent of the "shot heard 'round the world," it did get the attention of the government community. Prior to that decision, governments drafting statutes and regulations regularly relied upon such stereotyped beliefs as "girls are poor at mathematics," "men think with their heads, women with their hearts," and "women are baffled by financial matters." After *Reed,* they could no longer be confident that this casual reliance on such stereotypes would survive judicial scrutiny.

The decision in *Reed* is clearer than the reasons supporting it. When the Court announced that sex is a classification "subject to scrutiny under the Equal Protection Clause," it meant subject to *special* scrutiny. The standard of review used here was clearly not the rational basis standard. Although the Court acknowledged that the statutory objective was legitimate and that the sex-based classification did advance that objective, it nevertheless declared that the arrangement violated the Equal Protection Clause.

If sex-based classifications were not to be reviewed under the rational basis standard, what standard would be used? The only alternative identified at the time was the strict scrutiny standard used in race, alienage, and national origin cases. Did *Reed* signal that sex is a suspect classification and, like race, triggers strict judicial scrutiny? Feminists had argued since the mid-1960s that sex and race discrimination are analogous. The Court's response came two years later in *Frontiero v. Richardson.*

The Court's answer was that it does not. The justices were badly split in this case. Four voted to recognize sex an a suspect classification, requiring strict judicial scrutiny, and to overturn the statute. These were Justices Brennan, Douglas, Marshall, and White. Four also voted to overturn the statute but not to recognize sex as a suspect classification. These were Chief Justice Burger and Justices Stewart, Powell, and Blackmun. Justice Rehnquist, who had joined the Court in January 1972, replacing Justice Harlan, and who had not taken part in the *Reed* decision, voted to uphold the statute. Thus, although the statute was invalidated by a vote of 8–1, only the Brennan minority endorsed the use of strict scrutiny for sex-based laws. Had one more justice joined the Brennan opinion, thereby making it a majority rather than a plurality opinion, the views announced in it would have had precedential value, binding on the Court in future decisions.

Frontiero v. Richardson

Supreme Court of the
United States, 1973.
411 U.S. 677, 39 S.Ct. 1764,
36 L.Ed.2d 583.

Mr. Justice BRENNAN announced the judgment of the Court and an opinion in which Mr. Justice DOUGLAS, Mr. Justice WHITE, and Mr. Justice MARSHALL join.

The question before us concerns the right of a female member of the uniformed services to claim her spouse as a "dependent" for the purposes of obtaining increased quarters allowances and medical and dental benefits . . . on an equal footing with male members. Under these statutes, a serviceman may claim his wife as a "dependent" without regard to whether she is in fact dependent upon him for any part of her support. A servicewoman, on the other hand, may not claim her husband as a "dependent" under these programs unless he is in fact dependent upon her for over one-half of his support. Thus, the question for decision is whether this difference in treatment constitutes an unconstitutional discrimination against servicewomen in violation of the Due Process Clause of the Fifth Amendment. A three-judge District Court for the Middle District of Alabama, one judge dissenting, rejected this contention and sustained the constitutionality of the provisions of the statutes making this distinction. . . .

In an effort to attract career personnel through re-enlistment, Congress established . . .

a scheme for the provision of fringe benefits to members of the uniformed services on a competitive basis with business and industry. Thus, . . . a member of the uniformed services with dependents is entitled to an increased "basic allowance for quarters" and . . . a member's dependents are provided comprehensive medical and dental care.

Appellant Sharon Frontiero, a lieutenant in the United States Air Force, sought increased quarters allowances, and housing and medical benefits for her husband, appellant Joseph Frontiero, on the ground that he was her "dependent." Although such benefits would automatically have been granted with respect to the wife of a male member of the uniformed services, appellant's application was denied because she failed to demonstrate that her husband was dependent on her for more than one-half of his support.[4] Appellants then commenced this suit, contending that, by making this distinction, the statutes unreasonably discriminate on the basis of sex in violation of the Due Process Clause of the Fifth Amendment. In essence, appellants asserted that the discriminatory impact of the statutes is twofold: first, as a procedural matter, a female member is required to demonstrate her spouse's dependency, while no such burden is imposed upon male members; and, second, as a substantive matter, a male member who does not provide more than one-half of his wife's support receives benefits, while a similarly situated female member is denied such benefits. Appellants therefore sought a permanent injunction against the continued enforcement of these statutes and an order directing the appellees to provide Lieutenant Frontiero with the same housing and medical benefits that a similarly situated male member would receive.

Although the legislative history of these statutes sheds virtually no light on the purposes underlying the differential treatment accorded

male and female members, a majority of the three-judge District Court surmised that Congress might reasonably have concluded that, since the husband in our society is generally the "breadwinner" in the family—and the wife typically the "dependent" partner—"it would be more economical to require married female members claiming husbands to prove actual dependency than to extend the presumption of dependency to such members." Indeed, given the fact that approximately 99% of all members of the uniformed services are male, the District Court speculated that such differential treatment might conceivably lead to a "considerable saving of administrative expense and manpower."

At the outset, appellants contend that classifications based upon sex, like classifications based upon race, alienage, and national origin, are inherently suspect and must therefore be subjected to close judicial scrutiny. We agree and, indeed, find at least implicit support for such an approach in our unanimous decision only last Term in *Reed v. Reed*. . . .

There can be no doubt that our Nation has had a long and unfortunate history of sex discrimination. Traditionally, such discrimination was rationalized by an attitude of "romantic paternalism" which, in practical effect, put women, not on a pedestal, but in a cage. . . .

As a result of notions such as these, our statute books gradually became laden with gross, stereotyped distinctions between the sexes and, indeed, throughout much of the 19th century the position of women in our society was, in many respects, comparable to that of blacks under the pre-Civil War slave codes. Neither slaves nor women could hold office, serve on juries, or bring suit in their own names, and married women traditionally were denied the legal capacity to hold or convey property or to serve as legal guardians of their own children.

It is true, of course, that the position of women in America has improved markedly in recent decades. Nevertheless, it can hardly be doubted that, in part because of the high visibility of the sex characteristic, women still face pervasive, although at times more subtle, discrimination in our educational institutions, in the job market and, perhaps most conspicuously, in the political arena. . . .

---

[4] *Appellant Joseph Frontiero is a full-time student at Huntingdon College in Montgomery, Alabama. According to the agreed stipulation of facts, his living expenses, including his share of the household expenses, total approximately $354 per month. Since he receives $205 per month in veterans' benefits, it is clear that he is not dependent upon appellant Sharon Frontiero for more than one-half of his support.*

Moreover, since sex, like race and national origin, is an immutable characteristic determined solely by the accident of birth, the imposition of special disabilities upon the members of a particular sex because of their sex would seem to violate "the basic concept of our system that legal burdens should bear some relationship to individual responsibility. . . ." And what differentiates sex from such nonsuspect statutes as intelligence or physical disability, and aligns it with the recognized suspect criteria, is that the sex characteristic frequently bears no relation to ability to perform or contribute to society. As a result, statutory distinctions between the sexes often have the effect of invidiously relegating the entire class of females to inferior legal status without regard to the actual capabilities of its individual members.

We might also note that, over the past decade, Congress has itself manifested an increasing sensitivity to sex-based classifications. In Title VII of the Civil Rights Act of 1964, for example, Congress expressly declared that no employer, labor union, or other organization subject to the provisions of the Act shall discriminate against any individual on the basis of "race, color, religion, *sex,* or national origin." Similarly, the Equal Pay Act of 1963 provides that no employer covered by the Act "shall discriminate . . . between employees on the basis of *sex.*" And § 1 of the Equal Rights Amendment, passed by Congress on March 22, 1972, and submitted to the legislatures of the States for ratification, declares that "[e]quality of rights under the law shall not be denied or abridged by the United States or by any State on account of sex." Thus, Congress itself has concluded that classifications based upon sex are inherently invidious, and this conclusion of a coequal branch of Government is not without significance to the question presently under consideration.

With these considerations in mind, we can only conclude that classifications based upon sex, like classifications based upon race, alienage, or national origin, are inherently suspect, and must therefore be subjected to strict judicial scrutiny. Applying the analysis mandated by that stricter standard of review, it is clear that the statutory scheme now before us is constitutionally invalid.

The sole basis of the classification established in the challenged statutes is the sex of the individuals involved. . . .

Moreover, the Government concedes that the differential treatment accorded men and women under these statutes serves no purpose other than mere "administrative convenience." In essence, the Government maintains that, as an empirical matter, wives in our society frequently are dependent upon their husbands, while husbands rarely are dependent upon their wives. Thus, the Government argues that Congress might reasonably have concluded that it would be both cheaper and easier simply conclusively to presume that wives of male members are financially dependent upon their husbands, while burdening female members with the task of establishing dependency in fact. . . .

We therefore conclude that, by according differential treatment to male and female members of the uniformed services for the sole purpose of achieving administrative convenience, the challenged statutes violate the Due Process Clause of the Fifth Amendment insofar as they require a female member to prove the dependency of her husband.

Reversed.

Mr. Justice STEWART concurs in the judgment, agreeing that the statutes before us work an invidious discrimination in violation of the Constitution. *Reed v. Reed.*

Mr. Justice POWELL, with whom The Chief Justice and Mr. Justice BLACKMUN join, concurring in the judgment.

I agree that the challenged statutes constitute an unconstitutional discrimination against servicewomen in violation of the Due Process Clause of the Fifth Amendment, but I cannot join the opinion of Mr. Justice Brennan, which would hold that all classifications based upon sex, "like classifications based upon race, alienage, and national origin," are "inherently suspect and must therefore be subjected to close judicial scrutiny." It is unnecessary for the Court in this case to characterize sex as a suspect classification, with all of the far-reaching implications of such a holding. *Reed v. Reed* which abundantly supports our decision today, did not add sex to the narrowly limited group of classifications which are inherently suspect. In my view, we can and should decide this case on the authority of *Reed* and reserve for the future any expansion of its rationale.

There is another, and I find compelling, reason for deferring a general categorizing of sex classifications as invoking the strictest test of judicial scrutiny. The Equal Rights Amendment, which if adopted will resolve the substance of this precise question, has been approved by the Congress and submitted for ratification by the States. If this Amendment is duly adopted, it will represent the will of the people accomplished in the manner prescribed by the Constitution. By acting prematurely and unnecessarily, as I view it, the Court has assumed a decisional responsibility at the very time when state legislatures, functioning within the traditional democratic process, are debating the proposed Amendment. It seems to me that this reaching out to pre-empt by judicial action a major political decision which is currently in process of resolution does not reflect appropriate respect for duly prescribed legislative processes.

There are times when this Court, under our system, cannot avoid a constitutional decision on issues which normally should be resolved by the elected representatives of the people. But democratic institutions are weakened, and confidence in the restraint of the Court is impaired, when we appear unnecessarily to decide sensitive issues of broad social and political importance at the very time they are under consideration within the prescribed constitutional processes.

Mr. Justice Rehnquist dissents for the reasons stated by Judge Rives in his opinion for the District Court, *Frontiero v. Laird*, 341 F Supp 201 (1972).

STUDY QUESTIONS

1. What two burdens did the statute place upon women but not on men? What reasons did the Congress have for introducing this differential treatment into this statute?
2. The plurality opinion preferred a strict scrutiny standard of review for all sex-based statutes, at least those understood to hurt women. It saw an analogy between sex and race discrimination. Do you think that is a fair reading of the experiences of racial minorities and majority women? What about minority women? Are there important-differences as well as similarities? What consequences should follow from those differences?
3. Were Justices Stewart and Powell right to believe that the standard adopted in *Reed* was sufficient to resolve this case?

Several aspects of the concurring opinions take on special significance as a result of subsequent developments. By declining to join Justice Brennan's opinion, Justices Powell and Blackmun and Chief Justice Burger made clear that they preferred to allow the shift to strict judicial scrutiny for sex-based classifications to come about with the ratification of the federal Equal Rights Amendment (ERA), which in 1973 seemed inevitable. How these justices would have voted had the ERA not been on the horizon, of course, is complete speculation.

Justice Rehnquist was appointed chief justice on September 17, 1986, replacing the retiring Chief Justice Burger. As a result, his views on all areas of the law are especially important. His dissent in *Frontiero* is the first intimation from the bench of his reluctance to acknowledge the law's role in perpetuating and eliminating sex discrimination. This dissent is difficult to interpret with certainty. In it, he endorsed the arguments of the lower court judge. Judge Rives had upheld the statute because the statutory scheme, as he saw it, was not based on sex but on the relationship between service people and their dependents. As it did not discriminate invidiously against women in any event, he applied the rational basis standard and found for the government. By endorsing this line of reasoning, Justice Rehnquist hinted that he would not be prepared to submit a sex-based law to more than minimum scrutiny unless it was shown to be motivated by prejudice—unless it was indivious.

From *Reed* we learned that the standard of equal protection review applicable to gender classifications is not the rational basis standard. From *Frontiero* we learned that it is not the strict scrutiny standard either. Presumably the standard for sex-based classifications is somewhere in between these. Two questions remained open after *Frontiero*: What is the standard of review for laws that classify on the basis of sex, and why does the Court consider that standard more appropriate than either of the others?

intermediate

The year after *Frontiero* was decided, the Court addressed a different question, viz., when is a classification sex-based? The case involved a comprehensive, government-sponsored disability insurance plan that excluded normal pregnancy and childbirth from coverage.

The decision in that case was significant for a number of reasons. Pregnancy discrimination has long been a major practical problem. The income and job continuity of countless women who work outside the home are directly affected. Their spouses and families are also affected, although indirectly. Cases involving pregnancy discrimination have also posed significant analytical problems for courts. Should pregnancy-based classifications be considered sex-based and reviewed closely to determine whether they result in a close enough fit between the targeted and relevant populations? Is the principle of gender equality embedded in the equal protection guarantee violated whenever pregnancy is invoked as a reason for treating men and women differently? Those who, like the Court in the following case, do not perceive discrimination based on pregnancy as belonging to the same category as sex discrimination usually deny that pregnancy classifications place the principle of gender equality in peril. For some, that position seems plausible, particularly when stated in the abstract, but the concrete arguments offered by the Court in its support strike many observers as exceedingly odd.

Geduldig v. Aiello

Supreme Court of the
United States, 1974.
417 U.S. 484, 94 S.Ct. 2485,
41 L.Ed.2d 256.

Mr. Justice STEWART delivered the opinion of the Court.

For almost 30 years California has administered a disability insurance system that pays benefits to persons in private employment who are temporarily unable to work because of disability not covered by workmen's compensa-

tion. The appellees brought this action to challenge the constitutionality of a provision of the California program that, in defining "disability," excludes from coverage certain disabilities resulting from pregnancy. . . .

California's disability insurance system is funded entirely from contributions deducted from the wages of participating employees. Participation in the program is mandatory unless the employees are protected by a voluntary private plan approved by the State. Each employee is required to contribute one percent of his salary, up to an annual maximum of $85. . . .

In return for his one-percent contribution to the Disability Fund, the individual employee is insured against the risk of disability stemming from a substantial number of "mental or physical illness[es] and mental or physical injur[ies]." Cal. Unemp. Ins. Code § 2626. It is not every disabling condition, however, that triggers the obligation to pay benefits under the program. ... § 2626 of the Unemployment Insurance Code excludes from coverage certain disabilities that are attributable to pregnancy. It is this provision that is at issue in the present case. ...

It is clear that California intended to establish this benefit system as an insurance program that was to function essentially in accordance with insurance concepts. Since the program was instituted in 1946, it has been totally self-supporting, never drawing on general state revenues to finance disability or hospital benefits. ...

Over the years California has demonstrated a strong commitment not to increase the contribution rate above the one-percent level. The State has sought to provide the broadest possible disability protection that would be affordable by all employees, including those with very low incomes. Because any larger percentage or any flat dollar-amount rate of contribution would impose an increasingly regressive levy bearing most heavily upon those with the lowest incomes, the State has resisted any attempt to change the required contribution from the one-percent level. The program is thus structured, in terms of the level of benefits and the risks insured, to maintain the solvency of the Disability Fund at a one-percent annual level of contribution. ...

[A three-judge District Court found that the program denied equal protection, and the state appealed.]

The essential issue in this case is whether the Equal Protection Clause requires such policies to be sacrificed or compromised in order to finance the payment of benefits to those whose disability is attributable to normal pregnancy and delivery.

We cannot agree that the exclusion of this disability from coverage amounts to invidious discrimination under the Equal Protection Clause. California does not discriminate with respect to the persons or groups which are eligible for disability insurance protection under the program. The classification challenged in this case relates to the asserted underinclusiveness of the set of risks that the State has selected to insure. Although California has created a program to insure most risks of employment disability, it has not chosen to insure all such risks, and this decision is reflected in the level of annual contributions exacted from participating employees. ...

It is evident that a totally comprehensive program would be substantially more costly than the present program and would inevitably require state subsidy, a higher rate of employee contribution, a lower scale of benefits for those suffering insured disabilities, or some combination of these measures. There is nothing in the Constitution, however, that requires the State to subordinate or compromise its legitimate interests solely to create a more comprehensive social insurance program than it already has.

The State has a legitimate interest in maintaining the self-supporting nature of its insurance program. Similarly, it has an interest in distributing the available resources in such a way as to keep benefit payments at an adequate level for disabilities that are covered, rather than to cover all disabilities inadequately. Finally, California has a legitimate concern in maintaining the contribution rate at a level that will not unduly burden participating employees, particularly low-income employees who may be most in need of the disability insurance.

These policies provide an objective and wholly noninvidious basis for the State's decision not to create a more comprehensive insurance program than it has. There is no evidence in the record that the selection of the risks insured by the program worked to discriminate against any definable group or class in terms of the aggregate risk protection derived by that group or class from the program.[20] There is no

---

[20]*The dissenting opinion to the contrary, this case is thus a far cry from cases like* Reed v. Reed, *404 U.S. 71 (1971), and* Frontiero v. Richardson, *411 U.S. 677 (1973), involving discrimination based upon gender as such. The California insurance program does not exclude anyone from benefit eligibility because of gender but merely removes one physical condition—pregnancy—from the list of compensable disabilities. While it is true that only women can become pregnant, it does not follow that every legislative classification concerning pregnancy is a sex-based classification like those considered in* Reed, *supra, and* Frontiero, *supra.*

risk from which men are protected and women are not. Likewise, there is no risk from which women are protected and men are not.

The appellee simply contends that, although she has received insurance protection equivalent to that provided all other participating employees, she has suffered discrimination because she encountered a risk that was outside the program's protection. For the reasons we have stated, we hold that this contention is not a valid one under the Equal Protection Clause of the Fourteenth Amendment.

The stay heretofore issued by the Court is vacated, and the judgment of the District Court is

Reversed.

Mr. Justice BRENNAN, with whom Mr. Justice DOUGLAS and Mr. Justice MARSHALL join, dissenting.

. . . [C]ompensation is paid for virtually all disabling conditions without regard to cost, voluntariness, uniqueness, predictability, or "normalcy" of the disability. Thus, for example, workers are compensated for costly disabilities such as heart attacks, voluntary disabilities such as cosmetic surgery or sterilization, disabilities unique to sex or race such as prostatectomies or sickle-cell anemia, pre-existing conditions inevitably resulting in disability such as degenerative arthritis or cataracts, and "normal" disabilities such as removal of irritating wisdom teeth or other orthodontia.

Normal pregnancy is an objectively identifiable physical condition with unique characteristics. Absent a showing that distinctions involving pregnancy are mere pretexts designed to effect an invidious discrimination against the members of one sex or the other, lawmakers are constitutionally free to include or exclude pregnancy from the coverage of legislation such as this on any reasonable basis, just as with respect to any other physical condition.

The lack of identity between the excluded disability and gender as such under this insurance program becomes clear upon the most cursory analysis. The program divides potential recipients into two groups—pregnant women and nonpregnant persons. While the first group is exclusively female, the second includes members of both sexes. The fiscal and actuarial benefits of the program thus accrue to members of both sexes.

Despite the Code's broad goals and scope of coverage, compensation is denied for disabilities suffered in connection with a "normal" pregnancy—disabilities suffered only by women. Disabilities caused by pregnancy, however, like other physically disabling conditions covered by the Code, require medical care, often include hospitalization, anesthesia and surgical procedures, and may involve genuine risk to life. Moreover, the economic effects caused by pregnancy-related disabilities are functionally indistinguishable from the effects caused by any other disability: wages are lost due to a physical inability to work, and medical expenses are incurred for the delivery of the child and for postpartum care. In my view, by singling out for less favorable treatment a gender-linked disability peculiar to women, the State has created a double standard for disability compensation: a limitation is imposed upon the disabilities for which women workers may recover, while men receive full compensation for all disabilities suffered, including those that affect only or primarily their sex, such as prostatectomies, circumcision, hemophilia, and gout. In effect, one set of rules is applied to females and another to males. Such dissimilar treatment of men and women, on the basis of physical characteristics inextricably linked to one sex, inevitably constitutes sex discrimination. . . .

STUDY QUESTIONS

1. Which standard did the Court use to review the operation of the California plan? Who had the burden of proof in this instance?

2. In footnote 20, Justice Stewart declared that the classification here was not sex-based. In dissent, Justice Brennan declared that it was. Who do you think was right? Why?

3. Do you think that in this case the legislature intended to harm women by excluding pregnancy from coverage? Should that make a difference? Did it intend harm to women in *Reed* and *Frontiero?*

The rationale that apparently guided the Court's decision in *Geduldig* is that the equal protection guarantee does not forbid governments from treating men and women differently if physical differences are directly involved. The Court appears to have concluded that pregnancy-based discrimination does not violate that guarantee because the capacity to become pregnant is unique to women. In focusing so narrowly on that physical difference, the Court neglected to recognize that pregnant workers denied benefits under the plan were as unable to work as were those workers who received disability benefits.

The Court's treatment of policies and practices affecting pregnancy, however, has not been as consistent as this decision suggests. A few months before *Geduldig* was decided, the Court ruled that dismissing school teachers or placing them on forced leave of absence in the early stages of pregnancy violated their fundamental due process rights to make procreative choices, *Cleveland Board of Education v. LaFleur*, 414 U.S. 632 (1973). In 1975, the Court declared, again on due process grounds, that pregnant women who are ready, willing, and able to work may not be denied unemployment compensation when they are denied jobs, *Turner v. Department of Employment Security*, 423 U.S. 44. A year later, however, the Court followed the *Geduldig* rationale. It ruled that Title VII of the Civil Rights Act of 1964 is not violated by an employer who excludes women unable to work due to pregnancy or childbirth from disability insurance coverage, *General Electric Co. v. Gilbert*, 429 U.S. 125 (1976). (See Chapter 3.) The Court held there that the differentiation on the basis of pregnancy was not discrimination because of sex. The next year, however, in another pregnancy case, the Court appeared to change its position again. The Court found that a program that imposed a mandatory leave upon pregnant employees, without pay or benefits and with loss of accumulated seniority, did violate Title VII, *Nashville Gas Co. v. Satty*, 434 U.S. 136 (1977). In 1978, Congress disagreed with the *Gilbert* decision and amended Title VII to make clear that the statutory definition of sex discrimination includes pregnancy discrimination.

When is disadvantageous treatment of pregnant workers impermissible? *Geduldig* and *Gilbert* appear to say "never"; *LaFleur* and *Turner* appear to say "always"; *Nashville Gas* appears to say "sometimes." How are these apparently divergent conclusions to be reconciled? Then judge, now Justice, Ruth Bader Ginsburg suggested that the explanation for the divergence is to be found elsewhere than in the Court's opinions.

> It may be that a factor not fully acknowledged in the written opinions, and based more on the justices' life experiences than legal analysis, accounts for the divergent responses in *LaFleur, Turner,* and *Nashville Gas* on the one hand, *Aiello [Geduldig]* and *General Electric* [*Gilbert*] on the other. Perhaps the able pregnant woman seeking only to do a day's work for a day's pay, or the woman seeking to return to her job relatively soon after childbirth, is a credible figure to the Court, while the woman who asserts she is disabled by pregnancy is viewed with suspicion. Is she really incapitated physically or is she malingering so that she may stay "where [some think] she belongs"—at home tending baby?
> *Ruth Bader Ginsburg. "The Burger Court's Grappling with Sex Discrimination." In* The Burger Court: The Counter Revolution That Wasn't, *edited by V. Blasi. New Haven, Conn.: Yale University Press, 1983. P. 150.*

If Justice Ginsburg's speculation is correct, then the decision in *Geduldig* is directly related to the rationale of the *Muller* decision discussed in Chapter 1. There, as here, differential treatment of men and women was permitted. In both cases, the justification appeared to be based solely on physical characteristics unique to women. In both, however, physical characteristics were given legal significance because of the special place maternity is understood to have in the human scheme of existence. Seen in this light, *Geduldig* confuses a physical characteristic with the significance given that characteristic within the prevailing cultural ideology. It is one thing to allude to the undisputed fact that only women can become pregnant; it is quite another to rely on that fact as though it has legal significance independent of some cultural and ideological frame of reference. *Geduldig* thus reveals a much broader exception to the principle of gender equality announced in *Reed* and *Frontiero* than may have been apparent at the time. It signaled that any physical differences, the ideological coloration of which appears valid to a majority of the Court, can justify treating women and men differently.

Although the insurance plan upheld in *Geduldig* did not protect pregnant women—indeed, it denied them protection—the decision nevertheless reflects a view of women very much akin to that used to sustain the protective labor legislation in *Muller*. *Geduldig,* like *Muller,* turns on the assumption that woman's primary role is as childbearer and child rearer. For this reason, it is acceptable in *Geduldig* to treat workers disabled by pregnancy differently from all other workers for purposes of apportioning benefits, just as it was acceptable in *Muller* to treat women workers differently from other workers for purposes of limiting hours.

Two decisions handed down during the mid-1970s can be seen as extending the compensatory theme that had rationalized granting special benefits to women since at least the *Breedlove* decision in 1937. (See Chapter 1). In the first of these cases, *Kahn v. Shevin,* 416 U.S. 351 (1974), the Court addressed a challenge to a Florida law that gave a tax exemption to widows but not widowers. Acknowledging that the law was overtly sex-based, the Court nevertheless invoked the rational basis standard and upheld the law. The more lenient standard was applied because elderly women bear a special hardship as a result of sex discrimination in the workplace that victimized them during their working years.

The difference between the sexes relied upon in *Geduldig* was a physical difference—only women can become pregnant. The difference relied upon in *Kahn* was clearly not physical. Women are victims of past and present discrimination; men are not. Here the Court accepted the compensatory rationale asserted by the state as defining the statutory objective. Indeed, it accepted that assertion without serious question, even though the law that was enacted in 1885 gave only a fifteen-dollar tax break and grouped women together with the blind and totally disabled.

When discussing some of the decisions in Chapter 1, we observed that accommodating the special circumstances of or according "special consideration" to women has several unfortunate consequences. It tends to undercut the urgency of the call to eradicate the wrongful practice that gave rise to the demand for the compensatory measure in the first place. It is inevitably used as an excuse for denying still other privileges to the beneficiaries of special considerations. It places a disproportionate burden on all men, even those who have not directly benefited from past discrimination against women. The following decision illustrates how a policy of "benign discrimination" can have these same consequences. Here, too, the Court invoked the rational basis standard to review a sex-based statute that was seen as affording special treatment to women because they labor under special burdens.

Schlesinger v. Ballard

Supreme Court of the
United States, 1975.
419 U.S. 498, 95 S.Ct. 572, 42 L.Ed.2d
610.

Mr. Justice STEWART delivered the opinion of the Court.

Appellee Robert C. Ballard is a lieutenant in the United States Navy. After more than nine years of active service as a commissioned officer, he failed, for a second time, to be selected for promotion to the grade of lieutenant commander, and was therefore subject to mandatory discharge under 10 U. S. C. § 6382 (a). He brought suit in federal court claiming that if he had been a woman officer, he would have been subject to a different separation statute, 10 U. S. C. § 6401, under which he would have been entitled to 13 years of commissioned service before a mandatory discharge for want of promotion. He claimed that the application of § 6382 to him, when compared with the treatment of women officers subject to § 6401, was an unconstitutional discrimination based on sex in violation of the Due Process Clause of the Fifth Amendment.

The District Judge issued a temporary restraining order prohibiting Ballard's discharge. Subsequently, a three-judge District Court was convened to hear the claim. . . . Relying upon *Frontiero v. Richardson,* and concluding that the challenged mandatory-discharge provisions are supported solely by considerations of fiscal and administrative policy, the court held that § 6382 is unconstitutional because the 13-year tenure provision of § 6401 discriminates in favor of women without sufficient justification. Accordingly, the court enjoined the Navy from discharging Ballard for failure to be promoted to the grade of lieutenant commander before the expiration of 13 years of commissioned service. . . .

Because the Navy has a pyramidal organizational structure, fewer officers are needed at each higher rank than are needed in the rank below. In the absence of some mandatory attrition of naval officers, the result would be stagnation of promotion of younger officers and disincentive to naval service. If the officers who failed to be promoted remained in the service, the promotion of younger officers through the ranks would be retarded. Accordingly, a basic "up or out" philosophy was developed to maintain effective leadership by heightening competition for the higher ranks while providing junior officers with incentive and opportunity for promotion. It is for this reason, and not merely because of administrative or fiscal policy considerations, that § 6382 (a) requires that lieutenants be discharged when they are "considered as having failed of election for promotion to the grade of lieutenant commander . . . for the second time." Similar selection-out rules apply to officers in different ranks who are twice passed over for promotion. . . .

It is against this background that we must decide whether, agreeably to the Due Process Clause of the Fifth Amendment, the Congress may accord to women naval officers a 13-year tenure of commissioned service under § 6401 before mandatory discharge for want of promotion, while requiring under § 6382 (a) the mandatory discharge of male lieutenants who have been twice passed over for promotion but who, like Ballard, may have had less than 13 years of commissioned service. In arguing that Congress has acted unconstitutionally, appellee relies primarily upon the Court's recent decisions in *Frontiero v. Richardson* and *Reed v. Reed.*

In both *Reed* and *Frontiero* the challenged classifications based on sex were premised on overbroad generalizations that could not be tolerated under the Constitution. In *Reed,* the assumption underlying the Idaho statute was that men would generally be better estate administrators than women. In *Frontiero,* the assumption underlying the Federal Armed Services benefit statutes was that female spouses of servicemen would normally be dependent upon their husbands, while male spouses of servicewomen would not. . . .

In contrast, the different treatment of men and women naval officers under §§ 6382 and 6401 reflects, not archaic and overbroad generalizations, but, instead, the demonstrable fact that male and female line officers in the Navy are *not* similarly situated with respect to opportunities for professional service. Appellee has not challenged the current restrictions on women officers' participation in combat and in most sea duty. Specifically, "women may not be assigned to duty in aircraft that are engaged in combat missions nor may they be assigned to duty on vessels of the Navy other than hospital ships and transports." 10 U. S. C. § 6015. Thus, in competing for promotion, female lieutenants will not generally have compiled records of seagoing service comparable to those of male lieutenants. In enacting and retaining § 6401, Congress may thus quite rationally have believed that women line officers had less opportunity for promotion than did their male counterparts, and that a longer period of tenure for women officers would, therefore, be consistent with the goal to provide women officers with "fair and equitable career advancement programs." . . .

The judgment is reversed.

Mr. Justice BRENNAN, with whom Mr. Justice DOUGLAS and Mr. Justice MARSHALL join, dissenting.

. . . [T]he Court goes far to conjure up a legislative purpose which *may* have underlain the gender-based distinction here attacked. I find nothing in the statutory scheme or the legislative history to support the supposition that Congress intended, by assuring women but not men line lieutenants in the Navy a 13-year tenure, to compensate women for other forms of disadvantage visited upon them by the Navy. Thus, the gender-based classification of which appellee complains is not related, rationally or otherwise, to any legitimate legislative purpose fairly to be inferred from the statutory scheme or its history, and cannot be sustained.

The Court suggests no purpose other than compensation for disadvantages of women

which might justify this gender-based classification. I agree that the "up or out" philosophy "was developed to maintain effective leadership by heightening competition for the higher ranks while providing junior officers with incentive and opportunity for promotion." But the purpose behind the "up or out" philosophy applies as well to women as to men. The issue here is not whether the treatment accorded either women or men under the statutory scheme would, if applied evenhandedly to both sexes, forward a legitimate or compelling state interest, but whether the *differences* in the provisions applicable to men and women can be justified by a governmental purpose. . . .

STUDY QUESTIONS

1. The dissenters spoke of the statutory provision as compensating women officers for other forms of disadvantage. What evidence was introduced to establish that the purpose of Congress was compensatory? Did the majority rely on a compensatory rationale?

2. The Court argued that women officers did not have equal employment opportunities in the Navy because Section 6015 prohibited their serving aboard most ships and aircraft in the Navy. If the women officers were wronged sufficiently to deserve compensatory treatment, should not Congress be required to remove the offending provision? If not, why do the women officers deserve special treatment?

3. Is the preferential treatment granted in Section 6401 apt to relieve the discontent of women officers prompted by Section 6015? Might it also delay legal challenge to that section? Is it likely to retard the advancement of junior male officers? Are personnel policies such as this likely to promote or inhibit good working relationships among men and women who work for the same employer?

We have already seen a number of cases in which sex-based classifications were defended on the basis that women were entitled to benign preference. In its 1978 decision in *University of California Bd. of Regents v. Bakke,* 438 U.S. 265, the Supreme Court finally reached the question of benign preferences based on racial classifications. Although the Court struck down the special admission program of the Medical School of the University of California at Davis, it did not produce a unified opinion setting out the standard of review to be used in such cases. Four justices found that the Davis plan violated a federal statute and did not reach the constitutional question. Justice Brennan, joined by three other justices, found it inappropriate to submit those classifications to the strict scrutiny standard where they harmed whites since whites have not suffered the same historical disadvantages as blacks. On the other hand, Brennan argued, the fact that race-based classifications, like sex-based classifications, may reinforce debilitating stereotypes indicates that they should be subjected to the intermediate standard used in gender cases. By contrast, Justice Powell, who provided the swing vote in *Bakke,* saw no analogy between race and sex classifications. He stressed the diversity of racial and ethnic groups in this country and announced that "the perception of racial classifications as inherently odious stems from a lengthy and tragic history that gender-based classifications do not share."

When thinking about what level of scrutiny to advocate in preferential treatment cases involving sex-based laws, consider the following questions:

1. What do you believe are the benefits and dangers of benign preference?
2. In view of what you know about the history of race and sex discrimination, do you believe programs of preferential treatment present the same mix of advantages and disadvantages for women as for minorities?
3. Is it important that benign classifications for minorities and women be judged by the same standard? If not, which should be subjected to the more careful review?

III. SETTING THE STANDARD

During the early years of the *Reed* era, the Court began to articulate its attitude toward laws and government programs that used sex to classify people. Sex-based statutes and programs came to be judged by a standard that is stricter than the rational basis test but not as stern as the strict scrutiny test. Had the Court uniformly followed that orientation, a significant break with the "romantic paternalism" of the past would have been accomplished. Men as well as women could have looked forward to having much greater opportunity to develop their abilities and explore their individual potential, unencumbered by the baggage of ancient custom.

By the mid-1970s, however, the Court acknowledged two broad exceptions to that general approach. The first, announced in *Kahn* and *Ballard,* permits a sex-based statute designed to compensate women for past and present discrimination to be given only minimal scrutiny under the rational basis standard, even where the government itself is responsible for the disadvantageous position of women. As we will see, the viability of this exception is doubtful. The second exception, illustrated by *Geduldig,* permits a classification predicated upon distinctions the Court regards as real differences between the sexes to be subjected to only minimal scrutiny. This exception appears to have persisted.

Three main questions continued to warrant attention after these decisions. What does the intermediate standard of review applied to most sex-based classifications require? How broad are the two exceptions fashioned by the Court? How will the Court decide whether invidious intent motivated the adoption of laws that impose a disproportionate disadvantage upon women or men? During the following five years, the Court seemed to achieve a consensus in responding to these questions.

In 1976, the Court finished fashioning a formula that captures the "intermediate" standard that it is prepared to use when reviewing laws it sees as sex-based. As has so often been the case, the Court was considering complaints by men that sex discrimination had violated their equal protection rights. When reading this opinion, be careful not to overlook the significance of the standard used in deciding the validity of this relatively trivial statute.

Craig v. Boren

Supreme Court of the
United States, 1976.
429 U.S. 190, 97 S.Ct. 451, 50 L.Ed.2d
397.

Mr. Justice BRENNAN delivered the opinion of the Court.

The interaction of two sections of an Oklahoma statute Okla. Stat., Tit. 37, §§ 241 and 245 (1958 and Supp. 1976), prohibits the sale of "nonintoxicating" 3.2% beer to males under the age of 21 and to females under the age of 18. The question to be decided is whether such a gender-based differential constitutes a denial to males 18–20 years of age of the equal protection of the laws in violation of the Fourteenth Amendment. . . .

Before 1972, Oklahoma defined the commencement of civil majority at age 18 for females and age 21 for males. In contrast, females were held criminally responsible as adults at age 18 and males at age 16. After the Court of Appeals for the Tenth Circuit held in 1972, on the authority of *Reed v. Reed,* that the age distinction was unconstitutional for purposes of establishing criminal responsibility as adults, the Oklahoma Legislature fixed age 18 as applicable to both males and females. In 1972, 18 also was established as the age of majority for males and females in civil matters, except that §§ 241 and 245 of the 3.2% beer statute were simultaneously codified to create an exception to the gender-free rule.

Analysis may appropriately begin with the reminder that *Reed* emphasized that statutory classifications that distinguish between males and females are "subject to scrutiny under the Equal Protection Clause." To withstand constitutional challenge, previous cases establish that classifications by gender must serve important governmental objectives and must be substantially related to achievement of those objectives. . . .

We turn then to the question whether, under *Reed,* the difference between males and females with respect to the purchase of 3.2% beer warrants the differential in age drawn by the Oklahoma statute. We conclude that it does not. . . .

We accept for purposes of discussion the District Court's identification of the objective underlying §§ 241 and 245 as the enhancement of traffic safety. Clearly, the protection of public health and safety represents an important function of state and local governments. However, appellees' statistics in our view cannot support the conclusion that the gender-based distinction closely serves to achieve that objective and therefore the distinction cannot under *Reed* withstand equal protection challenge.

The appellees introduced a variety of statistical surveys. First, an analysis of arrest statistics for 1973 demonstrated that 18–20-year-old male arrests for "driving under the influence" and "drunkenness" substantially exceeded female arrests for that same age period. Similarly, youths aged 17–21 were found to be overrepresented among those killed or injured in traffic accidents, with males again numerically exceeding females in this regard. Third, a random roadside survey in Oklahoma City revealed that young males were more inclined to drive and drink beer than were their female counterparts. Fourth, Federal Bureau of Investigation nationwide statistics exhibited a notable increase in arrests for "driving under the influence." Finally, statistical evidence gathered in other jurisdictions, particularly Minnesota and Michigan, was offered to corroborate Oklahoma's experience by indicating the pervasiveness of youthful participation in motor vehicle accidents following the imbibing of alcohol. Conceding that "the case is not free from doubt," the District Court nonetheless concluded that this statistical showing substantiated "a rational basis for the legislative judgment underlying the challenged classification."

Even were this statistical evidence accepted as accurate, it nevertheless offers only a weak answer to the equal protection question presented here. The most focused and relevant of the statistical surveys, arrests of 18–20-year-olds for alcohol-related driving offenses, exemplifies the ultimate unpersuasiveness of this evidentiary record. Viewed in terms of the correlation between sex and the actual activity that Oklahoma seeks to regulate—driving while under the influence of alcohol—the statistics broadly establish that .18% of females and 2% of males in that age group were arrested for that offense. While such a disparity is not trivial in a statistical sense, it hardly can form the basis for employment of a gender line as a classifying device. Certainly if maleness is to serve as a proxy for drinking and driving, a correlation of 2% must be considered an unduly tenuous "fit." . . .

We conclude that the gender-based differential contained in Okla. Stat., Tit. 37, § 245 (1976 Supp.) constitutes a denial of the equal protection of the laws to males aged 18–20[23] and reverse the judgment of the District Court.

It is so ordered.

STUDY QUESTIONS

1. Why do you suppose the Oklahoma legislature kept this exception to the uniform rule of eighteen years as the age of majority? Could traditional stereotypes of women have played a role?
2. What is the standard of review announced here? Which of its two prongs did the Oklahoma statute fail to meet?
3. Compare the "Craig standard" with the rational basis and strict scrutiny standards. What is the difference between a legitimate, an important, and a compelling government interest? Between a rational, a substantial, and a necessary relationship? How do these standards differ in terms of burden of proof? What is it that triggers the use of each of these standards?

---

[23]*Insofar as* Goesaert v. Cleary, *335 U.S. 464 (1948), may be inconsistent, that decision is disapproved. . . .*

The decision in *Craig* is the closest the Court has yet come to agreeing upon a formula for the standard used to review sex-based laws. In order to prevail under the intermediate standard announced here, the government has the burden to prove that the use of sex as a classifying tool is substantially related to the advancement of an important government objective. The element that is added by *Craig* to the standard sketched first in *Reed* is that the statutory objective must be an important one. Table 2.2 shows the ways in which this standard compares with the lenient and strict standards developed in previous years.

In formulating the intermediate standard more precisely than it had in previous decisions, the Court appeared to suggest that it had achieved firm agreement on its approach to sex-based laws. That appearance was reinforced by the following decision, which, in applying the intermediate standard, added to it in two ways. On the one hand, the Court in *Orr* required that the government show that a less discriminatory alternative is unavailable when it seeks to use sex-based laws. This is the import of "carefully tailored," a phrase that recurs in more recent decisions. On the other, it further diminished the prospects for the compensatory exception to the

TABLE 2.2 Comparison of Equal Protection Standards

Constitutional Standard	Burden of Proof	Objective Must Be:	Classification Must Be:
Rational Basis	Challenger	Legitimate	Rationally Related
Intermediate	Government	Important	Substantially Related
Strict Scrutiny	Government	Compelling	Necessary

intermediate standard. Movement in that direction was signaled a few years earlier when, in *Weinberger v. Wiesenfeld,* 420 U.S. 636, 648 (1975), the Court indicated, in a departure from its previous practice, that "the mere recitation of a benign, compensatory purpose is not an automatic shield which protects against any inquiry into the actual purposes underlying a statutory scheme."

Orr v. Orr

Supreme Court of the
United States, 1979.
440 U.S. 268, 99 S.Ct. 1102,
59 L.Ed.2d 306.

Mr. Justice BRENNAN delivered the opinion of the Court.

The question presented is the constitutionality of Alabama alimony statutes which provide that husbands, but not wives, may be required to pay alimony upon divorce.

On February 26, 1974, a final decree of divorce was entered, dissolving the marriage of William and Lillian Orr. That decree directed appellant, Mr. Orr, to pay appellee, Mrs. Orr, $1,240 per month in alimony. On July 28, 1976, Mrs. Orr initiated a contempt proceeding in the Circuit Court of Lee County, Ala., alleging that Mr. Orr was in arrears in his alimony payments. On August 19, 1976, at the hearing on Mrs. Orr's petition, Mr. Orr submitted in his defense a motion requesting that Alabama's alimony statutes be declared unconstitutional because they authorize courts to place an obligation of alimony upon husbands but never upon wives. The Circuit Court denied Mr. Orr's motion and entered judgment against him for $5,524, covering back alimony and attorney fees. Relying solely upon his federal constitutional claim, Mr. Orr appealed

the judgment. On March 16, 1977, the Court of Civil Appeals of Alabama sustained the constitutionality of the Alabama statutes. . . .

In authorizing the imposition of alimony obligations on husbands, but not on wives, the Alabama statutory scheme "provides that different treatment be accorded . . . on the basis of . . . sex; it thus establishes a classification subject to scrutiny under the Equal Protection Clause," *Reed v. Reed.* The fact that the classification expressly discriminates against men rather than women does not protect it from scrutiny. *Craig v. Boren.* "To withstand scrutiny" under the equal protection clause, " 'classifications by gender must serve important governmental objectives and must be substantially related to achievement of those objectives'. " We shall, therefore, examine the three governmental objectives that might arguably be served by Alabama's statutory scheme.

Appellant views the Alabama alimony statutes as effectively announcing the State's preference for an allocation of family responsibilities under which the wife plays a dependent role, and as seeking for their objective the reinforcement of that model among the State's citizens. We agree, as he urges, that prior cases settle that this purpose cannot sustain the statutes. *Stanton v. Stanton,* 421 U.S. 7 (1975) . . . If the statute is to survive constitutional attack, therefore, it must be validated on some other basis.

The opinion of the Alabama Court of Civil Appeals suggests other purposes that the statute may serve. Its opinion states that the Alabama statutes were "designed" for "the wife of a broken marriage who needs financial assistance." This may be read as asserting either of two legislative objectives. One is a legislative purpose to provide help for needy spouses, using sex as a proxy for need. The other is a goal of compensating women for past discrimination during marriage, which assertedly has left them unprepared to fend for themselves in the working world following divorce. We concede, of course, that assisting needy spouses is a legitimate and important governmental objective. We have also recognized "[r]eduction of the disparity in economic condition between men and women caused by the long history of discrimination against women . . . as . . . an important governmental objective." It only remains, therefore, to determine whether the classification at issue here is "substantially related to achievement of those objectives."

Ordinarily, we would begin the analysis of the "needy spouse" objective by considering whether sex is a sufficiently "accurate proxy" for dependency to establish that the gender classification rests " 'upon some ground of difference having a fair and substantial relation to the object of the legislation.' "

Similarly, we would initially approach the "compensation" rationale by asking whether women had in fact been significantly discriminated against in the sphere to which the statute applied a sex-based classification, leaving the sexes "*not* similarly situated with respect to opportunities" in that sphere. . . .

But in this case, even if sex were a reliable proxy for need, and even if the institution of marriage did discriminate against women, these factors still would "not adequately justify the salient features of" Alabama's statutory scheme. Under the statute, individualized hearings at which the parties' relative financial circumstances are considered *already* occur. There is no reason, therefore, to use sex as a proxy for need. Needy males could be helped along with needy females with little if any additional burden on the State. In such circumstances, not even an administrative convenience rationale

exists to justify operating by generalization or proxy. Similarly, since individualized hearings can determine which women were in fact discriminated against vis à vis their husbands, as well as which family units defied the stereotype and left the husband dependent on the wife, Alabama's alleged compensatory purpose may be effectuated without placing burdens solely on husbands. Progress toward fulfilling such a purpose would not be hampered, and it would cost the State nothing more, if it were to treat men and women equally by making alimony burdens independent of sex. "Thus, the gender-based distinction is gratuitous; without it the statutory scheme would only provide benefits to those men who are in fact similarly situated to the women the statute aids," *Wiesenfeld*, and the effort to help those women would not in any way be compromised. . . .

Legislative classifications which distribute benefits and burdens on the basis of gender carry the inherent risk of reinforcing stereotypes about the "proper place" of women and their need for special protection. Thus, even statutes purportedly designed to compensate for and ameliorate the effects of past discrimination must be carefully tailored. Where, as here, the State's compensatory and ameliorative purposes are as well served by a gender-neutral classification as one that gender-classifies and therefore carries with it the baggage of sexual stereotypes, the State cannot be permitted to classify on the basis of sex. . . .

Reversed.

STUDY QUESTIONS

1. Identify the three possible governmental objectives served by Alabama's statutory scheme. What reasons did the Court give for rejecting each of these?
2. The Court announced that sex-based statutes, even those aimed at compensating women for past discrimination, must be "carefully tailored." What does that expression mean? Why was a "carefully tailored" sex-based alimony statute unnecessary here?

In many ways, *Orr* was an easy case. Like *Craig,* it dealt with an outmoded stereotype. It was easy enough to impose a more demanding standard of review where the stereotype was outmoded and to demand careful tailoring where alternative means of identifying who is needy and who deserves compensation were readily at hand. The Court later faced cases in which the stereotypes were not outmoded and the use of sex-based classifications appeared to be the most efficient means at hand.

Two close decisions in the same year show that the Court was still grappling with the concept of sex discrimination. Both dealt with the rights of unmarried fathers. Together, they reveal the difficulty the Court experiences in distinguishing between impermissible sex-role stereotypes and sex differences regarded as legitimate.

These cases presented more difficult problems than had *Craig* and *Orr* because they involved illegitimacy. The Court had been solicitous for some time to relieve children of the legal consequences of the stigma of illegitimacy. The Court had also been solicitous about the legal consequences of the stigma that attaches to fathers of out-of-wedlock children. In *Stanley v. Illinois,* 405 U.S. 645 (1972), the Court struck down, on due process grounds, a state statute that presumed such fathers to be unfit for custody of their children.

One of the two 1979 cases, *Caban v. Mohammed,* 441 U.S. 380, involved a New York law that permitted the adoption of out-of-wedlock children without their father's consent, although it required their mother's consent. The statute was invalidated in a 5–4 decision on equal protection grounds. As Justice Powell wrote for the majority:

> . . . § 111 is another example of "overbroad generalizations" in gender-based classifica-
> tions. The effect of New York's classification is to discriminate against unwed fathers even
> when their identity is known and they have manifested a significant paternal interest in the
> child. The facts of this case illustrate the harshness of classifying unwed fathers as being
> invariably less qualified and entitled than mothers to exercise a concerned judgment as to
> the fate of their children. Section 111 both excludes some loving fathers from full
> participation in the decision whether their children will be adopted and, at the same time,
> enables some alienated mothers arbitrarily to cut off the paternal rights of fathers. We
> conclude that this undifferentiated distinction between unwed mothers and unwed
> fathers, applicable in all circumstances where adoption of a child of theirs is at issue, does
> not bear a substantial relationship to the State's asserted interests. . . .

Justice Stewart's dissenting opinion, however, demonstrated a greater willingness to regard men and women as situated differently. Here, those differences derived mainly from role expectations then current in the culture.

> . . . Gender, like race, is a highly visible and immutable characteristic that has historically
> been the touchstone for pervasive but often subtle discrimination. Although the analogy to
> race is not perfect and the constitutional inquiry therefore somewhat different, gender-
> based statutory classifications deserve careful constitutional examination because they
> may reflect or operate to perpetuate mythical or stereotyped assumptions about the proper
> roles and the relative capabilities of men and women that are unrelated to any inherent
> differences between the sexes. Sex-based classifications are in many settings invidious
> because they relegate a person to the place set aside for the group on the basis of an
> attribute that the person cannot change. Such laws cannot be defended, as can the bulk of
> the classifications that fill the statute books, simply on the ground that the generalizations
> they reflect may be true of the majority of members of the class, for a gender-based

classification need not ring false to work a discrimination that in the individual case might be invidious. Nonetheless, gender-based classifications are not invariably invalid. When men and women are not in fact similarly situated in the area covered by the legislation in question, the Equal Protection Clause is not violated.

In my view, the gender-based distinction drawn by New York falls in this latter category. With respect to a large group of adoptions—those of newborn children and infants—unwed mothers and unwed fathers are simply not similarly situated. . . . Our law has given the unwed mother the custody of her illegitimate children precisely because it is she who bears the child and because the vast majority of unwed fathers have been unknown, unavailable, or simply uninterested. This custodial preference has carried with it a correlative power in the mother to place her child for adoption or not to do so.

In the second case, also dealing with the rights of unmarried fathers as regards their children, the Court leaned in the other direction. In a 5–4 decision, with Justice Powell concurring in the judgment, the Court approved a Georgia statute that permitted mothers but not fathers of unlegitimated children to sue for the wrongful death of their children.

Parham v. Hughes

Supreme Court of the
United States, 1979.
441 U.S. 347, 99 S.Ct. 1742,
60 L.Ed.2d 269.

Mr. Justice STEWART announced the judgment of the Court and an opinion in which The Chief Justice, Mr. Justice REHNQUIST, and Mr. Justice STEVENS join.

Under § 105-1307 of the Georgia Code (hereinafter the "Georgia statute"), the mother of an illegitimate child can sue for the wrongful death of that child. A father who has legitimated a child can also sue for the wrongful death of the child if there is no mother. A father who has not legitimated a child, however, is precluded from maintaining a wrongful death action. . . .

The appellant was the biological father of Lemeul Parham, a minor child who was killed in an automobile collision. The child's mother, Cassandria Moreen, was killed in the same collision. The appellant and Moreen were never married to each other, and the appellant did not legitimate the child as he could have done under Georgia law. The appellant did, however, sign the child's birth certificate and contribute to his support. The child took the appellant's name and was visited by the appellant on a regular basis.

After the child was killed in the automobile collision, the appellant brought an action seeking to recover for the allegedly wrongful death. The complaint named the appellee (the driver of the other automobile involved in the collision) as the defendant, and charged that negligence on the part of the appellee had caused the death of the child. . . .

The appellee filed a motion for summary judgment in the present case, asserting that under the Georgia statute the appellant was precluded from recovering for his illegitimate child's wrongful death. The trial court held that the Georgia statute violated both the Due Process and Equal Protection Clauses of the Fourteenth Amendment and, accordingly, denied a summary judgment in favor of the appellee. On appeal, the Georgia Supreme Court reversed the ruling of the trial court. The appellate court found that the statutory classification was rationally related to three legitimate state interests: (1) the interest in avoiding difficult problems of proving paternity in wrongful death actions; (2) the interest in promoting a legitimate family unit; and (3) the interest in setting a standard of morality by not according to the father of an illegitimate child the statutory right to sue for the child's death. Accordingly, the court held that the statute did not violate either the Equal

Protection or Due Process Clauses of the Fourteenth Amendment. . . .

The Court has . . . held that certain classifications based upon sex are invalid under the Equal Protection Clause. . . .Underlying these decisions is the principle that a State is not free to make overbroad generalizations based on sex which are entirely unrelated to any differences between men and women or which demean the ability or social status of the affected class. . . .

In cases where men and women are not similarly situated, however, and a statutory classification is realistically based upon the differences in their situations, this Court has upheld its validity. . . .

With these principles in mind, it is clear that the Georgia statute does not invidiously discriminate against the appellant simply because he is of the male sex. The fact is that mothers and fathers of illegitimate children are not similarly situated. Under Georgia law, only a father can by voluntary unilateral action make an illegitimate child legitimate. Unlike the mother of an illegitimate child whose identity will rarely be in doubt, the identity of the father will frequently be unknown. By coming forward with a motion under § 74-103 of the Georgia Code, however, a father can both establish his identity and make his illegitimate child legitimate.

Thus the conferral of the right of a natural father to sue for the wrongful death of his child only if he has previously acted to identify himself, undertake his paternal responsibilities, and make his child legitimate, does not reflect any overbroad generalizations about men as a class, but rather the reality that in Georgia only a father can by unilateral action legitimate an illegitimate child. Since fathers who do legitimate their children can sue for wrongful death in precisely the same circumstances as married fathers whose children were legitimate ab initio, the statutory classification does not discriminate against fathers as a class but instead distinguishes between fathers who have legitimated their children and those who have not. Such a classification is quite unlike those condemned in the *Reed, Frontiero,* and *Stanton* cases which were premised upon overbroad generalizations and excluded all members of one sex even though they were similarly situated with members of the other sex. . . .

For these reasons, the judgment of the Supreme Court of Georgia is affirmed.

STUDY QUESTIONS

1. Is the statutory classification here sex-based? Was the approach endorsed in *Craig* followed here?
2. Why do you suppose the Georgia legislature decided to withhold the right at issue from fathers but not mothers of unlegitimated children?
3. The plurality stressed that men and women are not similarly situated with respect to the Georgia statute. Why is that? Does it result from physical differences between the sexes? Is the dissimilarity of the situations of mothers and fathers of illegitimate children a consequence of the operation of the very statute under challenge here? Is the plurality's argument circular?

Stanley and *Craig* showed that the Court applies a more demanding standard of review to sex-based laws when it sees them as based on outmoded stereotypes. These decisions consolidate and develop the themes that first appeared in *Reed* and *Frontiero. Caban* and *Parham* show that the Court still finds merit in an approach followed in *Geduldig:* where the differences between the sexes are not rooted in myth and outmoded stereotype, a less demanding standard of review is used. This approach clearly echoes earlier decisions, e.g., *Quong Wing.* There is, however, one important difference between the approach taken in *Geduldig* and the one in *Parham.* In the former, the difference was physical—only women can become pregnant; in the latter, the difference was legal—in Georgia, only fathers can legitimate a child born out-of-wedlock.

Standing alone, *Parham* might have signaled either a deterioration in the Court's willingness to eliminate restrictions for both men and women or a willingness to accept the burdens imposed on fathers of illegitimate children in limited situations. Another decision that same year, however, lent more credence to the deterioration theory. It addressed a new question of far-reaching importance.

Most of the statutes and government programs challenged in the cases from *Reed* through *Craig* employed sex as an explicit statutory classification. These openly imposed special burdens upon or granted special privileges to people because of their sex. There is no difficulty in discerning that such statutes discriminate on the basis of sex. However, statutes can have the same effect even though they do not expressly use sex as a statutory classification. Suppose that 90 percent of women and only 10 percent of men are less than 5'6" tall. If a statute were to impose a special burden, e.g., a tax, on anyone under 5'6" tall, the weight of that burden would be felt disproportionately by women. Such statutes are said to be neutral on their face, even though they have a disparate impact on women. Do such statutes discriminate on the basis of sex? Should the equal protection guarantee permit such laws?

In 1971, the Court ruled in *Griggs v. Duke Power Co.,* 401 U.S. 424. (See Chapter 4), a landmark decision under the Civil Rights Act of 1964, that facially neutral practices that have a disparate impact on African-Americans do violate that statute, even though they do not flow from discriminatory intentions. Five years later, in *Washington v. Davis,* 426 U.S. 229 (1976), the Court ruled that a similar practice did not violate the equal protection guarantee. The practice challenged in *Davis,* like that challenged in *Griggs,* did not explicitly classify people on the basis of race but did disproportionately exclude African-Americans from jobs. Writing for the Court in *Davis,* Justice White announced that the equal protection guarantee, unlike the civil rights statute, is violated only if ". . . the invidious quality of the law . . . [is] ultimately traced to a . . . discriminatory purpose." That same rationale was followed and further developed in a later decision that addressed a challenge to a facially neutral state statute that disproportionately disadvantaged women.

Personnel Adm'r of Mass. v. Feeney

Supreme Court of the
United States, 1979.
442 U.S. 256, 99 S.Ct. 2282,
60 L.Ed.2d 870.

Mr. Justice STEWART delivered the opinion of the Court.

This case presents a challenge to the constitutionality of the Massachusetts Veterans Preference Statute on the ground that it discriminates against women in violation of the Equal Protection Clause of the Fourteenth Amendment. Under ch. 31, § 23, all veterans who qualify for state civil service positions must be considered for appointment ahead of any qualifying nonveterans. The preference operates overwhelmingly to the advantage of males.

The appellee Helen B. Feeney is not a veteran. She brought this action pursuant to 42 U. S. C. § 1983 alleging that the absolute preference formula established in ch. 31, § 23 inevitably operates to exclude women from consideration for the best Massachusetts civil service jobs and thus unconstitutionally denies them the equal protection of the laws. The three-judge District Court agreed, one judge dissenting. . . .

The veterans' hiring preference in Massachusetts, as in other jurisdictions, has traditionally been justified as a measure designed to reward veterans for the sacrifice of military service, to ease the transition from military to civilian life, to encourage patriotic service, and to attract loyal and well disciplined people to civil service occupations. . . .

At the outset of this litigation the State conceded that for "many of the permanent positions for which males and females have competed" the veterans' preference has "resulted in a substantially greater proportion of female eligibles than male eligibles" not being certified for consideration. The impact of the veterans' preference law upon the public employment opportunities of women has thus been severe. This impact lies at the heart of the appellee's federal constitutional claim.

The sole question for decision on this appeal is whether Massachusetts, in granting an absolute lifetime preference to veterans, has discriminated against women in violation of the Equal Protection Clause of the Fourteenth Amendment. . . . [The Court next reviewed its decision in *Davis*.]

The dispositive question, then, is whether the appellee has shown that a gender-based discriminatory purpose has, at least in some measure, shaped the Massachusetts veterans' preference legislation. As did the District Court, she points to two basic factors which in her view distinguish ch. 31, § 23 from the neutral rules at issue in the *Washington v. Davis*. . . . The first is the nature of the preference, which is said to be demonstrably gender-biased in the sense that it favors a status reserved under federal military policy primarily to men. The second concerns the impact of the absolute lifetime preference upon the employment opportunities of women, an impact claimed to be too inevitable to have been unintended. The appellee contends that these factors, coupled with the fact that the preference itself has little if any relevance to actual job performance, more than suffice to prove the discriminatory intent required to establish a constitutional violation. . . .

. . . The District Court's conclusion that the absolute veterans' preference was not originally enacted or subsequently reaffirmed for the purpose of giving an advantage to males as such necessarily compels the conclusion that the State intended nothing more than to prefer "veterans." Given this finding, simple logic suggests that an intent to exclude women from significant public jobs was not at work in this law. To reason that it was, by describing the preference as "inherently non-neutral" or "gender-biased," is merely to restate the fact of impact, not to answer the question of intent. . . .

The appellee's ultimate argument rests upon the presumption, common to the criminal and civil law, that a person intends the natural and foreseeable consequences of his voluntary actions. . . .

. . . The decision to grant a preference to veterans was of course "intentional." So, necessarily, did an adverse impact upon nonveterans follow from that decision. And it cannot seriously be argued that the legislature of Massachusetts could have been unaware that most veterans are men. It would thus be disingenuous to say that the adverse consequences of this legislation for women were unintended, in the sense that they were not volitional or in the sense that they were not foreseeable.

"Discriminatory purpose," however, implies more than intent as volition or intent as awareness of consequences. It implies that the decisionmaker, in this case a state legislature, selected or reaffirmed a particular course of action at least in part "because of," not merely "in spite of," its adverse effects upon an identifiable group. Yet nothing in the record demonstrates that this preference for veterans was originally devised or subsequently re-enacted because it would accomplish the collateral goal of keeping women in a stereotypic and predefined place in the Massachusetts Civil Service. . . .

. . . The substantial edge granted to veterans by ch. 31, § 23 may reflect unwise policy. The appellee, however, has simply failed to demonstrate that the law in any way reflects a purpose to discriminate on the basis of sex.

The judgment is reversed, and the case is remanded for further proceedings consistent with this opinion.

STUDY QUESTIONS

1. Did the Court give any weight to the fact that few women are veterans because of government restrictions on the number of women allowed in the armed forces? Was that consistent with the reasoning in *Parham?*

2. What language did the Court use to explain what it meant by "discriminatory intent"?

What sort of evidence would a challenger need to present in order to show intent in that sense? Is it enough that the consequences are foreseeable? Given that legislatures seldom act single-mindedly, is it, as a practical matter, possible to mount a successful equal protection challenge to a statute on grounds of disparate impact?

The decision in *Feeney* applied the approach of *Washington v. Davis* to laws that in fact treat women and men differently. Unless a facially neutral statute that imposes a disproportionate disadvantage on members of one sex or race can be shown to have been adopted intentionally, it will be reviewed under the rational basis standard. One of the considerations that led the Court to adopt this restrictive approach to equal protection challenges of laws that are facially neutral but have disparate impact was expressed in *Davis* and other cases. The Court clearly was concerned about the enormous number and variety of laws that would be affected if a broader approach were taken. Sales taxes, for example, arguably impose a disproportionate burden on minorities and women because they are disproportionately poorer than whites and men.

Just as *Washington v. Davis* was a sore disappointment to those interested in promoting justice between the races, so too was *Feeney* a sore disappointment to those interested in promoting justice between the sexes. The equal protection guarantee can be used as a basis for challenging facially neutral laws that have a disparate impact on women or minorities only if discriminatory purpose as defined in *Feeney* can be proven. Such proof may be particularly difficult in the case of sex discrimination where many laws and government practices are what Justice Stevens has called "the accidental by-product of a traditional way of thinking about females." Attitudes and predispositions rooted in such cultural stereotypes can be expressed both in overtly sex-based laws and in laws that are facially neutral but have a disparate impact on women. The latter, however, require only a minimal standard of equal protection review.

In retrospect, it appears that from *Reed* through *Craig,* sex-based classifications were generally reviewed under an intermediate standard. Two exceptions to this general practice were signaled in decisions handed down in the early 1970s. The first, invoked in *Kahn* and *Ballard,* permits sex-based laws represented by a state as designed to compensate women for past and present discrimination to be reviewed under the rational relation standard. The second, followed in *Geduldig,* permits the use of the rational basis standard if the Court regards the classification to be based on real differences between the sexes. The differences regarded as real in *Geduldig* were physical. The decision in *Parham* expanded the second type of exception by including differences in the legal status of men and women within the category of "real differences."

By the end of the 1970s, the Court substantially narrowed the first type of exception. In *Kahn* and *Ballard,* the Court accepted without serious questioning the claim of the governments that the challenged statutes were designed to compensate women for discrimination and applied the rational relation standard of review. In *Orr,* the Court announced that even where it is satisfied that the purpose of the state was compensatory, a heightened standard of review must be applied. Following the decision in *Orr,* the viability of the compensatory rationale as an independent mode of analysis came into serious doubt. On the other hand, the decision in *Parham* suggested that although the compensatory rationale was in jeopardy, the types of situations previously covered by it might be justified by the "real difference" exception. The decision expanded that exception to include differences in the legal status of men and women. While the utility of the compensatory exception appeared to be declining in the late 1970s, that of the real difference exception was secure.

IV. REFINING THE MODEL

By the time of the *Feeney* decision, the Court seemed to have consolidated the approach it would take toward laws that classify people on the basis of their sex. That approach involves a number of steps. The first question to be addressed when considering a challenge under the Equal Protection Clause, of course, is state action. If the state action requirement is satisfied, the next question is whether the classification is neutral on its face as regards sex. If it is, then the statute is reviewed under the rational basis standard, unless it is shown to have been adopted for the purpose of disadvantaging people on the basis of their sex. If the latter is shown or if the statute explicitly uses a sex-based classification, then it is reviewed under the intermediate standard formulated in *Craig,* and the state is required to show that the statute is carefully tailored to advance an important government interest. This model has one main exception. It does not apply where the Court perceives what it believes to be "real differences" between the sexes. In such situations, the rational basis standard is applied.

While the approach represented by this decision model went a long way toward systematizing the thinking of the Court on equal protection challenges to sex-based laws, it had yet to be applied to some of the most severely taxing questions. In 1981, two decisions addressing such questions were handed down. Both were authored by Justice Rehnquist, who had long opposed the use of any but the minimal standard of review for most laws that classify people on the basis of their sex. Both expand the "real differences" exception, relate to stereotypes that are not outmoded, and pose the question of whether men as well as women have equal protection rights against sex discrimination by governmental bodies.

Michael M. v. Super. Ct. of Sonoma Cty.

Supreme Court of the
United States, 1981.
450 U.S. 464, 101 S.Ct. 1200,
67 L.Ed.2d 437.

Justice REHNQUIST announced the judgment of the Court and delivered an opinion in which The Chief Justice, Justice STEWART, and Justice POWELL joined.

The question presented in this case is whether California's "statutory rape" law, § 261.5 of the California Penal Code, violates the Equal Protection Clause of the Fourteenth Amendment. Section 261.5 defines unlawful sexual intercourse as "an act of sexual intercourse accomplished with a female not the wife of the perpetrator, where the female is under the age of 18 years." The statute thus makes men alone criminally liable for the act of sexual intercourse.

In July 1978, a complaint was filed in the Municipal Court of Sonoma County, Cal., alleging that petitioner, then a 17 ½ year old male, had had unlawful sexual intercourse with a female under the age of 18, in violation of § 261.5. The evidence adduced at a preliminary hearing showed that at approximately midnight on June 3, 1978, petitioner and two friends approached Sharon, a 16 ½ year old female, and her sister as they waited at a bus stop. Petitioner and Sharon, who had already been drinking, moved away from the others and began to kiss. After being struck in the face for rebuffing petitioner's initial advances, Sharon submitted to sexual intercourse with petitioner. Prior to trial, petitioner sought to set aside the information on both state and federal constitutional grounds, asserting that § 261.5 unlawfully discriminated on the basis of gender. The trial court and the California Court of Appeal denied petitioner's request for relief and petitioner sought review in the Supreme Court of California.

The Supreme Court held that "Section 261.5 discriminates on the basis of sex because only females may be victims, and only males may violate the section." The court then subjected the classification to "strict scrutiny," stating that it must be justified by a compelling state interest. It found that the classification was "supported not by mere social convention but by the immutable physiological fact that it is the female exclusively who can become pregnant." Canvassing "the tragic human cost of illegitimate teenage pregnancies," including the large number of teenage abortions, the increased medical risk associated with teenage pregnancies, and the social consequences of teenage child bearing, the court concluded that the state has a compelling interest in preventing such pregnancies. Because males alone can "physiologically cause the result which the law properly seeks to avoid" the court further held that the gender classification was readily justified as a means of identifying offender and victim. . . .

. . . Unlike the California Supreme Court, we have not held that gender-based classifications are "inherently suspect" and thus we do not apply so-called "strict scrutiny" to those classifications. Our cases have held, however, that the traditional minimum rationality test takes on a somewhat "sharper focus" when gender-based classifications are challenged.

In *Reed v. Reed,* for example, the Court stated that a gender-based classification will be upheld if it bears a "fair and substantial relationship" to legitimate state ends, while in *Craig v. Boren,* the Court restated the test to require the classification to bear a "substantial relationship" to "important governmental objectives."

Underlying these decisions is the principle that a legislature may not "make overbroad generalizations based on sex which are entirely unrelated to any differences between men and women or which demean the ability or social status of the affected class." *Parham v. Hughes.* But because the Equal Protection Clause does not "demand that a statute necessarily apply equally to all persons" or require "things which are different in fact . . . to be treated in law as though they were the same," this Court has consistently upheld statutes where the gender classification is not invidious, but rather realistically reflects the fact that the sexes are not similarly situated in certain circumstances. As the Court has stated, a legislature may "provide for the special problems of women." *Weinberger v. Wiesenfeld.*

Applying those principles to this case, the fact that the California Legislature criminalized the act of illicit sexual intercourse with a minor female is a sure indication of its intent or purpose to discourage that conduct. . . .

The justification for the statute offered by the State, and accepted by the Supreme Court of California, is that the legislature sought to prevent illegitimate teenage pregnancies. That finding, of course, is entitled to great deference. . . .

We are satisfied not only that the prevention of illegitimate pregnancy is at least one of the "purposes" of the statute, but that the State has a strong interest in preventing such pregnancy. At the risk of stating the obvious, teenage pregnancies, which have increased dramatically over the last two decades, have significant social, medical and economic consequences for both the mother and her child, and the State. Of particular concern to the State is that approximately half of all teenage pregnancies end in abortion. And of those children who are born, their illegitimacy makes them likely candidates to become wards of the State.

We need not be medical doctors to discern that young men and young women are not similarly situated with respect to the problems and the risks of sexual intercourse. Only women may become pregnant and they suffer disproportionately the profound physical, emotional, and psychological consequences of sexual activity. The statute at issue here protects women from sexual intercourse at an age when those consequences are particularly severe.

The question thus boils down to whether a State may attack the problem of sexual intercourse and teenage pregnancy directly by prohibiting a male from having sexual intercourse with a minor female. We hold that such a statute is sufficiently related to the State's objectives to pass constitutional muster.

Because virtually all of the significant harmful and inescapably identifiable consequences of teenage pregnancy fall on the young female, a legislature acts well within its authority when it elects to punish only the participant who, by nature, suffers few of the consequences of his conduct. It is hardly unreasonable for a legislature acting to protect minor females to exclude them from punishment. Moreover, the risk of pregnancy itself constitutes a substantial deterrence to young females. No similar natural sanctions deter males. A criminal sanction imposed solely on males thus serves to roughly "equalize" the deterrents on the sexes.

We are unable to accept petitioner's contention that the statute is impermissibly underinclusive and must, in order to pass judicial scrutiny, be *broadened* so as to hold the female as criminally liable as the male. It is argued that this statute is not *necessary* to deter teenage pregnancy because a gender-neutral statute, where both male and female would be subject to prosecution, would serve that goal equally well. The relevant inquiry, however, is not whether the statute is drawn as precisely as it might have been, but whether the line chosen by the California Legislature is within constitutional limitations.

In any event, we cannot say that a gender-neutral statute would be as effective as the statute California has chosen to enact. The State persuasively contends that a gender-neutral statute would frustrate its interest in effective enforcement. Its view is that a female is surely less likely to report violations of the statute if she herself would be subject to criminal prosecution. In an area already fraught with prose-

cutorial difficulties, we decline to hold that the Equal Protection Clause requires a legislature to enact a statute so broad that it may well be incapable of enforcement.

We similarly reject petitioner's argument that § 261.5 is impermissibly overbroad because it makes unlawful sexual intercourse with prepubescent females, who are, by definition, incapable of becoming pregnant. Quite apart from the fact that the statute could well be justified on the grounds that very young females are particularly susceptible to physical injury from sexual intercourse, it is ludicrous to suggest that the Constitution requires the California Legislature to limit the scope of its rape statute to older teenagers and exclude young girls.

There remains only petitioner's contention that the statute is unconstitutional as it is applied to him because he, like Sharon, was under 18 at the time of sexual intercourse. Petitioner argues that the statute is flawed because it presumes that as between two persons under 18, the male is the culpable aggressor. We find petitioner's contentions unpersuasive. Contrary to his assertions, the statute does not rest on the assumption that males are generally the aggressors. It is instead an attempt by a legislature to prevent illegitimate teenage pregnancy by providing an additional deterrent for men. The age of the man is irrelevant since young men are as capable as older men of inflicting the harm sought to be prevented. . . .

Accordingly, the judgment of the California Supreme Court is affirmed.

Affirmed.

Justice BRENNAN, with whom Justices WHITE and MARSHALL join, dissenting.

It is disturbing to find the Court so splintered on a case that presents such a straightforward issue: whether the admittedly gender-based classification in Cal. Penal Code § 261.5 bears a sufficient relationship to the State's asserted goal of preventing teenage pregnancies to survive the "mid-level" constitutional scrutiny mandated by *Craig v. Boren.* Applying the analytical framework provided by our precedents, I am convinced that there is only one proper resolution of this issue: the classification must be declared unconstitutional. I fear that the plurality and Justices Stewart and Blackmun reach the opposite result by placing too much emphasis on the desirability of achieving the State's asserted statutory goal—prevention of teenage pregnancy—and not enough emphasis on the fundamental question of whether the sex-based discrimination in the California statute is *substantially* related to the achievement of that goal. . . .

The plurality assumes that a gender-neutral statute would be less effective than § 261.5 in deterring sexual activity because a gender-neutral statute would create significant enforcement problems. The plurality thus accepts the State's assertion that

> "a female is surely less likely to report violations of the statute if she herself would be subject to criminal prosecution. In an area already fraught with prosecutorial difficulties, we decline to hold that the Equal Protection Clause requires a legislature to enact a statute so broad that it may well be incapable of enforcement."

However, a State's bare assertion that its gender-based statutory classification substantially furthers an important governmental interest is not enough to meet its burden of proof under *Craig v. Boren.* Rather, the State must produce evidence that will persuade the Court that its assertion is true.

The State has not produced such evidence in this case. Moreover, there are at least two serious flaws in the State's assertion that law enforcement problems created by a gender-neutral statutory rape law would make such a statute less effective than a gender-based statute in deterring sexual activity.

First, the experience of other jurisdictions, and California itself, belies the plurality's conclusion that a gender-neutral statutory rape law "may well be incapable of enforcement." There are now at least 37 States that have enacted gender-neutral statutory rape laws. Although most of these laws protect young persons (of either sex) from the sexual exploitation of older individuals, the laws of Arizona, Florida, and Illinois permit prosecution of both minor females and minor males for engaging in mutual sexual conduct. California has introduced no evidence that those states have been handicapped by the enforcement problems the plu-

rality finds so persuasive. Surely, if those States could provide such evidence, we might expect that California would have introduced it.

In addition, the California Legislature in recent years has revised other sections of the Penal Code to make them gender-neutral. For example, Cal. Penal Code §§ 286 (b)(1) and 288a (b)(1), prohibiting sodomy and oral copulation with a "person who is under 18 years of age," could cause two minor homosexuals to be subjected to criminal sanctions for engaging in mutually consensual conduct. Again, the State has introduced no evidence to explain why a gender-neutral statutory rape law would be any more difficult to enforce than those statutes.

The second flaw in the State's assertion is that even assuming that a gender-neutral statute would be more difficult to enforce, the State has still not shown that those enforcement problems would make such a statute less effective than a gender-based statute in deterring minor females from engaging in sexual intercourse. Common sense, however, suggests that a gender-neutral statutory rape law is potentially a *greater* deterrent of sexual activity than a gender-based law, for the simple reason that a gender-neutral law subjects both men and women to criminal sanctions and thus arguably has a deterrent effect on twice as many potential violators. Even if fewer persons were prosecuted under the gender-neutral law, as the State suggests, it would still be true that twice as many persons would be *subject* to arrest. The State's failure to prove that a gender-neutral law would be a less effective deterrent than a gender-based law, like the State's failure to prove that a gender-neutral law would be difficult to enforce, should have led this Court to invalidate § 261.5.

Until very recently, no California court or commentator had suggested that the purpose of California's statutory rape law was to protect young women from the risk of pregnancy. Indeed, the historical development of § 261.5 demonstrates that the law was initially enacted on the premise that young women, in contrast to young men, were to be deemed legally incapable of consenting to an act of sexual intercourse. Because their chastity was considered particularly precious, those young women were felt to be uniquely in need of the State's protection. In contrast, young men were assumed to be capable of making such decisions for themselves; the law therefore did not offer them any special protection.

It is perhaps because the gender classification in California's statutory rape law was initially designed to further these outmoded sexual stereotypes, rather than to reduce the incidence of teenage pregnancies, that the State has been unable to demonstrate a substantial relationship between the classification and its newly asserted goal. But whatever the reason, the State has not shown that Cal. Penal Code § 261.5 is any more effective than a gender-neutral law would be in deterring minor females from engaging in sexual intercourse. It has therefore not met its burden of proving that the statutory classification is substantially related to the achievement of its asserted goal.

I would hold that § 261.5 violates the Equal Protection Clause of the Fourteenth Amendment and I would reverse the judgment of the California Supreme Court.

STUDY QUESTIONS

1. In so readily accepting the California Supreme Court's assurances about the legislative objective and the ineffectiveness of alternatives, did the Court apply the rational basis or the intermediate standard? Who had the burden of proof here?

2. Did the plurality find that the classification involved here treated similarly situated people differently? Why or why not? Are the differences perceived between men and women physical, legal, or cultural?

The message of the plurality in *Michael M.* seemed to be that governments ought to be permitted to enact sex-based statutes provided that they can colorably assert that the statutory objective is legitimate and that the classification reflects a physical difference between the sexes. In explaining why California was allowed to punish a male but not a female for engaging in sexual intercourse with another person, not a spouse, who is under the age of eighteen. Justice Rehnquist said that the differences reflected by the statute were only physical differences between the sexes—"Only women may become pregnant" and "males alone can 'physiologically cause [that] result'."

The approach taken in the plurality opinion in *Michael M.* strained the commitment of the Court to using the intermediate standard announced in *Craig* and refined in *Orr.* Specifically, the Court failed to honor the requirement of "narrow tailoring" that was endorsed in *Orr.* The following essay argues that the plurality's focus on physical differences obscures the social bases on which many assertedly protective statutes have relied over the past century.

Perspectives on Women's Subordination and the Role of Law

Nadine Taub and Elizabeth M. Schneider.
In *The Politics of Law,*
edited by D. Kairys.
New York: Pantheon, 1982. Pp. 132-35.

. . . The most recent expression of the Court's current ideology of equality is a 1981 Supreme Court case, *Michael M. v. Sonoma County,* upholding California's statutory rape law, challenged by a seventeen-year-old male, which punished males having sex with a female under eighteen. The thrust of his attack on the statute was that it denied him equal protection since he, not his partner, was criminally liable.

Statutory rape laws have rested historically on the legal fiction that young women are incapable of consent. They exalt female chastity and reflect and reinforce archaic assumptions about the male initiative in sexual relations and the weakness and naïveté of young women. Nevertheless, the Court in *Michael M.* found no violation of equal-protection guarantees and upheld the differential treatment as reasonably related to the goal of eliminating teenage pregnancy.

Although the Court in *Michael M.* cited its prior decisions rejecting sex-based classifications without proof of a "substantial relationship" to "important governmental objectives," it did not, in fact, apply them. No legislative history was produced in California or elsewhere to show that the purpose of the sex-based classification was to eliminate teenage pregnancy. Moreover, the experience of other jurisdictions showed that the criminalization of male, but not female, conduct bore little relation to the goal of eliminating teenage pregnancy. Instead, the Court simply stated that because females become pregnant and because they bear the consequences of pregnancy, "equalization" via differential punishment is reasonable. . . .

Yet, the classification at issue in *Michael M.* had very little to do with biological differences between the sexes. As is seen from the total absence of supportive legislative history, the statute was not designed to address the problem of teenage pregnancy. . . . The statute instead embodies and reinforces the assumption that men are always responsible for initiating sexual intercourse and females must always be protected against their aggression. Nevertheless, the Court's focus on the physical fact of reproductive capacity serves to obscure the social bases of its decision. Indeed, it is striking that the Court entirely fails to treat pregnancy as sex discrimination when discrimination really is in issue, while using it as a rationale in order to justify differential treatment when it is not in issue.

Like *Bradwell* and *Muller, Michael M.* affirms that there are differences between the sexes,

both the physical difference of childbearing capacity and women's social role, which should result in differential legal treatment. However, because this affirmation comes at the same time as the Court claims to reject "overbroad generalizations unrelated to differences between men and women or which demean [women's] ability or social status," the Court's approval of differential treatment is especially pernicious. The fact of and harms caused by teenage pregnancy are used by the Court to avoid close analysis of the stereotypes involved and careful scrutiny of the pregnancy rationale. The role that the challenged statute plays in reinforcing those harms is never examined. The Court accepts as immutable fact that men and women are not similarly situated, particularly when pregnancy is involved. The Court then appears to favor equal rights for women, but for one small problem—pregnancy.

As an ideological matter, the separation of pregnancy and childbearing capacity, social discrimination, and even legally imposed discrimination from "invidious" discrimination, in which differential treatment is unrelated to "real" differences between men and women, perform an important function of legitimizing discrimination through the language of equality. Although its doctrinal veneer is different, the Court's current approach has the same effect as *Bradwell* and *Muller.* If both pregnancy and socially imposed differences in role always keep men and women from being similarly situated—thereby excluding sex-based differences from the purview of equal protection—then the real substance of sex discrimination can still be ignored. Childbearing capacity is the single greatest basis of differential treatment for women—it is a major source of discrimination in both work and family life, and the critical distinction on which the ideology of both separate spheres and physical differences rests. Yet, by appearing to reject gross generalizations about proper roles of the sexes exemplified by both *Bradwell* and *Muller,* current ideology attempts to maintain credibility by "holding out the promise of liberation." By emphasizing its reliance on a reality that appears more closely tied to physical differences and the hard facts of social disadvantage, e.g., the consequences of teenage pregnancy for young girls, the Court appears sensible and compromising. Indeed, the message of the Court's approach is merely to reject "ultra feminist" androgyny while favoring equality generally. However, by excluding the core of sex discrimination, the Court is effectively removing women entirely from the reach of equal protection.

This new ideological approach must be viewed, as were *Bradwell* and *Muller,* in its historical context. Although the women's movement provided the triggering change in consciousness, and an understanding of the nature and forms of sex stereotyping on which the sex-discrimination challenges of this period have been based, many of the sex-discrimination cases decided by the Supreme Court have not arisen from feminist struggles and have been presented to the Court by men, not women. As a result, these cases, including *Michael M.,* did not always develop the harm perceived by women for the Court, either as a factual or legal matter. Moreover, in the absence of a sustained mass movement, the Supreme Court has been able to use feminist formulations to justify the status quo. Over the last several years, with the advent of a visible right-wing, anti-feminist, and anti-abortion movement, the women's movement appears to be garnering less public support. Indeed, a strategy of these groups to separate superficial claims for parity, such as equal pay, from more fundamental demands, such as the Equal Rights Amendment and reproductive control, has already had some impact on the women's movement, where issues of reproductive control have not always been viewed as sex discrimination. The Court's new approach tends to strengthen this separation of issues within the women's movement and reward the most conservative tendencies.

Although the legal ideology of equality shows some progression from *Bradwell* to *Michael M.,* there is less than might be expected. Certainly the Court's view of women, and the ways in which it sees the sexes, has moved from an overt view of women's separate roles to a more subtle view of limited differences, but this new view is more dangerous precisely because it appears so reasonable. The Court's perception of differences that suffice to justify discrimination has altered somewhat, but it remains equally fixed. The Court continues to validate inequality by legitimizing differential treatment.

STUDY QUESTIONS

1. What assumptions traditionally underlie statutory rape laws? Do these relate to physical differences between men and women or to cultural differences in our expectations about the behavior of women and men? Should these, even where they are widely believed and followed, be permitted to guide and justify criminal laws?

2. Does the failure of the Court's plurality to recognize the function of cultural stereotypes relating to pregnancy and childbearing effectively remove women "entirely from the reach of equal protection"? How severely does it limit the equal protection rights of women?

3. Some feminists take the position that societal practices that give men power over women should be restrained by sex-based laws. Do you think that cultural differences, such as males taking the initiative in sexual relations, are sufficient to justify sex-based laws?

The decision in *Michael M.* brings into focus one of the main problems with the "real differences" exception. *Geduldig (physical differences), Parham (legal differences),* and now *Michael M. (cultural differences)* show that the Court is willing to permit laws that treat men and women differently if they are based on any difference between the sexes, provided that those differences appear valid to a majority of the justices. In each of these decisions, the justices reinforced ideological frameworks that lend signficance to these various differences between women and men. In each, they appear to have relied upon what Justice Ginsburg, in her remarks relating to *Geduldig,* called their "life experiences." Seen in this context, *Michael M.* raises two general questions about this entire approach. First, is there an objective and logically consistent basis for distinguishing between those differences beween the sexes that are "real" and those that are not, or does that distinction depend solely upon the "life experiences" of those individuals that become justices? Second, if there is such a basis, is that basis itself rooted in outmoded cultural stereotypes? Most of the justices have yet to face these questions squarely.

Another perplexing aspect of the plurality's opinion here is its attitude toward sex discrimination against men. The Court held from *Stanley* through *Orr* that laws seen to discriminate against men would be reviewed in the same way as those that discriminate against women. Here, the plurality speaks of that protection as a "provision for the special problems of women." Is sex discrimination constitutionally objectionable only when it burdens women? Is it even possible for sex-based laws to burden only one sex? The second key decision handed down in 1981 seems to add to that apprehension. In that decision, Justice Rehnquist spoke for the majority.

Rostker v. Goldberg

Supreme Court of the
United States, 1981.
453 U.S. 57, 101 S.Ct. 2646,
69 L.Ed.2d 478.

Justice REHNQUIST delivered the opinion of the Court.

The question presented is whether the Military Selective Service Act, 50 U.S.C. App. § 451 *et seq.,* violates the Fifth Amendment to the United States Constitution in authorizing the President to require the registration of males and not females.

Congress is given the power under the Constitution "To raise and support Armies," "To provide and maintain a Navy," and "To make Rules for the Government and Regulation of the land and naval Forces." Art. I, § 8, cls. 12–14. Pursuant to this grant of authority Congress has enacted the Military Selective Service Act, 50 U.S.C. App. § 451 *et seq.* ("the MSSA" or "the Act"). Section 3 of the Act, empowers the President, by proclamation, to require the registration of "every male citizen" and male resident aliens between the ages of 18 and 26. The purpose of this registration is to facilitate any eventual conscription. . . .

Registration for the draft under § 3 was discontinued in 1975. In early 1980, President Carter determined that it was necessary to reactivate the draft registration process. The immediate impetus for this decision was the Soviet armed invasion of Afghanistan. . . .

Congress agreed that it was necessary to reactivate the registration process, and allocated funds for that purpose in a joint resolution which passed the House on April 22 and the Senate on June 12. The resolution did not allocate all the funds originally requested by the President, but only those necessary to register males. . . .

These events of last year breathed new life into a lawsuit which had been essentially dormant in the lower courts for nearly a decade. It began in 1971 when several men subject to registration for the draft and subsequent induction into the Armed Services filed a complaint in the United States District Court for the Eastern District of Pennsylvania challenging the MSSA on several grounds. A three-judge district court was convened in 1974 to consider the claim of unlawful gender-based discrimination which is now before us. . . . Nothing more happened in the case for five years. . . .

On Friday, July 18, 1980, three days before registration was to commence, the District Court issued an opinion finding that the Act violated the Due Process Clause of the Fifth Amendment and permanently enjoined the Government from requiring registration under the Act. . . . Applying the "important government interest" test articulated in *Craig v. Boren,* the court struck down the MSSA. The court stressed that it was not deciding whether or to what extent women should serve in combat, but only the issue of registration, and felt that this "should dispel any concern that we are injecting ourselves in an inappropriate manner in military affairs." . . .

Whenever called upon to judge the constitutionality of an Act of Congress—"the gravest and most delicate duty that this Court is called upon to perform," the Court accords "great weight to the decisions of Congress." . . .

This is not, however, merely a case involving the customary deference accorded congressional decisions. The case arises in the context of Congress' authority over national defense and military affairs, and perhaps in no other area has the Court accorded Congress greater deference. . . .

Not only is the scope of Congress' constitutional power in this area broad, but the lack of competence on the part of the courts is marked. . . .

None of this is to say that Congress is free to disregard the Constitution when it acts in the area of military affairs. In that area as any other Congress remains subject to the limitations of the Due Process Clause, but the tests and limitations to be applied may differ because of the military context. . . .

This case is quite different from several of the gender-based discrimination cases we have considered in that, despite appellees' assertions, Congress did not act "unthinkingly" or "reflexively and not for any considered reason." . . .

The House declined to provide for the registration of women when it passed the Joint Resolution allocating funds for the Selective Service System. When the Senate considered the Joint Resolution, it defeated, after extensive debate, an amendment which in effect would have authorized the registration of women. As noted earlier, Congress in H. R. J. Res. 521 only authorized funds sufficient to cover the registration of males. . . .

Congress determined that any future draft, which would be facilitated by the registration scheme, would be characterized by a need for combat troops. The Senate Report explained, in a specific finding later adopted by both Houses, that "if mobilization were to be ordered in a wartime scenario, the primary manpower need would be for combat replacements." . . . The purpose of registration, therefore, was to prepare for a draft of combat troops.

Women as a group, however, unlike men as a group, are not eligible for combat. The restrictions on the participation of women in combat in the Navy and Air Force are statutory. Under 10 U.S.C. § 6015 "women may not be assigned to duty on vessels or in aircraft that are engaged in combat missions," and under 10 U.S.C. § 8549 female members of the Air Force "may not be assigned to duty in aircraft engaged in combat missions." The Army and Marine Corps preclude the use of women in combat as a matter of established policy. Congress specifically recognized and endorsed the exclusion of women from combat in exempting women from registration. . . .

The existence of the combat restrictions clearly indicates the basis for Congress' decision to exempt women from registration. The purpose of registration was to prepare for a draft of combat troops. Since women are excluded from combat, Congress concluded that they would not be needed in the event of a draft, and therefore decided not to register them. . . .

The reason women are exempt from registration is not because military needs can be met by drafting men. This is not a case of Congress arbitrarily choosing to burden one of two similarly situated groups, such as would be the case with an all-black or all-white, or an all-Catholic or all-Lutheran, or an all-Republican or all-Democratic registration. Men and women, because of the combat restrictions on women, are simply not similarly situated for purposes of a draft or registration for a draft.

Congress' decision to authorize the registration of only men, therefore, does not violate the

Due Process Clause. The exemption of women from registration is not only sufficiently but closely related to Congress' purpose in authorizing registration. . . .

In light of the foregoing, we conclude that Congress acted well within its constitutional authority when it authorized the registration of men, and not women, under the Military Selective Service Act. The decision of the District Court holding otherwise is accordingly

Reversed.

STUDY QUESTIONS

1. What standard of review did the Court use here? Did it require that sex-based classifications be shown by convincing evidence to be carefully tailored to the advancement of any objective whatsoever? Did it require that a sex-neutral classification be shown to be too ineffective?

2. Does the outcome in this case turn on the fact that it involved the military? Has the Court always exercised minimal scrutiny when sex discrimination challenges were brought against a branch of the armed forces?

———————————— ❧ ————————————

In *Rostker,* the Court upheld the challenged provision because Congress saw the sex-based classification as closely related to the achievement of the government's asserted purpose of preparing for the draft of combat troops. This reasoning was severely criticized by the dissenting justices. Justice White pointed out that the military draft has consistently been used not only "to fill combat positions and those noncombat positions that must be filled by combat-trained men, but also to secure personnel needed for jobs that can be performed by persons ineligible for combat. . . ." Justice Marshall pointed out that according to the intermediate standard adopted in *Craig,* the Court addressed the wrong question. The question, in his view, is not whether "a gender-neutral classification would substantially advance an important government interest" but whether "excluding women" would advance such interests.

Justice Marshall also observed: "The Court today places its imprimatur on one of the most potent remaining public expressions of 'ancient canards about the proper role of women.'" He was referring, of course, to the themes that were explored in Chapter 1, to the traditional exclusion of women from civic responsibilities through the ideology of separate spheres and the cult of true womanhood. The district court in *St. Clair* reminded us, also in regard to the military draft, of "the teachings of history that if a nation is to survive, men must provide the first line of defense while women keep the home fires burning."

As the following comment shows, the decision in *Rostker* can be read on several levels.

On the surface, the highly publicized *Rostker* case appears to favor women—allowing them to volunteer for the military or not as they so choose, while subjecting men to involuntary registration and perhaps involuntary servitude in the military. This facile conclusion vanishes when one asks why males are subjected to this burden. The answer that our government gives the recalcitrant young man is: "It is your duty as a United States citizen." The message to young women is: "Your citizenship duty is optional, while your brother's (the real citizen) is mandatory." The analogy in the jury system, first upheld in *Hoyt v. Florida,* and later invalidated in *Taylor v. Louisiana,* is apparent.

Arnold H. Loewy. "*Returned to the Pedestal—The Supreme Court and Gender Classification Cases: 1980 Term.*" 60 North Carolina Law Review 87, 95–6 (1981).

In Loewy's interpretation, *Rostker* failed to recognize that the differential treatment of women and men as regards draft registration flows from the same dual classes of citizenship that pervaded the law during the centuries before *Reed*. These are the "ancient canards" alluded to by Justice Marshall.

Taub and Schneider suggested that the women's movement make a concerted effort to sensitize the Court to the cultural stereotypes that hamper the advancement of equality of the sexes. Although NOW and other women's groups urged the Court to strike down the male-only draft registration provision at issue in *Rostker,* feminists disagree over the *Rostker* decision. Ellie Smeal, then head of NOW, for example, expressed relief that "at least we can save our daughters." On the other hand, she also expressed regret that "they have taken away our voice of protest. We can't even say, 'Hell no, we won't go.'" Some feminists saw more clearly the sinister implications of both the *Michael M.* and *Rostker* decisions. In an essay published shortly after these decisions were handed down, law professor Wendy Williams pointed out how these decisions damage the interests of women.

> The single-sex laws upheld in *Michael M.* and *Rostker* ultimately do damage to women. For one thing, they absolve women of personal responsibility in the name of protection. There is a sense in which women have been victims of physical aggression in part because they have not been permitted to act as anything but victims. For another, do we not acquire a greater right to claim our share from society if we too share its ultimate jeopardies? To me, *Rostker* never posed the question of whether women should be forced as men now are to fight wars, but whether we, like them, must take the responsibility for deciding whether or not to fight, whether or not to bear the cost of risking our lives, on the one hand, or resisting in the name of peace, on the other. And do we not, by insisting upon our differences at these crucial junctures, promote and reinforce the us-them dichotomy that permits the Rehnquists and Stewarts to resolve matters of great importance and complexity by the simplistic, reflexive assertion that men and women "are simply not similarly situated"?
>
> *Wendy Williams, "The Equality Crisis: Some Reflections on Culture, Courts, and Feminism." 7 Women's Rights Law Reporter 175–200 (1982), at 189–90.*

In the decade following the *Rostker* decision, the resistance of the American military to women serving in combat positions began to soften. During the 1991 Persian Gulf War, thirty-five thousand women served as pilots, mechanics, intelligence specialists, truck drivers, ground personnel, and so on. Two were captured by the Iraqis. Fourteen were killed in action. Nor was this the first time in recent memory that American women saw action in military service to their country. Six hundred took part in the military action in Panama in 1989. More than seventy-four thousand women served during the Korean War. A quarter of a million served during the Vietnam War, seventy-five hundred "in country." Eight of their names are engraved on the Vietnam Memorial in Washington, D.C. During World War II, 350,000 served mainly as nurses but also as Air Force service pilots. What was different in 1991 was that Congress recognized the value of the contributions made by women as well as men. It did so by repealing section 8549 and amending section 6015, thereby removing the bar to assigning women to fly combat aircraft for the Air Force and Navy.

These changes were not gracefully received by the military leadership. In November 1992, a presidential commission reacted by recommending that the repealed sections be reinstated and that the Army's policy of excluding women from combat be written into law but that Navy combat ships be opened to women with the exception of submarines and amphibious vessels. Those recommendations were not influential with the newly elected Clinton administration, which declared itself in favor of expanding the opportunities of women as well as gays and lesbians in the military. In April, 1993, Secretary of Defense Les Aspin ordered all the services to drop restrictions on women flying combat missions and serving aboard most warships. Whether and when other combat roles, including those in ground combat units, will be made available to women remains an open question at this writing.

At the end of the 1980–81 term, Justice Stewart retired from active duty on the Court. He was replaced by the first woman ever to serve on that Court, Justice Sandra Day O'Connor. During her first term on the Court, Justice O'Connor's presence was felt in a sex discrimination case. The case involved the exclusion of one sex from a state-run school that prepared people for careers in a profession traditionally associated with the other sex. In this case, the profession was nursing, and those excluded were men. The challenge to this instance of single-sex public schools might have raised the more general issue of whether state-sponsored, sex-segregated schools are permitted by the equal protection guarantee. Just six years earlier, the Court faced that question in *Vorchheimer v. School District of Philadelphia* (see Chapter 6). It affirmed a lower court decision that held that they are but did so by a 4-4 vote (Justice Rehnquist did not participate) and issued no opinion explaining the significance of that decision. In *Hogan,* as indicated in footnote 1, the Court steered clear of the more general issue and focused instead on the narrower question of whether the Equal Protection Clause bars states from excluding one sex from schools provided for the other.

Miss. Univ. for Women v. Hogan

Supreme Court of the
United States, 1982.
458 U.S. 718, 102 S.Ct. 3331,
73 L.Ed.2d 1090.

Justice O'CONNOR delivered the opinion of the Court.

This case presents the narrow issue of whether a state statute that excludes males from enrolling in a state-supported professional nursing school violates the Equal Protection Clause of the Fourteenth Amendment.

The facts are not in dispute. In 1884, the Mississippi legislature created the Mississippi Industrial Institute and College for the Education of White Girls of the State of Mississippi, now the oldest state-supported all-female college in the United States. The school, known

today as Mississippi University for Women (MUW), has from its inception limited its enrollment to women.[1]

In 1971, MUW established a School of Nursing, initially offering a two-year associate degree. Three years later, the school instituted a four-year baccalaureate program in nursing and today also offers a graduate program. The School of Nursing has its own faculty and administrative officers and establishes its own criteria for admission.

Respondent, Joe Hogan, is a registered nurse but does not hold a baccalaureate degree in nursing. Since 1974, he has worked as a nursing supervisor in a medical center in Columbus, the city in which MUW is located. In 1979, Hogan applied for admission to the MUW School of Nursing's baccalaureate program. Although he

---

[1] *Mississippi maintains no other single-sex public university or college. Thus, we are not faced with the question of whether States can provide "separate but equal" undergraduate institutions for males and females. Cf. Vorchheimer v. School District of Philadelphia.*

was otherwise qualified, he was denied admission to the School of Nursing solely because of his sex. School officials informed him that he could audit the courses in which he was interested, but could not enroll for credit.

Hogan filed an action in the United States District Court for the Northern District of Mississippi, claiming the single-sex admissions policy of MUW's School of Nursing violated the Equal Protection Clause of the Fourteenth Amendment. Hogan sought injunctive and declaratory relief, as well as compensatory damages.

Following a hearing, the District Court denied preliminary injunctive relief. The court concluded that maintenance of MUW as a single-sex school bears a rational relationship to the state's legitimate interest "of providing the greatest practical range of educational opportunities for its female student population." Furthermore, the court stated, the admissions policy is not arbitrary because providing single-sex schools is consistent with a respected, though by no means universally accepted, educational theory that single-sex education affords unique benefits to students. Stating that the case presented no issue of fact, the court informed Hogan that it would enter summary judgment dismissing his claim unless he tendered a factual issue. When Hogan offered no further evidence, the District Court entered summary judgment in favor of the State.

The Court of Appeals for the Fifth Circuit reversed, holding that, because the admissions policy discriminates on the basis of gender, the District Court improperly used a "rational relationship" test to judge the constitutionality of the policy. Instead, the Court of Appeals stated, the proper test is whether the State has carried the heavier burden of showing that the gender-based classification is substantially related to an important governmental objective. Recognizing that the State has a significant interest in providing educational opportunities for all its citizens, the court then found that the State had failed to show that providing a unique educational opportunity for females, but not for males, bears a substantial relationship to that interest. . . .

We begin our analysis aided by several firmly-established principles. Because the challenged policy expressly discriminates among applicants on the basis of gender, it is subject to scrutiny under the Equal Protection Clause of the Fourteenth Amendment. *Reed v. Reed.* That this statute discriminates against males rather than against females does not exempt it from scrutiny or reduce the standard of review, *Orr v. Orr.* Our decisions also establish that the party seeking to uphold a statute that classifies individuals on the basis of their gender must carry the burden of showing an "exceedingly persuasive justification" for the classification, *Feeney.* The burden is met only by showing at least that the classification serves "important governmental objectives and that the discriminatory means employed" are "substantially related to the achievement of those objectives." *Wengler v. Druggists Mutual Ins. Co.,* 446 U.S. 142 (1980). . . .

The State's primary justification for maintaining the single-sex admissions policy of MUW's School of Nursing is that it compensates for discrimination against women and, therefore, constitutes educational affirmative action. As applied to the School of Nursing, we find the State's argument unpersuasive.

In limited circumstances, a gender-based classification favoring one sex can be justified if it intentionally and directly assists members of the sex that is disproportionately burdened. See *Schlesinger v. Ballard.* However, we consistently have emphasized that "the mere recitation of a benign, compensatory purpose is not an automatic shield which protects against any inquiry into the actual purposes underlying a statutory scheme." *Weinberger v. Wiesenfeld.* The same searching analysis must be made, regardless of whether the State's objective is to eliminate family controversy, *Reed,* to achieve administrative efficiency, *Frontiero,* or to balance the burdens borne by males and females. . . .

Mississippi has made no showing that women lacked opportunities to obtain training in the field of nursing or to attain positions of leadership in that field when the MUW School of Nursing opened its door or that women currently are deprived of such opportunities. In fact, in 1970, the year before the School of Nursing's first class enrolled, women earned 94 percent of the nursing baccalaureate degrees conferred in Mississippi and 98.6 percent of the degrees earned nationwide. . . . That year was not an aberration; one decade earlier, women had earned all the nursing degrees conferred in Mississippi and 98.9 percent of the degrees conferred nationwide. As one would expect, the labor force reflects the same predominance of women in nursing. When MUW's School of Nursing began operation, nearly 98 percent of all employed registered nurses were female.

Rather than compensate for discriminatory barriers faced by women, MUW's policy of excluding males from admission to the School of Nursing tends to perpetuate the stereotyped view of nursing as an exclusively woman's job. By assuring that Mississippi allots more openings in its state-supported nursing schools to women than it does to men, MUW's admissions policy lends credibility to the old view that women, not men, should become nurses, and makes the assumption that nursing is a field for women a self-fulfilling prophecy. Thus, we conclude that, although the State recited a "benign, compensatory purpose," it failed to establish that the alleged objective is the actual purpose underlying the discriminatory classification.

The policy is invalid also because it fails the second part of the equal protection test, for the State has made no showing that the gender-based classification is substantially and directly related to its proposed compensatory objective. To the contrary, MUW's policy of permitting men to attend classes as auditors fatally undermines its claim that women, at least those in the School of Nursing, are adversely affected by the presence of men. . . .

Thus, considering both the asserted interest and the relationship between the interest and the methods used by the State, we conclude that the State has fallen far short of establishing the "exceedingly persuasive justification" needed to sustain the gender-based classifica-

tion. Accordingly, we hold that MUW's policy of denying males the right to enroll for credit in its School of Nursing violates the Equal Protection Clause of the Fourteenth Amendment.[17] . . .

Because we conclude that the State's policy of excluding males from MUW's School of Nursing violates the Equal Protection Clause of the Fourteenth Amendment, we affirm the judgment of the Court of Appeals.

It is so ordered.

STUDY QUESTIONS

1. What standard of review did the Court use here? Did the Court simply accept the claimed objective or require the state to show that the legislature actually attempted to further that aim? If the statute in *Michael M.* had been subjected to the same degree of searching analysis as was used in *Hogan,* would the result there have been different? What about the one in *Rostker?*
2. How narrow is the rationale for this decision? Under it, could Joe Hogan be denied admission to a state medical school for women? Could a state open a nursing school for men only? How about a graduate school of business administration limited to women students? Under this decision, could a state provide "separate but equal" high schools for boys and girls?

---

[17]*Justice Powell's dissent suggests that a second objective is served by the gender-based classification in that Mississippi has elected to provide women a choice of educational environments. Since any gender-based classification provides one class a benefit or choice not available to the other class, however, that argument begs the question. The issue is not whether the benefited class profits from the classification, but whether the State's decision to confer a benefit only upon one class by means of a discriminatory classification is substantially related to achieving a legitimate and substantial goal.*

A number of interesting and crucial points were made in *Hogan*. The obvious one is that men are also protected against sex discrimination under the Equal Protection Clause. After *Michael M.* and *Rostker,* the extent of that protection was in doubt. Another substantial point in *Hogan* is that the Court again asserted that when it applies an intermediate test, that test has teeth. Whether that standard is referred to in the language of *Craig* or merely as "heightened scrutiny," it requires that sex-based laws have an "exceedingly persuasive justification." In reiterating this point, the Court relieved the suspicion that the standard had been weakened in *Michael M.*

By far the most significant point made in *Hogan* is the Court's insistence that the compensatory objective of a sex-based program must be demonstrated by rigorous and convincing evidence. Justice O'Connor found the arrangement here to be oriented more to reinforcing a sex-role stereotype than to compensating women for past discrimination. This appears to reassert the "careful tailoring" requirement that surfaced in *Orr* in connection with purportedly compensatory laws. The Court seems ready to disentangle the threads of latent cultural stereotypes from genuine compensatory projects, and once again to place the burden of proving the aptness of such projects on the government.

A recent application of *Hogan* in the lower courts also involved the exclusion of one sex from a state-run school that prepared people for careers in a profession traditionally associated with the other sex. In this case, the profession involved was the military, and those excluded were women. The male-only admissions policy of the Virginia Military Institute (VMI), one of two public institutions of higher education that still refused to admit women to their undergraduate programs on a full-time basis in the early 1990s, was successfully challenged on equal protection grounds. (See Chapter 6.)

For now, *Hogan* is the leading Supreme Court decision interpreting the Equal Protection Clause as it relates to sex-based laws. The Court's reiteration of the intermediate standard there was helpful, but it should not be mistaken for a solid commitment to a uniform standard of review. As we have seen throughout this chapter, the different members of the Court divide differently on the various issues posed by sex-based laws at different times. Thus, in *Frontiero,* Justice Brennan spoke for only a plurality in calling for special scrutiny of such laws because sex, like race, is "an immutable characteristic determined solely by accident of birth" that "frequently bears no relation to ability to perform or contribute to society" and that often has had "the effect of invidiously relegating the entire class of females to inferior legal status without regard to the actual capabilities of its individual members." Likewise, in *Michael M.,* Justice Rehnquist spoke for only a plurality when he indicated that the objective of sex-based laws is to "provide for the special problems of women" by avoiding "overbroad generalizations based on sex which are entirely unrelated to any differences between men and women or which demean the ability or social status of the affected class." Neither of these views has yet gained a consistent majority of the justices.

Compounding this uncertainty is the change in personnel on the Court. Since 1982, five of the nine justices on the *Hogan* Court have retired and been replaced. Most significant, of course, was the replacement of Chief Justice Burger by Chief Justice Rehnquist. Justice Rehnquist's seat was filled by Justice Scalia. In addition, four key associate justices retired—Justices Powell, Brennan, Marshall, and White— and were replaced by Justices Kennedy, Souter, Thomas and Ginsburg. Just how the "life experiences" of these justices will affect the way the Court approaches equal protection challenges to sex-based laws will be the source of intense interest.

V. THE CONSTITUTIONAL AMENDMENT ALTERNATIVE

Within the U.S. legal system, those interested in abolishing laws and government practices that assign rights and responsibilities on the basis of sex may rely on one or more of three main strategies. First, they may appeal to the legislative and executive branches of government at the various levels in order to revise existing statutes, regulations, programs, and practices individually or in small packages of related measures. This piecemeal approach has been in use at least since the adoption of the Married Women's Property Acts of the mid-nineteenth century. A second strategy involves challenging sex-based laws and practices under the various guarantees of the federal and state constitutions. This approach has been widely used since the *Reed* decision in 1971. As we have seen, however, the Supreme Court appears willing to apply heightened scrutiny to sex-based laws only in a limited range of situations. The third strategy is that of amending federal and state constitutions. It was this approach that finally accomplished the extension of the franchise to women. The drive to erect a constitutional guarantee of equal rights for women and men is popularly thought to have been an episode mainly of the 1970s that focused solely on an amendment to the federal constitution. In fact, this strategy has been deployed since 1923 and also affects state constitutions. In this section, we briefly explore the experience and lessons of the strategy.

The Federal ERA Experience

When the Congress passed the ERA on March 22, 1972, it was understood to have fairly specific objectives. The operative provision of the ERA read: "Equality of rights under the law shall not be denied or abridged by the United States or by any State on account of sex." The leading analysis of the ERA argued for securing an equal rights amendment in addition to equal protection litigation and statutory reform because it would be, relative to the other alternatives, swift, economical, and thorough. Unlike the other strategies, a constitutional amendment would express a permanent, uniform, and national standard for eliminating sex discrimination by government at all levels.

Under that analysis, the ERA would absolutely bar the use of sex-based classifications by governmental bodies, except in rare and readily identifiable situations involving either physical characteristics unique to one sex or privacy rights independently protected by the Constitution. Unlike the views expressed by Justice Powell in his concurring opinion in *Frontiero,* this analysis called for a standard of review even more stringent than the strict scrutiny test developed by the Court for race-based classifications. This analysis anticipated that the ERA would work major changes in the way government programs and agencies were structured, programs such as Social Security and agencies such as the Department of Defense. It also anticipated that the ERA would require the states to make major adjustments in family and criminal law and to eliminate protective labor laws that had proliferated from the early years of this century. (See Brown, Emerson, Falk and Freeman, "The Equal Rights Amendment: A Constitutional Basis for Equal Rights for Women," 80 *Yale Law Journal* 871 (1971).)

As we noted earlier in this chapter, the 1970s saw an expansion of constitutional protections under the equal protection guarantee. During that same period, the implementation of statutory protections improved as well. These developments undercut the arguments advanced by both ERA proponents and opponents. The following selection sketches the history of the ERA at the federal level, from its beginnings in the 1920s through its latest stages.

The ERA Experience and Its Lessons

Jane J. Mansbridge,
Why We Lost the ERA.
Chicago: University of Chicago Press,
1986. Pp. 8–14, 187–99.

The major women's organizations were able to persuade two-thirds of the states to approve women's suffrage in 1920. In the same year these organizations began to discuss an Equal Rights Amendment. Alice Paul and her militant National Woman's Party had gained national notoriety by picketing the White House and staging hunger strikes for women's suffrage. Now the same group proposed a constitutional amendment, introduced in Congress in 1923, that read: "Men and women shall have equal rights throughout the United States and in every place subject to its jurisdiction. Congress shall have power to enforce this article by appropriate legislation."

From the beginning, "equal rights" meant "ending special benefits." An ERA would have made unconstitutional the protective legislation that socialists and social reformers like Florence Kelley, frustrated by the lack of a strong working-class movement in America, had struggled to erect in order to protect at least women and children from the worst ravages of capitalism. Against Kelley and women like her, the National Woman's Party leaders, primarily professional and upper- or upper-middle-class women, argued that "a maximum hour law or a minimum wage law which applied to women but not to men was bound to hurt women more than it could possibly help them." Kelley in turn dubbed the ERA "topsy-turvy feminism," and declared that "women cannot achieve true equality with men by securing identity of treatment under the law."

After a 1921 meeting between Alice Paul, Florence Kelley, and others, the board of directors of the National Consumers' League voted to oppose the Equal Rights Amendment. The League, a powerful Progressive organization of which Kelley was general secretary, thereafter made opposition to the ERA a consistent plank in its program. The strong opposition of Progressive and union feminists meant that when the Equal Rights Amendment was introduced in Congress in 1923 it was immediately opposed by a coalition of Progressive organizations and labor unions. And although the Amendment was introduced in every subsequent Congress for the next twenty years, opposition from this coalition and from most conservatives ensured its repeated defeat.

During the 1930s, the National Association of Women Lawyers and the National Federation of Business and Professional Women's Clubs (BPW) decided to sponsor the ERA, and in 1940 the Republican party revitalized the ERA by placing it in the party's platform. In 1944, despite strong opposition from labor, the Democratic party followed suit. Nonetheless, the ERA never came close to passing until 1950 and 1953, when the U.S. Senate passed it, but with the "Hayden rider," which provided that the Amendment "shall not be construed to impair any rights, benefits, or exemptions now or hereinafter conferred by law upon persons of the female sex." In both years the House of Representatives recessed without a vote. Because the women's organizations supporting the ERA knew that special benefits were incompatible with equal rights, they had tried to block the amended ERA in the House and were relieved when their efforts succeeded.

Support widened during the 1950s—primarily among Republicans, although among the Democrats Eleanor Roosevelt and some other prominent women dropped their opposition to the ERA in order to support the United Nations charter, which affirmed the "equal rights of men and women." In 1953 President Dwight Eisenhower replaced the unionist head of the Federal Women's Bureau with a Republican businesswoman who, having sponsored Connecticut's equal pay law, moved the bureau from active opposition into a neutral position regarding the ERA. In later speeches Eisenhower also stressed the pro-ERA planks of both parties and stated his support for "equal rights" for women. In 1963, however, labor struck back when President John Kennedy's Commission on the Status of Women—created under labor influence partly to siphon off pressure for an ERA—concluded that "a constitutional amendment need not now be sought in order to establish this principle [equal rights for women]."

The crucial step in building progressive and liberal support for the ERA was the passage of Title VII of the Civil Rights Act of 1964, which prohibited job discrimination on the basis of sex. Title VII had originally been designed to prevent discrimination against blacks, but a group of southern congressmen added a ban on discrimination against women in a vain effort to make the bill unacceptable to northern conservatives. Initially, Title VII had no effect on "protective" legislation. Unions, accordingly, continued to oppose the ERA because they thought it would nullify such legislation. In 1967, when the newly formed National Organization for Women (NOW) gave the ERA first place on its Bill of Rights for Women, several union members immediately resigned. But by 1970 both the federal courts and the Equal Employment Opportunity Commission (EEOC) had interpreted Title VII as invalidating protective legislation, and had extended most traditional protections to men rather than removing them for women. With their long-standing concern now for the most part made moot, union opposition to the ERA began to wane.

In 1970, the Pittsburgh chapter of NOW took direct action. The group disrupted Senator Birch Bayh's hearings on the nineteen-year-old vote, getting Bayh to promise hearings on the ERA the following spring. This was the moment. Labor opposition was fading, and, because few radical claims had been made for the ERA, conservatives had little ammunition with which to oppose it. In April, the United Auto Workers' convention voted to endorse the ERA. In May, Bayh began Senate hearings on the ERA, and for the first time in its history the U.S. Department of Labor supported the ERA. In June, Representative Martha Griffiths succeeded in collecting enough signatures on a discharge petition to pry the ERA out of the House

Judiciary Committee, where for many years the liberal chair of the committee, Emanuel Celler, had refused to schedule hearings because of the persistent opposition by labor movement traditionalists. After only an hour's debate, the House of Representatives passed the ERA by a vote of 350 to 15. . . .

. . . .On March 22, 1972, the ERA passed the Senate of the United States with a vote of 84 to 8.

. . .[O]n the very day that the U.S. Senate passed the ERA, Hawaii became the first state to ratify. Delaware, Nebraska, and New Hampshire ratified the next day, and on the third day Idaho and Iowa ratified. Twenty-four more states ratified in 1972 and early 1973. The very earliest states to ratify were all unanimous, and in the other early states the votes were rarely close. . . .

By late 1973, however, the ERA's proponents had lost control of the ratification process. While the national offices of the various pro-ERA organizations could relatively easily coordinate their Washington activities to get the ERA through Congress, they were slow in organizing coalitions in the states. At the end of the 1973 state legislative sessions, only a few states even had active ERA coalitions.

Moreover, in 1973 the Supreme Court decided, in *Roe v. Wade,* that state laws forbidding abortion violated the "right to privacy" implicit in the Constitution. Although the ERA had no obvious direct bearing on whether "abortion is murder," the two issues nonetheless became politically linked. The *Roe* decision took power out of the hands of relatively parochial, conservative state legislators and put it in the hands of a relatively cosmopolitan, liberal U.S. Supreme Court. The ERA would have done the same thing. Furthermore, both were sponsored by what was at that time still called the "women's liberation" movement. Traditionalists saw the "women's libbers" both as rejecting the notion that motherhood was a truly important task and as endorsing sexual hedonism instead of moral restraint. The *Roe* decision seemed to constitute judicial endorsement for these values. Since NOW was not only the leading sponsor of the ERA but the leading defender of abortion on demand, conservative activists saw abortion and the ERA as two prongs of the "libbers' " general strategy for undermining traditional American values. Unable to overturn the *Roe* decision directly, many conservatives sought to turn the ERA into a referendum on that decision. To a significant degree, they succeeded. The opponents began to organize and convinced the first of several states to rescind ratification—a move that had no legal force but certainly made a political difference in unratified states.

Three more states ratified in 1974, one in 1975, and one—Indiana—in 1977, bringing the total to thirty-five of the required thirty-eight. No state ratified after 1977 despite the triumph of ERA proponents in 1978 in getting Congress to extend the original 1979 deadline until 1982. In 1982 this extension ran out, and the Amendment died. Alabama, Arizona, Arkansas, Florida, Georgia, Illinois, Louisiana, Mississippi, Missouri, Nevada, North Carolina, Oklahoma, South Carolina, Utah, and Virginia had not ratified. All were Mormon or southern states, except Illinois, which required a three-fifths majority for ratifying constitutional amendments and which had a strongly southern culture in the third of the state surrounded by Missouri and Kentucky. . . .

In January 1983, the ERA was reintroduced in the U.S. House of Representatives. After hearings in the spring, Republican representatives proposed a series of amendments to the ERA, providing that it would not require public funding for abortion, would not draft women, would not send women into combat, and would not jeopardize the tax-exempt status of all-male and all-female schools and colleges. To avoid discussing or voting on these amendments, the Democratic Speaker of the House suspended normal rules when the issue came to the floor in November, limited debate to forty minutes, and barred any modifications of the measure on the floor. The Speaker took this action because, he said, he "doubted very, very much" that all of the proposed amendments could have been defeated. In these circumstances the ERA garnered 278 votes for passage and 147 against. It thus fell six votes short of the two-thirds majority needed for a constitutional amendment. Since the Senate is currently more conservative than the House, and since state legislators are far more conservative than Congress on this issue, it seems clear that an ERA of the kind Congress passed in 1972 has virtually no chance of being ratified in the near future.

The political demise of the ERA poses a number of questions. First, with the wisdom born of hindsight, feminists must ask themselves a strategic question: Was the struggle worth the enormous effort they poured into it? Second, anyone involved in the political process can fruitfully ask tactical questions about the struggle: Were any "mistakes" made in the campaign from which all political activists can learn? Finally, there is the question of what to do in the future: Should feminists continue the struggle for the ERA, or abandon it, at least for the moment? . . .

Although the ERA provoked little informed or subtle debate regarding its own impact, it did foster discussion of women's issues more generally. For ten years the ERA focused public attention on women's disadvantage in the workplace, the home, and the streets. The effect was probably greatest in those states that did not ratify, for issues like these had not previously had a large role in the public life of these states. . . .

The ERA ratification campaign brought many women on the Left and the Right into active politics for the first time in their lives. It more than trebled the membership of NOW, making it stronger today than its counterpart in almost any other country. . . .

The attempt to put an ERA in the Constitution also produced important changes in political and judicial practice. At the federal level, the fact that Congress passed the ERA almost certainly encouraged the Supreme Court to interpret the Fourteenth Amendment as barring many varieties of discrimination against women, although uncertainty about the ERA's prospects for ratification may have later discouraged the Court from making gender a suspect classification.

On the state level, the campaign's impact varied greatly from one state to another. In many states, adopting a state ERA, or sometimes even ratifying the federal ERA, led the legislators to review state laws and rewrite them in "gender-neutral" form. . . .

The campaign had costs, but they were not excessive. Because the ratification campaign lost, feminists perhaps lost some political credibility. But the defeat came by a very narrow margin. At least in the key unratified states, legislators were impressed by the duration and intensity of the political effort that both sides mounted. . . .

In some cases, no doubt, the ratification battle also diverted energy from other feminist causes. But there is no fixed supply of activist talent and energy that NOW or other groups can allocate as they see fit. The ratification campaign in the 1970s and early 1980s dramatically increased both the numbers of feminist activists and the money available to them. . . .

All political activists will have gained something worthwhile from these ten years if the history of the ERA ratification campaign can teach more general lessons about politics and voluntary organizations. The major lesson of this book, which applies not only to women's groups but to all volunteers who work for a political cause, is that the very structure of a voluntary political organization tends to produce an inability to hear or understand what others are saying. This is, almost by definition, an unconscious error. And the first step toward correcting such errors is to make them conscious.

This book has shown how volunteer activity encourages ideological purity and allows individuals to make choices for which they are not accountable. It also has shown how decisions by accretion accentuate the impact of unconscious assumptions. Forewarned, anyone who volunteers for political activity can perceive, and begin to resist, the psychological temptations of dividing the world into the pure and impure. Activists can learn to ask to what degree their having freely volunteered their time exonerates them from accountability to others. And they can learn to watch for the inevitable tendency of every organization to drift into decisions without realizing that a decision is even being made.

Committed activists also need to question their almost automatic rejection of the muddled thinking and compromises that characterize mainstream discussions of most issues. The muddled middle is often muddled, not because it is composed of morons, lunatics, or unprincipled opportunists but because it is composed of people trying to reconcile conflicting principles and commitments that are all quite legitimate. Activists who are aware of the way their self-selection, sacrifice, and exposure to others like themselves encourages them to oversimplify should become more willing to listen to legislators, churches, and other groups that are sympathetic to their views but not totally committed to them.

While the decade of agitation for and against the ERA on balance raised the consciousness of many Americans on matters relating to women as well as producing significant concrete gains, continuing this particular struggle now would probably yield diminishing returns and might become counterproductive.

During this moratorium, feminists will need to discuss what would be best for all women in the realms of combat, school athletics, prisons, and sex-blind legislation generally. Since about 1980, as more women have experienced the results of gender-neutral legislation like no-fault divorce laws and joint custody, some feminists have begun to articulate a critique of egalitarianism that looks much like Marx's critique of bourgeois equality. They argue that in a society where one group holds most of the power, "neutral" laws usually benefit the powerful group. . . .

. . .Whatever the reasons, the years immediately after 1982 saw the start of a lively, thought-provoking debate among feminist lawyers on, among other issues, how thoroughly the law should embrace strict gender neutrality It also saw the publication of several books by feminists that took seriously the concerns of those who opposed traditional feminist positions. . . .

. . .In ten or twenty years it may be possible to pass an ERA that expresses the principle of equality between the sexes in language as simple and unadorned as that of the Bill of Rights and the Fourteenth Amendment. It may even be possible at that time to develop a different legislative history that would extend the Amendment to prohibit some of the laws that discriminate in fact, and not just in intent, against women. But if this book indicates anything, it is that persuad-

THE CONSTITUTIONAL AMENDMENT ALTERNATIVE **99**

ing state legislators to vote for such an Amendment would require a major change in political climate.

STUDY QUESTIONS

1. According to this account, what were the reasons that the ERA was initially opposed? What subsequent developments undercut

that opposition? Did those same developments also undercut the need for an ERA?

2. In what way did the pro-ERA coalition lose control of the ratification process? Had it been more astute organizationally, would that have changed the outcome?

3. In what ways was the ratification drive worthwhile? What lessons does the ERA experience hold for us?

———————————————— ੨੧ ————————————————

In November 1992, the voters of Iowa rejected an initiative that would have added an Equal Rights Amendment to their state constitution by 52 percent to 48 percent. This adds to the credibility of Mansbridge's judgment that the political climate is not yet ripe for a reiteration of the constitutional amendment strategy. Even so, it is worth noting and remembering that an ERA would probably have generated results that are difficult to accomplish otherwise. During the congressional ERA hearings held in 1983, legal experts testified that the ERA would generate different results than had the Equal Protection Clause in a number of the cases that we have studied in this chapter. They reasoned that the ERA would have brought about a different outcome in *Geduldig, Ballard, Feeney,* and *Rostker.* If that logic is sound, the need for an ERA has not been entirely preempted by the developments of the past two decades.

The State ERA Experience

One by-product of the federal ERA ratification drive, as Mansbridge noted, was the adoption of equal rights amendments to several state constitutions. During the 1970s, nine states added amendments to their constitutions nearly identical to the proposed federal ERA. These states included: Pennsylvania (1971), Colorado, Hawaii, Maryland, Texas, Washington (1972), New Mexico (1973), New Hampshire (1974), and Massachusetts (1976). These amendments to state constitutions are of interest for three reasons: they show how additional avenues can be used to vindicate the rights of victims of sex discrimination; they shed light on the likely consequences of adopting the ERA at the federal level; and they suggest what an ERA can accomplish that an Equal Protection Clause cannot.

The interpretations given by state courts to these ERAs fall across a spectrum. Some endorse an absolute bar to the use of any sex-based classification; others impose only strict scrutiny. This section explores the experience of one state on the strictest end of that spectrum—Pennsylvania.

The Pennsylvania Equal Rights Amendment
Equality of rights under the law shall not be denied or abridged in the Commonwealth of Pennsylvania because of the sex of the individual.
Pa. Const., Art. I, Sec. 28 [previously Sec. 27].

As required by its state constitution, the Pennsylvania ERA was passed by two consecutive sessions of the state legislature and was submitted for ratification to the voters in a statewide referendum. On March 18, 1971, that referendum was approved by the voters by an overwhelming margin while the U.S. Senate was still debating the federal ERA. As a result of early judicial activism, a strong stand by the executive branch, an energetic family law and public interest bar, and active participation by women's organizations, Pennsylvania quickly experienced a variety of ERA-related developments. In the first of a series of ERA cases, the state's supreme court declared, in *Henderson v. Henderson,* 327 A.2d 60 (1974), that "the sex of citizens of this Commonwealth is no longer a permissible factor in the determination of their legal rights and legal responsibilities." In that same year, it reiterated the point when it announced in *Commonwealth v. Butler,* 328 A.2d 851, that the purpose of the state ERA was to eliminate sex as a "classifying tool." In early 1975, the same court struck down a presumption then common in family law. In the case that follows, the Pennsylvania Supreme Court held that the common law doctrine, rooted in coverture, that presumes that the husband owns the property of a married couple is invalid on the ground that it is clearly sex-based. The second aspect of the decision, however, has even greater significance. The court also found invalid the trial court's presumption that the purchaser of marital property is its owner. The presumption incorporates a classification that is neutral on its face but disproportionately disadvantages women. In that respect, the decision appears to indicate that the ERA in this state goes beyond the requirements of the federal Equal Protection Clause because it does not require a showing of purposeful discrimination (see *Pers. Admin. of Mass. v. Feeney* in this chapter).

DiFlorido v. DiFlorido

Supreme Court of Pennsylvania, 1975.
459 Pa. 641, 331 A.2d 174.

JONES, Chief Justice.

The parties in this case, appellee, Rose A. DiFlorido, and appellant, Noe A. DiFlorido, were married on September 17, 1960. Thereafter, Mr. and Mrs. DiFlorido resided together as husband and wife until their separation on October 15, 1970. Subsequently, on June 18, 1971, the DiFloridos were divorced. . . . The trial judge . . . directed the appellant to pay over to the appellee one-half of the appraised value of certain property consisting of household goods and furnishings. . . .

The appellant now contends that the preceding dispositions were improper for the following reasons: . . . (4) since the appellant was the sole provider during the marriage and since household goods found in the joint possession of husband and wife *presumptively* belong to the husband, the appellee should have been found to have no interest in those household goods. . . .

In order to ascertain the ownership of these household items, the lower court traced the source of funds used in purchasing the contested property and then, *presuming* the *purchaser* to be the owner, placed the burden on the other party to show that a gift to the marital unit had been made. . . .

Turning, for the moment, to the lower court's approach of determining the *actual* purchaser, we note that such approach eliminates the injustice of initially presuming that the husband purchased *all* property intimately associated with the marriage. Nevertheless, we can not accept an approach that would base ownership of household items on proof of funding alone, since to do so would necessitate an itemized accounting whenever a dispute over household goods arose and would fail to acknowledge the *equally important* and often substantial non-monetary contributions made by either spouse.

With the passage of the Equal Rights Amendment, this Court has striven to insure the equality of rights under the law and to eliminate sex as a basis for distinction. Since "the law will not impose different benefits or different burdens upon the members of a society based on the fact that they may be man or woman" Henderson v. Henderson, we unhesitatingly discard the one-sided presumption confronted today. Furthermore, having found that the husband is no longer necessarily the "sole provider" and noting that even where he is, it is likely that both spouses have contributed in some way to the acquisition and/or upkeep of, and that both spouses intend to benefit by the use of, the goods and furnishings in the household, we will not burden either party with proving that such household items were donated to the marital unit.

We conclude, therefore, that for the purpose of determining title of household goods and furnishings between husband and wife, the property that has been acquired in anticipation of or during marriage, and which has been possessed and used by both spouses, will, in the absence of evidence showing otherwise, be presumed to be held jointly by the entireties. Since in this case, there was no proof of title to overcome such presumption, and since, in any

event, the only evidence adduced at trial comported with a finding of joint ownership, we will not disturb the lower court's findings.

Order and decree affirmed.

STUDY QUESTIONS

1. Which of the presumptions used by the trial court was rejected here?
2. What contributions by the wife did this presumption neglect? Should such contributions be recognized as equivalent to monetary contributions to the family unit? Why?
3. Is the classification used by this presumption sex-neutral? If the law were to honor this presumption, would it impose "different benefits or different burdens upon members of society based on the fact that they may be man or woman"?

Using the state ERA, the Pennsylvania courts abolished or substantially altered many other common law doctrines and government practices. Some of these decisions might have been reached under the Equal Protection Clause. For example, in *Hopkins v. Blanco,* 320 A.2d 139 (1974), the state supreme court considered the common law rule that dated back to coverture permitting husbands, but not wives, to recover damages for the loss of their spouses' services, especially their sexual services. The court found that rule in conflict with the state ERA and extended the right of recovery to the wife. Similarly, in *Commonwealth v. Carson,* 368 A.2d 635 (1977), the state supreme court invalidated the "tender years" doctrine as inconsistent with the ERA. That doctrine required courts hearing child custody cases to presume that the mother of young children is better suited to care for the child's needs than the father. The doctrine of "coercion" was another principle of common law abandoned under the ERA, *Commonwealth v. Santiago,* 340 A.2d 440 (Sup. Ct. of Pa. 1975). Under that doctrine, wives who commit crimes jointly with their husbands were immune from prosecution because they are presumed to be under the power and authority of their husbands. This too was a relic of the age in which coverture was predominant.

Some decisions reached under the Pennsylvania ERA produced results that are not currently available under the federal Equal Protection Clause. *DiFlorido's* invalidation of the facially sex-neutral presumption that the purchaser of property is its owner represents one of these. Two other decisions rejected the "separate but equal" doctrine as applied to sex segregation in public schools, even though the federal courts had reached a contrary result under the Fourteenth Amendment in *Vorchheimer v. School District of Philadelphia.* (See Chapter 6.) In *Commonwealth v. P.I.A.A.* (see Chapter 6), an appellate court found sex-segregated school sports in violation of the ERA. Likewise, a trial court found an all-male admissions policy for a public high school invalid under the state ERA. (See *Newberg v. Bd. of Educ.* in Chapter 6.)

Another result that probably could not have been reached under the federal Equal Protection Clause came from a sequence of cases that extended throughout the 1980s and ended in the abolition of the use of sex-based rate schedules by private insurance companies operating within the state. In 1980, a state appellate court held that the reach of the state's ERA was restricted by the "state action" limitation, just as is the federal Equal Protection Clause, which imposes constitutional limits only on governmental conduct. As a result, a man suing under the ERA could not have a private insurance company enjoined from charging him more for his auto insurance policy because of his sex. Four years later, the state supreme court reversed that decision. Thereafter, the state legislature enacted a statute, over the governor's veto, that specifically authorized sex-based insurance rate tables. That act, in turn, was successfully challenged in the following case.

Bartholomew v. Foster

Commonwealth Court of Pennsylvania, 1988. 541 A.2d 393. Affirmed by an equally divided vote of the Pennsylvania Supreme Court, 563 A.2d 1390 (1989).

COLINS, Judge

Before the Court in its original jurisdiction are cross-motions for summary judgment seeking to determine the validity of Section 3(e) of The Casualty and Surety Rate Regulatory Act (Rate Act) which provides for gender-based automotive insurance rates.

Section 3 of the Rate Act, entitled "Making of rates," lists the various provisions under which all rates shall be determined. Subsection (e) of that provision, enacted on April 14, 1986, states:

> This section shall not be construed to prohibit rates for automobile insurance which are based, in whole or in part, on factors, including, but not limited to, sex, if the use of such a factor is supported by sound actuarial principles or is related to actual or reasonably anticipated experience; however, such factors shall not include race, religion or national origin.

Ann and Craig Bartholomew (petitioners) brought this action on behalf of themselves and their then seventeen year old son, Jonathan, to enjoin the Insurance Commissioner of Pennsylvania (Insurance Commissioner or respondent) from enforcing the 1986 amendment to the Rate Act. Petitioners were insured by the Erie Insurance Group, which insurer, along with National Mutual Insurance Company and State Farm Mutual Automobile Insurance Company, was granted intervenor status in this matter.

Intervenor, Erie Insurance, bases its insurance rates for passenger cars driven by persons under the age of twenty-four at least in part on the sex of the individual driver. Petitioners, accordingly, were charged a higher premium for their son's auto insurance than would be a similar family insuring a teenage daughter. They seek an order declaring Section 3(e) of the Rate Act violative of article I, § 28 of the Pennsylvania Constitution (Pennsylvania Equal Rights Amendment) and further enjoining the Commissioner from otherwise enforcing the Rate Act. Respondent seeks a contrary declaration and contends that Section 3(e) of the Rate Act is constitutional because the gender-based insurance rates charged by the respective companies are founded upon sound actuarial principles. . . .

The petitioners argue that they are entitled to judgment as a matter of law because Section 3(e) of the Rate Act clearly violates the constitutional mandate of the Pennsylvania Equal Rights Amendment and the case law interpreting that provision. To support their proposition, petitioners cite *Henderson v. Henderson*. . . .

The respondent attempts to counter petitioners' argument by stating that the Pennsylvania Equal Rights Amendment only prohibits sex discrimination under law. In other words, according to respondent, this constitutional provision applies only to action attributable to the state and not to insurance rates charged by private companies to private policyholders. Respondent argues that there is no state action involved in the matter sub judice. It submits that the Rate Act itself does not create sexual classifications in insurance rates but permits insurance companies to structure their rates on gender classifications so long as such classifications are actuarially sound. . . .

The respondent's lengthy discussion of the federal concept of state action is inappropriate here. In *Hartford Accident & Indemnity v. Insurance Comm'r,* 482 A.2d 542 (1984), the Supreme Court found:

> The "state action" test is applied by the courts in determining whether, in a given case, a state's involvement in private activity is sufficient to justify the application of a federal constitutional prohibition of state action to that conduct. The rationale underlying the "state action" doctrine is irrelevant to the interpretation of the scope of the Pennsylvania Equal Rights Amendment, a state constitutional amendment adopted by the Commonwealth as part of its own organic law. The

language of that enactment, not a test to measure the extent of federal constitutional protections, is controlling. *Id.* at 549 (emphasis added).

In order to invoke the provisions of the Pennsylvania Equal Rights Amendment, we conclude that there is no requirement of state action as arguably found under the proposed Equal Rights Amendment to the United States Constitution. . . .

. . . Accordingly, we must declare that sex-based gender classifications pertaining to insurance rates are unconstitutional. . . .

. . .[P]etitioners' Motion for Summary Judgment . . . is hereby granted. The respondent's and intervenors' Cross-Motion for Summary Judgment is hereby denied. . . .

STUDY QUESTIONS

1. What reasons did the Bartholomews propose for overturning the Rate Act? What reasons did the group of insurance companies propose in its support?
2. Which of these arguments did the court accept? Why? Had this challenge been brought under the Equal Protection Clause, would the result have been different?

This is not to suggest that the full protections envisioned by the defenders of the federal ERA are already in place in Pennsylvania or any of the other states that have such constitutional provisions. The clearest exception, of course, is the Abortion Control Act that was upheld by the U.S. Supreme Court in the 1992 *Casey* decision. In a 1985 decision, the Pennsylvania Supreme Court upheld a provision of that act that limits public funding of abortions to those that are necessary to save the life of the mother and to pregnancies that resulted from rape or incest. The court rejected an ERA challenge to that limitation. (See Chapter 8 for *Casey* and other decisions on public funding of abortions.) Even though all medically necessary services for men were reimbursable, while a medically necessary abortion, which by its nature can only affect women, was not reimbursable, the court declared, in language reminiscent of *Geduldig,* that "the distinction here is not sex but abortion, and the statute does not accord varying benefits to men and women because of their sex, but accords varying benefits to one class of women, as distinct from another, based on a voluntary choice made by the women." (*Fischer v. Comm. Dept. of Public Welfare* 502 A.2d 114, 314 (1985).)

The state judiciary was not the only branch of government involved in implementing the state's ERA. Shortly after the state supreme court handed down the decision in *Henderson,* implementation of the ERA began in the other branches of state government. The main impetus came when the governor issued an executive order charging the Commission for Women with the responsibility of analyzing existing statutes and recommending changes consistent with the mandate of the ERA. Three years later, following a computer search of all statutes then in force, the commission proposed a package of twenty-six major bills to the legislature. Most of these were approved by the legislature and signed into law by the governor within four years.

The legislature took action on specific statutory provisions and on entire codes. It extended the special tax privilege of widows to widowers, revised the bases for temporary alimony awards—formerly granted only to wives, now available to economically dependent spouses of either sex—and recognized that the testimony of rape victims is as credible as the testimony of male victims of violent crimes. Entire sections of the Pennsylvania Code underwent significant revision. These included the Criminal, Probate, Judicial, Military, Public School, and Partnership Codes. Major amendments were also adopted in the laws regarding tax, child labor, welfare, landlords and tenants, and employment.

Under the mandate of the ERA, state agencies issued new regulations. Public schools are now required to open all classes, programs, and activities to both sexes. This regulation had significant effect on physical and vocational education programs. Although all physical education classes at the elementary level are co-ed, as are selected classes at the secondary level, boys and girls are not required to share locker rooms. Banks subject to state regulation are now on notice to end sex discrimination in all their dealings, including employment and credit. Anyone licensed to sell liquor in the state must now serve both men and women and may not discriminate in employment.

Finally, the attorney general of the state issued opinions to implement the ERA. These directed various state agencies, bureaus, and commissions to terminate sexually discriminatory practices. In the area of employment, the attorney general declared invalid statutes that barred the payment of unemployment benefits to women who are unable to continue on their jobs during the thirty days before and after childbirth, that limited newspaper delivery to boys, and that limited cosmetologists to working only on female customers' hair. The attorney general also declared invalid a proposed minimum height requirement for state police and limitation on police employment and the newspaper practice of listing sex-segregated "help wanted" advertisements. In other areas, the attorney general directed state agencies and departments to avoid providing grants or financial assistance to any organization—public or private—that limited membership to one sex. Another opinion declared invalid a statute that provided fewer benefits to widowers than widows of former state employees who died in the line of duty. Another removed bureaucratic barriers to married women using their birth names.

Not all state constitutions contain ERAs or similar provisions. Nine states adopted their own ERAs in the early 1970s. Seven others have constitutional provisions that closely approximate the language of the federal ERA. Although not all of these states have adopted the strict standard of review or the activist posture found in Pennsylvania, the Pennsylvania ERA experience may be a good predictor of what can result from the adoption of an ERA at the federal level. What are the lessons of the Pennsylvania experience?

The Pennsylvania experience makes several points with crystal clarity. First, the legal chaos anticipated by many opponents of the federal ERA did not occur. Public toilets are still sex-segregated. The ERA has not caused a greater instability in family life. The abandonment of sex-segregated schools and school sport programs has not resulted in a decline in academic or athletic performance or in unisex locker rooms, and homosexual marriage has not increased due to the ERA.

A second point made clear by the Pennsylvania experience is that the implementation of an ERA requires an enormous commitment. The time and energy of citizens has been and continues to be required to realize the promise of the ERA. The hidden costs of the strategy needed to achieve justice between the sexes by means of a constitutional amendment are significant.

The final lesson is that the reach of an Equal Rights Amendment can be significantly broader than that of the Equal Protection Clause. In *DiFlorido,* we saw that a facially neutral principle that has disparate impact on women can be successfully challenged under an ERA. Earlier in this chapter, however, we saw in *Feeney* that an equal protection challenge of such a principle fails unless it is shown to have been adopted for an invidious purpose. We also noted earlier that the federal Equal Protection Clause is limited by "state action"—only governments can violate its guarantee.

Three important points emerge when we combine the lessons of the federal ERA experience, as developed by Mansbridge, and the lessons of the Pennsylvania experience with a state ERA listed above. Important results can be accomplished better by a constitutional amendment. An ERA can be a catalyst for thoroughly overhauling the common law doctrines, agency regulations, and government practices that litter the legal landscape. The organization and commitment of a wide spectrum of the public and elected officials are necessary ingredients for exploiting the full potential of this strategy. The window of opportunity for developing that organization and that commitment on a broad enough scale to reap the benefits of a federal ERA, in all likelihood, will not open again at least for another decade or so.

3 Evolving Feminist Perspectives

I n Chapter 1, we noted with historian Gerda Lerner that patriarchy involves pervasive male dominance in both the public and the private spheres. An important mechanism for maintaining that pattern is permanent heterosexual marriage. In that relationship, the man's role is to provide resources and protection for the woman and children in the household, and the woman's role centers on bearing and rearing children and serving the man. Although women under patriarchy may not be totally powerless and exploited, they are consistently subordinated to men. Moreover, they generally must exercise the limited power available to them by indirect manipulation or by making appeals based on their special circumstances. As Abigail Adams and Catherine Beecher observed, these powers can be quite effective in improving women's conditions. These same themes of protection and appeal to special circumstances survive in our century and have played a formative role in constitutional litigation. The brief submitted by Louis Brandeis in *Muller v. Oregon* illustrates the former, and the decision by the Supreme Court in *Hoyt v. Florida* illustrates the latter.

Women have always struggled to improve their own condition and that of their loved ones. Until the nineteenth century, that struggle was typically carried on from within the patriarchal order. Feminists also struggle to improve the condition of women and their loved ones. The distinctive feature of feminism, however, is the rejection of the patriarchal order. Beginning with the Grimké sisters and the Seneca Falls Declaration of Sentiments, feminists have worked to replace the patriarchal pattern of relationship with another order of things.

I. ALTERNATIVE APPROACHES

Questions bearing on what the new relationship among the sexes should be, on how that objective is best advanced within existing circumstances, and on what role law ought to play in the process have been controversial among feminists from the beginning. Like all activists, feminists maintain a lively debate over both the means and the goals of their struggle. One persistent pattern in the controversy for the past century and a half that is of particular interest in the feminist legal community relates to legal strategies, viz., what changes in law are most likely to lead to significant improvement in the condition of women. Two alternatives are perennially discussed.

One, which might be called *the asymmetrical approach,* contends that it is crucial to recognize women's unique needs and to value their special contributions. It argues that the best way to do this is by means of sex-specific laws and policies that treat women differently than men. The other, which might be called *the symmetrical approach,* argues that women are best served by making sex irrelevant to all decisions governing opportunities available to women and men. It contends that the best way to secure this is through sex-neutral statutes and regulations that stress the analogies between the life situations of women and men.

The asymmetrical-symmetrical debate over feminist goals and strategies has continued since the Grimké sisters first advocated the moral rights of women. We also noticed in Chapter 1 that, to achieve the franchise, Elizabeth Cady Stanton and mainstream feminists of the late nineteenth and early twentieth centuries increasingly abandoned the drive for equal rights in solidarity with men and women of color in favor of arguments from expediency that focused on the special needs of women. We saw that many feminists, impressed by the urgency of the needs of women and impatient with more general reform initiatives, supported both protective and compensatory measures during the first six decades of the twentieth century. As an example of the contest between the asymmetical and symmetrical approaches, consider the following debate over the merits of the ERA that occurred shortly after the ratification of the Nineteenth Amendment, which extended the franchise to women. The affirmative side of the debate defended a symmetrical approach, while the negative side took an asymmetrical approach.

Shall Women Be Equal before the Law?

The Nation (April 12, 1922).
Pp. 419–21.

YES!

By Elsie Hill

The removal of all forms of the subjection of women is the purpose to which the National Woman's Party is dedicated. Its present campaign to remove the discriminations against women in the laws of the United States is but the beginning of its determined effort to secure the freedom of women, an integral part of the struggle for human liberty for which women are first of all responsible. Its interest lies in the final release of woman from the class of a dependent, subservient being to which early civilization committed her.

The laws of various States at present hold her in that class. [The article then lists provisions in state laws that disadvantage women.] . . .

The National Woman's Party believes that it is a vital social need to do away with these discriminations against women and is devoting its energies to that end. The removal of the discriminations and not the method by which they are removed is the thing upon which the Woman's Party insists. [Next, the text of an early draft of the ERA was included.] . . .

There are two ways by which discriminations against women may be removed and by which equal rights before the law may be conferred. One method is by a general enactment, such as the law to which I refer, and the other method is by amending a multiplicity of special statutes on a variety of subjects treated in the statutes. The first method is simple and direct; the second cumbersome, complicated, and inconsistent with the amendment to the Federal Constitution granting full privileges and rights by the fundamental law.

Our experience, therefore, convinces us that the general enactment is in complete harmony with the Federal amendment, and directly effective in establishing full equality of men and women before the law. . . .

NO!

By Florence Kelley

Sex is a biological fact. The political rights of citizens are not properly dependent upon sex, but social and domestic relations and industrial activities are. All modern-minded people desire that women should have full political equality and like opportunity in business and the professions. No enlightened person desires that they should be excluded from jury duty or denied the equal guardianship of children, or that unjust inheritance laws or discriminations against wives should be perpetuated.

The inescapable facts are, however, that men do not bear children, are freed from the burdens of maternity, and are not susceptible, in the same measure as women, to poisons now increasingly characteristic of certain industries, and to the universal poison of fatigue. These differences are so far reaching, so fundamental, that it is grotesque to ignore them. Women cannot be

made men by act of the legislature or by amendment of the Federal Constitution. This is no matter of today or tomorrow. The inherent differences are permanent. Women will always need many laws different from those needed by men.

The effort to enact the blanket bill in defiance of all biological differences recklessly imperils the special laws for women as such, for wives, for mothers, and for wage-earners. . . .

If women are subject to the *same* freedom of contract as men, will not women wage-earners lose the statutory eight-hour day, rest at night, and one day's rest in seven, which they now have under statutes that, *pro tanto,* limit their freedom of contract? . . . Why should wage-earning women be thus forbidden to get laws for their own health and welfare and that of their unborn children? Why should they be made subject to the preferences of wage-earning men? . . .

If there were no other way of promoting more perfect equality for women, an argument could perhaps be sustained for taking these risks. But why take them when every desirable measure attainable through the blanket bill can be enacted in the ordinary way? . . .

The contest between the two approaches heated up once again at the end of the twentieth century. Although there are similarities among the debates over feminist legal strategy that have occurred over the past century and a half, they each had their distinctive character and pragmatic focus. The following selection explores the nature of the debate in the feminist legal community during the 1980s.

Thoughts on Living and Moving with the Recurring Divide

Nadine Taub.
24 *Georgia Law Review* 965–69 (1990).

This article was originally published at 24 Ga. L. Rev. 965 and is reprinted with permission.

. . . The concrete issues splitting legal feminists have involved pressing problems. Among them

are whether women should be drafted, whether pregnant women should be accorded special job guarantees and other work-related benefits, whether women should be given an edge in child custody disputes through the use of primary caretaker standards, whether ordinances should be enacted to provide civil actions against pornographers and whether birthmothers should always be preferred in contract parenthood disputes.

Underlying these issue-oriented disputes are more theoretical controversies. Do women share traits as a group that exceed their differences? To what extent are the differences between women and men biological and immutable? To what extent are they socially constructed and subject to change? To what extent is such change desirable? Will insisting on mixed gender activities—particularly political activities—destroy women's special sensibility and solidarity? When is sex-based legislation or other governmental action acceptable? Is it more important to encourage women and men to assume different roles or to reward women who have fulfilled traditional expectations? What role does the law play in shaping sex-based attitudes and behaviors? Is sexuality, the sexual division of labor, or some other factor the key to women's oppression? How critical is male involvement in childrearing?

A common thread runs through these theoretical controversies. To a large extent, it is a dispute that goes to the permanency and desirability of differences between women and men. For some, reducing difference means eliminating rules and practices that have constrained and continue to constrain women, thus expanding the options available to them as individuals. For others, recognizing women's contributions and identity as valuable is the priority, and retaining difference is critical to that recognition. As positions have solidified, the debate over minimizing or maximizing this difference has solidified into a recurring divide running through the feminist legal community.

Today's feminist disputes have involved—and often have confused—three different levels of struggle. First is the identity question, frequently key to political action. With whom do we sympathize? For example, does one have an immediate tendency to side with Mary Beth Whitehead irrespective of one's view of contract parenthood or surrogacy? Whose actions are we moved to join? For instance, whether or not we perceive peace as a women's issue, do we seek women-only groups to contest military hegemony?

The related issue of maximizing our effectiveness goes to the second strategic level. How are we most likely to make the changes that will lead us to liberation? How will we best be heard? Do we emphasize the uniqueness of pregnancy, for example, or do we point out what it has in common with other conditions in various contexts?

The third level of struggle involves defining our ultimate goal. What is liberation? What is equality? Do we seek equal power, dignity and respect for women who will remain—for biological or other reasons—significantly different from men? Or do we seek a world in which one's situation and choices are determined as much as possible independent of sex? What one thinks one ultimately wants varies with time and circumstance and is obviously difficult, if not impossible, to foresee clearly under conditions that both oppress women and fail to acknowledge, let alone value, our contributions. Yet the question "[i]n an ideal world, what would [women's] situation look like?" continues to be asked and different visions continue to be offered. . . .

STUDY QUESTIONS

1. Identify the concrete issues that were debated among feminists during the 1980s. Which of these issues are still controversial? Where do you stand on the issues that are still "hot"?
2. What were the three levels of struggle that Taub distinguished? Are these levels interrelated? Should our commitment to particular goals be determined by whom we sympathize with in specific conflicts, or should it be the other way around?
3. On which of the levels of struggle distinguished by Taub would you locate the debate between Hill and Kelley?

———————————— ❧ ————————————

In this chapter, we trace the evolution of the current debate within the feminist legal community by focusing on one problem—pregnancy in the workplace. In the next section, we trace the approach taken to this problem by the Supreme Court and Congress. In the final section we will trace the debate prompted among feminists by these legal developments.

II. PREGNANCY IN THE WORKPLACE

Much of the initial phase of feminism's second wave sought to achieve gender equality and women's liberation by eliminating arbitrary restraints that preserved male dominance in the public sphere. Thus, as we saw in Chapter 2, constitutional challenges were generally successful when they demonstrated that women were similarly situated to men and therefore entitled to the same positions, compensation, and benefits as men. However, as we see in this chapter, when advocates for women sought to analogize temporary incapacities due to pregnancy and childbirth to temporary incapacities suffered by men as well as women, their court challenges failed. Subsequent legislative actions and theoretical developments prompted intense debate over the best way for the law to treat pregnancy and childbearing.

Pregnancy-related policies in the workplace were the focus of these developments. These policies too often assumed that women's primary commitment was to homemaking, with the result that women were turned away from jobs and the needs of those women who remained were ignored.

> . . . [M]any employers either would not hire married women, or would not hire married women with young children. When women workers became pregnant, they faced a range of adverse consequences. Often, it was simply understood that they would quit, and the lack of any maternity leave policies usually assured that this would be so. Other women were fired, or relegated to less desirable jobs. . . . [M]any women faced mandatory maternity leaves that were unrelated to their ability or desire to work and that adversely affected their benefits and future job prospects. . . . While on leave, usually without income, women in some states found that they could not receive unemployment compensation, because the state defined them as unable to work by the very fact of their new motherhood.
>
> *Lucinda M. Finley. "Transcending Equality Theory: A Way Out of the Maternity and the Workplace Debate." 86* Columbia Law Review *1118, at 1123–25 (1986).*

State and federal statutes frequently reinforce such expectations and policies on the part of employers, and there is at present little prospect that the courts will overturn them on equal protection grounds. Indeed, the only successful constitutional challenges to pregnancy-related employment policies argued that a state's mandatory leave policies unduly burdened the fundamental right to bear a child. (See *Cleveland Board of Education v. LaFleur,* 414 U.S. 632 (1974).) The *Geduldig* ruling, by contrast, emphasized that the capacity to become pregnant is unique to women. It is, therefore, a real difference between women and men and justifies their different treatment.

The principal vehicle used in the past three decades to reform employer's discriminatory policies toward pregnant workers has been Title VII of the Civil Rights Act of 1964, which prohibits, among other things, discrimination by employers "because of sex." The act, as will be discussed in detail in Chapters 4 and 5, has played a major role in eliminating unfair constraints on women's occupational opportunities. However, as originally enacted, Title VII was silent as to whether employment decisions based on pregnancy were to be understood as sex discrimination for the purposes of Title VII. Two years after the Supreme Court ruled in *Geduldig* that pregnancy-based classifications are not sex-based for the purposes of equal protection considerations, the question was posed as to whether pregnancy discrimination is discrimination "because of sex" under Title VII. The Court's answer was the same.

General Electric Co. v. Gilbert

Supreme Court of the United States, 1976. 429 U.S. 125, 97 S.Ct. 401, 50 L.Ed.2d 343.

MR. JUSTICE REHNQUIST delivered the opinion of the Court.

Petitioner, General Electric Co., provides for all of its employees a disability plan which pays weekly nonoccupational sickness and accident benefits. Excluded from the plan's coverage, however, are disabilities arising from pregnancy. Respondents, on behalf of a class of women employees, brought this action seeking, inter alia, a declaration that this exclusion constitutes sex discrimination in violation of Title VII of the Civil Rights Act of 1964. The District Court for the Eastern District of Virginia, following a trial on the merits, held that the exclusion of such pregnancy-related disability benefits from General Electric's employee disability plan violated Title VII. The Court of Appeals affirmed. . . .

Section 703(a)(1) provides in relevant part that it shall be an unlawful employment practice for an employer

> "to discriminate against any individual with respect to his compensation, terms, conditions, or privileges of employment, because of such individual's race, color, religion, sex, or national origin."

While there is no necessary inference that Congress, in choosing this language, intended to incorporate into Title VII the concepts of discrimination which have evolved from court decisions construing the Equal Protection Clause of the Fourteenth Amendment, the similarities between the congressional language and some of those decisions surely indicate that the latter are a useful starting point in interpreting the former. Particularly in the case of defining the term "discrimination," which Congress has nowhere in Title VII defined, those cases afford an existing body of law analyzing and

discussing that term in a legal context not wholly dissimilar to the concerns which Congress manifested in enacting Title VII. We think, therefore, that our decision in *Geduldig v Aiello* dealing with a strikingly similar disability plan, is quite relevant in determining whether or not the pregnancy exclusion did discriminate on the basis of sex. . . .

Since it is a finding of sex-based discrimination that must trigger, in a case such as this, the finding of an unlawful employment practice under § 703(a)(1), *Geduldig* is precisely in point in its holding that an exclusion of pregnancy from a disability-benefits plan providing general coverage is not a gender-based discrimination at all. . . .

The instant suit was grounded on Title VII rather than the Equal Protection Clause, and our cases recognize that a prima facie violation of Title VII can be established in some circumstances upon proof that the *effect* of an otherwise facially neutral plan or classification is to discriminate against members of one class or another. . . .

As in *Geduldig,* respondents have not attempted to meet the burden of demonstrating a gender-based discriminatory effect resulting from the exclusion of pregnancy-related disabilities from coverage. Whatever the ultimate probative value of the evidence introduced before the District Court on this subject in the instant case, at the very least it tended to illustrate that the selection of risks covered by the Plan did not operate, in fact, to discriminate against women. . . . The Plan, in effect (and for all that appears), is nothing more than an insurance package, which covers some risks, but excludes others. The "package" going to relevant identifiable groups we are presently concerned with—General Electric's male and female employees—covers exactly the same categories of risk, and is facially nondiscriminatory in the sense that "[t]here is no risk from which men are protected and women are not. Likewise, there is no risk from which women are protected and men are not." As there is no proof that the package is in fact worth more to men than to women, it is impossible to find any gender-based discriminatory effect in this scheme simply because women disabled as a result of pregnancy do not receive benefits; that is to say, gender-based discrimination does not result simply because an employer's disability-benefits plan is less than all-inclusive.[17] For all that appears, pregnancy-related disabilities constitute an *additional* risk, unique to women, and the failure to compensate them for this risk does not destroy the presumed parity of the benefits, accruing to men and women alike, which results from the facially evenhanded *inclusion* of risks. To hold otherwise would endanger the commonsense notion that an employer who has no disability benefits program at all does not violate Title VII even though the "underinclusion" of risks impacts, as a result of pregnancy-related disabilities, more heavily upon one gender than upon the other. Just as there is no facial gender-based discrimination in that case, so, too, there is none here. . . .

We therefore agree with petitioner that its disability-benefits plan does not violate Title VII because of its failure to cover pregnancy-related disabilities. The judgment of the Court of Appeals is reversed.

MR. JUSTICE STEVENS, dissenting.

. . . *Geduldig v Aiello*, does not control the question of statutory interpretation presented by this case. . . . We are, therefore, presented with a fresh, and rather simple, question of statutory construction: Does a contract between a company and its employees which treats the risk of absenteeism caused by pregnancy differently from any other kind of absence discriminate against certain individuals because of their sex? . . .

. . . [T]he rule at issue places the risk of absence caused by pregnancy in a class by itself.[5] By definition, such a rule discriminates on account of sex; for it is the capacity to become pregnant which primarily differentiates the female from the male. The analysis is the same whether the rule relates to hiring, promotion, the acceptability of an excuse for absence, or an exclusion from a disability insurance plan. Accordingly, . . . I conclude that the language of the statute plainly requires the result which the Courts of Appeals have reached unanimously.

STUDY QUESTIONS

1. The Court concluded that the General Electric plan did not "operate, in fact, to discriminate against women." What could the Court have meant by that in the light of the fact that the plan covered all disability claims of male employees but only some disability claims of female employees?
2. The Court spoke of pregnancy-related disability as an "*additional* risk" and of benefits covering that risk as "extra compensation." To what set of risks and what compensation level were these believed to be additional and extra? Is there a normal or standard risk and compensation level to which these were being implicitly compared? If so, what were they? Who best exemplifies them?
3. Do you find Justice Rehnquist's or Justice Stevens's description of the problem posed here to be more plausible?

17. *Absent proof of different values, the cost to "insure" against the risks is, in essence, nothing more than extra compensation to the employees, in the form of fringe benefits. If the employer were to remove the insurance fringe benefits and, instead, increase wages by an amount equal to the cost of the "insurance," there would clearly be no gender-based discrimination, even though a female employee who wished to purchase disability insurance that covered all risks would have to pay more than would a male employee who purchased identical disability insurance, due to the fact that her insurance had to cover the "extra" disabilities due to pregnancy. . . . The District Court was wrong in assuming, as it did, 375 F Supp, at 383, that Title VII's ban on employment discrimination necessarily means that "greater economic benefit[s]" must be required to be paid to one sex or the other because of their differing roles in "the scheme of human existence."*

5. *It is not accurate to describe the program as dividing " 'potential recipients into two groups—pregnant women and nonpregnant persons.' " Insurance programs, company policies, and employment contracts all deal with future risks rather than historic facts. The classification is between persons who face a risk of pregnancy and those who do not.*

Nor is it accurate to state that under the plan " '[t]here is no risk from which men are protected and women are not.' " Ibid. If the word "risk" is used narrowly, men are protected against the risks associated with a prostate operation whereas women are not. If the word is used more broadly to describe the risk of uncompensated unemployment caused by physical disability, men receive total protection . . . against that risk whereas women receive only partial protection.

Two points in particular emerge from *Gilbert.* Both reflect and reinforce cultural stereotypes about the place of pregnancy and childbirth in "the scheme of human existence." As it had in *Geduldig,* the Court once again implicitly relied upon controversial ideological doctrines when it reasserted that programs that deny benefits to people because of pregnancy do not discriminate "because of sex." A newer emphasis came with a second point. Here, the Court asserted that a benefit package that supports all the needs of male employees and all the needs of female employees that are comparable to those of men, is, by that very fact, evenhanded and sex-neutral. The point here is initially difficult to grasp, but careful attention to Justice Rehnquist's language, especially the references to "additional risk" and "extra compensation," led one commentator to the following conclusions about the stereotypes that underlie this second point:

> Pregnancy, for Rehnquist, is an "extra," special problem of women. Equality does not contemplate handing out benefits for extras—indeed, to do so would be to grant special benefits to women, possibly discriminating against men. The fact that men were compensated under the program for disabilities unique to their sex troubled his analysis not at all. . . . [The Court] makes man the standard (whatever disabilities men suffer will of course be compensated) and measures women against that standard (as long as she is compensated for anything he is compensated for, she is treated equally). For Rehnquist, as long as women get treated in the same way as men in the areas where they are like a man—in the disability program this would mean coverage for things like heart attacks, broken bones, appendicitis—that's equality. To the extent the Court will consider the equities with respect to childbearing capacity, it will consider them only in the category where they belong—extra, separate, different. A family, marital or reproductive right, yes, in appropriate circumstances. A matter of the public equality and equal protection of women—no.
>
> *Wendy Williams. "Equality's Riddle: Pregnancy and the Equal Treatment/Special Treatment Debate." 13* New York University Review of Law and Social Change *325, 345–46 (1984–85).*

The year after *Gilbert* was decided, the Court confronted another pregnancy-based benefits package challenged under Title VII (*Nashville Gas Co. v. Satty,* 434 U.S. 136 (1977)). In that case, the employer required pregnant employees, but not employees disabled for other reasons, to take unpaid leaves of absence and further provided that employees returning from maternity leaves lose all accumulated job seniority. The Court permitted the mandatory unpaid maternity leave policy but found the loss of seniority provision in violation of Title VII. Here again, the difference seems to turn on a male standard. Being required to take an unpaid leave is not discriminatory because those employees are pregnant. Sick pay for them, presumably, would be "extra compensation." Denial of accumulated seniority to employees returning from maternity leave is discriminatory because they are no longer pregnant and so should be treated as well as men. Although the result in *Satty* is, in part at least, different from the result in *Gilbert,* the rationale seems to be the same.

In *Geduldig* and again in *Gilbert,* the Court declared that there is no question of discrimination because the capacity to become pregnant is unique to women. According to this approach to discrimination, where there are "real differences," there can be no question of inequality. Inequality presupposes comparability, and a finding of uniqueness denies that comparisons are possible.

This, however, is not the only approach that different justices have taken toward barring sex discrimination. As the dissenting justices in these cases pointed out, when pregnancy causes an inability to work, that inability is analogous to inabilities caused by other temporary physical conditions. Viewed in that way, the fact that pregnancy-related incapacities are singled out for less advantageous treatment does not reflect biological difference but rather a stereotyped conviction that women are not "regular workers"—that their primary commitments lie in the home.

Two years after the *Gilbert* decision, Congress effectively reversed that decision by enacting the Pregnancy Discrimination Act of 1978 (PDA). In doing so, it followed an approach similar to the one espoused by the dissenting justices. That act amended Title VII by adding what is now section 701(k), which reads in part as follows:

> The terms "because of sex" or "on the basis of sex" include, but are not limited to, because of or on the basis of pregnancy, childbirth or related medical conditions; and women affected by pregnancy, childbirth, and related medical conditions shall be treated the same for all employment-related purposes, including receipt of benefits under fringe benefit programs, as other persons not so affected but similar in their ability or inability to work. . . .

The PDA rejects the *Geduldig* and *Gilbert* holdings completely. Its first sentence answers the question posed in *Gilbert* by adjusting the definitions section of the statute to make clear that decisions taken because of pregnancy are taken "because of sex" for the purposes of Title VII. The second sentence also makes clear that the PDA rejects the uniqueness approach to pregnancy endorsed by the Court in *Geduldig* and *Gilbert*" by declaring that pregnancy and related conditions must be treated the same as other conditions that may affect the ability to work.

Another way to understand the PDA approach involves looking again at the notion of similarity and difference. Similarities and differences emerge only where things are compared. Comparisons, however, always occur within some particular context of analysis that gives a point to making the comparisons. Thus, when assembling a basketball team, differences related to motor coordination and vision are germane, whereas those related to race and national origin are not. Title VII is concerned with eliminating artificial barriers to employment opportunities. In that context, pregnancy is germane because it can occasion work interruptions or a changed ability to perform on the job. As such, it is comparable to other conditions that have the same impact on employment decisions. For the purposes of Title VII, then, pregnant workers are not to be considered as unique. They can, and according to the second sentence, must be compared to others who are similar in their ability or inability to perform on the job. Seen in this light, the PDA mandates that people who are similar in job-related characteristics be treated similarly, regardless of their sex.

The Supreme Court endorsed this way of conceptualizing the treatment of pregnancy under Title VII when it first interpreted the PDA in a case involving the denial of pregnancy benefits to the spouses of male employees. *Newport News Shipbuilding and Dry Dock Co. v. EEOC,* 462 U.S. 669 (1983). The employer's benefits package included benefits for all its employees and for their families as well. As part of that package, pregnancy benefits were included, but only for employees. Thus, all the health needs of the families of female employees were met by the package, but not all the health needs of the families of male employees. The Court found this arrangement in violation of the PDA.

After *Newport News,* it seems clear that employer disability programs that provide for all needs of male employees and all needs of female employees, except those arising from physical characteristics unique to women—pregnancy, childbirth and related medical conditions—violate the PDA and must be altered so as to extend coverage to those risks unique to women. The requirement of equal treatment announced in the second clause of the PDA seems to require no less.

A second problem addressed in the context of the PDA appeared to challenge the viability of the equal treatment ideal. The PDA does not permit employers to treat pregnant workers more harshly than other workers, but does it also forbid that they be treated less harshly? For example, may an employer provide disability leaves for childbearing but not otherwise? The opportunity to address this question came to the Supreme Court in the following case. California was one of four states that, by the mid-1980s had laws in force requiring employers to provide reasonable maternity leaves and benefits for pregnant employees. The others were Connecticut, Massachusetts and Montana. The practice at issue in the California case was the reinstatement of a woman who returned from a childbearing leave. Does Title VII permit a state to require this of employers even when it does not require them to reinstate workers returning from other forms of disability leave?

California Federal Savings & Loan v. Guerra

Supreme Court of the United States, 1987. 479 U.S. 272, 107 S.Ct. 683, 93 L.Ed.2d 613.

JUSTICE MARSHALL delivered the opinion of the Court.

The question presented is whether Title VII of the Civil Rights Act of 1964, as amended by the Pregnancy Discrimination Act of 1978, pre-empts a state statute that requires employers to provide leave and reinstatement to employees disabled by pregnancy.

I

California's Fair Employment and Housing Act (FEHA) is a comprehensive statute that prohibits discrimination in employment and housing. In September 1978, California amended the FEHA to proscribe certain forms of employment discrimination on the basis of pregnancy.[1] Subdivision (b)(2)—the provision at issue here—is the only portion of the statute that applies to employers subject to Title VII. . . . Accordingly, the only benefit pregnant workers actually derive from § 12945(b)(2) is a qualified right to reinstatement. . . .

II

Petitioner California Federal Savings and Loan Association (Cal Fed) is a federally chartered savings and loan association based in Los Angeles; it is an employer covered by both Title VII and § 12945(b)(2). Cal Fed has a facially neutral leave policy that permits employees who have completed three months of service to take unpaid leaves of absence for a variety of reasons, including disability and pregnancy. Although it is Cal Fed's policy to try to provide an employee taking unpaid leave with a similar position upon returning Cal Fed expressly reserves the right to terminate an employee who has taken a leave of absence if a similar position is not available.

Lillian Garland was employed by Cal Fed as a receptionist for several years. In January 1982, she took a pregnancy disability leave. When she was able to return to work in April of that

---

1. Section 12945(b)(2) provides, in relevant part:
"It shall be an unlawful employment practice unless based upon a bona fide occupational qualification:

. . . . .

"(b) For any employer to refuse to allow a female employee affected by pregnancy, childbirth, or related medical conditions. . . ."

. . . . .

"(2) To take a leave on account of pregnancy for a reasonable period of time; provided, such period shall not exceed four months. . . . Reasonable period of time means that period during which the female employee is disabled on account of pregnancy, childbirth, or related medical conditions. . . ."
"An employer may require any employee who plans to take a leave pursuant to this section to give reasonable notice of the date such leave shall commence and the estimated duration of such leave."

year, Garland notified Cal Fed, but was informed that her job had been filled and that there was no receptionist or similar positions available. Garland filed a complaint with respondent Department of Fair Employment and Housing, which issued an administrative accusation against Cal Fed on her behalf. Respondent charged Cal Fed with violating § 12945(b)(2) of the FEHA. Prior to the scheduled hearing before respondent Fair Housing and Employment Commission, Cal Fed, joined by petitioners Merchants and Manufacturers Association and the California Chamber of Commerce, brought this action in the United States District Court for the Central District of California. They sought a declaration that § 12945(b)(2) is inconsistent with and pre-empted by Title VII and an injunction against enforcement of the section. The District Court granted petitioners' motion for summary judgment. Citing *Newport News Shipbuilding & Dry Dock Co. v. EEOC,* the court stated that "California employers who comply with state law are subject to reverse discrimination suits under Title VII brought by temporarily disabled males who do not receive the same treatment as female employees disabled by pregnancy. . . ." On this basis, the District Court held that "California state law and the policies of interpretation and enforcement . . . which require preferential treatment of female employees disabled by pregnancy, childbirth, or related medical conditions are preempted by Title VII and are null, void, invalid and inoperative under the Supremacy Clause of the United States Constitution."

III

A

. . . In two sections of the 1964 Civil Rights Act, §§ 708 and 1104, Congress has indicated that state laws will be pre-empted only if they actually conflict with federal law. Section 708 of Title VII provides:

> "Nothing in this title shall be deemed to exempt or relieve any person from any liability, duty, penalty, or punishment provided by any present or future law of any State or political subdivision of a State, other than any such law which purports

to require or permit the doing of any act which would be an unlawful employment practice under this title." . . .

Title VII, as amended by the PDA, and California's pregnancy disability leave statute share a common goal. The purpose of Title VII is "to achieve equality of employment opportunities and remove barriers that have operated in the past to favor an identifiable group of . . . employees over other employees." . . . Rather than limiting existing Title VII principles and objectives, the PDA extends them to cover pregnancy. As Senator Williams, a sponsor of the Act, stated: "The entire thrust . . . behind this legislation is to guarantee women the basic right to participate fully and equally in the workforce, without denying them the fundamental right to full participation in family life." 123 Cong. Rec. 29658 (1977).

Section 12945(b)(2) also promotes equal employment opportunity. By requiring employers to reinstate women after a reasonable pregnancy disability leave, § 12945(b)(2) ensures that they will not lose their jobs on account of pregnancy disability. . . .

We emphasize the limited nature of the benefits § 12945(b)(2) provides. The statute is narrowly drawn to cover only the period of *actual physical disability* on account of pregnancy, childbirth, or related medical conditions. Accordingly, unlike the protective labor legislation prevalent earlier in this century, § 12945(b)(2) does not reflect archaic or stereotypical notions about pregnancy and the abilities of pregnant workers. A statute based on such stereotypical assumptions would, of course, be inconsistent with Title VII's goal of equal employment opportunity. . . .

C

Moreover, even if we agreed with petitioners' construction of the PDA, we would nonetheless reject their argument that the California statute requires employers to violate Title VII. Section 12945(b)(2) does not prevent employers from complying with both the federal law (as petitioners construe it) and the state law. This is not a case where "compliance with both federal and state regulations is a physical impossibility," . . . or where there is an "inevitable collision between the two schemes of regulation." Section 12945(b)(2) does not compel California employers to treat pregnant workers *better* than other disabled employees; it merely establishes benefits that employers must, at a minimum, provide to pregnant workers. Employers are free to give comparable benefits to other disabled employees, thereby treating "women affected by pregnancy" no better than "other persons not so affected but similar in their ability or inability to work." Indeed, at oral argument, petitioners conceded that compliance with both statutes "is theoretically possible."

IV

Thus, petitioners' facial challenge to § 12945(b)(2) fails. The statute is not pre-empted by Title VII, as amended by the PDA, because it is not inconsistent with the purposes of the federal statute, nor does it require the doing of an act which is unlawful under Title VII.

The judgment of the Court of Appeals is

Affirmed.

STUDY QUESTIONS

1. On what grounds did Cal Fed argue that compliance with Section 12945(b)(2) would be in violation of Title VII? Had the Court endorsed this line of reasoning, would the goal of equal employment opportunity have been advanced or retarded? Why?

2. Does compliance with Section 12945(b)(2) necessarily involve treating pregnant workers more favorably than other disabled workers? How can that be avoided?

The *Cal Fed* decision admits of a number of readings. On the one hand, it appears to validate the notion that the PDA permits special pregnancy-based policies that benefit women, even though it prohibits pregnancy-based policies that disadvantage women. On the other hand, the Court noted in *Cal Fed* that the combination of state and federal statutes did not place employers in a double bind. Employers may observe the requirements of both by the simple expedient of affording more adequate disability leaves for all who are temporarily unable to satisfy the ordinary requirements of their job.

The *Cal Fed* litigation, together with a parallel case bearing on a Montana statute and culminating in the decision in *Miller-Wohl Company v. Commissioner of Labor and Industry*, 479 U.S. 1050 (1987), became the focus of intense feminist debates. Feminists filed briefs on all sides in both streams of the litigation. Although all shared the goal of attaining workplace protection for all workers—pregnant and otherwise—feminists differed over the most effective strategy to achieve that goal. Those taking the symmetrical approach analogized the problems of pregnant workers to those of others. They sought to strengthen women's positions by emphasizing the commonalities in the working lives of all workers. They argued for extending disability benefits to all workers who are temporarily disabled for whatever reason. Those taking the asymmetrical approach saw the explicit recognition of women's unique maternal role as essential to their equal treatment and believed that women are more likely to benefit by stressing their uniqueness. They argued in favor of permitting special provisions for pregnancy in the workplace, even where no provision was made for workers unable to work for other reasons. "As long as fetal development occurs *in utero* and breast-feeding proves advantageous for newborn infants," observed Deborah Rhode, "mothers will experience a conflict between their productive and reproductive roles that fathers will not." They concluded that since employer no-leave policies place a heavier burden on female than on male employees, employers should be permitted to make special provisions for female employees to compensate for those heavier burdens. Once women gained benefits, they argued, benefits for others would follow. They were also concerned with arguments that seemed to call pregnancy a disability.

Proponents of the symmetrical alternative saw the need for that approach as very important for making progress on another pregnancy-related issue of the 1970s and '80s. That issue involved a "protection" argument for restricting women's employment opportunities. As employers found women entering the skilled trades in greater numbers, they raised questions about the exposure to toxic substances that had regularly threatened the health of male workers. Focusing solely on the threats to the health of children conceived during and after their mothers' exposure to such toxins, employers sought to limit women's employment opportunities in the name of "fetal protection." Presumably in response to their possible liability, employers sought to justify denying fertile women jobs by pointing to their unique ability to become pregnant.

Women faced with the choice of sterilization or lower wages argued that these fetal protection policies violate Title VII. Arguing against these policies, feminists who favored the symmetrical approach sought to show that toxic working environments often pose a health threat to the future children of both male and female workers. For that reason, they argued that Title VII requires that this safety issue be addressed in a gender-neutral fashion. In the first case to reach a federal court of appeals, the employer was permitted to continue its fetal protection program on the grounds that "the safety of unborn children of workers would seem no less a matter of legitimate business concern than the safety of the traditional business licensee or invitee upon an employer's premises." *Wright v. Olin,* 697 F.2d 1172, 1189 (4th Cir. 1982). The second fetal protection case to reach a federal court of appeals turned out quite differently. Applying the symmetrical approach, the court in *Hayes v. Shelby Memorial Hospital,* 726 F.2d 1543 (11th Cir. 1984), ruled against the employer. The court insisted that differential treatment on the basis of pregnancy is a facial violation of Title VII "unless the employer shows a direct relationship between the policy and the actual ability of a pregnant fertile female to perform her job." As we will see in Chapter 4, when this issue came before the Supreme Court in the *Johnson Controls* case, the Court too relied on the symmetrical approach and ruled against the employer, because "women as capable of doing their jobs as their male counterparts may not be forced to choose between having a child and having a job."

Another legal development, favored by proponents of the symmetrical approach, also raised hopes for realizing improvement for women through more general reforms. The enactment of the Family and Medical Leave Act of 1993 (FMLA), which requires large employers to allow their employees to take up to three months' unpaid leave for family caretaking, provides many of the protections demanded by advocates of the asymmetrical approach but without claiming that pregnancy and child rearing are special cases. By recognizing that men as well as women have important responsibilities in their families and that women as well as men have important responsibilities on the job, the FMLA addresses one of the most pressing unfinished agenda items of our era, the reintegration of the values and structures of the public sphere of work and the private sphere of families.

III. CONTEMPORARY THEORETICAL DEBATES

Earlier in this chapter, we saw how the first wave of feminism divided over ways the law might best advance the condition of women. At first, the dominant preference was for a symmetrical approach that endorsed gender-neutral laws. Later, that approach was challenged by an asymmetrical preference that favored female-specific laws. The Hill-Kelley debate illustrates the contest between these perspectives. In the last section, we reviewed the legal developments relating to pregnancy in the workplace during the 1970s and '80s. These generated the most sustained and searching theoretical debates among feminist legal theorists during the second wave of feminism. In this section, we explore the main lines of those debates in greater depth.

During the second wave of feminism, the initial policy preference once again favored the symmetrical approach. At first, the effort was to improve the condition of women by eliminating arbitrary restraints that preserve male dominance in the public sphere. Arguments generally relied on the concept of formal justice, which requires that like cases be treated alike. However, the consensus behind the symmetrical approach weakened as the Court handed down it decisions in *Geduldig* and *Gilbert*. In these, the Court showed that although it was willing to require that women be treated in the same ways as men when women function in the same ways as men, it would not do so where it saw them as different from men. Moreover, it made clear that women were inevitably different from men in their capacity to become pregnant.

One response to this problem proposed to add a limited modification to a generally sex-neutral approach. Thus, for example, law professor Herma Hill Kay argued that sex should not be a consideration that has any moral or legal consequences *except* where biological sex differences are directly implicated. Sex-based barriers that prevent people from performing according to their abilities must be removed, but biological differences that may keep a woman from using her abilities during pregnancy should not be ignored. Kay applied her approach to the employment context in this way:

> Let us postulate two workers, one female, the other male, who respectively engage in reproductive conduct. Assume as well that prior to this activity, both were roughly equal in their ability to perform their similar jobs. The consequence of their having engaged in reproductive behavior will be vastly different. The man's ability to perform on the job will be largely unaffected. The woman's ability to work, measured against her prior performance, may vary with the physical and emotional changes she experiences during pregnancy. At times, her ability to work may be unaffected by the pregnancy; at other times, she may be temporarily incapacitated by it. Ultimately, she may require medical care to recover from miscarriage, or to complete her pregnancy by delivery, or to terminate it earlier by induced abortion. In order to maintain the woman's equality of opportunity during her pregnancy, we should modify as far as reasonably possible those aspects of her work where her job performance is adversely affected by the pregnancy. Unless we do so, she will experience employment disadvantages arising from her reproductive activity that are not encountered by her male coworker.
>
> *Herma Hill Kay. "Equality and Difference: The Case of Pregnancy." 1* Berkeley Woman's Law Journal *1, 26–7 (1985).*

While feminists like Kay generally advocate retaining the symmetrical approach but insist that exceptions must be made in the area of reproduction lest women be placed as a disadvantage in the workplace, others have taken more extreme positions. Thus, some critics during the early 1980s argued that the decisions in *Geduldig* and *Gilbert* show that the symmetrical approach is fatally compromised. Pointing out that women are frequently different from men, especially as regards reproduction, they concluded that, inasmuch as women cannot and should not be assimilated into the life patterns of men, a different, sex-specific approach must be taken to legal reform. An example of this approach is the bivalent model proposed by a prominent feminist philosopher in an influential book that appeared at the beginning of the 1980s. The introduction explains her central argument.

Equality and the Rights of Women

Elizabeth H. Wolgast.
Ithaca, NY: Cornell University Press,
1980. Pp. 13–17.

Where there is equality, can there fail to be justice? Can we take for granted that equal treatment will remedy injustice?

Running through our political tradition is the idea that, underneath, people are the same: the wealthy and the poor, the owner of slaves and the slave, a man in authority and a man under it. We are inclined to say that, stripped of the accidents and trappings brought about by chance, these individuals could change places. The slave and slaveowner might, but for accidents of fate, be in each other's shoes. The prince might change places with the pauper. This view of society encourages us to think of any person as having only the essential characteristics, needs, and concerns of all the rest.

But when we substitute "woman" for "slave" and "pauper" in such traditional formulas, the result is implausible. It is not obvious that, accidents and trappings aside, women share the set of their basic interests with men. And if women are irreducibly different in respect to some of these, then to the degree of the difference, the places cannot be changed. The prince who can change places with a pauper may be unable to change places with a princess.

Arguments supporting equal rights for men and women often stress the similarity of their needs and concerns. And if justice means providing equal rights to all, then, by implication, such rights must be appropriate to everyone. But what if the needs and concerns are different?

Among the forces that push us and shape us are the concepts we are accustomed to using. They, like psychological forces and social mores, shape our reasoning, our expectations, and so our form of life. In this way, arguing for women's rights under the banner of equality encourages women to identify their interests with those of men. What is good for men, this reasoning requires, must be good for women too. To bear babies, since it does not pertain also to men, does not figure in the equalitarian's vision. For women to identify themselves as women—therefore different from men—changes the logical basis of the reasoning, and so undermines what appears the best argument they have for their rights. In asserting their difference, it seems, women are courting their own disadvantage.

When we think about justice in terms of equality, a consequence appears that whatever is not an instance of equality seems to be one of *in*equality. And to our ears inequality has the ring of injustice, of unfairness and discrimination. What, we wonder, could possibly justify the claim of human inequality?

It is my thesis that a profound difficulty for the advance of women's rights is conceptual. We need an alternative to egalitarian reasoning. One such alternative would be a bivalent form of thinking, a form that distinguishes between the interests of men and the interests of women. Women, it could be argued, need to represent their own concerns and should not expect them to be represented by men. This is clearest in matters of family and maternity care, but a case could also be made in regard to the economic dependence of women, their opportunities for employment, and provisions for their later years. Such a bivalent view provides a justification for affirmative action policies because it rejects a neutral perspective from which the concerns of both sexes can be seen "objectively." It supports the idea that women contribute distinctively to their professions and fields of interest, to the diversity of our culture and the richness of its values. And it casts suspicion on the idea that women's qualifications for various endeavors should be judged exclusively by men.

But I do not think this bivalent view can give the full solution to the problems raised by the atomistic-egalitarian model. For an adequate solution, it would be necessary to replace this model by one that gives emphasis to human connections, to forms of human interdependence, and to the needs that lead to them. Many important facts should be taken into account: that a baby needs someone's time-consuming love and care; that elderly persons are unable to compete for their sustenance; that childbearing and child-nurturing are not primarily ways to satisfy self-oriented desires; that families are not associations of individuals who join together for their mutual benefit. A model that cannot reasonably represent these facts is just not an acceptable model of human society.

If men and women have somewhat different perspectives and concerns, as I argue, then it seems reasonable that a new model of society would profit from contributions by women, even though some of these contributions may be ajar with tradition. In that cause, truly, this work has been written.

STUDY QUESTIONS

1. What is identified as the main premise of the egalitarian approach to justice and equal rights? What difficulties are identified with that view?
2. What alternative is proposed? How does it seek to avoid the difficulties that attend the egalitarian approach? Is the proposed approach itself incomplete? In what ways?

Some feminists, like Wolgast, would totally abandon the symmetrical approach because it calls for comparing women *and* men, and that, they say, means inevitably adopting "the male standard" by comparing women *to* men. As law professor Ann Scales expressed this concern, "[I]f women ask to be treated the same as men on the grounds that we *are* the same, then we concede that we have no claim to equality in contexts where we are *not* the same." "Feminist Legal Method: Not So Scary?" 2 *UCLA Women's Law Journal* 1, 11 (1992). The decisions in *Geduldig* and *Gilbert* illustrate how that can happen.

The symmetrical approach was delineated and defended against these and other objections in the following essay.

Equality's Riddle: Pregnancy and the Equal Treatment/ Special Treatment Debate

Wendy Williams. 13 *New York University Review of Law and Social Change* 325–32, 380 (1984–85).

The legal battle for gender equality gave birth, in the early 1970's, to a riddle. Faced with the pervasive and profound effect of employer responses to women's reproductive function on their status and opportunity in the paid workforce, feminist litigators asked how laws or rules based on a capacity unique to women—the capacity to become pregnant and give birth— could be susceptible to challenge under any equality doctrine the courts of this country might realistically be persuaded to employ. In response to that question, the proponents of gender equality developed a theory which has been used with moderate success in scores of cases challenging pregnancy rules under Title VII and, for a time, under the equal protection clause as well. Most of these cases have arisen in the employment context; courts have been asked to compare an employer's treatment of pregnancy to its treatment of other physical conditions with similar workplace consequences. The approach has been, in the words of the 1978 Pregnancy Discrimination Act (PDA), to require that "women affected by pregnancy, childbirth or related medical conditions. . . be treated the same for all employment related purposes . . . as other persons not so affected but similar in their ability or inability to work."

Today, commentators have raised questions about the wisdom and propriety of this "equal treatment" approach to pregnancy rules and laws. [This paper discusses the comments of Ann Scales, Linda Krieger, and Patricia Cooney at length.] . . .

. . . [A]t least superficially, the dispute centers on whether pregnancy should be viewed as comparable to other physical conditions or as unique and special. On a deeper level, the dispute is about whether pregnancy "naturally" makes women unequal and thus requires special legislative accommodation to it in order to equalize the sexes, or whether pregnancy can or should be visualized as one human experience which in many contexts, most notably the workplace, creates needs and problems similar to those arising from causes other than pregnancy, and which can be handled adequately on the same basis as are other physical conditions of employees. On the deepest level, the debate may reflect a demand by special treatment advocates that the law recognize and honor a separate identity which women themselves consider special and important and, on the equal treatment side, a commitment to a vision of the human condition which seeks to uncover commonality rather than difference.

The critics believe that the "equal treatment model" precludes recognition pregnancy's uniqueness, and thus creates for women a Procrustean bed—pregnancy will be treated as if it were comparable to male conditions when it is not, thus forcing pregnant women into a workplace structure designed for men. Such a result, they believe, denies women's special experience and does not adequately respond to the realities of women's lives.

The proponents of the equal treatment model are also concerned with ensuring that workplace pregnancy rules do not create structural barriers to the full participation of women in the workplace. Unlike the critics, however, they are prepared to view pregnancy as just one of the physical conditions that affect workplace participation for men and women. From their perspective, the objective is to readjust the general rules for dealing with illness and disability to ensure that the rules can fairly account for the whole range of workplace disabilities that confront employed people. Pregnancy creates not "special" needs, but rather exemplifies typical basic needs. If these particular typical needs are not met, then pregnant workers simply become part of a larger class of male and female workers, for whom the basic fringe benefit structure is inadequate. The solution, in that view, is to solve the underlying problem of inadequate fringe benefits rather than to respond with measures designed especially for pregnant workers. . . .

I propose to further the debate by offering a rationale for the "equal treatment" approach to pregnancy (and other characterisitics unique to one sex) in the terms in which its proponents would present it. I do so as one who has participated, almost from the beginning, in the development of the model now under attack. If that model is to be rejected, it should be relinquished with a full understanding of what it is and how it works. . .

The first proposition essential to this analysis is that sex-based generalizations are generally impermissible whether derived from physical differences such as size and strength, from cultural role assignments such as breadwinner or homemaker, or from some combinations of innate and ascribed characteristics, such as the greater longevity of the average woman compared to the average man. Instead of classifying on the basis of sex, lawmakers and employers must classify on the basis of the trait or function or behavior for which sex was used as a proxy. Strength, not maleness, would be the criterion for certain jobs; economic dependency, not femaleness, the criterion for alimony upon divorce. The basis for this proposition is a belief that a dual system of rights inevitably produces gender hierarchy and, more fundamentally, treats women and men as statistical abstractions rather than as persons with individual capacities, inclinations and aspirations—at enormous cost to women and not insubstantial cost to men.

The second essential proposition is that laws and rules which do not overtly classify on the basis of sex, but which have a disproportionately negative effect upon one sex, warrant, under appropriate circumstances, placing a burden of justification upon the party defending the law or rule in court. In the view of its proponents, the proposition is an essential companion to the first proposition and is necessary for the ultimate equality of the sexes. Society has been tailored to predefined sex roles not only through overt gender classification, but also through laws and rules neutral on their face but inspired by the same assumptions, stereotypes and ideologies as sex-based classifications.

The goal of the feminist legal movement that began in the early seventies is not and never was the integration of women into a male world any more than it has been to build a separate but better place for women. Rather, the goal has been to break down the legal barriers that restricted each sex to its predefined role and created a hierarchy based on gender. The ability to challenge covert as well as overt gender sorting laws is essential both for challenging in court a male defined set of structures and institutions and for requiring their reconstitution to reflect the full range of our human concerns. The first proposition (sex classifications are generally impermissible) facilitates the elimination of legislation that overtly classifies by sex. The second proposition (perpetrators of rules with a disparate effect must justify them) provides a doctrinal tool with which to begin to squeeze the male tilt out of a purportedly neutral legal structure and thus substitute genuine for merely formal gender neutrality.

How does pregnancy fit into this general framework? The short answer is that the general framework applies, with minor alteration, to laws or rules based on physical characteris-

tics unique to one sex. The proponents contend that classifications based on such characteristics, of which pregnancy is the central example, are sex-based. Under the equal protection clause, the consequence of that conclusion would be that the intermediate standard of review applicable to gender-based classifications would apply to pregnancy classifications. The Supreme Court rejected that position in 1974 in *Geduldig v. Aiello*. Under Title VII, the consequence of characterizing pregnancy classifications as sex-based is that pregnancy-based employer rules constitute unlawful sex discrimination unless the employer can establish that its pregnancy rule is, in the words of the statute, a "bona fide occupational qualification reasonably necessary to the normal operation of that particular business or enterprise." This interpretation of Title VII was adopted by the lower federal courts, ignored by the Supreme Court in 1976 in *General Electric Company v. Gilbert,* and finally imposed by Congress through the amendment known as the Pregnancy Discrimination Act, a 1978 amendment to Title VII. The principle that discrimination based on pregnancy (or other physical characteristics unique to one sex) should be treated as sex discrimination would also be recognized under the Equal Rights Amendment, and classifications grounded on such characteristics would be subjected to strict judicial scrutiny.

The approach in all three legal contexts assumes that for some purposes, sex-unique physical characteristics and capacities are comparable to other characteristics and capacities. Where the purposes of the legislation render them comparable, classifications which single them out for unfavorable treatment would be invalid. Where they are not comparable, such classifications would be upheld. Under this approach, all the classifications would be scrutinized by the courts, and the burden (defined somewhat differently in the three different legal contexts) would be on the party defending the classification to justify its existence.

The companion principle—that neutral laws and rules which have a disproportionately negative effect upon one sex, may warrant shifting the burden of justification to the party defending the law or rule—would apply to "neutral" rules whose disproportionate effects on one sex were due to pregnancy. That principle was recognized for Title VII purposes in the original EEOC guidelines on pregnancy and reiterated in the post-Pregnancy Discrimination Act guidelines. Because of the Supreme Court's insistence in equal protection cases on the existence of an intent to discriminate, narrowly defined, the theory is not available in sex discrimination cases brought under the Fourteenth Amendment. If the proponents' interpretation is adopted by the courts, however, it may well be available under an Equal Rights Amendment. . . .

The "equal treatment" model is designed to discourage employers and the state from creating or maintaining rules that force people to structure their family relationships upon traditional sex-based lines and from refusing to respond to pregnancy as within the normal range of events which temporarily affect workers. . . .

When we get past the simplistic assertion that pregnancy is different and cannot be compared to anything else, is there anything left of objections to "equal treatment"? The answer to that question is clearly yes. Exploration of "what is left" requires a more detailed exposition of the critics' views.

Professor Ann Scales . . . [l]ooking at the *Geduldig-Gilbert* outcome, . . . concludes that it is the attempt to analogize pregnancy to any other condition or enterprise that is the problem. To do so, she thinks, permits maleness to be the norm. But the Court preserved the male model by *failing* to take seriously the similarity in the position of pregnant disabled workers and other disabled workers. It preserved the discontinuity between motherhood and workforce participation by failing to understand that the stake of pregnant workers in such benefits was like other workers' stakes—and thus failed to require that women be integrated fully into the basic system of worker protections. Scales's insistence on the uniqueness of pregnancy would not "direct opposite results from those reached by the Supreme Court in the pregnancy cases," but rather the same results. Scales fails to see that her incorporationist vision—a vision of the inclusion and proper accounting for pregnancy in the public sphere—is best served

by the equal treatment approach. It is precisely that vision that gave birth to the equal treatment model in the first place. The model was proposed in the context of an exclusionary workplace, and it was urged to promote the "normalization" of pregnancy. In the litigation context, the model was the basis for insisting on the incorporation of pregnancy into existing benefit schemes. The litigators sought incorporation not by insisting that pregnancy was "the same" as other physical events but that the position of the pregnant worker was analogous to the position of other workers. The approach was based on the notion that the pregnant woman is entitled to respect and dignity as a worker and that the stake a woman shares with other workers in job security and economic viability does not suddenly evaporate when she becomes pregnant. It sought to overcome the definition of the prototypical worker as male and to promote an integrated—and androgynous—prototype. . . .

Krieger and Cooney's view leads them to assert that pregnancy is a difference which must be "accommodated," in the manner that Title VII requires employer accommodation to religious practices, or federal regulations require accommodation to employee handicaps. However, the Supreme Court has interpreted accommodation requirements very narrowly. It has little sympathy for provisions which make employers go out of their way for the atypical worker. This result seems predictable. Special "favors" for such workers are viewed as an imposition unconnected to the employer's business needs and interests. In contrast, provisions for the "typical" worker are more easily seen as necessary or desirable responses to the nature of the workforce which may increase employee loyalty and productivity. Moreover, the special treatment approach for women will always embroil its proponents in a debate about whether they are getting more or not enough. Finally, such provisions are a double-edged sword for their beneficiaries because they impose upon employers special costs and obligations in connection with pregnant workers, rendering them less desirable employees and creating an incentive to discriminate against them. By contrast, the equal treatment approach, premised squarely on an androgynousnous rather than a male prototype and reaching for an incorporationist rather than accommodationist vision, seeks to avoid these consequences by requiring a fundamental reorganization of the way the presence of pregnant working women in the workplace is understood. . . .

The dispute among feminists about whether women and men are essentially similar or dissimilar as to their stake in the workplace is as old as feminism itself. Assumptions about similarities and differences yield different theories of what will break down gender hierarchy and promote equality between women and men. The vigorous dispute among those feminists who supported and those who attacked protective labor legislation earlier in this century has been replaced by the debate over whether the fact of pregnancy should be given "equal treatment" or "special treatment" in workplace policies to promote the ultimate equality of women. I have contended here that the "equal treatment" approach to preg-

nant wage workers, both as a litigative and legislative matter, is demonstrably the better approach. . . .

STUDY QUESTIONS

1. What are the two essential premises of the "equal treatment" approach? What is its main goal? Do you share Williams's goal of overcoming the definition of the prototypical worker as male and promoting an integrated, androgynous prototype instead?
2. How does Williams reply to the charge that her sex-neutral approach accepts the male standard? Why did Williams reject the bivalent or dual system of rights model?
3. How does this sex-neutral approach apply to pregnancy in the workplace? Do you agree that treating neutral-seeming rules that have a disproportionately negative impact on women as violations of equality guarantees is an effective way to challenge male norms?

Williams and other proponents of symmetrical approaches have two basic reservations about asymmetrical strategies. One is principled, the unfairness of special pleading. Williams stated that concern briefly in an earlier essay.

> . . . [T]reating pregnancy as a special case divides us in ways that I believe are destructive in a particular political sense as well as a more general sense. On what basis can we fairly assert, for example, that the pregnant woman fired by Miller-Wohl deserved to keep her job when any other worker who got sick for any other reason did not? Creating special privileges of the Montana type has, as one consequence, the effect of shifting attention away from the employer's inadequate sick leave policy or the state's failure to provide important protections to all workers and focusing it upon the unfairness of protecting one class of worker and not others.
>
> *Wendy Williams. "The Equality Crisis: Some Reflections on Culture, Courts, and Feminism." 7* Women's Rights Law Reporter *175, 196 (1982).*

The other reservation warns of the risks that attend attaching legal consequences to differences between women and men. Doing so, Williams suggests, reinforces employers' stereotypes of women in a way that is too reminiscent of the protective and compensatory strategies of earlier generations, strategies that we have come to regret. Treating pregnancy or any of the other distinctive aspects of women's experience as a special case has a history that has repeatedly shown it to be a double-edged sword, more often wielded at the expense of women than to their advantage. (See Chapters 1 and 2.)

Williams's argument in favor of the symmetrical approach, however, is not without its critics. Many feminists are uneasy about her willingness to speak of women who are unable to work at times during their pregnancies in the same breath as the larger group of workers who are temporarily incapacitated. Although Williams stresses that she is only talking about pregnant workers who are actually unable to meet the requirements of their jobs, there is concern that she creates the image of pregnancy as a disability. "In some feminists' view," reports Deborah Rhode, "even to speak of pregnancy in terms of disability distorts its meaning." *Justice and Gender*, Cambridge: Harvard University Press, 1989, p. 121.

Other objections to the symmetrical approach highlight possible losses to women. The following selection argues that one pitfall of sex neutrality is that it ensnares us in a tendency to confuse the inclusion of some men in a program with making that program more inclusive—a confusion that all too often works to the disadvantage of women. The example chosen to illustrate this tendency is the Family and Medical Leave Act of 1990 (FMLA), which was vetoed by President George Bush.

Does It Still Make Sense to Talk about "Women"?

Christine Littleton.
1 *UCLA Women's Law Journal* 15,
32–37 (1991).

... [I]nclusion is considered in most feminist circles to be an unalloyed good, exclusion to be either politically incorrect or at best a necessary evil to be practiced sparingly and temporarily. Rather than challenge this general premise, the next several paragraphs question the content of inclusion and exclusion contained in the FMLA. This analysis indicates that by self-consciously shifting the focus from debates over female employees' needs for, among other things, pregnancy disability leave, to a focus on female and male needs for family and medical leave, feminist supporters ironically ended up supporting the same kind of "half a loaf" measure that they had criticized in the litigation arena—only it was a different "half." My assertion is that, had the bill focused on all women, it would have included many more people among its beneficiaries. Thus what looked like more inclusion ("let's add men") could, from a women-centered perspective, be seen as exclu-

sion ("what about the women we've left out?"). . . .

The FMLA excludes women in two ways: eligibility and impact. Under the bill, an eligible employee would be entitled to twelve work weeks of leave during any twelve-month period. The right to take a leave can be exercised in the event of the birth of an employee's child or because of the placement with the employee of a child for adoption [or] foster care. Additionally, an employee is entitled to take a leave in order to care for her or his son, daughter, spouse, or parent who has a serious health condition. Finally, an employee can take a leave during her or his own illness, injury or other disabling condition.

The most obvious exclusion in this legislative scheme is, of course, lesbians—whose partners cannot be "spouses" under any existing state law. In addition, only one of two lesbian co-parents can be genetically related to the child at birth. Existing law does not allow adoption by the nongenetic mother, and is only beginning to allow joint adoption of unrelated children. Thus many lesbians would also be prevented from using the leave to care for their children, who are not *legally* their sons and daughters.

Women living in extended or nontraditional families are not eligible for leave to care for the relatives (such as aunts, uncles or grandparents) or legally unrelated family members with whom they actually live. Since women of color and recent immigrant women are more likely to be in such a family setting, this exclusion also has racial, ethnic, and class dimensions. Indeed, even though we know that women overwhelmingly perform the caretaking functions in families, such women would not be eligible for leave to care for their extended family members or even for their spouse's parents, but only for their own.

Census information reveals that the above-mentioned exclusions are numerically significant. Over a million women live in a household with an unrelated adult of the other sex, and another 726,000 live with a partner of the same sex. None of these women are eligible for leave to care for their domestic partners. Additionally, 2.5 percent of all children in this country live with persons other than their father or mother. Only 1.5 percent of white children live with other relatives or nonrelatives, but 7.5 percent of Black children and 2.4 percent of Hispanic children do so. The women caring for these children are not eligible for child care leave, since the children are not legally related to them.

While these express exclusions from eligibility are both numerically significant and symbolically troubling, the greatest number of women are likely to be excluded from leave, not because they are ineligible, but because they simply cannot afford to take advantage of it. Under section 102 (c) of the FMLA, employers would be required only to provide *unpaid* leave. Although the employee may elect to use paid vacation, personal or family leave instead, such an option depends on the employer already having a voluntary program of such other paid leaves. As indicated earlier, women may be less able to bargain for such voluntary programs, and thus will be less able to avail themselves of this option under the FMLA.

Not only will many working women be unable to afford foregoing income for any significant period of time, but in addition the lack of paid leave will affect decisions about caretaking responsibility in families with two workers eligible for caretaking leaves. Because men's wages continue to be significantly higher than women's, it would be economically rational for a married women to take the leave alone, as she would forgo a smaller income than her husband would, and his larger income would continue. Thus the vision of allowing for more shared responsibility in child caretaking is unlikely to be achieved, regardless of its theoretical possibility, until more parity in wages has been won.

The lesson I draw from the preceding account of the history and politics of the Family and Medical Leave Act is that focusing on *women* can lead to a *more* inclusive focus, rather than a less inclusive one. A Women's Family and Medical Leave Act would provide for leave to care for domestic partners, regardless of marital status. It would provide for leave to care for healthy infants and sick children according to actual responsibility rather than legal relationship. It would allow for leave to care for elderly relatives of *either* the female employee *or* her partner. Male employees would thus be able to take care of their female domestic partners when they were ill. The Act would also require leave when male employees actually had responsibility for the care of children, elderly members of the household, or same-sex domestic partners, so that female relatives and friends would not feel pressured to pick up the burden. To prevent disincentives for families that decide either to share the burdens of caretaking between male and female members or to shift the burden to male members, all employees should be subject to the same documentation requirements. Finally, the bill would at least start its legislative life with a requirement of paid leave, so that its sponsors could agree to drop that demand only if and when necessary in order to assure passage of the rest of the measure. . . .

STUDY QUESTIONS

1. In what ways does Littleton think the FMLA fell short? Do you think that these shortcomings were due to following a symmetrical approach? Might these shortcomings have as easily escaped the grasp of those who follow an asymmetrical approach? Are they more readily cured by either of these approaches?

2. As we saw earlier in this chapter, a later version of the FMLA was finally passed and signed by President Bill Clinton in 1993. Do you believe its enactment will make it more likely or less likely that other laws will be passed that provide the expanded coverage Littleton seeks?

Others, moving beyond the question of pregnancy, question the very idea of neutrality that is central to the symmetrical approach. Law professor Martha Fineman suggests "that gender neutrality may ultimately be as oppressive to the interests of women as the creation of differences exemplified by the *Bradwell* opinion."

> Neutral treatment in a gendered world or within a gendered institution does not operate in a neutral manner. There are more and more empirical studies that indicate that women's relative positions have worsened in our new ungendered doctrine world. Ignoring differences in favor of assimilation has not made the differences in gender expectations disappear. They operate to disadvantage women as the material implications of motherhood, for example, are realized in the context of career development and opportunity. Furthermore, even for women choosing to forgo gendered roles and to accept the male worker standard as the norm, entry into previously male-dominated institutions does not guarantee equality. Many such women encounter incremental obstacles to their advancement as glass ceilings and other impediments appear.
>
> *Martha Fineman. "Feminist Theory in Law: The Difference It Makes." 2* Columbia Journal of Gender and Law *1, 12 (1992).*

Fineman went on to advance a proposal that is reminiscent of an argument defended by Florence Kelley a half century earlier. The social and cultural assumptions and expectations that accompany the sexes' different reproductive roles have significant material consequences that are harmful to women. Instead of pressing for sex neutrality in that cultural context, Fineman favors "a concept of gendered life" that recognizes these contemporary differences and calls for "differentiated treatment to rectify [this] existing pervasive social and legal inequality."

In the mid-1980s, the main lines of the theoretical discussions among feminist legal scholars were cast as a debate opposing what was then called the "equal treatment" camp to the "different treatment" camp. By the end of the decade, these discussions were increasingly marked by a recognition of the need to transcend these simple dichotomies, to open new horizons of theory and fresh approaches to improving the condition of women.

A concern heard toward the end of the 1980s was that both the symmetrical and the asymmetrical approaches tend to work to the disadvantage of women. One feminist legal theorist who has been highly critical of both the equal treatment and different treatment camps is Catharine MacKinnon. She submits that both approaches measure women by the male standard. The equal treatment approach does so openly by incorrectly arguing that women are not different from men. The different treatment approach avoids that mistake, insists that women are different from men, and urges that we "value or compensate women for what we are or have become distinctively as women . . . under existing conditions." (*Feminism Unmodified.* Cambridge: Harvard University Press, 1987, p. 33). However, in her view, the different treatment approach also relies on the male standard. It does so by asserting that it is women's differences from men that justify preferential treatment. Instead of pursuing either of these approaches, MacKinnon favors focusing on male dominance. She urges feminists instead to address male supremacy and female subordination, which, for her, centers on sexually oppressive practices, such as rape, battering, and pornography.

Another important feminist theorist has pointed out that in the context of gendered institutions both equal treatment and different treatment approaches are harmful to women, minorities and, indeed, everyone perceived as "different." The following selection discusses this "dilemma of difference" in the context of bilingual and special education. The same patterns, however, apply wherever we attempt to remedy inequalities.

Making All the Difference: Inclusion, Exclusion, and American Law

Martha Minow.
Ithaca, NY: Cornell University Press,
1990. Pp. 20–21.

Perhaps ironically, . . . educational policymakers and law reformers during the 1970s and 1980s switched allegiance to bilingual programs that pull students at least part time from the mainstream classroom, while simultaneously sponsoring special education programs that integrate handicapped students into either the mainstream classroom or the "least restrictive alternative." The apparent contrast between these two responses to students who differ from their peers, however, suggests a deeper similarity. Schools, parents, and legal officials confront in both contexts the difficult task of remedying inequality. With both bilingual and special education, schools struggle to deal with children defined as "different" without stigmatizing them. Both programs raise the same question: when does treating people differently emphasize their differences and stigmatize or hinder them on that basis? and when does treating people the same become insensitive to their difference and likely to stigmatize or hinder them on *that* basis?

I call this question "the dilemma of difference." The stigma of difference may be recreated both by ignoring and by focusing on it. Decisions about education, employment, benefits, and other opportunities in society should not turn on an individual's ethnicity, disability, race, gender, religion, or membership in any other group about which some have deprecating or hostile attitudes. Yet refusing to acknowledge these differences may make them continue to matter in a world constructed with some groups, but not others, in mind. The problems of inequality can be exacerbated both by treating members of minority groups the same as members of the majority and by treating the two groups differently.

The dilemma of difference may be posed as a choice between integration and separation, as a choice between similar treatment and special treatment, or as a choice between neutrality and accommodation. Governmental neutrality may be the best way to assure equality, yet governmental neutrality may also freeze in place the past consequences of differences. Do the public schools fulfill their obligation to provide equal opportunities by including all students in the same integrated classroom, or by offering some students special programs tailored to their needs? Special needs arise from "differences" beyond language proficiency and physical or mental disability. Religious differences also raise questions of same versus different treatment. Students who belong to religious minorities may seek exemption from courses in sex education or other subjects that conflict with their religious teachings. Religiously observant students may ask to use school time and facilities to engage in religious activities, just as other students engage in other extracurricular activities. But the legal obligation of neutrality is explicit here, in a polity committed to separating church and state. Do the schools remain neutral toward religion by balancing the teaching of evolution with the teaching of scientific arguments about creation? Or does this accommodation of a religious viewpoint depart from the requisite neutrality?

The difference dilemma also arises beyond the schoolhouse. If women's biological differences from men justify special benefits in the workplace—such as maternity leave—are women thereby helped or hurt? Are negative stereotypes reinforced, in violation of commitments to equality? Or are differences accommodated, in fulfillment of the vision of equality? Members of religious groups that designate Saturday as the Sabbath may desire accommodation in the workplace. Is the commitment to a norm of equality advanced through such an accommodation, or through neutral application of a Saturday work requirement that happens to burden these individuals differently from others? These knotty problems receive diverse labels and inconsistent treatment in the legal system. The dilemma of difference—sometimes treated as a constitutional question of equal protection, due process, or religious freedom; sometimes

treated as a problem of statutory interpretation in civil rights, education, employment, housing, or income maintenance benefits—produces heated legal controversies that reverberate beyond courtrooms and legislatures. They occupy the attention of students and teachers, parents and neighbors, mass media and scholars. These controversies enact the political dramas of a diverse society committed to equality and to pluralism.

STUDY QUESTIONS

1. How are school policies that favor bilingual education said to be similar to policies that favor mainstreaming special education students?
2. Describe the horns of the dilemma on which school officials dealing with these problems

are caught. What application does this analysis have to the problem of childbearing and careers at issue in *Cal Fed*?
3. Discuss one experience that you have had with the "dilemma of difference."

As the 1990s began, a variety of fresh perspectives was offered by feminist theorists. In the remainder of this chapter, we sample three of these initiatives. In the first selection, law professor Joan Williams uses a postmodern approach in an effort to dissolve the dichotomy between sameness and difference. In this way, she seeks to refocus attention and energies on the pragmatic strategies that are likely to be most productive.

Dissolving the Sameness/Difference Debate: A Post-Modern Path Beyond Essentialism in Feminist and Critical Race Theory

Joan C. Williams.
1991 *Duke Law Journal* 296, 306–11, 322–3 (1991).

. . . Although both sameness and difference arguments have potential as strategies of trans-

formation, both need to be reformulated to avoid their potential to reinforce the status quo. Let me start the process of reformulating sameness and difference with a story. I was having lunch with a friend at the faculty club of my university. At the time, he and his wife had two children under three years of age, an experience that struck both of us as miserable. Yet the more he talked, the more I felt how "male" his reaction was. I am not sure why anymore, but it had something to do with his attitudes towards work and family. Then the topic shifted to birth control; his reaction struck me as shockingly Catholic. We proceeded through the lunch line and he bantered with the cashier—and I recognized a mixture of tension and camaraderie that I attributed to the complex dynamic between privileged and working-class blacks, complicated by a sexual flirtation that I had never seen before, though I had often been through the line with white male colleagues. (There was probably more camaraderie and less tension in

Joan C. Williams, Dissolving the Sameness/Difference Debate: A Post Modern Path Beyond Essentialism in Feminist and Critical Race Theory, *1991 Duke L.J. 297.*

the reaction I saw because my friend is handsome and personable.) Then we sat down, talked about scholarship for a while and he struck me as just another upper-middle-class academic like myself.

For me, that lunch dissolved the sameness/difference debate. On the one hand, it dramatized the truth of anti-essentialism. My friend does not have "a" minority perspective, he has many different perspectives: male, Catholic, upper-middle-class black, upper-middle-class generic, upper-middle-class academic. Which one is relevant depends on the situation: what he is discussing or doing, and with whom. To reify his viewpoint as "black" (or "male") is to make a set of extremely troubling value choices by silencing all the ways in which his life is shaped by forces other than his race (or sex). Now, at some level, one can interpret every other category in terms of his race and say he reacted as a black Catholic, a black academic, etc. And sometimes I do feel that he is reacting as a black Catholic, but not always. Note that the only context in which I felt the need to use what I think of as "junction categories" was to describe his interaction with a fellow African-American of lower status. This is a concrete way to illustrate my rejection of a single African-American voice, much less one minority voice, because the interaction of two Hispanics or two Asian-Americans would have been unutterably different.

Yet if my analysis dramatizes the contingency of categories, and warns against reifying any one category as being always of interpretive importance, it also expresses certain value judgments about what are the most useful categories for interpreting this sequence of events. The categories that I chose do not strike me as controversial (though I am not the best judge of this; I chose them because they seemed "obvious" to me). But it is useful to note that I focused on race, class, and gender—the traditional troika of American social commentary—with religion added, an overlooked but vital engine of American life. The traditional troika reflects the realities of power in American life, and thus dramatizes Foucault's insistence on the links between knowledge and power. My choice of those categories suggests a new way to interpret difference. Claims of difference simply mean that *in some contexts* gender or race may shape (or even determine) one's outlook. This reformulation of difference, which we could call post-modern difference, avoids essentialism because it refuses to concede that race, gender—or, indeed, *any* given category—will always be determinative. It allows us to argue that, although race and gender may prove determinative *in some particular context*, this is a far cry from a reified "minority perspective" or "women's voice" that determines how a given individual will react in every situation.

This post-modern approach starts from the notion of a fragmented and shifting self. Sometimes I feel like a white, sometimes a heterosexual, sometimes a Jew, sometimes a lawyer, sometimes an Episcopalian. Often I feel simply like my mother's daughter. A post-modern approach to difference highlights that each person is embedded in a matrix of social and psychological factors that interact in different contexts. Essentialism dissolves before the notion of a shifting, constantly reconfigured self, shaped but not determined by membership in sets of social categories that crystallize power relations in America.

A. Reformulating Sameness

The basic problem with sameness arguments is the claim that people who are as "obviously" different as men and women or blacks and whites are actually the same. This embarrassment is easy to solve if we stress not sameness but equal dignity. The basic claim ("I'm just as good as you!") need not entail a claim that I am the *same* as you. One only needs to say that "I will fulfill the conventional requirements for excellence in my own way—which, after all, is all anyone can ever do."

Once reformulated in this way, "sameness" entails not a claim that A and B are the same, instead, it entails the assertion that the differences that exist should be irrelevant in this particular context. This approach links equality with questions of policy rather than biology. Ultimately, one is left with disagreements not about who is similar to whom, but about which differences should matter in which contexts.

This approach to sameness reflects a post-modern sensitivity to the constructedness of categories. After all, no two people are truly "the same." Thus, when we call Person A the same as Person B we are constructing a cat-egory of "sameness" that ignores a whole series of differences for strategic reasons. The asser-tion that A and B are "the same" is not merely an assertion of *fact*. Instead, it is an argument that the characteristics that A and B share are more important for the purpose at issue than the ones they do not share.

Post-modern sameness makes it easier to see that, where women or minorities are not "the same," their failure often reflects their inability to measure up to a standard stacked against them. The "ideal worker" standard is stacked against women; elite schools' standards for law professors are stacked against those who lack access to cultural and class privileges that shape the usual path to academic "merit." This ap-proach links sameness with power: We as out-siders are not the same because we are disin-herited by our own tradition. Post-modern sameness cannot be reversed for use against outsiders because it does not make misleading claims that people as "obviously" different as blacks and whites, women and men, are the same. Neither is it content to leave intact sup-posedly neutral standards such as that of the ideal worker. Post-modern sameness makes ex-plicit outsiders' demand not to be disadvan-taged by physical (or social) characteristics that should be irrelevant when it comes to distribut-ing societal benefits.

B. Reformulating Difference

Because sameness feminism has been under siege for nearly a decade, the leading sameness advocate has reformulated sameness along post-modern lines. Difference feminists have generally not done the same with difference, despite the growing anti-essentialists critique. Thus far, the leading anti-essentialists have gen-erally focused on the fact that descriptions of women's "difference" tend to describe white women.

Beyond critiquing existing descriptions of dif-ference, how can we reformulate difference in ways that are true to outsiders' experience while avoiding essentialism? We begin once again with a post-modern sensitivity to the constructedness of categories. Traditional epistemology assumed the existence of a firm foundation, a "God's eye

point of view," a truth not dependent upon hu-man strivings. Non-foundationalists since the late nineteenth century have stressed the inevitability of different perspectives and different truths, start-ing from the axiom that things look different from different points of view. Non-foundationalists ar-gue that because every interpretation entails a viewpoint, no interpretation is final or objective. Different interpretations serve different purposes.

This outlook offers a way to dissolve differ-ence in much the same way that it dissolved sameness. Post-modern sameness translated ar-guments about physical or cultural *similarity* into arguments about which differences are relevant in which contexts. Post-modern differ-ence dissolves claims about *difference* into ar-guments about which differences should matter in which contexts. Once reformulated, differ-ence dissolves into sameness and vice versa.

One advantage of this reformulation of sameness and difference is that it shows how one can be a sameness feminist, or a Randall Kennedy, and still acknowledge difference. One can believe that gender or race is not the operative category in a range of contexts with-out claiming that gender or race is *never* deter-minative. This is an important point because of the widespread sense that sameness feminism has been discredited because "women and men obviously aren't the same."

A second advantage of a post-modern refor-mulation of sameness and difference is that it suggests that sameness advocates acknowledge differences and that difference advocates ac-knowledge sameness. The basic claim of post-modern sameness feminism is not that men and women (or whites and blacks) are *identical*, but that the importance of gender is at times over-shadowed by race, class, personality, or any of a number of other factors. This is a position with which, I suspect, most difference advocates would agree.

If sameness and difference feminists agree to this extent, are their disagreements illusory? Alas, no. . . .

Disagreement Over Strategy. One important disagreement is over strategy. Here I will limit my discussion to the feminist context, although many of the same issues arise in the context of race.

Both sameness and difference advocates advocate dismantling of facially-neutral standards that are in fact molded around the life patterns and self-image of males. Yet sameness and difference advocates disagree on how to proceed if an immediate change of the male standard is unattainable. Difference advocates opt for "special treatment"; sameness advocates opt for identical treatment. Sameness advocates charge that "special treatment" reinforces women's traditional disadvantage; difference advocates charge that denying women special treatment hurts women even more. In fact, both positions reinforce women's marginalization. Special treatment reinforces the message that "real" workers do not need pregnancy benefits; only "special" (more expensive, and therefore less desirable) workers do. Equal treatment reinforces women's marginalization to the extent it silences and privatizes the costs of a standard designed to privilege men.

What I have been describing, of course, is the *California Federal* debate. That decision has been widely considered a crisis for sameness feminism, because it revealed that women were "really" different. In fact, it showed the deep split among feminists about what to do when they are forced to settle (as they often must) for half a loaf. I strongly suspect that the sameness and difference proponents could have agreed that the *optimal* solution entailed redefining the ideal worker as one who shoulders simultaneous parental and job responsibilities. The disagreement emerged because that solution was perceived as unattainable. In that context sameness proponents argued that employers, to meet the requirements of the law, had to offer disability benefits (including, but not limited to, maternity leaves) for both men and women. In effect, they argued that a change in a "male" standard was the only acceptable solution. Presumably, difference advocates disagreed because they felt that the courts were too likely to treat women "the same" not by giving disability benefits to *both* men and women, but giving them to *neither* (thereby leaving women without maternity leaves).

Which position is more persuasive? This is a thorny issue. But it is a very different issue than

deciding whether men and women are "really" alike or "really" different. Dissolving the difference debate allows us to focus on issues of strategy instead of on fruitless discussions about the essential nature of outsiders. . . .

IV. CONCLUSION

A post-modern approach to the debate ultimately dissolves the traditional dichotomy between sameness and difference. Sameness claims are best viewed as policy arguments about which categories applicable to a given individual ought to matter in a specific context. This revamping of the sameness argument makes it easier to link assertions about sameness with the need for transformation. If I cannot be "the same" in a context in which equality depends on sameness, this means that the "neutral" standard that I cannot live up to is not, in fact, neutral.

Post-modern difference also begins from the notion that a myriad of possible categories are applicable to any individual. Assertions about difference are arguments that a given category—sex, race, class, etc.—is likely to yield powerful interpretive results in a particular context. The categories that crystallize power relations in America (race, sex, class) will often prove indispensable to analysis of sameness. This is not to say, though, that any category will always prove important, or even relevant. Women do not *always* react as women; sometimes they react as Democrats, lesbians, bigots, or blacks. This formulation of difference shows that any assertion of a unified outlook entails an interpretive decision to reify gender, or race, or some other characteristic, to assert that the particular characteristic *always* overrides all other possible characteristics in importance. Without a biological link to render such an interpretive decision "objective," this approach will normally prove repressive of the complex and changing forces that shape individuals.

This analysis helps us to understand that sameness and difference are not arguments about the essential nature of human beings. Instead, they are questions that stem from the fact that "neutral" standards systematically disadvantage outsiders: The "ideal worker" standard disadvantages women; conventional notions of merit disadvantage African-Americans; and both institutions and physical structures disadvantage the disabled.

If we insist on changing these standards, the need for outsiders to claim sameness or difference will disappear. Once the standard is designed with them in mind, they will simply meet it. Unfortunately, this solution is tidy in theory but difficult in practice, as Martha Minow's work has explored in such eloquence and depth. Until we can teach the whole class sign-language, the difference dilemma will persist.

Although we will not soon escape the difference dilemma, we can try to avoid diverting our energy into arguments amongst ourselves over whether outsiders are "really" the same or "really" different. Reformulating sameness and difference along post-modern lines largely dissolves the divergence between these two positions. Such reformulations can help refocus our attention onto two topics of abiding concern. The first is how to describe differences between outsiders and the mainstream in ways that do not reinforce stereotypes. The second is to forge working agreements on the most effective strategies to pursue in the face of the supposedly "neutral" standards of a tradition that disinherits us.

STUDY QUESTIONS

1. What truth of antiessentialism was dramatized by the luncheon conversation? What broader point associated with postmodern analysis was drawn from that illustration?
2. Contrast the ways that sameness and difference are cast in the essentialist and postmodern approaches. Which seems more familiar? Which seems more defensible?
3. Discuss the application of this postmodern perspective to the strategic debates over the situation in *Cal Fed*.

Another criticism of efforts to identify and protect women as a special class is that they gloss over differences among women. According to this view, much is to be gained from recognizing very real and important race, class, and other differences. Law professor Angela Harris explains this perspective.

Race and Essentialism in Feminist Legal Theory

Angela P. Harris.
42 *Stanford Law Review* 581, 585–57, 605–13 (1990).

. . . In this article, I discuss some of the writings of feminist legal theorists Catharine MacKinnon and Robin West. I argue that their work, though powerful and brilliant in many ways, relies on what I call gender essentialism—the notion that

a unitary, "essential" women's experience can be isolated and described independently of race, class, sexual orientation, and other realities of experience. The result of this tendency toward gender essentialism, I argue, is not only that some voices are silenced in order to privilege others (for this is an inevitable result of categorization, which is necessary both for human communication and political movement), but that the voices that are silenced turn out to be the same voices silenced by the mainstream legal voice of "We the People"—among them, the voices of black women.

This result troubles me for two reasons. First, the obvious one: As a black woman, in my opinion the experience of black women is too often ignored both in feminist theory and in legal theory, and gender essentialism in feminist legal theory does nothing to address this problem. A second and less obvious reason for my criticism of gender essentialism is that, in my view, contemporary legal theory needs less abstraction and not simply a different sort of abstraction. To be fully subversive, the methodology of feminist legal theory should challenge not only law's content but its tendency to privilege the abstract and unitary voice, and this gender essentialism also fails to do. . . .

The need for multiple consciousness in feminist movement—a social movement encompassing law, literature, and everything in between—has long been apparent. Since the beginning of the feminist movement in the United States, black women have been arguing that their experience calls into question the notion of a unitary "women's experience." In the first wave of the feminist movement, black women's realization that the white leaders of the suffrage movement intended to take neither issues of racial oppression nor black women themselves seriously was instrumental in destroying or preventing political alliances between black and white women within the movement. In the second wave, black women are again speaking loudly and persistently, and at many levels our voices have begun to be heard. Feminists have adopted the notion of multiple consciousness as appropriate to describe a world in which people are not oppressed only or primarily on the basis of gender, but on the bases of race, class, sexual orientation, and other categories in inextricable webs. Moreover, multiple consciousness is implicit in the precepts of feminism itself. In Christine Littleton's words, "[f]eminist method starts with the very radical act of taking women seriously, believing that what we say about ourselves and our experience is important and valid, even when (or perhaps especially when) it has little or no relationship to what has been or is being said about us." If a unitary "women's experience" or "feminism" must be distilled, feminists must ignore many women's voices. [Williams next discusses the work of MacKinnon and West.] . . .

If gender essentialism is such a terrible thing, why do two smart and politically committed feminists like Catharine MacKinnon and Robin West rely on it? In this section I want to briefly sketch some of the attractions of essentialism.

First, as a matter of intellectual convenience, essentialism is easy. Particularly for white feminists—and most of the people doing academic feminist theory in this country at this time are white—essentialism means not having to do as much work, not having to try and learn about the lives of black women, with all the risks and discomfort that that effort entails. Essentialism is also intellectually easy because the dominant culture is essentialist—because it is difficult to find materials on the lives of black women, because there is as yet no academic infrastructure of work by and/or about black women or black feminist theory. Second, and more important, essentialism represents emotional safety. Especially for women who have relinquished privilege or had it taken away from them in their struggle against gender oppression, the feminist movement comes to be an emotional and spiritual home, a place to feel safe, a place that must be kept harmonious and free of difference. . . .

Third, feminist essentialism offers women not only intellectual and emotional comfort, but the opportunity to play all-too-familiar power games both among themselves and with men. Feminist essentialism provides multiple arenas for power struggle which cross-cut one another in complex ways. The gameswomanship is palpable at any reasonably diverse gathering of feminists with a political agenda. The participants are busy constructing hierarchies of oppression, using their own suffering (and consequent innocence) to win the right to define "women's experience" or to demand particular political concessions for their interest group. White women stress women's commonality, which enables them to control the group's agenda; black women make reference to 200 years of slavery and argue that their needs should come first. Eventually, as the group seems ready to splinter into mutually suspicious and self-righteous factions, someone reminds the group that after all, women are women and we are all oppressed by men, and solidarity reappears through the threat of a common enemy. These are the strategies of zero-sum games; and feminist essentialism, by purveying the notion that there is only one "women's experience," perpetuates these games.

Finally, as Martha Minow has pointed out, "Cognitively, we need simplifying categories, and the unifying category of 'woman' helps to organize experience, even at the cost of denying some of it." Abandoning mental categories completely would leave us . . . terrorized by the sheer weight and particularity of experience. No categories at all, moreover, would leave nothing of a women's movement, save perhaps a tepid kind of "I've got my oppression, you've got yours" approach. . . .

In this part of the article, I want to talk about what black women can bring to feminist theory to help us move beyond essentialism and toward multiple consciousness as feminist and jurisprudential method. In my view, there are at least three major contributions that black women have to offer post-essentialist feminist theory: the recognition of a self that is multiplicitous, not unitary; the recognition that differences are always relational rather than inherent; and the recognition that wholeness and commonality are acts of will and creativity, rather than passive discovery.

A. THE ABANDONMENT OF INNOCENCE

Black women experience not a single inner self (much less one that is essentially gendered), but many selves. This sense of a multiplicitous self is not unique to black women, but black women have expressed this sense in ways that are striking, poignant, and potentially useful to feminist theory. bell hooks describes her experience in a creative writing program at a predominantly white college, where she was encouraged to find "her voice," as frustrating to her sense of multiplicity.

It seemed that many black students found our situations problematic precisely because our sense of self, and by definition our voice, was not unilateral, monologist, or static but rather multi-dimensional. We were as at home in dialect as we were in standard English. Individuals who speak languages other than English, who speak patois as well as standard English, find it a necessary aspect of self-affirmation not to feel compelled to choose one voice over another, not to claim one as more authentic, but rather to construct social realities that celebrate, acknowledge, and affirm differences, variety. . . .

B. STRATEGIC IDENTITIES AND "DIFFERENCE"

A post-essentialist feminism can benefit not only from the abandonment of the quest for a unitary self, but also from Martha Minow's realization that difference—and therefore identity—is always relational, not inherent. Zora Neale Hurston's work is a good illustration of this notion.

In an essay written for a white audience, ["]How It Feels to Be Colored Me,["] Hurston argues that her color is not an inherent part of her being, but a response to her surroundings. She recalls the day she "became colored"—the day she left her home in an all-black community to go to school: "I left Eatonville, the town of the oleanders, as Zora. When I disembarked from the river-boat at Jacksonville, she was no more. It seemed that I had suffered a sea change. I was not Zora of Orange County any more, I was now a little colored girl." But even as an adult, Hurston insists, her colored self is always situational: "I do not always feel colored. Even now I often achieve the unconscious Zora of Eatonville before the Hegira. I feel most colored when I am thrown against a sharp white background." . . .

C. INTEGRITY AS WILL AND IDEA

. . . Finally, black women can help feminist movement beyond its fascination with essentialism through the recognition that wholeness of the self and commonality with others are asserted (if never completely achieved) through creative action, not realized in shared victimization. Feminist theory at present, especially feminist legal theory, tends to focus on women as passive victims. For example, for MacKinnon, women have been so objectified by men that the miracle is how they are able to exist at all. Women are the victims, the acted-upon, the helpless, until by radical enlightenment they are somehow empowered to act for themselves. Similarly, for West, the "fundamental fact" of women's lives is pain—"the violence, the danger, the boredom, the ennui, the non-productivity, the poverty, the fear, the numbness, the frigidity, the isolation, the low self-esteem, and the pathetic attempts to assimilate."

This story of woman as victim is meant to encourage solidarity by emphasizing women's shared oppression, thus denying or minimizing difference, and to further the notion of an essential woman—she who is victimized. But as bell hooks has succinctly noted, the notion that women's commonality lies in their shared victimization by men "directly reflects male supremacist thinking. Sexist ideology teaches women that to be female is to be a victim." Moreover, the story of woman as passive victim denies the ability of women to shape their own lives, whether for better or worse. It also may thwart their abilities. Like Minnie Bruce Pratt, reluctant to look farther than commonality for fear of jeopardizing the comfort of shared experience, women who rely on their victimization to define themselves may be reluctant to let it go and create their own self-definitions. . . .

STUDY QUESTIONS

1. What are the contributions that Harris says black women can make to post essentialist feminist theory? Do you agree that they are valid? Do you see them as important?
2. Do you agree that there are dangers in seeing women primarily as victims? Is there a danger in refusing to recognize women's shared oppression?
3. What were Harris's two worries about essentialism? What are the attractions of essentialism? Does Littleton's focus on women suffer from these problems?

The final selection, by one of the country's most eminent feminist philosophers, draws attention to a different dimension. It focuses on processes, not only those that generate differences and make them matter in our culture but also the processes of feminist consciousness. It urges the development of both the pragmatic and the utopian strands of feminist consciousness that the author sees as having been at odds throughout the debates of the 1980s.

Sexual Difference and Sexual Equality

Alison M. Jaggar. In D. Rhode (ed.), Theoretical Perspectives on Sexual Difference.
Cambridge: Harvard University Press, 1990. Pp. 239–54.

The persistence and intensity of the perennial interest in sexual difference is not sustained by simple curiosity. Instead, it derives from an urgent concern with issues of sexual justice. For almost two and a half millennia, ever since Aristotle articulated the intuition central to the western concept of justice with his pithy but enigmatic dictum that justice consists in treating like cases alike and different cases differently, men and later women have debated the nature, extent, and even existence of the differences between the sexes and reflected on their relevance for the just organization of society. . . .

EQUALITY

Western feminists have not always been unanimous in demanding sexual equality. Even though this ideal inspired not only some of the earliest English feminists but also participants in the U.S. Seneca Falls Convention of 1848, most nineteenth-century feminists in the United States did not endorse such a radical demand, preferring instead to retain membership in women's separate sphere. Despite the ideology of separate spheres, however, feminist challenges to such inequities in the legal system as women's inability to vote or to control their own property on marriage developed eventually into demands for identity of legal rights for men and women or, as it came to be called, equality before the law. By the end of the 1960s, mainstream feminists in the United States had come to believe that the legal system should be sex-blind, that it should not differentiate in any way between women and men. This belief was expressed in the struggle for an Equal Rights Amendment to the U.S. Constitution, an amendment that, had it passed, would have made any sex-specific law unconstitutional. . . .

Within the last ten or fifteen years, increasing numbers of feminists have been challenging the assumption that sexual equality always requires sex-blindness. The growing public recognition that equality in areas other than gender relations is compatible with and may even require substantive differences in practical treatment adds plausibility to this challenge. For instance, equality in education ordinarily is taken to be compatible with, and even to require, the provision of different educational programs and bilingual or otherwise specially qualified teachers to serve the needs of children with varying abilities and disabilities. Similarly, there is increasing public willingness to provide special resources for people who are disabled or differently abled: readers for the blind, interpreters for the deaf, and adequate work space and access for those confined to wheelchairs.

Commitment to affirmative action in hiring probably constituted the first contemporary feminist challenge to the traditional sex-blind understanding of sexual equality. Affirmative action programs are generally uncontroversial among feminists because they are conceived as temporary expedients, as means rather than as ends. . . .

Most of the other proposals for achieving sexual equality through the recognition of sexual difference are considerably more controversial than affirmative action, even among feminists. One such proposal is that employers should be forbidden to terminate or refuse a reasonable leave of absence to workers disabled by pregnancy or childbirth even though such leaves may not be available to workers who are disabled for other reasons. The *Miller-Wohl* and *California Federal* cases, for instance, sharply divided the feminist legal community.

Even more controversial than special pregnancy maternity leaves are proposals to loosen the standard criteria of legal responsibility for women in some circumstances. For instance, there have been moves to recognize so-called premenstrual syndrome, which by definition afflicts only women, as a periodically disabling condition during which women enjoy diminished legal responsibility. Other feminist lawyers have proposed that there should be special criteria for identifying self-defense, criteria that go beyond immediate life-threatening danger, in the cases of women who kill their abusive husbands. . . .

It is easy to understand why most proposals for achieving sexual equality through the institutional recognition of sexual difference are controversial among feminists. The reason is that the supposed benefits of such recognition are bought only at a certain price to women. This price includes the danger that measures apparently designed for women's special protection may end up protecting them primarily from the benefits that men enjoy. This has happened frequently in the past. For instance, as [Wendy Williams] remarks,

> The protective labor legislation that limited the hours that women could work, prohibited night work and barred them from certain dangerous occupations such as mining may have promoted their health and safety and guaranteed them more time with their families. But it also precluded them from certain occupations requiring overtime, barred them from others where the entry point was the night shift, and may have contributed to the downward pressure on women's wages by creating a surplus of women in the jobs they were permitted to hold. . . .

A further problem with treating women differently from men is that it reinforces sexual stereotypes. Among the most familiar and pervasive of prevailing stereotypes are the correlative assumptions that men by nature are sexual aggressors and that women's very presence is sexually arousing and constitutes a temptation to aggression. In recent years these assumptions have been the basis of court decisions excluding women from the job of prison guard in Alabama maximum security prisons and even from the job of chaplain in a male juvenile institution. Such decisions have not only the direct consequence of "protecting" women from jobs that may be the best paid available to them (in the case of the prison guard) or to which they may even feel a religious calling (in the case of the chaplain); they also have far-reaching indirect consequences insofar as they perpetuate the dangerous and damaging stereotype that women by nature are the sexual prey of men. This cultural myth serves as an implicit legitimation for the prostitution, sexual harassment, and rape of women, because it implies that such activities are in some sense natural. Other legislation designed to draw attention to the need to protect women's sexuality, such as legislation defining the subjects in pornography paradigmatically as female, may well have similar consequences.

Legal recognition of women as a specially protected category may also encourage homogenization or "essentialism," the view that women are all alike. In one form, this point is more than a century old: liberal feminists since John Stuart Mill have argued that treating women as a homogeneous group is unfair to exceptional individuals, whose interests and capacities may be different from those of the majority of their sex. Increasing feminist sensitivity to differences between groups of women as well as to differences between individual women now requires further elaboration of Mill's anti-essentialist insight. As the present wave of feminism has rolled on, middle-class white feminists have been forced to recognize that their definitions of women's nature and women's political priorities too often have been biased by factors like race, class, age, and physical ability. Legislation that separates women into a single category inevitably will define that category in a way that makes a certain subgroup of women into the paradigm for the whole sex. . . .

When the risks involved in the sex-responsive approach to sexual equality become apparent, feminist theory arrives at an impasse. Both the sex-blind and the sex-responsive interpretations of equality seem to bear unacceptable threats to women's already vulnerable economic and social status. . . .

DIFFERENCE

In what follows, I outline an approach to understanding sexual difference that is more adequate to insights that feminists recently have emphasized. I focus especially on two characteristics of this approach. In saying that a more deeply feminist understanding of sexual difference must be dynamic rather than static, I mean that it must reflect the continually expanding feminist awareness of the ways in which the history of women's subordination, especially as this intersects with the history of other subordinated groups, has shaped and continues to shape both existing differences between the sexes and the ways in which we perceive and evaluate those differences.

A more fully feminist understanding of sexual difference does not deny that deep differences may exist between the sexes, but it does not assume that these differences are presocial or biological givens, unambiguous causes of women's apparently universal inequality and subordination. Instead, feminists must be committed to exploring the ways in which not only women's cognitive and emotional capacities, but even our bodies and our physical abilities, have been marked by a history of inequality and domination: a mark imposed not just on the development of individual women but on the whole evolution of our species. Thus the differences we perceive between men and women may be results as much as causes of sexual inequality. . . .

. . . [A]n adequate understanding of sexual difference must be sensitive to the differences between women and women as well as to the differences between women and men. Like the differences between women and men, the differences between women of varying classes, ages, racial and ethnic backgrounds, and so on are not given prior to society, nor are they static and unchanging. Instead they too are influenced by social forces. In consequence, feminists must be committed to investigating how these differences, too, as well as our perceptions of them, are shaped by the changing circumstances of age, class, race, and ethnicity. As a direct result of their awareness that social inequality has shaped not only perceptions of sexual difference and even difference itself but also the ways in which sexual difference has been valued, a number of feminists now are consciously reevaluating sexual difference.

In addition to challenging biologically reductionist accounts of sexual difference, they have begun to look at difference in a more woman-centered way, not just as evidence of women's weakness but as a possible source of women's strength.

The most evident difference between the sexes is women's capacity to become pregnant and give birth. Existing sex-responsive conceptions of sexual equality typically have viewed this capacity as a disability for which women deserve social compensation. But more feminists now are emphasizing that the ability to give birth is a uniquely valuable potential. Some claim it is a potential that is valuable not only in itself but in its giving rise to characteristically feminine ways of approaching and dealing with the world, ways that may provide a basis for feminist reconstruction. . . .

When sexual difference comes to be understood in ways that are dynamic and woman-affirming rather than static and woman-devaluing, a new light is thrown on the ideal of sexual equality.

A DIFFERENT FEMINISM

A dynamic approach to understanding sexual difference helps to explain the inadequacy of both the sex-blind and the sex-responsive ways of construing sexual equality. Because it recognizes the reality of sexual difference, such an approach shows why a sex-blind procedure may be unjust if it makes sexual inequality in outcome more likely. Simultaneously, through its recognition both of differences between women and of the social genesis of many inter- and intrasex differences, it shows the dangers of self-fulfilling prophecy that lurk in the sex-responsive approach to sexual equality. A dynamic understanding of sexual difference demonstrates why feminism must rethink traditional interpretations of sexual equality. Contemporary feminist revalorizations of sexual difference indicate some directions in which this rethinking may proceed. . . .

The ideal of equality gained its popularity in a period when caste and class divisions were extremely rigid and regulated every aspect of people's lives in a highly conspicuous way. In a situation where some groups have privileges that others lack, where certain groups are systematically restricted and repressed, the call for equality is voiced spontaneously. It provides a rallying cry to abolish privilege, to end oppression, to unite people against injustice and domination. This cry in the past has served women well, inspiring heroic and often victorious struggles against women's legal disabilities and forcing the opening up of economic, social, and educational opportunities for women. In a world where women (or certain groups of women) are still at the bottom of the pile, where women in full-time jobs earn on average less than two-thirds of the male wage and still do 70 percent of the housework (with husband and children averaging 15 percent each), where one girl in four is subjected to male incest, almost one woman in three to rape and half of all married women to domestic violence, in a world such as this, which is our world, feminists cannot afford to abandon the rhetoric of equality.

Equality, then, is a weapon that feminists seem forced to use, but some fear that it may turn against feminism. For some feminists, the language of equality is not women's "mother tongue"; instead, it is a language that some men developed at a particular point in European history, a language that western women have borrowed and sometimes put to good use. In its prevailing interpretations it is a language of impartiality and abstraction, a language of rational distance rather than of close connection. It presupposes scarcity and a preoccupation with getting one's fair share. It conjures up a rationalized and bureaucratic society of procedurally regulated competition, not an abundant, sensuous, and emotional world rich with human uniqueness and diversity.

Ruddick has written that "to mothers, the ideal of equality is a phantom." Certainly it is true that mothers typically are less concerned with abstract procedures or with merit than with individual need. They respond to the members of their families as concrete rather than as generalized individuals. Their actions are guided by intimate knowledge informed by feeling, not by abstract principle and emotional distance. This is why some see mothers as practicing an ethics of care rather than an ethics of justice.

There are unmistakable parallels between this (admittedly idealized) practice of mothers and the ideal of the classless society sketched by Marx in his *Critique of the Gotha Programme*. In such a society, according to Marx, an emphasis on equality of rights is likely to lead to inequality precisely because people differ from each other. In such a society, equal right becomes "*a right of inequality, in its content, like every right*" (italics original). It creates inequalities by ignoring differences between individuals. "To avoid all these defects, right instead of being equal would have to be unequal." Marx believed that these defects are unavoidable in the first phase of communist society but that in a higher phase the principle of communist distribution would be: "From each according to his [*sic*] ability, to each according to his [*sic*] needs." To apply this Marxist principle certainly would require a knowledge of individual circumstances at least as intimate as that which mothers have of their families, and in advocating this principle Marx, like mothers, often has been seen as abandoning the ideal of equality. Since equality, as we have seen, is a central feature in the western conception of justice, one who interpreted Marx in this way might even say, obviously anachronistically that Marx, like mothers, rejects an ethic of justice in favor of an ethic of care.

Alternatively, one might deny that either mothers or Marxists are unconcerned with equality. One might interpret them instead as reaching for a more determinate and substantive conception of equality, equality of outcome or condition rather than equality of procedure or opportunity. One might say that neither mothers nor Marxists are rejecting equality, but instead are groping toward a finer-grained and more adequate conception of equality, one that does not presuppose a framework where justice is wholly or even partially blind. One might even suggest that it is only by removing her blindfold completely, permitting her to see the full particularity of human individuals, that we enable justice to achieve full equality by making the discriminations necessary to treat genuinely like cases alike and genuinely different cases differently.

CONCLUSION: HAVING IT BOTH WAYS

No matter whether one construes mothers and Marxists as reinterpreting or transcending equality, there remains an enormous contrast between their radical vision, now being appropriated and developed by some contemporary feminists, and the currently limited conceptions of sexual equality employed in the daily struggle for sexual justice. Feminists seem caught in the dilemma of simultaneously demanding and scorning equality with men.

My own view is that feminists should embrace both horns of this dilemma, abandoning neither our short-term determination to reform existing society nor our long-term desire to transform it. We should develop both the pragmatic and the utopian strands in our thinking, in the hope that each may strengthen the other.

On the one hand, feminists should continue to struggle for women to receive a fair share of the pie, carcinogenic though it ultimately may be. They should use the rhetoric of equality in situations where women's interests clearly are being damaged by their being treated either differently from or identically with men. It seems likely that neither of the two prevailing interpretations of equality is best in all circumstances. Sometimes equality in outcome may be served best by sex-blindness, sometimes by sex-responsiveness— and sometimes by attention to factors additional to or other than sex. Because perceived sexual differences so often are the result of differences in treatment, it seems prudent to advocate only short-term rather than permanent protections for women. For example, affirmative action and special legal defenses for chronically abused women seem less dangerous to women's status than premenstrual exemptions from legal responsibility. Some questions that have been presented as issues of sexual equality, such as antipornography ordinances and moves to draft women, may be decided better by reference to considerations other than those of equality.

Throughout the battle for sexual equality, it is necessary to remain critical of the standards by which that equality is measured. In particular, feminists should be ready constantly to challenge norms that may be stated in gender-neutral language but that are established on the basis of male experience, and so likely to be biased in favor of men. One example of such a norm is the ordinance forbidding firefighters to breast-feed between calls; another is the minimum height requirement for airline pilots, a requirement based on the seemingly sex-blind concern that pilots be able to reach the instrument panel. Feminist challenges to such norms should mitigate at least to some extent the concern that sexual equality simply will "masculinize" women by assimilating them to male standards. The need to redesign the organization of both paid work and of domestic responsibility in order to avoid this kind of male bias must surely modify the extremes of gender polarization.

Simultaneously with insisting on sexual equality in a world presently racked by scarcity and injustice, feminists should develop their long-term visions of a world in which equality is less a goal than a background condition, a world in which injustice is not "the first virtue of social institutions," but in which justice and equality are overshadowed by the goods of mutual care. But this must be care in a new sense, not the feminized, sentimentalized, privatized care with which we are familiar; not care as a nonrational or even irrational feeling; not care as self-sacrifice (Noddings' "motivational displacement"), nor care as contrasted with justice. Feminists need to develop a distinctive conception of care, one that draws on but transcends women's traditional practice. Feminist care must be responsive both to our common humanity and our inevitable particularity. Neither narrowly personal nor blandly impersonal, it can consist neither in the mechanical application of abstract rules nor in an uncritical surge of feeling, but must transcend both rationalism and romanticism.

The development of such a conception of care is a practical and political as much as an intellectual project. It cannot take place in a world that is structured by domination, where the public sphere is separated sharply from the private, and where inequality is justified in terms of such familiar, gender-linked, western oppositions as culture/nature, mind/body, reason/emotion—dichotomies in which each of the first terms is associated with the masculine and considered superior to each of the second. Instead, experimentation with ways of transcending equality requires an enriched and in some ways protected environment, a consciously feminist community dedicated to discovering less rigid and less hierarchical ways of living and thinking. We need not fear that such an environment will be so sheltered as to produce a weakened, hothouse plant. Far from being sheltered from the cold winds of the larger world, alternative communities may be particularly vulnerable to them. It is stimulating but hardly comfortable to live daily with contradictions.

STUDY QUESTIONS

1. What features of the sex-blind and the sex-responsive ways of thinking about the goal of sexual equality are identified by Jaggar? What reasons are given for regarding each as inadequate?
2. What are the distinctive characteristics of the new approach advocated here? How does it avoid the inadequacies of the older perspectives?
3. What are the implications of the new approach for feminist litigation and legislative reform? Do you think the approach would avoid the problems of the equal treatment and special treatment approaches?

The theoretical debates traced in this chapter help us to see—and value—the ways women differ from men. They also help us see that women differ from one another in many ways and that we must learn from their different perspectives in the struggle for equality. Finally, they help us appreciate the different legal responses that are possible. Understanding the legal responses favored by different groups in particular situations often involves sorting out three levels of choices: What is the goal ultimately desired? What is the strategy seen as most likely to advance that goal? Who do those involved respond to emotionally?

As pregnancy-related cases and legislation have shown, concrete legal developments often affect the course of theoretical discussions. Moreover, theory may shape the legal changes that people strive to make. We have already seen how contested theoretical positions shed light on concrete policy questions. In Chapter 2, for example, we examined the question of whether women should be exempt from compulsory military service and from assignment, even voluntary, to combat roles. In the remainder of the book, we will encounter other issues over which these same debates are joined. These include: Should sex-segregated public schools and school athletic programs be permitted? Should women be given an edge in child custody disputes? Should birthmothers always be preferred in contract parenthood disputes? As you think through these and other concrete problems in the chapters ahead, consider the implications presented by the different theoretical perspectives outlined here.

4 Equal Employment Opportunity

F rom the beginning, one of the principal grievances of feminists has been sex
discrimination in employment. In 1848, the Seneca Falls Conference de-
nounced sex segregation in the workplace and the devaluation of work done
by women: "He [man] has monopolized nearly all the profitable employments and
from those she is permitted to follow, she receives but a scanty remuneration"
(*Declaration of Sentiments;* see Chapter 1).

The participation of women in the paid labor force has been restricted by a variety
of techniques. During the nineteenth and early twentieth centuries, laws excluded
women from particular occupations and limited the hours and times they could work.
As discussed in Chapter 1, these restrictions were justified by the separate spheres
ideology and later by the protective rationale. Throughout that period, women's
participation in the labor force was largely limited to low-paying jobs in textile
manufacturing, offices, teaching, and domestic service. Short-lived exceptions to this
pattern occurred during the two world wars, when the economy experienced personnel shortages in other labor sectors. Even then, however, women generally earned
substantially lower wages than did men in comparable positions.

Sex segregation in the workplace and devaluation of the work done by women
have a devastating impact. Although ancient in origin, these practices were not widely
acknowledged until the 1950s, when women's participation in the paid labor force
dramatically increased. Only 28 percent of adult women worked outside the home in
1950, and half of them on a part-time basis. Within four decades, a revolution in the
employment patterns of adult women occurred. By 1990, over 57 percent of adult
women worked outside the home, over 70 percent of them full-time. Whereas only
about 10 percent of women with preschool-age children were employed in 1950, over
two-thirds of such women were in the labor force in the early 1990s.

With this massive change in the rate at which adult women participate in the
labor force, the impact of sex discrimination in employment became recognized as
a problem of acute proportions. That problem is threefold. The first issue is the
"earnings gap." Full-time women workers as a group earn between 60 percent and
70 percent as much as full-time men workers as a group. This ratio has held constant
throughout our century in spite of the change in labor force participation by women
and in spite of major legal measures adopted in the 1960s and 1970s. The second
dimension is sex segregation in the workplace. In the early 1990s, three-fifths of all
working women held jobs in stereotypically female occupations. They were nurses,
librarians and clerical workers, and as many as 20 percent more worked in other jobs

where nine out of ten of their peers were women. The "feminization of poverty" is the final dimension of the problem. Due to a number of factors, including increases in the divorce rate, families with children are increasingly headed by single females. Conditions in the early 1990s were captured in a number of statistical measures. Over 37 percent of families with children were headed by women—more than three times the rate reported in 1960. This phenomenon, combined with the continuing segregation of women into low paying, dead-end jobs, has served to produce the feminization of poverty. A child who lived with its divorced mother was six times more likely to live in poverty than a child who lived with the father or both parents. The poverty effect of sex discrimination in employment is not restricted to young women with children. Since Social Security and pensions generally are keyed to past income levels, elderly women are also affected. Over 15 percent of women sixty-five years and older lived below the poverty line. Elderly black women were especially hard hit, with 37.9 percent in poverty.

These effects of sex discrimination in employment, discussed at greater length in Chapters 5 and 7, received attention by the legislative and executive branches of government at the state and federal levels in the 1960s and early 1970s. The statutes enacted are usually referred to as Fair Employment Practice (FEP) laws. State FEP laws were generally understood to be patterned after those at the federal level. There, the main measures were the Equal Pay Act of 1963 and Title VII of the Civil Rights Act of 1964. Of these, Title VII has been the bulwark of antisex-bias practices in employment. This chapter will introduce the principal features of that statute. The other measures will be discussed in Chapter 5.

I. AN INTRODUCTION TO TITLE VII

The History of Title VII

Title VII of the Civil Rights Act of 1964 (42 U.S.C. § 2000e) is the most comprehensive equal employment opportunity statute ever adopted by the federal government. The struggle to enact it was long and bitter. Its proponents sought to eliminate the effects of racial bias from hiring and promotion decisions in private-sector employment. Bills similar to Title VII had been introduced and routinely defeated since 1943—often by means of a Senate filibuster.

The main impetus to the passage of the 1964 bill came only a month after President John F. Kennedy was assassinated in November 1963. President Johnson dedicated the Civil Rights Act, then a series of bills in Congress, to the memory of his predecessor, saying: "We have talked long enough in this country about equal rights. . . . it is time now to write the next chapter, and to write it in the book of laws." The following June, President Johnson announced that the Senate filibuster had been broken. The Civil Rights Act was signed into law a month later and went into effect in July, 1965.

The story of how gender came to be included in Title VII as a prohibited basis of employment discrimination is anything but edifying. An amendment to the original bill adding "sex" to "race, color, religion and national origin" as a prohibited employment criterion was first proposed on the floor of the House of Representatives on the last day of debate on the bill. It was proposed by Representative Howard Smith of Virginia, chairman of the House Rules Committee, evidently for the purpose of blocking passage of the entire act. The only arguments favoring the amendment at the time were that sex discrimination was wrong and without the amendment, white women would be at a disadvantage in relation to African-American women. The amendment was opposed by the President's Commission on the Status of Women, the Women's Bureau of the Department of Labor, and the American Association of University Women. Even so, the amended bill passed. Representative Smith's ploy failed. One of the most powerful remedies for sex discrimination available today owes its origin to a misfired political tactic on the part of opponents of the act.

Title VII has been amended three times since it was initially enacted. The amendments of 1972 extended the powers of the Equal Employment Opportunity Commission (EEOC), expanded the coverage of the act to include public employers and educational institutions, and clarified a number of its terms and provisions. In 1978, the Pregnancy Discrimination Act amended Title VII by adding what is now section 701(k), which declares that classifications based on pregnancy and pregnancy-related disabilities fall within the meaning of "sex" as used in Title VII. The Civil Rights Act (CRA) of 1991 amended Title VII to reverse a series of recent Supreme Court decisions that threatened to cripple the enforcement of the civil rights protected by the statute. It also added several new provisions affecting remedies. Many of these changes will be mentioned in the course of this chapter.

Coverage

Title VII may be conveniently analyzed in three ways. In terms of its coverage, to whom are the statutes' prohibitions addressed? Who are the potential defendants in actions under this statute? Second, in terms of its scope, what behaviors are forbidden? Third, in terms of its remedies, what relief does the statute provide for the victims of prohibited behavior? This chapter and the next will focus on the scope of the statute. Remedies under Title VII will be discussed later in this chapter.

In Chapter 2, we noted that the Equal Protection Clause of the federal Constitution applies only where "state action" is found. That restriction does not apply to the statutes under discussion here. They extend to both the public and private sectors. Title VII prohibits discriminatory practices by employers, employment agencies, labor organizations, and training programs. Since similar principles apply to all these potential defendants, for purposes of clarity we will confine our attention to employers. An employer is defined in 701(b) as "a person engaged in an industry affecting commerce who has fifteen or more employees. . . ." Section 701(a) defines "persons" as including governments, corporations, and partnerships as well as individuals. The Supreme Court ruled in 1984 that a law partnership is an employer under Title VII, *Hishon v. King & Spaulding,* 467 U.S. 69.

Having identified employers, the statute goes on to declare that some employers are nevertheless exempt from the statute's prohibitions. Two of these are relevant to our discussion of sex discrimination. An employer is exempt from coverage under Title VII if it is a bona fide private membership club (701(b)). Finally, an employer is exempt from coverage of Title VII in the employment of aliens outside the United States (section 702). The CRA of 1991 amended the statute to make clear that U.S. citizens working abroad for U.S.-based employers are included within the coverage of Title VII.

Scope

The main prohibitions of the statute are stated in section 703(a).

It shall be an unlawful employment practice for an employer—
(1) to fail or refuse to hire or to discharge any individual, or otherwise to discriminate against any individual with respect to his compensation, terms, conditions, or privileges

of employment, because of such individual's race, color, religion, sex, or national origin:
or

(2) to limit, segregate, or classify his employees or applicants for employment in any way which would deprive or tend to deprive any individual of employment opportunities or otherwise adversely affect his status as an employee, because of such individual's race, color, religion, sex, or national origin.

Although attention will be concentrated on the prohibitions of section 703, those in 704(a) should not be ignored. There, the statute makes retaliation against those who oppose unlawful discrimination or participate in complaint proceedings a separate offense. This provision provides protection for those who come to the aid of their fellow workers.

Just as there are exemptions from the coverage, there are exceptions to the scope of the prohibitions. The main exception relevant to sex discrimination is the bona fide occupational qualification (BFOQ) (703(e)(1)). This exception will be discussed at some length later in this chapter. Others include veterans' preference (712); differential treatment based upon seniority, merit systems, productivity, and professionally developed ability tests (703(h)); and wage differentials authorized by the Equal Pay Act (703(h)). Other exceptions include the personal staff or policy-level appointees of elected political officials (701(f)) and individuals not covered for national security reasons (703(g)).

II. TWO CONCEPTS OF DISCRIMINATION

The Basic Ingredients

Title VII does not define the expressions "discrimination" or "because of sex." Congress left the task of interpreting the meaning of these expressions to the courts. Much of the litigation reviewed in this chapter can be read as clarifying the meaning of these expressions. To begin, we will examine practices that are clearly discriminatory and determine which of these are imposed "because of sex" as that expression is understood in the statute.

Discrimination against women and men takes many forms and is most often directed toward the enforcement of social norms that are keyed to the biological sex of individuals. Courts have understood Title VII to extend to only some of these forms of discrimination. Mandatory heterosexuality is one type that is not currently included within the scope of Title VII.

DeSantis v. Pacific Tel. & Tel. Co.

United States Court of Appeals,
Ninth Circuit, 1979.
608 F.2d 327.

CHOY, Circuit Judge.

. . . DeSantis, Boyle, and Simard, all males, claimed that Pacific Telephone & Telegraph Co. (PT&T) impermissibly discriminated against them because of their homosexuality. DeSantis alleged that he was not hired when a PT&T supervisor concluded that he was a homosexual. According to appellants' brief, "BOYLE was continually harrassed by his co-workers and had to quit to preserve his health after only three months because his supervisors did nothing to alleviate this condition." Finally, "SIMARD was forced to quit under similar conditions after almost four years of employment with PT&T, but he was harrassed by his supervisors [as well]. . . . In addition, his personnel file has been marked as not eligible for rehire, and his applications for employment were rejected by PT&T in 1974 and 1976." Appellants DeSantis, Boyle, and Simard also alleged that PT&T officials have publicly stated that they would not hire homosexuals. . . .

Lundin and Buckley, both females, were operators with PT&T. They filed suit in federal court alleging that PT&T discriminated against them because of their known lesbian relationship and eventually fired them. They also alleged that they endured numerous insults by PT&T employees because of their relationship. . . . Appellants sought monetary and injunctive relief. The district court dismissed their suit as not stating a claim upon which relief could be granted. . . .

Appellants argue first that the district courts erred in holding that Title VII does not prohibit discrimination on the basis of sexual preference. They claim that in prohibiting certain employment discrimination on the basis of "sex," Congress meant to include discrimination on the basis of sexual orientation. . . .

In *Holloway v. Arthur Andersen & Co.,* plaintiff argued that her employer had discriminated against her because she was undergoing a sex transformation and that this discrimination violated Title VII's prohibition on sex discrimination. This court rejected that claim, writing:

The cases interpreting Title VII sex discrimination provisions agree that they were intended to place women on an equal footing with men.

Giving the statute its plain meaning, this court concludes that Congress had only the traditional notions of "sex" in mind. Later legislative activity makes this narrow definition even more evident. Several bills have been introduced to *amend* the Civil Rights Act to prohibit discrimination against "sexual preference." None have [sic] been enacted into law. . . .

Following *Holloway,* we conclude that Title VII's prohibition of "sex" discrimination applies only to discrimination on the basis of gender and should not be judicially extended to include sexual preference such as homosexuality. . . .

Having determined that appellants' allegations do not implicate Title VII's prohibition on sex discrimination, we affirm the district court's dismissals of the Title VII claims. . . .

STUDY QUESTIONS

1. What were the forms of treatment complained of by the plaintiffs? Were the plaintiffs victims of discrimination?
2. What reasons did the court give for finding that the discrimination suffered by the plaintiffs is not within the scope of Title VII? In the light of those reasons, would it have been inappropriate for the court to have ruled differently?

Gay men and lesbian women are regularly required to endure practices similar to those alleged in *DeSantis* because they do not conform to societal norms for their gender. The consequences are devastating in economic and personal terms. Without accepting or denying those propositions, courts have regularly held that, although Title VII does prohibit discrimination because of gender, it does not prohibit discrimination because of sexual preference. In doing so, the courts typically understand the objective of the act in ways similar to the interpretation given in *DeSantis,* viz., "to place women on an equal footing with men."

Title VII prohibits discrimination in employment "because of sex." *DeSantis* shows that "sex" means gender. Before proceeding, however, we need clarification of the "because of" dimension. It isn't enough, after all, that women or men are victims of discrimination in the workplace. To establish a violation of Title VII, they must show that they have been victimized "because of" their sex.

The "because of" component can be understood in a variety of ways. Courts have considered two of these, rejecting the one and accepting the other. On one reading, an employment practice is prohibited by the statute where the sex of the victim is a sufficient condition for being treated in a discriminatory manner. In this "sufficient condition" interpretation, a discriminatory practice affecting women is prohibited only if all women are eligible for discriminatory treatment under it. The Supreme Court rejected that interpretation in 1971, *Phillips v. Martin Marietta Corp.*, 400 U.S. 542. There, the employer attempted to defend a policy of refusing to hire women for selected positions if they had preschool-age children at home. The employer unsuccessfully argued that since not all women were affected, the policy was not prohibited by Title VII.

A second interpretation of "because of" has been widely accepted by the courts. In that reading, an employment practice is prohibited by the statute where the sex of the victim is a necessary condition for being treated in a discriminatory manner. In this "necessary condition" interpretation, a discriminatory practice affecting women or men is prohibited only if they would not have been victimized had they not been female or male. In legal jargon, these people would not have been victims "but for" their gender. The following case illustrates the way the "necessary condition" or "but for" interpretation functions in a case and the type of evidence needed to support the claim of discrimination "because of sex."

EEOC v. Brown & Root, Inc.
United States Court of Appeals,
Fifth Circuit, 1982.
688 F.2d 338.

ALVIN B. RUBIN, Circuit Judge:

. . . The following facts are undisputed: Sarah Joan Boyes was employed by Brown & Root as an electrician's helper. Brown & Root is a construction company and Ms. Boyes was assigned to work on an overhead steel beam that was part of a structure being erected at Escatawpa, Mississippi. She became paralyzed by fear and was unable to move, a condition known as "freezing." It was necessary physically to assist her to climb down. Brown & Root discharged Ms. Boyes from her job for the stated reason that she was "not capable of performing assigned work." After she was fired, another female worker was hired to fill the position of electrician's helper.

What is disputed is whether men who manifested the same acrophobia were also discharged. In opposition to the motion for summary judgment, the Equal Employment Opportunity Commission offered the affidavit of its investigator. To

this were attached copies of statements taken from four male employees, each of whom stated that he or some other worker had at some prior time frozen on the beams, could not get down without help, and was not discharged. One statement referred also to a male worker who was kept on the ground because he was afraid of heights. There was also attached an "EEOC affidavit" from a male employee stating that he had "frozen" and had not been discharged. [The district court granted summary judgment for the defendant.]

While neither the pleadings nor the proof in opposition to the motion for summary judgment frame the issue as directly as would be desirable, the disputed issue was not whether Ms. Boyes was unable to work at heights, a fact that was, indeed, undisputed, or whether she was replaced by a male, another fact that was not disputed, but whether, had she been a man, she would have suffered dismissal as a result of her phobia. . . .

If an employee is discharged under circumstances in which an employee of another sex would not have been discharged, an inference of discrimination arises irrespective of the gender of the employee's replacement. . . .

The summary judgment is REVERSED and the case is REMANDED for further proceedings consistent with this opinion.

STUDY QUESTIONS

1. Why was the plaintiff fired? Does it appear that defendant was merely using the episode as an excuse to keep women out of the electricians' trade?

2. Had defendant also fired acrophobic men, would the decision in this case have been different?

Men and women are treated differently in many ways in employment settings. The reasons offered in justification frequently give expression to ancient, often tradition-based, stereotypes. The objective of Title VII is to counteract the impact of these cultural stereotypes. Employer decisions that work to the disadvantage of women, however, are sometimes based upon true generalizations about differences between men and women. Does Title VII bar employment decisions that treat men and women workers differently if those decisions are based not on outmoded stereotypes but on true generalizations? In the decision that follows, the Supreme Court addressed that question.

Los Angeles Dept. of Water & Power v. Manhart

Supreme Court of the United States, 1978.
435 U.S. 702, 98 S.Ct. 1370,
55 L.Ed.2d 657.

Mr. Justice STEVENS delivered the opinion of the Court.

As a class, women live longer than men. For this reason, the Los Angeles Department of Water and Power required its female employees to make larger contributions to its pension fund than its male employees. We granted certiorari to decide whether this practice discriminated against individual female employees because of their sex in violation of § 703 (a) (1) of the Civil Rights Act of 1964, as amended.

For many years the Department has administered retirement, disability, and death-benefit programs for its employees. Upon retirement each employee is eligible for a monthly retirement benefit computed as a fraction of his or her salary multiplied by years of service. The monthly benefits for men and women of the same age, seniority, and salary are equal. Benefits are funded entirely by contributions from the employees and the Department, augmented by the income earned on those contributions. No private insurance company is involved in the administration or payment of benefits.

Based on a study of mortality tables and its own experience, the Department determined that its 2,000 female employees, on the average, will live a few years longer than its 10,000 male employees. The cost of a pension for the average retired female is greater than for the average male retiree because more monthly payments must be made to the average woman. The Department therefore required female employees to make monthly contributions to the fund which were 14.84% higher than the contributions required of comparable male employees. Because employee contributions were withheld from paychecks, a female employee took home less pay than a male employee earning the same salary.[5]

. . . On a motion for summary judgment, the District Court held that the contribution differ-

---

[5] The significance of the disparity is illustrated by the record of one woman whose contributions to the fund (including interest on the amount withheld each month) amounted to $18,171.40; a similarly situated male would have contributed only $12,843.53.

ential violated § 703 (a) (1) and ordered a refund of all excess contributions made before the amendment of the plan. The United States Court of Appeals for the Ninth Circuit affirmed. . . .

There are both real and fictional differences between women and men. It is true that the average man is taller than the average woman; it is not true that the average woman driver is more accident prone than the average man. Before the Civil Rights Act of 1964 was enacted, an employer could fashion his personnel policies on the basis of assumptions about the differences between men and women, whether or not the assumptions were valid.

It is now well recognized that employment decisions cannot be predicated on mere "stereotyped" impressions about the characteristics of males or females. Myths and purely habitual assumptions about a woman's inability to perform certain kinds of work are no longer acceptable reasons for refusing to employ qualified individuals, or for paying them less. This case does not, however, involve a fictional difference between men and women. It involves a generalization that the parties accept as unquestionably true: Women, as a class, do live longer than men. The Department treated its women employees differently from its men employees because the two classes are in fact different. It is equally true, however, that all individuals in the respective classes do not share the characteristic that differentiates the average class representatives. Many women do not live as long as the average man and many men outlive the average woman. The question, therefore, is whether the existence or nonexistence of "discrimination" is to be determined by comparison of class characteristics or individual characteristics. A "stereotyped" answer to that question may not be the same as the answer that the language and purpose of the statute command.

The statute makes it unlawful "to discriminate against any *individual* with respect to his compensation, terms, conditions, or privileges of employment, because of such *individual's* race, color, religion, sex, or national origin." The statute's focus on the individual is unambiguous. It precludes treatment of individuals as simply components of a racial, religious, sexual,

or national class. If height is required for a job, a tall woman may not be refused employment merely because, on the average, women are too short. Even a true generalization about the class is an insufficient reason for disqualifying an individual to whom the generalization does not apply.

That proposition is of critical importance in this case because there is no assurance that any individual woman working for the Department will actually fit the generalization on which the Department's policy is based. Many of those individuals will not live as long as the average man. While they were working, those individuals received smaller paychecks because of their sex, but they will receive no compensating advantage when they retire.

It is true, of course, that while contributions are being collected from the employees, the Department cannot know which individuals will predecease the average woman. Therefore, unless women as a class are assessed an extra charge, they will be subsidized, to some extent, by the class of male employees. It follows, according to the Department, that fairness to its class of male employees justifies the extra assessment against all of its female employees.

But the question of fairness to various classes affected by the statute is essentially a matter of policy for the legislature to address. Congress has decided that classifications based on sex, like those based on national origin or race, are unlawful. Actuarial studies could unquestionably identify differences in life expectancy based on race or national origin, as well as sex. But a statute that was designed to make race irrelevant in the employment market could not reasonably be construed to permit a take-home-pay differential based on a racial classification.

Even if the statutory language were less clear, the basic policy of the statute requires that we focus on fairness to individuals rather than fairness to classes. Practices that classify employees in terms of religion, race, or sex tend to preserve traditional assumptions about groups rather than thoughtful scrutiny of individuals. The generalization involved in this case illustrates the point. Separate mortality tables are easily interpreted as reflecting innate differences between the sexes; but a significant part of the longevity differential may be explained by the social fact that men are heavier smokers than women.

Finally, there is no reason to believe that Congress intended a special definition of discrimination in the context of employee group insurance coverage. It is true that insurance is concerned with events that are individually unpredictable, but that is characteristic of many employment decisions. Individual risks, like individual performance, may not be predicted by resort to classifications proscribed by Title VII. Indeed, the fact that this case involves a group insurance program highlights a basic flaw in the Department's fairness argument. For when insurance risks are grouped, the better risks always subsidize the poorer risks. Healthy persons subsidize medical benefits for the less healthy; unmarried workers subsidize the pensions of married workers; persons who eat, drink, or smoke to excess may subsidize pension benefits for persons whose habits are more temperate. Treating different classes of risks as though they were the same for purposes of group insurance is a common practice that has never been considered inherently unfair. To insure the flabby and the fit as though they were equivalent risks may be more common than treating men and women alike; but nothing more than habit makes one "subsidy" seem less fair than the other. . . .

Although we conclude that the Department's practice violated Title VII, we do not suggest that the statute was intended to revolutionize the insurance and pension industries. All that is at issue today is a requirement that men and women make unequal contributions to an employer-operated pension fund. Nothing in our holding implies that it would be unlawful for an employer to set aside equal retirement contributions for each employee and let each retiree purchase the largest benefit which his or her accumulated contributions could command in the open market. Nor does it call into question the insurance industry practice of considering the composition of an employer's work force in determining the probable cost of a retirement or death benefit plan. Finally, we recognize that in a case of this kind it may be necessary to take special care in fashioning appropriate relief.

There can be no doubt that the prohibition against sex-differentiated employee contributions represents a marked departure from past practice. Although Title VII was enacted in 1964, this is apparently the first litigation challenging contribution differences based on valid actuarial tables. Retroactive liability could be devastating for a pension fund. The harm would fall in large part on innocent third parties. If, as the courts below apparently contemplated, the plaintiffs' contributions are recovered from the pension fund, the administrators of the fund will be forced to meet unchanged obligations with diminished assets. If the reserve proves inadequate, either the expectations of all retired employees will be disappointed or current employees will be forced to pay not only for their own future security but also for the unanticipated reduction in the contributions of past employees.

. . . [I]t was error to grant such relief in this case. Accordingly, although we agree with the Court of Appeals' analysis of the statute, we vacate its judgment and remand the case for further proceedings consistent with this opinion.

It is so ordered.

STUDY QUESTIONS

1. Was the pension plan unfair to women as a class or only to those women who outlive the average woman? What question did the Court regard as central to this case?
2. Explain the department's complaint that the Court's solution would be unfair to its male employees. Is that a valid complaint?
3. What reason did the Court offer in support of its decision here? Do you think it reached the correct decision? Suppose that white males have greater life expectancy than black males. Would Title VII permit differentiation in pension payments for them?

The *Manhart* decision, however sweeping its endorsement of the principle of fairness to individuals, was limited in two respects. It dealt only with pension plans that provide for equal payments to women and men after retirement but require unequal payments by participating men and women workers prior to retirement. Most pension plans work the other way around, i.e., they require equal payments into the plan by all workers but provide lower payments to female than male retirees. After *Manhart,* the status of those pension plans remained in doubt. That doubt was removed in 1983 when the Court held in *Arizona Governing Committee v. Norris,* 463 U.S. 1073, that an employer-sponsored pension plan of the latter description violates Title VII.

The *Manhart* decision is also limited in that it applies only to employer-sponsored pension or insurance plans. This limitation is implicit in Title VII, which, you will recall, only covers conduct by employers, employment agencies, labor organizations, and training programs. Insurance and pension plans sponsored and marketed independently of employers and other parties who fall within the coverage of Title VII are not affected by this act.

The Equal Protection Clause affords no protection against sex-based rate schedules in privately issued insurance and pension programs because no state action is involved. It is worth noting once again that state law sometimes affords a remedy where federal law does not. For example, in 1988, a Pennsylvania appellate court found that the sex-based rate schedules used by a private automobile insurance company were in violation of the Equal Rights Amendment to that state's constitution, even though no state action was involved (*Bartholomew v. Foster,* see Chapter 2).

Title VII bars discrimination in employment on the bases of both race and sex. On casual inspection, that may seem to afford an extra measure of protection to women of color. Law professor Kimberlè Crenshaw points out in the following essay that in practice, Title VII often affords less rather than more protection for African-American women. This is because they live at the intersection of the two antidiscrimination principles.

A Black Feminist Critique of Antidiscrimination Law and Politics

Kimberlè Crenshaw. In *The Politics of Law,* edited by David Kairys. Rev. ed. New York: Pantheon Books, 1990. Pp. 195–202.

The title of one of the very few Black women's studies books, *All the Women Are White, All the*

Blacks Are Men, But Some of Us Are Brave, sets forth a problematic consequence of the tendency to treat race and gender as mutually exclusive categories of experience and analysis. This tendency is perpetuated by a single-axis framework dominant in antidiscrimination law and reflected in feminist theory and antiracist politics that distorts the multidimensionality of Black women's experiences and undermines efforts to broaden feminist and antiracist analyses.

One way to approach the problem at the intersection of race and sex is to examine how courts frame and interpret the stories of Black women plaintiffs. Indeed, the way courts interpret claims made by Black women is itself part of Black women's experience; consequently, a cursory review of cases involving Black female plaintiffs is quite revealing. To illustrate the difficulties inherent in judicial treatment of intersectionality, I will consider three employment discrimination cases: *DeGraffenreid v. General Motors, Moore v. Hughes Helicopter and Payne v. Travenol.*

In *DeGraffenreid,* five Black women brought suit against General Motors, alleging that the employer's seniority system perpetuated the effects of past discrimination against Black women. Although General Motors did not hire Black women prior to 1964, the court noted that "General Motors has hired . . . female employees for a number of years prior to the enactment of the Civil Rights Act of 1964." Because General Motors did hire women—albeit *white women*—during the period that no Black women were hired, there was, in the court's view, no sex discrimination that the seniority system could conceivably have perpetuated. Moreover, reasoning that Black women could choose to bring either a sex or a race discrimination claim, but not both, the court stated:

> The legislative history surrounding Title VII does not indicate that the goal of the statute was to create a new classification of "black women" who would have greater standing than, for example, a black male. The prospect of the creation of new classes of protected minorities, governed only by the mathematical principles of permutation and combination, clearly raises the prospect of opening the hackneyed Pandora's box.

The court's conclusion that Congress did not intend to allow Black women to make a compound claim arises from its inability to imagine that discrimination against Black women can exist independently from the experiences of white women or of Black men. Because the court was blind to this possibility, it did not question whether Congress could have meant to leave this form of discrimination unredressed. Assuming therefore that there was no distinct discrimination suffered by Black women, the court concluded that to allow plaintiffs to make a compound claim would unduly advantage Black women over Black men or white women. . . .

Moore v. Hughes Helicopters, Inc. presents a different way in which courts fail to understand or recognize Black women's claims. *Moore* is typical of cases in which courts refused to certify Black females as class representatives in

race *and* sex discrimination actions. In *Moore,* the plaintiff alleged that the employer, Hughes Helicopter, practiced race and sex discrimination in promotions to upper-level craft positions and to supervisory jobs. Moore introduced statistical evidence establishing a significant disparity between men and women, and somewhat less of a disparity between Black and white men in supervisory jobs.

Affirming the district court's refusal to certify Moore as the class representative in the sex discrimination complaint on behalf of all women at Hughes, the Ninth Circuit noted approvingly:

> . . . Moore had never claimed before the EEOC that she was discriminated against as a female, *but only* as a Black female. . . .[T]his raised serious doubts as to Moore's ability to adequately represent white female employees. . . .

The *Moore* court also denied the plaintiffs' bid to represent Black males, leaving Moore with the task of supporting her race and sex discrimination claims with statistical evidence of discrimination against Black females alone. Because she was unable to represent white women or Black men, she could not use overall statistics on sex disparity at Hughes, nor could she use statistics on race. Proving her claim using statistics on Black women alone was no small task, due to the fact that she was bringing the suit under a disparate impact theory of discrimination.

The court's rulings on Moore's sex and race claim left her with such a small statistical sample that even if she had proved that there were qualified Black women, she could not have shown discrimination under a disparate impact theory. *Moore* illustrates yet another way that antidiscrimination doctrine essentially erases Black women's distinct experiences and, as a result, deems their discrimination complaints groundless.

Finally, Black female plaintiffs have sometimes encountered difficulty in their efforts to win certification as class representatives in some race discrimination actions. This problem typically arises in cases where statistics suggest significant disparities between Black and white workers and further disparities between Black men and Black women. Courts in some cases have denied certification based on logic that mirrors the rationale in *Moore:* The sex disparities between Black men and Black women created such conflicting interests that Black women could not possibly represent Black men adequately. In one such case, *Payne v. Travenol,* two Black female plaintiffs alleging race discrimination brought a class action suit on behalf of all Black employees at a pharmaceutical plant. The court refused, however, to allow the plaintiffs to represent Black males and granted the defendant's request to narrow the class to Black women only. Ultimately, the district court found that there had been extensive racial discrimination at the plant and awarded back pay and constructive seniority to the class of Black female employees. But, despite its finding of general race discrimination, the court refused to extend the remedy to Black men for fear that their conflicting interests would not be adequately addressed; the Fifth Circuit affirmed.

Even though *Travenol* was a partial victory for Black women, the case specifically illustrates how antidiscrimination doctrine generally creates a dilemma for Black women. It forces them to choose between specifically articulating the intersectional aspects of their subordination, thereby risking their ability to represent Black men, or ignoring intersectionality in order to state a claim that would not lead to the exclusion of Black men. When one considers the political consequences of this dilemma, there is little wonder that many people within the Black community view the specific articulation of Black women's interests as dangerously divisive.

In sum, several courts have proved unable to deal with intersectionality, although for contrasting reasons. In *DeGraffenreid,* the court refused to recognize the possibility of compound discrimination against Black women and analyzed their claim using the employment of white women as the historical base. As a consequence, the employment experiences of white women obscured the distinct discrimination that Black women experienced.

Conversely, in *Moore,* the court held that a Black woman could not use statistics reflecting the overall sex disparity in supervisory and upper-level labor jobs because she had not claimed discrimination as a woman, but "only" as a Black woman. The court would not entertain the notion that discrimination experienced by Black women is indeed sex discrimination—provable through disparate impact statistics on women.

Finally, courts such as the one in *Travenol* have held that Black women cannot represent an entire class of Blacks due to presumed class conflicts in cases where sex additionally disadvantaged Black women. As a result, in the few cases where Black women are allowed to use overall statistics indicating racially disparate treatment, Black men may not be able to share in the remedy. . . .

. . .The point is that Black women can experience discrimination in any number of ways and that the contradiction arises from our assumptions that their claims of exclusion must be unidirectional. Consider an analogy to traffic in an intersection, coming and going in all four directions. Discrimination, like traffic through an intersection, may flow in one direction, and it may flow in another. If an accident happens in an intersection, it can be caused by cars traveling from any number of directions and, sometimes, from all of them. Similarly, if a Black woman is harmed because she is in the intersection, her injury could result from sex discrimination or race discrimination or both.

Providing legal relief only when Black women prove that their claims are based on race or on sex is analogous to calling an ambulance for the victim only after the driver responsible for the injuries is identified. But it is not always easy to identify the driver: sometimes the skid marks and the injuries simply indicate that they occurred simultaneously, frustrating efforts to determine which driver caused the harm. In these cases the tendency seems to be that no driver is held responsible, no treatment is administered, and the involved parties simply get back in their cars and zoom away.

I am suggesting that Black women can experience discrimination in ways that are both similar to and different from those experienced by white women and Black men. Black women sometimes experience discrimination in ways similar to white women's experiences; sometimes they share very similar experiences with Black men. Yet often they experience double discrimination—the combined effects of practices which discriminate on the basis of race, and on the basis of sex. And sometimes, they experience discrimination as Black women— not the sum of race and sex discrimination, but as Black women. . . .

STUDY QUESTIONS

1. Discuss the disadvantages that women of color experience under antidiscrimination laws, drawing on the metaphor of an accident at the intersection of two roads.

2. Where do you think the courts in these cases went wrong? On what grounds could they have reached more satisfactory decisions?

When drafting Title VII, Congress did not define the term "discrimination." That task was left to the courts. The meaning of that term emerges from court decisions relating to questions of proof—what is sufficient to establish a violation of the statute?—and questions of procedure—what order of proof is used when analyzing Title VII cases? In the course of addressing these questions, the Supreme Court recognized two concepts of discrimination. These were first explicitly formulated in a footnote to an important race discrimination decision:

> "Disparate treatment" . . . is the most easily understood type of discrimination. The employer simply treats some people less favorably than others because of their race, color, religion, sex, or national origin. Proof of discriminatory motive is critical, although it can in some situations be inferred from the mere fact of differences in treatment. . . . Claims of disparate treatment may be distinguished from claims that stress "disparate impact." The latter involve employment practices that are facially neutral in their treatment of different groups but that in fact fall more harshly on one group than another and cannot be justified by business necessity. Proof of discriminatory motive, we have held, is not required under a disparate impact theory. . . .
> International Brotherhood of Teamsters v. U.S., *431 U.S. 324, fn. 15 (1977)*.

Disparate Treatment

Discrimination in the disparate treatment sense is, as the Court indicated, similar to the everyday notion of biased or prejudiced treatment, differential treatment that is motivated by prejudice. Sometimes discrimination in this sense can be directly inferred from the employer's behavior, e.g., *EEOC v. Brown and Root*. More often, however, discrimination is not so easily proven. Employment decisions that affect only one or a few persons present especially difficult problems of proof. One such situation was faced by the Supreme Court in the following case. There, the Court summarized its instructions on how proof of discrimination must proceed in disparate treatment cases.

Texas Dept. of Community Affairs v. Burdine

Supreme Court of the United States, 1981.
450 U.S. 248, 101 S.Ct. 1089, 67 L.Ed.2d 207.

Justice POWELL delivered the opinion of the Court.

. . . Petitioner, the Texas Department of Community Affairs (TDCA), hired respondent, a female, in January 1972, for the position of accounting clerk in the Public Service Careers Division (PSC). PSC provided training and employment opportunities in the public sector for unskilled workers. When hired, respondent possessed several years' experience in employment training. She was promoted to Field Services Coordinator in July 1972. Her supervisor resigned in November of that year, and respondent was assigned additional duties. Although she applied for the supervisor's position of Project Director, the position remained vacant for six months. . . .

After consulting with personnel within TDCA, [B.R. Fuller, then Executive Director of TDCA] hired a male from another division of the agency as Project Director. In reducing the PSC staff, he fired respondent along with two other employees, and retained another male, Walz, as the only professional employee in the division. It was undisputed that respondent had maintained her application for the position of Project Director and had requested to remain with TDCA. Respondent soon was rehired by TDCA and assigned to another division of the agency. She received the exact salary paid to the Project Director at PSC, and the subsequent promotions she has received have kept her salary and responsibility commensurate with what she would have received had she been appointed Project Director.

Respondent filed this suit in the United States District Court for the Western District of Texas. She alleged that the failure to promote and the subsequent decision to terminate her had been predicated on gender discrimination in violation of Title VII. After a bench trial, the District Court held that neither decision was based on gender discrimination. . . .

. . . The Court of Appeals, however, reversed the District Court's finding that Fuller's testimony sufficiently had rebutted respondent's prima facie case of gender discrimination in the decision to terminate her employment at PSC. The court reaffirmed its previously announced views that the defendant in a Title VII case bears the burden of proving by a preponderance of the evidence the existence of legitimate nondiscriminatory reasons for the employment action and that the defendant also must prove by objective evidence that those hired or promoted were better qualified than the plaintiff. The court found that Fuller's testimony did not carry either of these evidentiary burdens. It, therefore, reversed the judgment of the District Court and remanded the case for computation of backpay. . . .

In *McDonnell Douglas Corp. v. Green,* we set forth the basic allocation of burdens and order of presentation of proof in a Title VII case alleging discriminatory treatment. First, the plaintiff has the burden of proving by the preponderance of the evidence a prima facie case of discrimination. Second, if the plaintiff succeeds in proving the prima facie case, the burden shifts to the defendant "to articulate some legitimate, nondiscriminatory reason for the employee's rejection." Third, should the defendant carry this burden, the plaintiff must then have an opportunity to prove by a preponderance of the evidence that the legitimate reasons offered by the defendant were not its true reasons, but were a pretext for discrimination.

The nature of the burden that shifts to the defendant should be understood in light of the plaintiff's ultimate and intermediate burdens. The ultimate burden of persuading the trier of fact that the defendant intentionally discriminated against the plaintiff remains at all time with the plaintiff. . . .

The burden of establishing a prima facie case of disparate treatment is not onerous. The plaintiff must prove by a preponderance of the evidence that she applied for an available position, for which she was qualified, but was rejected under circumstances which give rise to an inference of unlawful discrimination.[6] The prima facie case serves an important function in the litigation: it eliminates the most common nondiscriminatory reasons for the plaintiff's rejection. As the Court explained in *Furnco*

---

[6] *In McDonnell Douglas* we described an appropriate model for a prima facie case of racial discrimination. The plaintiff must show: "(i) that he belongs to a racial minority; (ii) that he applied and was qualified for a job for which the employer was seeking applicants; (iii) that, despite his qualification, he was rejected; and (iv) that, after his rejection, the position remained open and the employer continued to seek applicants from persons of complainant's qualifications."

We added, however, that this standard is not inflexible, as "[t]he facts necessarily will vary in Title VII cases, and the specification above of the prima facie proof required from respondent is not necessarily applicable in every respect in differing factual situations."

In the instant case, it is not seriously contested that respondent has proved a prima facie case. She showed that she was a qualified woman who sought an available position, but the position was left open for several months before she finally was rejected in favor of a male, Walz, who had been under her supervision.

Construction Co. v. Waters, the prima facie case "raises an inference of discrimination only because we presume these acts, if otherwise unexplained, are more likely than not based on the consideration of impermissible factors." Establishment of the prima facie case in effect creates a presumption that the employer unlawfully discriminated against the employee. If the trier of fact believes the plaintiff's evidence, and if the employer is silent in the face of the presumption, the court must enter judgment for the plaintiff because no issue of fact remains in the case.

The burden that shifts to the defendant, therefore, is to rebut the presumption of discrimination by producing evidence that the plaintiff was rejected, or someone else was preferred, for a legitimate, nondiscriminatory reason. The defendant need not persuade the court that it was actually motivated by the proffered reasons. It is sufficient if the defendant's evidence raises a genuine issue of fact as to whether it discriminated against the plaintiff. To accomplish this, the defendant must clearly set forth, through the introduction of admissible evidence, the reasons for the plaintiff's rejection. The explanation provided must be legally sufficient to justify a judgment for the defendant. If the defendant carries this burden of production, the presumption raised by the prima facie case is rebutted, and the factual inquiry proce[e]ds to a new level of specificity. Placing this burden of production on the defendant thus serves simultaneously to meet the plaintiff's prima facie case by presenting a legitimate reason for the action and to frame the factual issue with sufficient clarity so that the plaintiff will have a full and fair opportunity to demonstrate pretext. The sufficiency of the defendant's evidence should be evaluated by the extent to which it fulfills these functions.

The plaintiff retains the burden of persuasion. She now must have the opportunity to demonstrate that the proffered reason was not the true reason for the employment decision. This burden now merges with the ultimate burden of persuading the court that she has been the victim of intentional discrimination. She may succeed in this either directly by persuading the court that a discriminatory rea-

son more likely motivated the employer or indirectly by showing that the employer's proffered explanation is unworthy of credence. . . .

The Court of Appeals has misconstrued the nature of the burden that *McDonnell Douglas* and its progeny place on the defendant. . . .

The court placed the burden of persuasion on the defendant apparently because it feared that "[i]f an employer need only *articulate*—not prove—a legitimate, nondiscriminatory reason for his action, he may compose fictitious, but legitimate, reasons for his actions." We do not believe, however, that limiting the defendant's evidentiary obligation to a burden of production will unduly hinder the plaintiff. First, as noted above, the defendant's explanation of its legitimate reasons must be clear and reasonably specific. This obligation arises both from the necessity of rebutting the inference of discrimination arising from the prima facie case and from the requirement that the plaintiff be afforded "a full and fair opportunity" to demonstrate pretext. Second, although the defendant does not bear a formal burden of persuasion, the defendant nevertheless retains an incentive to persuade the trier of fact that the employment decision was lawful. Thus, the defendant normally will attempt to prove the factual basis for its explanation. Third, the liberal discovery rules applicable to any civil suit in federal court are supplemented in a Title VII suit by the plaintiff's access to the Equal Employment Opportunity Commission's investigatory files concerning her complaint. Given these factors, we are unpersuaded that the plaintiff will find it particularly difficult to prove that a proffered explanation lacking a factual basis is a pretext. We remain confident that the *McDonnell Douglas* framework permits the plaintiff meriting relief to demonstrate intentional discrimination. . . .

In summary, the Court of Appeals erred by requiring the defendant to prove by a preponderance of the evidence the existence of nondiscriminatory reasons for terminating the respondent and that the person retained in her stead had superior objective qualifications for the position. When the plaintiff has proved a prima facie case of discrimination, the defendant bears only the burden of explaining clearly the nondiscriminatory reasons for its actions. The judgment of the Court of Appeals is vacated and the case is remanded for further proceedings consistent with this opinion.

It is so ordered.

STUDY QUESTIONS

1. Women who work in environments where men are predominately the supervisors often suspect that they are being discriminated against because of their sex. Most frequently, such suspicions are discounted and dismissed as misunderstandings on their own part. How should women who find themselves in Burdine's position evaluate such suspicions? What role might networking play in situations like these?

2. Burdine was certain that her suspicions were true. How should a court decide whether her allegations are true? What additional difficulties does that present?

As we saw, the disparate treatment concept of discrimination bears upon differential treatment that is motivated by biased intentions. In *Burdine,* the Court indicated how discriminatory intent can be proven. It is worth noting that the understanding of intent that the Court relies on here is not nearly so narrow as was used in *Feeney* when interpreting the Equal Protection Clause. (See Chapter 2.) There, to establish that a course of action was intentional, the complainant had to show that it was undertaken "at least in part 'because of,' not merely 'in spite of,' its adverse effects upon an identifiable group." In *Burdine,* the demands on the plaintiff are considerably less prodigious. Here, the Court indicated the three-step pattern of proof that is typically required under Title VII. In the first step, called the prima facie case, the courts consider whether the plaintiff has "eliminated the most common reasons for plaintiff's rejection." The plaintiff succeeds in establishing her prima facie case if she raises an inference of discrimination. In footnote 6, the Court recalled from an earlier decision a typical way of establishing a prima facie case. Two points about this step should be kept in mind. The requirement of raising the inference of discrimination is not difficult to satisfy. In the Court's words, it is not "onerous." The other point is that the four-stage model outlined in *McDonnell Douglas* is one way, but not the only way, to meet that requirement.

Once they are satisfied that the plaintiff has raised an inference of discrimination, the courts take the second step and look to the defendant for rebuttal. To meet that burden, the employer must articulate a legitimate, nondiscriminatory reason for the employment decision. In *Burdine,* the Court was at pains to indicate that the employer need not show that it was "actually motivated by the proffered reasons." Rather, the defendant needs only introduce evidence that the decision could have been based upon legitimate, nondiscriminatory grounds. The Court carefully noted, however, that this must be done with sufficient clarity to give the plaintiff a fair opportunity to show that the proffered reasons were a pretext.

When they are satisfied that the defendant has articulated legitimate, nondiscriminatory reasons for the challenged employment decision, the courts' third step is to consider whether the plaintiff has shown that those reasons represent a pretext, i.e., that they are used as a ploy to mask discriminatory intent. The plaintiff may show pretext in either of two ways. She may do so "either directly by persuading the court that a discriminatory reason more likely motivated the employer or indirectly by showing that the employer's proffered explanation is unworthy of credence." Although, as we shall see, not all disparate treatment cases turn on a showing of

TABLE 4.1 Order of Proof in Disparate Treatment Cases

Stage	Burden on	To
Prima facie case	Plaintiff	Eliminate the most common reasons for the plaintiff's rejection
Rebuttal	Defendant	Articulate a nondiscriminatory reason that may have motivated the decision
Pretext	Plaintiff	Show, either directly or indirectly, that the explanation proposed by the defendant was not the true reason for the employment decision

pretext, this is often the crux of the disparate treatment approach to proving discrimination. Table 4.1 may help to organize the elements of a disparate treatment case.

When enacting the Civil Rights Act of 1991, Congress established a commission to study the effects of "the glass ceiling." This initiative followed through on a Department of Labor report issued in August 1991. This initiative is discussed at length at the end of Chapter 5. In that report, "glass ceiling" was defined as "artificial barriers based upon attitudinal or organizational bias that prevent qualified minorities and women from advancing into mid- and senior-management positions." As the work of this commission proceeds, the organizational dynamics that contribute to the denial of promotions to well-qualified women and minorities may become clearer. Some aspects of that dynamic have already been identified by means of litigation. Title VII plaintiffs often allege that they are passed over for promotion into management positions because of their sex. These claims are frequently analyzed as disparate treatment. Where that pattern is followed, the decisions most frequently turn on the establishment of pretext. Accordingly, the following cases illustrate both the dynamics of the glass ceiling and the various ways in which pretext is established under the disparate treatment approach to discrimination under Title VII.

As indicated in *Burdine,* pretext can be shown either directly or indirectly. Direct methods attempt to persuade the court that a discriminatory reason was more likely to have motivated the employer than the nondiscriminatory reason that was offered in rebuttal. Indirect methods attempt to discredit the nondiscriminatory explanation that was offered by the employer. The following cases illustrate each of these techniques—*Hopkins,* the direct; *Lindahl,* the indirect.

Price Waterhouse v. Hopkins

Supreme Court of the
United States, 1989.
490 U.S. 228, 104 L.Ed.2d 268,
109 S.Ct. 1775.

Justice BRENNAN announced the judgment of the Court and delivered an opinion, in which Justice MARSHALL, Justice BLACKMUN, and Justice STEVENS join. [Justice WHITE and Justice O'CONNOR filed opinions concurring in the judgment.]. . . .

At Price Waterhouse, a nationwide professional accounting partnership, a senior manager becomes a candidate for partnership when the partners in her local office submit her name as a candidate. All of the other partners in the firm are then invited to submit written comments on each candidate. . . . After reviewing the comments and interviewing the partners who submitted them, the firm's Admissions Committee makes a recommendation to the Policy Board. This recommendation will be either that the firm accept the candidate for partnership, put her applicant on "hold," or deny her the promotion outright. . . .

Ann Hopkins had worked at Price Waterhouse's Office of Government Services in Washington, D.C., for five years when the partners in that office proposed her as a candidate for partnership. Of the 662 partners at the firm at that time, 7 were women. Of the 88 persons proposed for partnership that year [1982], only 1—Hopkins—was a woman. Forty-seven of these candidates were admitted to the partnership, 21 were rejected, and 20—including Hopkins—were "held" for reconsideration the following year. Thirteen of the 32 partners who had submitted comments on Hopkins supported her bid for partnership. Three partners recommended that her candidacy be placed on hold, eight stated that they did not have an informed opinion about her, and eight recommended that she be denied partnership.

In a jointly prepared statement supporting her candidacy, the partners in Hopkins' office showcased her successful 2-year effort to secure a $25 million contract with the Department of State, labeling it "an outstanding performance" and one that Hopkins carried out "virtually at the partner level.". . .

The partners in Hopkins' office praised her character as well as her accomplishments, describing her in their joint statement as "an outstanding professional" who had a "deft touch," a "strong character, independence and integrity." Clients appear to have agreed with these assessments. . . .

On too many occasions, however, Hopkins' aggressiveness apparently spilled over into abrasiveness. Staff members seem to have borne the brunt of Hopkins' brusqueness. . . . Both "[s]upporters and opponents of her candidacy," stressed [District Court] Judge Gesell,

"indicated that she was sometimes overly aggressive, unduly harsh, difficult to work with and impatient with staff."

There were clear signs, though, that some of the partners reacted negatively to Hopkins' personality because she was a woman. One partner described her as "macho"; another suggested that she "overcompensated for being a woman"; a third advised her to take "a course at charm school." Several partners criticized her use of profanity; in response, one partner suggested that those partners object to her swearing only "because it[']s a lady using foul language." Another supporter explained that Hopkins "ha[d] matured from a tough-talking somewhat masculine hard-nosed mgr to an authoritative, formidable, but much more appealing lady ptr candidate." But it was the man who, as Judge Gesell found, bore responsibility for explaining to Hopkins the reasons for the Policy Board's decision to place her candidacy on hold who delivered the coup de grace: in order to improve her chances for partnership, Thomas Beyer advised, Hopkins should "walk more femininely, talk more femininely, dress more femininely, wear make-up, have her hair styled, and wear jewelry.".

In previous years, other female candidates for partnership also had been evaluated in sex-based terms. As a general matter, Judge Gesell concluded, "[c]andidates were viewed favorably if partners believed they maintained their femin[in]ity while becoming effective professional managers"; in this environment, "[t]o be identified as a 'women's lib[b]er' was regarded as [a] negative comment." In fact, the judge found that in previous years "[o]ne partner repeatedly commented that he could not consider any woman seriously as a partnership candidate and believed that women were not even capable of functioning as senior managers—yet the firm took no action to discourage his comments and recorded his vote in the overall summary of the evaluations."

Judge Gesell found that Price Waterhouse legitimately emphasized interpersonal skills in its partnership decisions, and also found that the firm had not fabricated its complaints about Hopkins' interpersonal skills as a pretext for discrimination. Moreover, he concluded, the firm did not give decisive emphasis to such traits only because Hopkins was a woman; although there were male candidates who lacked these skills but who were admitted to partnership, the judge found that these candidates possessed other, positive traits that Hopkins lacked.

The judge went on to decide, however, that some of the partners' remarks about Hopkins stemmed from an impermissibly cabined view of the proper behavior of women, and that Price Waterhouse had done nothing to disavow reliance on such comments. He held that Price Waterhouse had unlawfully discriminated against Hopkins on the basis of sex by consciously giving credence and effect to partners' comments that resulted from sex stereotyping. Noting that Price Waterhouse could avoid equitable relief by proving by clear and convincing evidence that it would have placed Hopkins' candidacy on hold even absent this discrimination, the judge decided that the firm had not carried this heavy burden.

The Court of Appeals affirmed the District court's ultimate conclusion. . . .

The District Court found that sex stereotyping "was permitted to play a part" in the evaluation of Hopkins as a candidate for partnership. Price Waterhouse disputes both that stereotyping occurred and that it played any part in the decision to place Hopkins' candidacy on hold. In the firm's view, in other words, the District Court's factual conclusions are clearly erroneous. We do not agree." . . .

. . . It takes no special training to discern sex stereotyping in a description of an aggressive female employee as requiring "a course at charm school." Nor, turning to Thomas Beyer's memorable advice to Hopkins, does it require expertise in psychology to know that, if an employee's flawed "interpersonal skills" can be corrected by a soft-hued suit and a new shade of lipstick, perhaps it is the employee's sex and not her interpersonal skills that had drawn the criticism. . . .

Price Waterhouse appears to think that we cannot affirm the factual findings of the trial court without deciding that, instead of being overbearing and aggressive and curt, Hopkins is in fact kind and considerate and patient. If this is indeed its impression, petitioner misunderstands the theory on which Hopkins prevailed. The District Judge acknowledged that Hopkins' conduct justified complaints about her behavior as a senior manager. But he also concluded that the reactions of at least some of the partners were reactions to her as a *woman* manager. Where an evaluation is based on a subjective assessment of a person's strengths and weaknesses, it is simply not true that each evaluator will focus on, or even mention, the same weaknesses. Thus, even if we knew that Hopkins had "personality problems," this would not tell us that the partners who cast their evaluations of Hopkins in sex-based terms would have criticized her as sharply (or criticized her at all) if she had been a man. It is not our job to review the evidence and decide that the negative reactions to Hopkins were based on reality; our perception of Hopkins' character is irrelevant. We sit not to determine whether Ms. Hopkins is nice, but to decide whether the partners reacted negatively to her personality because she is a woman.

We hold that when a plaintiff in a Title VII case proves that her gender played a motivating part in an employment decision, the defendant may avoid a finding of liability only by proving by a preponderance of the evidence that it would have made the same decision even if it had not taken the plaintiff's gender into account. Because the courts below erred by deciding that the defendant must make this proof by clear and convincing evidence, we reverse the Court of Appeals' judgment against Price Waterhouse on liability and remand the case to that court for further proceedings.

It is so ordered.

STUDY QUESTIONS

1. What nondiscriminatory reason did Price Waterhouse propose as motivating its decision to put Hopkins's promotion on hold? In what language did the partners describe Hopkins's interpersonal skills?

2. How did Hopkins show that discriminatory reasons also motivated the decision? The court spoke of stereotyping that affected the partners' decision. Discuss what stereotyping involves and why it is not permitted under Title VII.

Hopkins addressed what is often called the "mixed motive" situation, i.e., one in which an employment decision is motivated both by discriminatory and nondiscriminatory considerations. There, the Court held that such employment decisions are permitted only if the employer can show that the same decision would have been made in the absence of the discriminatory considerations. The Civil Rights Act of 1991 overturned that decision. The key language in the statute makes clear that "an unlawful employment practice has been established when the complaining party demonstrates that race, color, religion, sex, or national origin was a motivating factor for any employment practice, even though other factors also motivated the practice."

Like *Hopkins*, the following case also illustrates the glass ceiling, the ways that attitudinal factors limit the upward mobility of talented women. Here, the plaintiff used an indirect method of showing pretext by arguing that employer's explanation was unworthy of credence. When studying this case, consider what factors brought these biased attitudes to light. Had Lindahl not seized the initiative and pressed for satisfactory explanations, would Air France have even noticed its own biases?

Lindahl v. Air France

United States Court of Appeals,
Ninth Circuit, 1991.
930 F.2d 1434.

RYMER, Circuit Judge:

Michelle Lindahl . . . worked as a Customer Promotion Agent in Air France's Los Angeles office. The office had two groups of employees to handle sales activities, Customer Promotion Agents and Sales Representatives. Sales Representatives worked mostly in the field promoting sales, while the Customer Promotion Agents worked inside, providing backup to the Sales Representatives.

In 1982, the District Manager, Karl Kershaw, told the Customer Promotion Agents that Air France was planning to create a new position of Senior Customer Promotion Agent and invited all of them to apply for the position. After considering their qualifications, Kershaw told Lindahl that she was the most qualified and would be given the promotion. Subsequently, however, Air France decided not to create the position, and Lindahl did not get the promotion.

In 1987, without any prior notification to the Customer Promotion Agents, Kershaw announced that he had chosen Edward Michels to fill a new Senior Customer Promotion Agent position. At that time, there were four eligible can-

didates: two women over age 40 (including Lindahl), and two men under age 40 (including Michels).

Lindahl, upset about the decision, decided to pursue Air France's grievance procedure. First, she asked Kershaw to give an explanation. After about six weeks, he responded that Michels had the "best overall qualifications." Unsatisfied, she wrote to Regional Manager Robert Watson. Watson responded by affirming Kershaw's decision. Finally, Lindahl had her attorney take her grievance to Personnel Services Manager Eugene Carrara. At this time, she made clear that she felt that the decision was the product of age and sex discrimination. Carrara held a hearing and decided to reject her claim because he believed the promotion decision was reasonable. In his decision, he stated that Michels's computer expertise was the principal reason for selecting him. . . .

. . . After exhausting her administrative remedies, she filed suit in the district court, alleging age and sex discrimination. . . . Air France moved for summary judgment on both causes of action.

The district court granted summary judgment on the ground that Lindahl had not raised a genuine issue of material fact as to whether Air France's legitimate, nondiscriminatory explanations are pretexts for discrimination. . . . She now appeals. . . .

The district court concluded, and the parties do not dispute, that Lindahl made out a prima facie case of discrimination. She is a woman over age 40 who, in effect, applied for a promotion, was qualified for it, but lost it to a man under age 40. The parties also do not dispute that Air France met its burden of producing legitimate, nondiscriminatory reasons for promoting Michels and not Lindahl. Air France points to the deposition testimony of Watson and Kershaw, indicating that their reasons for promoting Michels were (1) his computer proficiency, and (2) his leadership abilities as they related to Air France's need to establish order, rules, and regulations in a chaotic office. . . .

As to Air France's explanation that Michels was chosen for his computer proficiency, Lindahl argues that it is not credible because neither Kershaw nor Watson (the ones most closely associated with the decision) mentioned it as the reason for choosing Michels. Kershaw had said only that Michels had "the best overall qualifications to lead the group," and Watson had simply affirmed Kershaw's decision. The computer explanation did not come out until Personnel Services Manager Carrara, who was not involved with the decision, mentioned it four months later in response to a letter from Lindahl's attorney. . . .

Moreover, computer expertise was not clearly related to the leadership position. Indeed, computer proficiency had never been listed as a qualification for the position of Senior Customer Promotion Agent. While Michels's computer knowledge might have been helpful to Air France generally, it is not clear that it made him a better candidate to lead the Customer Promotion Group.

Lindahl also challenges the credibility of Air France's explanation that Michels was chosen for his leadership abilities. Kershaw testified in his deposition that "being accepted" is an important part of being a leader, but he admitted that Michels "was not well liked by the group." By contrast, Kershaw described Lindahl as having "a good relationship with the staff."

Lindahl also stated that Michels was preoccupied with the computer and neglected his duties backing up the Sales Representatives and that these backup duties were traditionally part of the Customer Promotion Group's responsibilities. Finally, the record shows that Michels was the most junior member of the Customer Promotion Group. . . .

Moreover, even if Kershaw did make his decision based on leadership abilities, other evidence could suggest that his evaluation of leadership ability was itself sexist. Lindahl points out that Kershaw made statements about the candidates' relative qualifications that reflect male/female stereotypes. Kershaw testified in his deposition that he believed that both female candidates get "nervous" and that the other female candidate "gets easily upset [and] loses control." By contrast, Kershaw described Michels's leadership qualities as "not to back away from a situation, to take hold immediately of the situation, to attack the situation right away, to stay cool throughout the whole process." He went on to comment that "sitting and griping and getting emotional is not contributing to, No. 1, getting the job done, number two, to the morale and atmosphere of the group."

The Supreme Court has made clear that sex stereotyping can be evidence of sex discrimination, especially when linked to the employment decision. *Price Waterhouse v. Hopkins.* Kershaw apparently saw Michels as aggressive and cool (in addition to being the one who could impose order), while he saw the female candidates as nervous and emotional. His comments could suggest that Kershaw made his decision on the basis of stereotypical images of men and women, specifically that women do not make good leaders because they are too "emotional."

Finally, Lindahl points to evidence showing that Air France handled the promotion decision differently when only women were eligible than when young men were eligible. In 1982, when the possibility of an opening for Senior Customer Promotion Agent position first arose, the only eligible candidates for the position were women. Kershaw told all of them about the possible opening and that they would have to take a test. Air France abandoned the idea to add the position. In 1987, two men under age 40 and two women over age 40 were eligible. Kershaw did not tell the candidates about the position, and Michels got the promotion without taking a test or having an interview. This difference in treatment might further support an inference that Air France was discriminating against older women.

While not overwhelming, Lindahl's evidence of discriminatory motive is sufficient to raise a genuine issue of fact. She has pointed to facts that could call into question the credibility of Air France's nondiscriminatory explanations and could suggest discriminatory motives. Whether the facts do indicate discrimination is a question that should ordinarily be resolved by a factfinder, and we believe it is possible that a reasonable trier of fact could find that Air France discriminated against Lindahl in promoting Michels. We therefore conclude that summary judgment should not have been granted.

Reversed and remanded.

STUDY QUESTIONS

1. Did Lindahl's immediate supervisor give her a specific explanation of why she was denied the promotion? Who did give her a specific explanation? Why do you suppose that the employer felt compelled to give a specific explanation for its decision?

2. What circumstances surrounding the promotion decision persuaded this court that the employer's nondiscriminatory explanation of its decision was not credible? Have you noticed any similar circumstances in jobs that you or your friends have held?

The courts in *Hopkins* and *Lindahl* found that the employers had relied upon stereotypes when denying promotions to women professionals. Here is an especially clever comparison of common stereotypes about men and women office workers. Can you think of other stereotypes that work to the disadvantage of women who work in blue-collar jobs? What stereotypes work to the disadvantage of men who work in the health professions? What stereotypes work to the disadvantage of women of color, single mothers, divorced women?

He Works, She Works

Natasha Josefowitz.
"Impressions from an Office."
Paths to Power. Addison-Wesley
Publishing Co., 1980. P. 60.

The family picture is on HIS desk:
Ah, a solid, responsible man.

HIS desk is cluttered:
He's obviously a hard worker and a busy man.

HE is talking with his co-workers:
He must be discussing the latest deal.

HE's not at his desk:
He must be at a meeting.

HE's not in the office:
He's meeting customers.

HE's having lunch with the boss:
He's on his way up.

The family picture is on HER desk:
Umm, her family will come before her career.

HER desk is cluttered:
She's obviously a disorganized scatterbrain.

SHE is talking with her co-workers:
She must be gossiping.

SHE's not at her desk:
She must be in the ladies' room.

SHE's not in the office:
She must be out shopping.

SHE's having lunch with the boss:
They must be having an affair.

Reprinted with permission.

The boss criticized HIM:
He'll improve his performance.
HE got an unfair deal:
Did he get angry?
HE's getting married:
He'll get more settled.
HE's having a baby:
He'll need a raise.
HE's going on a business trip:
It's good for his career.
HE's leaving for a better job:
He knows how to recognize a good opportunity.

The boss criticized HER:
She'll be very upset.
She got an unfair deal:
Did she cry?
SHE's getting married:
She'll get pregnant and leave.
SHE's having a baby:
She'll cost the company money in maternity benefits.
SHE's going on a business trip:
What does her husband say?
SHE's leaving for a better job:
Women are undependable.

Disparate Impact

One sense in which discrimination because of sex is prohibited by Title VII is the familiar and straightforward "disparate treatment" discussed above. Early in Title VII litigation, the Supreme Court distinguished a second: the disparate impact concept of discrimination. This type of discrimination involves "employment practices that are facially neutral in their treatment of different groups, but that, in fact, fall more harshly on one group than another and cannot be justified by business necessity."

The basic idea behind the disparate impact concept of discrimination derives from elementary statistics. Random selection procedures yield samples that tend to replicate the composition of the populations from which they were drawn. Selection procedures that do not produce such samples are said to be biased. Suppose that you want to estimate the proportion of blue marbles in a pail. One easy way to do that is to use a color-blind technique to select a certain number of marbles from the pail. Once that is done, inspect the sample, determine the proportion of blue marbles in it, and infer that blue marbles are present in that same proportion in the pail.

Like the sampling technique, the statistical concept at the root of disparate impact analysis involves three elements: the general population, the sample population, and the selection procedure. If you know the value of any two of these elements, you can infer the value of the other. In the marble example, we knew the value of the sample population and the selection procedure and inferred the value of the general population. The point of interest for the law of sex discrimination is that if we know the value of the general and the sample populations, we can infer the value of the selection procedure, i.e., we can determine whether it is biased. If that sounds strange to you, consider the following fable.

The Fable of the Fox and the Stork

Cooper, Rabb, and Rubin.
Fair Employment Litigation.
St. Paul, Minn.: West Publishing Company, 1975. P. xxxii.

A Fox one day invited a Stork to dinner, and being disposed to divert himself at the expense of his guest, provided nothing for the entertainment but some thin soup in a shallow dish. This the Fox lapped up very readily, while the Stork, unable to gain a mouthful with her long narrow bill, was as hungry at the end of dinner as at the beginning. The Fox meanwhile professed his regret at seeing his guest eat so sparingly, and feared that the dish was not seasoned to her liking. The Stork said little but begged that the Fox would do her the honor of returning her visit. Accordingly, he ageed to

dine with her on the following day. He arrived true to his appointment and the dinner was ordered forthwile. But when it was served up he found to his dismay that it was contained in a narrow necked vessel, down which the Stork readily thrust her long neck and bill, while the Fox was obliged to content himself with licking the neck of the jar.

Reprinted with permission of the West Publishing Company.

෨

Bias is the common element of the two concepts of discrimination used in Title VII analysis. The disparate treatment concept is the more familiar because it is quite similar to the everyday concept of discrimination—the motive of the person who makes the selections is biased. The disparate impact concept of discrimination relies upon a statistical concept of bias. There, it is not the motive but the selection procedure that is biased. The disparate impact concept of discrimination was developed and endorsed by a unanimous Supreme Court in the following case.

When studying *Griggs,* it is well to notice the contrast between the Court's rulings under Title VII and those under the Equal Protection Clause. We saw in the *Feeney* decision in Chapter 2 that it is discriminatory intent that renders differential treatment of women and men to be a violation of our equal protection rights. There, the Court explicitly rejected the extension of the disparate impact concept of discrimination to constitutional interpretation. In *Griggs,* the argument that later prevailed in *Feeney* was endorsed by the lower courts only to be rejected by a unanimous Supreme Court in favor of the disparate impact concept of discrimination. As you study this case, notice the factors that motivated the Court to adopt this interpretation of the statute. Also try to imagine what employers such as the Duke Power Company would probably have done had the Court affirmed the interpretation developed by the circuit court.

Griggs v. Duke Power Co.

Supreme Court of the United States, 1971. 401 U.S. 424, 91 S.Ct. 849, 28 L.Ed.2d 158.

Mr. Chief Justice BURGER delivered the opinion of the Court.

We granted the writ in this case to resolve the question whether an employer is prohibited by the Civil Rights Act of 1964, Title VII, from requiring a high school education or passing of a standardized general intelligence test as a condition of employment in or transfer to jobs when (a) neither standard is shown to be significantly related to successful job performance, (b) both requirements operate to disqualify Negroes at a substantially higher rate than white applicants, and (c) the jobs in question formerly had been filled only by white employees as part of a longstanding practice of giving preference to whites.

Congress provided, in Title VII of the Civil Rights Act of 1964, for class actions for enforcement of provisions of the Act and this proceeding was brought by a group of incumbent Negro employees against Duke Power Company. All the petitioners are employed at the Company's Dan River Steam Station, a power generating facility located at Draper, North Carolina. At the time this action was instituted, the Company had 95 employees at the Dan River Station, 14 of whom were Negroes; 13 of these are petitioners here.

The District Court found that prior to July 2, 1965, the effective date of the Civil Rights Act of 1964, the Company openly discriminated on the basis of race in the hiring and assigning of employees at its Dan River plant. The plant was organized into five operating departments: (1) Labor, (2) Coal Handling, (3) Operations, (4) Maintenance, and (5) Laboratory and Test. Negroes were employed only in the Labor Department where the highest paying jobs paid less than the lowest paying jobs in the other four "operating" departments in which only whites were employed. Promotions were normally made within each department on the basis of job seniority. Transferees into a department usually began in the lowest position.

In 1955 the Company instituted a policy of requiring a high school education for initial assignment to any department except Labor, and for transfer from the Coal Handling to any "inside" department (Operations, Maintenance, or Laboratory). When the Company abandoned its policy of restricting Negroes to the Labor Department in 1965, completion of high school also was made a prerequisite to transfer from Labor to any other department. From the time the high school requirement was instituted to the time of trial, however, white employees hired before the time of the high school education requirement continued to perform satisfactorily and achieve promotions in the "operating" departments. Findings on this score are not challenged.

The Company added a further requirement for new employees on July 2, 1965, the date on which Title VII became effective. To qualify for placement in any but the Labor Department it became necessary to register satisfactory scores on two professionally prepared aptitude tests, as well as to have a high school education. . . . In September 1965 the Company began to permit incumbent employees who lacked a high school education to qualify for transfer from Labor or Coal Handling to an "inside" job by passing two tests—the Wonderlic Personnel Test, which purports to measure general intelligence, and the Bennett Mechanical Comprehension Test. Neither was directed or intended to measure the ability to learn to perform a particular job or category of jobs. The requisite scores used for both initial hiring and transfer approximated the national median for high school graduates.

The District Court had found that while the Company previously followed a policy of overt racial discrimination in a period prior to the Act, such conduct had ceased. . . .

The Court of Appeals was confronted with a question of first impression, as are we, concerning the meaning of Title VII. After careful analysis a majority of that court concluded that a subjective test of the employer's intent should govern, particularly in a close case, and that in this case there was no showing of a discriminatory purpose in the adoption of the diploma and test requirements. On this basis, the Court of Appeals concluded there was no violation of the Act. . . .

The objective of Congress in the enactment of Title VII is plain from the language of the statute. It was to achieve equality of employment opportunities and remove barriers that have operated in the past to favor an identifiable group of white employees over other employees. Under the Act, practices, procedures, or tests neutral on their face, and even neutral in terms of intent, cannot be maintained if they operate to "freeze" the status quo of prior discriminatory employment practices.

The Court of Appeals' opinion . . . agreed that, on the record in the present case, "whites register far better on the Company's alternative requirements" than Negroes. This consequence would appear to be directly traceable to race. Basic intelligence must have the means of articulation to manifest itself fairly in a testing process. Because they are Negroes, petitioners have long received inferior education in segregated schools. . . . Congress did not intend by Title VII, however, to guarantee a job to every person regardless of qualifications. In short, the Act does not command that any person be hired simply because he was formerly the subject of discrimination, or because he is a member of a minority group. Discriminatory preference for any group, minority or majority, is precisely and only what Congress has proscribed. What is required by Congress is the removal of artificial, arbitrary, and unnecessary barriers to employment when the barriers operate invidiously to discriminate on the basis of racial or other impermissible classification.

Congress has now provided that tests or criteria for employment or promotion may not provide equality of opportunity merely in the sense of the fabled offer of milk to the stork and the fox. On the contrary, Congress has now required that the posture and condition of the job-seeker be taken into account. It has—to resort again to the fable—provided that the vessel in which the milk is proffered be one all seekers can use. The Act proscribes not only overt discrimination but also practices that are fair in form, but discriminatory in operation. The touchstone is business necessity. If an employment practice which operates to exclude Negroes cannot be shown to be related to job performance, the practice is prohibited.

On the record before us, neither the high school completion requirement nor the general intelligence test is shown to bear a demonstrable relationship to successful performance of the jobs for which it was used. Both were adopted, as the Court of Appeals noted, without meaningful study of their relationship to job-performance ability. Rather, a vice president of the Company testified, the requirements were instituted on the Company's judgment that they generally would improve the overall quality of the work force. . . .

The Court of Appeals held that the Company had adopted the diploma and test requirements without any "intention to discriminate against Negro employees." We do not suggest that either the District Court or the Court of Appeals erred in examining the employer's intent; but good intent or absence of discriminatory intent does not redeem employment procedures or testing mechanisms that operate as "built-in headwinds" for minority groups and are unrelated to measuring job capability.

The Company's lack of discriminatory intent is suggested by special efforts to help the undereducated employees through Company financing of two-thirds the cost of tuition for high school training. But Congress directed the thrust of the Act to the *consequences* of employment practices, not simply the motivation. More than that, Congress has placed on the employer the burden of showing that any given requirement must have a manifest relationship to the employment in question.

The facts of this case demonstrate the inadequacy of broad and general testing devices as well as the infirmity of using diplomas or degrees as fixed measures of capability. History is filled with examples of men and women who rendered highly effective performance without the conventional badges of accomplishment in terms of certificates, diplomas, or degrees. Diplomas and tests are useful servants, but Congress has mandated the commonsense proposition that they are not to become masters of reality. . . .

Nothing in the Act precludes the use of testing or measuring procedures; obviously they are useful. What Congress has forbidden is giving these devices and mechanisms controlling force unless they are demonstrably a reasonable measure of job performance. Congress has not commanded that the less qualified be preferred over the better qualified simply because of minority origins. Far from disparaging job qualifications as such, Congress has made such qualifications the controlling factor, so that race, religion, nationality, and sex become irrelevant. What Congress has commanded is that any tests used must measure the person for the job and not the person in the abstract.

The judgment of the Court of Appeals is, as to that portion of the judgment appealed from, reversed.

STUDY QUESTIONS

1. What did the Supreme Court understand to be the objective of Title VII? Precisely what does it proscribe? What does it require? Is that a fair reading of the statute? Should an employer be found in violation of an antidiscrimination statute where there is no proof of prejudice or biased motives?

2. What does "business necessity" mean? What is its role in the order of proof discussed here? Did the employer prove business necessity here?

3. Critics have argued that the disparate impact analysis of Title VII implicitly obligates employers to use employment quotas. Under that analysis, so the critics argue, employment policies that do not grant benefits to people of color and whites in a given pattern place the employer at risk of liability. On the Court's reading of Title VII, are employers required to hire, promote, etc., people of color, even though better qualified whites are available?

Following the *Griggs* decision, the courts found many facially neutral employment policies and practices in violation of Title VII on the grounds of disparate impact. These include using subjective employment and promotion criteria, imposing various educational requirements, and rejecting applicants with criminal records.

Minimum height and weight requirements are among the most common work requirements that exclude women to a much greater extent than men. Just such a requirement was challenged in the following case. This was the first time that the Supreme Court applied disparate impact analysis in a sex case. There, the Court developed a three-step approach to disparate impact analysis that parallels the one developed for disparate treatment cases. In this case, the Court addressed two aspects of Title VII that are of central importance, viz., the disparate impact challenge and a challenge based on the BFOQ exception. The latter will be discussed in section III of this chapter.

Dothard v. Rawlinson

Supreme Court of the
United States, 1977.
433 U.S. 321, 97 S.Ct. 2720,
53 L.Ed.2d 786.

Mr. Justice STEWART delivered the opinion of the Court.

Appellee Dianne Rawlinson sought employment with the Alabama Board of Corrections as a prison guard, called in Alabama a "correctional counselor." After her application was rejected, she brought this class suit under Title VII of the Civil Rights Act of 1964 . . . alleging that she had been denied employment because of her sex in violation of federal law. A three-judge Federal District Court for the Middle District of Alabama decided in her favor. . . .

At the time she applied for a position as correctional counselor trainee, Rawlinson was a 22-year-old college graduate whose major course of study had been correctional psychology. She was refused employment because she failed to meet the minimum 120-pound weight requirement established by an Alabama statute. The statute also establishes a height minimum of 5 feet 2 inches. . . .

In enacting Title VII, Congress required "the removal of artificial, arbitrary, and unnecessary barriers to employment when the barriers operate invidiously to discriminate on the basis of racial or other impermissible classification." *Griggs v. Duke Power Co.* The District Court found that the minimum statutory height and weight requirements that applicants for employment as correctional counselors must meet constitute the sort of arbitrary barrier to equal employment opportunity that Title VII forbids. The appellants assert that the District Court erred both in finding that the height and weight standards discriminate against women, and in its refusal to find that, even if they do, these standards are justified as "job related."

The gist of the claim that the statutory height and weight requirements discriminate against women does not involve an assertion of purposeful discriminatory motive. It is asserted, rather, that these facially neutral qualification standards work in fact disproportionately to exclude women from eligibility for employment by the Alabama Board of Corrections. We dealt in *Griggs v. Duke Power Co.*, and *Albemarle Paper Co. v. Moody,* with similar allegations that facially neutral employment standards disproportionately excluded Negroes from employment, and those cases guide our approach here.

Those cases make clear that to establish a prima facie case of discrimination, a plaintiff need only show that the facially neutral standards in question select applicants for hire in a significantly discriminatory pattern. Once it is thus shown that the employment standards are discriminatory in effect, the employer must meet "the burden of showing that any given requirement [has] a manifest relationship to the employment in question." *Griggs.* If the employer proves that the challenged requirements are job related, the plaintiff may then show that other selection devices without a similar discriminatory effect would also "serve the employer's legitimate interest in 'efficient and trustworthy workmanship.' "

Although women 14 years of age or older compose 52.75% of the Alabama population and 36.89% of its total labor force, they hold only 12.9% of its correctional counselor positions. In considering the effect of the minimum height and weight standards on this disparity in rate of hiring between the sexes, the District Court found that the 5´2´´-requirement would operate to exclude 33.29% of the women in the United States between the ages of 18–79, while excluding only 1.28% of men between the same ages. The 120-pound weight restriction would exclude 22.29% of the women and 2.35% of the men in this age group. When the height and weight restrictions are combined, Alabama's statutory standards would exclude 41.13% of the female population while excluding less than 1% of the male population. Accordingly, the District Court found that Rawlinson had made out a prima facie case of unlawful sex discrimination. . . .

For these reasons, we cannot say that the District Court was wrong in holding that the statutory height and weight standards had a discriminatory impact on women applicants. . . .

We turn, therefore, to the appellants' argument that they have rebutted the prima facie case of discrimination by showing that the height and weight requirements are job related. These requirements, they say, have a relationship to strength, a sufficient but unspecified amount of which is essential to effective job performance as a correctional counselor. In the District Court, however, the appellants produced no evidence correlating the height and weight requirements with the requisite amount of strength thought essential to good job performance. Indeed, they failed to offer evidence of any kind in specific justification of the statutory standards.

If the job-related quality that the appellants identify is bona fide, their purpose could be achieved by adopting and validating a test for applicants that measures strength directly. Such a test, fairly administered, would fully satisfy the standards of Title VII because it would be one that "measure[s] the person for the job and not the person in the abstract." But nothing in the present record even approaches such a measurement.

For the reasons we have discussed, the District Court was not in error in holding that Title VII of the Civil Rights Act of 1964, as amended, prohibits application of the statutory height and weight requirements to Rawlinson and the class she represents.

STUDY QUESTIONS

1. How did Rawlinson establish a prima facie case here?
2. Suppose that the state of Alabama had introduced convincing evidence that the statutory requirements are job-related. What could Rawlinson have argued in order to prevail?

Disparate impact cases are often class actions, i.e., actions brought by representative members of a protected group on behalf of all members of that group. These cases are analyzed by the courts in three stages that bear a surface resemblance to the three stages of analysis under disparate treatment (see *Burdine*). In the prima facie case, the plaintiff class has the burden of proving that the challenged employment practice disproportionately disadvantages women or men. Often, as in *Dothard,* straightforward statistical analysis is sufficient to establish a prima facie case.

Once a court is satisfied that the plaintiff class has shown that the practice has disparate impact, it looks to the defendant for rebuttal. Here, the employer has the burden of persuading the court that the challenged practice is a "business necessity," i.e., "has . . . a manifest relationship to the employment in question."

If the defendant succeeds in showing that the challenged policy or practice is a business necessity, rather than merely a "business convenience," the court considers whether the plaintiff class has shown that there exist "other selection devices without similar discriminatory effect [that] would also 'serve the employer's legitimate interest in efficient and trustworthy workmanship.' " In *Dothard,* the Court indicated that a test that measures the strength of individuals would be a less discriminatory alternative. Table 4.2 shows the elements of a disparate impact case.

In the years following these decisions, the federal courts have handed down some decisions in disparate impact cases that eroded the very strong stance taken in *Griggs* and *Dothard.* Some lower courts weakened the business necessity requirements out of consideration for the interests of employers in avoiding the costs of accommodating women. One circuit court approved a minimum height requirement for airline pilots not because being over five-foot-seven tall bears a manifest relation to the safe and efficient operation of an airplane but because airplane cockpits were designed for people whose physical stature is that of the average male. Instead of requiring the employer to reconfigure the physical layout of the workplace to accommodate qualified women, the court lightened the business necessity burden (*Boyd v. Ozark Air Lines, Inc.,* 568 F.2d 50 (8th Cir. 1977).) Another circuit court approved an employer policy limiting the coverage of the employer's medical insurance to heads of households, even though 89 percent of male and only 13 percent of female employees qualified. The reason given was that the policy was a cost-saving measure for the employer (*Wambheim v. J. C. Penney Co.,* 705 F.2d 1492 (9th Cir. 1983), cert. denied, 467 U.S. 1255 (1984)).

After these decisions, the most devastating blows to Title VII came a few years after Justice Kennedy joined the Court, filling the vacancy left by the retirement of Justice Powell in 1987. A series of decisions handed down during the 1988–1989

TABLE 4.2 Order of Proof in Disparate Impact Cases

Stage	Burden on	To Show
Prima facie case	Plaintiff	The facially neutral practice disproportionately disadvantages women or men.
Rebuttal	Defendant	Business necessity, i.e., the practice has a manifest relationship to the employment in question
Pretext	Plaintiff	Equally efficient but less discriminatory alternatives are available to the employer

term substantially reversed two decades of positive enforcement of civil rights laws. The decision that did the most to cripple Title VII came in the case of *Wards Cove Packing Co. v. Antonio,* 490 U.S. 642 (1989). In that decision, the Court substantially altered its unanimous 1971 *Griggs v. Duke Power Co.* decision establishing the disparate impact approach to employment discrimination. In *Wards Cove,* the Court ruled that no matter how extreme the impact on a protected class, an employer has no obligation to establish the need for the challenged practice; indeed, the victims of discrimination were required to prove that no legitimate reason justifies its use.

Both of these judicial trends were reversed by Congress. On November 21, 1991, President George Bush signed into law the Civil Rights Act of 1991, ending a two-and-a-half year campaign by civil rights advocates to reverse *Wards Cove* and other decisions that threatened to gut Title VII and other civil rights laws. Until then, the Bush administration had resisted such efforts under the guise of opposing any measures that would promote the use of quotas. In the end, civil rights advocates asserted, the president relented because of the political climate created in part by the Anita Hill-Clarence Thomas hearings and the surprisingly strong showing by past Klu Klux Klan leader David Duke in the Republican primary election in Louisiana.

The CRA went into effect on the day it was signed. One of its effects was to reverse *Wards Cove* and the drift toward a lighter standard of business necessity that was noted above in the lower courts. Section 105 of the act reaffirms the integrity of the disparate impact analysis as it had developed from *Griggs* and other decisions prior to *Wards Cove.* The key language in this section provides that an unlawful practice is established when "a complaining party demonstrates that a respondent uses a particular employment practice that causes a disparate impact on the basis of race, color, religion, sex, or national origin and the respondent fails to demonstrate that the challenged practice is job related for the position in question and consistent with business necessity." Like all statutory provisions, this section too is subject to judicial interpretation. Future decisions alone will show whether the CRA ended the erosion of civil rights enforcement.

III. BONA FIDE OCCUPATIONAL QUALIFICATIONS

When discussing the ways that violations of Title VII can be established, the Supreme Court typically distinguishes three patterns of litigation. Two were discussed in the preceding section, viz., disparate treatment and disparate impact. These involve differential treatment of men and women that stems from biased motives and differential treatment that stems from the use of biased selection procedures. There is yet another pattern, one that the Court usually calls overt or facial discrimination. Employer practices are overtly discriminatory if by their very terms they establish one policy for employees or applicants for employment who are women and another for those who are men, regardless of whether they were motivated by benign or prejudiced motive.

Where a case is analyzed as one of overt discrimination, there is no need to pause over what would be a phase parallel to the prima facie case in disparate treatment and disparate impact cases. In facially discriminatory situations, either the employers concede that they discriminate because of sex or it is evident from their policies and practices that they do. In these cases, the courts move directly to the phase that parallels that of rebuttal or business necessity. The only way that an employer engaging in overt discrimination can escape liability under Title VII is by successfully establishing that the policy is a "bona fide occupational qualification" (BFOQ). Congress established this exception by adding the following language to the statute. Note that this exception does not extend to facial racial discrimination.

> Notwithstanding any other provision of this subchapter. (1) it shall not be an unlawful employment practice for an employer to hire and employ employees . . . on the basis of his religion, sex, or national origin in those certain instances where religion, sex, or national origin is a bona fide occupational qualification reasonably necessary to the normal operation of that particular business or enterprise. . . . (703(e)(1)).

The Equal Employment Opportunity Commission (EEOC) quickly recognized that, like any exception, this one too could defeat the rule if understood broadly. If interpreted to included a wide spectrum of situations, it could, in the EEOC's words, swallow the rule. To forestall that result, the commission urged that the BFOQ be interpreted quite narrowly.

> *29 C.F.R. § 1604.2. Sex as a bona fide occupational qualification.*
>
> (a) The commission believes that the bona fide occupational qualification exception as to sex should be interpreted narrowly. Label—"Men's jobs" and "Women's jobs"—tend to deny employment opportunities unnecessarily to one sex or the other.
>
> (1) The Commission will find that the following situations do not warrant the application of the bona fide occupational qualification exception:
>
> (i) The refusal to hire a woman because of her sex based on assumptions of the comparative employment characteristics of women in general. For example, the assumption that the turnover rate among women is higher than among men.
>
> (ii) The refusal to hire an individual based on stereotyped characterizations of the sexes. Such stereotypes include, for example, that men are less capable of assembling intricate equipment: that women are less capable of aggressive salesmanship. The principle of nondiscrimination requires that individuals be considered on the basis of individual capacities and not on the basis of any characteristics generally attributed to the group.
>
> (iii) The refusal to hire an individual because of the preferences of coworkers, the employer, clients or customers except as covered specifically in paragraph (a)(2) of this section.
>
> (2) Where it is necessary for the purpose of authenticity or genuineness, the Commission will consider sex to be a bona fide occupational qualification, e.g., an actor or actress.

The courts have generally heeded that counsel but not without some difficulty. New stereotypes as well as old ones in unexpected contexts continue to be uncovered by litigants claiming and contesting BFOQs. In this section, we will explore some of the more interesting and important aspects of that litigation.

Developing the Standard

Before the courts could confidently apply this exception, they had first to agree on the meaning of the statuatory language. By what standard were the courts to interpret "reasonably necessary to the normal operation of that particular business . . ."? A second preliminary issue was the burden of proof. Who must prove that this exception applies or does not apply to the situation? The following case shows how the lower courts reached preliminary accord on the meaning of that language as well as the burden of proof. In *Cheatwood,* the court considered the merits of two interpretations. One was endorsed by the Fifth Circuit Court of Appeals in *Weeks v.*

Southern Bell T. & T. The other was adopted by another district court in the case of *Bowe v. Colgate-Palmolive Co.* As you read this case, consider what would probably have happened to the frequency of sex discrimination had the *Bowe* standard been widely adopted by the courts.

Cheatwood v. So. Cent. Bell Tel. & Tel. Co.

United States District Court, Northern District of Alabama, 1969. 303 F.Supp. 754.

FRANK M. JOHNSON, Jr., Chief Judge.

In this action Mrs. Claudine B. Cheatwood charges her employer, South Central Bell Telephone & Telegraph Company, with discrimination on the basis of sex in filling a vacancy for the job classification of commercial representative in Montgomery, Alabama, in violation of Title VII. . . .

It is admitted that the plaintiff and two other female employees submitted timely bids for the vacancy, that Employer declined to consider the bids of the female employees without considering their individual qualifications, and that the job was awarded to the only male applicant. . . .

Employer has, in effect, admitted a prima facie violation . . . [but] has consistently contended, however, that the position of commercial representative fits within the [BFOQ] exception. . . .

In a recent case quite similar to the one *sub judice,* the Court of Appeals for the Fifth Circuit made clear that the burden of proof is on the employer to demonstrate that a given position fits within the bona fide occupational qualification exception. *Weeks v. Southern Bell Telephone & Telegraph Co.,* 408 F.2d 228 (5th Cir. 1969). The court in *Weeks* went on to explain the extent of the showing required to satisfy that burden:

> "In order to rely on the bona fide occupational qualification exception, an employer has the burden of proving that he had reasonable cause to believe, that is, a factual basis for believing, that all or substantially all women would be unable to perform safely and efficiently the duties of the job involved."

The only issues in this case, then, are determining the duties of a commercial representative and determining whether or not all or substantially all women would be unable to perform those duties safely and efficiently.

The official job description in effect at the time this dispute arose provides:

> "COMMERCIAL REPRESENTATIVE—(9/49) Handles commercial matters primarily outside the Company's office, such as visits to customers' premises in connection with criticisms, facilities, securing signed applications where required, credit information, deposits, advance payments, coin telephone inspections, and visits in connection with live and final account treatment work. May also be assigned to work inside the office pertaining to service and collections."

The testimony at trial produced more specific descriptions of these duties and revealed certain additional duties that go with the job in Montgomery, Alabama:

1. Rural canvassing for new customers and mileage checks for billing purposes.
2. Relief of the coin telephone collector on an average of about two days per week.
3. Destroying certain of employer's records on a monthly and annual basis.
4. Handling current record of billing stubs and handling supply requisitions in the office.
5. Performing the biennial furniture inventory.

Defendant contends that several features of these duties make them inappropriate for performance by women. With respect to the rural canvassing, it suggests the possibilities that tires will need to be changed and that restroom facilities are occasionally inaccessible. These contentions can be regarded as little more than makeweights. There is no proof that all or nearly all women would be unable to cope with these difficulties. They do, of course, render the position somewhat unromantic. But as was said in *Weeks,* Title VII "vests individual women with the power to decide whether or not to take on unromantic tasks."

Employer also contends that the duties of commercial representative would subject a female employee to harassment and danger. This is based partly on problems arising from the collection of over due bills and partly on the fact that when acting as a substitute coin collector, the employee must make collections in bars, poolrooms, and other such locations. Again, however, there is nothing in the record to indicate that these features of the position are functionally related to sex. They mean nothing more than that some women, and some men, might not wish to perform such tasks. Here, however, the record is clear that one obtains this position by bidding for it and that if one is dissatisfied it is possible to request a transfer or a return to the former position.

Employer has consistently placed principal reliance on the fact that certain aspects of the job as performed in Montgomery require lifting of weights. Although other aspects of the job require occasional lifting, the alleged strenuousness of the position relates primarily to the work involved in relieving the coin collector. The evidence reflects that other commercial representatives in Montgomery have spent an average of two days per week on this relief work. In a normal day of this work a commercial representative would collect approximately 45 coin boxes from pay stations on his route. As they are collected, these coin boxes are placed in a small metal case which is compact and relatively easy to handle. Each case will hold up to nine coin boxes. A case weighs approximately 6 pounds empty, and the estimates of its weight when full varied from 45 to 80 pounds. An actual random sample indicated that the average on a particular day in Montgomery was 60 ¾ pounds. Occasionally, a case will weigh over 90 pounds. In a given day, from five to nine cases must be handled, and each case must be lifted and/or carried full in, out or around the collection truck four times a day. . . .

. . . Employer relies upon a statement in *Bowe v. Colgate-Palmolive Co.,* 272 F.Supp. 332, 365 (S.D.Ind.1967), for the proposition that such a showing is sufficient to rely upon the bona fide occupational qualification exception:

> "Generally recognized physical capabilities and physical limitations of the sexes may be made the basis for occupational qualifications in generic terms."

As indicated above, however, Employer faces a more substantial burden. The language quoted from *Bowe* was specifically rejected in *Weeks* for the Fifth Circuit and the [EEOC] is urging on appeal that it be rejected by the Seventh Circuit—in both instances for the very good reason that if it were followed the bona fide occupational exception would swallow the rule against discrimination. . . .

Weeks requires Employer to show that all or substantially all women would be unable to perform safely and efficiently the duties of the position involved. While it may be that, in terms of lifting weights, the duties of this position begin to approach the outer limits of what women should undertake, this Court firmly concludes that Employer has not satisfied its burden of proof. . . . Nor is the fact that pregnant women should not perform the job of crucial importance. Employer can have a rule against pregnant women being considered for this position, but Title VII surely means that all women cannot be excluded from consideration because some of them may become pregnant. . . .

Accordingly, this Court now specifically finds and concludes that the male sex is not a bona fide occupational qualification for the position of commercial representative in Montgomery, Alabama.

STUDY QUESTIONS

1. What is the difference between the *Weeks* and *Bowe* standards for interpreting the BFOQ? What reason did the court give for preferring the *Weeks* standard?
2. Why did the court discount the employer's solicitude for women being inconvenienced by the unavailability of restrooms and its concern for the safety of its women employees? Does Title VII require that employers stop being gallant? How can the convenience and safety of women workers be protected?

3. Why did the court reject the argument from weight lifting ability? How can an employer, without relying on size and gender, decide who is capable of safely lifting sixty to ninety pounds?

What accommodation for pregnancy did the court indicate would be acceptable? Would that accommodation be acceptable after the adoption of the Pregnancy Discrimination Act?

The district court in *Cheatwood* and the Fifth Circuit Court of Appeals in *Weeks* placed the burden of proof on the employer who claims a BFOQ to produce a factual basis for believing that all or substantially all women will be unable to safely and efficiently perform the job in question. That approach was also followed by the Ninth Circuit Court of Appeals in *Rosenfeld v. Southern Pacific Co.,* 444 F.2d 1219 (1971). There, the employer attempted to defend a policy of excluding women from selected jobs on two grounds: the jobs were deemed unsuitable for women because they involved irregular hours and lifting weights of up to twenty-five pounds; and state laws limited the maximum hours and weight lifting that an employer was permitted to require of female employees. The court decided that neither ground established a BFOQ. That decision is widely regarded as having established that "protective" labor laws similar to those that survived constitutional challenges from *Muller v. Oregon* onward (see Chapter 1) violate Title VII. They violate the statute because, by relying upon gender stereotypes, they discriminate against individuals because of their sex.

These decisions effectively rejected the use of stereotypes relating to the relative preferences and abilities of women and men as a basis for this exception. We saw in *Manhart* that the scope of Title VII prohibitions is not restricted to decisions rooted in stereotyping. They also extend to true generalizations about a sexual group that do not apply to the individuals affected by the employer's decisions. The following case addressed a BFOQ defense based not on stereotyped assumptions but on factual findings.

Diaz v. Pan Am. World Airways, Inc.

United States Court of Appeals,
Fifth Circuit, 1971.
442 F.2d 385, *cert. denied,*
404 U.S. 950 (1971).

TUTTLE, Circuit Judge:

. . . The facts in this case are not in dispute. Celio Diaz applied for a job as flight cabin attendant with Pan American Airlines in 1967. He was rejected because Pan Am had a policy of restricting its hiring for that position to females. . . .

Pan Am admitted that it had a policy of restricting its hiring for the cabin attendant position to females. Thus, both parties stipulated that the primary issue for the District Court was whether, for the job of flight cabin attendant, being a female is a "bona fide occupational qualification (hereafter BFOQ) reasonably necessary to the normal operation" of Pan American's business.

The trial court found that being a female was a BFOQ. . . .

We note, at the outset, that there is little legislative history to guide our interpretation. The amendment adding the word "sex" to "race, color, religion and national origin" was adopted one day before House passage of the Civil Rights Act. It was added on the floor and engendered little relevant debate. In attempting to read Congress' intent in these circumstances, however, it is reasonable to assume, from a reading of the statute itself, that one of Congress' main goals was to provide equal access to the job market for both men and women. Indeed, as this court in *Weeks v. Southern Bell Telephone and Telegraph Co.,* 5 Cir., 408 F.2d 228 at 235 clearly stated, the purpose of the Act was to provide a foundation in the law for the principle of nondiscrimination. Construing the statute as embodying such a principle is based on the assumption that Congress sought a formula that would not only achieve the optimum use of our labor resources but, and more importantly, would enable individuals to develop as individuals.

Attainment of this goal, however, is, as stated above, limited by the bona fide occupational qualification exception in section 703(e). In construing this provision, we feel, as did the court in *Weeks, supra,* that it would be totally anomalous to do so in a manner that would, in effect, permit the exception to swallow the rule. Thus, we adopt the EEOC guidelines which state that "the Commission believes that the bona fide occupational qualification as to sex should be interpreted narrowly." . . . [T]he trial court's conclusion was based upon (1) its view of Pan Am's history of the use of flight attendants; (2) passenger preference; (3) basic psychological reasons for the preference; and (4) the actualities of the hiring process.

Having reviewed the evidence submitted by Pan American regarding its own experience with both female and male cabin attendants it had hired over the years, the trial court found that Pan Am's current hiring policy was the result of a pragmatic process, "representing a judgment made upon adequate evidence acquired through Pan Am's considerable experience, and designed to yield under Pan Am's current operating conditions better *average* performance for its passengers than would a policy of mixed male and female hiring." (emphasis added) The performance of female attendants was *better* in the sense that they were *superior* in such non-mechanical aspects of the job as "providing reassurance to anxious passengers, giving courteous personalized service and, in general, making flights as pleasurable as possible within the limitations imposed by aircraft operations."

The trial court also found that Pan Am's passengers overwhelmingly preferred to be served by female stewardesses. Moreover, on the basis of the expert testimony of a psychiatrist, the court found that an airplane cabin represents a unique environment in which an air carrier is required to take account of the special psychological needs of its passengers. These psychological needs are better attended to by females. This is not to say that there are no males who would not have the necessary qualities to perform these non-mechanical functions, but the trial court found that the actualities of the hiring process would make it more difficult to find these few males. Indeed, "the admission of men to the hiring process, in the present state of the art of employment selection, would have increased the number of unsatisfactory employees hired, and reduced the average levels of performance of Pan Am's complement of flight attendants." . . .

Because of the narrow reading we give to section 703(e), we do not feel that these findings justify the discrimination practiced by Pan Am.

We begin with the proposition that the use of the word "necessary" in section 703(e) requires that we apply a business *necessity* test, not a business *convenience* test. That is to say, discrimination based on sex is valid only when the *essence* of the business operation would be undermined by not hiring members of one sex exclusively.

The primary function of an airline is to transport passengers safely from one point to another. While a pleasant environment, enhanced by the obvious cosmetic effect that female stewardesses provide as well as, according to the finding of the trial court, their apparent ability to perform the non-mechanical functions of the job in a more effective manner than most men, may all be important, they are tangential to the essence of the business involved. No one has suggested that having male stewards will so seriously affect the operation of an airline as to jeopardize or even minimize its ability to provide safe transportation from one place to another. Indeed the record discloses that many airlines including Pan Am have utilized both men and women flight cabin attendants in the past and Pan Am, even at the time of this suit, has 283 male stewards employed on some of its foreign flights. . . .

While we recognize that the public's expectation of finding one sex in a particular role may cause some initial difficulty, it would be totally anomalous if we were to allow the preferences and prejudices of the customers to determine whether the sex discrimination was valid. Indeed, it was, to a large extent, these very prejudices the Act was meant to overcome. Thus, we feel that customer preference may be taken into account only when it is based on the company's inability to perform the primary function or service it offers.

Of course, Pan Am argues that the customers' preferences are not based on "stereotyped thinking," but the ability of women stewardesses to better provide the non-mechanical aspects of the job. Again, as stated above, since these aspects are tangential to the business, the fact that customers prefer them cannot justify sex discrimination.

The judgment is reversed and the case is remanded for proceedings not inconsistent with this opinion.

STUDY QUESTIONS

1. Would the four reasons offered in support of the restriction here have satisfied the *Weeks* standard? Why did this court reject those reasons?
2. How did the court interpret the word "necessary"? Are courts qualified to decide what the "essence of the business operation" is and to draw a line between it and "tangential" operations? What is the alternative?
3. Assuming that it was right about the preferences of its customers, was Pan Am likely to lose customers to other airlines as a result of this decision? Did this decision affect only Pan Am?

The question of the meaning of the BFOQ first reached the Supreme Court in the following case. There, the Court endorsed the narrow standard developed by lower courts in earlier BFOQ cases but appeared to find a factual basis for concluding that all, or substantially all, otherwise qualified women would be unable to safely and efficiently perform the duties of a guard in Alabama maximum-security prisons housing male inmates. The Court's decision, although limited to the facts of this particular situation, is highly controversial. The more controversial points are reviewed by Justice Marshall in his dissenting opinion.

In *Dothard,* the Court addressed two important aspects of Title VII: the BFOQ exception and the disparate impact theory of discrimination. Those elements of the decision relating to the disparate impact theory were discussed in section II of this chapter.

Dothard v. Rawlinson

Supreme Court of the
United States, 1977.
433 U.S. 321, 97 S.Ct. 2720,
53 L.Ed.2d 786.

Mr. Justice STEWART delivered the opinion of the Court.

Appellee Dianne Rawlinson sought employment with the Alabama Board of Corrections as a prison guard, called in Alabama a "correctional counselor." After her application was rejected, she brought this class suit under Title VII of the Civil Rights Act of 1964 . . . alleging that she had been denied employment because of her sex in violation of federal law. A three-judge Federal District Court for the Middle District of Alabama decided in her favor. . . .

At the time she applied for a position as correctional counselor trainee, Rawlinson was a 22-year-old college graduate whose major course of study had been correctional psychology. She was refused employment because she failed to meet the minimum 120-pound weight requirement established by an Alabama statute. The statute also establishes a height minimum of 5 feet 2 inches.

After her application was rejected because of her weight, Rawlinson filed a charge with the Equal Employment Opportunity Commission, and ultimately received a right-to-sue letter. She then filed a complaint in the District Court on behalf of herself and other similarly situated women, challenging the statutory height and weight minima as violative of Title VII and the Equal Protection Clause of the Fourteenth Amendment. A three-judge court was convened. While the suit was pending, the Alabama Board of Corrections adopted Administrative Regulation 204, establishing gender criteria for assigning correctional counselors to maximum-security institutions for "contact positions," that is, positions requiring continual close physical proximity to inmates of the institution. Rawlinson amended her class-action complaint by adding a challenge to Regulation 204 as also violative of Title VII and the Fourteenth Amendment.

Like most correctional facilities in the United States, Alabama's prisons are segregated on the basis of sex. . . . The Julia Tutwiler Prison for Women and the four male penitentiaries are maximum-security institutions. Their inmate living quarters are for the most part large dormitories, with communal showers and toilets that are open to the dormitories and hallways. . . .

A correctional counselor's primary duty within these institutions is to maintain security and control of the inmates by continually supervising and observing their activities. .

Unlike the statutory height and weight requirements, Regulation 204 explicitly discriminates against women on the basis of their sex. In defense of this overt discrimination, the appellants rely on § 703 (e). . . .

The District Court rejected the bona-fide-occupational-qualification (bfoq) defense, relying on the virtually uniform view of the federal courts that § 703 (e) provides only the narrowest of exceptions to the general rule requiring equality of employment opportunities. This view has been variously formulated. In *Diaz v. Pan American World Airways,* the Court of Appeals for the Fifth Circuit held that "discrimina-

tion based on sex is valid only when the essence of the business operation would be undermined by not hiring members of one sex exclusively." In an earlier case, *Weeks v. Southern Bell Telephone and Telegraph Co.* the same court said that an employer could rely on the bfoq exception only by proving "that he had reasonable cause to believe, that is, a factual basis for believing, that all or substantially all women would be unable to perform safely and efficiently the duties of the job involved." But whatever the verbal formulation, the federal courts have agreed that it is impermissible under Title VII to refuse to hire an individual woman or man on the basis of stereotyped characteristics of the sexes, and the District Court in the present case held in effect that Regulation 204 is based upon just such stereotyped assumptions.

We are persuaded—by the restrictive language of § 703 (e), the relevant legislative history, and the consistent interpretation of the Equal Employment Opportunity Commission—that the bfoq exception was in fact meant to be an extremely narrow exception to the general prohibition of discrimination on the basis of sex. In the particular factual circumstances of this case, however, we conclude that the District Court erred in rejecting the State's contention that Regulation 204 falls within the narrow ambit of the bfoq exception.

The environment in Alabama's penitentiaries is a peculiarly inhospitable one for human beings of whatever sex. Indeed, a Federal District Court has held that the conditions of confinement in the prisons of the State, characterized by "rampant violence" and a "jungle atmosphere," are constitutionally intolerable. *Pugh v. Locke.* The record in the present case shows that because of inadequate staff and facilities, no attempt is made in the four maximum-security male penitentiaries to classify or segregate inmates according to their offense or level of dangerousness—a procedure that, according to expert testimony, is essential to effective penological administration. Consequently, the estimated 20% of the male prisoners who are sex offenders are scattered throughout the penitentiaries' dormitory facilities.

In this environment of violence and disorganization, it would be an oversimplification to characterize Regulation 204 as an exercise in "romantic paternalism." In the usual case, the argument that a particular job is too dangerous for women may appropriately be met by the rejoinder that it is the purpose of Title VII to allow the individual woman to make that choice for herself. More is at stake in this case, however, than an individual woman's decision to weigh and accept the risks of employment in a "contact" position in a maximum-security male prison.

The essence of a correctional counselor's job is to maintain prison security. A woman's relative ability to maintain order in a male, maximum-security, unclassified penitentiary of the type Alabama now runs could be directly reduced by her womanhood. There is a basis in fact for expecting that sex offenders who have criminally assaulted women in the past would be moved to do so again if access to women were established within the prison. There would also be a real risk that other inmates, deprived of a normal heterosexual environment, would assault women guards because they were women.[22] In a prison system where violence is the order of the day, where inmate access to guards is facilitated by dormitory living arrangements, where every institution is understaffed, and where a substantial portion of the inmate population is composed of sex offenders mixed at random with other prisoners, there are few visible deterrents to inmate assaults on women custodians.

Appellee Rawlinson's own expert testified that dormitory housing for aggressive inmates poses a greater security problem than single-cell lockups, and further testified that it would be unwise to use women as guards in a prison where even 10% of the inmates had been convicted of sex crimes and were not segregated from the other prisoners.[23] The likelihood that inmates would assault a woman because she

was a woman would pose a real threat not only to the victim of the assault but also to the basic control of the penitentiary and protection of its inmates and the other security personnel. The employee's very womanhood would thus directly undermine her capacity to provide the security that is the essence of a correctional counselor's responsibility.

There was substantial testimony from experts on both sides of this litigation that the use of women as guards in "contact" positions under the existing conditions in Alabama maximum-security male penitentiaries would pose a substantial security problem, directly linked to the sex of the prison guard. On the basis of that evidence, we conclude that the District Court was in error in ruling that being male is not a bona fide occupational qualification for the job of correctional counselor in a "contact" position in an Alabama male maximum-security penitentiary.

The judgment is accordingly affirmed in part and reversed in part, and the case is remanded to the District Court for further proceedings consistent with this opinion.

It is so ordered.

Mr. Justice MARSHALL, with whom Mr. Justice BRENNAN joins, concurring in part and dissenting in part.

. . . The Court is unquestionably correct when it holds "that the bfoq exception was in fact meant to be an extremely narrow exception to the general prohibition of discrimination on the basis of sex." I must, however, respectfully disagree with the Court's application of the bfoq exception in this case. . . .

What would otherwise be considered unlawful discrimination against women is justified by the Court, however, on the basis of the "barbaric and inhumane" conditions in Alabama prisons, conditions so bad that state officials have conceded that they violate the Constitution. To me, this analysis sounds distressingly like saying two wrongs make a right. It is refuted by the plain words of § 703 (e). The statute requires that a bfoq be "reasonably necessary to the normal operation of that particular business or enterprise." But no governmental "business"

---

[22] *The record contains evidence of an attack on a female clerical worker in an Alabama prison, and of an incident involving a woman student who was taken hostage during a visit to one of the maximum-security institutions.*

[23] *Alabama's penitentiaries are evidently not typical. Appellee Rawlinson's two experts testified that in a normal, relatively stable maximum-security prison—characterized by control over the inmates, reasonable living conditions, and segregation of dangerous offenders—women guards could be used effectively and beneficially. Similarly, an amicus brief filed by the State of California attests to that State's success in using women guards in all-male penitentiaries.*

may operate "normally" in violation of the Constitution. Every action of government is constrained by constitutional limitations. While those limits may be violated more frequently than we would wish, no one disputes that the "normal operation" of all government functions takes place within them. A prison system operating in blatant violation of the Eighth Amendment is an exception that should be remedied with all possible speed, as Judge Johnson's comprehensive order in *Pugh v. Locke* is designed to do. In the meantime, the existence of such violations should not be legitimatized by calling them "normal." Nor should the Court accept them as justifying conduct that would otherwise violate a statute intended to remedy age-old discrimination.

The Court's error in statutory construction is less objectionable, however, than the attitude it displays toward women. Though the Court recognizes that possible harm to women guards is an unacceptable reason for disqualifying women, it relies instead on an equally speculative threat to prison discipline supposedly generated by the sexuality of female guards. There is simply no evidence in the record to show that women guards would create any danger to security in Alabama prisons significantly greater than that which already exists. All of the dangers—with one exception discussed below—are inherent in a prison setting, whatever the gender of the guards.

The Court first sees women guards as a threat to security because "there are few visible deterrents to inmate assaults on women custodians." In fact, any prison guard is constantly subject to the threat of attack by inmates, and "invisible" deterrents are the guard's only real protection. No prison guard relies primarily on his or her ability to ward off an inmate attack to maintain order. Guards are typically unarmed and sheer numbers of inmates could overcome the normal complement. Rather, like all other law enforcement officers, prison guards must rely primarily on the moral authority of their office and the threat of future punishment for miscreants. As one expert testified below, common sense, fairness, and mental and emotional stability are the qualities a guard needs to cope with the dangers of the job. Well qualified and properly trained women, no less than men, have these psychological weapons at their disposal.

The particular severity of discipline problems in the Alabama maximum-security prisons

is also no justification for the discrimination sanctioned by the Court. The District Court found in *Pugh v. Locke* that guards "must spend all their time attempting to maintain control or to protect themselves." If male guards face an impossible situation, it is difficult to see how women could make the problem worse, unless one relies on precisely the type of generalized bias against women that the Court agrees Title VII was intended to outlaw. For example, much of the testimony of appellants' witnesses ignores individual differences among members of each sex and reads like "ancient canards about the proper role of women." The witnesses claimed that women guards are not strict disciplinarians; that they are physically less capable of protecting themselves and subduing unruly inmates; that inmates take advantage of them as they did their mothers, while male guards are strong father figures who easily maintain discipline, and so on. Yet the record shows that the presence of women guards has not led to a single incident amounting to a serious breach of security in any Alabama institution. And, in any event, "[g]uards rarely enter the cell blocks and dormitories," *Pugh v. Locke,* where the danger of inmate attacks is the greatest.

It appears that the real disqualifying factor in the Court's view is "[t]he employee's very womanhood." The Court refers to the large number of sex offenders in Alabama prisons, and to "[t]he likelihood that inmates would assault a woman because she was a woman." In short, the fundamental justification for the decision is that women as guards will generate sexual assaults. With all respect this rationale regrettably perpetuates one of the most insidious of the old myths about women—that women, wittingly or not, are seductive sexual objects. The effect of the decision, made I am sure with the best of intentions, is to punish women because their very presence might provoke sexual assaults. It is women who are made to pay the price in lost job opportunities for the threat of depraved conduct by prison inmates. . . .

The Court points to no evidence in the record to support the asserted "likelihood that inmates would assault a woman because she was a woman." Perhaps the Court relies upon common sense, or "innate recognition." But the danger in this emotionally laden context is that common sense will be used to mask the " 'romantic paternalism' " and persisting discriminatory attitudes that the Court properly eschews. To me, the only matter of innate recognition is that the incidence of sexually motivated attacks on guards will be minute compared to the "likelihood that inmates will assault" a *guard* because he or she is a *guard*.

The proper response to inevitable attacks on both female and male guards is not to limit the employment opportunities of law-abiding women who wish to contribute to their community, but to take swift and sure punitive action against the inmate offenders. Presumably, one of the goals of the Alabama prison system is the eradication of inmates' antisocial behavior patterns so that prisoners will be able to live one day in free society. Sex offenders can begin this process by learning to relate to women guards in a socially acceptable manner. To deprive women of job opportunities because of the threatened behavior of convicted criminals is to turn our social priorities upside down.[5]

Although I do not countenance the sex discrimination condoned by the majority, it is fortunate that the Court's decision is carefully limited to the facts before it. I trust the lower courts will recognize that the decision was impelled by the shockingly inhuman conditions in Alabama prisons, and thus that the "extremely narrow [bfoq] exception" recognized here, . . . will not be allowed "to swallow the rule" against sex discrimination. Expansion of today's decision beyond its narrow factual basis would erect a serious roadblock to economic equality for women.

STUDY QUESTIONS

1. What did Regulation 204 provide? On what grounds was it defended?
2. What reasons were cited for allowing a BFOQ in this case? What would have been lost by following the rationale indicated in *Cheatwood* and allowing the individual job applicant to balance the risk of injury against the benefits of the job?
3. What objections were raised by the dissenters to the Court's willingness to view a guard's "very womanhood" as an impediment to her safe and efficient performance of her job?
4. Does this decision reject the standard developed by the lower courts for interpreting the BFOQ exception or only authorize a narrow departure from that standard in this case?

---

[5]*The appellants argue that restrictions on employment of women are also justified by consideration of inmates' privacy. It is strange indeed to hear state officials who have for years been violating the most basic principles of human decency in the operation of their prisons suddenly become concerned about inmate privacy. It is stranger still that these same officials allow women guards in contact positions in a number of nonmaximum security institutions, but strive to protect inmates' privacy in the prisons where personal freedom is most severely restricted. I have no doubt on this record that appellants' professed concern is nothing but a feeble excuse for discrimination.*

As the District Court suggested, it may well be possible, once constitutionally adequate staff is available, to rearrange work assignments so that legitimate inmate privacy concerns are respected without denying jobs to women. Finally, if women guards behave in a professional manner at all times, they will engender reciprocal respect from inmates, who will recognize that their privacy is being invaded no more than if a woman doctor examines them. The suggestion implicit in the privacy argument that such behavior is unlikely on either side is an insult to the professionalism of guards and the dignity of inmates.

The decision in *Dothard* as regards the BFOQ exception can be confusing on first reading. The result of the decision was that Alabama was permitted to discriminate against qualified women who applied for the positions at issue here, at least until the unconstitutionally violent conditions of its prisons were corrected. In this respect, several points should be noted. One is that the Court itself emphasized that its ruling here was limited to those unusual circumstances. Another is that very few other prisons have been successful in enlisting the ruling in *Dothard* in support of excluding women from security positions in all other prisons.

More important, however, the Court in *Dothard* approved the narrow interpretation given by the EEOC and the lower courts to the BFOQ exception. In the longer term, therefore, *Dothard* can be understood as indicating that, although there can very well be situations in which differential treatment of women and men in an employment setting is "reasonably necessary to the normal operation of that particular business," those situations are likely to be very rare.

That such situations, however rare they may be, must be tolerated is surely regrettable. The justification offered for the facially discriminatory practices that were present in the Alabama prisons, as Justice Marshall correctly observed, "sounds distressingly like saying two wrongs make a right." Even if it were true that Alabama could not give reasonable assurances to inmates of their safety in part because it could not control those who are prone to violence, it surely does not follow that denial of equal employment opportunities to qualified women who elect to contribute their services in such circumstances is acceptable. This line of justification is reminiscent of traditional attitudes and strategies—woman as temptress and blaming the victim. In the end, the only consolation there may be for accommodating ourselves to such practices is that they are few and far between.

Accommodating Safety, Efficiency, and Privacy Interests

The language of the statute allows overt sex discrimination by an employer where it is "reasonably necessary to the normal operation of that particular business or enterprise." The EEOC specifically rejected "the preferences of coworkers, the employer, clients or customers" (except for the purposes of authenticity or genuineness) as grounds for a BFOQ. In *Dothard,* the Court approved the narrow emphasis recommended by the EEOC, as well as the *Weeks* and *Diaz* standards for interpreting the language of the BFOQ exception. In *Weeks,* the circuit court placed the burden on the employer that invokes a BFOQ defense of proving that "he had reasonable cause to believe, that is, a factual basis for believing, that all or substantially all women would be unable to perform safely and efficiently the duties of the job involved." The Court has since repeated that commitment on several occasions. Several issues remain unclear. How closely must the sex of an employee be related to the job that she performs? Would increased costs to the employer's overall operation suffice as a justification? What type of considerations give an employer reasonable cause to believe that sex is related to job performance? Must such a belief be documented by empirical evidence? Are all types of third party preferences for being served by people of one sex to be rejected as grounds for a BFOQ? Are there no circumstances in which the customary standards of modesty carry sufficient weight to excuse sex discrimination in employment? The following cases illustrate the state of the questions on these issues.

In *Johnson Controls,* the Supreme Court addressed the BFOQ in the context of a safety issue. The safety concern here was not like that in *Cheatwood,* where the employer argued that the safety of the employee was at risk. Here, as in *Dothard,* the risk was to the safety of potential third parties, i.e., to fetuses of women who conceived while working in toxic environments created by the employer.

U. A. W. v. Johnson Controls, Inc.

United States Supreme Court, 1991.
___ U.S. ___, 111 S.Ct 1196, 113 L.Ed.2d 158.

Justice BLACKMUN delivered the opinion of the Court.

. . . Respondent Johnson Controls, Inc., manufactures batteries. In the manufacturing process, the element lead is a primary ingredient. Occupational exposure to lead entails health risks, including the risk of harm to any fetus carried by a female employee . . . .

. . . [I]n 1982, Johnson Controls . . . announc[ed] a broad exclusion of women from jobs that exposed them to lead: ". . . [I]t is [Johnson Controls'] policy that women who are pregnant or who are capable of bearing children will not be placed into jobs involving lead exposure or which could expose them to lead through the exercise of job bidding, bumping, transfer or promotion rights." The policy defined "women . . . capable of bearing children" as "[a]ll women except those whose inability to bear children is medically documented." . . .

The District Court granted summary judgment for defendant-respondent Johnson Controls. . . . The Court of Appeals for the Seventh Circuit, sitting en banc, affirmed the summary judgment by a 7-to-4 vote. [This was the first ruling by a Circuit Court] to hold that a fetal-protection policy directed exclusively at women could qualify as a BFOQ. . . .

The bias in Johnson Controls' policy is obvious. Fertile men, but not fertile women, are given a choice as to whether they wish to risk their reproductive health for a particular job. . . . Respondent's fetal-protection policy explicitly discriminates against women on the basis of their sex. The policy excludes women with childbearing capacity from lead-exposed jobs and so creates a facial classification based on gender. . . .

. . . [T]he Court of Appeals assumed . . . that sex-specific fetal-protection policies do not involve facial discrimination. [It] analyzed the policies as though they were facially neutral, and had only a discriminatory effect upon the employment opportunities of women. Consequently, the [court] looked to see [the] employer . . . had established that its policy was justified as a business necessity. The business necessity standard is more lenient for the employer than the statutory BFOQ defense. . . . The court assumed that because the asserted reason for the sex-based exclusion (protecting women's unconceived offspring) was ostensibly benign, the policy was not sex-based discrimination. That assumption, however, was incorrect.

. . . Johnson Controls' policy is facially discriminatory because it requires only a female employee to produce proof that she is not capable of reproducing.

. . . We hold that Johnson Controls' fetal-protection policy is sex discrimination forbidden under Title VII unless respondent can establish that sex is a "bona fide occupational qualification" [BFOQ]. . . .

Johnson Controls argues that its fetal-protection policy falls within the so-called safety exception to the BFOQ. Our cases have stressed that discrimination on the basis of sex because of safety concerns is allowed only in narrow circumstances. . . .

Our case law [*Dothard* and other of our decisions] makes clear that the safety exception is limited to instances in which sex or pregnancy actually interferes with the employee's ability to perform the job. This approach is consistent with the language of the BFOQ provision itself, for it suggests that permissible distinctions based on sex must relate to ability to perform the duties of the job. Johnson Controls suggests, however, that we expand the exception to allow fetal-protection policies that mandate particular standards for pregnant or fertile women. We decline to do so. Such an expansion contradicts not only the language of the BFOQ and the narrowness of its exception but the plain language and history of the Pregnancy Discrimination Act [PDA].

The PDA's amendment to Title VII contains a BFOQ standard of its own: unless pregnant employees differ from others "in their ability or inability to work," they must be "treated the same" as other employees "for all employment-related purposes." This language clearly sets forth Congress' remedy for discrimination on the basis of pregnancy and potential pregnancy. Women who are either pregnant or potentially pregnant must be treated like others "similar in their ability . . . to work." In other words, women as capable of doing their jobs as their male counterparts may not be forced to choose between having a child and having a job. . . .

We have no difficulty concluding that Johnson Controls cannot establish a BFOQ. Fertile women, as far as appears in the record, participate in the manufacture of batteries as efficiently as anyone else. Johnson Controls' professed moral and ethical concerns about the welfare of the next generation do not suffice to establish a BFOQ of female sterility. Decisions about the welfare of future children must be left to the parents who conceive, bear, support, and raise them rather than to the employers who hire those parents. Congress has mandated this choice through Title VII, as amended by the Pregnancy Discrimination Act. . . .

The judgment of the Court of Appeals is reversed and the case is remanded for further proceedings consistent with this opinion.

STUDY QUESTIONS

1. Compare the issues raised in this case with those raised in *Muller,* as well as the way they were decided. In both, women and men risked safety hazards. In both, job opportunities were denied women. In both, the asserted motivation is to protect the interests of some individuals from the hazards of particular workplaces. Who has Congress entrusted with the prerogative of deciding whether the risk is to be undertaken where the hazard is to the employee? Who is entrusted with that prerogative where the hazard is to future possible children? Do you agree with that decision? What are the alternatives?

2. The Court decided here that no sex-specific fetal protection policy can be defended as a BFOQ. The Court noted in the course of its decision that the employer had not examined evidence showing that fetal damage can result from the exposure of male as well as female parents to lead. Had the employer imposed this job restriction on anyone capable of reproducing, would the outcome have been different? Would you approve of that result?

The decision in *Johnson Controls* was unanimous. The lower courts' decision to grant summary judgment to the employer was overturned without a dissenting vote. Notwithstanding, this was a close decision on one issue of lasting significance. Just how narrow an exception is the BFOQ? Justice Blackmun, writing for a majority of five justices, declared that it is narrowly focused on the ability to perform the specific job in question. An important part of the rationale supporting that view was introduced through the discussion of the Pregnancy Discrimination Act.

Four justices disagreed. Justices White and Kennedy and Chief Justice Rehnquist declared that the PDA has to do with the definition of "because of sex" and is not relevant to determining the scope of the BFOQ exception. These justices, along with Justice Scalia, rejected the view that BFOQs can be justified only by the linkage of employee ability to the specific job. According to these four justices, the contribution of employees to the employer's cost of doing business is also germane and could sometimes be controlling. Thus, Justice Scalia indicated, "I think, for example, that a shipping company may refuse to hire pregnant women as crew members on long voyages because the on-board facilities for foreseeable emergencies, though quite feasible, would be inordinately expensive." As several justices who voted in the majority in this case have since retired from the Court, the balance of the justices on the delicate question of whether the scope of the BFOQ exception is the same or narrower than that of "business necessity" in the disparate impact pattern of litigation is far from settled.

Commitment to the requirements of the *Weeks* standard has shown signs of waning over the past few years. The latest evidence of this at the circuit court level came in a case that approved a BFOQ on the basis of general understandings and opinions of management, rather than, as *Weeks* required, on "a factual basis" for believing that only women could efficiently perform the duties of the job involved.

This drift toward a broader interpretation of the BFOQ exception brings to mind the concern voiced by the *Cheatwood* court and echoed in *Dothard* that the exception so understood could swallow the rule.

Torres v. Wisconsin Dept. of Health and Social Services

United States Court of Appeals, Seventh Circuit, 1988.
859 F.2d 1523.

RIPPLE, Circuit Judge.

. . . .

Facts

TCI [Taycheedah Correctional Institution] has three buildings for housing inmates. Each building has three residence floors, and the inmates live in single, double, or multiple occupancy rooms. The rooms are not cells with bars, but are more akin to college dormitory rooms. Each room has a solid door with a clear glass window at eye level that is approximately four inches by six inches. The rooms have one bed per inmate, a desk, chair, light, toilet, and wash basin. In two buildings, privacy curtains have been installed around the toilets. When an inmate is behind the curtain, only her feet are visible. At the time of trial, TCI had plans to install privacy curtains in the other residence building soon.

From 6 A.M. until 9 P.M., inmates may place "privacy cards" inside the door windows so that they can use the toilet or change their clothes without being observed. TCI's rules allow the privacy cards to be up for only ten minutes per day per inmate. In multiple inmate rooms, this means that the cards can be up permissibly for as much as thirty or forty minutes. However, the testimony offered at trial suggests that correctional officers are not able to keep careful track of the time that a privacy card has been in place, and that inmates sometimes leave their cards up for more than ten minutes per inmate.

On one occasion, two inmates used their privacy card to facilitate an escape, and on another occasion an inmate beat up her roommate while the privacy card covered the window.

From 9 P.M. until 6 A.M., inmates may not place their privacy card on the inside of their window, but they may place their card outside the window all night long in order to prevent light from entering the room. Correctional officers then lift up the card for body counts and inspections. TCI's rules require that the officers conduct a body count each day at 7:30 A.M., 12:30 P.M., 5:30 P.M., 9:30 P.M., and once each hour between 10 P.M. and 6 A.M. Inmates know this schedule. TCI provides appropriate sleepwear for the inmates but they are not required to wear it. The guards are required to see the inmates' skin or hair during nighttime body counts.

Each floor of the residence buildings has a shower room. Inmates must sign up with their floor officer before taking a shower, and they are required to wear some sort of clothing when walking to the shower room. Testimony at trial suggested that guards normally do not enter the shower rooms when occupied. The doors to the shower rooms are solid, although some contain windows that have been rendered opaque. The shower rooms have one to three shower stalls, one to three toilets, and some have one or more bathtubs. The showers and toilets have privacy curtains or privacy doors. Only one inmate may occupy the shower room at a time, except that roommates may enter together. TCI allows each inmate fifteen minutes in the shower room.

The Wisconsin Administrative Code allows prison officials to perform four types of inmate searches. Wis. Admin. Code § HSS 306.16 (1987). Correctional officers may perform pat searches at any time. During a pat search, inmates empty their pockets and the officer runs his or her hands over the inmates' entire body. The custom at TCI is that only female guards perform pat searches. The second type of allowable search is the strip search. Strip searches must be authorized by a supervisor and performed in private by an officer of the same sex, except during emergencies. The third type of search is the body cavity search. Body cavity searches are only performed by medical personnel in special circumstances. The fourth permissible search is a body content search, such as urinalysis or blood analysis. Under this regulation, body content searches are permitted only in extreme circumstances. In addition, correctional officers are expected to search occasionally inmates' rooms and the shower rooms when they are unoccupied.

Ms. Switala became superintendent of TCI in 1978. She previously had worked for three years as treatment director at TCI and for eight years as a probation and parole agent with the Wisconsin Division of Corrections. Ms. Switala, her superiors at the DHSS, and her personnel at TCI, soon began discussions regarding TCI's staffing needs. It ultimately was decided, principally by Ms. Switala, that certain positions at TCI should be staffed only by female correctional officers. It is clear from Ms. Switala's testimony at trial that the principal reason for this decision was her concern for inmate rehabilitation and security. TCI's administrators then advised all correctional officers in 1980 that a BFOQ program would be implemented gradually in the next two years.

TCI has three different ranks for its correctional officers. The lowest position is a correctional officer 1 (CO-1), followed by correctional officer 2 (CO-2) and correctional officer 3 (CO-3). The CO-3 in charge of a living unit is a "sergeant." The positions to be affected by the BFOQ plan were nineteen of the twenty-seven correctional officer positions in the living units, including all of the CO-3 posts in the living units. As a result of the plan, only three CO-3 positions at TCI would be open to men. The three plaintiffs, Mr. Torres, Mr. Utz, and Mr. Schmit, were all CO-3's prior to implementation of the BFOQ plan. Because of the limited number of available CO-3 positions, the three plaintiffs were required to accept CO-2 positions, although this demotion resulted in no loss of pay. The plaintiffs presently work under female CO-3's who have less seniority and experience. . . .

[The district court found TCI in violation of Title VII because it failed to establish that sex was a BFOQ for these correctional officer positions on security, rehabilitation or privacy grounds. A panel of the Seventh Circuit Court of Appeals affirmed. Upon rehearing the appeal *en banc,* the full appellate court reversed, focusing on rehabilitation.]

Ms. Switala, the superintendent of TCI, made a professional judgment that giving women prisoners a living environment free from the presence of males in a position of authority was necessary to foster the goal of rehabilitation. This decision was based on Ms. Switala's professional expertise and on her interviews and daily contact with female prisoners. She also based her decision on the fact that a high percentage of female inmates has been physically and sexually abused by males. Indeed, she noted that sixty percent of TCI's inmates have been so abused.

There can be no question that the proposed BFOQ is directly related to the "essence" of the "business"—the rehabilitation of females incarcerated in a maximum security institution. As we already have noted, the Wisconsin legislature has mandated that rehabilitation is one of the objectives of that state's prison system. Therefore, we stress that this is not a case where the interest of the plaintiffs in their continued employment simply conflicts with the basic privacy rights of the inmates. Here, the interest of the plaintiffs conflicts with the task of the administrators to rehabilitate the inmates for whom they are responsible. . . .

The more difficult question is whether the proposed BFOQ was "reasonably necessary" to furthering the objective of rehabilitation. The defendants can establish that the BFOQ was reasonably necessary only if they "had reasonable cause to believe, that is, a factual basis for believing, that all or substantially all [men] would be unable to perform safely and efficiently the duties of the job involved."

The district court determined that the defendants had not met this hurdle because "[t]hey offered no objective evidence, either from empirical studies or otherwise, displaying the validity of their theory." We respectfully differ with our colleagues in the district court as to the legal appropriateness of this standard. Certainly, there is no general requirement that the necessity of a BFOQ be established by this type of evidence. In *Dothard,* the Supreme Court determined that Alabama prison officials were justified in removing female guards from the state's "peculiarly inhospitable" penitentiaries. The Court said that "[t]here is a basis in fact for expecting that sex offenders who have criminally assaulted women in the past would be moved to do so again if access to women were established within the prison." The Court also said that there would "be a real risk that other inmates, deprived of a normal heterosexual environment, would assault women guards because they were women." These appraisals were not based on objective, empirical evidence, but instead on a common-sense understanding of penal conditions, and, implicitly, on a limited degree of judicial deference to prison administrators. . . .

Reversed and Remanded

STUDY QUESTIONS

1. Was the requirement of the *Weeks* standard met by this decision? Do you approve or disapprove? Did the court require the employer to produce "a factual basis for believing" that men could not effectively perform the duties of these jobs?

2. The justification given by the employer in this case mainly involves matters of efficiency. What did the employer argue would be less efficiently done by males if the BFOQ program were not instituted? Is this type of consideration part of the "essence of the business"?

3. One of the reasons that the EEOC rejected reliance on the preferences of employers is that, however well meaning they might be, they very often rely on stereotypes. Might Ms. Switala be relying on stereotyped views of both male guards and female prisoners?

In the years since *Dothard,* a number of social scientists have studied the consequences of employing women as correctional officers in all-male prisons. These show that where women held these jobs, the male inmates believed that their presence increased the livability of the institutions and also improved the behavior of the inmates. A recent study found similar results for male officers guarding female inmates. Linda Zupan concluded her study by pointing out that all but two of the sixty-four maximum- and medium-security women's prisons in her study employed men as correctional officers and in all but eight, "men were routinely assigned to supervise female inmates in the housing units." One of her conclusions is relevant to the *Torres* decision:

> In regard to reaction of female prisoners to the presence of male officers in the living units, the findings of this study suggest that inmate resistance is minimal. In general, female inmates at the women's prisons in this study expressed a preference for supervision by male officers. The inmates also noted a change in the behavior of other residents in the presence of male officers. They observed that the appearance and grooming of some inmates improved and that inmates were more obedient to the commands of male officers than they were to the commands of female officers.
> *Linda L. Zupan, "Men Guarding Women." 20 Journal of Criminal Justice 297–309 (1992), 308.*

Another of Zupan's findings was that both male and female inmates object strongly to the deployment of opposite-sexed guards in assignments that require direct physical contact or visual observation of a personal nature, e.g., pat or strip searches and supervision of toilet areas. This leads to a third major area of BFOQ decisions, viz., those that relate to privacy interests. These arise in institutional settings involving intimate care and/or close, round-the-clock observation. Prisons, hospitals, and nursing facilities are most frequently the employers that invoke the privacy interests of their clients as grounds for BFOQs. Here, the issue is whether demands for a same-sex service provider based on customs of personal modesty are to be regarded as a protected interest that is closely enough involved in the essence of the business to warrant a BFOQ or as just another type of customer preference that is not permitted to interfere with the equal employment opportunities of qualified women and men.

The privacy interest was raised in footnote 5 of Justice Marshall's dissent in *Dothard*. There, he endorsed the customer preference approach to these claims and dismissed such complaints as "an insult to the professionalism of guards and the dignity of inmates." Thereafter, the decisions of the lower courts have gone both ways as regards prison inmates. Then, in 1984, the Supreme Court ruled that prisoners do not have a reasonable expectation of privacy in their cells that is sufficient to entitle them to Fourth Amendment protection against unreasonable searches. According to the Court, the interest of prisoners in privacy must give way to the interest of society in the security of its penal institutions, *Hudson v. Palmer*, 468 U.S. 517 (1984). That decision makes it unlikely that prisons can justify single-sex BFOQs by invoking a privacy interest on behalf of inmates.

Prisons are not the only institutional settings in which asserted privacy interests can come into conflict with equal employment opportunity. The following case addresses that same conflict in a hospital setting. Although the decision was later vacated because the plaintiff voluntarily resigned from the hospital, it illustrates the rationale and result that lower courts typically reach when hospitals and nursing facilities assert a BFOQ on the basis of patient privacy interests.

Backus v. Baptist Medical Ctr.

United States District Court, Eastern District of Arkansas, 1981.
510 F.Supp. 1191, *vac'd and dismissed as moot*, 671 F.2d 1100 (8th Cir. 1982).

ROY, District Judge.

Plaintiff Gregory Backus is an adult male who was graduated as a registered nurse (R.N.) and certified by the State of Arkansas to perform nursing services in May 1978. At the time of his graduation he was already training as a student nurse at the Baptist Medical Center Hospital in Little Rock, Arkansas, assigned to the obstetrics and gynecology department (OB–GYN) of the hospital as a student nurse.

Defendant Baptist Medical Center is a private hospital incorporated pursuant to the laws of the State of Arkansas, and it provides extensive medical services, among which are gynecological and obstetrical care.

Defendant makes its facilities available to physicians practicing throughout the community. Currently there are eleven physicians who are actually involved in the delivery of babies, and of these eleven, two are female. Defendant also provides a support staff which includes nurses and orderlies.

On April 19, 1978, plaintiff Backus requested placement as a full-time registered nurse in the labor and delivery section of the OB–GYN department. On April 24, 1978, the Assistant Administrator of the Nursing Division refused his request. Plaintiff appealed to J. A. Gilbreath, Executive Director of the Baptist system, and was again refused. Plaintiff did begin work as an R.N. in the intensive care nursery, a part of the OB–GYN department.

On January 3, 1979, Backus renewed his request to work in the labor and delivery section of the OB–GYN department. He was refused his request on January 5, 1979, on the basis that the hospital "did not employ male R.N.'s in the OB–GYN positions because of the concern of our female patients for privacy and personal dignity which make it impossible for a male employee to perform the duties of this position effectively."

. . . There are few duties which a registered nurse can perform in relation to an obstetrical patient which are not sensitive or intimate. Among the duties performed by the nurse in the labor room are the following: checking the cervix for dilation, shaving the perineum, giving an enema, assisting in the expulsion of the enema and sterilizing the vaginal area. In the recovery room the nurse checks the patient for bleeding, gives massages to the uterus, and changes perineal pads.

At Baptist Medical Center obstetrical patients are randomly assigned to a nurse upon admittance to the hospital. This nurse is not selected by the patient and is a stranger to her. The labor and delivery nurses perform intimate functions. Defendant contends that if a male nurse is performing these duties, the patient's constitutional right to privacy is violated. We agree with the defendant.

The Court finds merit in defendant's contention that the majority of women patients will object to intimate contact with a member of the opposite sex. Once a patient becomes dissatisfied with a service that the defendant offers, it is probable that the patient will seek future medical care elsewhere. In addition to offending future patients, a male nurse would necessitate the presence of a female nurse to protect the hospital from charges of molestation. This unnecessary duplication of manpower would result in higher salary costs. . . .

Due to the intimate touching required in labor and delivery, services of all male nurses are inappropriate. Male nurses are not inadequate due to some trait equated with their sex; rather, it is their very sex itself which makes all male nurses unacceptable.

. . . The fact that the plaintiff is a health care professional does not eliminate the fact that he is an *unselected individual* who is intruding on the obstetrical patient's right to privacy. The male nurse's situation is not analogous to that of the male doctor *who has been selected* by the patient.

It follows that requiring labor and delivery nurses to be female is a bona fide occupational qualification (BFOQ) which is "reasonably necessary to the normal operation of [its] particular business or enterprise." . . .

Plaintiff's complaint is hereby dismissed with prejudice.

STUDY QUESTIONS

1. What reason did Judge Roy cite in support of the conclusion that the interest at stake here is the constitutional right of privacy, rather than customer preference?

2. Had the court ruled in favor of Mr. Backus, would this hospital have been put at a competitive disadvantage to other medical facilities in the area? Would the decision affect only Baptist Medical Center?

3. In *Dothard,* the Supreme Court found that in the situation of the Alabama prisons of the time, the "very womanhood" of the complaining parties prevented them from effectively performing their duties. Did the court here make a similar argument about Backus's "very manhood"? Was Backus being regarded as a nurse or as a sex object? Does Justice Marshall's remark about "professionalism" in footnote 5 of his dissent in *Dothard* apply here?

IV. REMEDIES

A paramount practical concern of parties who litigate disputes under fair employment practices (FEP) laws is the sanctions that courts are likely to impose once violations are found. It is the prospect of benefiting from such sanctions that provides the motivation for aggrieved parties to bring actions and carry them through to completion. It is the prospect of being burdened by such sanctions that provides the motivation for employers to vigorously defend themselves in these actions.

The sanctions that courts are authorized to impose for discrimination in an employment context differ somewhat depending on the statute or statutes under which the violation is found. There are, as we have seen, a number of statutes prohibiting employment discrimination at both federal and state levels. Our discussion will focus primarily on the sanctions available under Title VII. Success in obtaining remedies available under Title VII requires compliance with the particular procedures set out in the statute.

Three themes run through those subsections of the statute that deal with procedure. First, they give high priority to resolving complaints by means of conciliation, rather than litigation. For this reason, a person is not permitted to file a Title VII action in federal court until the EEOC has had the opportunity to investigate the charge and to eliminate the problem by means of persuasion. The second is one of accommodation to the interests of states in promoting equal employment opportunity. Thus, those states that have their own FEP laws must be allowed the opportunity to act on their own FEP laws before the EEOC can assert jurisdiction. The third theme concerns timeliness. All steps have deadlines. For example, a victim has 180 days to file a charge with the EEOC (300 if it occurred in a state with its own FEP laws). The CRA of 1991 added a provision clarifying when the clock begins to run on some of these deadlines. An intentionally discriminatory seniority system can be challenged within 180 (300) days either of its initial adoption, when it becomes applicable to the complaining party, or when the complaining party is injured by its application. A victim may demand a "right to sue letter" 180 days after the charge is filed with the EEOC, even if the EEOC has not taken action on it, but must generally file a suit in federal court within 90 days of receipt of that letter.

One of the most important procedural points to remember is where to file a complaint. If the employer suspected of violating a provision of Title VII is the federal government, the complaint must be filed with the Civil Service Commission. If the employer is not a unit of the federal government, the complaint must be filed with the EEOC. Initiation of a complaint with the EEOC requires the completion of a simple form by the person who claims to have been victimized. Although this phase of proceedings under Title VII may be completed without the assistance of a lawyer, that assistance is often helpful.

The primary source of the authority of the courts to impose sanctions under Title VII is section 706(g). The original language of that section is as follows:

> If the court finds that the respondent has intentionally engaged in or is intentionally engaging in an unlawful employment practice charged in the complaint, the court may enjoin the respondent from engaging in such unlawful employment practice, and order such affirmative action as may be appropriate, which may include, but is not limited to, reinstatement or hiring of employees, with or without back pay . . . or any other equitable relief as the court deems appropriate.

In general, the sanctions imposed under Title VII are designed to offset the harm suffered as a result of violations. Although the language of section 706(g) restricts remedies to "intentional" violations, in this context, the term "intentional" has been interpreted to mean simply that the practice was not accidental, *Rowe v. General*

Motors Corp., 457 F.2d 348 (5th Cir. 1972). The type of sanction imposed corresponds to the type of violation found: where the defendant has refused to hire the plaintiff on unlawful grounds, the courts have ordered that the plaintiff be hired; where the plaintiff has been fired on discriminatory grounds, the courts have ordered reinstatement; and where the employer has paid the plaintiff at a lower rate in violation of the statute, the courts have ordered back pay. Where the plaintiff has unlawfully been denied a promotion to a better paying job, but promotion cannot be ordered because the position is filled, the courts have ordered front pay, i.e., a cash award equal to the difference between the victim's future earnings in her present job and what she would have earned in the position unlawfully denied her. For plaintiffs unlawfully denied seniority, the courts have ordered these rights restored. As indicated in section 706(g), the courts may issue court orders or injunctions to prevent unlawful employment practices from occurring and from continuing. These are the main forms of relief granted by courts in Title VII cases where the plaintiff prevails. Others will be discussed in the course of this section.

Sanctions imposed by the law are sometimes discussed in terms of the purposes they are designed to serve. Three such purposes are often distinguished. As we will see, a given form of relief might be ordered for more than one of these purposes. The first purpose is to compensate the victim of wrongdoing, to make the victim whole, to restore the victim to her or his "rightful place," i.e., the status that the victim would have enjoyed had she or he not been wronged. Back pay is often ordered for a compensatory purpose. Other types of compensatory remedies include monetary awards for emotional stress and humiliation or actual expenses incurred as a result of discrimination. Another form of monetary relief regularly awarded to plaintiffs who prevail under Title VII is attorney's fees. This type of remedy requires the defendant to pay the reasonable attorney's fees incurred by the plaintiff. These awards are specifically provided by the statute in section 706(k).

A second purpose for imposing sanctions is to penalize a wrongdoer. Examples of sanctions imposed for this purpose are usually found in the context of criminal law, although punitive damages are sometimes awarded in civil contexts. These remedies are ordinarily not available under Title VII or most state antidiscrimination laws.

The third purpose for imposing legal sanctions is the least familiar to the general public. It is to prevent a wrong from occurring. Remedies imposed for that purpose are called "prophylactic remedies." The best example of such a remedy is the traditional equitable remedy, an injunction. This is a court order directing the employer to avoid engaging in the challenged practice. These orders may bind the employer either temporarily until the dispute is settled at trial or permanently. Permanent injunctions are imposed after a trial on the merits. Injunctions are regularly issued under Title VII and state fair employment provisions.

Just as legal sanctions can be understood from the perspective of the purposes for which they are imposed, they can also be understood from the perspective of the consequences they produce. The consequences provide incentives for future behavior. The concept of prophylactic remedies relies on this. Unless the prospect of being held in contempt of court provides an incentive for a party to comply with an injunction, such a remedy will not prevent the occurrence of wrongful acts. The same can be said for at least one theory of punitive remedies as well, viz., the deterrence theory of punishment.

Compensatory remedies also create incentives. In the following decision, the Supreme Court indicated how back pay remedies available under Title VII are to be awarded for both compensatory and prophylactic purposes. The Court indicated that the expectation of a back pay award provides an incentive, "a spur or catalyst," for employers to examine their practices and to eliminate those that might lay them open to liability under Title VII. It should also be noted that the expectation of back pay provides incentive for victims of employment discrimination to complain to the EEOC and to bring suit under Title VII. Such remedies provide an answer to the "What's in it for me?" question, whether asked by employer or employee. Indeed, it is the availability of remedies that makes a practical difference in the type and frequency of discriminatory behavior.

The courts have broad discretion under the authority of section 706(g) in fashioning remedies for the relief of those who have been unlawfully denied employment opportunities. The term "equitable relief" in the statute refers to a longstanding distinction between "legal" remedies and "equitable" remedies dating back to early English practices. Legal remedies, for example, awards of money damages, are those that have historically been available in the King's "law courts," while equitable remedies, for example, injunctions, are those that have historically been available "in equity," that is, from the King's Chancellor. Equity traditionally was more flexible and more concerned with doing justice. Today, most American jurisdictions have combined their law and equity courts. The distinction, nevertheless, continues to have important consequences. One of these is that the right of a jury trial guaranteed by the constitution is limited to claims that would traditionally have been tried in law courts. Claims for equitable relief are heard by judges sitting alone.

One deficiency in the original design of Title VII was that it provided for the award of make-whole remedies but not monetary damages. In this respect, it contrasted unfavorably with the 1866 Civil Rights Act (section 1981), which afforded compensatory and punitive damages to individuals who successfully claimed that they had suffered from intentional racial discrimination in employment settings. The CRA of 1991 partially removed that asymmetry by providing that a victim of intentional discrimination on the basis of race, color, religion, sex, or national origin who cannot recover damages under section 1981 may recover compensatory and punitive damages under Title VII in addition to make-whole relief.

The 1991 act placed a cap on the amount of monetary damages available to those victims, depending on the size of the employer's workforce. These range from fifty thousand dollars where the business employees one hundred or fewer people (95 percent of all businesses) to a maximum of three hundred thousand dollars for those that employ over five hundred. No such cap affects damage awards under section 1981. Legislation was introduced in both houses of Congress in 1992 to remove this cap on damage awards.

At the same time, the CRA of 1991 provided for trial by jury in Title VII cases where intentional discrimination is claimed and damages are demanded. Some knowledgeable practitioners believe that, of all the provisions of the CRA, this one will have the most favorable impact on the interests of complaining parties. The expectation is that the jury trial option will make favorable findings both as to liability and amount of damages much more likely.

In the case that follows, the Supreme Court identified the primary objective of Title VII remedies. In its opinion, the Court indicated the rationale that is to guide lower courts as they fashion remedies appropriate to successful plaintiffs. The decision also brings into focus many of the distinctions discussed in these introductory remarks.

Albemarle Paper Co. v. Moody

Supreme Court of the
United States, 1975.
422 U.S. 405, 95 S.Ct. 2362,
45 L.Ed.2d 280.

Mr. Justice STEWART delivered the opinion of the Court.

. . . The respondents—plaintiffs in the District Court—are a certified class of present and former Negro employees at a paper mill in Roanoke Rapids, N. C.; the petitioners—defendants in the District Court—are the plant's owner, the Albemarle Paper Co., and the plant employees' labor union, Halifax Local No. 425. In August 1966, after filing a complaint with the Equal Employment Opportunity Commission (EEOC), and receiving notice of their right to sue, the respondents brought a class action in the United States District Court for the Eastern District of North Carolina, asking permanent injunctive relief against "any policy, practice, custom or usage" at the plant that violated Title VII. The respondents assured the court that the suit involved no claim for any monetary awards on a class basis, but in June 1970, after several years of discovery, the respondents moved to add a class demand for backpay. The court ruled that this issue would be considered at trial.

At the trial, in July and August 1971, the major issues were the plant's seniority system, its program of employment testing, and the question of backpay. In its opinion of November 9, 1971, the court found that the petitioners had "strictly segregated" the plant's departmental "lines of progression" prior to January 1, 1964, reserving the higher paying and more skilled lines for whites. The "racial identifiability" of whole lines of progression persisted until 1968, when the lines were reorganized under a new collective-bargaining agreement. The court found, however, that this reorganization left Negro employees " 'locked' in the lower paying job classifications." The formerly "Negro" lines of progression had been merely tacked on to the bottom of the formerly "white" lines, and promotions, demotions, and layoffs continued to be governed—where skills were "relatively equal"—by a system of "job seniority." Because of the plant's previous history of overt segregation, only whites had seniority in the higher job categories. Accordingly, the court ordered the petitioners to implement a system of "plantwide" seniority.

The court refused, however, to award backpay to the plaintiff class for losses suffered under the "job seniority" program. . . .

. . . Relying directly on *Newman v. Piggie Park Enterprises,* the Court of Appeals reversed, holding that backpay could be denied only in "special circumstances." The petitioners argue that the Court of Appeals was in error—that a district court has virtually unfettered discretion to award or deny backpay, and that there was no abuse of that discretion here.

Piggie Park Enterprises is not directly in point. The Court held there that attorneys' fees should "ordinarily" be awarded—*i. e.,* in all but "special circumstances"—to plaintiffs successful in obtaining injunctions against discrimination in public accommodations, under Title II of the Civil Rights Act of 1964. While the Act appears to leave Title II fee awards to the district court's discretion, the court determined that the great public interest in having injunctive actions brought could be vindicated only if successful plaintiffs, acting as "private attorneys general," were awarded attorneys' fees in all but very unusual circumstances. There is, of course, an equally strong public interest in having injunctive actions brought under Title VII, to eradicate discriminatory employment practices. But this interest can be vindicated by applying the *Piggie Park* standard to the *attorneys' fees* provision of Title VII. For guidance as to the granting and denial of *backpay,* one must, therefore, look elsewhere.

The petitioners contend that the statutory scheme provides no guidance, beyond indicating that backpay awards are within the District Court's discretion. We disagree. It is true that backpay is not an automatic or mandatory remedy; like all other remedies under the Act, it is one which the courts "may" invoke. The scheme implicitly recognizes that there may be cases calling for one remedy but not another, and—owing to the structure of the federal judiciary—these choices are, of course, left in the first instance to the district courts. However, such discretionary choices are not left to a court's "inclination, but to its judgment; and its judgment is to be guided by sound legal principles." The power to award backpay was bestowed by Congress, as part of a complex legislative design directed at a historic evil of national proportions. A court must exercise this power "in light of the large objectives of the Act." . . .

The District Court's decision must therefore be measured against the purposes which inform Title VII. As the Court observed in *Griggs v. Duke Power Co.,* the primary objective was a prophylactic one:

> "It was to achieve equality of employment opportunities and remove barriers that have operated in the past to favor an identifiable group of white employees over other employees."

Backpay has an obvious connection with this purpose. If employers faced only the prospect of an injunctive order, they would have little incentive to shun practices of dubious legality. It is the reasonably certain prospect of a backpay award that "provides[s] the spur or catalyst which causes employers and unions to self-examine and to self-evaluate their employment practices and to endeavor to eliminate, so far as possible, the last vestiges of an unfortunate and ignominious page in this country's history."

It is also the purpose of Title VII to make persons whole for injuries suffered on account of unlawful employment discrimination. This is shown by the very fact that Congress took care to arm the courts with full equitable powers. For it is the historic purpose of equity to "secur[e] complete justice." "[W]here federally protected rights have been invaded, it has been the rule from the beginning that courts will be alert to adjust their remedies so as to grant the necessary relief." Title VII deals with legal injuries of an economic character occasioned by racial or other antiminority discrimination. The terms "complete justice" and "necessary relief" have acquired a clear meaning in such circumstances. Where racial discrimination is concerned, "the [district] court has not merely the

power but the duty to render a decree which will so far as possible eliminate the discriminatory effects of the past as well as bar like discrimination in the future." And where a legal injury is of an economic character.

> "[t]he general rule is, that when a wrong has been done, and the law gives a remedy, the compensation shall be equal to the injury. The latter is the standard by which the former is to be measured. The injured party is to be placed, as near as may be, in the situation he would have occupied if the wrong had not been committed." . . .

. . . Congress' purpose in vesting a variety of "discretionary" powers in the courts was not to limit appellate review of trial courts, or to invite inconsistency and caprice, but rather to make possible the "fashion[ing] [of] the most complete relief possible."

It follows that, given a finding of unlawful discrimination, backpay should be denied only for reasons which, if applied generally, would not frustrate the central statutory purposes of eradicating discrimination throughout the economy and making persons whole for injuries suffered through past discrimination. The courts of appeals must maintain a consistent and principled application of the backpay provision, consonant with the twin statutory objectives, while at the same time recognizing that the trial court will often have the keener appreciation of those facts and circumstances peculiar to particular cases. . . .

[Vacated and remanded.]

STUDY QUESTIONS

1. Explain how the prospect of a back pay award provides "the spur and catalyst" for the employer mentioned by the Court.
2. Explain how the magnitude of a compensatory or make-whole remedy is to be decided and measured. What is the doctrine of "rightful place"?
3. What rule did the Court adopt for back pay awards under Title VII? Do you think that provides adequate incentive for employers? Does it provide incentive for employees who believe they have been unlawfully treated?

In *Albemarle,* the Court emphasized that the primary objective of Title VII was preventive or "prophylactic." The strong emphasis on compensatory or make-whole remedies derives from that objective. These latter remedies, such as back pay, put victims in their "rightful places." Such remedies also motivate employers to prevent violations from occurring. In this way, back pay and other compensatory remedies further the prophylactic objective of the statute. A similar argument can be made for the award of compensatory damages, i.e., cash awards used to compensate victims for such injuries as mental distress and the expense of seeking other employment. A further deterrent might include punitive damages, i.e., cash awards that express condemnation of the employer for malicious conduct. Since the statutory authority for awarding damages was enacted only in 1991, the courts will probably require a few years to develop the standards that will govern their award.

In *Albemarle,* the Court endorsed the principle that, in relevant cases, back pay may be denied only where consistent with the strong prophylactic objective of the statute. One year later, the Court asserted the same principle regarding the award of seniority denied to victims of unlawful discrimination in hiring, *Franks v. Bowman Transportation Co.,* 424 U.S. 747 (1976).

In its discussion of *Piggie Park,* the Court referred to another type of remedy available under Title VII, viz., attorney's fees. This remedy, authorized by section 706(k), was developed by the Congress to encourage aggrieved employees to bring actions against employers that they believe have violated the statute. This is the "private attorneys general" theory of this remedy. Potential plaintiffs are provided an extra incentive to sue by raising the prospect of having the fees of their attorneys paid by the defendant if their suit is successful. The Court also allows the award of attorney's fees to a prevailing defendant where the plaintiff's action is found to be "frivolous, unreasonable, and without foundation," *Christianburg Garment Co. v. EEOC,* 434 U.S. 412 (1978).

In considering sanctions that the courts may impose for a violation of Title VII, it is essential to keep two points in mind. On the one hand, although trial courts have broad discretion in these matters, their discretion is limited by legal principles deriving from the objective of the statute. On the other hand, decisions about remedies are not, in the words of the Court in *Albemarle,* "automatic or mandatory." The language of section 706(g) underscores the fact that in deciding what sanctions will be imposed, trial courts are concerned to "secure complete justice." In so doing, they must fashion remedies in particular situations that balance three concerns: the concern for vindicating the rights of plaintiffs who prevail on the merits; the concern for securing the rights of defendants against sanctions not warranted by the facts of the case; and the concern for avoiding unnecessary sacrifice of the interests of third parties. The following case illustrates these points.

Mitchell v. Mid-Continent Spring Co.

United States Court of Appeals, Sixth Circuit, 1978.
583 F.2d 275, *cert. denied,* 441 U.S. 922 (1979).

WEICK, Circuit Judge.

This class action was brought in the District Court by plaintiff-appellee, Mrs. Jane Mitchell (Mitchell), against defendant-appellant, Mid-Continent Spring Company of Kentucky (Mid-Continent), a corporation, her employer, alleging sex discrimination against her and on account of her discharge for engaging in protected activity, in violation of § 703(a) of Title VII

VII of the Civil Rights Act of 1964, and requesting equitable relief. . . .

Following a bench trial the District Court found in favor of Mitchell and her class, in all respects. The issue of back pay was referred to a Special Master, who recommended that Mitchell recover on her individual claim $24,528.86 in back pay, and that an additional $222,885 be divided among all members of the plaintiff class, according to a formula and certain qualifying criteria. The Court accepted these recommendations and entered judgment therefor, and ordered Mitchell reinstated if she desired; and, in addition, the Court awarded Mitchell and the class a total of $75,000 in attorneys' fees, plus expenses of $2,427.32. Finally, the Court ordered injunctive relief against further discrimination and imposed an affirmative action plan, including the imposition of a quota of 33 ⅓% of all new female employees to be assigned to formerly male job classifications, for the next five years, and 33 ⅓% of all newly hired males to be assigned to formerly female job classifications for the next five years. Mid-Continent was also required to make reports to plaintiff's attorneys.

For the reasons that follow, we are of the view that the judgment of the District Court should be affirmed only with respect to relief granted plaintiff Mitchell, individually, and the injunction against further discrimination. We reverse the judgment with respect to the issue of class-wide liability for back pay, totaling $222,885, the affirmative action plan involving quotas, and the award of attorneys' fees plus expenses.

I

Mitchell was first employed by Mid-Continent on August 6, 1962. In early 1969 she contacted the Wage and Hour Division of the United States Department of Labor, alleging that the Company discriminated against female production workers. An investigation was made during the period of July 2–18, 1969, by Compliance Officer Herbert L. Livingston. At the conclusion of his investigation Livingston advised Louis Langhi, President of Mid-Continent, that although no violations of the Equal Pay Act had been found to exist, the Company's practice of assigning higher-paying jobs exclusively to males (which will be discussed further, below)

appeared in his opinion to be in violation of Title VII. Livingston recommended that Langhi contact the EEOC for assistance in bringing the company into compliance.

Langhi became incapacitated subsequently in 1971, because of brain surgery which left him virtually unable to speak, and partially paralyzed. His wife then assumed control of the company.

On or about July 29, 1969 Mitchell mailed a letter of complaint to the Cleveland Regional Office of the EEOC. This letter constituted a charge of discrimination under EEOC guidelines. The EEOC replied on August 1, enclosing two blank EEOC charge forms, one for plaintiff's use and one for the possible use of employee, Louise McGehee, who had been promoted from her lower-paying machine operator position to a higher-paying inspection position, immediately after the Wage and Hour investigation.

On August 7 Mitchell approached McGehee, while in the company parking lot, before working hours, and asked her if she would like to make a complaint. McGehee refused, and reported to her foreman, Clyde Warren, that Mitchell had asked her to sign a complaint regarding wages, which complaint was to be sent to the federal government.

On August 11, 1969, Jane Mitchell was instructed to come to the office of Ward Mitchell (no relation to Jane), the company's plant superintendent. Clyde Warren and others were present at the meeting. There was discussion about the Government papers that Mitchell had been circulating, after which Ward Mitchell took from his desk drawer Jane Mitchell's final paycheck, which was already prepared. In Mitchell's words, he said, "I'm going to tell you, you are a good worker, but you're a trouble maker. . . . I'm going to have to let you go."

On August 14, Jane Mitchell made a second complaint to the EEOC, charging a retaliatory discharge. She was granted leave by the EEOC to file this suit.

On the basis of this evidence the District Court found that Mitchell was fired in retaliation for having engaged in protected activity in violation of § 704(a) of Title VII. She was awarded back pay of $24,528.86, and, if she so desired, was ordered reinstated in her previous employment with full seniority and benefits. . . .

II

Mid-Continent is a manufacturer of precision springs. The plant contains fifteen departments, each headed by a foreman, and each department consists of a separate job category. The manufacturing process begins when wire of the proper specifications is sent to the coiling department, where the machines are "set up" to produce springs according to customer specifications. After coiling, the springs are tempered by heat-treatment and then tested. At this point the springs are sent to other various departments for further processing: to Secondary Operations for sizing on a "kick press," if needed; to the grinding room; to "hopper-looper," where loops are placed on the ends of the springs; to "four-slide," where angles are formed in the springs; to torsion, which further coils springs and attaches "legs"; or to the paint department.

In both Secondary and Grinding operations the work is light, and the female machine operators in these departments remain seated while working. In Secondary, the female workers operate kick presses, and in Grinding they load and unload grinding machines, both relatively unskilled tasks. In the other departments, however, the work is heavier and is more difficult. In the set-up functions, workers are required to make precise, mathematical computations and adjustments with complex machinery in accordance with both blueprints and written specifications. These functions require skill and training, which many women either do not possess or do not desire to undertake. Other positions require various amounts of lifting of heavy coils of wire and quantities of springs, exposure to high temperatures, and untidy work conditions. These departments also require employees to work during the second or night shift when necessary to fill customers' orders. Married women who have young children, or who live in the country, did not like the night shift.

Consequently, employees who perform these more difficult jobs are higher paid than are machine operators in the Secondary and Grinding departments. These more difficult jobs have been performed traditionally by men employed by the company. As of August 6, 1973, machine operators started at $2.10 per hour and reached a maximum of $2.35 per hour after eighteen months. Set-up jobs, on the other hand, paid $2.20 per hour to start and reached a maximum of $2.95 per hour after four years. The remaining job classifications at Mid-Continent were also higher-paid than machine operators, starting at $2.20 per hour and reaching $2.75 per hour after four years. . . .

The [District] Court concluded that the practice of steering females into the lowest-paying positions constituted discrimination and segregation on the basis of sex in violation of § 703(a) of Title VII. The company's discriminatory shift-transfer and seniority policies were held to be further violations.

We affirm these holdings as supported by substantial evidence. . . .

III

[The court next reversed the award of classwide back pay because the lower court had erroneously placed the burden of proof for each claimant's ineligibility for back pay on the employer.]

IV

In its conclusions of law entered November 22, 1974, the District Court held:

> 20. The Court is aware that affirmative relief will be required to insure equal job opportunities at the Mid-Continent plant for present female employees and to insure that future hires will be assigned on a non-discriminatory basis.
>
> 21. The Court is further aware that affirmative action on the part of Mid-Continent is essential to remedy the continuing consequences of past discrimination, and to insure that all employees understand that Mid-Continent is henceforth committed to equality of employment opportunity without regard to the sex of the employee.

Accordingly, the Court in its judgment of October 14, 1976, properly enjoined Mid-Continent from further discriminatory classifications and practices. The Court went further, however, and ordered an affirmative action plan as well. The Court ordered that for five years all vacancies in previously all-male positions were to be first offered to current female employees in order of seniority, and at least one-third of those persons transferring into such positions were to be female. Also, for a period of five years one-third of all newly-hired females were to be assigned to previously all male jobs, and one-third of all newly-hired males were to be assigned to previously all-female jobs. This plan was stayed by the District Court pending appeal.

We reverse this portion of the judgment, finding nothing in the record to justify such affirmative relief. Indeed, the Court's 1974 conclusion that affirmative action would be necessary is undercut by the subsequent findings of its Special Master. On May 13, 1976, in denying back pay for 1975 and succeeding years, the Special Master stated:

> The evidence presented at the hearing before the Special Master indicates that the defendant made several more bonafide [sic] offers for job transfers to female employees during 1975 and 1976 [in addition to those in 1974], and that female employees began to bid on these jobs during 1975. Currently, two female employees are working in what were formerly male jobs. The Special Master has determined that *the "residual effects" of the company's prior practices and policies diminished greatly in 1975* as female employees began to realize that *formerly male jobs were, in fact, open to them.* [Emphasis added.]

The Special Master added that although no injunction had at that time been issued by the District Court, it was the Special Master's belief that the Court's 1974 findings against the defendant "may have had some effect" in eliminating the residual effects of defendant's prior discrimination.

In view of the eventual issuance of the injunctive relief and the finding that all jobs were, in fact, open to females, we see no factual justification for the imposition of the affirmative action plan.

V

We also vacate the allowance of attorneys' fees of $75,000 and expenses in the amount of $2,427.32. . . .

The judgment of the District Court is affirmed in part, reversed in part, and vacated in part, as hereinbefore ordered, and is remanded with instructions to conduct further proceedings consistent with this opinion. Costs in connection with Mitchell's individual claim are to be assessed against Mid-Continent as well as costs incurred by it.

[Upon rehearing the court reinstated the award of attorney's fees. 587 F.2d. 841(1978).]

STUDY QUESTIONS

1. List the types of remedies awarded by the district court.
2. For what violation was Jane Mitchell awarded back pay and reinstatement? Do those remedies appear well designed to return her to her "rightful place"? Might they also deter Ward Mitchell from retaliatory behavior in the future?
3. What purpose led the district court to issue an injunction? To impose an "affirmative action plan"? Why was one upheld on appeal and the other rejected? Was that reasonable?

The relief granted here include an injunction, back pay, reinstatement, and attorney's fees. Affirmative action promotion quotas were rejected by the appellate court. Each of these remedies was fashioned to balance the concerns of the complainant to be restored to her rightful place, of the employer to avoid sanctions that were not warranted by its violations, and of present and future employees to be treated by their employer without regard to their sex. The prospect of an award of back pay and of attorney's fees and the opportunity of reinstatement were designed to put Mitchell in the position that she would have occupied had she not been the victim of unlawful sexual discrimination and retaliation. The injunction, in addition to the other measures, was designed to force the employer to stop engaging in unlawful sex discrimination. The affirmative action measure was rejected because it was unnecessary to accomplish the prophylactic purposes of the statute.

5 Working Conditions and Compensation

This chapter treats two strategically important problem areas. These problems, sexual harassment on the job and the earnings gap, are well known. Both affect us all, men as well as women, directly or indirectly, whether we are in the full-time labor force or not. This chapter reviews the principal legal methods and strategies that have been developed over the past two decades for dealing with these forms of sex discrimination.

The principal legal instruments for combating sex discrimination in employment are statutes. At the federal level, the base of the push for more equal employment opportunities is Title VII of the Civil Rights Act of 1964. The main aspects of that statute, the principles used by the courts to interpret it, and remedies available to victims of unlawful employment practices under it were discussed in Chapter 4.

I. SEXUAL HARASSMENT

Discussions of this topic often founder on the way that the phrase is used. For now, we can adopt a working definition of sexual harassment simply as any unwelcome sexual attention. A moment's reflection reveals that sexual harassment is everywhere and extends over a broad spectrum of behavior from forcible rape and unwanted touching to rude inquiries and crude boasting. As in other contexts, sexual harassment in the workplace can be blatant—"have sex with me or you're fired"—or more subtle—comments on the anatomy of one's fellow workers. Although debate persists about the magnitude of the problem, an increasing body of information supports the contention that the frequency of sexual harassment in the workplace is very significant.

How Pervasive Is Sexual Harassment?

Charles S. Clark, "Sexual Harassment."
1 *CQ Researcher* 539, 542–3 (1991).

Reprinted by permission of publisher

Gauging the actual incidence of sexual harassment is difficult, both because definitions of the term are mercurial and, according to some critics, because the problem's seriousness may be exaggerated by ideologues or management consultants who specialize in sexual harassment cases.

Several surveys covering disparate sectors of society have varied widely in their findings.

The first broadscale effort to measure sexual harassment was conducted by *Redbook* magazine, which surveyed 9,000 women in 1976. Eighty-eight percent of the respondents said they had been victims of harassment and 52 percent said they had been fired or induced to quit a job because of it.

In 1980, a survey was conducted among 20,000 federal workers by the U.S. Merit Systems Protection Board (MSPB), the grievance arbitration board for government employees. Forty-two percent of the females and 15 percent of the males responding said they had been sexually harassed. (An updated, smaller survey conducted by the board in 1987 produced nearly identical results.) According to the MSPB, victims of harassment tended to be young, not married, college-educated, members of a minority racial or ethnic group (if male), in a trainee position (or office/clerical positions, if male), in a non-traditional position (female law enforcement officers or male secretaries), to have an immediate supervisor of the opposite sex or to have an immediate work group composed predominantly of the opposite sex.

The most recent large-scale survey of sexual harassment was released in September 1990 by the Department of Defense. Of 20,000 U.S. military respondents around the world, 64 percent of the females reported having been sexually harassed, some directly, others in subtler ways such as being subjected to catcalls, dirty looks and teasing. (Only 17 percent of the males reported being harassed.) Of those women reporting direct harassment, 38 percent said they had been touched or "cornered," 15 percent said they had been pressured for sexual favors (compared with only 2 percent of males) and 5 percent said they had been victims of rape or attempted rape.

In the corporate world, recent surveys indicate that 15 percent of women have been sexually harassed within the past year, according to Freada Klein, an organizational development expert who specializes in sexual harassment.

Surveys on college campuses show the number of respondents reporting to have been sexually harassed ranging from 40–70 percent.

Bernice R. Sandler, a college specialist at the Center for Women Policy Studies in Washington, says only 2 percent of campus harassment cases involve a professor demanding sex in return for a good grade. Most sexual harassment on campus involves male and female students, she says. On several campuses recently, college men have been taken to task for a practice known as "scoping"—loudly rating the physical attributes of women as they walk by. Sometimes the men will surround a woman and demand that she bare her breasts.

The steadiest barometer of the ebbs and flows of sexual harassment is the number of such complaints filed with EEOC offices. The number of complaints (of which those found to have merit is a fraction) has risen slightly in recent years, reaching 5,557 in 1990. The 1986 Supreme Court decision expanding the definition of sexual harassment to include incidents that create a hostile work environment may account for some of the increase. . . .

Women's groups and others who favor an activist approach to combating sexual harassment say the incidence is significantly underreported. "Women used to think there was nothing they could do about it," says Isabelle Katz Pinzler, director of the women's rights project at the ACLU. Many women decline to file charges for fear of confronting superiors, being labeled a troublemaker or subjecting their personal lives to scrutiny.

The American population at large does not appear to believe that sexual harassment is rampant. Only 26 percent of the women responding to a national survey conducted in September 1986 said they had experienced sexual harassment at work. Only 17 percent of the women and 16 percent of the men thought sexual harassment was "a big problem"; 67 percent of both men and women said it was "somewhat of a problem."

STUDY QUESTIONS

1. What proportion of women employees reported to the MSPB that they were victims of sexual harassment? How did that survey characterize the typical victim? Does the MSPB survey hold any surprises for you?

2. What forms do harassing behaviors take in the military? On college and university campuses?

3. As of August 1986, what proportion of the public thought that sexual harassment was a "big problem"?

———————————— ৰ্ছ ————————————

Although sexual harassment is commonplace, it had not been widely acknowledged, even among those whose lives were most severely affected by it. It was one of the dirty secrets of our culture. That changed on October 11, 1991. On that day, law professor Anita Hill broke the silence. Testifying at a nationally televised hearing of the all-male Senate Judiciary Committee, Hill alleged in vivid detail how Supreme Court nominee Clarence Thomas had sexually harassed her in the early 1980s when he was her supervisor in the Department of Education and the EEOC.

The sharp contrast between the poise and courage shown by Hill and the obtuse and often mean-spirited response of committee members staggered a great many viewers, both women and men. It was clear that the Senators did not comprehend the seriousness and pervasiveness of sexual harassment. Two types of reactions were common among viewers. "They just don't get it, the men, they just don't get it!" was a widespread sentiment. Women and men apparently do not perceive sexual harassment in the same way. Another common reaction took the form of self-examination: Has this happened to me? Have I done this to someone else? As these questions were pursued, the nation began to glimpse the dimensions of the problem.

A second watershed event affecting the nation's consciousness of sexual harassment took place in 1991. The annual convention of the Tailhook Association, a professional organization of active duty and retired Navy flying officers, held that year in a Las Vegas hotel from September 4th to 7th, was the scene of massive sexual harassment. After repeated attempts to hide the ugly details by Navy officials at various levels, the Pentagon's inspector general released the final report of his investigation in April 1993. According to the report, 83 women and seven men were sexually assaulted during the drunken revel. The report said that as many as 175 officers may face disciplinary action as a result of their involvement and suggested that the cases of 30 Navy admirals and 2 Marine generals present at the meeting be reviewed. The adverse publicity received by the Navy and the military generally over the two year period leading up to the final report prompted a commitment on the part of the Clinton administration to fundamentally changing the culture of the military from one that condones, if not encourages, sexual harassment of women to one that respects and values women who serve their country in the uniform of the military services.

Clark noted that sexual harassment in the workplace was not widely acknowledged as "a big problem" as of September 1986. Since the Hill-Thomas hearings and the Tailhook scandal, that has changed sharply. One measure is the volume of complaints alleging sexual harassment filed with the EEOC. These doubled in the six months following the hearing. Another indication of changed attitudes is political activity. In November 1992, a record eleven women stood for election to the U.S. Senate. In addition, 107 women were on the ballot for the House of Representatives, a 54 percent increase over 1990.

As these reactions spread, a new level of intensity was introduced into an already ongoing course of legal events. The following selection reviews the ways that individual activists, feminist organizations, and legal scholars contributed to these developments.

How We Got Here: From Carmita Wood to Anita Hill

Susan Brownmiller and
Dolores Alexander.
Ms., January/February 1992. Pp. 70–1.

Professor Anita Hill's testimony last October at the Senate Judiciary Committee hearing may have been some people's first exposure to the legal concept of sexual harassment on the job, but the issue had been named and developed in the mid 1970s.

The women's movement was full blown by the time Lin Farley, a 29-year-old activist, was teaching an experimental course on women and work at Cornell University in 1974. During a consciousness-raising session with her class, students talked about disturbing behavior they had been subjected to on summer jobs; in all the cases, the women had been forced off the job by these unwanted advances.

Coincidentally, Carmita Wood, a 44-year-old administrative assistant, walked out of the office a Cornell physicist after becoming physically ill from the stress of fending off his advances. When Ms. Wood filed for unemployment compensation in Ithaca, New York, claiming it wasn't her fault she had quit her job, the nascent movement acquired its first heroine, as well as a clear delineation of a problem as endemic as the abuse itself. The credibility of an office worker, a mother of four, was pitted against the reputation of an eminent scientist whose status was—and remains—so lofty that to this day his name has not appeared in accounts of her case.

Farley and two Cornell colleagues, Susan Meyer and Karen Sauvigné, found a lawyer for Wood and brainstormed to invent a name for their newly identified issue: "sexual harassment." The young feminists and their complainant proceeded to hold a movement-style speak-

out (a technique that had been used effectively to articulate the issues of abortion and rape) in a community center in Ithaca in May 1975. A questionnaire collected after the meeting showed that an astonishing number of women had firsthand experience to contribute.

Eleanor Holmes Norton, then chair of the New York City Commission on Human Rights, was conducting hearings on women and work that year. Farley came to testify, half expecting to be laughed out of the hearing room. "The titillation value of sexual harassment was always obvious," Farley recalls. "But Norton treated the issue with dignity and great seriousness." Norton, who had won her activist spurs in the civil rights movement, was to put her understanding of sexual harassment to good use during her later tenure in Washington, D.C., as head of the Equal Employment Opportunity Commission (EEOC). But we are moving ahead of our history.

Reporter Enid Nemy covered the Human Rights Commission hearings for the New York *Times.* Her story, "Women Begin to Speak Out Against Sexual Harassment at Work," appeared in the *Times* on August 19, 1975, and was syndicated nationally, to a tidal wave of response from women across the country.

Sauvigné and Meyer set up the Working Women's Institute in New York City as a clearinghouse for inquiries, and to develop a data bank with an eye toward public policy. Wood lost her case; the unemployment insurance appeals board ruled her reasons for quitting were personal. Lin Farley's breakthrough book, *Sexual Shakedown: The Sexual Harassment of Women on the Job,* was published by McGraw-Hill in 1978—after 27 rejections. "I thought my book would change the workplace," Farley says. "It is now out of print."

Things had begun to percolate on the legal front. Working with a large map and color-coded pushpins, Sauvigné and Meyer matched up complainants with volunteer lawyers and crisis counselors. Initially, aggrieved women sought redress by filing claims for unemployment insurance after they'd quit their jobs under duress, or by bringing their complaints to local human rights commissions. Ultimately the most important means of redress became the EEOC, the federal agency charged with investigating and mediating discrimination cases under Title VII of the 1964 Civil Rights Act. (The inclusion of sex discrimination in the 1964 act had been introduced at the last minute in an attempt to defeat the bill.)

By 1977, three cases argued at the appellate level (*Barnes* v. *Costle; Miller* v. *Bank of America; Tomkins* v. *Public Service Electric & Gas*) had established a harassed woman's right, under Title VII, to sue the corporate entity that employed her. "A few individual women stuck their necks out," says Nadine Taub, the court-appointed attorney for Adrienne Tomkins against the New Jersey utilities company.

The Tomkins case, in particular, made it clear that the courts would no longer view harassment as a personal frolic, but as sex discrimination for which the employer might be held responsible. A young woman named Catharine MacKinnon had followed these cases with avid interest while a law student at Yale; later she published an impassioned, if somewhat obfuscating, treatise, *Sexual Harassment of Working Women,* in 1979.

Job-threatening though it was, sexual harassment remained on a back burner of the public conscience, as life-threatening issues—rape, battery, child abuse, and the ongoing pro-choice battle—continued to dominate feminist activity and media attention.

"We felt so alone out there," remembers Freada Klein, whose Boston area advocacy group was called the Alliance Against Sexual Coercion. "There was a *Redbook* survey in 1976 and a *Ms.* speakout and cover story in 1977. That was all." Peggy Crull, director of research for the New York City Commission on Human Rights, recalls that by the close of the decade, however, "every women's magazine had run a piece."

Slowly and quietly, case law broadened the definition of unlawful harassment. As women entered the work force in greater numbers, committing themselves not only to jobs but to careers, new cases went beyond those situations in which a boss suggested sex to a subordinate as a quid pro quo for keeping her job or getting a promotion. A court decision in Minnesota established

that coworker harassment was as inimical to working conditions as harassment by a boss. A New York decision held that a receptionist could not be required to wear revealing clothes that brought her unwanted attention.

Meanwhile, a clerk-typist named Karen Nussbaum was pursuing her own mission to organize women office workers through a national network she called 9 to 5. An old friend from the antiwar movement, Jane Fonda, visited her headquarters in Cleveland with the idea of making a movie about underpaid and unappreciated secretaries in a large U.S. corporation.

9 to 5, produced by Fonda's IPC Films, and starring Fonda, Lily Tomlin, and Dolly Parton, was released in 1980, with Parton playing the plucky secretary who fends off her lecherous boss. The loopy movie, a commercial success, used broad comedic strokes to highlight the woman's perspective.

In the waning days of the Carter administration, when Eleanor Holmes Norton was chair of the EEOC, she seized the initiative by issuing a set of federal guidelines on sexual harassment. The guidelines, a single-page memorandum issued on November 10, 1980, as Norton's tenure was running out, stated with admirable brevity that sexual activity as a condition of employment or promotion was a violation of Title VII. The creation of an intimidating, hostile, or offensive working environment was also a violation. Verbal abuse alone was deemed sufficient to create a hostile workplace. The guidelines encouraged corporations to write their own memoranda and inform employees of appropriate means of redress.

Guidelines are interpretations of existing statutes and do not have the full authority of law. But in 1981 (while Anita Hill was working for Clarence Thomas at the Department of Education), the EEOC was required to defend itself in *Bundy* v. *Jackson,* said the former EEOC general counsel Leroy D. Clark. The District of Columbia circuit court ruled in favor of Sandra Bundy, a corrections department employee, and accepted the EEOC's guidelines as law, holding that Title VII could be violated even if a woman remained on the job.

Employers who were caught off guard were in for another surprise. During that same first year of the Reagan administration, the Merit

Systems Protection Board, a regulatory agency that seldom makes news, released the results of a random survey of 20,100 federal employees. The findings revealed that a staggering 42 percent of the government's female workers had experienced an incident of sexual harassment on the job in the previous two years. "It was the first decent methodological study," says Freada Klein, who served as an adviser. "They did it again in 1988 and came up with the same figures."

It took the U.S. Supreme Court until 1986 to affirm unanimously, in *Meritor Savings Bank* v. *Vinson,* that sexual harassment even without economic harm was unlawful discrimination, although the court drew back in some measure from employer liability in hostile-environment cases.

Five years later, Anita Hill's testimony to 14 white male senators, and the merciless attacks on her credibility, echoed the agonies of her predecessors from Carmita Wood to Mechelle Vinson, who came forward at the risk of ridicule to tell about an abuse of power by a favored, institutionally protected, high-status male.

Detractors of the feminist role in social change have sought to create the impression that sexual harassment is yet another nefarious plot cooked up by an elite white movement to serve middle-class professionals. As it happens, veterans of the battle have been struck time and again by the fact that the plaintiffs in most of the landmark cases, brave women every one, have been workingclass and African American: Paulette Barnes, payroll clerk; Margaret Miller, proofing machine operator; Diane Williams, Justice Department employee; Rebekah Barnett, shop clerk; Mechelle Vinson, bank teller trainee.

We collected many speculations as to why black women have led this fight, but the last word goes to Eleanor Holmes Norton, who said, succinctly, "With black women's historic understanding of slavery and rape, it's not surprising to me."

STUDY QUESTIONS

1. How was the phenomenon of "sexual harassment" first brought to public awareness? Who coined the phrase?
2. What was the role of activists in pressing and framing the legal issues? Who were the plaintiffs in the landmark cases? What might account for their courage?

Catherine MacKinnon's book, *The Sexual Harassment of Working Women* (New Haven, Conn.: Yale University Press, 1979), helped to focus attention on legal and conceptual advances already worked out by others. In particular, she drew attention to a distinction that feminist activists had made between two types of sexual harassment. The first, quid pro quo harassment, "is defined by the more or less explicit exchange: the woman must comply [with a demand for a sexual service] or forfeit an employment benefit" (p. 32). In these situations, a supervisor makes submission to his sexual demands a prerequisite for an employment benefit, such as being hired, promoted, given a wage increase, or even simply retained. The other, most frequently called the hostile environment form of harassment, "is the situation in which sexual harassment simply makes the work environment unbearable" (p. 40). In these cases, the harasser, who may be a supervisor, a co-worker, or even a customer, engages in sexual advances or other verbal or physical conduct of a sexual nature that is so unwelcome as to create an intimidating, hostile, or offensive working environment.

As Brownmiller and Alexander indicated, the main impetus for the legal developments came as a result of litigation by the feminist bar beginning in the early 1970s. When the issue was first raised in the early 1970s, the courts refused to recognize unwanted sexual attentions toward women such as ogling, patting, brushing against, propositioning, grabbing, etc., by supervisors, co-workers, and customers, as violations of Title VII. This resistance reflected male attitudes on the part of the courts. First, such behavior was seen as a private matter, an innocent intrusion of sexual byplay into the workplace. It was viewed as an innocuous, if unproductive interlude. Second, even if working women sustained harm as a result of such treatment, the courts could not bring themselves to make employers liable for it. They believed this form of maltreatment almost invariably occurred without the knowledge of higher management and contrary to its policies. Finally, the courts were concerned lest they adopt a legal doctrine that would be ridiculed by their peers. In particular, they were slow to acknowledge that sexual harassment is imposed "because of sex." One common worry was that a defense of bisexuality would become available, i.e., the claim that the plaintiff would have been subject to the same treatment even if she had been a man. See, for example, *Corne v. Bausch & Lomb,* 390 F.Supp. 161 (D. Ariz. 1975).

Courts first held that the sexual harassment of employees violates Title VII in the mid-1970s. *Tomkins* was one of the first of these decisions. Over the next ten years, culminating in the Supreme Court's decision in *Vinson,* a number of the key features of Title VII law as it relates to sexual harassment were established. One is the distinction between the quid pro quo and the hostile environment types of sexual harassment. *Tomkins* illustrates the quid pro quo type of sexual harassment.

Tomkins v. Public Service Electric & Gas Co.

United States Court of Appeals, Third Circuit, 1977. 568 F.2d 1044.

ALDISERT, Circuit Judge.

. . . Taken as true, the facts set out in appellant's complaint demonstrate that Adrienne Tomkins was hired by PSE&G in April 1971, and progressed to positions of increasing responsibility from that time until August 1973, when she began working in a secretarial position under the direction of a named supervisor. On October 30, 1973, the supervisor told Tomkins that she should have lunch with him in a nearby restaurant, in order to discuss his upcoming evaluation of her work, as well as a possible job promotion. At lunch, he made advances toward her, indicating his desire to have sexual relations with her and stating that this would be necessary if they were to have a satisfactory working relationship. When Tomkins attempted to leave the restaurant, the supervisor responded first by threats of recrimination against Tomkins in her employment, then by threats of physical force, and ultimately by physically restraining Tomkins. During the incident, he told her that no one at PSE&G would help her should she lodge a complaint against him. . . .

Tomkins' complaint alleges that PSE&G and certain of its agents knew or should have known that such incidents would occur, and that they nevertheless "placed [Tomkins] in a position where she would be subjected to the aforesaid conduct of [the supervisor] and failed to take adequate supervisory measures to prevent such incidents from occurring." It further alleged that on the day following the lunch, Tomkins expressed her intention to leave PSE&G as a result of the incident. She agreed to continue work only after being promised a transfer to a comparable position elsewhere in the company. A comparable position did not become available, however, and Tomkins was instead placed in an inferior position in another department. There, she was subjected to false and adverse employment evaluations, disciplinary lay-offs, and threats of demotion by various PSE&G employees. Tomkins maintains that as a result of the supervisor's conduct and the continued pattern of harassment by PSE&G personnel, she suffered physical and emotional distress, resulting in absenteeism and loss of income.

In January 1975, PSE&G fired Tomkins. Following her dismissal, she filed an employment discrimination complaint with the Equal Employment Opportunity Commission, which ultimately issued a Notice of Right to Sue. After Tomkins filed suit in district court, PSE&G moved to dismiss the complaint. . . . [T]he company's motion to dismiss Tomkins' claim against PSE&G for his actions was granted for failure to state a claim. The latter judgment was determined final by the district court . . . and this appeal followed. . . .

Tomkins claims that the sexual demands of her supervisor imposed a sex-based "term or condition" on her employment. She alleges that her promotion and favorable job evaluation were made conditional upon her granting sexual favors, and that she suffered adverse job consequences as a result of this incident. In granting appellees' motion to dismiss, however, the district court characterized the supervisor's acts as "abuse of authority . . . for personal purposes." The court thus overlooked the major thrust of Tomkins' complaint, i.e., that her employer, either knowingly or constructively, made acquiescence in her supervisor's sexual demands a necessary prerequisite to the continuation of, or advancement in, her job.

The facts as alleged by appellant clearly demonstrate an incident with employment ramifications, one within the intended coverage of Title VII. The context within which the sexual advances occurred is itself strong evidence of a job-related condition: Tomkins was asked to lunch by her supervisor for the express purpose of discussing his upcoming evaluation of her work and possible recommendation of her for a promotion. But one need not infer the added condition from the setting alone. It is expressly alleged that the supervisor stated to Tomkins

that her continued success and advancement at PSE&G were dependent upon her agreeing to his sexual demands. The demand thus amounted to a condition of employment, an additional duty or burden Tomkins was required by her supervisor to meet as a prerequisite to her continued employment. . . .

. . . The courts have distinguished between complaints alleging sexual advances of an individual or personal nature and those alleging direct employment consequences flowing from the advances, finding Title VII violations in the latter category. This distinction recognizes two elements necessary to find a violation of Title VII: first, that a term or condition of employment has been imposed and second, that it has been imposed by the employer, either directly or vicariously, in a sexually discriminatory fashion. Applying these requirements to the present complaint, we conclude that Title VII is violated when a supervisor, with the actual or constructive knowledge of the employer, makes sexual advances or demands toward a subordinate employee and conditions that employee's job status—evaluation, continued employment, promotion, or other aspects of career development—on a favorable response to those advances or demands, and the employer does not take prompt and appropriate remedial action after acquiring such knowledge. . . .

We do not agree with the district court that finding a Title VII violation on these facts will result in an unmanageable number of suits and a difficulty in differentiating between spurious and meritorious claims. The congressional mandate that the federal courts provide relief is strong; it must not be thwarted by concern for judicial economy. More significant, however, this decision in no way relieves the plaintiff of the burden of proving the facts alleged to establish the required elements of a Title VII violation. Although any theory of liability may be used in vexatious or bad faith suits, we are confident that traditional judicial mechanisms will separate the valid from the invalid complaints.

The judgment of the district court will be reversed and the cause remanded for further proceedings.

STUDY QUESTIONS

1. In what sense were the advances Tomkins allegedly endured a "condition of employment"? Would they have been a condition of employment if no job-related consequences were threatened?
2. What standard did the court use for establishing employer liability? If Tomkins's supervisor had not threatened reprisal if she refused, would she have prevailed in this court? If the person who took her to lunch on the fateful day had not been Tomkins' supervisor but rather a co-worker, would she have prevailed?
3. Answer the critic who proclaims that: "This has gone too far! After all, no one was hurt. There's no harm in asking, right? Only a prude would advocate the removal of all sexual give and take from the workplace. Hey, loosen up."

When first confronted with complaints alleging that sexual harassment violates Title VII, the courts did not treat them seriously. They continued to perceive such situations as innocuous until the plight of the victims was made abundantly clear. They then recognized that sexual harassment in an employment setting is very harmful to its victims. The early cases, such as *Tomkins,* focused primarily upon the harm suffered in terms of income, job security, and career advancement. These are substantial harms, but they are not the entire story.

Stress is another direct consequence of sexual harassment. The Working Women's Institute analyzed letters from victims of sexual harassment on the job and found that the resulting stress affected the work performance, the psychological well-being, and the physical health of the victims.

> Even though women express pride at being able to do their jobs despite harassment, 46 percent of the 518 cases said it interfered with their work performance. The two most common effects on work performance were that the women were distracted from their tasks and dreaded coming to work. . . .
>
> The negative effects of sexual harassment are not limited to the work setting. They invade every aspect of the woman's life and often are manifested as general psychological stress symptoms. At least one negative effect was reported by over 94 percent of the women in our sample. The reaction most often mentioned was excessive tension. . . .
>
> About 36 percent of the women involved in our study pointed out physical ailments they thought had been brought about by sexual harassment. The most prevalent ones were nausea, tiredness (a frequent sign of depression), and headaches. . . .
>
> *Peggy Crull. "Sexual Harassment and Women's Health." In* Double Exposure: Women's Health Hazards on the Job and in the Home, *edited by W. Chavkin. New York: Monthly Review Press, 1983. Pp. 107–109.*

Beyond the financial, career, and stress effects of sexual harassment in the workplace, there is the perhaps even more crushing emotional harm occasioned by the message such treatment inevitably conveys in our culture. The attorney who argued Tomkins's case described that harm as follows:

> Sexual references, as well as explicit demands for sexual cooperation, convey the message that a woman is a sexual object before she is a contributing worker, and whether it is consciously undertaken or not, such behavior serves to reinforce woman's sexual role. Indeed, such behavior is probably the quintessential expression of stereotypic role

expectations. Like other expressions of stereotypic expectations occurring at the work place, it is dysfunctional in two respects. Whether or not perceived as flattering by women, sexual advances remind women of a societally-imposed incongruity between their role as worker and as woman. By thus arousing role conflict in women, advances interfere with their performance. By underscoring their sexual identity in the eyes of male supervisors, sexual advances make it less likely that women will be viewed as persons capable of performing a demanding task, and consequently, less likely that they will have the opportunity to try to do so. . . .

The situation in which a person is asked to exchange sexual services for continued employment is uniquely disturbing to women. It is a reminder, a badge or incident of a servile status, which women are striving to leave behind.

Nadine Taub. "Keeping Women in Their Place: Stereotyping Per Se as a Form of Employment Discrimination." 21 Boston College Law Review *345, 361, 368 (1980).*

In order to prevail under Title VII, a plaintiff who alleges sexual harassment on the job must show that the employer is responsible for the imposition of a special condition of employment upon the plaintiff because of her sex. *Tomkins* and similar decisions during the late 1970s laid the foundations for later refinements by the EEOC and the federal courts.

The court in *Tomkins* took the view that sexual harassment on the job is "a condition of employment" in the sense of a "prerequisite" for some employment benefit. This no doubt resulted from the fact that Tomkins's harassment was of that nature. Still, until that conception of "condition of employment" was expanded, harassment by co-workers, as well as other dimensions of this problem, were beyond the reach of Title VII.

Tomkins also addressed the issue of employer liability. There, the court held the employer responsible for the sexual harassment of female employees by their male supervisors on the basis of something like a *negligence standard* (the employer knew or should have known of the conduct and taken immediate and appropriate corrective action). Other courts facing quid pro quo situations at about the same time used a stricter standard of employer liability. In *Miller v. Bank of America,* 600 F.2d 211 (9th Cir. 1979), the court used what appears to be a *strict liability standard* (the employer is unconditionally responsible for the torts that employees commit in the course of their employment). After these decisions, the courts were faced with the question of which standard of responsibility applies to employers in Title VII actions alleging sexual harassment. The next major step came in November 1980, when the EEOC, then under the leadership of Eleanor Holmes Norton, published its Guidelines on Sexual Harassment.

29 C.F.R. § 1604.11 Sexual harassment.

(a) Harassment on the basis of sex is a violation of Sec. 703 of Title VII. Unwelcome sexual advances, requests for sexual favors, and other verbal or physical conduct of a sexual nature constitute sexual harassment when (1) submission to such conduct is made either explicitly or implicitly a term or condition of an individual's employment, (2) submission to or rejection of such conduct by an individual is used as the basis for employment decisions affecting such individual, or (3) such conduct has the purpose or effect of unreasonably interfering with an individual's work performance or creating an intimidating, hostile, or offensive working environment.

(b) In determining whether alleged conduct constitutes sexual harassment, the Commission will look at the record as a whole and at the totality of the circumstances, such as the nature of the sexual advances and the context in which the alleged incidents occurred. The determination of the legality of a particular action will be made from the facts, on a case by case basis.

(c) Applying general Title VII principles, an employer, employment agency, joint apprenticeship committee or labor organization (hereinafter collectively referred to as "employer") is responsible for its acts and those of its agents and supervisory employees with respect to sexual harassment regardless of whether the specific acts complained of were authorized or even forbidden by the employer and regardless of whether the employer knew or should have known of their occurrence. The Commission will examine the circumstances of the particular employment relationship and the job functions performed by the individual in determining whether an individual acts in either a supervisory or agency capacity.

(d) With respect to conduct between fellow employees, an employer is responsible for acts of sexual harassment in the workplace where the employer (or its agents or supervisory employees) knows or should have known of the conduct, unless it can show that it took immediate and appropriate corrective action.

(e) An employer may also be responsible for the acts of non-employees, with respect to sexual harassment of employees in the workplace, where the employer (or its agents or supervisory employees) knows or should have known of the conduct and fails to take immediate and appropriate corrective action. In reviewing these cases the Commission will consider the extent of the employer's control and any other legal responsibility which the employer may have with respect to the conduct of such non-employees.

(f) Prevention is the best tool for the elimination of sexual harassment. An employer should take all steps necessary to prevent sexual harassment from occurring, such as affirmatively raising the subject, expressing strong disapproval, developing appropriate sanctions, informing employees of their right to raise and how to raise the issue of harassment under Title VII, and developing methods to sensitize all concerned.

(g) Other related practices: Where employment opportunities or benefits are granted because of an individual's submission to the employer's sexual advances or requests for sexual favors, the employer may be held liable for unlawful sex discrimination against other persons who were qualified for but denied that employment opportunity or benefit.

The EEOC guidelines provided bold leadership in formulating the main elements of Title VII law as it relates to sexual harassment. They are regularly cited with approval by the courts and relied upon by employers. The definition set out in section (a) is widely used in both the public and the private sectors. It incorporates both the quid pro quo and the hostile environment forms of harassment. The standards of employer liability for each of the forms of harassment are set out in sections (c) and (d). The EEOC endorsed strict liability in cases of quid pro quo harassment. The negligence standard is endorsed for hostile environment situations.

The guidelines also broke new ground in sections (e) and (g). In the former, the EEOC recommended treating the sexual harassment of employees by customers and clients as a form of hostile environment and therefore subject to the negligence standard. The advance in section (g) was even more subtle. Sometimes people who resist sexual advances in an employment setting fear that they will lose advancement opportunities to others who are less qualified but more sexually accommodating. Although the number of people who "get ahead on their backs" and the advancement achieved in that way is greatly exaggerated by office mythology, the fear of that type of competition is real and extensive. The guidelines made provision for allaying those fears by making the employer liable for granting employment benefits in those situations.

Shortly after the EEOC guidelines were issued, the Circuit Court of Appeals of the District of Columbia handed down a decision that gave effect to the approach to the hostile environment type of sexual harassment endorsed by these guidelines.

Bundy v. Jackson

United States Court of Appeals for the District of Columbia, 1981.
641 F.2d 934.

J. SKELLY WRIGHT, Chief Judge.

In *Barnes v. Costle,* we held that an employer who abolished a female employee's job to retaliate against the employee's resistance of his sexual advances violated Title VII of the Civil Rights Act of 1964. . . . [A]ppellant asks us to extend *Barnes* by holding that an employer violates Title VII merely by subjecting female employees to sexual harassment, even if the employee's resistance to that harassment does not cause the employer to deprive her of any tangible job benefits.

The District Court in this case made an express finding of fact that in appellant's agency "the making of improper sexual advances to female employees [was] standard operating procedure, a fact of life, a normal condition of employment," and that the director of the agency, to whom she complained of the harassment, failed to investigate her complaints or take them seriously. Nevertheless, the District Court refused to grant appellant any declaratory or injunctive relief, concluding that sexual harassment does not in itself represent discrimination "with respect to . . . terms, conditions, or privileges of employment" within the meaning of Title VII. . . .

Appellant Sandra Bundy is now, and was at the time she filed her lawsuit, a Vocational Rehabilitation Specialist, level GS–9, with the District of Columbia Department of Corrections (the agency). . . . In recent years Bundy's chief task has been to find jobs for former criminal offenders.

The District Court's finding that sexual intimidation was a "normal condition of employment" in Bundy's agency finds ample support in the District Court's own chronology of Bundy's experiences there. Those experiences began in

1972 when Bundy, still a GS–5, received and rejected sexual propositions from Delbert Jackson, then a fellow employee at the agency but now its Director and the named defendant in this lawsuit in his official capacity. It was two years later, however, that the sexual intimidation Bundy suffered began to intertwine directly with her employment when she received propositions from two of her supervisors, Arthur Burton and James Gainey.

Burton became Bundy's supervisor when Bundy became an Employment Development Specialist in 1974. Shortly thereafter Gainey became her first-line supervisor and Burton her second-line supervisor, although Burton retained control of Bundy's employment status. Burton began sexually harassing Bundy in June 1974, continually calling her into his office to request that she spend the workday afternoon with him at his apartment and to question her about her sexual proclivities. Shortly after becoming her first-line supervisor Gainey also began making sexual advances to Bundy, asking her to join him at a motel and on a trip to the Bahamas. Bundy complained about these advances to Lawrence Swain, who supervised both Burton and Gainey. Swain casually dismissed Bundy's complaints, telling her that "any man in his right mind would want to rape you," and then proceeding himself to request that she begin a sexual relationship with him in his apartment. Bundy rejected his request.

We add that, although the District Court made no explicit findings as to harassment of other female employees, its finding that harassment was "standard operating procedure" finds ample support in record evidence that Bundy was not the only woman subjected to sexual intimidation by male supervisors.

In denying Bundy any relief, the District Court found that Bundy's supervisors did not take the "game" of sexually propositioning female employees "seriously," and that Bundy's rejection of their advances did not evoke in them any motive to take any action against her. The record, however, contains nothing to support this view, and indeed some evidence directly belies it. . . .

We thus readily conclude that Bundy's employer discriminated against her on the basis of sex. What remains is the novel question whether the sexual harassment of the sort Bundy suffered amounted by itself to sex discrimination with respect to the *"terms, conditions, or privileges of employment."* Though no court has as yet so held, we believe that an affirmative answer follows ineluctably from numerous cases finding Title VII violations where an employer created or condoned a substantially discriminatory work *environment,* regardless of whether the complaining employees lost any tangible job benefits as a result of the discrimination.

Bundy's claim on this score is essentially that "conditions of employment" include the psychological and emotional work environment— that the sexually stereotyped insults and demeaning propositions to which she was indisputably subjected and which caused her anxiety and debilitation, illegally poisoned that environment. . . .

The employer can thus implicitly and effectively make the employee's endurance of sexual intimidation a "condition" of her employment. The woman then faces a "cruel trilemma." She can endure the harassment. She can attempt to oppose it, with little hope of success, either legal or practical, but with every prospect of making the job even less tolerable for her. Or she can leave her job, with little hope of legal relief and the likely prospect of another job where she will face harassment anew.

Bundy proved that she was the victim of a practice of sexual harassment and a discriminatory work environment permitted by her employer. Her rights under Title VII were therefore violated. We thus reverse the District Court's holding on this issue and remand it to that court so it can fashion appropriate injunctive relief.

STUDY QUESTIONS

1. What did the district court mean when it said that the supervisors didn't take the "game" of sexually propositioning female employees seriously? If they didn't take it seriously, why did Bundy?
2. Was Judge Wright correct in describing this behavior as "sexual intimidation"? Is being subjected to such treatment likely to affect one's job performance? Is that apt to affect one's success in a career? Is it likely to affect the employer's productivity?
3. What was the "cruel trilemma" that faced Bundy? What enabled the others to place her in that position? Who was best situated to prevent such manipulation from occurring?

———————————— ❧ ————————————

In 1982, the Circuit Court of Appeals for the Eleventh Circuit drew together the strands of previous rulings and set out the principles and standards that apply to sexual harassment claims under Title VII in an orderly fashion. In *Henson v. City of Dundee,* 682 F.2d 897 (1982), the court gave judicial approval, at least in the Eleventh Circuit, to most of the principles and standards proposed in the EEOC guidelines. It recognized both the quid pro quo and the hostile environment forms of sexual harassment and specified the same standards of employer liability for them as had the EEOC guidelines. The *Henson* court agreed that the hostile environment form of sexual harassment violates Title VII on the basis of an analogy with racial harassment. "Surely, a requirement that a man or woman run a gauntlet of sexual abuse in return for the privilege of being allowed to work and make a living can be as demeaning and disconcerting as the harshest of racial epithets." It went on to defend a stricter standard of employer liability for quid pro quo than for hostile environment harassment on the grounds that in a case of quid pro quo harassment, "the supervisor relies on his apparent or actual authority to extort sexual consideration from an employee." Those who create a hostile working environment by means of sexual harassment, however, do not need to rely on the authority of the employer.

The standards applying Title VII to allegations of sexual harassment in the workplace were developed over the course of a decade by the federal circuit courts and the EEOC. In its first decision on a sexual harassment case under Title VII, the Supreme Court unanimously signaled general approval of these standards. Of particular interest was its approval of the "hostile environment" theory of liability and the centrality of "unwanted" in the definition of sexual harassment. The decision in *Vinson,* however, reserved judgment on the standards of employer liability developed by the EEOC and the lower courts.

Meritor Savings Bank v. Vinson

Supreme Court of the
United States, 1986.
477 U.S. 57, 106 S.Ct. 2399, 91 L.Ed.2d 49.

Justice REHNQUIST delivered the opinion of the Court. . . .

In 1974, respondent Mechelle Vinson met Sidney Taylor, a vice president of what is now petitioner Meritor Savings Bank (the bank) and manager of one of its branch offices. When respondent asked whether she might obtain employment at the bank, Taylor gave her an application, which she completed and returned the next day; later that same day Taylor called her to say that she had been hired. With Taylor as her supervisor, respondent started as a teller-trainee, and thereafter was promoted to teller, head teller, and assistant branch manager. She worked at the same branch for four years, and it is undisputed that her advancement there was based on merit alone. In September 1978, respondent notified Taylor that she was taking sick leave for an indefinite period. On November 1, 1978, the bank discharged her for excessive use of that leave.

Respondent brought this action against Taylor and the bank, claiming that during her four years at the bank she had "constantly been subjected to sexual harassment" by Taylor in violation of Title VII. She sought injunctive relief, compensatory and punitive damages against Taylor and the bank, and attorney's fees.

At the 11-day bench trial, the parties presented conflicting testimony about Taylor's behavior during respondent's employment. Respondent testified that during her probationary period as a teller-trainee, Taylor treated her in a fatherly way and made no sexual advances. Shortly thereafter, however, he invited her out to dinner and, during the course of the meal, suggested that they go to a motel to have sexual relations. At first she refused, but out of what she described as fear of losing her job she eventually agreed. According to respondent, Taylor thereafter made repeated demands upon her for sexual favors, usually at the branch, both during and after business hours; she estimated that over the next several years she had intercourse with him some 40 or 50 times. In addition, respondent testified that Taylor fondled her in front of other employees, followed her into the women's restroom when she went there alone, exposed himself to her, and even forcibly raped her on several occasions. These activities ceased after 1977, respondent stated, when she started going with a steady boyfriend. . . .

Taylor denied respondent's allegations of sexual activity, testifying that he never fondled her, never made suggestive remarks to her, never engaged in sexual intercourse with her and never asked her to do so. He contended instead that respondent made her accusations in response to a business-related dispute. The bank also denied respondent's allegations and asserted that any sexual harassment by Taylor was unknown to the bank and engaged in without its consent or approval.

The District Court denied relief, but did not resolve the conflicting testimony about the existence of a sexual relationship between respondent and Taylor. It found instead that

> "If [respondent] and Taylor did engage in an intimate or sexual relationship during the time of [respondent's] employment with [the bank], that relationship was a voluntary one having nothing to do with her continued employment at [the bank] or her advancement or promotions at that institution."

The court ultimately found that respondent "was not the victim of sexual harassment and was not the victim of sexual discrimination" while employed at the bank.

Although it concluded that respondent had not proved a violation of Title VII, the District Court nevertheless went on to address the bank's liability. After noting the bank's express policy against discrimination, and finding that neither respondent nor any other employee had ever lodged a complaint about sexual harassment by Taylor, the court ultimately concluded that "the bank was without notice and cannot be held liable for the alleged actions of Taylor."

The Court of Appeals for the District of Columbia Circuit reversed. . . .

Respondent argues, and the Court of Appeals held, that unwelcome sexual advances that create an offensive or hostile working environment violate Title VII. Without question, when a supervisor sexually harasses a subordinate because of the subordinate's sex, that supervisor "discriminate[s]" on the basis of sex. Petitioner apparently does not challenge this proposition. It contends instead that in prohibiting discrimination with respect to "compensation, terms, conditions, or privileges" of employment, Congress was concerned with what petitioner describes as "tangible loss" of "an economic character," not "purely psychological aspects of the workplace environment.". . . .

We reject petitioner's view. First, . . .[p]etitioner has pointed to nothing in the Act to suggest that Congress contemplated the limitation urged here.

Second, in 1980 the EEOC issued guidelines specifying that "sexual harassment," as there defined, is a form of sex discrimination prohibited by Title VII. The EEOC guidelines fully support the view that harassment leading to noneconomic injury can violate Title VII. . . .

Since the guidelines were issued, courts have uniformly held, and we agree, that a plaintiff may establish a violation of Title VII by proving that discrimination based on sex has created a hostile or abusive work environment. As the Court of Appeals for the Eleventh Circuit wrote in *Henson v. Dundee*:

> "Sexual harassment which creates a hostile or offensive environment for members of one sex is every bit the arbitrary barrier to sexual equality at the workplace that racial harassment is to racial equality. Surely, a requirement that a man or woman run a gauntlet of sexual abuse in return for the privilege of being allowed to work and make a living can be as demeaning and disconcerting as the harshest of racial epithets." . . .

The question remains, however, whether the District Court's ultimate finding that respondent "was not the victim of sexual harassment," effectively disposed of respondent's claim. The Court of Appeals recognized, we think correctly, that this ultimate finding was likely based on one or both of two erroneous views of the law. First, the District Court apparently believed that a claim for sexual harassment will not lie absent an *economic* effect on the complainant's employment. . . . Since it appears that the District Court made its findings without ever considering the "hostile environment" theory of sexual harassment, the Court of Appeals' decision to remand was correct.

Second, the District Court's conclusion that no actionable harassment occurred might have rested on its earlier "finding" that "[i]f [respondent] and Taylor did engage in an intimate or sexual relationship . . . , that relationship was a voluntary one." But the fact that sex-related conduct was "voluntary," in the sense that the complainant was not forced to participate against her will, is not a defense to a sexual harassment suit brought under Title VII. The gravamen of any sexual harassment claim is that the alleged sexual advances were "unwelcome." 29 CFR § 1604.11(a) (1985). While the question whether particular conduct was indeed unwelcome presents difficult problems of proof and turns largely on credibility determinations committed to the trier of fact, the District Court in this case erroneously focused on the "voluntariness" of respondent's participation in the claimed sexual episodes. The correct inquiry is whether respondent by her conduct indicated that the alleged sexual advances were unwelcome, not whether her actual participation in sexual intercourse was voluntary. . . .

Although the District Court concluded that respondent had not proved a violation of Title VII, it nevertheless went on to consider the question of the bank's liability. Finding that "the bank was without notice" of Taylor's alleged conduct, and that notice to Taylor was not the equivalent of notice to the bank, the court concluded that the bank therefore could not be held liable for Taylor's alleged actions. The Court of Appeals took the opposite view, holding that an employer is strictly liable for a hostile environment created by a supervisor's sexual advances, even though the employer neither knew nor reasonably could have known of the alleged misconduct. . . .

[The] debate over the appropriate standard for employer liability has a rather abstract quality about it given the state of the record in this case. We do not know at this stage whether Taylor made any sexual advances toward respondent at all, let alone whether those advances were unwelcome. . . .

We therefore decline the parties' invitation to issue a definitive rule on employer liability, but

we do agree with the EEOC that Congress wanted courts to look to agency principles for guidance in this area. While such common-law principles may not be transferable in all their particulars to Title VII, Congress' decision to define "employer" to include any "agent" of an employer, surely evinces an intent to place some limits on the acts of employees for which employers under Title VII are to be held responsible. For this reason, we hold that the Court of Appeals erred in concluding that employers are always automatically liable for sexual harassment by their supervisors. For the same reason, absence of notice to an employer does not necessarily insulate that employer from liability. . . .

Accordingly, the judgment of the Court of Appeals reversing the judgment of the District Court is affirmed, and the case is remanded for further proceedings consistent with this opinion.

STUDY QUESTIONS

1. What reason did the Court give for rejecting voluntariness as a defense in sexual harassment suits brought under Title VII? How would the Court have strengthened the position of would-be harassers had it allowed this defense? Think about the cruel trilemmas faced by the plaintiffs in the foregoing cases.

2. The District Court held that employer liability is limited to situations of which it has actual notice. What standard of employer liability was adopted in *Henson* for the type of situation described in Vinson's testimony? By the EEOC? By the Supreme Court? Which do you favor?

After *Vinson*, the key issues that remained to be worked out were the standard of employer liability in cases that allege quid pro quo harassment and the standard for assessing whether the behavior complained of in cases alleging hostile environment harassment rises to the level of being hostile, offensive, or intimidating. Since *Vinson*, the main developments have been on the latter issue.

In *Vinson*, the Court outlined the pattern of proof for hostile environment situations. To establish a prima facie case, the plaintiff must show that: (1) she was subjected to unwelcome sexual conduct; (2) these were based on her sex; (3) they were sufficiently pervasive or severe to create an abusive or hostile work environment; and (4) the employer knew or should have known of the harassment and failed to take prompt and appropriate remedial action. Fashioning a test for these elements poses special problems. Subsequent decisions by lower courts have clarified the first and third of these elements.

When assessing whether the plaintiff, in the words of the Court, "by her conduct indicated that the alleged sexual advances were unwelcome" and whether the harassment is so pervasive and abusive as to create a hostile environment, courts usually applied a reasonableness test from the perspective of the actor. Would a "reasonable person" in the harasser's position have known that the behavior was unwelcome? In practice, this approach typically trivializes the seriousness of sexual harassment because harassers ordinarily are men, and men, as we have seen, have had great difficulty in appreciating the harm done to female victims of sexual harassment. The feminist bar has long argued that harassing conduct must be assessed from the victim's perspective. The emphasis on harassment as "unwelcome" behavior in *Vinson* was an advance in that direction. The next advance came when circuit courts began to apply the reasonableness standard from the perspective of the victim. Would "a reasonable person" in the victim's position have regarded the behavior as unwelcome? The court in the following case took that approach in endorsing the "reasonable victim" standard.

Ellison v. Brady

United States Court of Appeals,
Ninth Circuit, 1991.
924 F.2d 872

BEEZER, Circuit Judge:

. . . Kerry Ellison worked as a revenue agent for the Internal Revenue Service [IRS] in San Mateo, California. During her initial training in 1984 she met Sterling Gray, another trainee, who was also assigned to the San Mateo office. The two co-workers never became friends, and they did not work closely together.

. . . In June of 1986 when no one else was in the office, Gray asked Ellison to lunch. She accepted. . . .

Ellison alleges that after the June lunch Gray started to pester her with unnecessary questions and hang around her desk. [Over the next four months, Gray's unwelcome attentions escalated. He continued to ask Ellison out and to send her notes and letters that expressed affection for her. She rejected all of Gray's attentions.] . . .

Explaining her reaction [to a three-page letter], Ellison stated: "I just thought he was crazy. I thought he was nuts. I didn't know what he would do next. I was frightened."

She immediately telephoned [Bonnie] Miller [who supervised both Ellison and Gray]. Ellison told her supervisor that she was frightened and really upset. She requested that Miller transfer either her or Gray because she would not be comfortable working in the same office with him. . . .

. . . Gray subsequently transferred to the San Francisco office. . . .

After three weeks in San Francisco, Gray filed union grievances requesting a return to the San Mateo office. The IRS and the union settled the grievances in Gray's favor, agreeing to allow him to transfer back to the San Mateo office provided that he spend four more months in San Francisco and promise not to bother Ellison. On January 28, 1987, Ellison first learned of Gray's request in a letter from Miller explaining that Gray would return to the San Mateo office. The letter indicated that management decided to resolve Ellison's problem with a six-month separation, and that it would take additional action if the problem recurred.

After receiving the letter, Ellison was "frantic." She filed a formal complaint alleging sexual harassment on January 30, 1987 with the IRS. She also obtained permission to transfer to San Francisco temporarily when Gray returned. . . .

[The Treasury Department, the EEOC, and the district court all found in favor of the government, and Ellison appealed.]

The parties ask us to determine if Gray's conduct, as alleged by Ellison, was sufficiently severe or pervasive to alter the conditions of Ellison's employment and create an abusive working environment. The district court, with little Ninth Circuit case law to look to for guidance, held that Ellison did not state a prima facie case of sexual harassment due to a hostile working environment. It believed that Gray's conduct was "isolated and genuinely trivial." We disagree.

. . . The Supreme Court in *Meritor* explained that courts may properly look to guidelines issued by the Equal Employment Opportunity Commission (EEOC) for guidance when examining hostile environment claims of sexual harassment. The EEOC guidelines describe hostile environment harassment as "conduct [which] has the purpose or effect of unreasonably interfering with an individual's work performance or creating an intimidating, hostile, or offensive working environment." The EEOC, in accord with a substantial body of judicial decisions, has concluded that "Title VII affords employees the right to work in an environment free from discriminatory intimidation, ridicule, and insult."

The Supreme Court cautioned, however, that not all harassment affects a "term, condition, or privilege" of employment within the meaning of Title VII. For example, the "mere utterance of an ethnic or racial epithet which engenders offensive feelings in an employee" is not, by itself, actionable under Title VII. To state a claim under Title VII, sexual harassment "must be sufficiently severe or pervasive to alter the conditions of the victim's employment and create an abusive working environment." . . .

[W]e believe that in evaluating the severity and pervasiveness of sexual harassment, we should focus on the perspective of the victim. If we only examined whether a reasonable person

would engage in allegedly harassing conduct, we would run the risk of reinforcing the prevailing level of discrimination. Harassers could continue to harass merely because a particular discriminatory practice was common, and victims of harassment would have no remedy. . . .

In order to shield employers from having to accommodate the idiosyncratic concerns of the rare hyper-sensitive employee, we hold that a female plaintiff states a prima facie case of hostile environment sexual harassment when she alleges conduct which a reasonable woman[11] would consider sufficiently severe or pervasive to alter the conditions of employment and create an abusive working environment.[12]

We adopt the perspective of a reasonable woman primarily because we believe that a sex-blind reasonable person standard tends to be male-biased and tends to systematically ignore the experiences of women. The reasonable woman standard does not establish a higher level of protection for women than men. Instead, a gender-conscious examination of sexual harassment enables women to participate in the workplace on an equal footing with men. By acknowledging and not trivializing the effects of sexual harassment on reasonable women, courts can work toward ensuring that neither men nor women will have to "run a gauntlet of sexual abuse in return for the privilege of being allowed to work and make a living."

We note that the reasonable victim standard we adopt today classifies conduct as unlawful sexual harassment even when harassers do not realize that their conduct creates a hostile working environment. Well-intentioned compliments by co-workers or supervisors can form the basis of a sexual harassment cause of action if a reasonable victim of the same sex as the plain-

---

[11] *Of course, where male employees allege that co-workers engage in conduct which creates a hostile environment, the appropriate victim's perspective would be that of a reasonable man.*

[12] *We realize that the reasonable woman standard will not address conduct which some women find offensive. Conduct considered harmless by many today may be considered discriminatory in the future. Fortunately, the reasonableness inquiry which we adopt today is not static. As the views of reasonable women change, so too does the Title VII standard of acceptable behavior.*

tiff would consider the comments sufficiently severe or pervasive to alter a condition of employment and create an abusive working environment.[13]

We cannot say as a matter of law that Ellison's reaction was idiosyncratic or hypersensitive. We believe that a reasonable woman could have had a similar reaction. . . .

We next must determine what remedial actions by employers shield them from liability under Title VII for sexual harassment by co-workers. . . .

Ellison maintains that the government's remedy was insufficient because it did not discipline Gray and because it allowed Gray to return to San Mateo after only a six-month separation. Even though the hostile environment had been eliminated when Gray began working in San Francisco, we cannot say that the government's response was reasonable under Title VII. The record on appeal suggests that Ellison's employer did not express strong disapproval of Gray's conduct, did not reprimand Gray, did not put him on probation, and did not inform him that repeated harassment would result in suspension or termination. Apparently, Gray's employer only told him to stop harassing Ellison. Title VII requires more than a mere request to refrain from discriminatory conduct. Employers send the wrong message to potential harassers when they do not discipline employees for sexual harassment. If Ellison can prove

on remand that Gray knew or should have known that his conduct was unlawful and that the government failed to take even the mildest form of disciplinary action, the district court should hold that the government's initial remedy was insufficient under Title VII. At this point, genuine issues of material fact remain concerning whether the government properly disciplined Gray. . . .

We reverse the district court's decision that Ellison did not allege a prima facie case of sexual harassment due to a hostile working environment, and we remand for further proceedings consistent with this opinion. . . .

STUDY QUESTIONS

1. The court here intended to shield employers from liability by not accommodating the sensibilities of idiosyncratic and hypersensitive individuals. Do you think the reactions of Kerry Ellison were extreme and unreasonable? Do the men and women in your class agree about that? To what do you attribute that disagreement? In your discussions of this case, has anyone's views changed? How did that come about?

2. If it is true, for now at least, that men and women often do not agree that some forms of sexual conduct are deeply offensive, why should the law adopt the perspective of the victim? Why not adopt the perspective of the "reasonable harasser" instead? Which perspective are employers likely to prefer? Is employee productivity apt to be affected even if the men "don't get it"?

[13.] *If sexual comments or sexual advances are in fact welcomed by the recipient, they, of course, do not constitute sexual harassment. Title VII's prohibition of sex discrimination in employment does not require a totally desexualized workplace.*

One of the concerns left by the *Ellison* decision is how courts are to determine what the reasonable person in the plaintiff's circumstances would have felt. At about the same time that the Ninth Circuit Court of Appeals decided the *Ellison* case, a district court in Florida, using the same standard, handed down its ruling in the following case. Two features are significant about the *Robinson* case. It is the first sexual harassment case in which expert witnesses played an important role. It is also the first case in which the display of pornography in the workplace was found to have created a sufficiently hostile working environment to violate Title VII. Apparently the impact of pornography in the workplace is quite different when viewed from the perspective of the reasonable woman and that of the "reasonable harasser."

Robinson v. Jacksonville Shipyards, Inc.

United States District Court,
Florida, 1991.
760 F.Supp. 1486.

MELTON, D.J.

This action was commenced by plaintiff Lois Robinson pursuant to Title VII of the Civil Rights Act of 1964, as amended. . . . Plaintiff asserts defendants created and encouraged a sexually hostile, intimidating work environment. Her claim centers around the presence in the workplace of pictures of women in various stages of undress and in sexually suggestive or submissive poses, as well as remarks by male employees and supervisors which demean women. Defendants dispute plaintiff's description of the work environment and maintain that, to the extent the work environment may be found to satisfy the legal definition of a hostile work environment, they are not liable for the acts that give rise to such a description. . . .

Plaintiff Lois Robinson ("Robinson") is a female employee of Jacksonville Shipyards, Inc. ("JSI"). She has been a welder since September 1977. Robinson is one of a very small number of female skilled craftworkers employed by JSI. Between 1977 and the present, Robinson was promoted from third-class welder to second-class welder and from second-class welder to her present position as a first-class welder. . . .

Pictures of nude and partially nude women appear throughout the JSI workplace in the form of magazines, plaques on the wall, photographs torn from magazines and affixed to the wall or attached to calendars supplied by advertising tool supply companies ("vendors' advertising calendars"). Two plaques consisting of pictures of naked women, affixed to wood and varnished, were introduced into evidence and identified by several witnesses as having been on display for years at JSI in the fab[rication] shop area under the supervision of defendant Lovett. . . .

Robinson's testimony provides a vivid description of a visual assault on the sensibilities of female workers at JSI that did not relent during working hours. She credibly testified that the pervasiveness of the pictures left her unable to recount every example, but those pictures which she did describe illustrate the extent of this aspect of the work environment at JSI. She testified to seeing in the period prior to April 4, 1984, the three hundredth day prior to the filing of her EEOC charge: (a) a picture of a woman, breasts and pubic area exposed, inside a dry-dock area in 1977 or 1978. (b) a picture of a nude Black woman, pubic area exposed to reveal her labia, seen in the public locker room. (c) drawings and graffiti on the walls, including a drawing depicting a frontal view of a nude female torso with the words "USDA Choice" written on it, at the Commercial Yard in the late 1970's or early 1980's, in an area where Robinson was assigned to work. (d) a picture of a woman's pubic area with a meat spatula pressed on it, observed on a wall next to the sheetmetal shop at Mayport in the late 1970's. . . .

Robinson's testimony concerning visual harassment in the period commencing April 4, 1984, includes: (a) a picture of a nude woman with long blonde hair wearing high heels and holding a whip, waved around by a coworker, Freddie Dixon, in 1984, in an enclosed area where Robinson and approximately six men were working. Robinson testified she felt particularly targeted by this action because she has long blonde hair and works with a welding tool known as a whip. . . .

Robinson also testified about comments of a sexual nature she recalled hearing at JSI from coworkers. In some instances these comments were made while she also was in the presence of the pictures of nude or partially nude women. Among the remarks Robinson recalled are: "Hey pussycat, come here and give me a whiff"; "The more you lick it, the harder it gets"; "I'd like to get in bed with that,"; "I'd like to have some of that"; "Black women taste like sardines," . . .

Robinson testified concerning the presence of abusive language written on the walls in her working areas in 1987 and 1988. Among this graffiti were the phrases "lick me you whore dog bitch," "eat me," and "pussy." This first phrase appeared on the wall over a spot where

Robinson had left her jacket. The second phrase was freshly painted in Robinson's work area when she observed it. The third phrase appeared during a break after she left her work area to get a drink of water. . . .

The Court heard testimony from two of Robinson's female coworkers, Lawanna Gail Banks ("Banks") and Leslie Albert ("Albert"), concerning incidents of sexual harassment to which they were subjected, including incidents that did not occur in Robinson's presence. . . .

Based on the foregoing, the Court finds that sexually harassing behavior occurred throughout the JSI working environment with both frequency and intensity over the relevant time period. Robinson did not welcome such behavior. . . .

. . . To affect a "term, condition, or privilege" of employment within the meaning of Title VII, the harassment "must be sufficiently severe or pervasive 'to alter the conditions of [the victim's] employment and create an abusive working environment.'" "This test may be satisfied by a showing that the sexual harassment was sufficiently severe or persistent 'to affect seriously [the victim's] psychological well being.'" This "is a question to be determined with regard to the totality of the circumstances." . . .

Element four must be tested both subjectively and objectively. Regarding the former, the question is whether Robinson has shown she is an "affected individual," that is, she is at least as affected as the reasonable person under like circumstances. The evidence reflects the great upset that Robinson felt when confronted with individual episodes of harassment and the workplace as a whole. Further, the impact on her work performance is plain. . . .

The objective standard asks whether a reasonable person of Robinson's sex, that is, a reasonable woman, would perceive that an abusive working environment has been created. The severity and pervasiveness aspects form a structure to test this hypothesis. . . .

A reasonable woman would find that the working environment at JSI was abusive. This conclusion reaches the totality of the circumstances, including the sexual remarks, the sexual jokes, the sexually-oriented pictures of women, and the nonsexual rejection of women by coworkers. The testimony by Dr. Fiske and Ms. Wagner [expert witnesses for the plaintiff] provides a reliable basis upon which to conclude that the cumulative, corrosive effect of this work environment over time affects the psychological well-being of a reasonable woman placed in these conditions. . . .

This Court must "render a decree which will so far as possible eliminate the discriminatory effects of the past as well as bar like discrimination in the future." *Albemarle Paper Co.* Ms. Wagner endorsed plaintiff's proposed sexual harassment policy and procedures as an effective remedy for the work environment at JSI. The Court agrees with her assessment. The Court notes the use of education, training and the development of effective complaint procedures as an appropriate remedy in prior hostile work environment sexual harassment cases. The Court adopts the policy and procedures proposed by plaintiff. . . .

STUDY QUESTIONS

1. Do you agree that the reasonable person in the plaintiffs' circumstances would have found this working environment to be hostile and offensive? Do the men and women in your class agree on this?

2. Do you find the observations of Dr. Fiske and Ms. Wagner credible? If it had been shown that Lois Robinson was as tolerant of pornography in other settings as the average person, would your views of her complaints here be any different? Does the social context in which pornography is viewed affect the extent to which it is taken as threatening?

The reasonable woman standard was used by these courts to alter, not reinforce, prevailing stereotypes—to combat generally tolerated, if not accepted, discriminatory practices. Their decisions declare that even if the form of harassment is commonplace, it nevertheless violates Title VII if it is sufficiently severe or pervasive in the eyes of the reasonable woman. The hope here is that this process will contribute to changing the prevailing stereotypes and customary practices of those in power in the workplaces of the nation. The hope is that one day, soon, the men will "get it."

The particular outcome in *Robinson,* however, is troublesome for many observers. This decision, like so many before it that have attempted to restrict the availability and use of pornography, raises free speech concerns. More directly, the question that *Robinson* raises is whether the First Amendment's guarantee of free speech permits the Congress to make a law, such as Title VII, that restricts people in making the utterances and gestures and in distributing the printed materials that were the basis of the complaint in this case. This concern was raised but not confronted in connection with the "hate speech" provisions of college disciplinary codes. (See Chapter 6.) The Court may reach this issue when it decides the appeal of *Harris v. Forklift Systems, Inc.* (976 F.2d 733 (6th Cir. 1992), *Cert. granted,* 113 S. Ct. 1382 (1993) during the 1993-94 term. There, the question is whether, to prevail on a hostile environment approach, a woman who was offended by conduct that would have offended a reasonable person must also show that she sustained "severe psychological injury."

Over the past three decades, feminists have worked to eliminate sexual harassment from our culture and in particular from our workplaces. The focus in this section has been on litigative approaches to that goal. The following selection identifies additional ways to advance the same objective.

Techniques for Preventing Sexual Harassment

Kathryn Abrams,
"Gender Discrimination and the Transformation of Workplace Norms." 42 *Vanderbilt Law Review* 1183, 1215–20 (1989).

. . . Although revising Title VII standards is a crucial step toward reshaping the norms governing personal exchange in the workplace, it would be unwise to rely on litigation as the sole, or even primary, means of reform. Litigation is vastly disruptive of the plaintiffs' relations with others in the workplace. . . . The sexual harassment plaintiff typically is subjected to further or intensified harassment as she pursues her claim, and her relationships with both men and women in the workplace may be

Reprinted by permission of Vanderbilt Law Review

severed beyond repair, a form of damage that even legal victory cannot undo. Moreover, changes in behavior that are compelled by judicial decree, rather than voluntarily introduced and advocated by the employer, may produce lingering resentment among male workers that affects not only their receptivity to subsequent female coworkers, but also their behavior toward the other women in their lives. Strategies to end sexual harassment should not require all women to make the difficult choice between enduring continued harassment and seeking costly victory in the courts.

Litigation can also be a comparatively blunt tool for producing changes in workplace norms. Judgments—and even opinions—in sexual harassment cases give employers only an anecdotal notion of what behavior is unacceptable, and otherwise fail to direct employers toward more satisfactory behavior. Nor do these decisions, in and of themselves, organize or educate employees to produce the necessary changes in conduct. An adverse judgment also may put supervisors on the defensive, rather than engaging them as participants in bringing about change. For the protection of women and the education of those who victimize them, it is necessary to explore less coercive means of normative change.

Reliance on nonadjudicative means should not, and need not, alter the focus of enforcement against sexual harassment. Two nonadjudicative strategies might offer an even more effective means of targeting and ameliorating devaluative sexual conduct in the workplace. First, enforcement efforts by the EEOC provide an avenue for reform that is less adversarial in nature than a full-blown private action. Were the EEOC to conciliate . . . , it could investigate devaluative sexual conduct and seek agreements to reform workplace behavior that would provide a comprehensive education to members of the defendant's workforce. Conciliation . . . also would be less coercive than judicial intervention, and would produce few of the costs to the complaint that arise from pressing and testifying in her own litigation.

Another promising approach is for employers to implement the proposed Title VII standards through voluntary compliance programs. Compliance programs have been adopted widely by large and small firms in areas such as antitrust, in which the consequences of legal liability are potentially great. Although treble damages and criminal sanctions do not threaten defendants in Title VII cases, other factors might make compliance programs attractive to employers. . . . A well-administered compliance program reduces the likelihood that an employer will be held liable for harassing conduct, and should reduce the likelihood that such harassment will occur at all. Moreover, a well-publicized program could be an effective recruitment tool for an employer seeking to increase the number of women in its workforce, notwithstanding the possible ambivalence of some of its male employees. An effective compliance program might also bring broader competitive advantages, as it would reduce a source of tension that saps employees' productivity, and might improve the position of the firm in the labor market and among certain groups of consumers.

Although compliance programs do not carry the force of legal sanctions, they have several features that better enable them to modify those norms giving rise to sexual harassment. First, they can provide guidelines for employees regarding proper and improper behavior in a context less emotionally charged, and more accessible to employees, than a court battle. . . .

Perhaps the greatest asset of a compliance program is the opportunity it provides for sustained re-education of a workforce. A judicial decree awards only reinstatement, back pay, or attorney's fees; the preceding litigation may highlight only a few offensive practices. Neither the decree nor the litigation helps employers or employees understand the injury that the legal standard is intended to prevent, nor do they help workers learn more acceptable forms of conduct. Most authors of legal compliance programs insist that the element most important to the programs' success is a face-to-face education of the workforce at their inception. Thorough introductions accompanied by small-group question and answer sessions can provide new perspectives on widely accepted conduct. Readings, films, or simulations—varying perhaps with the background of the workforce—can help perpetrators to recognize potential violations and help victims to stand firm in their resistance. These opportunities for exchange can be of crucial value when the goal is to create an awareness of divergent viewpoints.

While a change in the adjudicative approach to sexual harassment is essential, it need not be the only arrow in the quiver of feminists advocating change. The precise guidelines, shared responsibility, and comprehensive education that compliance programs can provide make them a nondivisive, fine-tuned supplement to adjudicative enforcement.

STUDY QUESTIONS

1. What reasons were given against complete reliance on litigation to eliminate sexual harassment from workplaces? What alternative techniques are discussed?

2. What incentives do employers have for implementing voluntary compliance programs designed to end sexual harassment in their workplaces? What interest do victims and potential victims have in supporting such programs? Are such programs likely to escape the problems faced by the litigative approach?

II. PAY EQUITY

Of all the issues that have arisen in the area of sex discrimination in employment, the most heated and enduring relates to the compensation differential between men and women. In the remainder of this chapter, we will explore some of the many dimensions of that issue and examine the main legal responses available under federal law.

The Earnings Gap

> The Lord said to Moses, "Say to the people of Israel, When a man makes a special vow of persons to the Lord at your valuation, then your valuation of a male from twenty years old up to sixty years old shall be fifty shekels of the sanctuary. If the person is a female, your valuation shall be thirty shekels."
> *Lev. 27:1–4.*

Over the past three decades, the gender composition of the labor force has undergone an unprecedented transformation. What has occurred might be called the feminization of the workforce. The U.S. Department of Labor reports that in 1960, one in three full-time workers was a woman. In 1990, women made up 57.5 percent of the workforce. Since 1960, the participation of married women in the labor force, including those with children in the home, has dramatically increased. In 1992, almost three of every five married women whose husband was present in the household worked full-time. In that same group, two of every three who had children under eighteen years old at home were in the labor force full-time in 1992. This compared with 31 percent and 28 percent, respectively, in 1960.

Of course, other changes occurred during that same period. In 1960, one in ten households, just over 5 million families, was maintained by women—no spouse present. By 1991, that number had tripled, and 18 percent of all households were headed by women. One of the consequences of these developments is reflected in the poverty rates. In 1990, as reported by the U.S. Department of Commerce, 37.4 percent of all families with children under eighteen years old were female-headed, no spouse present. One of the groups to feel the impact of this was our children. Of the 33.6 million poor in this country in 1990, 40 percent of them were children under eighteen years of age. As Figure 5.1 shows, this effects people differently across racial and ethnic groups.

Certainly, one of the principal factors that generates these poverty effects from the feminization of the labor force is what has come to be known as the "earnings gap." As Table 5.1 indicates, the pattern has been remarkably consistent.

We saw in Chapter 4 that a much larger proportion of adult women are in the work force in the mid-1980s than in the mid-1950s, when only one in three worked outside the home. Now more than half are in the work force. During those three decades, however, the differential between male and female earnings remained the same as the one mentioned by Moses. Throughout that period, women earned three-fifths as much as men. The constancy of that differential over these decades is startling.

One of the dimensions of the earnings gap that is frequently overlooked when considering such gross measures is the different ways it affects minority women and men. As Figure 5.2 shows, men in each racial/ethnic category earn more than women in the same category. However, compare the earnings of white women to men in different racial/ethnic groups.

FIGURE 5.1. Families in Poverty—1991, Women in Households With Children

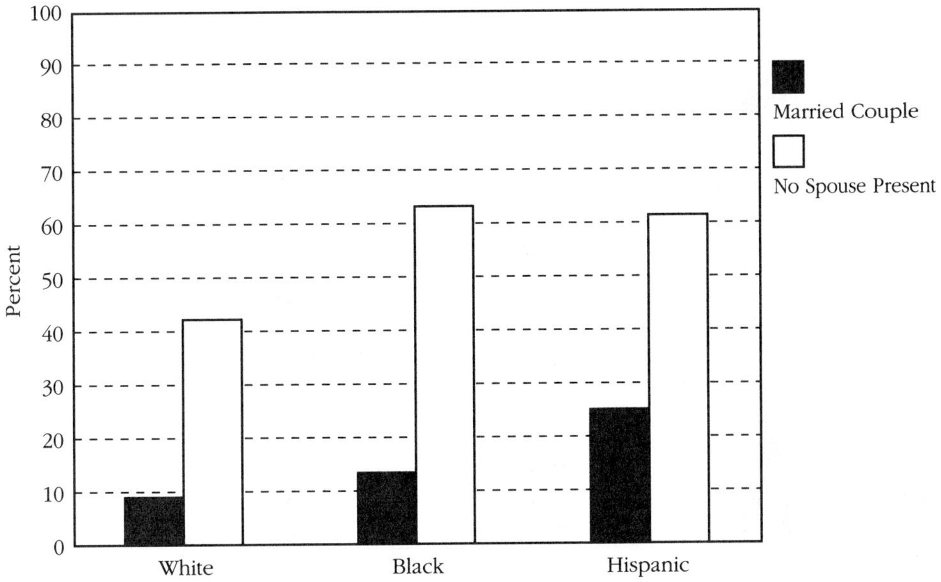

SOURCE: *U.S. Census Bureau.* Current Population Reports, *series P-60, no. 181. Washington, D.C.: Government Printing Office, August 1992. Table 21.*

What explains the earnings gap? Why does it exist at all, and what makes it so persistent? One of the most frequently voiced explanations is that women bring a different and less valued set of personal characteristics, such as skills and work experience, to the workplace than do men.

Educational attainment is frequently cited as one of the differences between males and females, as groups, in the labor force. Many who urge women to seek ever more education at ever more advanced levels proceed on this premise—the thought being that education is the great equalizer. Consider Table 5.2 to see if that premise is borne out by the data.

TABLE 5.1. Median Annual Earnings of Year-Round Full-Time Workers, 15 Years and Over, by Sex, 1955–91

Year	Men	Women	Women's Earnings as % of Men's
1991	$30,331	$21,245	70.0%
1990	28,979	20,591	71.1
1985	24,999	16,252	65.0
1980	19,173	11,591	60.5
1975	12,934	7,719	59.7
1970	9,184	5,440	59.2
1965	6,598	3,816	57.8
1960	5,434	3,296	60.7
1955	4,241	2,735	64.5

SOURCE: *U.S. Census Bureau.* Current Population Reports, *series P-60, no. 180. Washington, D.C.: Government Printing Office, August 1992. Table 24.*

FIGURE 5.2. The earnings gap—1991, by ethnic group

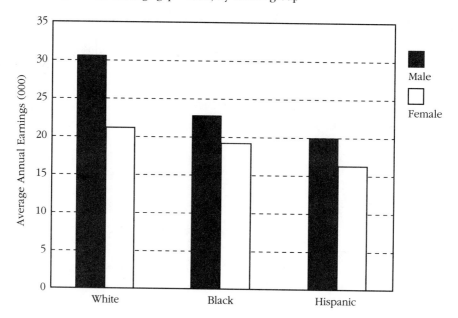

SOURCE: *U.S. Census Bureau.* Current Population Reports, *series P-60, no. 180. Washington, D.C.: Government Printing Office, August 1992. Table 24.*

The contrast here is not limited to the comparison between males and females who have roughly the same educational attainment. In Figure 5.3, these same data enable us to compare the average earnings of males and females who have different educational attainment. Notice the relationship between females who have graduated from high school (twelve years) and college (sixteen years) with males of lesser attainment! Does this indicate that education is the great equalizer?

Worker characteristics explain a part of the earnings gap. Researchers have confirmed that as much as 44 percent of the earnings gap can be explained by the different characteristics of men and women workers. (See, e.g., the Treiman and Hartman study later in this chapter.) Even allowing for that, however, more than half of the earnings gap remains unexplained. What else might account for the differential earnings of women and men who work full-time and year-round?

TABLE 5.2. Earnings Gap and Education—1991

	Average Annual Earnings ($000)		
Years of School	Female	Male	% of Male
<9	$12.07	$17.62	68.5%
10–11	14.46	21.40	67.5
12	18.84	26.78	70.3
13–15	22.14	31.66	70.0
16	29.09	40.91	71.1
17+	34.94	49.73	70.3

SOURCE: *U.S. Census Bureau.* Current Population Reports, *series P-60, no. 181. Washington, D.C.: Government Printing Office, August 1992. Table 24.*

FIGURE 5.3. Earnings Gap and Education

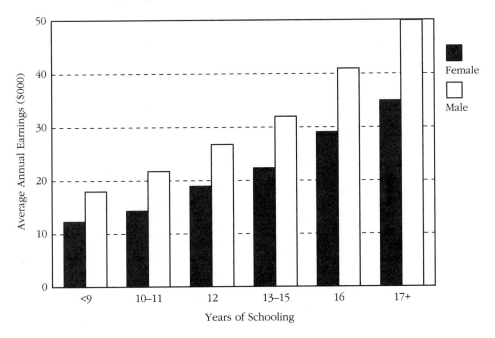

SOURCE: *U.S. Census Bureau.* Current Population Reports, *series P-60, no. 180. Washington, D.C.: Government Printing Office, August 1992. Table 24.*

The Equal Pay Act

Wage and salary discrimination is a second explanation that is commonly advanced to account for the earnings gap. In this view, a substantial proportion of the remaining wage gap might be explained by sex discrimination on the part of employers. Even though the language of Title VII includes such discrimination within the scope of its prohibitions, the main burden of preventing pay discrimination based on sex has been assumed by the Equal Pay Act.

The first major legal measure at the federal level attempting to remedy the substantial and unexplained wage differential was the Equal Pay Act of 1963 (29 U.S.C. § 206(d)(1)). As originally enacted, the act contained an exemption for "employees employed in a bona fide executive, administrative, or professional capacity. . . ." This exemption was removed by an amendment added by the 92nd Congress in 1972. The full text of the amended act reads as follows:

> *No employer* having employees subject to any provisions of this section *shall* discriminate, within any establishment in which such employees are employed, between employees on the basis of sex by paying wages to employees in such establishment at a rate less than the rate at which he pays wages to employees of the opposite sex in such establishment for equal work on jobs the performance of which requires equal skill, effort, and responsibility, and which are performed under similar working conditions,
>
> *except where* such payment is made pursuant to (i) a seniority system; (ii) a merit system; (iii) a system which measures earnings by quantity or quality of production; or (iv) a differential based on any other factor other than sex:

Provided, That an employer who is paying a wage rate differential in violation of this subsection shall not, in order to comply with the provisions of this subsection, reduce the wage rate of any employee. (Emphasis added.)

As you can see, the statute contains three main provisions. These are ordinarily referred to as the equal pay for equal work formula, the four affirmative defenses, and the limitation on remedies. The principles used to interpret these provisions were developed by the courts in the cases that follow. You can see from the table at the beginning of this section that the wage differential has not changed since the adoption of the Equal Pay Act. As you study these cases, see if you can explain why the act has had no measurable effect.

The "equal pay for equal work" provision of the act prohibits employers from paying employees of opposite sexes at different rates for jobs that are equivalent in terms of skill, effort, responsibility, and working conditions. The violation envisioned by this provision is paying women in a job classification less than men in the same classification. Such practices are banned by the act, whether blatantly exploitive of women or rationalized as granting preference to men as the alleged primary providers for the nation's households. In this sense, the act directly confronted the most blatant and overt instances of sex discrimination in matters of compensation. Congress, however, carefully limited the scope of this prohibition. The prohibition applies only where the jobs held by women and those held by better paid men are "equal." The prohibition of the Equal Pay Act does not reach differentiation in the rates of pay among different job classifications. The courts, however, have interpreted this prohibition to include jobs in distinct classifications where the work performed by women workers is "substantially equal" to that performed by better paid men in the respects listed in the act. (*Shultz v. Wheaton Glass Co.* 421 F.2d 259 (3d Cir. 1970).) This extension was evidently intended to thwart more subtle forms of wage discrimination in which refinements of job descriptions are used to mask sex discrimination.

In *Wheaton Glass,* the appellate court extended the reach of the act to include "substantially equal" work. In 1974, the Supreme Court followed a similar approach in the decision that follows. In the course of upholding a judgment against an employer, the Court also clarified the order of proof used in the analysis of equal pay litigation.

Corning Glass Works v. Brennan

Supreme Court of the
United States, 1974.
417 U.S. 188, 94 S.Ct. 2223,
41 L.Ed.2d 1.

Mr. Justice MARSHALL delivered the opinion of the Court.

These cases arise under the Equal Pay Act of 1963 which added to the Fair Labor Standards Act the principle of equal pay for equal work regardless of sex. The principal question posed is whether Corning Glass Works violated the Act by paying a higher base wage to male night shift inspectors than it paid to female inspectors performing the same tasks on the day shift, where the higher wage was paid in addition to a separate night shift differential paid to all employees for night work. In No. 73–29, the Court of Appeals for the Second Circuit, in a case involving several Corning plants in Corning, New York, held that this practice violated the Act. In No. 73–695, the Court of Appeals for the Third Circuit, in a case involving a Corning plant in Wellsboro, Pennsylvania, reached the opposite conclusion. We granted certiorari and consolidated the cases to resolve this unusually direct conflict between two circuits. . . .

Prior to 1925, Corning operated its plants in Wellsboro and Corning only during the day and all inspection work was performed by women. Between 1925 and 1930, the company began to introduce automatic production equipment which made it desirable to institute a night shift. During this period, however, both New York and Pennsylvania law prohibited women from working at night. As a result, in order to fill inspector positions on the new night shift, the company had to recruit male employees from among its male dayworkers. The male employees so transferred demanded and received wages substantially higher than those paid to women inspectors engaged on the two day shifts. During this same period, however, no plant-wide shift differential existed and male employees working at night, other than inspectors, received the same wages as their day shift counterparts. Thus a situation developed where the night inspectors were all male, the day inspectors all female, and the male inspectors received significantly higher wages.

In 1944, Corning plants at both locations were organized by a labor union and a collective-bargaining agreement was negotiated for all production and maintenance employees. This agreement for the first time established a plant-wide shift differential, but this change did not eliminate the higher base wage paid to male night inspectors. Rather, the shift differential was superimposed on the existing difference in base wages between male night inspectors and female day inspectors.

Prior to June 11, 1964, the effective date of the Equal Pay Act, the law in both Pennsylvania and New York was amended to permit women to work at night. It was not until some time after the effective date of the Act, however, that Corning initiated efforts to eliminate the differential rates for male and female inspectors. Beginning in June 1966, Corning started to open up jobs on the night shift to women. Previously separate male and female seniority lists were consolidated and women became eligible to exercise their seniority, on the same basis as men, to bid for the higher paid night inspection jobs as vacancies occurred.

On January 20, 1969, a new collective-bargaining agreement went into effect, establishing a new "job evaluation" system for setting wage rates. The new agreement abolished for the future the separate base wages for day and night shift inspectors and imposed a uniform base wage for inspectors exceeding the wage rate for the night shift previously in effect. All inspectors hired after January 20, 1969, were to receive the same base wage, whatever their sex or shift. The collective-bargaining agreement further provided, however, for a higher "red circle" rate for employees hired prior to January 20, 1969, when working as inspectors on the night shift. This "red circle" rate served essentially to perpetuate the differential in base wages between day and night inspectors.

The Secretary of Labor brought these cases to enjoin Corning from violating the Equal Pay Act and to collect back wages allegedly due female employees because of past violations. Three distinct questions are presented: (1) Did Corning ever violate the Equal Pay Act by paying male night shift inspectors more than female day shift inspectors? (2) If so, did Corning cure its violation of the Act in 1966 by permitting women to work as night shift inspectors? (3) Finally, if the violation was not remedied in 1966, did Corning cure its violation in 1969 by equalizing day and night inspector wage rates but establishing higher "red circle" rates for existing employees working on the night shift?

Congress' purpose in enacting the Equal Pay Act was to remedy what was perceived to be a serious and endemic problem of employment discrimination in private industry—the fact that the wage structure of "many segments of American industry has been based on an ancient but outmoded belief that a man, because of his role in society, should be paid more than a woman even though his duties are the same." The solution adopted was quite simple in principle: to require that "equal work will be rewarded by equal wages."

The Act's basic structure and operation are similarly straightforward. In order to make out a case under the Act, the Secretary must show that an employer pays different wages to employees of opposite sexes "for equal work on jobs the performance of which requires equal skill, effort, and responsibility, and which are performed under similar working conditions." Although the Act is silent on this point, its legislative history makes plain that the Secretary has the burden of proof on this issue, as both of the courts below recognized.

The Act also establishes four exceptions— three specific and one a general catchall provision—where different payment to employees of opposite sexes "is made pursuant to (i) a seniority system; (ii) a merit system; (iii) a system which measures earnings by quantity or quality of production; or (iv) a differential based on any other factor other than sex." Again, while the Act is silent on this question, its structure and history also suggest that once the Secretary has carried his burden of showing that the employer pays workers of one sex more than workers of the opposite sex for equal work, the burden shifts to the employer to show that the differential is justified under one of the Act's four exceptions. . . .

While a layman might well assume that time of day worked reflects one aspect of a job's "working conditions," the term has a different and much more specific meaning in the language of industrial relations. As Corning's own representative testified at the hearings, the element of working conditions encompasses two subfactors: "surroundings" and "hazards." "Surroundings" measures the elements, such as toxic chemicals or fumes, regularly encountered by a worker, their intensity, and their frequency. "Hazards" takes into account the physical hazards regularly encountered, their frequency, and the severity of injury they can cause. This definition of "working conditions" is not only manifested in Corning's own job evaluation plans but is also well accepted across a wide range of American industry.

Nowhere in any of these definitions is time of day worked mentioned as a relevant criterion. The fact of the matter is that the concept of "working conditions," as used in the specialized language of job evaluation systems, simply does not encompass shift differentials. . . . We agree with the Second Circuit that the inspec-

tion work at issue in this case, whether performed during the day or night, is "equal work" as that term is defined in the Act. . . .

. . . [The next] question is whether the company remedied the specific violation of the Act which the Secretary proved. We agree with the Second Circuit, as well as with all other circuits that have had occasion to consider this issue, that the company could not cure its violation except by equalizing the base wages of female day inspectors with the higher rates paid the night inspectors. This result is implicit in the Act's language, its statement of purpose, and its legislative history. . . .

The Equal Pay Act is broadly remedial, and it should be construed and applied so as to fulfill the underlying purposes which Congress sought to achieve. If, as the Secretary proved, the work performed by women on the day shift was equal to that performed by men on the night shift, the company became obligated to pay the women the same base wage as their male counterparts on the effective date of the Act. To permit the company to escape that obligation by agreeing to allow some women to work on the night shift at a higher rate of pay as vacancies occurred would frustrate, not serve, Congress' ends. . . .

The judgment in No. 73–29 is affirmed. The judgment in No 73–695 is reversed and the case remanded to the Court of Appeals for further proceedings consistent with this opinion.

It is so ordered.

STUDY QUESTIONS

1. What did the Court declare to have been Congress' purpose in enacting the Equal Pay Act?
2. On what grounds did the Court find that the jobs of day inspector and night inspector were performed under "similar working conditions"?

— ❧ —

In *Corning Glass,* the Court indicated the order of proof to be followed in Equal Pay Act cases. If the government shows that the employer used different wage rates for employees of opposite sexes for jobs that are substantially equal in skill, effort, responsibility, and working conditions, the burden of proof shifts to the employer to show that one of the four affirmative defenses listed in the statute apply to the situation. If the employer does not succeed, the government prevails.

The affirmative defenses afforded employers by the Act function as exceptions to the rule stated in the "equal pay for equal work" provision. As such, they create the same concern as those created by Title VII, i.e., that the exceptions might be interpreted so broadly as to "swallow the rule." This is especially important for the fourth affirmative defense—"any other factor other than sex." In the following case, the court construed that exception rather broadly.

Hodgson v. Robert Hall Clothes, Inc.

United States Court of Appeals,
Third Circuit, 1973.
473 F.2d 589, *cert. denied,*
414 U.S. 866 (1973).

JAMES HUNTER, III, Circuit Judge.

The Robert Hall store in question is located in Wilmington, Delaware. It sells clothing, and contains a department for men's and boys' clothing and another department for women's and girls' clothing. The store is a one-floor building, and the departments are in separate portions of it.

The merchandise in the men's department was, on the average, of higher price and better quality than the merchandise in the women's department; and Robert Hall's profit margin on the men's clothing was higher than its margin on the women's clothing. Consequently, the men's department at all times showed a larger dollar volume in gross sales, and a greater gross profit. Breaking this down, the salespeople in the men's department, on the average, sold more merchandise in terms of dollars and produced more gross profit than did the people in the women's department per hour of work.

The departments are staffed by full and part-time sales personnel. At all times, only men were permitted to work in the men's department and only women were permitted to work in the women's department. The complaint is not addressed to the propriety of such segregated employment.

The salespeople receive a base salary and can earn additional incentive payments. Various factors relating to the garment sold determine the amount of incentive payments. At all times, the salesmen received higher salaries than the saleswomen. Both starting salaries and periodic increases were higher for the males. The amount of incentive compensation was very slightly greater for the men.

After a trial in late 1970, the district court filed its opinion on April 16, 1971. The court found that Robert Hall had a valid business reason for segregating its sales personnel, i.e., "the frequent necessity for physical contact between the sales persons and the customers which would embarrass both and would inhibit sales unless they were of the same sex." . . . It proceeded to hold that the sales personnel of each department performed equal work within the meaning of § 206(d)(1).

The question then facing it was whether Robert Hall could prove that the wage "differential was based on any other factor other than sex." . . .

[The Secretary of Labor] argues that "any other factor" does not mean *any* other factor. Instead he claims it means any other factor other than sex which "is related to job performance or is typically used in setting wage scales." He contends that economic benefits to an employer do not fall within this exception.

He recognizes that the men's department produces a greater profit for Robert Hall. His contention is that the salesmen have nothing to do with producing this benefit since the district court found that the salesmen and saleswomen performed equal work. Since the saleswomen cannot sell the higher-priced clothing sold in the men's department, this cannot be used as a factor on which to base a wage differential. Otherwise, "the exception could swallow the rule."

Robert Hall does not argue that "any other" means "any other" either. It claims that a wage differential is permissible if based on a legitimate business reason. As the district court found, economic benefits could justify a wage differential. We need go no further than to say the district court was correct to hold in this case that economic benefits to an employer can justify a wage differential.

The Secretary's argument is incorrect for several reasons. It ignores the basic finding of the district court that Robert Hall's segregation of its work force was done for legitimate business purposes. It is also inconsistent with the wording of the statute.

In providing for exceptions, the statute states that they will apply when the males and females are doing equal work. Congress thus intended to allow wage differentials even though the contrasted employers were performing equal work.

The next question is whether Robert Hall proved that it received the economic benefits upon which it claimed it based its salary differentials. It is well-settled that the employer has the burden of proof on this issue. . . .

The overwhelming evidence which showed that the men's department was more profitable than the women's was sufficient to justify the differences in base salary. These statistics proved that Robert Hall's wage differentials were not based on sex but instead fully supported the reasoned business judgment that the sellers of women's clothing could not be paid as much as the sellers of men's clothing. Robert Hall's executives testified that it was their practice to base their wage rates on these departmental figures.

While no business reason could justify a practice clearly prohibited by the act, the legislative history set forth above indicates a Congressional intent to allow reasonable business judgments to stand. It would be too great an economic and accounting hardship to impose upon Robert Hall the requirement that it correlate the wages of each individual with his or her performance. This could force it toward a system based totally upon commissions, and it seems unwise to read such a result into § 206(d)(1)(iv). . . .

Affirmed.

STUDY QUESTIONS

1. Robert Hall did not show that the greater profits in the men's department were due to more productive efforts of the individual salespeople in that department. How, then, did it persuade the court that the wage differential was due to a "factor other than sex"?

2. What "factor other than sex" justified the wage differential that existed here? Did the court reach the correct result?

3. Should the courts accept "reasoned business judgment," i.e., "economic benefits," as an exception to the principle of equal pay for equal work? Do you suppose that in the past, employers would have supported discriminatory wages in the absence of such benefits? If the courts were to understand economic benefits as a "factor other than sex," would the rule be in danger of being swallowed by the exception?

The decision in *Robert Hall* permitted an exception to the principle of equal pay for equal work because the differential was based upon "reasoned business judgment." This interpretation of the "any factor other than sex" provision broadened this exception to such an extent that many feared, with Secretary of Labor Peter J. Brennan, that it practically rendered the Equal Pay Act a dead letter. In the absence of a definitive decision on the meaning of this affirmative defense by the Supreme Court, the circuit courts are left to seek consensus on their own. Although the "reasoned business judgment" interpretation of *Robert Hall* is not popular among the circuit courts, it remains a viable alternative. More recently, debate over the interpretation of this defense has centered on "market force theory." The following decision reflects the features of that theory, as well as the considerations that proponents find compelling and critics find disturbing.

Glenn v. General Motors Corp.

United States Court of Appeals, Eleventh Circuit, 1988. 841 F.2d 1567., *Cert. denied,* 488 U.S. 948 (1988).

JOHNSON, Circuit Judge:

Sheila Ann Glenn, Patricia Johns, and Robbie Nugent filed suit against General Motors Corporation (GM) and its Saginaw Steering Gear Division, alleging violation of the Equal Pay Act. The United States District Court for the Northern District of Alabama found for the appellees and awarded damages. . . .

The three appellees are employed in the Materials Management Department (previously Tool Stores Department) of the Saginaw Division of GM in three different plants near Athens, Alabama. The appellees currently work in the positions of Materials Management Expediter and Materials Follow-up Clerk, previously designated Follow-up and Associate Follow-up Tool and Die respectively. A follow-up basically ensures that adequate supplies of tools and operating materials are on hand in the GM plants to meet the minimum levels necessary to keep the plants running. Normally, each plant has three follow-ups, although GM has used less than three at times. Up to the time of suit, four women, including the appellees, (as well as men) had worked in the follow-up position. Appellee Nugent was hired in 1975, the first person to hold a follow-up position.

No doubt exists that through 1985 all three appellees earned less than all their male comparators in the follow-up position in the Tool Stores Department. In fact, the most highly paid appellee made less through 1985 than the lowest paid man. In addition, all the appellees received lower starting salaries as compared to those received by men hired near the same time.

In the present case, Nugent was hired "off the street" as a salaried follow-up, Glenn and Johns transferred from their salaried secretarial positions. In contrast, the male comparators transferred from hourly wage jobs. GM contends that to encourage people to move out of hourly wage jobs into salaried tracks, it maintains a longstanding, unwritten, corporate-wide policy against requiring an employee to take a cut in pay when transferring to salaried positions such as those at issue in the present case. GM thus argues that this "policy" constitutes a "factor other than sex" and legitimizes the pay disparity.

> The district court found that the "policy" suffered from a fatal flaw:
>
> [T]his so-called salary "policy" is in fact not a policy at all, but merely one aspect of a practice. In practice GM simply pays Follow-Ups what it takes to induce them to accept the employment. The court notes that historically companies may and do hire women at lower sta[r]ting salaries. The court is thus unconvinced of GM's attempted justification for the pay disparity. The three female plaintiffs are being paid less money than their male counterparts for equal work without justification.

Consequently, the district court held that GM had failed to prove an affirmative defense justifying the pay disparity.

We affirm the district court. GM seeks to defend that pay disparity as a result of the market force theory. This Court and the Supreme Court have long rejected the market force theory as a "factor other than sex": "[T]he argument that supply and demand dictates that women qua women may be paid less is exactly the kind of evil that the [Equal Pay] Act was designed to eliminate, and has been rejected."

We recognize that our holding may contradict the Seventh Circuit's holding in *Covington v. Southern Illinois University,* 816 F.2d 317 (7th Cir. 1987). In *Covington,* the defendant university argued that its salary retention policy, its financial emergency, and the male comparator's education and experience justified the pay disparity. The Seventh Circuit agreed with the university, and examined whether the salary retention policy alone could be a "factor other than sex."

The university had a sex-neutral policy of maintaining an employee's salary upon a change of assignment within the university. Covington argued that

> factors other than sex for purposes of the [Equal Pay Act] . . . are limited either to business-related reasons or, more narrowly, to factors that relate to the requirements of the job or to the individual's performance of that job. Covington contend[ed] that [the university]'s policy of retaining the salary of employees who change assignments does not fall within either of these categories.

The Seventh Circuit rejected Covington's argument. The flaws of the *Covington* decision are that the Seventh Circuit implicitly used the market force theory to justify the pay disparity and that the Seventh Circuit ignored congressional intent as to what is a "factor other than sex." Consequently, we reject *Covington* because it ignores that prior salary alone cannot justify pay disparity. . . .

STUDY QUESTIONS

1. What is the "market force theory" as described by the district court? What flaw was found with that approach to interpreting the "any other factor" defense?
2. Why do you suppose the Seventh Circuit Court of Appeals accepted the "market force" defense in the *Covington* case? Which of these approaches—the "reasoned business judgment" or the "market force theory"—is more in keeping with our form of economic system?

As indicated at the beginning of this section, the bulk of litigation regarding pay inequity has been governed by the Equal Pay Act. This resulted from an exception to Title VII known as the "Bennett Amendment" (section 703(h)), which provides:

> It shall not be an unlawful employment practice under this subchapter for any employer to differentiate upon the basis of sex in determining the amount of the wages or compensation paid or to be paid to employees of such employer if such differentiation is authorized by the provisions of section 206 (d) of Title 29 [The Equal Pay Act]. . . .

In its 1981 decision in *County of Washington v. Gunther* (452 U.S. 161), the Supreme Court declared that the Bennett Amendment is to be understood as incorporating not the equal pay for equal work formula but only the four affirmative defenses of the Equal Pay Act into Title VII. This decision has the effect of making any of these four defenses a complete shield against liability for pay discrimination under Title VII. We saw in *Robert Hall* just how broad the fourth of these defenses can be. When that is combined with the Bennett Amendment as interpreted by *Gunther,* we are in a position to appreciate just why it is that so few inroads have been made in the wage gap under existing laws. Consider the following decision in which the "any other factor" defense was used to defeat the "head of household rule."

Colby v. J. C. Penney Co.

United States Court of Appeals,
Seventh Circuit, 1991.
926 F.2d 645.

CUMMINGS, Circuit Judge.

. . . Plaintiff is a married employee of defendant which has more than 100 employees at its Niles, Illinois, store. Plaintiff sued as a member of a class of married female Penney employees complaining of a head of household requirement for determining spousal eligibility for coverage in its medical and dental plans. These plans deny coverage to an employee's spouse who is the "head of household." The plans provide that an employee may only obtain coverage for his or her spouse if the employee is the "head of household." That term is defined as any person who contributes more than 50% of the combined annual wage earnings of the employee and spouse. . . .

The plaintiff alleged that the "head of household" rule has an unlawful disparate impact and that the eligibility requirements for spousal coverage also constitute disparate treatment of Penney's female employees. . . .

. . . [T]he district court granted summary judgment to defendant. There the court found that Penney's "head of household" rule under which only employees making more money than their spouses can elect spousal coverage was formulated for a legitimate business reason. The purpose of the rule was to provide medical and dental insurance coverage for as many employees as possible. Because unrebutted evidence showed that Penney relied on a factor other than gender in formulating its policy, it had an affirmative defense to plaintiff wife's claims of disparate treatment and disparate impact. The Bennett Amendment incorporates into Title VII of the Civil Rights Act of 1964 the affirmative defenses set out in the Equal Pay Act of 1963 and thus excuses a compensation "differential based on any factor other than sex." The district court granted summary judgment for Penney and decertified the class on the ground that it was inadequately represented. Colby does not challenge the decertification of the class. . . .

[A document admitted at trial] supports the legitimacy of the head of household rule because it revealed that the primary purpose was "to provide benefits for as many Penney associates [employees] as possible." In the affidavit

Messinger added that "restricting spousal coverage under the head of household provision ensures that coverage is afforded to spouses who are dependent upon the associate [employee]." In view of these uncontested reasons for its plan, there was no violation of Title VII of the Civil Rights Act of 1964, for the Bennett Amendment provides that it is not an unlawful employment practice if the compensation differentiation upon the basis of sex is authorized by the Equal Pay Act. That Act permits any compensation "differential based on any other factor other than sex." 29 U.S.C. s 206(d)(1)(iv). Consequently the district court properly held that Penney was entitled to summary judgment on Colby's disparate treatment claims.

. . . Since Colby introduced no facts suggesting that Penney's head of household rule is pretextual or that Penney has less discriminatory means of achieving its broad beneficial purposes, summary judgment was appropriate on the disparate impact claims under our previous decision upholding the defense of a good business justification.

The . . . summary judgment for the defendant is affirmed.

STUDY QUESTIONS

1. On the disparate treatment allegation, what reason did the court give for finding in favor of the defendant? Why did the "any other factor" defense under the Equal Pay Act figure in this decision at all? Did the lower court apply a standard similar to the one endorsed in *Robert Hall?*
2. On the disparate impact allegation, what reason was given for finding for the defendant? Was the defense of "a good business justification" similar to the "market forces theory" discussed in *Glenn?*
3. What facts might Colby have introduced to support a different outcome?

Occupational Segregation

So far, we have considered two possible explanations of the earnings gap. The first was that women workers, as a group, possess a different and less valuable set of employment skills than do men workers as a group. We saw that research shows that this can explain less than half the difference in the average earnings of women and men. The second was that the difference was the result of overt sex discrimination on the part of employers that pay their women employees less than their men employees who do the same kind of work. The experience with the Equal Pay Act, which targets exactly that type of discrimination, suggests that this hypothesis has little explanatory power.

The tables at the beginning of section II demonstrate that the earnings gap has not measurably changed in the twenty years since the Equal Pay Act went into effect. That might be interpreted in several ways. One might suspect that the act has not been vigorously enforced—it's only been window dressing. Not even the harshest critics suggest that this is the entire explanation.

An alternative explanation is that the Equal Pay Act does not reach the principal factors responsible for the wage differential. One popular version of this theory proposes that working women as a group earn substantially less than working men as a group primarily because women workers tend to be concentrated in lower-paying occupations than men. If this is the principal explanation of the earnings gap, the act will not help, because it applies only to jobs that are substantially equal.

The occupational segregation explanation of the earnings gap has two parts, each of which is well-supported by Labor Department data. First, women and men are concentrated in different occupations (See Table 5.3).

The second part of the occupational segregation explanation of the earnings gap is that the occupations in which women cluster are lower paid than are those in which men predominate. This too is amply supported by 1991 Labor Department data that shows an inverse relationship of female concentration within an industry and average hourly earnings within that industry (see Figure 5.4).

Since the mid-1970s, feminists have insisted on the centrality of occupational segregation as a key factor in the eradication of the earnings gap. Since then, researchers have shown that occupational segregation accounts for a sizable portion of the earnings gap. Jerry Jacobs, in *Revolving Doors: Sex Segregation and Women's Careers* (Stanford, Calif.: Stanford University Press, 1989), reported that between 25 percent and 40 percent of the gap is explained by the direct effects of the

TABLE 5.3. Three-Fifths of all Women Workers are Concentrated in Occupations That are Predominantly Female

% of Female Labor Force	Occupation	% Female
26%	Clerical	80%
10%	Nurses, therapists and other health technicians	87%
8%	Food, child care, and other service occupations	82%
7%	Sales clerks and cashiers	77%
6%	Teachers (precollege)	74%
3%	Dress makers and sewing machine operators	76%
1%	Social and recreational workers	74%
62%	Total	

SOURCE: *U.S. Department of Labor, Bureau of Labor Statistics.* Employment and Earnings. *Washington, D.C.: Government Printing Office, July 1992.*

FIGURE 5.4. Earnings Decrease as Female Concentration in Industries Increases

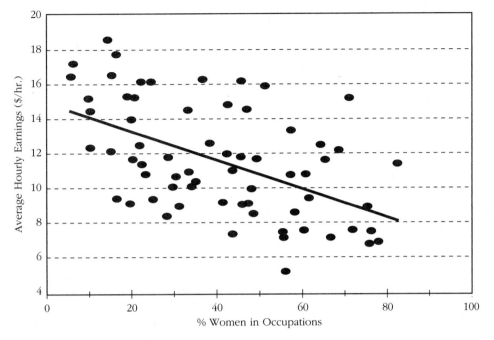

SOURCE: *Unpublished data. U.S. Department of Labor. August 1992.*

sex-segregated labor force. When the indirect effects are included, its explanatory power exceeds 50 percent.

The issue of interest in the context of this book is whether legal remedies are available where earnings differences are attributable to occupational segregation. This question has ordinarily been posed in the context of Title VII and resolved differently by different courts, depending, as Law professor Vicki Schultz points out, on the story that is told about why women tend to be concentrated in different occupations than men.

Telling Stories about Women and Work

Vicki Schultz.
103 *Harvard Law Review* 1749 (1990).

How do we make sense of that most basic feature of the world of work, sex segregation on the job? That it exists is part of our common understanding. Social science research has doc-umented, and casual observation confirmed, that men work mostly with men, doing "men's work," and women work mostly with women, doing "women's work." We know also the serious negative consequences segregation has for women workers. Work traditionally done by women has lower wages, less status, and fewer opportunities of advancement than work done by men. Despite this shared knowledge, however, we remain deeply divided in our attitudes toward sex segregation on the job. What divides us is how we interpret this reality, the stories we tell about its origins and meaning. Why does sex segregation on the job exist? Who is responsible for it? Is it an injustice, or an inevitability?

In *EEOC v. Sears, Roebuck & Co.*, the district court interpreted sex segregation as the expression of women's own choice. The Equal Employment Opportunity Commission (EEOC) sued Sears under Title VII of the Civil Rights Act of 1964. The EEOC claimed that Sears had engaged in sex discrimination in hiring and promotion into commission sales jobs, reserving these jobs mostly for men while relegating women to much lower-paying noncommission sales jobs. Like most employment discrimination plaintiffs, the EEOC relied heavily on statistical evidence to prove its claims. The EEOC's statistical studies showed that Sears had significantly underhired women sales applicants for the more lucrative commission sales positions, even after controlling for potential sex differences in qualifications.

Although the statistical evidence exposed a long-standing pattern of sex segregation in Sears' salesforce, the judge refused to attribute this pattern to sex discrimination. The judge concluded that the EEOC's statistical analyses were "virtually meaningless," because they were based on the faulty assumption that female sales applicants were as "interested" as male applicants in commission sales jobs. Indeed, the EEOC had "turned a blind eye to reality," for Sears had proved that women sales applicants preferred lower-paying noncommission sales jobs. The judge credited various explanations for women's "lack of interest" in commission sales, all of which rested on conventional images of women as "feminine" and nurturing, unsuited for the vicious competition in the male-dominated world of commission selling. In the court's eyes, Sears had done nothing to segregate its salesforce; it had merely honored the preexisting employment preferences of working women themselves. . . .

[Professor Schultz characterized this court and others that rely on the "lack of interest" explanation of work force sex segregation as "conservative." She went on to contrast that analysis with those of other "liberal" courts that rejected the "lack of interest" explanation.] Even though both explanations rest in a common evidentiary framework, each of them also stands as a separate narrative that justifies a different legal outcome. I refer to the rhetorical justification used by courts who have accepted the lack of interest argument . . . as the conservative story of choice, and to the one used by courts who have rejected that argument as the liberal story of coercion. . . .

The critical assumption that binds the two stories within a single interpretive universe is the assumption that women form stable job preferences, independently of employer action, in early social realms. In the conservative story, this assumption is accompanied by a naturalized, totalizing account of gender. Sex segregation exists because women are "feminine," and the feminine role is so all-encompassing that it implies by definition a preference for "feminine" work. In the liberal story of coercion, by contrast, the assumption that women's job preferences are fixed before they begin working means that gender difference must be suppressed. Liberal courts can justify holding employers liable only to the extent that judges can represent women as "ungendered" subjects who emerge from a gender-free social order with the same aspirations and values as men.

That these two stories constitute the entire interpretive universe creates problems for plaintiffs challenging sex segregation. By accepting the premise that only women who escape early sex-role socialization can aspire to nontraditional jobs, the liberal story reinforces the conservative one. By failing to develop an account of how employers create jobs and job aspirations along gendered lines, both stories ultimately assume away the major problem Title VII should be addressing: the organization of work structures and workplace cultures to disempower large numbers of women from aspiring to and succeeding in more highly rewarded nontraditional work. . . .

. . . The partial truth of the conservative story is that people and jobs are gendered. But they are not naturally or inevitably so. To provide an adequate explanation for sex segregation, one must account for how employers arrange work systems so as to construct work and work aspirations along gendered lines. The liberal story fails to develop such an account because it shares the conservative assumption that women form their work preferences exclusively in early pre-work realms. This assumption, in turn, leads the liberal approach to adopt an overly restrictive view of the role Title VII can play in dismantling sex segregation in the work-place. If women have already formed their job preferences before seeking work, the most the law can do is to ensure that employers do not erect formal barriers to prevent women from realizing their preexisting preferences.

There is a need for a new story to make sense of sex segregation in the workplace. Gender conditioning in pre-work realms is too slender a reed to sustain the weight of sex segregation. To explain sex segregation, the law needs an account of how employers actively construct gendered job aspirations—and jobs—in the workplace itself. . . .

The current judicial framework proceeds from the view that women bring to the labor market stable, fixed preferences for certain types of work. . . .

[This conviction] . . . depends on two different sets of assumptions. The first is the assumption that young women emerge from early life experiences articulating preferences for different types of work than young men. This assumption is correct. There is, however, nothing "natural" about the process through which young people come to express gendered job aspirations. Girls and boys are regularly subjected to sex-role conditioning in the family, the schools, and other early realms of life; they are constantly bombarded with messages that link "femininity" or "masculinity" to sex-appropriate work. It is therefore unsurprising that numerous studies have documented sex differences in the vocational aspirations of children, adolescents, teenagers, and young adults.

This evidence alone, however, is insufficient to support the claim that workplace segregation exists because women have been socialized to prefer traditionally female jobs. . . .

Recent sociological research has demonstrated the weakness of this link. In his book *Revolving Doors*, sociologist Jerry Jacobs presents the most comprehensive quantitative analyses of these issues to date. Jacobs' research presents three propositions that refute the claim that workplace segregation is attributable to women's pre-labor market preferences. First, the sex-type of the work to which young women initially aspire does not remain stable over time, but changes substantially after they start working. For the more than eighty percent of young women who changed their aspirations between 1970 and 1980, the sexual composition of the occupation to which they aspired in 1970 was only very weakly associated with the sexual composition of the occupation to which they aspired ten years later. Second, the sex-type of the work to which young women initially aspire does not predict the sex-type of the work they do as their careers unfold. For the eighty percent of young women who changed occupations, the sexual composition of the occupations they said they desired in 1970 was not correlated with the sexual composition of the occupations they actually held in 1980. Third, the sex-type of women's early work does not predict the type of work they do later in life. For those who changed occupations, there was no correlation between the sexual composition of the occupations in which they began and the sexual composition of the occupations in which they were employed a decade later. . . . Furthermore, not only young women change the sex-type of their occupations over time; older women do also. Mature women who move into nontraditional occupations mid-career are almost equally likely to move into them from male-dominated, female-dominated, and more sexually integrated occupations.

Taken together, Jacobs' analyses provide strong evidence that workplace segregation cannot be attributed solely to women's pre-labor market preferences. Even if young women's early preferences perfectly predicted the sex-type of their first jobs, the sex-type of the occupations to which they aspire changes substantially over time. . . .

. . . Even if the main thrust of women's early training is to reward them for appropriate sex-role behavior, socialization is not a straitjacket that predetermines that adult women will aspire only to work defined by the dominant culture as feminine.

[Schultz next reviewed the results of sociological research bearing on career choice among women workers and concluded that] the sociological literature provides an alternative to the pre-labor market explanation for sex segregation in the workplace. This alternative perspective begins from the premise that people's work aspirations are shaped by their experiences in the workworld. It examines how structural features of work organizations reduce women's incentive to pursue nontraditional work and encourage them to display the very work attitudes and behavior that come to be viewed as preexisting gender attributes. . . .

This perspective sheds light on the workplace dynamics that limit women's ability to claim higher-paid nontraditional work as their own. Women's patterns of occupational movement suggest that there are powerful disincentives for women to move into and to remain in nontraditional occupations. The mobility studies show that women in higher-paying, male-dominated occupations are much less likely to remain in such occupations over time than are women in lower-paying, female-dominated occupations, who are more likely to stay put. Thus, just as employers appear to have begun opening the doors to nontraditional jobs to women, almost as many women have been leaving those jobs as have been entering them. To the extent that women have been given the formal opportunity to do nontraditional work, something is preventing them from realizing that opportunity.

[This new] perspective instructs us to look beyond formal labor market opportunity and to ask what it is about the workplace itself that disempowers women from permanently seizing that opportunity. . . . [Schultz goes on to analyze] two structural features of work organizations that discourage women from pursuing nontraditional work. These two structural features interact dynamically to construct work and workers along gendered lines—the first on the "female" side and the second on the "male" side.

It is an old insight that people who are placed in jobs that offer little opportunity for growth or upward mobility will adapt to their situations by lowering their work aspirations and turning their energies elsewhere. Decades ago, researchers documented this phenomenon among male workers. Indeed, men in low-mobility positions display orientations toward work that conventional stereotypes reserve for women. . . .

While separate-but-unequal job structures encourage women to lower their work aspira-

tions, they also imply that segregation is natural in a way that encourages male workers to adopt proprietary attitudes toward "their" jobs. These attitudes encapsulate male-dominated jobs in a web of social relations that are hostile and alienating to women who dare to upset the "natural" order of segregation. I refer to the entire bundle of practices and processes through which these relations are created and sustained as harassment. Overtly sexual behavior is only the tip of a tremendous iceberg that confronts women in nontraditional jobs. They face a wide-ranging set of behaviors and attitudes by their male supervisors and co-workers that make the culture of nontraditional work hostile and alienating. . . .

This analysis of the relationship between harassment and the "masculinity" of nontraditional work makes clear why many women are reluctant to apply for such work. Women understand that behind the symbolism of masculinized job descriptions lies a very real force: the power of men to harass, belittle, ostracize, dismiss, marginalize, discard, and just plain hurt them as workers. . . .

The legal system thus places women workers in a Catch-22 situation. Women are disempowered from pursuing or staying in higher-paid nontraditional jobs because of the hostile work cultures. The only real hope for making those work cultures more hospitable to women lies in dramatically increasing the proportion of women in those jobs. Eliminating those imbalances is, of course, what Title VII lawsuits challenging segregation promise. But when women workers bring these suits, too often the courts tell them that they are under-represented in nontraditional jobs not because the work culture is threatening or alienating, but rather because their own internalized sense of "femininity" has led them to avoid those jobs.

And so the cycle continues. A few women continue to move in and out the "revolving door," with little being done to stop them from being shoved back out almost as soon as they enter. The majority of working women stand by as silent witnesses, their failure to enter used to confirm that they "chose" all along to remain on the outside. There is no need for a sign on the door. Women understand that they enter at their own risk. . . .

I have elaborated a new account of the dynamics of job segregation in the hope of challenging—but also offering something positive to replace—the images of women and work that inform this fatalistic choice explanation. . . .

The central insight of the new account is that working women do not bring with them to the workworld fixed preferences for traditionally female or traditionally male work. Rather, the workplace is a central site of development for women's aspirations and identities as workers. In a very real sense, employers create women's job preferences. Once judges realize that women's preferences are unstable and always potentially in transition depending on work conditions, it will no longer do to imagine that women have a static set of "true" preferences independent of employer action that courts can discover as a factual matter and use to ground legal decisionmaking. Indeed, the notion that women have stable preferences

for traditional or nontraditional work becomes a legal fiction that is plausible only by accepting as given the very structural features of the workplace that women seek to challenge through the lawsuit. . . .

STUDY QUESTIONS

1. What are the "lack of interest" and the "coercion" stories about why women workers tend to be concentrated in lower-paying occupations? What objections did Schultz raise to each of these explanations? Do you find her objections persuasive?

2. What story does she propose in their place? In this account, what factors inhibit women from moving out of female-intensive, lower-paying jobs? What factors encourage women to leave better-paying, male-intensive occupations? Might the presence of any of these factors constitute a violation of Title VII?

In the remainder of this chapter, we review the two main legal strategies used over the past decade to lessen the impact of occupational segregation on the earnings of women. Given that women are concentrated in different and lower-paying occupations than men, women's pay, prestige, and opportunities can be increased in two principal ways: (1) arrange to increase the pay for workers in female-intensive occupations and (2) encourage outward mobility from the "pink-collar ghetto." The comparable worth approach matches the first strategy; affirmative action, the second.

III. COMPARABLE WORTH

An explanation of the inverse relation of female concentration in occupations and average hourly earnings that is commonly mentioned is, as Schultz pointed out, that the work preferences of men and women differ. Women, for example, may place greater emphasis on occupations that allow flexibility and permit intermittent participation. To the extent that preferences of this type are more common among women, occupations that provide these features will be oversupplied with applicants, thus driving the price of labor lower than it would otherwise be. In this explanation, earnings in occupations are directly proportional to male concentration only incidentally. The rate of compensation in these markets is determined as it is in any other, by supply and demand.

A second explanation accepts the first as far as it goes but asserts that it does not go to the root of the matter. Oversupply does not explain, for example, why nurses, who in some parts of the country are in critically short supply, earn significantly less than common laborers, who are in plentiful supply. The second explanation proposes that wages for jobs held predominantly by women are "undervalued," i.e., artificially depressed relative to what they would be if the jobs were held by men. The suggestion central to this explanation is that the lower-paying jobs typically held by women are paid less *because* they are typically held by women.

The second explanation began to be articulated in the mid-1970s and achieved greater prominence in policy discussions during the early 1980s. It was inspired by the recalcitrance of the earnings gap to remedial measures previously available. Instead of combating the earnings gap by promoting upward mobility out of the "pink-collar ghetto," supporters of the comparable worth approach aim at raising the wage rates of women who find themselves in low-paid, female-intensive occupations. The credibility of this strategy was greatly advanced by a study conducted by a National Academy of Science team in the early 1980s. The summary of that study's conclusions follows.

Women, Work, and Wages: Equal Pay for Jobs of Equal Value

Donald J. Treiman and
Heidi I. Hartman, eds.
Washington, D.C.: National Academy Press, 1981. Pp. 91–96.

This report has been concerned with two questions: To what extent does the fact that women and minorities are on the average paid less than nonminority men reflect discrimination in the way jobs are compensated? If wage discrimination exists, what can be done about it?

On the basis of a review of the evidence, our judgment is that there is substantial discrimination in pay. Specific instances of discrimination are neither easily identified nor easily remedied because the widespread concentration of women and minorities into low-paying jobs makes it difficult to distinguish discriminatory from nondiscriminatory components of compensation. One approach, which needs further development but shows some promise, is to use existing job evaluation plans as a standard for comparing the relative worth of jobs.

This chapter summarizes the evidence leading to these conclusions. . . .

THE EXTENT AND THE SOURCES OF PAY DIFFERENTIALS

It is well established that in the United States today women earn less than men and minority men earn less than nonminority men. Among year-round full-time workers, the annual earnings of white women in the late 1970s averaged less than 60 percent of those of white men, while the earnings of black men averaged 70–75 percent of those of white men.

Such differential earnings patterns have existed for many decades. They may arise in part because women and minority men are paid less than white men for doing the same (or very similar) jobs within the same firm, or in part because the job structure is substantially segregated by sex, race, and ethnicity and the jobs held mainly by women and minority men pay less than the jobs held mainly by nonminority men. Since passage of the Equal Pay Act of 1963 and Title VII of the 1964 Civil Rights Act, legal remedies have been available for the first source of wage differentials. Although the committee recognizes that instances of unequal pay for the same work have not been entirely eliminated, we believe that they are probably not now the major source of differences in earnings.

With respect to the second source of wage differentials, the disparate distribution of workers among jobs and the concentration of women and minority men in low-paying jobs, the data are clear. Women and minorities are differentially concentrated not only by occupation but also by industry, by firm, and by division within firms. Moreover, the evidence shows that this differential concentration has persisted, at least with respect to women, over a substantial period of time. In the face of this differential concentration, then, the question of whether pay differentials are discriminatory can be stated quite simply: Would the low-paying jobs be low-paying regardless of who held them, or are they low-paying because of the sex, race, or ethnic composition of their incumbents?

To be able to state the question simply, however, is not to be able to answer it simply. In the committee's judgment, a correct response recognizes that both elements account for observed earnings differentials. Our economy is structured so that some jobs will inevitably pay less than others, and the fact that many such jobs are disproportionately filled by women and minorities may reflect differences in qualifications, interests, traditional roles, and similar factors; or it may reflect exclusionary practices with regard to hiring and promotion; or it may reflect a combination of both. However, several types of evidence support our judgment that it is also true in many instances that jobs held mainly by women and minorities pay less at least in part *because* they are held mainly by women and minorities. First, the differentials in average pay for jobs held mainly by women and those held mainly by men persist when the characteristics of jobs thought to affect their value and the characteristics of workers thought to affect their productivity are held constant. Second, prior to the legislation of the last two decades, differentials in pay for men and women and for minorities and nonminorities were often acceptable and were, in fact, prevalent. The tradition embodied in such practices was built into wage structures, and its effects continue to influence these structures. Finally, at the level of the specific firm, several studies show that women's jobs are paid less on the average than men's jobs with the same scores derived from job evaluation plans. The evidence is not complete or conclusive, but the consistency of the results in many different job categories and in several different types of studies, the size of the pay differentials (even after worker and job characteristics have been taken into account), and the lack of evidence for alternative explanations strongly suggest that wage discrimination is widespread.

IDENTIFYING AND ELIMINATING PAY DISCRIMINATION

The identification and correction of particular instances of pay discrimination are, however, not easy tasks. One procedure that has been suggested is to compare the actual rates of pay of jobs with the relative worth of jobs; wage discrimination would be suspected whenever jobs are not paid in accordance with their relative worth. This relative (or comparable) worth approach in turn requires a generally acceptable standard of job worth and a feasible procedure for measuring the relative worth of jobs. In our judgment no universal standard of job worth exists, both because any definition of the "relative worth" of jobs is in part a matter of values and because, even for a particular definition, problems of measurement are likely. . . .

JOB EVALUATION PLANS

Although no universal standard of job worth exists, job evaluation plans do provide standards and measures of job worth that are used to estimate the relative worth of jobs within many firms. In job evaluation plans, pay ranges for a job are based on estimates of the worth of jobs according to such criteria as the skill, effort, and responsibility required by the job and the working conditions under which it is performed. Pay for an individual, within the pay range, is set by the worker's characteristics, such as credentials, seniority, productivity, and quality of job performance. Job evaluation plans vary from firm to firm; both the criteria established and the compensable factors and relative weights used as measures of the criteria differ somewhat from plan to plan.

In our judgment job evaluation plans provide measures of job worth that, under certain circumstances, may be used to discover and reduce wage discrimination for persons covered by a given plan. Job evaluation plans provide a way of systematically rewarding jobs for their content—for the skill, effort, and responsibility they entail and the conditions under which they are performed. By making the criteria of compensation explicit and by applying the criteria consistently, it is probable that pay differentials resulting from traditional stereotypes regarding the value of "women's work" or work customarily done by minorities will be reduced.

But several aspects of the methods generally used in such plans raise questions about their ability to establish comparable worth. First, job evaluation plans typically ensure rough conformity between the measured worth of jobs and actual wages by allowing actual wages to determine the weights of job factors used in the plans. Insofar as differentials associated with sex, race, or ethnicity are incorporated in actual wages, this procedure will act to perpetuate them. Statistical techniques exist that may be able to generate job worth scores from which components of wages associated with sex, race, or ethnicity have been at least partly removed; they should be further developed.

Second, many firms use different job evaluation plans for different types of jobs. Since in most firms women and minority men are concentrated in jobs with substantially different tasks from those of jobs held by nonminority men, a plan that covers all jobs would be necessary in order to compare wages of women, minority men, and nonminority men. The selection of compensable factors and their weights in such a plan may be quite difficult, however, because factors appropriate for one type of job are not necessarily appropriate for all other types. Nevertheless, experiments with firm-wide plans might be useful in making explicit the relative weights of compensable factors, especially since they are already used by some firms.

Finally, it must be recognized that there are no definitive tests of the "fairness" of the choice of compensable factors and the relative weights given to them. The process is inherently judgmental and its success in generating a wage structure that is deemed equitable depends on achieving a consensus about factors and their weights among employers and employees.

The development and implementation of a job evaluation plan is often a lengthy and costly process. The underdeveloped nature of the technology involved, particularly the lack of systematic testing of assumptions, does not justify the universal application of such plans. In the committee's judgment, however, the plans have a potential that deserves further experimentation and development.

STUDY QUESTIONS

1. What analysis does this study suggest is most likely to explain the earnings gap? What evidence is cited in support of that suggestion? Does the study claim that this evidence is conclusive?

2. How does the study suggest that this type of analysis be used to identify and correct individual instances of pay discrimination? What difficulties inhibit widespread use of that technique?

The National Academy of Science study concluded that it is "true in many instances that jobs held mainly by women and minorities pay less at least in part *because* they are held mainly by women and minorities." This conclusion supports the comparable worth explanation that earnings in occupations are directly proportional to male-concentration; women working in female-intensive occupations probably earn less, in part at least, "because of their sex."

Initially, it was unclear just how instances are to be identified in which employers undervalue jobs done predominantly by women "because they are held mainly by women." The Academy study indicated that job evaluation plans be used to identify those jobs within a particular firm that would, absent discrimination, be paid equally.

Supporters found precedent for this proposal in the practice of the War Labor Board during World War II. Job evaluation plans describe the content of different jobs in terms of skill, effort, responsibility, and working conditions. They then assign a point value to each job in terms of these descriptions. Jobs with equal point values are regarded as of equal value to the employer. On this approach, and this is its key ingredient, jobs of equal value to an employer should, absent discrimination, be paid equally.

Once the methodological issues were understood, the comparable worth approach to pay equity became highly controversial. The short book by Michael Gold, *A Dialogue on Comparable Worth* (Ithaca, NY: Industrial Labor Relations Press, 1983), surveys the main themes in the controversy. Much of the controversy turns on whether it is even possible, in a nonsocialist economy, to make valid and detailed comparisons of the relative worth of different jobs, even when those jobs are within the same firm.

In the legal context, the debate over the comparable worth approach to pay equity came into focus as the question of whether an employer violates Title VII by failing to give equal pay to employees who perform jobs of comparable value to the employer, where that results in lower pay to those jobs that are predominantly held by women. The leading case addressing that issue was decided by the Ninth Circuit Court of Appeals in 1985. In an opinion authored by then Judge, now Justice, Anthony Kennedy, that court rejected the comparable worth approach as a viable method of establishing a violation of Title VII. There, the court represented comparable worth analysis as an invitation to serious governmental intervention into "the free market." The court declined the invitation.

AFSCME v. Washington

United States Court of Appeals,
Ninth Circuit, 1985.
770 F.2d 1401.

KENNEDY, C. J.

In this class action affecting approximately 15,500 of its employees, the State of Washington was sued in the United States District Court for the Western District of Washington. . . . The State of Washington has required salaries of state employees to reflect prevailing market rates. Throughout the period in question, comprehensive biennial salary surveys were conducted to assess prevailing market rates. The surveys involved approximately 2,700 employers in the public and private sectors. The results were reported to state personnel boards, which conducted hearings before employee representatives and agencies and made salary recommendations to the State Budget Director. The Director submitted a proposed budget to the Governor, who in turn presented it to the state legislature. Salaries were fixed by enactment of the budget.

In 1974 the State commissioned a study by management consultant Norman Willis to determine whether a wage disparity existed between employees in jobs held predominantly by women and jobs held predominantly by men. The study . . . found a wage disparity of about twenty percent, to the disadvantage of employees in jobs held mostly by women, for jobs considered of comparable worth. . . . The State of Washington conducted similar studies in 1976 and 1980, and in 1983 the State enacted legislation providing for a compensation scheme based on comparable worth. The scheme is to take effect over a ten-year period. . . .

. . . In 1982 AFSCME [the American Federation of State, County and Municipal Employees] brought this action in the district court, seeking immediate implementation of a system of compensation based on comparable worth. The district court ruled in favor of AFSCME and ordered injunctive relief and back pay. . . .

AFSCME alleges sex-based wage discrimination throughout the state system, but its explanation and proof of the violation is, in essence, Washington's failure as early as 1979 to adopt and implement at once a comparable worth compensation program. The trial court adopted this theory as well. The comparable worth theory, as developed in the case before us, postulates that sex-based wage discrimination exists if employees in job classifications occupied primarily by women are paid less than employees in job classifications filled primarily by men, if the jobs are of equal value to the employer, though otherwise dissimilar. . . . We must determine whether comparable worth, as presented in this case, affords AFSCME a basis for recovery under Title VII.

In the instant case, the district court found a violation of Title VII, premised upon both the disparate impact and the disparate treatment theories of discrimination. . . .

AFSCME's disparate impact argument is based on the contention that the State of Washington's practice of taking prevailing market rates into account in setting wages has an adverse impact on women, who, historically, have received lower wages than men in the labor market. Disparate impact analysis is confined to cases which challenge a specific, clearly delineated employment practice applied at a single point in the job selection process. . . .

The instant case does not involve an employment practice that yields to disparate impact analysis. . . . [T]he decision to base compensation on the competitive market, rather than on a theory of comparable worth, involves the assessment of a number of complex factors not easily ascertainable, an assessment too multifaceted to be appropriate for disparate impact analysis. In the case before us, the compensation system in question resulted from surveys, agency hearings, administrative recommendations, budget proposals, executive actions, and legislative enactments. A compensation system that is responsive to supply and demand and other market forces is not the type of specific, clearly delineated employment policy contemplated by *Dothard* and *Griggs;* such a compensation system, the result of a complex of market forces, does not constitute a single practice that suffices to support a claim under disparate impact theory. . . . Under these principles and precedents, we must reverse the district court's determination of liability under the disparate impact theory of discrimination.

We consider next the allegations of disparate treatment. Under the disparate treatment theory, AFSCME was required to prove a prima facie case of sex discrimination by a preponderance of the evidence. . . . In an appropriate case, the necessary discriminatory animus may be inferred from circumstantial evidence. Our review of the record, however, indicates failure by AFSCME to establish the requisite element of intent by either circumstantial or direct evidence.

AFSCME contends discriminatory motive may be inferred from the Willis study, which finds the State's practice of setting salaries in reliance on market rates creates a sex-based wage disparity for jobs deemed of comparable worth. AFSCME argues from the study that the market reflects a historical pattern of lower wages to employees in positions staffed predominantly by women; and it contends the State of Washington perpetuates that disparity, in violation of Title VII, by using market rates in the compensation system. The inference of discriminatory motive which AFSCME seeks to draw from the State's participation in the market system fails, as the State did not create the market disparity and has not been shown to have been motivated by impermissible sex-based considerations in setting salaries.

The requirement of intent is linked at least in part to culpability. . . . That concept would be undermined if we were to hold that payment of wages according to prevailing rates in the public and private sectors is an act which, in itself, supports the inference of a purpose to discriminate. Neither law nor logic deems the free market system a suspect enterprise. Economic reality is that the value of a particular job to an employer is but one factor influencing the rate of compensation for that job. Other considerations may include the availability of workers willing to do the job and the effectiveness of collective bargaining in a particular industry. . . . [E]mployers may be constrained by market forces to set salaries under prevailing wage rates for different job classifications. We find nothing in the language of Title VII or its legislative history to indicate Congress intended to abrogate fundamental economic principles such as the laws of supply and demand or to prevent employers from competing in the labor market.

While the Washington legislature may have the discretion to enact a comparable worth plan if it chooses to do so, Title VII does not obligate it to eliminate an economic inequality which it did not create.

We have recognized that in certain cases an inference of intent may be drawn from statistical evidence. We have admonished, however, that statistics must be relied on with caution. Though the comparability of wage rates in dissimilar jobs may be relevant to a determination of discriminatory animus, job evaluation studies and comparable worth statistics alone are insufficient to establish the requisite inference of discriminatory motive critical to the disparate treatment theory. The weight to be accorded such statistics is determined by the existence of independent corroborative evidence of discrimination. We conclude the independent evidence of discrimination presented by AFSCME is insufficient to support an inference of the requisite discriminatory motive under the disparate treatment theory. . . .

We also reject AFSCME's contention that, having commissioned the Willis study, the State of Washington was committed to implement a new system of compensation based on comparable worth as defined by the study. Whether comparable worth is a feasible approach to employee compensation is a matter of debate. . . . Assuming, however, that like other job evaluation studies it may be useful as a diagnostic tool, we reject a rule that would penalize rather than commend employers for their effort and innovation in undertaking such a study. . . .

We hold there was a failure to establish a violation of Title VII under the disparate treatment theory of discrimination, and reverse the district court on this aspect of the case as well. The State of Washington's initial reliance on a free market system in which employees in male-dominated jobs are compensated at a higher rate than employees in dissimilar female-dominated jobs is not in and of itself a violation of Title VII, notwithstanding that the Willis study deemed the positions of comparable worth. Absent a showing of discriminatory motive, which has not been made here, the law does not permit the federal courts to interfere in the market based system for the compensation of Washington's employees. . . .

Reversed.

STUDY QUESTIONS:

1. What did the court describe as the heart of the appellant's disparate impact argument? Why was it rejected? In *Griggs* (see Chapter 4), the Supreme Court found that where an employer hires and promotes using criteria that reflect societal racial bias, the employer violates Title VII unless business necessity is shown. What difference do you see between the situation in *Griggs* and that here?

2. What reasons did the court give for rejecting the disparate treatment argument? Why did it find that intent to discriminate had not been shown? How else might the court have explained the refusal of the state to rectify pay differences that it acknowledged to be based upon discrimination?

When the decade of the eighties opened, it was heralded as the decade of comparable worth. Since the *AFSCME* decision, it has been increasingly difficult to maintain confidence in the promise of the comparable worth approach to pay equity litigation. After that decision, its promise came to be seen as largely restricted to the areas of legislation and labor negotiation. Historian Sara Evans and political scientist Barbara Nelson summarize the potential of the comparable worth approach at the end of the decade in their book.

... [T]remendous momentum for comparable worth as a policy in state and local jurisdictions had been generated in the early 1980s. By August 1987, 28 states had begun the process of conducting job evaluation study and 20 had moved further to budgeting and implementation. In addition, 167 local jurisdictions outside Minnesota [where interest in comparable worth is widespread] had adopted comparable worth policies as well.

Waging Justice *(Chicago: University of Chicago Press, 1989), p. 41.*

IV. AFFIRMATIVE ACTION

We saw above that much, if not most, of the disparity between the earnings of women and men workers results from occupational segregation. Two strategies have been used over the past two decades to lessen the impact of occupational segregation on the earnings of women. The one, comparable worth, was specifically fashioned for this purpose. It aims at increasing the earnings of workers in female intensive occupations. The other, affirmative action, was fashioned for other purposes, but has its applications in this context as well. Here it is used to promote outward mobility from the "pink-collar ghetto." With the discouragement of the *AFSCME* decision for the comparable worth approach, the viability of affirmative action has once again come to into focus.

Affirmative action is a technical legal expression with a long history in the labor law of the early years of this century. In general, affirmative action consists of extra steps taken to ensure that a legally required result is actually produced. In ordinary terms, one takes affirmative action when one "goes the extra mile" to ensure that, e.g., equal employment opportunities are available to all employees. Affirmative action takes many forms, depending on the context. We will explore several of these in this section.

Questions relating to whether employers are legally obligated, or even permitted, to take affirmative action in the employment of women and minorities arise in a number of contexts. In this section, we review some of the principal features of litigation first under Title VII and then under the Equal Protection Clause.

Section 706(g) of Title VII specifically authorizes the courts to "order such affirmative action as may be appropriate." Under this provision, the district courts may, at their discretion, order employers found in violation of the statute to publicize their commitment to equal employment opportunity, to actively recruit minority and women applicants, and to develop training programs to improve the job qualifications of women and minorities. Of all the forms affirmative action has taken, the most controversial and difficult to understand involves the ordering of hiring and promotion ratios and goals based on race and sex.

Whenever such measures are adopted by an employer, whether as a result of a court order, a consent decree, or a provision of a contract with a governmental body, they can be expected to cause controversy. The dynamics of such debates are understandable. When extra steps are taken to contact, recruit, train, or hire some people, other people are left out. At first inspection, giving extra attention to some people puts those who do not receive that attention at a competitive disadvantage. This has raised objections couched in the familiar rhetoric of "reverse discrimination" and "quotas." As these concerns inevitably arise, it is essential that we attain a clear and accurate grasp of just what affirmative action does and does not involve, as well as its function within the legal system.

Affirmative action under Title VII is understood in the first instance as a remedy for violations of the statute. As such, affirmative relief might be fashioned to serve one or more of the three purposes—prevention, compensation, and punishment. We first encountered affirmative remedies in the *Mitchell* case in Chapter 4.

Until very recently, the courts spoke of affirmative action goals solely in terms of compensation for victims of past discrimination. So understood, these remedies were vulnerable to two weighty objections. First, the individuals hired or promoted under these orders were ordinarily not the same individuals as were the victims of the past discriminatory practices of the employer. In view of that fact, it is exceedingly difficult to see how such goals advance a bona fide compensatory purpose. Second, these remedies direct employers to use race- and sex-conscious selection procedures. That, however, seems to directly conflict with the central provisions of Title VII prohibiting hiring, etc., "because of . . . sex." In view of this, it seems strange indeed that an employer may, under Title VII, be ordered to engage in the very type of practice for which it was found in violation.

Beginning in the late 1970s, the courts began, partly due to these objections, to refine the discussion of affirmative action remedies under Title VII. Instead of viewing them as aiming at compensating victims of past discrimination, the courts began to speak of them as aimed primarily at preventing discriminatory employment practices from continuing into the future, i.e., as a supplement to cease and desist orders. This change in purpose addressed the first objection.

To see how affirmative action goals might work to advance a preventive objective, recall the discussion of the statistical ideas that lay at the basis of the concept of disparate impact. These were discussed in Chapter 4 in connection with the *Griggs* decision. Chief among these was the following: random selection procedures yield samples that replicate the composition of the populations from which they are drawn. The inference of a biased selection procedure from the lack of correspondence between the proportion of minorities or women hired or present in any employment category (work force ratio) and their proportions in the pool of qualified people in the relevant geographical area (availability ratio) is based on that principle. The key to understanding affirmative action goals as a preventive measure is the reverse of this inference. If a lack of correspondence between the work force and the availability ratios is evidence that the selection procedure is biased, then correspondence between them is evidence that the selection procedure is not biased. A court order directing the adoption of a hiring or promotional goal that is equal to the availability ratio, then, is another way to direct that the employer cease using biased selection procedures. It has an additional advantage over most injunctions in that it contains its own measurement of compliance.

The linkage of affirmative action goals to disparate impact analysis addresses the second of the objections raised above. The chief point of confusion here has been the assumption that these goals require the employer to grant preferential treatment to minorities and women. That assumption, however, neglects a key distinction relating to these goals. A hiring or promotional goal may be either impartial or preferential. A goal is impartial if it requires that the work force ratio equals the availability ratio. A goal of parity is impartial in the sense that it describes the result of selection procedures that do not give weight to the sex or minority status of candidates. Goals that aim only at the elimination of disparate impact are impartial in this sense. A goal is preferential if it requires that the work force ratio be greater than the availability ratio. Such a goal is preferential in the sense that it describes the result of selection procedures that do give weight to the sex and minority status of candidates. Goals that aim, in addition to eliminating disparate impact, at achieving a balanced work force typically impose hiring requirements that are preferential in this sense. If affirmative actions goals require only parity, then employers committed to them need not grant preferential treatment to anyone. Although they do require the use of sex- and race-conscious selection procedures, they do not require that the employment decisions be made "because of . . . sex." Indeed, the point of affirmative action goals as a preventive remedy is to ensure that the employer takes steps to implement selection procedures that do not give weight to the sex and race of candidates.

Two main concerns have dominated legal discussions of affirmative action in a Title VII context. The first is whether the act permits the courts to impose either impartial or preferential goals after a finding of a violation. When fashioning these, as other remedies, the courts have broad discretion and must balance concerns for three interests—the vindication of the rights of the victim, the protection of the rights of the employer, and the safeguarding of the interests of third parties. Although broad, the discretion of the courts here is limited by legal principles that derive from the primarily preventive objective of the statute. The second concern is whether the act permits employers voluntarily to initiate affirmative actions plans that include goals. The issue here is whether such goals may be used by employers at their own option, before being found to have discriminated against women or minorities.

The lower courts have generally followed a permissive policy on both of these concerns. Beginning with the election of Ronald Reagan and continuing throughout his presidency and that of George Bush (1980–1992), the executive branch pressed the courts to declare affirmative action goals of all types to be in violation of Title VII. This course of action was rooted in the administration's conviction that Title VII prohibits only the first type of discrimination distinguished in Chapter 4, i.e., discrimination that derives from prejudice. The courts were vigorously urged to reject the view endorsed by a unanimous Court in *Griggs* that Title VII also prohibits the use of biased employment procedures that are innocently adopted. Over a ten-year period, roughly corresponding to the Reagan and Bush presidencies, the Supreme Court responded to these concerns in a series of decisions that firmly endorsed the use of affirmative action remedies in a Title VII context. The first of the key decisions addressed a voluntary program adopted by a private employer.

United Steelworkers v. Weber

Supreme Court of the
United States, 1979.
443 U.S. 193, 99 S.CT. 2721, 61 L.Ed.2d 480.

Mr. Justice BRENNAN delivered the opinion of the Court.

. . . In 1974, petitioner United Steelworkers of America (USWA) and petitioner Kaiser Alumi-num & Chemical Corp. (Kaiser) entered into a master collective-bargaining agreement covering terms and conditions of employment at 15 Kaiser plants. The agreement contained, *inter alia,* an affirmative action plan designed to eliminate conspicuous racial imbalances in Kaiser's then almost exclusively white craft-work forces. Black craft-hiring goals were set for each Kaiser plant equal to the percentage of blacks in the respective local labor forces. To enable plants to meet these goals, on-the-job training programs were established to teach unskilled production workers—black and white—the skills necessary to become craft-workers. The plan reserved for black employees

50% of the openings in these newly created in-plant training programs.

This case arose from the operation of the plan at Kaiser's plant in Gramercy, La. Until 1974, Kaiser hired as craftworkers for that plant only persons who had had prior craft experience. Because blacks had long been excluded from craft unions, few were able to present such credentials. As a consequence, prior to 1974 only 1.83% (5 out of 273) of the skilled craftworkers at the Gramercy plant were black, even though the work force in the Gramercy area was approximately 39% black.

Pursuant to the national agreement Kaiser altered its craft hiring practice in the Gramercy plant. Rather than hiring already trained outsiders, Kaiser established a training program to train its production workers to fill craft openings. Selection of craft trainees was made on the basis of seniority, with the proviso that at least 50% of the new trainees were to be black until the percentage of black skilled craftworkers in the Gramercy plant approximated the percentage of blacks in the local labor force.

During 1974, the first year of the operation of the Kaiser-USWA affirmative action plan, 13 craft trainees were selected from Gramercy's production work force. Of these, seven were black and six white. The most senior black selected into the program had less seniority than several white production workers whose bids for admission were rejected. Thereafter one of those white production workers, respondent Brian Weber (hereafter respondent), instituted this class action in the United States District Court for the Eastern District of Louisiana.

The complaint alleged that the filling of craft trainee positions at the Gramercy plant pursuant to the affirmative action program had resulted in junior black employees' receiving training in preference to senior white employees, thus discriminating against respondent and other similarly situated white employees in violation of §§ 703 (a) and (d) of Title VII. The District Court held that the plan violated Title VII, entered a judgment in favor of the plaintiff class, and granted a permanent injunction prohibiting Kaiser and the USWA "from denying plaintiffs, Brian F. Weber and all other members of the class, access to on-the-job training pro-

grams on the basis of race." A divided panel of the Court of Appeals for the Fifth Circuit affirmed, holding that all employment preferences based upon race, including those preferences incidental to bona fide affirmative action plans, violated Title VII's prohibition against racial discrimination in employment.

We emphasize at the outset the narrowness of our inquiry. Since the Kaiser-USWA plan does not involve state action, this case does not present an alleged violation of the Equal Protection Clause of the Fourteenth Amendment. Further, since the Kaiser-USWA plan was adopted voluntarily, we are not concerned with what Title VII requires or with what a court might order to remedy a past proved violation of the Act. The only question before us is the narrow statutory issue of whether Title VII *forbids* private employers and unions from voluntarily agreeing upon bona fide affirmative action plans that accord racial preferences in the manner and for the purpose provided in the Kaiser-USWA plan. That question was expressly left open in *McDonald* v. *Santa Fe Trail Transp. Co.,* which held, in a case not involving affirmative action, that Title VII protects whites as well as blacks from certain forms of racial discrimination.

Respondent argues that Congress intended in Title VII to prohibit all race-conscious affirmative action plans. Respondent's argument rests upon a literal interpretation of §§ 703 (a) and (d) of the Act. Those sections make it unlawful to "discriminate . . . because of . . . race" in hiring and in the selection of apprentices for training programs. Since, the argument runs, *McDonald* v. *Santa Fe Trail Transp. Co.* settled that Title VII forbids discrimination against whites as well as blacks, and since the Kaiser-USWA affirmative action plan operates to discriminate against white employees solely because they are white, it follows that the Kaiser-USWA plan violates Title VII.

Respondent's argument is not without force. But it overlooks the significance of the fact that the Kaiser-USWA plan is an affirmative action plan voluntarily adopted by private parties to eliminate traditional patterns of racial segregation. In this context respondent's reliance upon a literal construction of §§ 703 (a) and (d) and upon *McDonald* is misplaced. It is a "familiar rule, that a thing may be within the letter of the statute and yet not within the statute, because not within its spirit, nor within the intention of its makers." The prohibition against racial discrimination in §§ 703 (a) and (d) of Title VII must therefore be read against the background of the legislative history of Title VII and the historical context from which the Act arose. Examination of those sources makes clear that an interpretation of the sections that forbade all race-conscious affirmative action would "bring about an end completely at variance with the purpose of the statute" and must be rejected.

Congress' primary concern in enacting the prohibition against racial discrimination in Title VII of the Civil Rights Act of 1964 was with "the plight of the Negro in our economy." . . .

Given this legislative history, we cannot agree with respondent that Congress intended to prohibit the private sector from taking effective steps to accomplish the goal that Congress designed Title VII to achieve. The very statutory words intended as a spur or catalyst to cause "employers and unions to self-examine and to self-evaluate their employment practices and to endeavor to eliminate, so far as possible, the last vestiges of an unfortunate and ignominious page in this country's history." *Albemarle Paper Co.* v. *Moody,* cannot be interpreted as an absolute prohibition against all private, voluntary, race-conscious affirmative action efforts to hasten the elimination of such vestiges. It would be ironic indeed if a law triggered by a Nation's concern over centuries of racial injustice and intended to improve the lot of those who had "been excluded from the American dream for so long," constituted the first legislative prohibition of all voluntary, private, race-conscious efforts to abolish traditional patterns of racial segregation and hierarchy.

Our conclusion is further reinforced by examination of the language and legislative history of § 703 (j) of Title VII. Opponents of Title VII raised two related arguments against the bill. First, they argued that the Act would be interpreted to *require* employers with racially imbalanced work forces to grant preferential treatment to racial minorities in order to integrate. Second, they argued that employers with racially imbalanced work forces would grant preferential

treatment to racial minorities, even if not required to do so by the Act. Had Congress meant to prohibit all race-conscious affirmative action, as respondent urges, it easily could have answered both objections by providing that Title VII would not require or *permit* racially preferential integration efforts. But Congress did not choose such a course. Rather, Congress added § 703 (j) which addresses only the first objection. The section provides that nothing contained in Title VII "shall be interpreted to *require* any employer . . . to grant preferential treatment . . . to any group because of the race . . . of such . . . group on account of" a *de facto* racial imbalance in the employer's work force. The section does *not* state that "nothing in Title VII shall be interpreted to *permit*" voluntary affirmative efforts to correct racial imbalances. The natural inference is that Congress chose not to forbid all voluntary race-conscious affirmative action.

The reasons for this choice are evident from the legislative record. Title VII could not have been enacted into law without substantial support from legislators in both Houses who traditionally resisted federal regulation of private business. Those legislators demanded as a price for their support that "management prerogatives, and union freedoms . . . be left undisturbed to the greatest extent possible." Section 703 (j) was proposed by Senator Dirksen to allay any fears that the Act might be interpreted in such a way as to upset this compromise. The section was designed to prevent § 703 of Title VII from being interpreted in such a way as to lead to undue "Federal Government interference with private businesses because of some Federal employee's ideas about racial balance or racial imbalance." Clearly, a prohibition against all voluntary, race-conscious, affirmative action efforts would disserve these ends. Such a prohibition would augment the powers of the Federal Government and diminish traditional management prerogatives while at the same time impeding attainment of the ultimate statutory goals. In view of this legislative history and in view of Congress' desire to avoid undue federal regulation of private businesses, use of the word "require" rather than the phrase "require or permit" in § 703 (j) fortifies the conclusion that Congress did not intend to limit traditional business freedom to such a degree as to prohibit all voluntary, race-conscious affirmative action.

We therefore hold that Title VII's prohibition in §§ 703 (a) and (d) against racial discrimination does not condemn all private, voluntary, race-conscious affirmative action plans.

We need not today define in detail the line of demarcation between permissible and impermissible affirmative action plans. It suffices to hold that the challenged Kaiser-USWA affirmative action plan falls on the permissible side of the line. The purposes of the plan mirror those of the statute. Both were designed to break down old patterns of racial segregation and hierarchy. Both were structured to "open employment opportunities for Negroes in occupations which have been traditionally closed to them."

At the same time, the plan does not unnecessarily trammel the interests of the white employees. The plan does not require the discharge of white workers and their replacement with new black hirees. Nor does the plan create an absolute bar to the advancement of white employees; half of those trained in the program will be white. Moreover, the plan is a temporary measure; it is not intended to maintain racial balance, but simply to eliminate a manifest

racial imbalance. Preferential selection of craft trainees at the Gramercy plant will end as soon as the percentage of black skilled craftworkers in the Gramercy plant approximates the percentage of blacks in the local labor force.

We conclude, therefore, that the adoption of the Kaiser-USWA plan for the Gramercy plant falls within the area of discretion left by Title VII to the private sector voluntarily to adopt affirmative action plans designed to eliminate conspicuous racial imbalance in traditionally segregated job categories. Accordingly, the judgment of the Court of Appeals for the Fifth Circuit is

Reversed.

STUDY QUESTIONS

1. Does it appear that the pre-1974 procedure for hiring craftworkers had disparate impact? Were the hiring goals in the Kaiser plan preferential or impartial? Was the goal for the training program preferential or impartial?
2. What consequences would have followed if the decision here had been to affirm? Would that result have discouraged employers from voluntarily undertaking action to correct the lingering effects of past discrimination?

In *Weber,* the Court ruled that Title VII permits private employers who have not been shown to have violated the act to adopt voluntary race-consciousness affirmative action plans to eliminate a manifest racial imbalance in traditionally segregated job categories. The arguments to the contrary were rejected because they relied on an interpretation of the language of the statute that was found to be in direct opposition to the statutory objective evidently endorsed by Congress. In reaching this decision, the Court carefully avoided setting limits to the range of permissible affirmative action plans. It did, however, observe that the Kaiser plan was found to be within the range of permissible plans because its purposes "mirror those of the statute," because it did not "unnecessarily trammel the interests of the white employees," and because the plan was "a temporary measure."

Undaunted by the *Weber* decision, the Reagan Justice Department continued to press the courts to change directions on affirmative action. It urged that more weight be given to the interests of white male employees, which were being displaced by the preference for those of women and minorities. Specifically, the administration's thesis was that Title VII permits only remedies that benefit identified victims of past employment discrimination. Among other actions taken, it asked the courts to overturn dozens of consent decrees that had been negotiated during the 1970s to settle bias complaints by women and minorities, consent decrees containing hiring and promotion goals. This confrontation reached its climax in the mid-1980s, when the issue was squarely joined in two cases argued before the Supreme Court.

In *Sheet Metal Workers International v. EEOC,* 478 U.S. 421 (1986), the Justice Department intervened on behalf of the union, arguing that the lower court had exceeded its authority under Title VII by imposing on the union a membership goal for minorities. The Court firmly rejected the administration's thesis that only actual victims of past employer discrimination may benefit from Title VII remedies. Pointing out that the district court had specifically found that the union had previously engaged in "bad faith attempts to prevent or delay [other forms of] affirmative action," the Court held that:

> 706(g) does not prohibit a court from ordering, in appropriate circumstances, affirmative race-conscious relief as a remedy for past discrimination. Specifically, we hold that such relief may be appropriate where an employer or a labor union has engaged in persistent or egregious discrimination, or where necessary to dissipate the lingering effects of pervasive discrimination. . . . (at 445)

The Court made clear in *Sheet Metal Workers* that Title VII permits the courts to impose impartial, flexible, and temporary affirmative action goals where evidence exists that the employer has engaged in persistent or egregious discrimination or that they are necessary to dissipate the lingering effects of pervasive discrimination. That decision is generally regarded as having provided a definitive answer to the first of the two main concerns about affirmative action goals in a Title VII context: whether and under what circumstances the act permits the courts to impose such remedies.

The second question, whether Title VII permits an employer to adopt voluntary affirmative action plans, was addressed as regards private employers in *Weber.* The Court took up this issue as regards public employers the next year in the first affirmative action case to involve a woman. The plan challenged in *Johnson v. Transportation Agency, Santa Clara Cty,* 480 U.S. 616 (1987), required that consideration be given to the sex of a candidate in employment decisions relating to traditionally segregated job categories where women are manifestly underrepresented. Writing for the Court, Justice Brennan approached this case by applying the principles developed in *Weber.* Noting that the plan was temporary and did not aim at maintaining a balanced work force, Justice Brennan concluded that the plan "embodies the contribution that voluntary employer action can make in eliminating the vestiges of discrimination in the workplace."

Justice O'Connor concurred in the judgment but in a separate opinion disapproved of the "expansive and ill-defined" approach endorsed in Justice Brennan's opinion.

> In my view, the proper initial inquiry in evaluating the legality of an affirmative action plan by a public employer under Title VII is no different from that required by the Equal Protection Clause. In either case . . . the employer must have had a firm basis for believing that remedial action was required. An employer would have such a firm basis if it can point to a statistical disparity sufficient to support a prima facie claim under Title VII. . . . (at 649)

The reference by Justice O'Connor provides a convenient transition to a review of the debate over whether government-imposed affirmative action plans, and specifically those features of the plans that involve goals and timetables, violate the Equal Protection Clause. The pivotal decision addressing that question was handed down the year after *Weber* was decided. In the following case, the Court upheld the challenged plan by a 6-3 vote. The justices voting in the majority, however, split over the standard by which affirmative action plans are reviewed under the Equal Protection Clause. The view that has prevailed as of this writing was announced by the chief justice.

Fullilove v. Klutznick

United States Supreme Court, 1980.
448 U.S. 448, 100 S.Ct. 2758,
65 L.Ed.2d 902.

Mr. Chief Justice BURGER announced the judgment of the Court and delivered an opinion, in which Mr. Justice WHITE and Mr. Justice POWELL joined. . . .

In May 1977, Congress enacted the Public Works Employment Act of 1977. . . . Section 103(f)(2) of the 1977 Act, referred to as the "minority business enterprise" or "MBE" provision, requires that:

"Except to the extent that the Secretary [of Commerce] determines otherwise, no grant shall be made under this Act for any local public works project unless the applicant gives satisfactory assurance to the Secretary that at least 10 per centum of the amount of each grant shall be expended for minority business enterprises. For purposes of this paragraph, the term 'minority business enterprise' means a business at least 50 per centum of which is owned by minority group members or, in case of a publicly owned business, at least 51 per centum of the stock of which is owned by minority group members. For the purposes of the preceding sentence minority group members are citizens of the United States who are Negroes, Spanish-speaking, Orientals, Indians, Eskimos, and Aleuts."

In late May 1977, the Secretary promulgated regulations governing administration of the grant program. . . .

On November 30, 1977, petitioners filed a complaint in the United States District Court for the Southern District of New York seeking declaratory and injunctive relief to enjoin enforcement of the MBE provision. . . . Petitioners are several associations of construction contractors and subcontractors, and a firm engaged in heating, ventilation, and air conditioning work. Their complaint alleged that they had sustained economic injury due to enforcement of the 10% MBE requirement and that the MBE [minority business enterprise] provision on its face violated the Equal Protection Clause of the Fourteenth Amendment, the equal protection component of the Due Process Clause of the Fifth Amendment, and various statutory antidiscrimination provisions.

. . . [T]he District Court . . . [upheld] the validity of the MBE program and . . . [denied] the injunctive relief sought.

The United States Court of Appeals for the Second Circuit affirmed. . . .

[The chief justice next conducted an extended review of the legislative and administrative deliberations surrounding this MBE program.] The clear objective of the MBE provision is . . . to ensure that, to the extent federal funds were granted under the Public Works Employment Act of 1977, grantees who elect to participate would not employ procurement practices that Congress had decided might result in perpetuation of the effects of prior discrimination which had impaired or foreclosed access by minority businesses to public contracting opportunities. The MBE program does not mandate the allocation of federal funds according to inflexible percentages solely based on race or ethnicity. . . .

. . . We recognize the need for careful judicial evaluation to assure that any congressional program that employs racial or ethnic criteria to accomplish the objective of remedying the present effects of past discrimination is narrowly tailored to the achievement of that goal. . . .

Our review of the regulations and guidelines governing administration of the MBE provision reveals that Congress enacted the program as a strictly remedial measure; moreover, it is a remedy that functions prospectively, in the manner of an injunctive decree. Pursuant to the administrative program, grantees and their prime contractors are required to seek out all available, qualified, bona fide MBE's; they are required to provide technical assistance as needed, to lower or waive bonding requirements where feasible, to solicit the aid of the Office of Minority Business Enterprise, the SBA [Small Business Administration], or other sources for assisting MBE's to obtain required working capital, and to give guidance through the intricacies of the bidding process. The program assumes that grantees who undertake these efforts in good faith will obtain at least 10% participation by minority business enterprises. It is recognized that, to achieve this target, contracts will be awarded to available, qualified, bona fide MBE's even though they are not the lowest competitive bidders, so long as their higher bids, when challenged, are found to reflect merely attempts to cover costs inflated by the present effects of prior disadvantage and discrimination. There is available to the grantee a provision authorized by Congress for administrative waiver on a case-by-case basis should there be a demonstration that, despite affirmative efforts, this level of participation cannot be achieved without departing from the objectives of the program. There is also an administrative mechanism, including a complaint procedure, to ensure that only bona fide MBE's are encompassed by the remedial program, and to prevent unjust participation in the program by those minority firms whose access to public contracting opportunities is not impaired by the effects of prior discrimination.

As a threshold matter, we reject the contention that in the remedial context the Congress must act in a wholly "color-blind" fashion. In *Swann v. Charlotte-Mecklenburg Board of Education,* 402 U.S. 1 (1971), we rejected this argument in considering a court-formulated school desegregation remedy on the basis that examination of the racial composition of student bodies was an unavoidable starting point and that racially based attendance assignments were permissible so long as no absolute racial balance of each school was required. . . .

Here we deal, as we noted earlier, not with the limited remedial powers of a federal court, for example, but with the broad remedial powers of Congress. It is fundamental that in no organ of government, state or federal, does there repose a more comprehensive remedial power than in the Congress, expressly charged by the Constitution with competence and authority to enforce equal protection guarantees. Congress not only may induce voluntary action to assure compliance with existing federal statutory or constitutional antidiscrimination provisions, but also, where Congress has authority to declare certain conduct unlawful, it may, as here, authorize and induce state action to avoid such conduct.

A more specific challenge to the MBE program is the charge that it impermissibly deprives nonminority businesses of access to at least some portion of the government contracting opportunities generated by the Act. It must be conceded that by its objective of remedying the historical impairment of access, the MBE provision can have the effect of awarding some contracts to MBE's which otherwise might be awarded to other businesses, who may themselves be innocent of any prior discriminatory actions. Failure of nonminority firms to receive certain contracts is, of course, an incidental consequence of the program, not part of its objective; similarly, past impairment of minority-firm access to public contracting opportunities may have been an incidental consequence of "business as usual" by public contracting agencies and among prime contractors.

It is not a constitutional defect in this program that it may disappoint the expectations of nonminority firms. When effectuating a limited and properly tailored remedy to cure the effects of prior discrimination, such "a sharing of the burden" by innocent parties is not impermissible. The actual "burden" shouldered by nonminority firms is relatively light in this connection when we consider the scope of this public works program as compared with overall construction contracting opportunities. Moreover, although we may assume that the complaining parties are innocent of any discriminatory conduct, it was within congressional power to act on the assumption that in the past some non-minority businesses may have reaped competitive benefit over the years from the virtual exclusion of minority firms from these contracting opportunities. . . .

Congress, after due consideration, perceived a pressing need to move forward with new approaches in the continuing effort to achieve the goal of equality of economic opportunity. In this effort, Congress has necessary latitude to try new techniques such as the limited use of racial and ethnic criteria to accomplish remedial objectives; this is especially so in programs where voluntary cooperation with remedial measures is induced by placing conditions on federal expenditures. That the program may press the outer limits of congressional authority affords no basis for striking it down.

Petitioners have mounted a facial challenge to a program developed by the politically responsive branches of Government. For its part, the Congress must proceed only with programs narrowly tailored to achieve its objectives, subject to continuing evaluation and reassessment; administration of the programs must be vigilant and flexible; and, when such a program comes under judicial review, courts must be satisfied that the legislative objectives and projected administration give reasonable assurance that the program will function within constitutional limitations. . . .

Affirmed.

STUDY QUESTIONS

1. Explain the Court's reasons for describing the minority set-aside at issue here as a preventive remedy, similar to an injunction.
2. Was the MBE provision in this case fashioned in a way that was consistent with the concerns emphasized by the Court in *Weber,* i.e., did the plan aim at fostering equal opportunity? Was it a temporary measure? Did it avoid unnecessarily trammeling the interests of whites?
3. What standard was endorsed by the chief justice for reviewing equal protection challenges to congressionally initiated affirmative action plans?

In *Fullilove,* the Court emphasized the comprehensive remedial powers of Congress. Toward the end of the decade, the Court addressed the same question in the context of state and local government powers and found them to be considerably less comprehensive. Speaking for a badly divided Court in the following decision, Justice O'Connor reiterated the position that she had indicated earlier in *Johnson.*

City of Richmond v. J. A. Croson Co.

United States Supreme Court, 1989.
454 U.S. 370, 109 S. Ct. 706, 102
L.Ed.2d 854.

Justice O'CONNOR announced the judgment of the Court and delivered the opinion of the Court with respect to Parts I, III-B, and IV, an opinion with respect to Part II, in which the Chief Justice and Justice WHITE join, and an opinion with respect to Parts III-A and V, in which the Chief Justice, Justice WHITE and Justice KENNEDY join. . . .

I

On April 11, 1983, the Richmond City Council adopted the Minority Business Utilization Plan (the Plan). The Plan required prime contractors to whom the city awarded construction contracts to subcontract at least 30% of the dollar amount of the contract to one or more Minority Business Enterprises (MBEs). The 30% set-aside did not apply to city contracts awarded to minority-owned prime contractors.

The Plan defined an MBE as "[a] business at least fifty-one (51) percent of which is owned and controlled . . . by minority group members." "Minority group members" were defined as "[c]itizens of the United States who are Blacks, Spanish-speaking, Orientals, Indians, Eskimos, or Aleuts." There was no geographic limit to the Plan; an otherwise qualified MBE from anywhere in the United States could avail itself of the 30% set-aside. The Plan declared that it was "remedial" in nature, and enacted "for the purpose of promoting wider participation by minority business enterprises in the construction of public projects." The Plan expired on June 30, 1988, and was in effect for approximately five years. . . .

The Plan was adopted by the Richmond City Council after a public hearing. . . . Proponents of the set-aside provision relied on a study which indicated that, while the general population of Richmond was 50% black, only .67% of the city's prime construction contracts had been awarded to minority businesses in the 5-year period from 1978 to 1983. It was also established that a variety of contractors' associations, whose representatives appeared in opposition to the ordinance, had virtually no minority businesses within their membership. The city's legal counsel indicated his view that the ordinance was constitutional under this Court's decision in *Fullilove* v. *Klutznick,* 448 U.S. 448 (1980). Councilperson Marsh, a proponent of the ordinance, made the following statement:

> "There is some information, however, that I want to make sure that we put in the record. I have been practicing law in this community since 1961, and I am familiar with the practices in the construction industry in this area, in the State, and around the nation. And I can say without equivocation, that the general conduct of the construction industry in this area, and the State, and around the nation, is one in which race discrimination and exclusion on the basis of race is widespread."

There was no direct evidence of race discrimination on the part of the city in letting contracts or any evidence that the city's prime contractors had discriminated against minority-owned subcontractors. ("[The public witnesses] indicated that the minority contractors were just not available. There wasn't a one that gave any indication that a minority contractor would not have an opportunity, if he were available"). . . .

On September 6, 1983, the city of Richmond issued an invitation to bid on a project for the provision and installation of certain plumbing fixtures at the city jail. . . .

. . . No MBE expressed interest in the project or tendered a quote. . . . On October 13, 1983, the sealed bids were opened. Croson turned out to be the only bidder, with a bid of $ 126,530. . . .

. . . The city informed Croson that it had decided to rebid the project. . . . Shortly thereafter Croson brought this action . . . in the Federal District Court for the Eastern District of Virginia, arguing that the Richmond ordinance was unconstitutional on its face and as applied in this case.

The District Court upheld the Plan in all respects. . . .

[A] divided panel of the [Fourth Circuit] Court of Appeals struck down the Richmond set-aside program as violating both prongs of strict scrutiny under the Equal Protection Clause of the Fourteenth Amendment. . . .

III

B

We think it clear that the factual predicate offered in support of the Richmond Plan suffers from the . . . two [fatal] defects. . . . [A] generalized assertion that there has been past discrimination in an entire industry provides no guidance for a legislative body to determine the precise scope of the injury it seeks to remedy. It "has no logical stopping point." . . .

While [t]here is no doubt that the sorry history of both private and public discrimination in this country has contributed to a lack of opportunities for black entrepreneurs, this observation, standing alone, cannot justify a rigid racial quota in the awarding of public contracts in Richmond, Virginia. . . .

It is sheer speculation how many minority firms there would be in Richmond absent past societal discrimination. . . . Defining these sorts of injuries as "identified discrimination" would give local governments license to create a patch-work of racial preferences based on statistical generalizations about any particular field of endeavor.

These defects are readily apparent in this case. The 30% quota cannot in any realistic sense be tied to any injury suffered by anyone. . . .

In sum, none of the evidence presented by the city points to any identified discrimination in the Richmond construction industry. We, therefore, hold that the city has failed to demonstrate a compelling interest in apportioning public contracting opportunities on the basis of race. To accept Richmond's claim that past societal discrimination alone can serve as the basis for rigid racial preferences would be to open the door to competing claims for "remedial relief" for every disadvantaged group. The dream of a Nation of equal citizens in a society where race is irrelevant to personal opportunity and achievement would be lost in a mosaic of shifting preferences based on inherently unmeasurable claims of past wrongs. . . .

IV

As noted by the court below, it is almost impossible to assess whether the Richmond Plan is narrowly tailored to remedy prior discrimination since it is not linked to identified discrimination in any way. We limit ourselves to two observations in this regard.

First, there does not appear to have been any consideration of the use of race-neutral means to increase minority business participation in city contracting. . . .

Second, the 30% quota cannot be said to be narrowly tailored to any goal, except perhaps outright racial balancing. It rests upon the "completely unrealistic" assumption that minorities will choose a particular trade in lockstep proportion to their representation in the local population. . . .

V

. . . Because the city of Richmond has failed to identify the need for remedial action in the awarding of its public construction contracts, its treatment of its citizens on a racial basis violates the dictates of the Equal Protection Clause. Accordingly, the judgment of the Court of Appeals for the Fourth Circuit is

Affirmed.

STUDY QUESTIONS

1. Does the MBE provision here seem to function in the same way as the one in *Fullilove*, i.e., as a preventive remedy? In view of the statements given at the public hearing, is it more accurate to describe the plan as aimed at preventing future discrimination or at "racial balancing"?

2. What was it that Justice O'Connor found missing in the city's defense of the provision under the narrow tailoring standard endorsed in *Fullilove?*

Although many legal issues relating to affirmative action are still in dispute, the question of whether it is permitted under Title VII and the Equal Protection Clause appears to be settled, at least in principle. Both permit the adoption of race- and sex-conscious affirmative action plans, at public and/or private initiative, where: (a) there is a firm basis to believe that the employer to which the plan applies has discriminated against the group favored by the plan in the past; (b) the plan is impartial, in the sense that it aims only to eliminate discriminatory practices; and (c) the plan is temporary.

As we indicated at the beginning of this discussion, affirmative action takes a variety of forms. The use of numerical goals is only one of them, the most controversial form. Recently, the Department of Labor has initiated another form of affirmative action aimed at identifying factors that inhibit the advancement of women into upper managerial positions in private industry. In the following selection, the Solicitor of Labor for the Bush Administration's Labor Department discusses that initiative.

The Department of Labor's Glass Ceiling Initiative

Marshall J. Berger.
Labor Law Journal (July 1992) 421–29.

The concept of a "glass ceiling" is not a new one. At the turn of the century, Marie Curie almost singlehandedly created the field of nuclear chemistry and forever changed the course of science and society. But even the ultimate scientific creativity award did not help her to crack the barrier of the science establishment. She received the Nobel Prize but was denied membership in the French Academie des Sciences because of her gender. It was only after her second Nobel Prize that the all male Academie reluctantly admitted her to the club. The problem that I have with this story is that a woman should not have to win a Nobel Prize to become a partner in a law firm or an executive in a corporation.

The development of glass ceiling issues at the Department of Labor did not require a radioactive discovery. Rather, the groundwork was laid several years ago, when we commissioned studies by the Hudson Institute on the demographics of the American work force in the year 2000. Those studies, and the reports that followed, demonstrated that a profound demographic change is taking place. By the year 2000, the overwhelming majority of new entrants into the work force will be minorities, women, and immigrants—white males will make up only 15 percent of this work force increase. So it is clear that to remain competitive corporate America will have to pick the best people from both the male and female graduates of our best universities. The companies that do not will not be around long.

Future trends do not address present problems, because it has also become clear that despite their dramatically increasing presence in the workplace, there is a dearth of women and minorities in the upper ranks of that work force. To put it another way, it has been said that the problem of the 1970s was bringing women and minorities into the corporation. The problem of the 1980s was keeping them there, and the challenge of the 1990s and beyond is to remove any artificial barriers impeding their upward mobility. Secretary of Labor Lynn Martin has made this one of her top priorities.

The Office of Federal Contract Compliance Programs at the Department of Labor (OFCCP) recently analyzed data from a sampling of 94 compliance reviews from Fortune 1000 companies (representing a total of 147,179 employees). It found that while women represented 37.2 percent of all companies' combined work force, only 16.9 percent of "officials and managers" working for these companies were women. And while minorities represented 15.5 percent of the companies' work force, only 6 percent of the companies' officials and managers were minorities. Furthermore, these numbers significantly overstate the percentage of women and minorities at executive-level, decision-making positions, since the category "officials and managers" includes people like the "head" of the janitorial staff and the "manager" of the clerical pool.

In terms of senior management (i.e., those at the level of assistant vice president and above), the compliance review pointed out that only 6.6 percent of those in senior management were women and 2.6 percent were minorities. Most of the individuals represented in these percentages, however, are in "velvet ghetto" staff jobs, such as human resources and public relations. These types of jobs usually do not put minorities or women on the fast track. So after moving up the ladder a few rungs, many women and minorities stop short and simply mark time.

There can, of course, be different reasons behind the relative scarcity of women and minorities in senior management positions. These reasons may include their relatively recent entry into the work force, coupled with the length of time necessary to reach senior management levels (estimated to be 20 years for a general

Reprinted with permission from Labor Law Journal, *July 1992, a Commerce Clearing House Publication.*

manager and 35 years for a CEO); the low turn-over rate at the management level; and, to a certain extent, personal choice, if not the—dare I say it—"Mommy Track." Yet it cannot be ignored that one of the most pervasive barriers to advancement is cultural attitudes toward women and minorities. Indeed, a recent poll of Fortune 1000 CEOs found that 81 percent believed "preconceptions by men" were major blocks to women reaching top levels of management.

Clearly, one reason for the scarcity of women and minorities at high levels can be actual discrimination. It is often a more subtle form of discrimination, referred to as sex stereotyping and recognized by the Supreme Court in the now famous case of *Price Waterhouse v. Hopkins,* where Justice Brennan stated: "In the specific context of sex stereotyping, an employer who acts on the basis of a belief that a woman cannot be aggressive, or that she must not be, has acted on the basis of gender. . . . An employer who objects to aggressiveness in women but whose positions require this trait, places women in an intolerable Catch 22: out of a job if they behave aggressively and out of a job if they don't." It is precisely this corporate attitude or culture that the Glass Ceiling Initiative is designed to detect and eliminate.

LAYING THE GROUNDWORK

One of the primary responsibilities of the OFCCP is to enforce Executive Order 11246. The Order and its implementing regulations prohibit government contractors and subcontractors from discriminating against any employee or applicant for employment, and it also requires such contractors to take affirmative action towards ensuring that employees and applicants are treated without regard to their race, color, religion, sex, or national origin. Traditionally, OFCCP's reviews of these contractors have tended to focus on entry-level positions. With the Glass Ceiling Initiative, we have begun to widen the scope of our attention to include barriers to advancement at all ranks of the work force, including its senior levels.

In 1988, OFCCP issued a policy directive entitled the Corporate Initiative. This initiative constituted a major new effort to encourage government contractors to increase their efforts in placing women and minorities in senior-level and executive-level positions. . . .

This directive laid the groundwork for the Glass Ceiling Initiative, which began with nine specially focused "pilot" corporate compliance reviews.

The major findings of these pilot reviews were summarized in the Secretary of Labor's Glass Ceiling Report, which was released in August 1991. The findings in this report confirmed what the studies had indicated. (1) There was definitely a level beyond which few minorities and women in each corporation had advanced. (2) We did not find that a hard line ran across each department, but the ceiling acted more like an undulating inversion layer. (3) The placement of the barrier varied according to function and salary level. Furthermore, the glass ceiling was at a level lower than anticipated. Indeed, the pilot reviews revealed much of the investigative questioning and many areas of prospective analysis to be irrelevant because there were no women or minorities at glass ceiling levels. Furthermore, minorities plateaued at a lower level than women. Generally, the highest-placed woman was at a higher reporting level to the CEO than the highest-placed minority.

The few women and minorities found at the highest levels tended to be in staff positions, such as human resources, research, or administration, rather than line positions, such as sales and production. Since line positions directly affect a company's bottom line, these positions are generally considered the path to the executive suite. . . .

The pilot reviews also revealed that organizations did not perceive equal opportunity and access principles as a broadbased corporate responsibility to be integrated throughout every level and area of the organization, but rather as the responsibility of one individual or division. Furthermore, there was generally no centralized means to monitor or track developmental opportunities and credential building experiences, such as training programs, developmental job rotations, and committee assignments, to ensure that all qualified employees were given consideration. . . .

Finally, the pilot reviews revealed that although a company that contracts with the government assumes an obligation to monitor its employment activities to ensure all employees and applicants are treated in a nondiscriminatory manner, many of the companies in the study did not have adequate EEO/affirmative action records concerning recruitment, employment, and developmental activities for management-type positions. Such records are essential for adequate monitoring of a company's fulfillment of its affirmative action responsibilities.

None of the nine companies in the pilot study was cited for discrimination. This does not mean that no violations were detected. Six of the companies entered into Conciliation Agreements for violation of recordkeeping requirements involving applicant flow, referrals, and placements. Two companies signed Letters of Commitment, also with regard to monitoring their recordkeeping and placement procedures. One company received a Letter of Compliance after addressing a problem in its pipeline leading to the executive suite. In addition, follow up to the original pilot study is now going on, since we are not only interested in what the companies accomplished in response to their regulatory requirements, but more importantly, what has been achieved through voluntary efforts since the reviews were conducted. . . .

I cannot underscore how important direct CEO involvement has been in the success of this initiative. What the pilot study showed was not some form of overt discrimination, but an attitude that led to minorities and women being overlooked for certain positions. . . .

Thus, while corporations cannot manage attitudes, they can manage behavior with accountability, rewards, and punishment. As in all other important areas of concern, what gets measured in business gets done, what is not measured is ignored. The Glass Ceiling Initiative has brought the issue to the forefront and has demonstrated to business the importance of shattering the barrier, so that it can no longer be ignored. And to assure that the issue remains on the front burner, the Civil Rights Act of 1991 established the Glass Ceiling Commission, which is to be chaired by the Secretary of Labor. . . .

Voluntary efforts play an important role in the glass ceiling endeavor. The heart of the Glass Ceiling Initiative is the promotion of equal opportunity, not mandated results. We encourage the promotion of good corporate conduct through an emphasis on cooperative, not just corrective, problem solving. We also believe in recognizing and rewarding those companies that are independently removing their own glass ceilings. Indeed, one of the most important benefits of the widespread publicity surrounding the Glass Ceiling Initiative has been the increasing corporate awareness of glass ceiling issues.

Since the release of the Report, many corporate executives have come forward to let the Department of Labor know what they are doing to remove their barriers. For example, some CEOs are making affirmative action a line item and holding managers personally responsible during the yearly appraisal process for affirmative action in their divisions. This is an example of managing behavior to produce positive results.

Voluntary compliance is also key for other reasons. Each corporate culture is distinct, and every company has its own approach to the development of a management team; therefore, businesses, not OFCCP, are best situated to determine the optimum means of ensuring that qualified women and minorities are being given the opportunity to advance. Businesses, not OFCCP, are best equipped to change the attitudes of managers who would cut short a person's career because he or she does not fit the manager's mold. And the ideal way to guarantee that this change in attitude happens is with a commitment from the CEO and other senior-level officers to make equal opportunity a key corporate objective toward becoming a premier employer.

Companies also need to recognize, especially given the changing demographics of the work force, that recruiting and developing well-trained women and minorities are essential if such companies are to remain competitive into the next century. Businesses with their eyes on the future understand the necessity of building a skilled and diverse work force throughout every level of the company. These businesses also know that a glass ceiling does not just prevent qualified women and minorities from reaching their full potential, it can also stunt the company's growth.

If the glass ceiling is allowed to remain, it effectively cuts the pool of potential corporate leaders by eliminating more than one half of the work force. It deprives business of new leaders, new sources of creativity, and would-be pioneers with entrepreneurial spirit. Personally, I believe the ceiling will be shattered, and I am pleased to be assisting Secretary Lynn Martin in wielding a hammer to that end.

STUDY QUESTIONS

1. What is meant by the "glass ceiling"? What evidence is there that a glass ceiling exists in American businesses?
2. What did Secretary Martin propose be done to correct this situation? Has calling for voluntary compliance on the part of the CEOs been tried in the past? Has it worked well? Does it seem to you to be an adequate response now?

6 Equal Educational Opportunity

M any of the instances of sex discrimination discussed in the preceding chapters have their roots in stereotyped attitudes toward what an earlier era called the nature, place, and proper destiny of men and women. The resiliance of these attitudes in the face of changes in the law and feminist critique is remarkable.

Schools are widely recognized as a central vehicle of culture in our country today. Undoubtedly, schools have contributed to the resiliancy of attitudes that cast men and women in different roles. Schools contribute to the process of sex-role socialization, however, not so much by initiating such roles and patterns of expectation as by reinforcing the attitudes already learned outside the school.

I. THE SOCIAL AND LEGAL CONTEXT

Since the early 1970s, courts and legislatures have become increasingly aware of the role that the schools play in denying girls and women equal access to important educational opportunities. The legal response to this increasing awareness came in the form of constitutional litigation in federal and state courts and new legislation from state legislatures and Congress. The courts began to apply the new *Reed* standard in equal protection cases to the schools. The main contribution by Congress is popularly known as Title IX. This chapter traces some of the more significant of these legal developments. Before turning to those, we consider the dimensions of the problem in historical context and briefly introduce Title IX.

Women's Education

Nona P. Lyons.
In *Encyclopedia of Educational Research*. 6th ed.
New York: Macmillan, 1992.
Pp. 1520–24.

In the past two decades women in the United States, like women around the world, have made startling achievements in gaining access to education. In the 1960s gender was the "single greatest predictor of educational access".[1] Today that

---

[1]G. P. Kelly (ed.), International Handbook of Women's Education. *New York: Greenwood, 1989.*

is not necessarily the case. The number of females in school worldwide is higher than at any previous time in history, reversing a trend that had characterized education in the United States in the first half of the twentieth century. By the 1970s, 7.5 million American women were in high school, roughly 80% of the high school-aged population, and the number of undergraduate women was growing four times as fast as the number of undergraduate men.[2] By the early 1980s:

> Women were earning more than half of all undergraduate and master's degrees, over 30 percent of all doctorates, a quarter of all medical degrees, and more than a third of all law degrees. The majority of a new, growing population of "nontraditional" older students returning to school were women.[3]

There is no question that major changes have taken place in women's education. Yet what educational access means for women in the 1990s is unclear in terms of power and authority in American society now or in the future, especially for women of color. Increasing educational access has not as a matter of course resulted in women's intellectual, political or social emancipation. . . .[4]

Although the education systems in the United States in 1990 provide 50% of the college-aged cohort with higher education and approach universal education at the secondary school level,[5] the situation for women remains problematic in several ways. Women continue to make better grades than men in high school, yet their scores on the Scholastic Aptitude Tests are lower in both verbal and math skills; they receive only 35% of the scholarships based on these scores.[6] And, according to Seller:

> Although women's educational attainment equals or exceeds men's at the bachelor's and master's levels, women, especially Blacks, Hispanics, and Asians are disproportionately concentrated in . . . community colleges and state teachers colleges and relatively scarce in prestigious research universities and technical institutes. . . .[7]

Perhaps most deeply troubling are high school dropout rates. Considering that women account for 60% of the total growth of the U.S. work force now and are expected to make up a similar percentage of entry-level workers through to the year 2000, tomorrow's workers are today's elementary and secondary school students.[8] "In the mid-1980s, the high school dropout rate of Hispanic women was more than double that of whites or blacks . . . and the high dropout rate of teenage mothers suggests the needs of these young women were not being met in traditional schools."[9]

Thus, in contrast to clear-cut gains in educational access in the last two decades, how these gains are being transformed into outcomes for women is decidedly not clear. Are they in fact helping women break out of traditional women's occupations, advance to top management, achieve comparable pay for comparable work, or change habits and policies or institutions? The statistics emphasize the paradoxical and contradictory nature of educational achievement for women. Has it always been so? A brief view of the history of women's education in the United States confirms a complex view. . . .

There are at least three key periods in the history of women in education: from the American Revolution to 1830, when women gained entry into academies and the common school and first became teachers in significant numbers; following the Civil War to the 1920s, when more women went to college for the first time

Copyright © 1992 by the American Educational Research Association. Reprinted from "Women's Education," Nona P. Lyons, Encyclopedia of Educational Research, Sixth Edition, edited by Marvin C. Alkin, Volume 4, 1520–1525. Excerpt with permission of Macmillan Publishing Company.

[2]*M. S. Seller, "The United States." In G. P. Kelly (ed.),* International Handbook of Women's Education. *New York: Greenwood, 1989.*

[3]Ibid., *p. 156.*

[4]*S. Schwager, "Educating Women in America." in E. Minnich, J. O'Barr, & R. Rosenfeld (eds.),* Reconstructing the Academy. *Chicago: University of Chicago Press, 1989, p. 156.*

[5]*G. P. Kelly, Op. Cit.*

[6]Ibid., *p. 74.*

[7]*M. S. Seller, Op. Cit., p. 535.*

[8]*A. M. Morrison & M. A. Von Glinow, "Women and Minorities in Management," 45* American Psychologist *200–208 (1990).*

[9]*M. S. Seller, Op. Cit., p. 537–538.*

in coeducational or single-gender institutions; and from the 1960s and 1970s to the present, when women's studies emerged in a flourish of scholarship, following a 30-year decline of women's educational advantages. . . .[10]

In the colonial period in American history, women and girls experienced schools and schooling before they were officially admitted to public schools, largely through their participation in the prevalent dame school. Public schools—mostly in New England— were predominately male centered. But in the years following the American Revolution, women's advocates—Benjamin Rush, Emma Willard, Catherine Beecher, and Horace Mann—made an unusual argument for women's education: Schooling would prepare women to be better mothers and wives, especially for their role in shaping the moral and civic character of the citizens of an expanding new nation. . . .[11]

The academies that emerged in the first decades after the Revolution made access to higher education available to young American middle-class women. Perhaps more importantly, historians now believe, they offered a new occupational role and identity for women as teachers, creating an early cohort of women leaders in education. For example, Scott, in tracing the history of the students of Emma Willard's school for girls (the Troy, New York Seminary, 1821), found that Emma Willard graduates established some 200 schools similar to the "Troy" seminary, as they went west and south across the United States. . . .

The great advance in women's education during and following the Civil War came with women's entry into higher education, a phenomenon fostered by the large number of men away at war.[12] Against virulent arguments positing that higher education was harmful to women physically and psychically—as G. S. Hall suggested, "The woman who uses her brain . . . has little hope to be other than a moral and medical freak"[13]—women slowly through their persistence gained access to coeducational as well as single-gender institutions of higher education. At first, women's colleges like the earlier academies shared a mission and, in some instances, a missionary zeal to encourage and prepare women for teaching. Graduates of Mt. Holyoke along with their largely New England sisters, like the graduates of Emma Willard's seminary, went to college and then west to teach. The 50 years from 1875 to 1925 witnessed gains in access to all kinds of educational institutions—state colleges, normal schools, etc. But whether women's entry into higher education in fact led to greater equality of outcome generally or merely reenforced traditional female roles is still debated by historians. . . .

Conway argues that neither early coeducational schools, such as Oberlin, the first college to admit women in 1830, or larger midwestern universities that burgeoned through the turn of the century, resulted in equality of intellectual or professional opportunity for women.[14] Studies of Stanford, Grinnell, Wisconsin, Cornell, and Berkeley suggest the struggle that women encountered in their exclusion from campus life or in their increasingly limited access to the disciplines they could study or the professions they could join. . . .

. . . [W]omen's studies have been a major factor shaping twentieth century educational experiences for women and men alike. Begun in the late 1960s and early 1970s, in response to the Civil Rights movement and the discovery of women's omission from most disciplines, the goal was the inclusion of women into the curriculum—in history, literature, sociology. As black Americans insisted on courses on the African-American experience, women demanded courses on female

---

[10]M. J. Boxer, "For and About Women: The Theory and Practice of Women's Studies in the United States." *13* Signs *661–695 (1982).*

[11]*M. S. Schwager,* Op. Cit.; *A. F. Scott, "The Ever Widening Circle: The Diffusion of Feminist Values from the Troy Female Seminary, 1822–1872." 19* History of Education Quarterly *3–25 (1979); B. M. Solomon,* In the Company of Educated Women. *New Haven, CT: Yale University Press, 1985; and T. Woody,* A History of Women's Education in the United States. *New York: Octagon Books, 1980. (Original work published 1929).*

---

[12]*P. A. Graham,* "Expansion and Inclusion: A History of Women in American Higher Education." *3 Signs 759–773 (1978).*

[13]*G. S. Hall,* Adolescence. *Vol. 11. New York: Appleton, 1905.*

[14]*J. K. Conway, "Coeducation and Women's Studies: Two Approaches to the Question of Women's Place in the Contemporary University." 103* Daedalus *239–249 (1974).*

experience. The movement had a clear political as well as educational end. Women's studies sought first to reclaim the past and second to analyze the causes of oppression. Simply by asking, "Where are the women?" a revolution was generated to excavate the history of one half of the human race.[15] By the mid-1980s, the number of courses and programs had grown to some 30,000—and, with them, scholarship that has dramatically revised or touched almost all the major disciplines. . . .

From all predictions, twenty-first century America will demand and offer unprecedented work and leadership opportunities for women. Yet, as some futurists argue, today's workplace is an anachronism, still defined by a time when men worked and women stayed at home. That is no longer likely, nor can it be ignored. But in light of known demands of tomorrow's workplace, skepticism about women's education for tomorrow is warranted—for several reasons.

The education of girls and women right now is problematic in terms of meeting their needs and in the quality of their educational experiences from the elementary grades through the professional schools.[16] Researchers report that boys and men speak more in class, that they are encouraged more at all levels, and that some women and girls look for different kinds of learning environments.[17] Research in psychol-ogy has only begun to map adolescent girls' development;[18] women's ways of knowing and approaches to learning[19] and the interdependence of students and teachers as knowers.[20] Despite growth in studies of African-American and Hispanic cultures, there is still too little research into these areas. There is a glaring lack of teachers or administrators of color currently in training. And all female students still receive less encouragement and have fewer science or math opportunities on the eve of a clearly technologically sophisticated workplace.

Women themselves need to participate in shaping their future, and educators, employers, and employees would, at this critical time, be wise to look for ways for that to happen as a new, unchartered future comes into being.

STUDY QUESTIONS

1. In what ways has the access of women to education changed in the past twenty years? In what ways has the meaning of education for women remained the same?

2. For what roles did education prepare women during the first two periods distinguished here? What are the educational aspirations of advocates of women's studies today?

3. In what ways does sex-role socialization in schools work to the disadvantage of girls and women? Of boys and men?

---

[15]C. R. Stimpson, Women's Studies in the United States. A Report to the Ford Foundation. *New York: Ford Foundation, 1986.*
[16]N. Noddings, "Feminist Critiques in the Professions." In C. B. Cazden (ed.), Review of Research in Education, 16. *Washington, D.C.: American Educational Research Association, 1990.*
[17]M. Sadker & D. Sadker, "Sexism in the Classroom: From Grade School to Graduate School." 67 Phi Delta Kappan *512–515 (1986).*

[18]C. Gilligan, N. Lyons, & T. Hanmer, Making Connections. *Cambridge, MA: Harvard University Press, 1990.*
[19]M. Belenky, B. Clinchy, N. Goldberger, & J. Tarule, Women's Ways of Knowing. *New York: Basic Books, 1986.*
[20]N. Lyons, "Dilemmas of Knowing: Ethical and Epistemological dimensions of Teachers' Work and Development." 60 Harvard Educational Review *159–180 (1990).*

The American Association of University Women issued a report in 1992 titled "How Schools Shortchange Girls" that reviewed the research finding of the past twenty years. It expanded on the list of problems cited by Lyons and concluded: "Whether one looks at preschool classrooms or university lecture halls, at female teachers or male teachers, research spanning the past twenty years consistently reveals that males receive more teacher attention than do females." Furthermore, the report said, "[t]he ways students treat each other during school hours is an aspect of the informal learning process, with significant negative implications for girls. There is mounting evidence that boys do not treat girls well." The findings reviewed in the AAUW report spurred a broader interest in lessening overt sex discrimination in the schools.

Under the impact of such legal measures as Title IX, the practice of overtly steering women students into traditional fields has declined. The result has not been a burgeoning enrollment of women in nontraditional courses of study. Part of the continued concentration of women in the more traditional fields can be explained by their own preferences. Student educational preferences continue to be formed by factors outside the control of schools and colleges. Nonetheless, differential treatment of students, even in mixed classrooms, continues to reinforce cultural stereotypes about the appropriate skills and aspirations of women and men. The following selection discusses some of the more subtle ways that women are steered into traditional roles.

The Classroom Climate: A Chilly One for Women

Roberta M. Hall, and Bernice R. Sandler. Project on the Status and Education of Women. Washington, D.C.: Association of American Colleges, 1982.

THE CLASSROOM CLIMATE

. . .Although many persons and experiences can help shape the campus climate, faculty attitudes and behaviors often have a profound effect—especially for women students. As Joseph Katz writes in *Men and Women Learning Together: A Study of College Students in the Late 1970's:*

> The newly raised consciousness of women [students] is in some respects fragile. In the intellectual and academic spheres there is still a tendency for women to think themselves as not quite on a par with men . . . there is some indication that women are meeting the challenge creatively, but they also could use more help from their teachers. . . .

In part because of the disproportionate number of male faculty at the college and university level, women may not always get this help. Several studies indicate that men faculty tend to affirm students of their own sex more than

students of the other sex, and often perceive women students primarily as sexual beings who are less capable and less serious than men students. Although these attitudes may be changing, a host of behaviors which can convey such attitudes are still prevalent in the academic setting.

Both men and women faculty—even those who are most concerned about sex discrimination—may inadvertently communicate to their students limiting preconceptions about appropriate and expected behaviors, abilities, career directions and personal goals which are based on sex rather than on individual interest and ability. For instance, some professors may habitually use classroom examples in which the man is always "the professional," the woman always the "client" or "patient," thus making it more difficult for women to imagine themselves in professional roles. Men and women faculty alike may ask questions and then look at men students only—as if no women were expected to respond. Some faculty may tend to ask women "lower order" factual questions ("When did Wordsworth write the first version of *The Prelude?*") and reserve "higher order" critical questions for men ("What do you see as the major thematic differences between the 1805 and the 1850 versions?") Others may make seemingly helpful comments which nevertheless imply that women in general are not as competent as men ("I know women have trouble with spatial concepts, but I'll be happy to give you extra help"). Some professors may be unaware that they interrupt women more often than men students, or allow women to be easily interrupted by others in class discussion. . . .

How a "Chilly" Climate for Women Affects All Students

Women Students. A chilling classroom climate puts women students at a significant educational disadvantage. Overtly disparaging remarks about women, as well as more subtle differential behaviors, can have a critical and lasting effect. When they occur frequently—especially when they involve "gatekeepers" who teach required courses, act as advisors, or serve as chairs of departments—such behaviors can have a profound negative impact on women's academic and career development by:

- discouraging classroom participation;
- preventing students from seeking help outside of class;
- causing students to drop or avoid certain classes, to switch majors or subspecialties within majors, and in some instances even to leave a given institution;
- minimizing the development of the individual collegial relationships with faculty which are crucial for future professional development;
- dampening career aspirations; and
- undermining confidence.

Instead of sharpening their intellectual abilities, women may begin to believe and act as though:

- their presence in a given class, department, program or institution is at best peripheral, or at worst an unwelcome intrusion;
- their participation in class discussion is not expected, and their contributions are not important;
- their capacity for full intellectual development and professional success is limited; and
- their academic and career goals are not matters for serious attention or concern.

Men Students. While women students may be most directly harmed by an inhospitable climate, men students are also affected. If limited views of women are overtly or subtly communicated by faculty, some men students may experience reinforcement of their own negative views about women especially because such views are confirmed by persons of knowledge and status. This may make it more difficult for men to perceive women students as full peers, to work with them in collaborative learning situations, and to offer them informal support as colleagues in the undergraduate or graduate school setting. Moreover, it may hamper men's ability to relate to women as equals in the larger world of work and family beyond the institution. . . .

HOW "SMALL" BEHAVIORS CREATE A CHILLY CLASSROOM CLIMATE

Devaluation, Evaluation and Doubt

The old saw that "a woman must be twice as good to get half as far as a man" still contains a core of truth: our society tends in many ways to value men more than it values women, and to assume that men's work and words are important, women's less so. . . .

. . .Thus, faculty may view and respond to the same behavior differently depending on the sex of the student. Males who act dispassionately may be viewed as "objective" but females as "cold." If a woman does exceptionally well, she may be praised for "thinking like a man"—a back-handed compliment which implies that there is something wrong with "thinking like a woman," which she is.

The devaluation of women's accomplishments is exacerbated by the related tendency to attribute males' success to skill or ability but females' success to luck or to lack of difficulty of the task to be performed. In one study, for example, adult tutors working with elementary school students who completed a preestablished assignment were most likely to tell high-achieving boys that they were competent, but to tell high-achieving girls that the assignment was easy. Thus, the cause for the children's identical achievement was viewed very differently—simply on the basis of the children's sex. . . .

If, as much research indicates, young women internalize this devaluation and "attribution" pattern of the larger society, they are likely to be especially prone to doubt their own competence and abilities. Indeed, women students themselves may be just as likely as males to downgrade "a woman's" academic work. In one study, for example, women college students rated scholarly articles higher if they believed they were written by a man than if they believed they were written by a woman. . . .

Colleges and universities ideally provide an environment that differentiates between students only on the basis of merit. However, faculty and students are not automatically immune from the limiting preconceptions held by the larger society or from the everyday behaviors by which different perceptions of men and women are reinforced and expressed. To the contrary, despite the increased enrollment of women students in recent years, college is often still considered a "masculine" environment where success depends on skills and abilities such as intellectual argumentation and competence in mathematics which women are viewed as lacking. As with work in society at large, academic work done by men may be valued more highly than that done by women; a woman student may have to outperform her male peers to be taken seriously by her professors.

Experiences in Early Schooling

Women and men students are likely to enter college with different educational histories—even if they have attended the same elementary and high schools. Ongoing research indicates, for example, that elementary teachers frequently treat boys and girls differently in everyday classroom interaction—often without knowing that they do so. Primary school teachers tend to:

☐ talk more to boys, ask them more "higher order" questions, and urge them to "try harder" if they are initially unsuccessful (thus imparting the message that they have the **ability** to succeed);

☐ give boys specific **instructions** on how to complete a project, but **show** girls how to do it—or, **do it for them;**

☐ talk to boys regardless of location in the classroom, but often only to girls who are nearby; and

☐ praise boys for the intellectual quality of their work and criticize them for lack of form and neatness, but do the opposite for girls.

Although there are obvious differences between colleges and elementary schools, some patterns of student-teacher interaction established at lower school levels may help set the stage for expectations and interactions in the college classroom.

THE POWER OF WORDS

Overtly discriminatory comments on the part of faculty are still surprisingly prevalent. These comments are often intentional—although those teachers who engage in them may be unaware of their potential to do real harm. They may occur not only in individual student-teacher interchanges, but also in classrooms, office consultations, academic advising situations and other learning contexts.

The individious nature of such comments can perhaps best be understood by comparing them to similar racial remarks. Few, if any, professors would make disparaging comments about blacks' seriousness of purpose or academic commitment, or use racist humor as a classroom device. (In order to experience the derogatory nature of such comments, the reader may wish to substitute the word "black" [or other minority] in the examples that follow):

☐ **comments that disparage women in general,** such as habitual references to "busy-body, middle-aged women," statements to the effect that "women are no good at anything," or the description of a class comprised solely of women as a "goddamn chicken pen."

☐ **comments that disparage women's intellectual ability,** such as belittling women's competencies in spatial concepts, math, etc., or making statements in class discussion such as "Well, you girls don't understand . . ."

☐ **comments that disparage women's seriousness and/or academic commitment,** such as "I know you're competent, and your thesis advisor knows you're competent. The question in our minds is, are you **really serious** about what you're doing?" or "You're so cute. I can't see you as a professor of anything."

☐ **comments that divert discussion of a woman student's work toward a discussion of her physical attributes or appearance,** such as cutting a student off in midsentence to praise her attractiveness, or suggesting that a student's sweater "looks big enough for both of us." (While such comments may seem harmless to some professors, and may even be made with the aim of complimenting the student, they often make women uncomfortable because essentially private matters related primarily to the sex of the student are made to take precedence over the exchange of ideas and information.)

☐ **comments about women faculty that define them in terms of their sex rather than their professional status** (e.g., "It must be that time of month") **or that disparage their professional accomplishments,** such as greeting the announcement of a female colleague's book with "After all, it's only her dissertation, and you know her [presumably male] advisor must have written most of that." (Such comments can be especially damaging, since the attitudes and behaviors of women faculty, and of male faculty toward them, is often "the most direct evidence available to students of both sexes of what it means to be a professional woman in our society.")

☐ **comments that refer to males as "men" but to females as "girls," "gals," etc. rather than "women."** This non-parallel terminology implies that women are viewed as similar to children and thus less serious or capable than men.

☐ **comments that rely on sexist humor as a classroom device,** either "innocently" to "spice up a dull subject," or with the conscious or unconscious motive of making women feel uncomfortable. Sexist humor can range from the blatantly sexual, such as a physics lecture in which the effects of a vacuum are shown by changes in the size of a crudely-drawn woman's "boobs," or the depiction of women in anatomy teaching slides as *Playboy* centerfolds, to "jokes about dating, about women students waiting to be called by men, etc.—i.e., the usual fooling around which relies on a certain bad taste (usually depicting women in a sexual context which is typically derogatory) in order to create a lively atmosphere in class."

☐ **comments that disparage scholarship about women, or that ridicule specific works because they deal with women's perceptions and feelings.** Such comments can reinforce students' perceptions that what men think, feel and do is important, while women's roles, actions, and feelings are not worth learning about.

Whether or not their intended purposes are "innocent," sexist humor and overtly sexist comments can interfere with classroom learning and have negative effects that go far beyond the immediate classroom or related learning situation.

THE CLASSROOM'S SILENT LANGUAGE

Like verbal behavior, nonverbal and other behaviors can also help shape classroom climate. A professor's nonverbal behavior can signal inclusion or exclusion of group members; indicate interest and attention or the opposite; communicate expectation of students' success or failure; and foster or impede students' confidence in their own abilities to learn specific tasks and procedures.

Faculty may treat men and women students differently in the following manner:

☐ **making eye contact more often with men than with women,** so that individual men students are more likely to feel recognized and encouraged to participate in class. (One teacher, for example, concerned because few women took part in discussion, learned from her students that she tended to ask a question and then to make eye contact with men only, as if only men students were expected to respond.)

☐ **nodding and gesturing more often in response to men's questions and comments than to women's.**

☐ **modulating tone** (for example, using a tone that communicates interest when talking with men, but a patronizing or impatient tone when talking with women).

☐ **assuming a posture of attentiveness** (for example, leaning forward) **when men speak, but the opposite** (such as looking at the clock) **when women make comments.**

☐ **habitually choosing a location near men students.** (Proximity in the college classroom may invite comments primarily from those sitting close by.)

☐ **excluding women from course-related activities, such as field trips, or attempting to discourage their participation because women are "too much trouble,"** etc. (Such exclusion is illegal under Title IX.)

☐ **grouping students according to sex, especially in a way which implies that women students are not as competent as or do not have status equal to men.** Women students, for example, have reported that some teachers insist there be no all-women lab teams because women cannot handle laboratory equipment on their own. (Other professors may group the women together "so they can help each other," or so that they "don't delay the men.") Some women have reported certain professors instruct male medical students to "scrub" with the faculty but women medical students with nurses. These kinds of arrangements may not only lead women students to doubt their competence, but also prevent women—for whom "hands-on experience" can be especially important in building confidence—from learning as much as men students.

  • if men students are expected to—and do—take over lab procedures, women are likely to be observers rather than participants.
  • "scrub" sessions may serve as informal learning circumstances from which women are excluded as learners and simultaneously "put in their place" as support professionals in the traditionally female field of nursing rather than as full colleagues.

☐ **favoring men in choosing student assistants.** In many institutions, men are still more likely than women to be chosen by faculty for these positions, which can provide students contact with faculty and opportunities for learning new skills and building confidence. Moreover, such course-related work experience with faculty can play a crucial role in sponsorship for jobs and admission to graduate and professional programs.

☐ **giving men detailed instructions in how to complete a particular problem or lab assignment in the expectation they will eventually succeed on their own, but doing the assignment for women—or allowing them to fail with less instruction.**

☐ **allowing women to be physically "squeezed out" from viewing a laboratory assignment or a demonstration.** This sort of physical exclusion can interfere with women students' opportunity to learn on their own.

☐ **making direct sexual overtures.** Direct sexual harassment by faculty can lead women students not only to feel threatened, but also to perceive that they are viewed by faculty primarily in sexual terms, rather than as individuals capable of scholastic and professional achievement. . . .

Outside the Classroom: A Chilly Campus Climate for Women?

Roberta M. Hall, and Bernice R. Sandler. Project on the Status and Education of Women. Washington, D.C.: Association of American Colleges, 1984.

Many experts in student development—and many college graduates—contend that what happens outside the classroom is as important for students' personal and intellectual growth as what happens inside the classroom. The wide range of activities and experiences involving all members of the campus community—faculty, staff and students—are not so much extra-curricular as co-curricular:

they are complementary and crucial parts of the learning process. Ideally, the college environment as a whole should help students acquire knowledge, build skills and confidence, learn how to make informed choices, and how to handle differences—including those of race, class and gender.

That colleges and universities too often fail to meet this challenge—especially in the case of women students—is underscored by findings of the most extensive longitudinal study of student development to date. It concludes that "[e]ven though men and women are presumably exposed to common liberal arts curriculum and other educational programs during the undergraduate years, it would seem that these programs serve more to preserve, rather than to reduce, stereotypic differences between men and women in behavior, personality, aspirations and achievement." . . .

Many factors, including familial and social expectations, may contribute to the preservation of these differences. However, the institutional "atmosphere," "environment" or "climate" also plays a crucial role in fostering or impeding women students' full personal, academic and professional development. As members of one institutional commission on campus life explain, although their college "houses a diverse group of people . . . [t]hat does not make it diverse . . . Many women and minority students think that both attitudinal and institutional factors relegate them to second-class status." From their standpoint, "this is . . . a fragmented community, dominated by a core group whose particular values are supported by the larger community and by the College itself." Traditionally geared to the intellectual and personal development of men from upper and middle class backgrounds, many colleges and universities may perpetuate an environment in which differences and divisions are inadvertently intensified rather than reduced. . . .

EVERYDAY INEQUITIES IN THE CAMPUS ENVIRONMENT

Small behaviors that often occur in the course of everyday interchanges—such as those in

which individuals are either singled out, or ignored and discounted because of sex, race or age—have been called "micro-inequities." Each instance—such as a disparaging comment or an oversight which affects only members of a given group—may in and of itself seem trivial, and may even go unnoticed. However, when taken together throughout the experience of an individual, these small differences in treatment can create an environment which "maintain[s] unequal opportunity. . . .

GENERAL BEHAVIORS THAT SINGLE OUT WOMEN

Typically, the more overt behaviors single out women because of their sex. These behaviors are often intentional—although those who engage in them may be unaware of their potential to do real harm. They include behaviors such as the following:

☐ disparaging women in general, women's intellectual abilities or women's professional potential;
☐ focusing attention on women's appearance or women's personal or family life as opposed to their performance;
☐ using sexist humor;
☐ grouping students by sex in a way which implies that women are not as competent or do not have status equal to men (as in campus employment, lab or field work);
☐ counseling women to lower their academic and career goals;
☐ engaging in verbal or physical sexual harassment; and
☐ making disparaging comments about lesbians, or using lesbianism as a label by which to accuse or threaten women. . . .

SUPPORT SERVICES, EMPLOYMENT AND COURSE-RELATED EXPERIENCES

Institutions clearly want to provide support services and out-of-class experiences fairly. However, the attitudes and behaviors of faculty, student services staff, other campus employees and student peers frequently determine how well—or how poorly—women students are served. . . .

Association of American Colleges, 1818 R. Street, N.W., Washington, D.C. 20009.

Admissions And Financial Aid

The way women are treated in the admissions and financial aid process sets the tone for their participation both within and beyond the institution. Yet, at both the undergraduate and graduate levels, students too often encounter personnel who may unwittingly communicate limited or outmoded preconceptions about women—and men—students. Admissions staff, for example, may inadvertently lead women to doubt their goals and question their potential; financial aid officers may see women's need for aid as less important than men's. The latter problem is particularly unfortunate, not only because of its economic implications, but also because receipt of aid has been shown to be closely connected with women students' intellectual self-esteem and academic persistence.

Health Care

The availability of appropriate health services such as gynecological care, rape treatment, and birth control information is just a starting point. Health care staff should avoid behaviors such as the following that can discourage women from using health services:

☐ automatically attributing women's concerns to "nervousness" or "emotional problems" and thus, for example, routinely prescribing tranquilizers for women when they would not be prescribed for men;

☐ providing information on contraception or abortion, or treatment for venereal disease, in a derisive or moralistic way;

☐ treating women in a patronizing manner ("Don't you worry your pretty little head about it.");

☐ responding to rape victims as if they were to blame for the assault;

☐ allowing stereotyped attitudes about sex— "appropriate" traits and behaviors as well as conventional attitudes about sexual preference—to shape treatment strategies and communicate approval or disapproval; and

☐ sexually harassing women. Several instances have been reported in which women students have refused to use college health clinics because of harassment by physicians and other staff.

Campus Safety

Safety has become an increasing concern on many campuses. Shuttle buses, escort services, buddy systems and other services are often available to students, many especially geared to women who use library, laboratory, computer and other facilities at night. However, campus safety personnel may inadvertently discourage women from using these services and seeking necessary help in a variety of ways such as:

☐ making light of women's hesitance to use college facilities or attend college functions at night;

☐ trivializing women's concerns when they report feeling threatened by dates or male classmates;

☐ taking a "boys-will-be-boys" attitude when male students, including members of fraternities, harass, frighten or threaten women;

☐ blaming women for instances of harassment or rape, either directly, or by commenting negatively on the circumstances and/or a woman's appearance; and

☐ responding to concerns raised by lesbian or gay students differently than to similar concerns raised by other students.

RESIDENTIAL, SOCIAL AND CULTURAL CLIMATE: A REEVALUATION

General Climate

As is the case with student services, colleges and universities across the country are examining the quality of residential, social and cultural life to see how well existing arrangements serve an increasingly diverse student population. Many campuses have begun to restructure residential systems away from the "anonymous dormitories" of the 60's and 70's and to diversify social and cultural offerings in order to increase faculty-student contact and to facilitate positive interchange between students from different backgrounds.

Of particular concern to many institutions is the role of the Greek system in shaping the general campus climate, especially at small colleges or institutions in small towns where alternative settings for social events are limited. Several colleges have concluded that fraternities, in particular, often build a bond among their own members largely by creating a divisive environment in the wider community that promotes exclusion and differential treatment based on class, race and especially on sex. Indeed, some fraternities have been called to task for "promoting sexist attitudes—actual harassment of women and, more generally, distrust between men and women." Sororities, too, may perpetuate a limited view of women and create divisiveness by choosing members largely on the basis of appearance, playing a "little sister" role in relation to fraternities, and generally reinforcing stereotyped gender roles.

These and other aspects of day-to-day life on campus can lead women to question their role in the college community. Women students may feel like interlopers on "male turf" when incidents and omissions like the following are commonplace, and/or tolerated by students, faculty and administrators when they do occur:

☐ "Petty" hostility toward women under the guise of "fun" is routinely expressed in social and residential settings—such as pouring drinks on women, beating women with celery sticks, or razzing women as they enter dining halls or lounges.

☐ Women are expected to perform stereotypically "feminine" roles in conjunction with social events and cooperative housing arrangements—such as preparing food and cleaning up—while men make tapes, provide entertainment or do maintenance work.

☐ Men dominate co-educational living units, by, for example, harassing women, creating a "locker room atmosphere," or loudly disrupting the floors at night.

☐ Residence hall advisers do not respond in a serious manner to dormitory climate and related concerns raised by women and/or do not refer women to campus services that can deal with their concerns.

☐ Housing options for women are more limited than those for men, or are subject to institutional control while men's are not. If, for example, fraternities manage themselves but sororities are required to have house mothers, women are treated as children while men are treated as adults. . . .

☐ Typical social activities and campus media demean women—as, for example, wet T-shirt contests, X-rated movies as fundraisers, or sexist articles and ads (such as a bikinied female torso surrounded by male heads and hands as an ad for a spring break trip) in the student newspaper or the college yearbook.

☐ Fraternities sponsor events which result in the harassment and degradation of women, or define women as sexual objects. On one Ivy League campus, for example, a recent fraternity "scavenger hunt" list included "xerox copies of female genitalia," "[X College] girls (brought willingly)," "women's underwear and related objects," each of which was assigned a "point value." . . .

Women may also feel like second-class citizens when campus women's organizations and activities are discounted in ways such as the following:

☐ Representatives of women's groups have little access to and/or no real input in dealing with top administrators on campus.

☐ Women students' organizations and activities receive little or no institutional support in the form of office space, funding, etc., or are offered space and support that identifies them with "fringe" organizations on campus.

☐ Activities sponsored by women students' organizations—such as lectures, workshops, films, or women's week activities—are avoided or belittled by faculty, staff and students.

☐ Women's concerns, women speakers and works dealing with women are omitted from university-sponsored cultural events, such as lecture series, art exhibits, and film series, or are seen as "controversial" or treated with ridicule.

☐ Women's studies programs and courses are disparaged.

☐ Women are rarely, if ever, awarded honorary degrees, chosen as commencement speakers, or named to prestigious chairs.

☐ There is no women's center—or the women's center is underfunded, understaffed and isolated from mainstream institutional services.

Athletics

Physical activity—whether jogging or gymnastics, hockey or hiking—can have a substantial impact on women's sense of self-confidence and mastery. Additionally, participation in team sports can build group skills, such as strategy development and leadership, and can also foster the capacity to respond to losing without a debilitating sense of personal failure.

Until fairly recently, however, women were all but excluded from serious athletic participation. Women were not expected to be interested in sports, and those who did show an interest or who joined a team were frequently discouraged from anything so "unfeminine." It is beyond the scope of this paper to detail the many inequities faced by women in sports. However, despite marked gains, women athletes often find their accomplishments are not taken seriously, and they themselves are subject to differential treatment of many kinds, such as the following:

☐ Faculty, administrators, peers and others may use stereotypic labels—like "tomboy" or "girl jock"—when describing women athletes.

☐ Those on campus may respond with surprise, disdain or ridicule when women express an interest in athletics.

☐ Female athletes' accomplishments may go unnoticed, while men's are the focus of discussion and praise. Campus publicity—both promotional and post-event coverage—may be less for women's than for men's matches.

☐ Faculty and student affairs personnel may suggest athletic participation to men, but not to women, as a form of recreation and an avenue for personal growth.

☐ Career counselors may provide information to men, but not to women, about opportunities involving athletics.

☐ Accusations of lesbianism may be used to discourage women from participating in or coaching sports, especially when they attempt to speak up about inequities.

☐ In coed recreational sports, men are likely to dominate.

STUDY QUESTIONS

1. What do the authors mean by a "chilly climate"? In what ways are women students treated differently in classrooms? In what ways are women students treated inequitably by admissions, campus security, and health care offices? What are some of the ways that the athletic climate of campuses discourages and devalues women students?

2. How are female students harmed as a result of the "chilly climate"? Are male students also harmed by it?

3. Where on your campus can you turn for help in eliminating practices that create a chilly climate for you and your friends?

Title IX

Over the past twenty years, the courts have applied constitutional provisions as well as the provisions of and regulations under Title IX to combat sex discrimination in education. We are already familiar, from Chapter 2, with the relevant developments in equal protection analysis and in state ERAs. Title IX, however, requires an introduction.

Title IX of the Educational Amendments of 1972, 20 U.S.C. Sec. 1681, was one of the first major legal steps taken to eliminate sex discrimination from the schools. It was passed by both houses of Congress after hearings, held in 1970, that documented the pervasiveness, perniciousness, and long-range consequences of sex discrimination in educational policy, practices, and attitudes. Regulations that interpret Title IX were issued three years later.

Since the enactment of Title IX, other federal statutes guaranteeing students equal educational opportunities without regard to their sex have been adopted. These include the Equal Educational Opportunities Act of 1974 and Title II of the Educational Amendments of 1976. Although some states have more stringent requirements, Title IX has served as a model for federal and state efforts to provide equal educational opportunities for men and women. The language of Title IX parallels that of Title VI of the Civil Rights Act of 1964, which prohibits racial discrimination in programs or activities receiving federal financial assistance.

Scope. Just as we found it helpful in Chapter 4 to analyze Title VII in terms of its coverage, scope, and remedies, so it is useful here to approach Title IX in the same way. In terms of its scope, i.e., what behaviors it prohibits, the statute provides:

> No person in the United States shall, on the basis of sex, be excluded from participation in, be denied the benefits of, or be subjected to discrimination under any education program or activity receiving Federal financial assistance. . . .

Regulations issued in support of Title IX amplify statutory requirements regarding admissions and recruitment and develop standards applicable to curriculum, research, extracurricular activities, student aid, student services, counseling and guidance, financial aid, housing, and athletics. Most observers agree that during the 1970s, performance in these areas by educational institutions vastly improved, and they credit Title IX with providing the impetus for that improvement. Between 1980 and 1988, the Reagan administration cut back on Title IX enforcement efforts with the result that much of the earlier momentum was lost. Interest in enforcement efforts was revived, however, with the passage of the Civil Rights Restoration Act of 1988 and with the 1991 Supreme Court decision in *Franklin v. Gwinnett,* both of which will be discussed later in this chapter.

Exceptions to the general prohibition of Title IX were included in both the statute itself and in the interpretative regulations. The main exception included in the statute relates to sex-based admission policies. The statute specifies eight types of educational institutions: 1) preschool; 2) elementary school; 3) secondary school; 4) vocational school; 5) private institution of undergraduate higher education; 6) public institution of undergraduate higher education; 7) professional school; and 8) graduate school. As a result of the exceptions written into the statute, the general prohibition against sex-based admissions policies applies only to four of these, viz., 4, 6, 7, and 8. The clear bar to sex-based admissions policies in vocational, professional, and graduate schools is generally credited as a significant move toward the integration of traditionally all-male fields, such as law, medicine, engineering, etc. Title IX, however, does not prohibit sex-based admissions in any public or private preschool, any public or private elementary school, any public or private secondary school, or any private college. By failing to mandate the sex integration of the schools across the board, Congress clearly compromised the principle of equal educational opportunity and missed an important opportunity to confront the ancient stereotypes as they surface in the formative childhood years.

Two other statutory exceptions pertain to material addressed in this chapter. One specifically declares that the sex-based admissions policies of any "public institution of undergraduate higher education which is an institution that traditionally and continually from its establishment has had a policy of admitting only students of one sex. . . ." do not violate the prohibition of sex-based admissions policies. At the time of this writing, the only schools that fit that description are Virginia Military Institute and the Citadel. The admissions policies of both of these schools were under equal protection challenge in the early 1990s. Another statutory exception to the general prohibition against sex discrimination in educational programs relates to social clubs. The statute excludes the membership policies of social fraternities and sororities from coverage under Title IX. As we will see, such organizations may be in jeopardy under other legal provisions addressing sex discrimination in public accommodations.

Title IX regulations introduce additional exceptions to the general prohibition against sex discrimination in educational programs. One of the distinguishing features of many of these exceptions is the use of the "separate but equal" approach that has long since been abandoned in the addressing racial discrimination in the educational context.

The regulations permit the provision of separate-but-equal housing, locker rooms, shower facilities, etc. These exceptions may be justified by appeal to considerations of personal privacy. Few would consider them to be departures from the principle of equal educational opportunity. The treatment of school athletics (45 C.F.R. § 86.41) is a different matter. The section opens with a sweeping prohibition:

> No person shall, on the basis of sex, be excluded from participation in, be denied the benefits of, be treated differently from another person or otherwise be discriminated against in any interscholastic, intercollegiate, club, or intramural athletics offered by a recipient, and no recipient shall provide any such athletics separately on such basis.

The section, however, immediately introduces a number of major exceptions to this general prohibition. Single-sex teams are permitted in the case of "contact sports," e.g., boxing, wrestling, rugby, football, basketball, and ice hockey. Schools are not required to sponsor female teams for contact sports. Single-sex teams are also permitted for noncontact sports if a team for the excluded sex is also sponsored in that sport. Thus a male tennis team is permitted if a female tennis team is also sponsored. The regulations, qualified in this way, require schools to permit females to try out for athletic teams previously dominated by males only in the case of noncontact sports and then only where a separate-but-equal female team is not provided.

Coverage. The prohibitions of Title IX are generally addressed to all educational institutions, including public and private preschool, elementary, secondary, vocational, graduate, and professional schools as well as colleges and universities, that receive federal financial assistance. The latter restriction is the key to grasping an important feature of Title IX, viz., that it imposes a contractual obligation upon recipients of federal largesse. The obligation to eliminate sex discrimination in educational institutions is a legal string that is attached to the funds that the schools receive from the federal government.

Several actions taken by the Supreme Court and Congress since the passage of Title IX have clarified the coverage of this statute. In 1984, the Supreme Court handed down two rulings in a case of key importance for the coverage of Title IX. On the one hand, it ruled that a private college that accepts no direct aid from the federal government but enrolls students who do receive federal grants that are used to defray tuition and fees at the school is a "recipient of federal financial assistance" for the purposes of Title IX and therefore is obligated to conform to its requirements

(*Grove City College v. Bell,* 465 U.S. 555). On the other hand, and in the same decision, the Court ruled that only the "educational program or activity" that benefits directly from the receipt of federal funds is under that obligation. In *Grove City,* that was the financial aid office of the college.

This latter aspect of the Court's decision in *Grove City* brought Title IX enforcement to a standstill for the next four years. The narrow construction given to the "program or activity" language of Title IX had an immediate chilling effect not only on Title IX but also on other civil rights statutes governing recipients of federal funds. Title VI, prohibiting discrimination on the basis of race and national origin; Section 504 of the Rehabilitation Act of 1973, protecting handicapped persons; and the Age Discrimination Act of 1975 are all severely impeded because the reach of these statutes is also limited by "program or activity" language. The decision in *Grove City* relating to that language was overturned by the Civil Rights Restoration Act. At the urging of the Reagan administration, the Republican-controlled Senate of the 98th and 99th Congresses rejected the act. In March 1988, it was passed by the Democrat-controlled 100th Congress over President Ronald Reagan's veto. Thereafter, enforcement efforts began to recover their earlier vigor.

Remedies. We saw above that the obligations imposed by Title IX are contractual in nature. Accordingly, the principal remedy initially envisioned for violations was the withholding of federal funds. Those schools that fail to avoid practices that discriminate on the basis of sex in the education of students or in dealing with employees are in jeopardy of having their federal funding cut off. We will see later in this chapter that the Supreme Court made clear that another remedy available to individuals who bring action under Title IX against schools is monetary damages. (See *Franklin v. Gwinnett Cty. Public Schools.*) Observers expect that the availability of damages will be a powerful incentive for schools to take more initiative in identifying and eliminating discriminatory practices in the future.

In the remainder of this chapter, we take up a number of themes that run through both litigation and legislation bearing on sex discrimination in the schools. Each illustrates that a variety of legal standards are frequently available to those who seek to enforce equality of educational opportunity.

II. SINGLE-SEX SCHOOLS

Title IX prohibits the segregation by sex of vocational, professional, and graduate schools and of those public undergraduate colleges and universities that have not barred admission to one sex continually from their founding. As indicated earlier, this prohibition was enormously influential in opening opportunities to women in these types of schools. Notwithstanding, many schools were not reached by Title IX because of specific statutory exclusions. As a result, the debate during the past several decades over whether sex segregation in the schools should be permitted has been framed mainly in terms of whether the Equal Protection Clause of the Fourteenth Amendment permits governments to support single-sex schools.

The leading arguments, pro and con, on equality of education and separate educational opportunities were first addressed in connection with racial segregation in the schools. It is worth reviewing these arguments here because they parallel the arguments we will encounter in the debate over sex-based segregation in the schools.

The Supreme Court first endorsed the "separate but equal" doctrine as it applied to racial segregation in *Plessy v. Ferguson*, 163 U.S. 537 (1896). In that case, the Court rejected an equal protection challenge to a Louisiana statute that provided for separate railway coaches for whites and blacks. The challenge was predicated upon the assumption that "the enforced separation of the two races stamps the colored race with a badge of inferiority." Applying the rational relation test, the Court rejected that argument and held that states are "at liberty to act with reference to the established usages, customs and traditions of the people, and with a view to the promotion of their comfort, and the preservation of the public peace and good order." Two grounds were given in support of that ruling. First, although blacks might *infer* a stigma from enforced separation, inferiority was not shown to have been *implied* by the legislature when it enacted the statute. The *Plessy* Court relied on the view that the social meaning of an action derives entirely from the intention of the actor, here the legislature. Second, traditional social attitudes are so deeply entrenched that the law "is powerless to eradicate racial instincts or to abolish distinctions based on physical differences. . . ." For that reason, the Court went on to assert that the Equal Protection Clause cannot have been intended "to abolish distinctions based upon color, or to enforce social, as distinguished from political equality, or a commingling of the two races upon terms unsatisfactory to either."

The "separate but equal" doctrine approved in *Plessy* permitted segregation of schools by race when the separate schools provided substantially equal facilities. The doctrine withstood over fifty years of argument and litigation. It was eaten away as part of legal campaign by the National Association for the Advancement of Colored People through intermediate decisions and was finally rejected outright in the landmark decision of *Brown v. Board of Education*, 347 U.S. 483 (1954). There, statutes of four states that provided for racially segregated public schools were challenged on equal protection grounds. The challenge was the same as the one that was rejected by the *Plessy* Court, i.e., enforced segregation imposes a stigma on the minority group.

Specifically, the question addressed by the *Brown* Court was: "Does segregation of children in public schools on the basis of race, even though the physical facilities and other 'tangible' factors may be equal, deprive the children of the minority group of equal educational opportunities?" A unanimous Court replied: "We believe that it does." In doing so, it rejected both of the grounds relied on by the *Plessy* Court. As to the first, the *Brown* Court pointed out that not only do black children who are forced to endure segregated schools experience a crippling "feeling of inferiority" but that enforced segregation is more generally "interpreted as denoting the inferiority of the negro group." No longer is the social meaning of a governmental action tied entirely to the supposed intention of the legislature. In *Brown*, the Court relied on a different approach to the interpretation of public actions. In this view, an action gives offense if, in the light of prevailing beliefs, it is generally understood in the community as an insult. The second of the *Plessy* Court's grounds was rejected outright. The law is not, the *Brown* Court insisted, powerless in the face of persistent social prejudice. That noble ambition was and is lauded by most, derided by a few, and is still undecided as a factual matter. "We conclude," wrote Chief Justice Warren, "that in the field of public education the doctrine of 'separate but equal' has no place. Separate educational facilities are inherently unequal."

Racially segregated schools were found in violation of the Equal Protection Clause because they enforce a larger social point about the inferior social place of racial minorities. Like so many other practices associated with the system of racial segregation in the United States—practices such as separate bathrooms, separate sleeping quarters, and separate sports leagues—separate schools also "imposed a badge of inferiority."

Lyons reminded us that sexually segregated schools were once commonplace. Like racially segregated schools, those schools also make a larger social point about boys and girls. Although sexually segregated schools were not as overtly hostile as those that were racially segregated, there is an important similarity. In this section, we consider the rationales used to justify sex segregation in the schools.

At first, the courts addressed equal protection challenges to single-sex schools by applying the same line of reasoning that was used in *Plessy*. The plaintiff had the burden of showing that the practice was arbitrary. That burden was not met where a usage, custom, or tradition of maintaining such schools could be cited. Equal facilities, however, had to be provided for all. The following decision, handed down before *Reed*, illustrates this approach.

Williams v. McNair

United States District Court,
South Carolina, 1970.
316 F.Supp. 134, *aff'd without opinion*,
401 U.S. 951 (1971).

DONALD RUSSELL, District Judge.

This is an action instituted by the plaintiffs, all males, suing on behalf of themselves and others similarly situated, to enjoin the enforcement of a State statute which limits regular admissions to Winthrop College, a State supported college located at Rock Hill, South Carolina, to "girls". They assert that, except for their sex, they fully meet the admission requirements of the college. . . .

It is clear from the stipulated facts that the State of South Carolina has established a wide range of educational institutions at the college and university level consisting of eight separate institutions, with nine additional regional campuses. The several institutions so established vary in purpose, curriculum, and location. Some are limited to undergraduate programs; others extend their offerings into the graduate field. With two exceptions, such institutions are co-educational. Two, by law, however, limit their student admissions to members of one sex. Thus the Citadel restricts its student admission to males and Winthrop, the college involved in this proceeding, may not admit as a reg-

ular degree candidate males. There is an historical reason for these legislative restrictions upon the admission standards of these two latter institutions. The first, the Citadel, while offering a full range of undergraduate liberal arts courses and granting degrees in engineering as well, is designated as a military school, and apparently, the Legislature deemed it appropriate for that reason to provide for an all-male student body. Winthrop, on the other hand, was designed as a school for young ladies, which, though offering a liberal arts program, gave special attention to many courses thought to be specially helpful to female students.[3]

The Equal Protection Clause of the Fourteenth Amendment does not require "identity of treatment" for all citizens, or preclude a state, by legislation, from making classifications and

---

[3] *See Section 401, Title 22, Code of South Carolina (1962):*
"*There shall be established an institution for the practical training and higher education of white girls which shall be known as Winthrop College. . . .*" *In Section 408, Title 22, the purpose of Winthrop College was stated to be:*
"*The establishment, conduct and maintenance of a first-class institution for the thorough education of the white girls of this State, the main object of which shall be (1) to give to young women such education as shall fit them for teaching and (2) to give instruction to young women in stenography, typewriting, telegraphy, bookkeeping, drawing (freehand, mechanical, architectural, etc.), designing, engraving, sewing, dressmaking, millinery, art, needlework, cooking, housekeeping and such other industrial arts as may be suitable to their sex and conducive to their support and usefulness. Said trustees may add, from time to time, such special features to the institution and may open such new departments of training and instruction therein as the progress of the times may require.*"

creating differences in the rights of different groups. It is only when the discriminatory treatment and varying standards, as created by the legislative or administrative classification are arbitrary and wanting in any rational justification that they offend the Equal Protection Clause. . . .

. . .Thus, the issue in this case is whether the discrimination in admission of students, created by the statute governing the operation of Winthrop and based on sex, is without rational justification.

It is conceded that recognized pedagogical opinion is divided on the wisdom of maintaining "single-sex" institutions of higher education but it is stipulated that there is a respectable body of educators who believe that "a single-sex institution can advance the quality and effectiveness of its instruction by concentrating upon areas of primary interest to only one sex." The idea of educating the sexes separately, the plaintiffs admit, "has a long history" and "is practiced extensively throughout the world". It is no doubt true, as plaintiffs suggest, that the trend in this country is away from the operation of separate institutions for the sexes, but there is still a substantial number of private and public institutions, which limit their enrollment to one sex and do so because they feel it offers better educational advantages. While history and tradition alone may not support a discrimination, the Constitution does not require that a classification "keep abreast of the latest" in educational opinion, especially when there remains a respectable opinion to the contrary; it only demands that the discrimination not be wholly wanting in reason. . . .

Under these circumstances, this Court cannot declare as a matter of law that a legislative classification, premised as it is on respectable pedagogical opinion, is without any rational justification and violative of the Equal Protection Clause. . . .

Let judgment be entered for the defendants.

STUDY QUESTIONS

1. What equal protection standard did the court apply here? Does the justification of the challenged practice cited by the court here draw upon the arguments used in *Plessy?*

2. In *Brown,* the Court observed that school segregation tends to promote feelings of inferiority among minority children. Would you expect to find similar effects among Winthrop students? If they were vehemently to deny such feelings, would you change your opinion?

3. Does the pedagogical opinion cited here in support of single-sex schools accord with your experience? Even if that opinion were demonstrably true, would it justify exclusion of students by law because of their sex?

Williams was decided before the Supreme Court handed down its decision in *Reed v. Reed.* In Chapter 2, we saw that the Court in *Reed* held that sex-based classifications are subject to heightened scrutiny under the Equal Protection Clause. After *Reed,* the rational relation test used in *Williams* would no longer suffice. Six years later, a circuit court upheld sex-segregated public high schools against an equal protection challenge assertedly applying a more stringent standard of review.

Vorchheimer v. Sch. Dist. of Philadelphia

United States Court of Appeals, Third Circuit, 1976.
532 F.2d 880, *aff'd by equally divided court,* 430 U.S. 703 (1977).

JOSEPH F. WEIS, Jr., Circuit Judge.

. . . Plaintiff is a teen-age girl who graduated with honors from a junior high school in Philadelphia. She then applied to Central High School, a public school in the city, but was refused admission because that institution is restricted to male students. . . .

Academic high schools have high admission standards and offer only college preparatory courses. There are but two such schools in Philadelphia, and they accept students from the entire city rather than operating on a neighborhood basis. Central is restricted to males, and Girls High School, as the name implies, admits only females.

Central High School was founded in 1836 and has maintained a reputation for academic excellence. For some years before 1939, it was designated a comprehensive rather than an academic high school as it is presently. Its graduates both before and after 1939 have made notable contributions to the professions, business, government and academe.

Girls High has also achieved high academic standing. It was founded in 1848 and became an academic school in 1893. Its alumnae have compiled enviable records and have distinguished themselves in their chosen diverse fields. It now has a faculty of more than 100 and a student body of approximately 2,000, about the same as those of Central.

. . . The Philadelphia school system does not have a co-ed academic school with similar scholastic requirements for admission.

The courses offered by the two schools are similar and of equal quality. The academic facilities are comparable, with the exception of those in the scientific field where Central's are superior. The district court concluded "that [generally] the education available to the female students at Girls is comparable to that available to the male students at Central." Moreover, "[g]raduates of both Central and Girls High, as well as the other senior high schools of Philadelphia," have been and are accepted by the most prestigious universities.

The plaintiff has stipulated that "the practice of educating the sexes separately is a technique that has a long history and world-wide acceptance." Moreover, she agrees that "there are educators who regard education in a single-sex school as a natural and reasonable educational approach." . . .

Before deciding which school she wished to attend, the plaintiff visited a number of them and developed some definite opinions. As to Girls High, she commented, "I just didn't like the impression it gave me. I didn't think I would be able to go there for three years and

not be harmed in any way by it." As to Central, she said, "I liked it there. I liked the atmosphere and also what I heard about it, about its academic excellence." She was somewhat dissatisfied with her education at George Washington High School because of her belief that the standards which the teacher set for the students were not high enough.

The trial judge found the gender based classification of students at the two schools to lack a "fair and substantial relationship to the School Board's legitimate interest" and enjoined the practice. . . .

The nature of the discrimination which the plaintiff alleges must be examined with care. She does not allege a deprivation of an education equal to that which the school board makes available to boys. Nor does she claim an exclusion from an academic school because of a quota system, or more stringent scholastic admission standards. Moreover, enrollment at the single-sex schools is applicable only to high schools and is voluntary, not mandatory. The plaintiff has difficulty in establishing discrimination in the school board's policy. If there are benefits or detriments inherent in the system, they fall on both sexes in equal measure. . . .

Equal educational opportunities should be available to both sexes in any intellectual field. However, the special emotional problems of the adolescent years are matters of human experience and have led some educational experts to opt for one-sex high schools. While this policy has limited acceptance on its merits, it does have its basis in a theory of equal benefit and not discriminatory denial. . . .

The record does contain sufficient evidence to establish that a legitimate educational policy may be served by utilizing single-sex high schools. The primary aim of any school system must be to furnish an education of as high a quality as is feasible. Measures which would allow innovation in methods and techniques to achieve that goal have a high degree of relevance. Thus, given the objective of a quality education and a controverted, but respected theory that adolescents may study more effectively in single-sex schools, the policy of the school board here does bear a substantial relationship. . . .

The judgment of the district court will be reversed.

GIBBONS, Circuit Judge (dissenting).

The majority opinion may be briefly summarized as follows:

> The object of the [14th] Amendment was undoubtedly to enforce the . . . equality of the two [sexes] before the law, but in the nature of things it could not have been intended to abolish distinctions based upon [sex], or to enforce social, as distinguished from political equality, or a commingling of the two [sexes] upon terms unsatisfactory to either. Laws permitting, and even requiring, their separation in places where they are liable to be brought into contact with each other do not necessarily imply the inferiority of either [sex] to the other, and have been generally, if not universally, recognized as within the competency of the state legislatures in the exercise of their police power. The most common instance of this is connected with the establishment of separate schools for [male] and [female] children, which has been held to be a valid exercise of the legislative power even by courts of States where the political rights of [women] have been longest and most earnestly enforced.

The quotation, with appropriate substitutions, will be recognized immediately as the analysis of Justice Brown, for the majority of the Supreme Court, in *Plessy v. Ferguson*. No doubt had the issue in this case been presented to the Court at any time from 1896 to 1954, a "separate but equal" analysis would have carried the day. I was under the distinct impression, however, that "separate but equal" analysis, especially in the field of public education, passed from the fourteenth amendment jurisprudential scene over twenty years ago. *See, e.g., Brown v. Board of Education.* . . .

Unlike the majority, I find it particularly difficult to say on the basis of the record in this case that the exclusion of females from Central bears a fair and substantial relationship to any of the Philadelphia School Board's legitimate objectives. Admittedly coeducation at the senior high school level has its supporters and its critics. The majority is also undoubtedly correct in suggesting that a legitimate educational policy may be served by utilizing single-sex high schools. But certainly that observation does not satisfy the substantial relationship test. Some showing must be made that a single-sex academic high school policy advances the Board's objectives in a manner consistent with the requirements of the Equal Protection Clause. *Reed v. Reed.* . . .

Because I agree with the district court that the Board has not made the required showing of a substantial relationship between its single-sex academic high school policy and its stated educational objectives, I would affirm the decision below. . . .

STUDY QUESTIONS

1. What standard of review was used here? Who had the burden of proof?
2. What do you suppose was meant by "the special emotional problems of the adolescent years"? How does the reference to those problems establish a reasonable basis for single-sex schools? Might one argue that these problems exist to a troublesome degree because boys and girls have been segregated too much rather than too little?
3. Was the dissenting judge right to characterize the test applied by the court here as the "separate but equal" doctrine?

Lyons alluded to the ideology of the social system that supported sex-segregated schools: females are intellectually inferior to males; they are too frail to withstand the rigors of mental training; and they are destined for social roles that do not require advanced studies. Judge Weis in *Vorchheimer* reminded us of another element of the ideology that supports the social system of sex segregation. The presence of girls in the same classroom as adolescent boys presents a distraction for the boys. That element, too, has a long history. It was represented in the Eden story (see Chapter 1).

When sex-segregated schools are viewed in the light of this social system and its ideology, we can easily see how it implies the inferiority of females: it too imposes "a badge of inferiority." The courts, however, have been reluctant to draw this parallel and address the question of whether "separate educational facilities are inherently unequal" where segregation is based on sex rather than race.

The segregation of Central and Girls high schools in Philadelphia was successfully challenged on equal protection and state ERA grounds in 1983 (*Newberg v. Board of Education,* 26 Pa. D & C 682). A trial-level court ruled that the educational opportunities afforded by the two schools were quite unequal and that the "theory that adolescents may study more effectively in single-sex schools" was contradicted by the actual experience of the Boston Latin School, which had recently admitted girls for the first time. In so ruling, the judge showed that sex-segregated schools can be found in violation even of the old "separate but equal" doctrine and that traditional theories lauding the merit of sex-segregated schools can be discredited when confronted with factual evidence.

The Supreme Court affirmed *Vorchheimer* by a 4-4 vote, without issuing an opinion. Six years later, the Court addressed another case involving sex segregation in an educational context. This time, it struck down the arrangement, although, as we noted in Chapter 2, on quite narrow grounds. Incorporated into the opinions in *Hogan* was a discussion of the merit and relevance of the arguments in support of sex-segregated colleges. We include parts of Justice Powell's dissent as well as footnote 17 of Justice O'Connor's opinion to show how the Court addressed those arguments. When considering these views, compare them with those expressed in the *McNair* and *Vorchheimer* decisions.

Miss. Univ. for Women v. Hogan

Supreme Court of the United States, 1982.
458 U.S. 718, 102 S.Ct. 3331, 73 L.Ed.2d 1090.

Justice O'CONNOR deliverd the opinion of the Court.

This case presents the narrow issue of whether a state statute that excludes males from enrolling in a state-supported professional nursing school violates the Equal Protection Clause of the Fourteenth Amendment.

The facts are not in dispute. In 1884, the Mississippi legislature created the Mississippi Industrial Institute and College for the Education of White Girls of the State of Mississippi, now the oldest state-supported all-female college in the United States. The school, known today as Mississippi University for Women (MUW), has from its inception limited its enrollment to women.[1]

In 1971, MUW established a School of Nursing, initially offering a two-year associate degree. Three years later, the school instituted a four-year baccalaureate program in nursing and today also offers a graduate program. The School of Nursing has its own faculty and administrative officers and establishes its own criteria for admission.

Respondent, Joe Hogan, is a registered nurse but does not hold a baccalaureate degree in nursing. Since 1974, he has worked as a nursing supervisor in a medical center in Columbus, the city in which MUW is located. In 1979, Hogan applied for admission to the MUW School of Nursing's baccalaureate program. Although he was otherwise qualified, he was denied admission to

---

[1] *. . . Mississippi maintains no other single-sex public university or college. Thus, we are not faced with the question of whether States can provide "separate but equal" undergraduate institutions for males and females. Cf. Vorchheimer v. School District of Philadelphia.*

the School of Nursing solely because of his sex. School officials informed him that he could audit the courses in which he was interested, but could not enroll for credit.

Hogan filed an action in the United States District Court for the Northern District of Mississippi, claiming the single-sex admissions policy of MUW's School of Nursing violated the Equal Protection Clause of the Fourteenth Amendment. Hogan sought injunctive and declaratory relief, as well as compensatory damages.

Following a hearing, the District Court denied preliminary injunctive relief. The court concluded that maintenance of MUW as a single-sex school bears a rational relationship to the state's legitimate interest "of providing the greatest practical range of educational opportunities for its female student population." Furthermore, the court stated, the admissions policy is not arbitrary because providing single-sex schools is consistent with a respected, though by no means universally accepted, educational theory that single-sex education affords unique benefits to students. Stating that the case presented no issue of fact, the court informed Hogan that it would enter summary judgment dismissing his claim unless he tendered a factual issue. When Hogan offered no further evidence, the District Court entered summary judgment in favor of the State.

The Court of Appeals for the Fifth Circuit reversed, holding that, because the admissions policy discriminates on the basis of gender, the District Court improperly used a "rational relationship" test to judge the constitutionality of the policy. Instead, the Court of Appeals stated, the proper test is whether the State has carried the heavier burden of showing that the gender-based classification is substantially related to an important governmental objective. Recognizing that the State has a significant interest in providing educational opportunities for all its citizens, the court then found that the State had failed to show that providing a unique educational opportunity for females, but not for males, bears a substantial relationship to that interest. . . .

We begin our analysis aided by several firmly-established principles. Because the challenged policy expressly discriminates among applicants on the basis of gender, it is subject to scrutiny under the Equal Protection Clause of the Fourteenth Amendment. *Reed v. Reed.* That this statute dis-

criminates against males rather than against females does not exempt it from scrutiny or reduce the standard of review. *Orr v. Orr.* Our decisions also establish that the party seeking to uphold a statute that classifies individuals on the basis of their gender must carry the burden of showing an "exceedingly persuasive justification" for the classification. *Feeney.* The burden is met only by showing at least that the classification serves "important governmental objectives and that the discriminatory means employed" are "substantially related to the achievement of those objectives." *Wengler v. Druggists Mutual Ins. Co.* . . .

The State's primary justification for maintaining the single-sex admissions policy of MUW's School of Nursing is that it compensates for discrimination against women and, therefore, constitutes educational affirmative action. As applied to the School of Nursing, we find the State's argument unpersuasive.

In limited circumstances, a gender-based classification favoring one sex can be justified if it intentionally and directly assists members of the sex that is disproportionately burdened. See *Schlesinger v. Ballard.* However, we consistently have emphasized that "the mere recitation of a benign, compensatory purpose is not an automatic shield which protects against any inquiry into the actual purposes underlying a statutory scheme." *Weinberger v. Wiesenfeld.* The same searching analysis must be made, regardless of whether the State's objective is to eliminate family controversy, *Reed,* to achieve administrative efficiency, *Frontiero,* or to balance the burdens borne by males and females. . . .

Mississippi has made no showing that women lacked opportunities to obtain training in the field of nursing or to attain positions of leadership in that field when the MUW School of Nursing opened its door or that women currently are deprived of such opportunities. In fact, in 1970, the year before the School of Nursing's first class enrolled, women earned 94 percent of the nursing baccalaureate degrees conferred in Mississippi and 98.6 percent of the degrees earned nationwide. . . . That year was not an aberration; one decade earlier, women had earned all the nursing degrees conferred in Mississippi and 98.9 percent of the degrees conferred nationwide. As one would expect, the labor force reflects the same predominance of women in nursing. When MUW's School of Nursing began operation, nearly 98 percent of all employed registered nurses were female.

Rather than compensate for discriminatory barriers faced by women, MUW's policy of excluding males from admission to the School of Nursing tends to perpetuate the stereotyped view of nursing as an exclusively woman's job. By assuring that Mississippi allots more openings in its state-supported nursing schools to women than it does to men, MUW's admissions policy lends credibility to the old view that women, not men, should become nurses, and makes the assumption that nursing is a field for women a self-fulfilling prophecy. Thus, we conclude that, although the State recited a "benign, compensatory purpose," it failed to establish that the alleged objective is the actual purpose underlying the discriminatory classification.

The policy is invalid also because it fails the second part of the equal protection test, for the State has made no showing that the gender-based classification is substantially and directly related to its proposed compensatory objective. To the contrary, MUW's policy of permitting men to attend classes as auditors fatally undermines its claim that women, at least those in the School of Nursing, are adversely affected by the presence of men. . . .

Thus, considering both the asserted interest and the relationship between the interest and the methods used by the State, we conclude that the State has fallen far short of establishing the "exceedingly persuasive justification" needed to sustain the gender-based classification. Accordingly, we hold that MUW's policy of denying males the right to enroll for credit in its School of Nursing violates the Equal Protection Clause of the Fourteenth Amendment.[17] . . .

Because we conclude that the State's policy of excluding males from MUW's School of Nurs-

ing violates the Equal Protection Clause of the Fourteenth Amendment, we affirm the judgment of the Court of Appeals.

It is so ordered.

Justice POWELL, with whom Justice Rehnquist joins, dissenting.

. . . Coeducation, historically, is a novel educational theory. From grade school through high school, college, and graduate and professional training, much of the Nation's population during much of our history has been educated in sexually segregated classrooms. At the college level, for instance, until recently some of the most prestigious colleges and universities . . . had long histories of single-sex education. As Harvard, Yale, and Princeton remained all-male colleges well into the second half of this century, the "Seven Sister" institutions established a parallel standard of excellence for women's colleges. . . .

The sexual segregation of students has been a reflection of, rather than an imposition upon, the preference of those subject to the policy. It cannot be disputed, for example, that the highly qualified women attending the leading women's colleges could have earned admission to virtually any college of their choice. Women attending such colleges have chosen to be there, usually expressing a preference for the special benefits of single-sex institutions. Similar decisions were made by the colleges that elected to remain open to women only.[4] . . .

The issue in this case is whether a State transgresses the Constitution when—within the context of a public system that offers a diverse range of campuses, curricula, and educational alternatives—it seeks to accommodate the legitimate personal preferences of those desiring the advantages of an all-women's college. In my view, the Court errs seriously by assuming—without argument or discussion—that the equal

---

[17]Justice Powell's dissent suggests that a second objective is served by the gender-based classification in that Mississippi has elected to provide women a choice of educational environments. Since any gender-based classification provides one class a benefit or choice not available to the other class, however, that argument begs the question. The issue is not whether the benefited class profits from the classification, but whether the State's decision to confer a benefit only upon one class by means of a discriminatory classification is substantially related to achieving a legitimate and substantial goal.

---

[4]In announcing Wellesley's decision in 1973 to remain a women's college, President Barbara Newell said that "[t]he research we have clearly demonstrates that women's colleges produce a disproportionate number of women leaders and women in responsible positions in society; it does demonstrate that the higher proportion of women on the faculty the higher the motivation for women students." . . .

protection standard generally applicable to sex discrimination is appropriate here. That standard was designed to free women from "archaic and overbroad generalizations. . . ." *Schlesinger v. Ballard*. . . .

By applying heightened equal protection analysis to this case, the Court frustrates the liberating spirit of the Equal Protection Clause. It prohibits the States from providing women with an opportunity to choose the type of university they prefer. And yet it is these women whom the Court regards as the victims of an illegal, stereotyped perception of the role of women in our society. The Court reasons this way in a case in which no woman has complained, and the only complainant is a man who advances no claims on behalf of anyone else. His claim, it should be recalled, is not that he is being denied a substantive educational opportunity, or even the right to attend an all-male or a coeducational college. It is only that the colleges open to him are located at inconvenient distances. . . .

In sum, the practice of voluntarily chosen single-sex education is an honored tradition in our country, even if it now rarely exists in state colleges and universities. Mississippi's accommo-dation of such student choices is legitimate because it is completely consensual and is important because it permits students to decide for themselves the type of college education they think will benefit them most. Finally, Mississippi's policy is substantially related to its long-respected objective. . . .

STUDY QUESTIONS

1. What standard of review was employed here? Justice Powell argued in dissent that sex discrimination raises a constitutional issue only when the rights of women are at issue. Did Justice O'Connor agree?
2. What were Justice Powell's reasons for upholding school sex segregation in this case? What advantages did he find accrue to the women who choose to attend all-women schools? Did Justice O'Connor deny that there are such advantages? What reason did she give for rejecting Justice Powell's line of argument in this case? Does the position that she defends here leave open the possibility that sex segregation in schools may be permissible in other contexts and for other reasons?

The debate between Justices O'Connor and Powell resurfaced in the early 1990s, when the lower courts were called upon to decide an equal protection challenge to the all-male admissions policy of Virginia Military Institute. VMI and the Citadel are exempt from coverage of Title IX's bar of single-sex admissions policies because both have been male-only schools continually from their founding. Echoing the arguments of Justice Powell, as well as those advanced in *McNair* and *Vorchheimer,* the district court declared that the maintenance of educational diversity was a sufficiently important government objective to justify the male-only admissions policy. The Fourth Circuit Court of Appeals neither affirmed nor reversed. Instead, it vacated the district court's order and returned the matter with instructions that many observers believe will eventually require Virginia to renounce the male-only admissions policy at VMI.

U.S. v. Virginia

United States Court of Appeals,
Fourth Circuit, 1992.
976 F.2d. 890, *cert. denied,*
_____ U.S. _____ , 113 S.Ct.2431 (1993).

NIEMEYER, Circuit Judge:

The male-only admissions policy of Virginia Military Institute (VMI), a state institution of higher education located in Lexington, Virginia, is challenged by the federal government under the Equal Protection Clause of the Fourteenth

Amendment and the jurisprudence of *Mississippi Univ. for Women v. Hogan.* . . .

Following a six-day trial and extensive findings of fact, the district court concluded that VMI's male-only policy "is fully justified" by a generally accepted benefit of single-sex education, and that the admission of women would "significantly" change the "methods of instruction and living conditions" at VMI. Having concluded that "diversity in education" was a legitimate state interest, the district court summarized, "I find that both VMI's single-sex status and its distinctive educational method represent legitimate contributions to diversity in the Virginia higher education system, and that excluding women is substantially related to this mission." . . .

The mission of VMI is to produce "citizen-soldiers, educated and honorable men who are suited for leadership in civilian life and who can provide military leadership when necessary." Focusing primarily on character development and leadership training through a unique and intense process, characterized as an "adversative" educational model drawn from earlier military training and English public schools, VMI's educational method emphasizes physical rigor, mental stress, absolute equality of treatment, absence of privacy, minute regulation of behavior, and indoctrination of values. The process is designed to foster in VMI cadets doubts about previous beliefs and experiences and to instill in cadets new values which VMI seeks to impart. . . .

VMI, with approximately 1,300 male students, has never accepted applications from women. During the two years preceding the filing of this action, it did, however, receive over 300 inquiries from women. Today, VMI is the only state-supported, single-sex college in Virginia, although historically most of Virginia's 15 public colleges were at one time single-sex institutions.

The government instituted this action on March 1, 1990 . . . on behalf of a female high school student who desired admission to VMI, contending that VMI's male-only admissions policy violates the Equal Protection Clause of the Fourteenth Amendment. . . .

[Relying on *Hogan,* the Court concluded that] . . . to conduct the appropriate Fourteenth Amendment analysis in this case, we must determine whether the state policy of excluding women from admission to VMI is substantially related to an important policy or objective of Virginia.

. . . [T]he record supports the district court's findings that at least these three aspects of VMI's program—physical training, the absence of privacy, and the adversative approach—would be materially affected by coeducation, leading to a substantial change in the egalitarian ethos that is a critical aspect of VMI's training. . . .

It is not the maleness, as distinguished from femaleness, that provides justification for the program. It is the homogeneity of gender in the process, regardless of which sex is considered, that has been shown to be related to the essence of the education and training at VMI.

. . . [T]he evidence in this case amply demonstrated that single-genderedness in education can be pedagogically justifiable. . . .

. . . The decisive question in this case therefore transforms to one of why the Commonwealth of Virginia offers the opportunity only to men. While VMI's institutional mission justifies a single-sex program, the Commonwealth of Virginia has not revealed a policy that explains why it offers the unique benefit of VMI's type of education and training to men and not to women. . . .

Virginia has committed the development of its educational policy in the first instance to the State Council of Higher Education for Virginia . . . [that] is charged with the responsibility of preparing plans, which it has done biennially. These plans articulate "access, excellence and accountability" as an overriding goal of Virginia's system of higher education, and they reaffirm a policy of autonomy and diversity to provide a variety of choice. . . .

Announcing a similar policy, a special commission legislatively established to chart the future goals of higher education in Virginia, the Commission on the University of the 21st Century, reported to the Governor and the General Assembly of Virginia in 1990 that the hallmarks of Virginia higher education, "autonomy and diversity," should be maintained. Within its report, the Commission indirectly reaffirmed the earlier stated policy of affording broad access to higher education in Virginia, and also observed: Because colleges and universities provide opportunities for students to develop values and learn from role models, it is extremely important that they deal with faculty, staff, and students without regard to sex, race, or ethnic origin. That statement is the only explicit one that we have found in the record in which the Commonwealth has expressed itself with respect to gender distinctions. Our inability to find a stated policy justifying single-sex education in state-supported colleges and universities is confirmed by the Virginia Attorney General's statement about the absence of such a state policy: "In the absence of a statute explicitly expressing the General Assembly's view on the policy issue, [the governor's] statement of the Commonwealth's policy [that 'no person should be denied admittance to a State supported school because of his or her gender'] is persuasive." . . .

If VMI's male-only admissions policy is in furtherance of a state policy of "diversity," the explanation of how the policy is furthered by affording a unique educational benefit only to males is lacking. A policy of diversity which aims to provide an array of educational opportunities, including single-gender institutions, must do more than favor one gender. . . .

We are thus left with three conclusions: (1) single-gender education, and VMI's program in particular, is justified by a legitimate and relevant institutional mission which favors neither sex; (2) the introduction of women at VMI will materially alter the very program in which women seek to partake; and (3) the Commonwealth of Virginia, despite its announced policy of diversity, has failed to articulate an important policy that substantially supports offering the unique benefits of a VMI-type of education to men and not to women. . . .

Although neither the goal of producing citizen soldiers nor VMI's implementing methodology is inherently unsuitable to women, the Commonwealth has elected, through delegation or inaction, to maintain a system of education which offers the program only to men. In the proceedings below, Virginia had the opportunity to meet its burden of demonstrating that it had made an important and meaningful distinction in perpetuating this condition. As the record stands, however, evidence of a legitimate and substantial state purpose is lacking.

In light of our conclusions and the generally recognized benefit that VMI provides, we do not order that women be admitted to VMI if alternatives are available. But VMI's continued status as a state institution is conditioned on the Commonwealth's satisfactorily addressing the findings we affirm and bringing the circumstances into conformity with the Equal Protection Clause of the Fourteenth Amendment. By commenting on the potential benefits of single gender education while discussing the alleged governmental interest in support of VMI's admissions policies, we do not mean to suggest the specific remedial course that the Commonwealth should or must follow hereafter. Rather, we remand the case to the district court to give to the Commonwealth the responsibility to select a course it chooses, so long as the guarantees of the Fourteenth Amendment are satisfied. Consistent therewith, the Commonwealth might properly decide to admit women to VMI and adjust the program to implement that choice, or it might establish parallel institutions or parallel programs, or it might abandon state support of VMI, leaving VMI the option to pursue its own policies as a private institution. While it is not ours to determine, there might be other more creative options or combinations.

Accordingly, we vacate the judgment and remand the case to the district court: (1) to require the defendants to formulate, adopt, and implement a plan that conforms with the Equal Protection Clause of the Fourteenth Amendment, (2) to establish appropriate timetables, and (3) to oversee the implementation of the plan.

Vacated and remanded for further proceedings.

STUDY QUESTIONS

1. What is VMI's educational mission? Why are women excluded from VMI? In what sense does VMI advance the goal of educational diversity in the state? Does Virginia make the benefits of this type of education available to both men and women?

2. Did Virginia meet its burden of proof under the *Hogan* standard? Why do you suppose that the court vacated the district court's decision, rather than simply reversing it?

3. In remanding this case, what options were left open to the state? In view of the statements of the governor and his commission, which of these options appears most likely to be adopted?

While the VMI case was on appeal, a class action suit was filed against the Citadel by two female Navy veterans who were denied admissions to the school's Veteran's Day Program. They challenged the all-male policy on equal protection grounds. The Day Program welcomed male veterans to summer and night classes and would have permitted the plaintiffs to pursue undergraduate degrees. Although the Day Program was distinct from the regular undergraduate program, a decision in that case about the one program may have had immediate effects on the other program as well. Accordingly, three months after the initial filing of the suit, the school announced that it had suspended the Veteran's Day Program. The action was reportedly taken in order to render the suit moot and thereby protect the integrity of its regular undergraduate program from challenge, at least for the time being.

Sex segregation in public education is almost extinct in our day. In 1991, only two publicly supported single-sex colleges survived—the Citadel and the Virginia Military Institute. In the private sector, single-sex schools are quickly becoming a rarity. At the college level, these schools are succumbing to financial pressures that have resulted from an overall decline in the numbers of college-age students and from changing educational preferences among high school graduates. In 1991, only four private all-men colleges remained in the United States, viz., Hampden-Sydney College (Virginia), Deep Springs College (California), Rose-Hulman Institute of Technology (Indiana), and Wabash College (Indiana). The picture for all-women schools is almost as extreme. Although there were 298 women's colleges in 1960, only 93 remained three decades later.

The question of whether women-only schools ought to be encouraged is hotly debated among feminists as well as the educational community. Here again, we find the same themes that divide sponsors of the equal treatment and sponsors of the different treatment approaches discussed in Chapter 3. Advocates of all-women schools emphasize the educational benefits available to women in supportive single-sex settings, in contrast with the "chilly climate" that so pervades coeducational schools. These arguments were stressed by Justice Powell in his *Hogan* dissent. The learning environment of women's colleges fosters self-confidence, intellectual self-esteem, and high aspirations among their students. They prepare women to assume positions of leadership in society. They encourage young women to pursue nontraditional fields of study, such as mathematics and the natural sciences. They provide resources that enable women to go on, after graduation, to promote equity for women in all walks of life. Studies showing that elite women's colleges have been historically more successful at producing career-oriented women graduates than have coeducational colleges and universities are adduced in support of these claims.

In *Hogan,* following the equal treatment approach, the Court rejected arguments very similar to these. The Court found that the all-women nursing school there had been defended on the grounds that "it was consistent with a respected, though by no means universally accepted, educational theory that single-sex education affords unique benefits to students." The Court did not challenge the truth of that theory, only its relevance to the equal protection issue. Thus, as Justice O'Connor stated, "The issue is not whether the benefited class profits from the classification, but whether the State's decision to confer a benefit only upon one class by means of a discriminatory classification is substantially related to achieving a legitimate and substantial goal." Advocates of special treatment of women students in all-women schools point to the ways that the women who are included benefit from inclusion. They have not yet shown that the denial of these benefits to the men who are excluded is substantially related to advancing an important state interest.

We recall from Chapter 2 that the Court invokes strict scrutiny when reviewing a racial classification but only a middle-level test for sex-based classifications. Thus, racial segregation of schools was declared "inherently unequal" in *Brown*. *Hogan*, applying a somewhat less demanding test, stopped short of declaring that sex segregation in schools is inherently unequal. What *Hogan* did do was to narrow the grounds that are available to justify government support of single-sex schools. The Fourth Circuit Court of Appeals left open the possibility that Virginia might be able to find an important government interest for affording the unique pedagogical approach to military training that is traditional at VMI and that it might be permitted to do so if it were also made available to women.

Other jurisdictions have explored approaches to single-sex education that may, in limited circumstances, satisfy the requirements of *Hogan*. Although race is a central feature of the following case, the single-sex issue was the deciding factor. Consider what might have happened if Detroit had established both male and female academies in the following situation.

Garrett v. Bd. of Educ. of the Sch. Dist. of Detroit

United States District Court, Michigan, 1991.
775 F.Supp. 1004.

WOODS,

Plaintiffs filed this suit on Monday, August 5, 1991, alleging the defendant Board of Education of the School District of the City of Detroit ("Board") violated the Fourteenth Amendment to the United States Constitution . . . through the establishment of male-only academies. Plaintiffs are girls enrolled in Detroit public schools and their parents. . . .

. . . The Court heard oral argument August 15, 1991 [on plaintiff's motion for a preliminary injunction], and issued its opinion from the bench. This written opinion supplements the bench order.

Three male academies ("Academies") are scheduled to open on August 26, 1991. The Academies will serve approximately 250 boys in preschool through fifth grade. Grades six through eight will be phased in over the next few years. The Academies offer special programs including

a class entitled "Rites of Passage", an Afrocentric (Pluralistic) curriculum, futuristic lessons in preparation for 21st century careers, an emphasis on male responsibility, mentors, Saturday classes, individualized counseling, extended classroom hours, and student uniforms.

Plaintiffs contend that these special offerings (1) do not require a uniquely male atmosphere to succeed; and (2) address issues that face all children and adolescents, including females. . . .

Plaintiffs allege in their complaint that the defendant has deliberately chosen to disregard the rights of girls in the public school system, despite the specific advice of state governmental authorities and the federal policy requiring equal educational opportunities without regard to sex. . . .

In *Mississippi v. Hogan,* the Supreme Court held that exclusion of an individual from a publicly-funded school because of his or her sex violates the Equal Protection Clause of the Fourteenth Amendment, unless the defendant can show the sex-based "classification serves 'important governmental objectives and that the discriminatory means employed'" are "substantially related to the achievement of those objectives."

Plaintiffs maintain the Board cannot meet this standard because the Board's policy of excluding girls inappropriately relies on gender as a proxy for "at-risk" students. The Academies were developed in response to the crisis facing

African-American males manifested by high homicide, unemployment, and dropout rates. While these statistics underscore a compelling need, they fall short of demonstrating that excluding girls is substantially related to the achievement of the Board's objectives. The Board has proffered no evidence that the presence of girls in the classroom bears a substantial relationship to the difficulties facing urban males.

Accordingly, plaintiffs conclude that the male academies improperly use gender as a "proxy for other, more germane bases of classification," in this instance, for "at-risk" students. Specifically, the gender specific data presented in defense of the Academies ignores the fact that all children in the Detroit public schools face significant obstacles to success. In fact, in its resolution establishing the Academies, the Board acknowledged an "equally urgent and unique crisis facing . . . female students." Urban girls drop out of school, suffer loss of self esteem and become involved in criminal activity. Ignoring the plight of urban females institutionalizes inequality and perpetuates the myth that females are doing well in the current system. . . .

Plaintiffs also assert that the special curriculum proposed for the Academies suggests a false dichotomy between the roles and responsibilities of boys and girls. For example, the Rites of Passage curriculum teaches that "men need a vision and a plan for living," "men master their emotions," and "men acquire skills and knowledge to overcome life's obstacles." These issues confront all adolescents and are not rites peculiarly male. Therefore, they are insufficient to justify gender-based classification.

Defendant responds that the validity of the objective of the male academies distinguishes the instant matter from the program found unconstitutional in *Hogan.* . . . In *Hogan,* the State attempted to justify the policy by proving it compensated for historical discrimination against women. The Court rejected this argument. In contrast, the defendant here argues it has confirmed the present delivery of education has resulted in substantially lower achievement levels for males than for females and that the Academies are the solution to this problem. The primary rationale for the Academies is simply that co-educational programs aimed at improving male performance have failed.

The Court is wary of accepting such a rationale. Although coeducational programs have failed, there is no showing that it is the coeducational factor that results in failure. Even more dangerous is the prospect that should the male academies proceed and succeed, success would be equated with the absence of girls rather than any of the educational factors that more probably caused the outcome.

Defendant argues that just because females also face academic performance problems does not weaken the importance of their objective in opening the male academies. Further, the Board states it has recognized the difficulties faced by urban females and developed alternative programs housed in single sex schools that specifically address the needs of females, such as pregnancy related programs. The Court does not find fault with this argument; the objective of the male academies is important; but, the degree of importance does not eliminate the defendant's burden of showing that the second prong of the *Hogan* test is met.

Defendant argues in the alternative that the second prong, "substantially related" is satisfied for three reasons. First, the establishment of male academies is critical to expeditiously determine what curriculum and training programs will work to keep urban males out of the City's morgues and prisons. Second, the Board has already reviewed smaller scale experimental programs at two schools that specifically addressed the special needs of urban males and found them successful in improving the overall academic and behavioral aspects of the urban males' life style. Third, the Board knows that current coed programs do not work. Consequently, the Board finds that research supports the establishment of an experimental school with a specialized curriculum to address the special needs of urban males.

None of these findings meet[s] the defendant's burden of showing how the exclusion of females from the Academies is necessary to combat unemployment, dropout and homicide rates among urban males. There is no evidence that the educational system is failing urban males because females attend schools with males. In fact, the educational system is also failing females. Thus, the Court concludes the application of the second prong of the *Hogan* test to the facts at hand, makes it likely that the plaintiffs will succeed on a constitutional argument. . . .

This Court views the purpose for which the Academies came into being as an important one. It acknowledges the status of urban males as an "endangered species." The purpose, however, is insufficient to override the rights of females to equal opportunities.

Now, therefore, this Court GRANTS plaintiffs, motion for preliminary injunction.

So ordered.

STUDY QUESTIONS

1. What is the important state interest that the court acknowledges in this case? Do you agree that this is indeed an important goal? If there was evidence that the male academy could address that goal, why did the court reject this initiative?
2. What assumptions did the plaintiffs identify in the board's initiative? Does that make it appear that the interests of the girls who are "at risk" were not as much in the forefront of the board's thinking as were the interests of the boys who are "at risk"?

The challenges faced by educational systems in our society are enormous. The effectiveness with which they are addressed has an enormous influence on the life prospects, not to mention the life expectancy, of rising generations. Accordingly, great care must be taken when restricting the types of experimental initiatives that schools are permitted to undertake. Lives literally depend on these initiatives. A central theme of this chapter, indeed of this book, is that a great deal turns on how these initiatives are designed and executed. They will no longer go unchallenged if the legitimate needs of our sons are addressed while those of our daughters are neglected. Surely, the habit of doing just that is at the very heart of the patriarchal order that has been under critique for the past century.

That approach has been constitutionally unacceptable at least since *Hogan*. The *Garrett* and *VMI* decisions follow *Hogan* in this respect, but they also show that *Hogan* leaves open the possibility that single-sex educational initiatives may be permissible in limited circumstances. If there is convincing evidence that an identifiable group of students are in serious jeopardy unless they receive special attention available only in a single-sex environment, it seems reasonably clear that equal protection considerations will not stand in the way of providing that special attention, provided that it is given equally to all those who are "at risk," both the male and the female students.

The main fault found with the Detroit academy plan and the VMI admissions policy was that the purported benefits of those arrangements were not made available to female students. What this shows is that the "separate but equal" doctrine survives as regards school segregation based on gender, provided that the dual programs can be shown to satisfy the intermediate standard of review.

One consideration that works against establishing and maintaining dual educational programs, whether they are entire school systems or only special opportunity programs within the same school, is the financial cost. The financial burden is the main factor that is driving women's colleges toward extinction. Many observers of the VMI situation doubt that the all-male admissions policy will survive, if for no other reason than because of the enormous costs that would be involved in opening a parallel military institute of comparable quality for women.

Because of the extra financial costs, then, dual programs for male and female students are likely to be increasingly rare. But undoubtedly there will be situations, such as Detroit, in which the alternative is still more expensive in terms of human costs. In school systems wracked by problems of the magnitude experienced by Detroit, the need to experiment with alternatives to the mainstream coeducational approach must be considered. Sound educational research may, in some circumstances, indicate that an important ingredient in any solution is to provide special programs for those who are "at risk," programs that are insulated from the mainstream classrooms. This technique of dealing with "at-risk" students is not novel. Schools have been using a combination of special and mainstream programs for the benefit of mentally and culturally challenged children for the past four decades. Whether schools and school districts will propose such initiatives and whether sufficiently convincing evidence can be adduced to show that they satisfy the standard of review endorsed in *Hogan,* of course, remains to be seen.

III. SCHOOL SPORTS

We saw above how the "chilly climate" in school athletic programs has worked to the disadvantage of female students. Title IX and its interpretative regulations prohibited discrimination in many aspects of school sport programs. The enforcement of Title IX, however, has been lax, especially during the Reagan and Bush administrations. As a result, the debate over sex discrimination in this area, like that over single-sex schools, has taken place within the framework of constitutional litigation. Once again, a review of the role that gender has played in the schools affords the context for the legal discussion.

Women and Sports

Susan L. Morse.
2 *CQ Researcher* 194–215 (1992).

The ancient Greeks didn't just exclude women from Olympic competition. They barred them from even viewing the games on pain of death. According to legend, those caught disobeying were hurled off the cliffs. But some plucky women established their own counterpart—the all-female Herean Games at Olympia, held a month before the Olympics. Females in Sparta, another macho Greek society, were encouraged to train from girlhood in running, jumping and javelin throwing, on the theory that athletics built better breeders.

It would be many grim centuries later before large numbers of women would experience such freedom again. In 19th-century America, the well-

to-do insisted on women's frailty, even while poor women lived lives of backbreaking toil. The modern concept of sports that formed by the end of the century excluded women. Popular leaders including Teddy Roosevelt glorified men's athleticism to combat what they saw as the "feminizing" effects of a more sedentary, post-industrial way of life. Sports, they said, built character, perseverance, strength and respect for authority—traits considered irrelevant for women.

But not all women thought so. Such women's colleges as Vassar began incorporating physical education into their curricula. And though critics warned physical exertion would damage women's reproductive capabilities and leave them too tired to fulfill their "womanly duties," students appeared to benefit. Other women followed suit, shedding tight corsets to gain freedom of movement.

For decades, the emphasis in women's gym classes was on play rather than competitive sport. Claiming women were more susceptible than men to heart strain, fatigue and other injury, educators changed game rules to restrict movement and vigorously opposed women's participation in Olympic games and tournaments. Athletic scholarships were rejected as potentially exploitative. "A game for every girl and a girl for every game," proclaimed the motto of the women's division of the National Amateur Athletic Federation in the 1930s. Women physical educators brandished the popular slogan to reassure women that all females would have an opportunity in sports, albeit not at a highly competitive level. The philosophy prevailed well into the 1960s.

In 1971 only 294,000 girls played high school sports, compared with nearly 2 million today. "Don't worry," parents of tomboys consoled one another. "They'll grow out of it." Most did. They had to. At colleges like the University of Michigan, the budget for women's sports was zero, and would-be athletes raised funds by selling apples at football games. Coeds' coaches—nearly all women—were unpaid, the equipment make-do and the practice time catch as catch can. Both in school, where gym classes were sex-segregated, and out, competition with boys was discouraged: Girls were routinely banned from Little League and other playing fields.

But the social revolution that was transforming the workplace, the family and education quickly spread to the gym, spurred by a new fitness craze and a potent federal law. Title IX of the Education Amendments of 1972 outlawed discrimination by sex in all schools receiving federal funds. The floodgates opened, and a new era in sports began.

Women today are roughly a third of all college athletes. They make up the majority of new participants in weight training, running, cycling and basketball. And more females than males swim, exercise aerobically and ride bicycles. Even such physically grueling contests as triathlons have seen jumps in female participation, from 1,200 women in 1982 to 72,000 in 1990.

More girls are exposed to sports at a young age, encouraged by a major shift in social attitudes: Nearly 90 percent of the 1,000 parents interviewed in a 1988 study viewed sports participation as important for their daughters as for their sons.

Female athletes' visibility and credibility have increased, too. While at annual sports rites like the Super Bowl women still appear only as nubile distractions, other audiences are learning that talented female players provide just as good entertainment as the men.

College basketball is a case in point. Last season, some 4 million fans attended women's games, more than double the attendance in 1981–82. CBS cameras followed the thrilling National Collegiate Athletic Association (NCAA) championship game on March 31, 1991, in which Tennessee squeaked past Virginia in triple overtime, 70–67. And just last month [February 1992] No. 2-ranked Virginia stole first place from Maryland before 14,500 fans—the fourth-largest regular season crowd in women's basketball history.

And talk about a steal. American women ran away with the gold this year at the Winter Olympics in Albertville, France, scooping up all five of the American team's first-place medals and nine of 11 U.S. medals overall.

But despite such gains, women's access still is severely limited: The playing field is far from level. "Sports in our society," says Donna Lopiano, director of intercollegiate athletics for women at the University of Texas at Austin, "is still a right for little boys and a privilege for little girls."

At the university level, equity in sports is regarded as something of a joke. Nationwide, female college athletes routinely get a third of the team spots, less than a third of the scholarship dollars and a mere fifth of the total athletic budget.

At the Olympic level, opportunities also are limited. Women's water polo, weightlifting, ice hockey, wrestling, soccer and pentathlon all have world championships—but no Olympic status, in most cases because the sports can't meet required participation levels. Men compete in all 33 Olympics sports categories, while women only compete in 24 of them. One-third of all events are for men only.

Fewer than ever female student athletes enter careers in physical education, and leadership ranks are shrinking. In 1972 women coached more than 90 percent of college women's sports teams and headed nearly all women's college athletic programs. Female coaches today head less than a quarter of all teams.

Female athletic directors, at 16 percent, are practically an endangered species.

The fight for women's sports is ultimately a fight for greater social access. "Sports has traditionally been used to train males for the competitive world of corporate games," says Lopiano. Sports, she says, teaches "loyalty, playing as a team, playing a role"—all with direct application in business. "When you remove sports from the training of women, you make them less competitive in other activities, including the work world."

STUDY QUESTIONS

1. What is involved in the "modern concept of sports," as articulated by Teddy Roosevelt? Have women's sports programs ever aspired to realizing that concept?
2. What have been some of the major changes in women's sports since the enactment of Title IX? What are some of the hurdles still standing in the way of equal opportunity in school sports?

Participation in athletics is recognized today as an important dimension of any healthy, vigorous life-style. Athletics have not always been viewed in that way. From earliest times, sport was represented as a form of combat, with victory over the adversary as the primary measure of accomplishment. Winning, as the best athletes and coaches stress, is not the only thing that is valued about athletics. Boys have traditionally been introduced to sports at an early age not only to urge upon them the skills and attitudes of combat but also so they will learn important lessons about self-discipline, self-confidence, leadership, and teamwork. These lessons are valuable to anyone who strives for achievement in a competitive environment, whether on the playing field or in the boardroom.

In our era, the lessons afforded by participation in sports are increasingly recognized as valuable for both boys and girls. Until quite recently, however, there was little commitment to afford athletic opportunities to girls. Even twenty years after the passage of Title IX, equity in school sports is not within sight. A 1990 survey of Michigan school districts revealed that 70 percent admitted to not providing girls with athletic opportunities comparable to those available to boys.

Even so, much has changed in the sports area for girls and women over the past two decades. The accomplishments of women athletes have been widely noted, participation rates of girls have soared, budgets for the programs that serve the interests of girls and women students have improved, and attendance and fan interest in women's athletics have also shown marked increases. Notwithstanding this, much remains to be done. Legal remedies already exist for taking down some of the remaining barriers. For others, legal remedies are being developed. This section explores some of these remedies.

Sex-Segregated Athletics

We saw in earlier sections of this chapter that, unlike race segregation in the schools, sex segregation can survive equal protection challenge. In that context, the "separate but equal" doctrine remains intact provided that single-sex programs can be shown to be substantially related to the advancement of important government interests. Courts have applied the same equal protection standard to sex segregation in school sports.

Sex stereotypes pervade debates over sports equity just as they do other educational contexts. The convictions that permeate discussions of girls and women participating in athletic programs include the following: (1) Girls and women are less athletically talented than are boys and men. Thus, in any competition involving both sexes, females as a group will do less well than will males as a group. (2) Girls and women are more likely to sustain injury in athletic competitions than are boys and men. This carries forward the Victorian image of girls and women as frail and delicate. (3) Sport masculinizes girls. This conviction draws on the concept of sport as combat mentioned by Morse, as well as the cultural association of aggressiveness with masculinity. As a result, the femininity of female athletes is placed in doubt, often overtly, as when women sports figures are ridiculed as lesbians. (4) People are not interested in women's sports. The plausibility of this conviction, which rationalized the status quo for decades, is becoming increasingly difficult to maintain in the light of attendance figures reviewed by Morse.

In each of the following four cases, a rule barring girls from participating with boys on sports teams was challenged on constitutional grounds. The first three were on equal protection grounds, the last on the basis of a state ERA. Notice the reasons offered in support of these rules. Notice also that the courts give different weight to these reasons depending on whether a parallel team for girls in the same sport is available and whether the activity in question is a contact sport.

Brenden v. Independent Sch. Dist. 742

United States Court of Appeals, Eighth Circuit, 1973.
477 F.2d 1292.

HEANEY, Circuit Judge.

. . . [T]he Minnesota State High School League . . . bars females from participating with males in high school interscholastic athletics. The rule states:

"Girls shall be prohibited from participation in the boys' interscholastic athletic program either as a member of the boys' team or a member of the girls' team playing the boys' team.

"The girls' team shall not accept male members." . . .

The complaint charges that this rule discriminates against females in violation of the Equal Protection Clause of the Fourteenth Amendment to the United States Constitution.

The plaintiffs are Peggy Brenden and Antoinette St. Pierre, female high school students at Minnesota public high schools. . . .

The plaintiffs desired to participate in noncontact interscholastic sports: Brenden in tennis; St. Pierre in cross-country skiing and cross-country running. Neither of their schools provided teams for females in the respective sports. They did, however, provide such teams for males. Both plaintiffs would have liked to qualify for positions on the teams which have been established for males, but they were precluded from doing so on the basis of the above quoted rule. The trial court found that both were excellent athletes, and that neither would be damaged by competition with males.

The court, after a trial on the merits, granted relief stating:

. . . [I]n these factual circumstances, the application of the League rules to Peggy Brenden and Tony St. Pierre is arbitrary and unreasonable, in violation of the equal protection clause of the fourteenth amendment. . . .

We believe that in view of the nature of the classification and the important interests of the plaintiffs involved, the High School League has failed to demonstrate that the sex-based classification fairly and substantially promotes the purposes of the League's rule.

First, we do not believe the High School League has demonstrated a sufficient rational basis for their conclusion that women are incapable of competing with men in non-contact sports. The trial court specifically found that the plaintiffs were capable of such competition and the evidence indicates that the class of women, like the class of men, includes individuals with widely different athletic abilities. . . .

Second, even if we assume, arguendo, that, on the whole, females are unlikely to be able to compete with males in non-contact interscholastic sports, this fact alone would not justify precluding qualified females like Brenden and St. Pierre from such competition. *Reed v. Reed.* . . .

. . . The failure to provide the plaintiffs with an individualized determination of their own ability to qualify for positions on these teams is, under *Reed,* violative of the Equal Protection Clause.

The High School League argues that invalidation of its rule will have an adverse impact on the future development of opportunities for females in interscholastic sports. This argument is too speculative to have merit. . . .

. . . This argument certainly cannot be used to deprive Brenden and St. Pierre of their rights to equal protection of the law. With respect to these two females, the record is clear. Their schools have failed to provide them with opportunities for interscholastic competition equal to those provided for males with similar athletic qualifications. Accordingly, they are entitled to relief.

Affirmed.

STUDY QUESTIONS

1. Why were Brenden and St. Pierre denied the opportunity to try out for the boys' tennis and ski teams?
2. What reasons did the league offer in justification of the rule? Do either of these reasons have merit? What do you suppose the court meant when it reported that the district court found that neither of the plaintiffs would be "damaged" by competition with males?

ᢒ᠖

In *Brenden,* female students were denied the opportunity of trying out for a non-contact school sport for which there was only one team. Applying heightened scrutiny, the court found a violation of the Equal Protection Clause. The league relied mainly on a policy of protection, one that was based squarely on the first of the stereotypes mentioned above. If the offending rule were dropped and school sports fully integrated, boys would tend to beat out girls for the spots on the teams. Without the rule protecting them from competition with the boys, the girls would have even fewer athletic opportunities. The court here parsed that argument into two segments and rejected both. It may be that girls as a group are less talented in cross-country skiing and running than are boys as a group, but that does not justify privileging a male athlete and marginalizing a female athlete to whom this generalization does not apply. On the authority of *Reed,* the court required that an individualized determination of ability be afforded to each athlete. The court rejected the predictions of a decline in girls' athletic opportunities as too speculative.

In *Brenden,* the court was not faced with the difficult questions of contact sports and separate but equal teams. In the following case, a district court addressed a situation similar in all relevant respects to *Brenden* except that it involved a contact sport.

Carnes v. Tenn. Secondary Sch. Athletic Assn.

United States District Court, Eastern District of Tennessee, 1976.
415 F.Supp. 569.

ROBERT L. TAYLOR, District Judge.

. . . Plaintiff Jo Ann Carnes is an eighteen-year-old female student at Central High School in Wartburg, Tennessee. Defendant Tennessee Secondary School Athletic Association (TSSAA) is a state-wide voluntary athletic association of which Central High School is a member. The TSSAA promulgates rules for participation in interscholastic high school athletics in Tennessee. . . .

Coach Kreis notified the student body at the high school in early March of this year that he sought prospective players for this year's team. Plaintiff was among the 35 or so applicants. At first the coach told plaintiff that she could participate in the baseball program if she was prepared to follow the normal rules applicable to the team. He told her that it would be necessary to have her hair cut to conform to team rules, and she complied.

After being advised by an official of the TSSAA that plaintiff was not eligible to play on the baseball team and that Central High School might be suspended from the association if it allowed plaintiff to participate in interscholastic baseball, Coach Kreis reversed his earlier position and informed plaintiff that she could not participate on the baseball team.

In a letter dated March 17, 1976 an official of the TSSAA communicated the following to the principal of Central High School:

> "This letter is to inform you that TSSAA does not permit girls to participate in baseball since baseball is a contact sport. Article II, Section 32 in the TSSAA Handbook entitled "Mixed Competition" states that boys and girls shall not be permitted to participate in interschool athletic games as mixed teams, nor shall boys' teams and girls' teams participate against each other in interschool athletic contests provided that this rule shall not apply to those sports which are not defined as collision sports or which do not involve physical contact. For purposes of this rule, collision sports and sports involving physical contact shall include, but not be limited to, football, baseball, basketball, and wrestling. . . .

A representative of the TSSAA stated at the hearing that at least two reasons exist for the collision vs. noncollision sport rule: (1) to protect females from exposure to an unreasonable risk of harm, and (2) to protect female sports programs from male intrusion.

TSSAA's first justification for its rule is questionable because it may be drawn too imprecisely to accomplish its avowed purpose. In other words, as applied to the facts of the present case, the rule may permit males who are highly prone to injury to play baseball at Central High School, while, at the same time, it may prevent females, whose physical fitness would make a risk of physical harm unlikely, from participating in the school's baseball program.

The proof showed that plaintiff was denied the opportunity to play baseball because of her sex and not because she may have been exposed to a risk of harm any greater than that to which the male players would have been exposed. She appeared physically suited to play baseball. Coach Kreis stated that she was baseball material, and that he knew of no physical reason why she could not play on the team. She has actively engaged in other sports without suffering any serious injuries and testified that, if given the opportunity to play, she would be willing to wear a chest protector specially designed for women.

The second avowed purpose of the rule, that of protecting female athletic programs from male intrusion, is also questionable. The separation of male and female interscholastic competition arguably bears a rational relation to a state interest in fostering equitable competition. Central High School, however, has no women's baseball team. Consequently, plaintiff either must play on Central's only baseball team or not play at all. Thus, rather than foster equitable competition, TSSAA's rule operates as a complete bar to plaintiff's opportunity to compete solely on the basis of her sex.

We recognize that little proof was heard on the TSSAA's justifications for its rule, and that legitimate reasons in support of it may exist. Assuming . . . that the State legitimately may discriminate between sexes when dealing with contact sports, the classification of a sport as a contact sport, nevertheless must be reasonable. Coach Kreis testified that the rules of baseball prohibit body checking and that base-runners are generally tagged with a glove. If the game is played properly, collisions at the plate are infrequent. Occasionally, a player is spiked, and a batter is hit by a wild pitch. It is questionable, therefore, whether TSSAA can reasonably classify baseball as a contact sport.

In this light, the Court finds that, on the question of injunctive relief, there is a likelihood that plaintiff will prevail on the merits. . . .

For the foregoing reasons, it is ordered that plaintiff's motion for a temporary injunction be, and the same hereby is, granted.

STUDY QUESTIONS

1. Why was Carnes denied the opportunity to play on the Central High baseball team? What reasons did the TSSAA offer in support of its rule?
2. What's so special about "contact sports"? What is the harm that is expected to follow bodily contact between boys and girls, but not between boys and boys or girls and girls, in the course of an athletic contest? Does it have more to do with "masculine" than with "contact" sports? Should any of these considerations be a basis for denying athletic opportunities to anyone?

In *Carnes,* the court issued a temporary injunction after finding that a female student, denied the opportunity of trying out for a contact school sport for which there was only one team, was likely to prevail in a trial on the merits. As had the league in *Brennan,* the TSSAA relied on protective arguments. In addition to protecting the athletic opportunities of girls, the association declared that the restrictive rule protects girls from "exposure to an unreasonable risk of harm." The first impression of this claim is that the TSSAA is concerned to protect girls from physical injury. That interpretation, however, is implausible. It is highly doubtful that adolescent females are more injury-prone than adolescent males. But even if that were true, that would be no reason to bar female athletes from risky activities but only to secure their informed consent, along with that of their parents. This is the procedure ordinarily followed for male athletes who are exposed to the risk of injury.

Two other forms of harm might be involved here, one affecting any coed sporting event, the other only coed contact sports. One might be called a social harm. What is at risk is damage not to the bodies of female athletes, should they compete with boys, but rather to their reputations. What may well be at risk is the femininity of the girls. This echoes the references in an earlier generation to such girls as "tomboys" and in ours as lesbians. Another form of harm that may be involved here might be called moral harm, moral in the sense of inappropriate sexual contact. The last study question intimated as much. This seems to be what is so special about contact sports. It takes no great stretch of one's imagination to anticipate that concerned parents may be repulsed by the prospect of adolescent boys and girls publicly touching one another's bodies in the course of any kind of event. In *Carnes,* the court did not address either of these types of harm, largely because it was not convinced that baseball is a contact sport.

The court in *Carnes,* however, was not faced with the more complex question of schools providing separate but equal teams in the sport. A few years later, another district court was faced with exactly that question.

O'Connor v. Board of Educ. of Sch. Dist. 23
United States District Court, Northern District of Illinois, 1982.
545 F.Supp. 376.

PRENTICE H. MARSHALL, District Judge.

Karen O'Connor is an extraordinarily gifted basketball player. She is also female. Therein lies the problem which gave rise to the instant case.

Since she was seven years old, Karen has played on organized basketball teams with boys. She has participated in programs run by the YMCA, the Arlington Heights Park District, the Arlington Heights Youth Basketball Association, and in the NBA-Pepsi Hotshot competition in Indianapolis, Indiana, and the Elks Hoop Shoot Contest. During this period, the teams Karen has played on have won 97 and lost only 17 games, Karen has frequently been the team's leading scorer, and she has received numerous awards recognizing her abilities. She has also gone to summer basketball camps, where she has been coached by Oscar Robertson, Digger Phelps and Lou Henson. In all of these programs, Karen played with boys. Karen has also played with boys in little league baseball and park district soccer and has excelled.

In the fall of 1980, Karen, now 11, enrolled in sixth grade at MacArthur Junior High School in Des Plaines, Illinois. She was then presented with her first opportunity to play interscholastic basketball (the lower grades do not have such teams). Naturally, she wanted to play with boys, feeling that only the boys' basketball team could provide her with a level of competition sufficiently high to enable her to develop her skills. As a result, Karen's father requested that she be permitted to try out for the boys' basketball team. Defendants in this case, the principal of the school, the superintendent and board of the school district which encompasses MacArthur, and the president of the principals' board of the Mid-Suburban Conference, an association of six schools organized to promote interscholastic activities to which the school belongs, all denied Karen permission to do so. . . .

We turn first to Karen's claim that she has been denied the equal protection of the laws in violation of the fourteenth amendment because defendants have subjected her to discrimination on the basis of her sex. Defendants concede that their refusal to permit Karen to try out for the boys' team is premised solely on her sex. When the state treats persons differently because of their sex, scrutiny of the differential treatment is required under the equal protection clause. . . . "To be constitutional, a gender-based discrimination must serve important governmental objectives. The discriminatory means must be substantially related to the achievement of those objectives." In this case, there is no dispute as to what the governmental objectives are

behind defendants' gender-based actions, or how their actions relate to the objectives.

Defendants' refusal to allow Karen to try out for the boys' team stems from their policy of maintaining separate basketball teams for boys and girls. Plaintiffs concede that defendants do this in order to maximize the participation of both sexes in interscholastic sports. Plaintiffs also concede that defendants' separate team policy is substantially related to this goal. Since boys, on the whole, are substantially better basketball players than are girls, then, . . . "[w]ithout a gender-based classification . . . there would be a substantial risk that boys would dominate the girls' program and deny them an equal opportunity to compete in interscholastic events." By maintaining separate programs, defendants enable girls to participate in interscholastic sports. On the other hand, defendants concede that their policy is arbitrary as applied to Karen. No claim is made that considerations of administrative convenience, prevention of harm to Karen or the boys in the program, or any other legitimate interests justify excluding Karen as a particular individual from the boys' tryouts. Neither do defendants dispute Karen's claim that only participation on the boys' team will provide her with a level of competition suited to her level of skills, and her needs for developing those skills. In short, defendants concede that there is no reason to keep Karen off the team apart from the general policy of separate teams.

. . . Because plaintiff does not dispute defendants' generalization about the relative basketball skills of boys and girls, or that the generalization is substantially related to an important governmental interest, defendants are entitled to summary judgment on plaintiff's equal protection claim. . . .

Defendants' motion for summary judgment is granted. Judgment to enter dismissing plaintiff's action with costs to defendants.

STUDY QUESTIONS

1. The separate-teams policy was described as aiming at increasing the athletic opportunities of girls rather than limiting them. Were the athletic opportunities of O'Connor under

the policy equal to those of less talented and experienced boys? Does this ruling square with the requirement of individualized determination in *Brenden* and in *Orr v. Orr* (see Chapter 2)?

2. The reasoning of the court implies that more boys would attain positions on the school's two basketball teams if spots on the second team were not reserved for girls. Does the separate-teams policy deny athletic opportunities to boys because of their sex? Should that be permitted under the Equal Protection Clause? Why?

In *O'Connor,* the defendants did not rely upon a rationale based on protecting female athletes. They succeeded in justifying sexually segregated sports teams by appeal to the policy of advancing equal opportunity for female students. That argument played a subsidiary role in *Brenden.* There, it was discounted as "too speculative to have merit." It was also raised in *Carnes* but discounted again because, there being no girls' team in the same sport, the challenged rule operated "as a complete bar to plaintiff's opportunity to compete." In *O'Connor,* the argument succeeded even though it retains an element of speculation. In contrast with *Carnes,* O'Connor was not completely barred from the sport. She could play on the girls' basketball team. The court saw this as the price that had to be paid in the circumstances for advancing equal opportunity for female athletes as a group. Apparently neither party raised the possibility of dividing the teams along height and weight lines rather than along gender lines. As a result, the court did not consider that alternative.

The court in *O'Connor* did not examine whether the opportunities afforded to the athletes on the girls' teams were in fact equal to those afforded to the athletes on the boys' teams. Neither did it address the central issue posed in any application of the "separate but equal" doctrine, viz., whether the very fact of being forced to play on a team that is generally regarded as less talented imposed a "badge of inferiority" on O'Connor solely because of her gender. This question had been addressed a few years earlier, although in the context of a state ERA.

Commonwealth of Pa., Packel v. Pa. Intersch. Ath. Assn.

Commonwealth Court, 1975.
18 Pa.C. 45, 334 A.2d 839.

BLATT, Judge.

On November 13, 1973 the Commonwealth of Pennsylvania, acting through its Attorney General initiated suit against the Pennsylvania Interscholastic Athletic Association (PIAA) by filing a complaint in equity in this Court. The PIAA is a voluntary unincorporated association whose members include every public senior high school in this Commonwealth, except for those in Philadelphia. It also includes some public junior high schools as well as some private schools. The PIAA regulates interscholastic competition among its members in the following sports: football, cross-country, basketball, wrestling, soccer, baseball, field hockey, lacrosse, gymnastics, swimming, volleyball, golf, tennis, track, softball, archery and badminton.

The complaint here specifically challenges the constitutionality of Article XIX, Section 3B of the PIAA By-Laws which states: "Girls shall not compete or practice against boys in any athletic contest." The Commonwealth asserts that this provision violates both the equal protection clause of the Fourteenth Amendment to the United States Constitution and also Article I, Section 28 of the Pennsylvania Constitution, the so-called Equal Rights Amendment (ERA), in that it denies to female student athletes the same opportunities which are available to males to practice for and compete in interscholastic sports. . . .

. . . It is asserted that there is no "legally cognizable right" to engage in interscholastic sports so that the PIAA By-Law does not fall within the purview of the ERA. We cannot accept this argument. The concept of "equality of rights *under the law*" (emphasis added) is at least broad enough in scope to prohibit discrimination which is practiced under the auspices of what has been termed "state action" within the meaning of the Fourteenth Amendment to the United States Constitution. In *Harrisburg School District v. Pennsylvania Interscholastic Athletic Association,* the activities of the PIAA were found to be state action in the constitutional sense because its membership consists primarily of public schools and because it is funded by the payment of membership fees from public school moneys, and so ultimately by the Commonwealth's taxpayers, and from the gate receipts of athletic events between public high schools, involving the use of state-owned and state-supplied facilities. We believe, therefore, that the PIAA By-Laws are subject to the scrutiny imposed by the ERA. There is no fundamental right to engage in interscholastic sports, but once the state decides to permit such participation, it must do so on a basis which does not discriminate in violation of the constitution.

The PIAA seeks to justify the challenged By-Law on the basis that men generally possess a higher degree of athletic ability in the traditional sports offered by most schools and that because of this, girls are given greater opportunities for participation if they compete exclusively with members of their own sex. This attempted justification can obviously have no validity with respect to those sports for which only one team exists in a school and that team's membership is limited exclusively to boys. Presently a girl who wants to compete interscholastically in that sport is given absolutely no opportunity to do so under the challenged By-Law. Although she might be sufficiently skilled to earn a position on the team, she is presently denied that position solely because of her sex. Moreover, even where separate teams are offered for boys and girls in the same sport, the most talented girls still may be denied the right to play at that level of competition which their ability might otherwise permit them. For a girl in that position, who has been relegated to the "girls' team", solely because of her sex, "equality under the law" has been denied.

The notion that girls as a whole are weaker and thus more injury-prone, if they compete with boys, especially in contact sports, cannot justify the By-Law in light of the ERA. Nor can we consider the argument that boys are generally more skilled. The existence of certain characteristics to a greater degree in one sex does not justify classification by sex rather than by the particular characteristic. If any individual girl is too weak, injury-prone, or unskilled, she may, of course, be excluded from competition on that basis but she cannot be excluded solely because of her sex without regard to her relevant qualifications. We believe that this is what our Supreme Court meant when it said in [*Commonwealth v.*] *Butler* that "sex may no longer be accepted as an exclusive classifying tool." 328 A.2d at 855 (1974). . . .

Although the Commonwealth in its complaint seeks no relief from discrimination against female athletes who may wish to participate in football and wrestling, it is apparent that there can be no valid reason for excepting those two sports from our order in this case.

For the foregoing reasons, therefore, we issue the following

ORDER

Now, the 19th day of March, 1975, the motion of the Commonwealth for summary judgment is granted to the extent that Article XIX, Section 3B of the Pennsylvania Interscholastic Athletic Association is hereby declared unconstitutional, and the Pennsylvania Interscholastic Athletic Association is hereby ordered to permit girls to practice and compete with boys in interscholastic athletics, this order to be effective for the school year beginning in the fall of 1975 and thereafter.

STUDY QUESTIONS

1. In *O'Connor,* the court found reason to believe that if girls were permitted to compete for places on boys' teams, the athletic opportunity

of the girls as a group would decline. But during the decades following the *PIAA* decision, the participation rates of girls in school sports in Pennsylvania increased sharply. What options did the earlier speculation ignore?

2. Does the bar to classification by sex when applied to wrestling and football create special problems? What are they? Are these likely to be insuperable? Is it sufficient that participation be voluntary?

In *PIAA,* Judge Blatt intimated that being "relegated to the girls' team" is stigmatizing. Part of the weight of that stigma, of course, is that the girls so relegated are represented as not good enough to make the team with the better players. There are, however, additional dimensions to that stigma:

> Certain sports are stigmatized by the people participating in them. Social suspicion of the female athlete is increased when the female is black, from a lower class, lesbian, or necessarily must develop characteristics that are defined as 'masculine,' such as strength. Thus, black women in track events; strong, muscular women in field events; lesbian women in team sports like softball and basketball, all face multiple problems of acceptance.
>
> Social approval is retained for sports in which the participants are all white, from higher social classes, and for whom there are no doubts about their sexual preference. Of all the stigmas noted, that of sexual preference has a special significance for sporting women. . . . The myth of masculinization of athletic women has always been a societal concern. Mere participation in sport can cast a woman's sexual preference into question, just as participation in ballet can for men.
>
> *Mary A. Boutilier, and Lucinda SanGiovanni.* The Sporting Woman. *Champaign, Illinois: Human Kinetics Publishers, 1982. P. 45.*

Since the mid-1970s, many schools have recognized that female students have been denied equal opportunity to participate in athletics and have committed to ending that practice. The impetus for change came from two directions. One was the passage of Title IX. The other was more immediate, a change in the preference of the parents. Whereas unequal athletic opportunities had been acceptable in the past, it is no longer. As Morse pointed out, 90 percent of parents surveyed in 1988 "viewed sports participation as important for their daughters as for their sons." The issue then became one of the means of equalizing athletic opportunities. The protection arguments articulated in *Brennan, Carnes,* and *O'Connor,* however, predicted that permitting girls to participate on boys' teams would result in decreased opportunities for girls. This argument assumes that if girls are permitted to play on boys' teams, boys will be permitted to play on girls' teams, where they would win spots more frequently than the girls would on the boys' teams. As the following case shows, another approach to advancing the athletic opportunities of girls is available, one that resembles affirmative action.

Clark v. Ariz. Intersch. Assn.

United States Court of Appeals, Ninth Circuit, 1982.
695 F.2d 1126.

NELSON, Circuit Judge.

. . . The Appellants, plaintiffs below, are students in Arizona High Schools, and have demonstrated their prowess in volleyball by participating on national championship teams sponsored by the Amateur Athletic Union. The plaintiffs have not, however, been able to participate on their high school volleyball teams. Their schools only sponsor interscholastic volleyball teams for girls, and a policy of the Arizona Interscholastic Association (the AIA) has been interpreted to preclude boys from playing on girls' teams, even though girls are permitted to participate on boys' athletic teams. The AIA's policy on matters relating to gender discrimination is set forth in its resolution of October 19, 1981: . . .

> 3. That the nondiscrimination policy of the AIA permits participation by girls on boys['] teams in non-contact sports in order to compensate for the girls['] historical lack of opportunity in interscholastic athletics, however, boys are not allowed to play on girls['] teams in non-contact sports since boys historically have had ample opportunity for participation and currently have available to them sufficient avenues for interscholastic participation, and since to allow boys to play on girls['] teams in non-contact sports would displace girls from those teams and further limit their opportunities for participation in interscholastic athletics.

The following stipulation was presented at trial:

> Generally, high school males are taller, can jump higher and are stronger than high school females. There are six basic skills necessary in volleyball—serving, passing, setting, digging, hitting and blocking. Of these skills, hitting and blocking are enhanced by physical size, strength and vertical jump. Males generally have the potential to be better hitters and blockers than females and thus may dominate these two skills in volleyball.

A second stipulation indicates that these physiologically-derived differences in athletic potential have real impact on the game of volleyball. Under the rules of the AIA, girls' volleyball teams use a net that is substantially lower than that used by boys' teams. According to the stipulated facts there seems to be no question, then, that boys will on average be potentially better volleyball players than girls. . . .

The trial court found that the rules and regulations of the AIA do not violate the equal protection clause of the fourteenth amendment. It held that the maintenance of a girls-only volleyball team "is substantially related to and serves the achievement of the important governmental objective" of: 1) promoting equal athletic opportunities for females in interscholastic sports, and 2) redressing the effects of past discrimination. . . .

The only issue presented on appeal is whether the trial court was correct in holding that the AIA's policy of prohibiting boys from playing on girls' volleyball teams did not deprive plaintiffs of equal protection under the fourteenth amendment. . . .

As discussed above, the governmental interest claimed is redressing past discrimination against women in athletics and promoting equality of athletic opportunity between the sexes. There is no question that this is a legitimate and important governmental interest.

The only question that remains, then, is whether the exclusion of boys is substantially related to this interest. The question really asks whether any real differences exist between boys and girls which justify the exclusion; i.e. are there differences which would prevent realization of the goal if the exclusion were not allowed.

The record makes clear that due to average physiological differences, males would displace females to a substantial extent if they were allowed to compete for positions on the volleyball team. Thus, athletic opportunities for women would be diminished. . . .

The situation here is one where there is clearly a substantial relationship between the exclusion of males from the team and the goal of redressing past discrimination and providing equal opportunities for women.

We recognize that specific athletic opportunities could be equalized more fully in a number of ways. For example, participation could be limited on the basis of specific physical characteristics other than sex, a separate boys' team could be provided, a junior varsity squad might be added, or boys' participation could be allowed but only in limited numbers. The existence of these alternatives shows only that the exclusion of boys is not *necessary* to achieve the desired goal. It does not mean that the required substantial relationship does not exist. . . .

In this case, the alternative chosen may not maximize equality, and may represent trade-offs between equality and practicality. But since absolute necessity is not the standard, and absolute equality of opportunity in every sport is not the mandate, even the existence of wiser alternatives than the one chosen does not serve to invalidate the policy here since it is substantially related to the goal. That is all the standard demands. While equality in specific sports is a worthwhile ideal, it should not be purchased at the expense of ultimate equality of opportunity to participate in sports. As common sense would advise against this, neither does the Constitution demand it.

Affirmed.

STUDY QUESTIONS

1. Did the AIA show preference for girl athletes here? Could the objection raised by the plaintiffs be described as one of reverse discrimination?
2. In *O'Connor,* a female athlete was excluded from a boys' team in order to advance the opportunities of girls as a group. Is the approach followed by the AIA a better way to advance that same objective? Does it avoid or compound the stigma identified in *PIAA?*

We have seen that much of the reluctance to adopt a coed team approach stems from the fear that the physiological differences between male and female athletes will result in a reduction in the overall level of athletic opportunity made available to the latter. The following two selections help us to reconsider some of the factors that have brought us to this juncture. The first proposes an approach that combines integration and segregation. The second proposes that as women's participation increases, the very character of athletics is being transformed.

Equity in School Athletics: A Guide

Joyce Countiss.
New Brunswick, NJ: Rutgers University Press, 1977. Pp. 8–10.

ORGANIZATIONAL PATTERNS FOR EQUITY IN INTERSCHOLASTIC ATHLETICS

Should there be separate sex teams, unitary teams (one team with both sexes), or a combination thereof? There are three possible options:

1. Integration of the entire program so that all teams will be unitary (open to both sexes).
2. Separate but equal teams coordinated in interscholastic competition through a joint scoring and scheduling system.

Reprinted with permission from: Equity in School Athletics: A Guide, *by Joyce R. Countiss, 1977, Consortium for Educational Equity, Rutgers, The State University of New Jersey.*

3. A combined approach in which both separate sex and unitary teams exist in some fairly equal mix in each season.

Unitary Teams

Some groups, such as the Pennsylvania NOW Sports Task Force, make a strong stand for immediate and total integration using unitary teams, because they believe the present sports structure which emphasizes differences between the sexes can never be truly equitable.

For example, those sports in which boys are encouraged to participate for the most part—football and basketball—accentuate the need for physical height and weight. Those sports in which girls are encouraged to participate—gymnastics and swimming—emphasize the need for grace and agility. The girls' picture is changing more rapidly than the boys' picture. More girls are being encouraged to take basketball and baseball. Boys are still not in any numbers going into gymnastics, etc. In fact, we have a system that favors a certain kind of boy who is abnormal in every dimension—he either has to be taller, heavier, or more combative than average.

The negative side of an all-unitary interscholastic athletics program is that, at present, girls are unable to qualify in large numbers for most such teams. Until remedial programs designed to emphasize those areas in which girls have received the least training are put into effect, girls would probably gain few places on most teams and would thereby lose most of the opportunities for participation they now have under the single sex approach. . . .

Separate but Equal Teams

The second option, separate but equal teams, would mean that in each school system a reassessment of the athletic goals and policies must occur so that equity in expenditures, game time, practice, equipment, and all other areas would be effected within a reasonable period of time. The immediate problem concerning equity is how to make the athletics budget, most of which has been devoted to one sex's teams, stretch to support two sets of teams in an equitable manner without a severe loss of funds and teams for males. One answer is the adoption of the Olympic scoring method in which separate teams compete against those of their sex, but do it together; in this system, both male and female team scores are combined to determine the winning school in any interscholastic competition. A detailed plan for such a system is proposed by Twin Cities NOW in "High School Athletics: A Strategy for Equality."

In team sports both teams would have the same set of coaches and same practice time. The two teams would play the same schedule of games. In basketball, for example, the girls' game would replace the junior varsity game, while in baseball the girls' game might be on a different field at the same time.

In individual sports, in addition to the single coaching staff, practice and competition schedule, there would also be only one team. Again, in actual competition one would compete against one's own sex, with girls' and boys' events either alternating or occurring concurrently. The winning team would be determined by totalling the points won by all the members, male and female.

Not only would this arrangement result in equity in scheduling, coaching, and equipment; it would also result in monetary savings in coaching salaries, maintenance and staffing of practice facilities, transportation, officials, and, finally, opening and staffing of game facilities.

A Combined Approach: Male, Female and Coeducational

A combined approach in which male, female, and co-educational teams are offered provides the best features of the unitary and separate team approaches because it overcomes the major defects of each of these organizational patterns: in the former, not enough participation for girls; and in the latter, total separation of the sexes. This plan allows for as many students as possible to participate, for some integration of the sexes (where it can be done equitably and profitably), and for some separation of the sexes (where it will benefit participation of both sexes). Although many schools claim to have a combined approach, most have labelled their programs incorrectly because of failure to understand this concept.

The combined approach would mean that substantially equal programs of separate sex and integrated sex teams would be offered in both the same and in some different sports in every season. . . .

If a school district were to adopt such a combined program to attain equity, it would set the following goals:

1. Accelerated introduction of female teams and co-ed teams to move toward equity for girls. All new sports introduced would be co-educational.
2. Along with the increased numbers of sports for girls, the district would provide increased practice time, equipment, and coaching for these teams to arrive at an equitable relationship with male teams.
3. The development of a program to seek out qualified women coaches for open positions on male, female, or co-ed teams.

The probable outcome of such a program would be: first, a greater range of options produced by the introduction of new sports, such as fencing, bowling, archery, offered on a co-ed basis. Second, an increase in the number, variety, and competitive levels of girls' teams. Third, a relative (not necessarily abso-lute) decrease in emphasis on boys' teams as the boys' teams are required to share funds, coaches, equipment, practice times, attention, publicity, facilities with the new girls' and co-ed teams. . . .

Countiss advocates a "combined approach" to athletics at the senior high school level and beyond because the physiological differences between male and female athletes in those age groups are substantial. Those physical sex differences, however, appear only after puberty. She sees no justification for the separation of the sexes in athletic contests prior to puberty. She therefore advocates "unitary teams" at the primary and junior high school levels. Grouping of athletes at these levels can, of course, be done on the basis of other factors, such as weight, height, and skill levels.

Organized sports have, for at least the last century, been dominated by what Morse called the combat model. Sports are about winning in a zero-sum contest of power over an opponent. As she indicated, women athletes and coaches have always been reluctant to be assimilated into that game. Instead, they have tradition-ally espoused a different approach to athletics. Author-athlete Mariah Burton Nelson interviewed women athletes, asking about their perception of sports. She discovered that a different model of sports is emerging.

Are We Winning Yet: How Women Are Changing Sports and Sports Are Changing Women

Mariah Burton Nelson.
New York: Random House, 1991.
Pp. 8–9.

As I listened to women athletes, through the diversity I began to hear a chorus singing the same song. Dismayed by the "winning is the only thing" ethic that presides over what Don Sabo calls "manstream" sport, many women are once again questioning the dualism and danger inher-ent in the male model. They're not just greedily gobbling up their thin slice of the sports pie. The old-school voices are resurfacing.

"Must we play as the men play?" they ask. "Should we celebrate women boxers? Should we take drugs? Must college athletes suffer so many injuries? What are we doing to ourselves in the name of winning? Are sports still fun?"

A new model of sport is emerging. I use the term "partnership model" to emphasize that teammates, coaches, and even opposing play-ers view each other as comrades rather than enemies. Players with disparate ability levels are respected as peers rather than ranked in a hierarchy, and athletes care for each other and their own bodies. "To compete" is understood from its Latin source, *competere:* "to seek together."

Contrast this to what I call the military model, characterized by obsessive ranking of teams and individuals according to playing statistics or earnings; authoritarian, derisive relationships between coaches and players; antagonism between opponents; and the inev-itable question, "Who won?" The language of the military model says it all: A quarterback's arm is his weapon. Opponents are to be feared and destroyed. Teams battle for honors. Even bowling can be a war. "Why does bowling satisfy?" wrote Art Plotnik in the *New York Times*. "Think of it. Ten bouncing, noisy maple pins tauntingly lined up at attention. Hit us! Hurt us! A shiny 16-pound cannonball all yours to fire at the enemy . . ."

The partnership model is a compassionate, egalitarian approach to sport in which athletes are motivated by love of themselves, of sports, and of each other. Power is understood not as power-over (power as dominance) but as power-to (power as competence). Like early physical educators, partnership athletes maintain that sport should be inclusive; in balance with other aspects of life; cooperative and social in spirit; and safe.

———————————— ❧ ————————————

Nelson is not so much advocating a change in the dominant ethic of athletics as she is reporting the direction in which sports are being transformed by the very persistent presence of serious and accomplished women athletes. Her observation is straightforward and insightful. "Women's presence in weight rooms and gyms, like women's presence in boardrooms and bars, is subtly and insistently challenging men to see women as peers, and to adapt their playing style to what women want and need." As Nelson says, "When a man sees a strong woman drive a golf ball, it changes the way he thinks about golf, and about women."

Inequitable Availability of Resources

The struggle for equitable treatment in athletics at the college and university level has proven a greater challenge than it was at the primary and secondary level. As Morse intimated, that is due in large part to the insinuation of professional sports interests at the college level. The dimensions and difficulty of this struggle are most evident in such mundane but vital issues as budgets, facilities, schedules, recruiting, and coaching. In these areas, although there has been substantial progress toward equity, much remains to be done.

Morse pointed out that in the early 1970s, many women's college teams had no budget at all. They typically relied on such traditional devices as bake sales to raise money for uniforms. It was not unusual for the coaches of the women's teams to volunteer their time, for the facilities to be unmaintained, and for scholarship aid to be entirely unavailable to women athletes. Just as in an earlier age girls and women were not taken seriously as students, so in the 1970s, they were seldom regarded as serious athletes. Indeed, at the time that Title IX was enacted, the very idea that women's sports should be afforded resources comparable with those provided for men's sports struck many collegiate officials as absurd. As women's sports historian Allen Guttmann reports, "At a time when Father Edmund M. Joyce, an executive vice-president of Notre Dame University, castigated Title IX as 'asinine,' his university allotted over $1 million for financial aid to male athletes and not a penny for the women."

Until quite recently, Title IX has afforded little effective recourse. Under the Reagan administration, and particularly in the wake of the *Grove City College* decision discussed above, the federal government did little to enforce the act's requirements. With the passage of the Civil Rights Restoration Act in March 1988, the courts became more engaged. Within months, Temple University settled an eight-year-old suit that focused on inequity in its sports programs. With the incentive of a restored Title IX, the university agreed to take a wide range of significant steps to place women's athletics on a par with men's programs. The provisions of the settlement included steps toward budget parity, new teams for women, increased coach and trainer staff serving women athletes, and a full-time publicist for women's programs. Temple's example, however, was not widely imitated.

In March 1992, the results of a National Collegiate Athletic Association (NCAA) study were released. That report documented just how poor compliance has been with the requirements of Title IX in the area of intercollegiate athletics. The study covered 646 colleges and universities and revealed that a huge gender gap in recruiting and funding sports programs on college campuses persists a full twenty years after Title IX was enacted. According to the report, on average, for every woman who gets a chance to play Division I college sports, 2.24 men do; for every dollar spent recruiting women athletes, $4.82 are spent recruiting men; for every woman who receives an athletic scholarship, 2.28 men do; for every dollar spent in support of women's sports, $3.42 are spent on men's sports; and, of course, for every dollar a men's basketball coach is paid, the women's coach is paid 55 cents.

In the wake of the NCAA report, both that organization and the Office of Civil Rights of the Department of Education pledged full support for correcting the inequities in collegiate athletics as required by Title IX. Past performance does not inspire confidence in these assurances. The Clinton administration, however, may bring a different and more constructive set of convictions to these concerns. It will certainly bear watching.

In the absence of enforcement leadership from the executive branch, the courts began to reach decisions that addressed this problem. Although suits alleging sports-related violations of Title IX have often been filed, few have been fully litigated. In the first such case to reach the circuit court level, the court signalled its determination to require equitable opportunities for both sexes in school athletics.

Cohen v. Brown University

United States Court of Appeals, First Circuit. 1993.
991 F.2d 888.

SELYA, Circuit Judge.

In this watershed case, defendants-appellants Brown University . . . appeal from the district court's issuance of a preliminary injunction ordering Brown to reinstate its women's gymnastics and volleyball programs to full intercollegiate varsity status pending the resolution of a Title IX claim. After mapping Title IX's rugged legal terrain and cutting a passable swath through the factual thicket that overspreads the parties' arguments, we affirm.

College athletics, particularly in the realm of football and basketball, has traditionally occupied a prominent role in American sports and American society. For college students, athletics offers an opportunity to execute leadership skills, learn teamwork, build self-confidence, and perfect self-discipline. In addition, for many student-athletes, physical skills are a passport to college admissions and scholarships, allowing them to attend otherwise inaccessible schools. These opportunities, and the lessons learned on the playing fields, are invaluable in attaining career and life successes in and out of professional sports.

The highway of opportunity runs in both directions. Not only student-athletes, but universities, too, benefit from the magic of intercollegiate sports. Successful teams generate television revenues and gate receipts which often fund significant percentages of a university's overall athletic program, offering students the opportunity to partake of sports that are not financially self-sustaining. Even those institutions whose teams do not fill the grandstands of cavernous stadiums or attract national television exposure benefit from increased student and alumni cohesion and the support it engenders. Thus, universities nurture the legends, great or small, inhering in their athletic past, polishing the hardware that adorns field-house trophy cases and reliving heroic exploits in the pages of alumni magazines.

In these terms, Brown will never be confused with Notre Dame or the more muscular members of the Big Ten. Although its football team did play in the 1916 Rose Bowl and its men's basketball team won the Ivy League championship as recently as 1986, Brown's athletic program has only occasionally achieved national prominence or, for that matter, enjoyed sustained success. Moreover, at Brown, as at most schools, women are a relatively inconspicuous part of the storied athletic past. Historically, colleges limited athletics to the male sphere, leaving those few women's teams that sprouted to scrounge for resources.

The absence of women's athletics at Brown was, until 1970, an ineluctable consequence of the absence of women; Brown sponsored a women's college—Pembroke—but did not itself admit women. In 1971, Brown subsumed Pembroke. Brown promptly upgraded Pembroke's rather primitive athletic offerings so that by 1977 there were fourteen women's varsity teams. In subsequent years, Brown added only one distaff team: winter track. Hence, in the 1991–92 academic year, Brown fielded fifteen women's varsity teams-one fewer than the number of men's varsity teams.

In the spring of 1991, Brown announced that it, like many other schools, was in a financial bind, and that, as a belt-tightening measure, it planned to drop four sports from its intercollegiate varsity athletic roster: women's volleyball and gymnastics, men's golf and water polo. The University permitted the teams to continue playing as "intercollegiate clubs," a status that allowed them to compete against varsity teams from other colleges, but cut off financial subsidies and support services routinely available to varsity teams (e.g., salaried coaches, access to prime facilities, preferred practice time, medical

trainers, clerical assistance, office support, admission preferences, and the like). Brown estimated that eliminating these four varsity teams would save $77,813 per annum, broken down as follows: women's volleyball, $37,127; women's gymnastics, $24,901; men's water polo, $9,250; men's golf, $6,545.

Before the cuts, Brown athletics offered an aggregate of 328 varsity slots for female athletes and 566 varsity slots for male athletes. Thus, women had 36.7% of the athletic opportunities and men 63.3%. Abolishing the four varsity teams took substantially more dollars from the women's athletic budget than from the men's budget, but did not materially affect the athletic opportunity ratios; women retained 36.6% of the opportunities and men 63.4%. At that time (and for a number of years prior thereto), Brown's student body comprised approximately 52% men and 48% women.

Following Brown's announcement of the cutbacks, disappointed members of the women's volleyball and gymnastics teams brought suit. . . . The plaintiffs charged that Brown's athletic arrangements violated Title IX's ban on gender-based discrimination, a violation that was allegedly exacerbated by Brown's decision to devalue the two women's programs without first making sufficient reductions in men's activities or, in the alternative, adding other women's teams to compensate for the loss.

. . . [A]fter hearing fourteen days of testimony from twenty witnesses, the [district court] judge granted a preliminary injunction requiring Brown to reinstate the two women's teams pending the outcome of a full trial on the merits. We stayed execution of the order and expedited Brown's appeal.

Title IX prohibits gender-based discrimination by educational institutions receiving federal financial support–in practice, the vast majority of all accredited colleges and universities. The statute sketches wide policy lines, leaving the details to regulating agencies. . . .

[The court next reviewed the provisions of Title IX and its implimenting regulations, focusing in particular upon an HEW policy interpretation that specifies] three major areas of regulatory compliance: "Athletic Financial Assistance (Scholarships)," "Equivalence in

Other Athletic Benefits and Opportunities," and "Effective Accommodation of Student Interests and Abilities." The court below . . . adopted this formulation and ruled that a university violates Title IX if it ineffectively accommodates student interests and abilities regardless of its performance in other Title IX areas.

Equal opportunity to participate lies at the core of Title IX's purpose. Because the third compliance area delineates this heartland, we agree with the district courts that have so ruled and hold that, with regard to the effective accommodation of students' interests and abilities, an institution can violate Title IX even if it meets the "financial assistance" and "athletic equivalence" standards. . . .

. . . The parties agree that the third compliance area is the field on which this appeal must be fought. In surveying the dimensions of this battleground, that is, whether an athletic program effectively accommodates students' interests and abilities, the Policy Interpretation maps a trinitarian model under which the university must meet at least one of three benchmarks: (1) Whether intercollegiate level participation opportunities for male and female students are provided in numbers substantially proportionate to their respective enrollments; or (2) Where the members of one sex have been and are underrepresented among intercollegiate athletes, whether the institution can show a history and continuing practice of program expansion which is demonstrably responsive to the developing interest and abilities of the members of that sex; or (3) Where the members of one sex are underrepresented among intercollegiate athletes, and the institution cannot show a continuing practice of program expansion such as that cited above, whether it can be demonstrated that the interests and abilities of the members of that sex have been fully and effectively accommodated by the present program. The first benchmark furnishes a safe harbor for those institutions that have distributed athletic opportunities in numbers "substantially proportionate" to the gender composition of their student bodies. Thus, a university which does not wish to engage in extensive compliance analysis may stay on the sunny side of Title IX simply by maintaining gender parity between its student body and its athletic lineup.

The second and third parts of the accommodation test recognize that there are circumstances under which, as a practical matter, something short of this proportionality is a satisfactory proxy for gender balance. For example, so long as a university is continually expanding athletic opportunities in an ongoing effort to meet the needs of the underrepresented gender, and persists in this approach as interest and ability levels in its student body and secondary feeder schools rise, benchmark two is satisfied and Title IX does not require that the university leap to complete gender parity in a single bound. Or, if a school has a student body in which one sex is demonstrably less interested in athletics, Title IX does not require that the school create teams for, or rain money upon, otherwise disinterested students; rather, the third benchmark is satisfied if the underrepresented sex's discernible interests are fully and effectively accommodated.

It seems unlikely, even in this day and age, that the athletic establishments of many coeducational universities reflect the gender balance of their student bodies. Similarly, the recent boom in Title IX suits suggests that, in an era of fiscal austerity, few universities are prone to expand athletic opportunities. It is not surprising, then, that schools more often than not attempt to manage the rigors of Title IX by satisfying the interests and abilities of the underrepresented gender, that is, by meeting the third benchmark of the accommodation test. Yet, this benchmark sets a high standard: it demands not merely some accommodation, but full and effective accommodation. If there is sufficient interest and ability among members of the statistically underrepresented gender, not slaked by existing programs, an institution necessarily fails this prong of the test.

Although the full-and-effective-accommodation standard is high, it is not absolute. Even when male athletic opportunities outnumber female athletic opportunities, and the university has not met the first benchmark (substantial statistical proportionality) or the second benchmark (continuing program expansion) of the accommodation test, the mere fact that there are some female students interested in a sport does not ipso facto require the school to provide a varsity team in order to comply with the third benchmark. Rather, the institution can satisfy the third benchmark by ensuring participatory opportunities at the intercollegiate level when, and to the extent that, there is "sufficient interest and ability among the members of the excluded sex to sustain a viable team and a reasonable expectation of intercollegiate competition for that team. . . ." Staying on top of the problem is not sport for the short-winded: the institution must remain vigilant, "upgrading the competitive opportunities available to the historically disadvantaged sex as warranted by developing abilities among the athletes of that sex," until the opportunities for, and levels of, competition are equivalent by gender. . . .

. . . In an era where the practices of higher education must adjust to stunted revenues, careening costs, and changing demographics, colleges might well be obliged to curb spending on programs, like athletics, that do not lie at the epicenter of their institutional mission. Title IX does not purport to override financial necessity. Yet, the pruning of athletic budgets cannot take place solely in comptrollers' offices, isolated from the legislative and regulatory imperatives that Title IX imposes.

This case aptly illustrates the point. Brown earnestly professes that it has done no more than slash women's and men's athletics by approximately the same degree, and, indeed, the raw numbers lend partial credence to that characterization. But, Brown's claim overlooks the shortcomings that plagued its program before it took blade in hand. If a school, like Brown, eschews the first two benchmarks of the accommodation test, electing to stray from substantial proportionality and failing to march uninterruptedly in the direction of equal athletic opportunity, it must comply with the third benchmark. To do so, the school must fully and effectively accommodate the underrepresented gender's interests and abilities, even if that requires it to give the underrepresented gender (in this case, women) what amounts to a larger slice of a shrinking athletic-opportunity pie.

The record reveals that the court below paid heed to these realities. It properly recognized that even balanced use of the budget-paring knife runs afoul of Title IX where, as here, the fruits of a university's athletic program remain ill-distributed after the trimming takes place. . . .

The preliminary injunction is affirmed, the temporary stay is dissolved, and the cause is remanded to the district court for further proceedings.

STUDY QUESTIONS

1. What led Brown University to decrease the size of its varsity athletic program? Did that decision disproportionately affect women athletes at Brown?
2. Discuss the three ways that colleges and universities have historically neglected athletic opportunities for women students? Why did the court find that Brown's action fell short when judged by these benchmarks?
3. What course of action is Brown permitted to take during years of shrinking resources?

IV. SEXUAL HARASSMENT OF STUDENTS

The Hall and Sandler selections make clear that the sexual harassment of students is one of the major contributors to the "chilly climate" for female students. In Chapter 5, we explored at length the forms and consequences of sexual harassment and the main legal remedies available for coping with it in an employment context. There we saw that the problem is widespread, serious, and unlawful. As schools and colleges are employment contexts, even for students engaged in work-study arrangements with their schools, some protection against sexual harassment is afforded by Title VII and other fair employment practices laws.

The issue of sexual harassment of students developed somewhat after it had in an employment context. In the school setting, too, the quid pro quo form of harassment was the first to be litigated. The *Alexander* case was the first circuit court decision to reach the question of whether the sexual harassment of students constitutes a violation of Title IX.

Alexander v. Yale University

United States Court of Appeals,
Second Circuit, 1980.
631 F.2d 178.

LUMBARD, Circuit Judge.

. . . [T]hree female students, two female graduates, and one male professor at Yale alleged that Yale's "failure to combat sexual harassment of female students and its refusal to institute mechanisms and procedures to address complaints and make investigations of such harassment interferes with the educational process and denies equal opportunity in education" in violation of Title IX and H.E.W.'s regulation. . . .

Ronni Alexander, a 1977 graduate of Yale College, alleged that she "found it impossible to continue playing the flute and abandoned her study of the instrument, thus aborting her desired professional career," because of the repeated sexual advances, "including coerced sexual intercourse," by her flute instructor, Keith Brion. Alexander further alleged that she attempted to complain to Yale officials about her harassment, but "was discouraged and intimidated by unresponsive administrators and complex and *ad hoc* methods."

Margery Reifler, a member of the Class of 1980, alleged that Richard Kentwell, coach of the field hockey team, "sexually harassed" her while she was working as that team's manager, and that she "suffered distress and humiliation. . . . and was denied recognition due her as team manager, all to her educational detriment." Reifler further alleged that she "wanted to complain to responsible authorities of defendant about said sexual harassment but was intimi-

dated by the lack of legitimate procedures and was unable to determine if any channels for complaint about sexual harassment were available to her."

Pamela Price, a member of the Class of 1979, alleged that one of her course instructors, Raymond Duvall, "offered to give her a grade of 'A' in the course in exchange for her compliance with his sexual demands," that she refused, and that she received a grade of "C" which "was not the result of a fair evaluation of her academic work, but the result of her failure to accede to Professor Duvall's sexual demands." She further alleges that she complained to officials of Yale who failed to investigate her complaint and told her that "nothing could be done to remedy her situation."

Lisa Stone, a member of the Class of 1978, alleged that her discussions with a woman student who had been sexually harassed and the absence of an "established, legitimate procedure" for complaints of such harassment caused her "emotional distress," deprived her of "the tranquil atmosphere necessary to her pursuit of a liberal education," and put her "in fear of her own associations with men in positions of authority at Yale."

Ann Olivarius, a 1977 graduate, alleged that the absence of a procedure for complaining about sexual harassment "forced [her] to expend time, effort and money in investigating complaints herself, preparing them to be presented to responsible officials of defendant, and attempting to negotiate the complexities of *ad hoc* 'channels.' " Olivarius further alleged that she was "subjected to threats and intimidation from individuals involved in her investigations and was given no protection or encouragement by responsible officials of defendant."

Then District Judge Newman, upon the opinion of Magistrate Latimer, dismissed all the plaintiffs but Price. . . . The court dismissed Stone and

Olivarius on the ground that they had not asserted claims "of personal exclusion from a federally funded education program or activity, or of the personal denial of full participation in the benefits of such a program or activity in any measurable sense.". . . The court dismissed Alexander, although she alleged a "personal experience of sexual harassment," on the ground that her graduation mooted her claim for equitable relief absent the "sheer conjecture" that she might someday wish to resume her flute studies. The court dismissed Reifler, although she too alleged a personal experience of sexual harassment, because she had not complained to anyone at Yale. . . . [T]he court concluded that Reifler's claim "that general university inertia should be equated with policy and has 'the effect of actively condoning . . . sexual harassment' is simply not adequate to show that Yale acted to deny her any right;" and the court further held that "the concept of mere *respondent superior* appears ill-adapted to the question of Title IX sex discrimination based on harassment incidents." As to Price, the court held that "academic advancement conditioned upon submission to sexual demands constitutes sex discrimination in education," and it therefore refused to dismiss Price. . . .

After the trial of Price's claim, Judge Burns found that "the alleged incident of sexual proposition did not occur and the grade of 'C' which Miss Price received on the paper submitted to Professor Duvall and the grade of 'C' which she received in his course did not reflect consideration of any factor other than academic achievement.". . .

The district court therefore entered judgment for Yale, and the five female plaintiffs (hereinafter "appellants") brought their appeal.

We first consider the claims raised by Olivarius, Stone, Alexander and Reifler. We find that the district court should be affirmed as to these plaintiffs because none of them presents a justiciable case or controversy. . . .

None of these plaintiffs at present suffers from the alleged injury. Nor would the grant of the requested relief aid these plaintiffs in the slightest. Thus their claims appear moot.

It is perhaps more important to note that, as Yale's counsel has assured us in brief and oral argument, Yale in fact has adopted a set of procedures for hearing such complaints. . . .

We thus agree with the district court that only plaintiff Price presented a justiciable claim for relief under Title IX. That claim, however, was tried and dismissed. We now turn to her assertions on appeal.

The district court found that Price failed at trial to prove that her alleged sexual harassment had in fact occurred. Price argues that, her failure to prove the incident of harassment notwithstanding, the district court should have enjoined Yale to adopt a complaint procedure. . . . We disagree. As Price failed to prove her case, she failed to prove any perceptible harm and therefore she lacks standing to attack Yale's failure to establish a complaint procedure. . . .

We affirm the judgment for Yale as to all of the plaintiffs.

STUDY QUESTIONS

1. Who won this appeal? Did the court indicate that sexual harassment can violate Title IX?
2. How do you think the court defined sexual harassment? Is it only the kind of quid pro quo advance that Price alleged, or does it somehow include problems later associated with hostile environment as well?
3. Does your college or university have an official policy, publicly announced, defining and disapproving sexual harassment of students? Have effective channels been established through which a victim can obtain assistance and the school can discipline an offender? If not, consult the appendix to *The Lecherous Professor* by Billie W. Dziech and Linda Weiner (Boston: Beacon Press, 1984), where model formats are presented.

A variety of studies conducted in the early 1980s confirmed the early impression that the incidence of sexual harassment of students is significant. These were local studies, conducted in university settings, using varying methodologies and definitions of sexual harassment. In general, they reported that of the women who responded, about 30 percent of the graduate students and 20 percent of the undergraduate students reported that they had experienced sexual harassment. These results, however distressing, underestimate the magnitude of the problem. At the time the surveys were taken, only the quid pro quo form of sexual harassment was widely recognized. Most of the definitions used in the surveys, accordingly, linked sexual harassment to those who were in a supervisory role relative to the respondents, i.e., to teachers and professors.

Later in the 1980s, courts began explicitly to apply the broader definition of sexual harassment that had been developed in the employment context to suits that arose in educational circumstances. In *Lipsett v. University of Puerto Rico,* 864 F.2d 881 (1988), the First Circuit Court of Appeals reversed a summary judgment favoring the university because the lower court had not taken seriously the plaintiff's evidence of both hostile environment and quid pro quo sexual harassment.

During the 1980s, attentions devoted to the sexual harassment of students, both by faculty and fellow students, were focused mainly on the college and professional school setting. Beginning with the following Supreme Court decision, the focus broadened to include sexual harassment in the primary and secondary schools as well. Just as rape is not confined to adults, neither is sexual harassment.

Franklin v. Gwinnett Cty. Public Schools

United States Supreme Court, 1991.
___U.S. ___, 112 S.Ct. 1028, 117 L.Ed.2d 208.

Justice WHITE delivered the opinion of the Court.

This case presents the question whether the implied right of action under Title IX of the Education Amendments of 1972 which this Court recognized in *Cannon v. University of Chicago,* 441 U.S. 677 (1979), supports a claim for monetary damages.

Petitioner Christine Franklin was a student at North Gwinnett High School in Gwinnett County, Georgia, between September 1985 and August 1989. Respondent Gwinnett County School District operates the high school and receives federal funds. According to the complaint filed on December 29, 1988 in the United States District Court for the Northern District of Georgia, Franklin was subjected to continual sexual harassment beginning in the autumn of her tenth grade year (1986) from Andrew Hill, a sports coach and teacher employed by the district. Among other allegations, Franklin avers that Hill engaged her in sexually-oriented conversations in which he asked about her sexual experiences with her boyfriend and whether she would consider having sexual intercourse with an older man; that Hill forcibly kissed her on the mouth in the school parking lot; that he telephoned her at her home and asked if she would meet him socially; and that, on three occasions in her junior year, Hill interrupted a class, requested that the teacher excuse Franklin, and took her to a private office where he subjected her to coercive intercourse. The complaint further alleges that though they became aware of and investigated Hill's sexual harassment of Franklin and other female students, teachers and administrators took no action to halt it and discouraged Franklin from pressing charges against Hill. On April 14, 1988, Hill resigned on the condition that all matters pending against him be dropped. The school thereupon closed its investigation.

In this action, the District Court dismissed the complaint on the ground that Title IX does not authorize an award of damages. The Court of Appeals affirmed. . . . In *Cannon,* the Court held that Title IX is enforceable through an implied right of action. We have no occasion here to reconsider that decision. Rather, in this case we must decide what remedies are available in a suit brought pursuant to this implied right. . . . [W]e presume the availability of all appropriate remedies unless Congress has expressly indicated otherwise. This principle has deep roots in our jurisprudence.

"[W]here legal rights have been invaded, and a federal statute provides for a general right to sue for such invasion, federal courts may use any available remedy to make good the wrong done." *Bell v. Hood,* 327 U.S. 678, 684 (1946). . . .

The *Bell* Court's reliance on this rule was hardly revolutionary. From the earliest years of the Republic, the Court has recognized the power of the judiciary to award appropriate remedies to redress injuries actionable in federal court, although it did not always distinguish clearly between a right to bring suit and a remedy available under such a right. In *Marbury v. Madison,* 5 U.S. (1 Cranch) 137 (1803), for example, Chief Justice Marshall observed that our government "has been emphatically termed a government of laws, and not of men. It will certainly cease to deserve this high appellation, if the laws furnish no remedy for the violation of a vested legal right." This prin-

ciple originated in the English common law, and Blackstone described "it is a general and disputable rule, that where there is a legal right, there is also a legal remedy, by suit or action at law, whenever that right is invaded."

In sum, we conclude that a damages remedy is available for an action brought to enforce Title IX. The judgment of the Court of Appeals, therefore, is reversed and the case is remanded for further proceedings consistent with this opinion.

So ordered.

STUDY QUESTIONS

1. In the *Cannon* decision, the Supreme Court declared that individual victims have a right to sue the offending school or educational program under Title IX. What remedy does this decision make available to individual plaintiffs?
2. By addressing the question as to available remedies, the Court is widely understood to have agreed that the behavior complained of by Franklin, if shown, does violate Title IX. What form of sexual harassment is alleged here?

In *Franklin,* the Court ruled that Title IX makes damages awards available to individual victims of sex discrimination, in that case, sexual harassment. Although Franklin claimed to have been the victim of quid pro quo harassment at the hands of a teacher, this ruling implies that the hostile environment form of harassment, at the hands of fellow students, also violates Title IX. This opens the door to suits by parents against schools in which their daughters are subjected to verbal and physical abuse because of their sex, what in the past was dismissed as "teasing."

In fact, such suits had already surfaced before *Franklin.* An eighth-grade girl in California reportedly settled a Title IX suit in which she complained of being subjected to a gauntlet of jeering boys throughout the school day for twenty thousand dollars. The Duluth School District settled a complaint filed with the Minnesota Department of Human Rights by paying fifteen thousand dollars in damages. In that case, a high school student had been the target of vulgar messages written on the bathroom wall. Since then, the department has been receiving an increasing flow of complaints from school girls and their parents.

These suits only began to gauge the magnitude of sexual harassment in primary and secondary schools. The first nationwide scientific survey of the problem, sponsored by the American Association of University Women and released in June,

1993, revealed that an astonishing 85 percent of girls and 76 percent of boys in grades eight through eleven reported that they had been subjected to " unwanted or unwelcome sexual behavior which interferes with [their lives]." The report entitled "Hostile Hallways," indicated that most harassment occurred in hallways and classrooms and that most harassers were fellow students. The most common form of harassment was sexual comments, jokes, gestures, and looks. However, more than half the students said that they were touched, grabbed, or pinched in a sexual way. The harassed students seldom reported these incidents to a parent, almost never to a school offical. Finally, most students admit to sexually harassing other students—66 percent of boys and 52 percent of girls. The AAUW described what the survey uncovered as a "sexual harassment epidemic."

Increased awareness of the problem of sexual harassment in the schools prompted some officials to go beyond prohibitions of physical assault and harassment. Some school districts, colleges and universities also started to include provisions in their codes of student conduct that prohibit verbal harassment on the basis of race and gender. These are often called "hate speech" codes. They attempt to deter the rising tide of verbal racist and sexist abuse on our campuses. The main concern of the colleges and universities is to prevent those who traffic in hate speech from creating a hostile learning environment for women and minorities. These codes, however, have come under increasing scrutiny because of their implications for First Amendment protections of speech. The following decision is representative of those that have been recently handed down by district courts.

The UWM Post, Inc. v. Bd. of Regents, Univ. of Wisc.

United States District Court, Wisconsin, 1991.
774 F.Supp. 1163.

WARREN, Senior District Judge.

On March 29, 1990, the UWM Post, Inc. and others ("plaintiffs") filed this action seeking that this Court enter a declaratory judgment that Wis.Admin.Code § UWS 17.06(2) (the "UW Rule") on its face violates: (1) plaintiffs' right of free speech guaranteed by the First Amendment to the United States Constitution. . . .

In May of 1988, the Board of Regents adopted "Design for Diversity," a plan to increase minority representation, multi-cultural understanding and greater diversity throughout the University of Wisconsin System's 26 campuses. Design for Diversity responded to concerns over an in-crease in incidents of discriminatory harassment [by enacting a rule that permitted the disciplining of students for racist or sexist expression in nonacademic settings]. For example, several highly publicized incidents involving fraternities occurred at the University of Wisconsin-Madison. In May of 1987, a fraternity erected a large caricature of a black Fiji Islander as a party theme. Later that year, there was a fight with racial overtones between members of two fraternities. In October of 1988, a fraternity held a "slave auction" at which pledges in black face performed skits parroting black entertainers. . . .

. . . [I]n order to be regulated under the UW Rule, a comment, epithet or other expressive behavior must: (1) Be racist or discriminatory; (2) Be directed at an individual; (3) Demean the race, sex, religion, color, creed, disability, sexual orientation, national origin, ancestry or age of the individual addressed; and (4) Create an intimidating, hostile or demeaning environment for education, university-related work, or other university-authorized activity. . . .

To date, at least nine students have been sanctioned under the UW Rule:

(2) The University of Wisconsin-Eau Claire found that plaintiff John Doe violated the UW Rule by yelling epithets loudly at a woman for approximately ten minutes, calling her a "fucking bitch" and "fucking cunt." Plaintiff John Doe was responding to statements the woman made in a university newspaper about the athletic department. The university placed the student on probation for a semester and required him to perform twenty hours of community service at a shelter for abused women.

(3) The University of Wisconsin-Oshkosh disciplined a student for angrily telling an Asian-American student: "It's people like you—that's the reason this country is screwed up" and "you don't belong here." The student also stated that "Whites are always getting screwed by minorities and some day the Whites will take over." The University placed the student on probation for seven months and required him to participate in alcohol abuse assessment and treatment. . . .

(6) The University of Wisconsin-Eau Claire disciplined a student under the UW Rule for sending a message that stated, "Death to all Arabs!! Die Islamic scumbags!" on a university computer system to an Iranian faculty member. The university formally reprimanded the student and placed him on probation for the remainder of the semester. . . .

(8) The University of Wisconsin-Oshkosh disciplined a female student under the UW Rule for referring to a black female student as a "fat-ass nigger" during an argument. The university found that the student violated the rule and another provision of the student code. The student, who was already on disciplinary probation, was required to view a video on racism and write an essay and a letter of apology and was reassigned to another residence hall.

(9) The University of Wisconsin-River Falls disciplined a male student under the UW Rule for yelling at a female student in public, "you've got nice tits." The university placed the student on probation for the remainder of his enrollment at the university and required him to apologize to the female student, to refrain from any further contact with her and to obtain psychological counseling. . . .

Although the First Amendment generally protects speech from content-based regulation, it does not protect all speech. The Supreme Court has removed certain narrowly limited categories of speech from First Amendment protection. These categories of speech are considered to be of such slight social value that any benefit that may be derived from them is clearly outweighed by their costs to order and morality. *Chaplinsky v. New Hampshire,* 315 U.S. 568 (1942). The categories include fighting words, obscenity and, to a limited extent, libel. . . .

. . . [T]he *Chaplinsky* Court set out a two-part definition for fighting words: (1) words which by their very utterance inflict injury and (2) words which by their very utterance tend to incite an immediate breach of the peace. The two parts of the fighting words definition correspond to different concerns regarding reactions to offensive expressions. . . .

Since *Chaplinsky,* the Supreme Court has narrowed and clarified the scope of the fighting words doctrine in at least three ways. First, the Court has limited the fighting words definition so that it now only includes its second half. Second, the Court has stated that in order for words to meet the second half of the definition they must "naturally tend to provoke violent resentment." Finally, the Court has held that fighting words must be "directed at the person of the hearer." . . .

. . . Since the elements of the UW Rule do not require that the regulated speech, by its very utterance, tend to incite violent reaction, the rule goes beyond the present scope of the fighting words doctrine.

The first element of the UW Rule, which requires that the speech be racist or discriminatory, describes the content of the speech regulated but does not state that the speech must tend to cause a breach of the peace. The second element, which requires that the speech be directed at an individual, meets the requirement . . . that the speech be "directed to the person of the hearer." In addition, the second element makes it likely that the rule will cover some speech which tends to incite violent reaction. Nevertheless, this element does not require that the regulated speech always tend to incite such reaction and is likely to allow the rule to apply to many situations where a breach of the peace is unlikely to occur.

The third element of the UW Rule requires that the regulated speech demean an individual's race, sex, religion, etc. This element addresses the concerns of the now defunct first half of the fighting words definition. Words which demean a person's race, sex, religion, etc. are likely to inflict injury and affect a person's sensibilities. Nonetheless, the third element of the UW Rule does not address the concerns of the second half of the fighting words definition. Speech may demean an individual's characteristics without tending to incite that individual or others to an immediate breach of the peace.

The fourth element of the UW Rule requires that the prohibited speech create an intimidating, hostile or demeaning environment. An intimidating, hostile or demeaning environment certainly "disturb[s] the public peace or tranquility enjoyed by the citizens of [a university] community." However, it does not necessarily tend to incite violent reaction. The creation of a hostile environment may tend to incite an immediate breach of peace under some circumstances. Nevertheless, the term "hostile" covers non-violent as well as violent situations. Moreover, an intimidating or demeaning environment is unlikely to incite violent reaction. To "intimidate" means to "make timid; threaten" or to "discourage or inhibit by or as if by threats." To "demean" is to "debase in dignity or stature." Given these definitions of "intimidate" and "demean," this Court cannot properly find that an intimidating or demeaning environment tends to incite an immediate breach of the peace. . . .

. . . Since the UW Rule covers a substantial number of situations where no breach of the peace is likely to result, the rule fails to meet the requirements of the fighting words doctrine. . . .

. . . The problems of bigotry and discrimination sought to be addressed here are real and truly corrosive of the educational environment. But freedom of speech is almost absolute in our land and the only restriction the fighting words doctrine can abide is that based on the fear of violent reaction. Content-based prohibitions such as that in the UW Rule, however well intended, simply cannot survive the screening which our Constitution demands.

. . . Accordingly, this Court ORDERS: (1) that a declaratory judgment be entered that the UW Rule on its face violates the overbreadth doctrine and is unduly vague; (2) that the Board of Regents and its agents and employees are permanently enjoined from enforcing the UW Rule and (3) that the Board of Regents is required to vacate the disciplinary action taken against plaintiff John Doe under the UW Rule and to expunge from his file all records related to that action. . . .

STUDY QUESTIONS

1. What types of behavior did the UW rule prohibit? Did the rule, as applied to these students, discourage sexual harassment? If students are protected from sexual harassment by Title IX, why did the Court enjoin its use and vacate the disciplinary actions taken under it?

2. Do the expressions for which the students were disciplined, by their very utterance, inflict injury? Does the First Amendment protect such expressions, however hateful, from government regulation? Should it?

3. Do the students' expressions naturally tend to provoke violent resentment? If not, is that because women and minorities are conditioned to endure gross insults?

The validity of school discipline codes directed at hate speech, such as the one struck down in *UWM Post,* was placed in even greater doubt when the Supreme Court handed down its decision in *R.A.V. v. St. Paul, Mn.,* ___U.S. ___, 112 S.Ct. 2538 (1992). The Court there unanimously invalidated a St. Paul ordinance that made it a misdemeanor to burn crosses or place swastikas on public or private property. Even though it accepted the Minnesota Supreme Court's interpretation that only "fighting words" were prohibited by the ordinance, the Court went on to strike it down. The flaw in the ordinance was that it criminalized only those forms of hate speech that are disfavored by the community—racist and anti-Semitic expression—but left unregulated other forms of hate speech that are currently in favor. Justice Scalia, writing for the Court, expressed confidence that legislatures can find ways to regulate disruptive behavior without singling out unpopular opinion for special treatment. If this confidence is well-taken, schools, universities, and employers may continue to prohibit behavior that creates a hostile or intimidating environment. What remains unclear after *R.A.V.* is whether all forms of sexual and racial harassment that take the form of expression are protected or whether some forms may be regulated, at least in some contexts.

V. ALL-MALE CLUBS

Boys and men, as a result of training and acculturation, come to perceive and treat girls and women as objects for their own gratification, as tools for advancing their own projects, and as instruments for the perpetuation of their genes. The central importance of sex-role socialization has long been the focus of feminist analysis. Attitudes and patterns of perception that sustain sexist practices from generation to generation are prompted and reinforced by a variety of cultural arrangements and institutions, including families, schools, and governments. Another traditional vehicle of cultural sexism is the all-male club. Throughout the 1980s, the exclusionary practices of such clubs were shown to place businesswomen at a distinct disadvantage in a number of contexts. In 1984, the New York City Council made clear how they work against women in the employment context when, in amending the city's ordinance prohibiting discrimination in public accommodations, the council extended its coverage to certain large private clubs.

> It is hereby found and declared that the city of New York has a compelling interest in providing its citizens an environment where all persons, regardless of race, creed, color, national origin or sex, have a fair and equal opportunity to participate in the business and professional life of the city, and may be unfettered in availing themselves of employment opportunities. Although city, state and federal laws have been enacted to eliminate discrimination in employment, women and minority group members have not attained equal opportunity in business and the professions. One barrier to the advancement of women and minorities in the business and professional life of the city is the discriminatory practices of certain membership organizations where business deals are often made and personal contacts valuable for business purposes, employment and professional advancement are formed. While such organizations may avowedly be organized for social, cultural, civic or educational purposes, and while many perform valuable services to the community, the commercial nature of some of the activities occurring therein and the prejudicial impact of these activities on business, professional and employment opportunities of minorities and women cannot be ignored.
>
> New York State Club Assn. v. City of New York, *487 U.S. 1, 5 (1988).*

As the range of organizations coming within the purview of public accommodations statutes has expanded, legal and political controversy has focused increasingly on the question of appropriate limits. Those seeking to limit the reach of public accommodations statutes often claim that these laws violate their constitutional right of free association. The Supreme Court has firmly rejected these arguments. In *Roberts v. U.S. Jaycees,* 468 U.S. 609 (1984), the Court upheld a requirement imposed under a Minnesota public accommodations statute that local clubs be permitted to extend full membership to women. In *Rotary International v. Rotary Club of Duarte,* 481 U.S. 537 (1987), the Court upheld a similar requirement under a California public accommodations law. Under the framework of analysis used by the Court in these cases, a constitutional right of association can be based either on the intrinsic value of an intimate association, such as the family, or on the instrumental value of an association for the exercise of First Amendment rights, such as freedom of speech and religion. The Court found that the Jaycees and the Rotary Club could not challenge state regulation of their membership policies on the intrinsic value of intimate association because their local clubs were not sufficiently small, selective, and exclusive. They could not ground their challenge on the second basis because states have a compelling interest in eliminating discrimination against women that justifies such limitations, even if they result in indirect restrictions on the right of association.

All-male clubs present a barrier to fair and equal educational and employment opportunities for girls and women. In schools and colleges, they limit access to important educational, athletic, and social opportunities to the males selected for membership. Studies continue to show that college fraternities are a prime vehicle for encouraging sexual abuse of college-age women. For these reasons, the integration or elimination of such clubs is a part of many feminist agendas. When enacting Title IX, Congress acknowledged that all-male clubs often obstruct equal educational opportunity for women. Under Title IX, colleges and universities that recognize single-sex clubs, other than social fraternities and sororities, risk losing federal funding. It was that consideration that led the University of Miami to decide to withdraw recognition of an all-male honor society unless it discontinued its practice of excluding female students from eligibility. (See *Iron Arrow Honor Society v. Heckler,* 702 F.2d 549 (5th Cir. 1983), *vacated,* 464 U.S. 61 (1983).)

As indicated, Title IX does not reach social fraternities and sororities. The statute explicitly exempts these tax-exempt, single-sex social clubs. As a result, federal law provides little basis for combating these vehicles of traditional sex-role socialization. Other legal resources, however, are often available, in particular state public accommodations laws. As the following case shows, public accommodations statutes may extend to all-male, tax-exempt social organizations on college and university campuses.

Frank v. Ivy Club

New Jersey Supreme Court, 1990.
576 A.2d 241, *cert. denied* 111 S.Ct.799 (1991).

GARIBALDI, J.

This appeal concerns whether the New Jersey Division on Civil Rights (Division) followed the proper administrative procedure in concluding that it had jurisdiction under the New Jersey Law Against Discrimination (LAD), over the Tiger Inn and Ivy Club (Clubs), all-male eating Clubs at Princeton University. Central to the resolution of the jurisdictional issue is whether the Clubs are "places of accommodation" within the meaning of LAD, or are exempt from LAD because they are "distinctly private." The Division found that the Clubs have an integral relationship of mutual benefit with Princeton which deprives them of private status and makes them subject to the Division's jurisdiction. . . .

. . . Princeton University is a private, non-sectarian institution of higher education, founded in 1746. The University is located in Princeton, New Jersey. From 1746 to 1968, Princeton University admitted only male students as undergraduates. In 1969, the University for the first time admitted women as undergraduate degree candidates.

From approximately 1803 to 1843, Princeton University required all undergraduate students to take their meals in commons operated by the college steward. In 1843, Princeton permitted its undergraduate students to board off-campus. The Princeton college refectory burned down in 1856 and was closed for fifty years. During that time, all students took their meals in boarding houses that were not affiliated with the college. In the mid-1800's several groups of Princeton students formed "select associations" to reduce the cost of their off campus living and dining expenses. By 1876 twenty five "select associations" or eating clubs were in existence.

The club system associated with Princeton University, which began with these "select associations," presently [sic] consists of thirteen clubs, eight of which are non-selective clubs and five of which are selective clubs. Campus, Charter, Cloister Inn, Colonial, Dial Lodge, Elm, Quadrangle and Terrace are the eight non-selective clubs. These clubs, formerly all male and selective, are now co-ed. The non-selective clubs offer social, recreational and dining activities. Admission to the non-selective or open clubs is by a lottery system. Students who are not accepted into the "open clubs" of their choice are given the opportunity to go through subsequent lottery rounds at any "open club" that has additional available contracts to offer.

The five selective clubs are Ivy, Cottage, Tiger Inn, Cap & Gown and Tower. The selective clubs also offer social, recreation and dining activities. Tower, Cap & Gown and Cottage accept male and female members. From their inception until the present, Ivy and Tiger have only accepted male members. . . .

Sally Frank was a student at Princeton University from September 1976 through June 1980, when she graduated. During that time

[she was refused membership in the Tower, Cap & Gown, Tiger Inn, Cottage, and Ivy clubs.] . . .

. . . [I]t is critical to understand that the Division rejected the theory that the Clubs themselves were places of accommodation. Instead, the Division premised its conclusion that the Clubs were not distinctly private on its finding that "the relationship between the Clubs and Princeton University is one of integral connection and mutual benefit." Jurisdiction over the Clubs is, essentially, based on jurisdiction over Princeton and supported by undisputed facts of the present day interdependence of the Clubs and Princeton. There no longer is any question that Princeton is a place of public accommodation under LAD. . . .

. . . [In reaching its decision] the Division gave little weight to the Clubs' present financial and legal independence from the University. Neither did it rely heavily on evidence of historical connections between the Clubs and the University. Instead, the Division drew from undisputed facts demonstrating that "the University and the Clubs are in reality integrally connected." Specifically, the Division relied upon three factual conclusions in coming to its determination:

(1) The Clubs are held out as part of a club system which serves Princeton students;
(2) The Clubs draw their membership almost exclusively from Princeton University students; and
(3) Princeton relies on the club system to feed a majority of its upperclass students. . . .

The finding of an integral and symbiotic relationship is based on the undisputed factual conclusions that the Clubs need the University and the University needs the Clubs, rather than on any particular act of control or integration. Where a place of public accommodation and an organization that deems itself private share a symbiotic relationship, particularly where the allegedly "private" entity supplies an essential service which is not provided by the public accommodation, the servicing entity loses its private character and becomes subject to laws against discrimination. It would be disingenuous for the Clubs to assert that they could ever exist apart from Princeton University. The Clubs gather their membership from Princeton and, in turn, provide the service of feeding Princeton students. Because of this, the Clubs lack the distinctly private nature that would exempt them from LAD.

The Division's conclusion that the Clubs are not distinctly private is based on undisputed evidence. . . .

Gender discrimination is contrary to the legislative policy of the State of New Jersey. "The eradication of 'the cancer of discrimination' has long been one of our State's highest priorities." The Legislature enacted LAD to reflect the belief that "discrimination threatens not only the rights and proper privileges of the inhabitants of the State but menaces the institutions of a free democratic state." The elimination of discrimination in educational institutions is particularly critical. The intent of the legislature to eliminate discrimination in educational institutions is evidenced by the designation in [the act], as a "place of accommodation," of any "college and university, or any educational institution under the supervision of the State Board of Education, or the Commissioner of Education of the State of New Jersey."

The Clubs have fiercely contested the threshold issue of jurisdiction because, once jurisdiction is established, there is no question that the Clubs discriminated against women. It is undisputed that the Clubs had a general policy that excluded females from consideration as members. It is also undisputed that the Clubs applied this policy to Frank when she attempted to [interview for membership] at the clubs. That policy constituted discrimination in violation of LAD. On the basis of the facts in this record, we agree with the Division that the Clubs cannot sever their ties to the University or remove themselves from the jurisdiction of the Division. Instead, the Clubs must obey this State's substantive legal proscriptions against discrimination and discontinue their practice of excluding women purely on the basis of gender.

We reverse the Appellate Division and reinstate the Order of the Division on Civil Rights dated May 26, 1987.

STUDY QUESTIONS

1. What aspect of freedom of association did the clubs claim prevented the application of the LAD to them? Why did the court reject that claim? What form did the interdependence between the clubs and the university take?

2. The New York City Council saw a link between membership in some private clubs and the availability of business and professional opportunities. Do you suppose that access to educational opportunities at Princeton is linked to membership in the eating clubs? That membership is linked to career and business consequences?

3. Based on its finding in Sally Frank's case, what would you expect the civil rights division to rule were it faced with a challenge involving single-sex dormatories? Fraternities? A campus women's center specializing in rape crisis counseling? Are there special arguments that would justify maintaining any of these facilities on a single-sex basis?

7 The Family

Unlike the public sphere of government and the marketplace, the family has long been considered an appropriate focus for women's interests and activities. Religion, culture, and law have routinely assigned family roles on the basis of sex, relegating women to a disproportionate share of child care and other domestic work.

Recall, for example, Blackstone's rendering of the common law doctrine of coverture and its consequences (see Chapter 1). Blackstone reported that at common law, the husband was accorded the role of head and master in the family. He owned the property, was entitled to the custody and labors of the children, owed support to the wife, and was responsible not only for her debts but also for her discipline. The wife, in turn, owed service and sexual fidelity to her husband. These legal disabilities and inequities were among the chief complaints of the early feminists in the 1848 Seneca Falls Declaration:

> The history of mankind is a history of repeated injuries and usurpations on the part of man toward woman, having in direct object the establishment of an absolute tyranny over her . . . He has made her, if married, in the eye of the law, civilly dead.
>
> In the covenant of marriage, [woman] is compelled to promise obedience to her husband, he becoming, to all intents and purposes, her master—the law giving him power to deprive her of her liberty, and to administer chastisement.
>
> He has so framed the laws of divorce, as to what shall be the proper causes, and in cases of separation, to whom guardianship of the children shall be given, as to be wholly regardless of the happiness of the woman—the law in all cases going upon the false supposition of the supremacy of man, and giving all power into his hands. . . .

As we saw in Chapter 1, some of these problems were remedied by the Married Women's Property Acts enacted in most states between 1840 and 1900. These laws made it possible for a woman to retain her wages from work outside the home, to manage and control her real property, and to sue and be sued.

These and other legal developments, primarily at the state level, have dispelled a number of the disabilities associated with coverture and have made it easier for women to escape from intolerable marriages. Nonetheless, problems persist. Assymetrical and, for some, oppressive, role expectations endure in family relationships. Women still have primary responsibility for the care of their husbands and their children, while men are expected to work outside the home. Women are often the subjects of sexual violence and other assaults by their husbands. As previous chapters have made clear, women's family obligations are frequently used to justify their exclusion from the public sphere. The myths and realities of women's domestic burdens, for example, have served as the basis for denying women employment and educational opportunities. Lingering notions of marital unity undercut married women's ability to establish credit in their own right. These inequalities in the public sphere, in turn, reinforce inequalities in the domestic sphere.

This chapter is divided into four sections, dealing with the marital relation, child care, the feminization of poverty, and relationships beyond the nuclear family. As you read them, think about the extent to which women still lose their identity on marrying.

I. THE MARITAL RELATION

The Heritage of Coverture

Marriage under the common law meant the imposition of fixed obligations on both spouses. These differences in duties and vulnerabilities continued long after many of the consequences of marriage were softened by the Married Women's Property Acts. The nature of these continuing marital obligations, the ways they can and cannot be enforced, and their continuing vitality are addressed in the next several cases. The first demonstrates the difficulties a wife faces in attempting to enforce the duty of support owed her during marriage.

McGuire v. McGuire

Supreme Court of Nebraska, 1953.
157 Neb. 226, 59 N.W.2d 336.

MESSMORE, Justice.

The plaintiff, Lydia McGuire, brought this action in equity in the district court for Wayne County against Charles W. McGuire, her husband, as defendant, to recover suitable maintenance and support money, and for costs and attorney's fees. Trial was had to the court and a decree was rendered in favor of the plaintiff. . . . [P]laintiff had been previously married. Her first husband died in October 1914, leaving surviving him the plaintiff and two daughters. He died intestate, leaving 80 acres of land in Dixon County. The plaintiff and each of the daughters inherited a one-third interest therein. At the time of the marriage of the plaintiff and defendant the plaintiff's daughters were 9 and 11 years of age. By working and receiving financial assistance from the parties to this action, the daughters received a high school education in Pender. One daughter attended Wayne State Teachers College for 2 years and the other daughter attended a business college in Sioux City, Iowa, for 1 year. Both these daughters are married and have families of their own.

On April 12, 1939, the plaintiff transferred her interest in the 80 acre farm to her two daughters. The defendant signed the deed.

At the time of trial plaintiff was 66 years of age and the defendant nearly 80 years of age. No children were born to these parties. The defendant had no dependents except the plaintiff.

The plaintiff testified that she was a dutiful and obedient wife, worked and saved, and cohabited with the defendant until the last 2 or 3 years. She worked in the fields, did outside chores, cooked, and attended to her household duties such as cleaning the house and doing the washing. For a number of years she raised as high as 300 chickens, sold poultry and eggs, and used the money to buy clothing, things she wanted, and for groceries. She further testified that the defendant was the boss of the house and his word was law; that he would not tolerate any charge accounts and would not inform her as to his finances or business; and that he was a poor companion. The defendant did not complain of her work, but left the impression to her that she had not done enough. On several occasions the plaintiff asked the defendant for money. He would give her very small amounts, and for the last 3 or 4 years he had not given her any money nor provided her with clothing, except a coat about 4 years previous. The defendant had purchased the groceries the last 3 or 4 years, and permitted her to buy groceries, but he paid for them by check. There is apparently no complaint about the groceries the defendant furnished. The defendant had not taken her to a motion picture show during the past 12 years. They did not belong to any organizations or charitable institutions, nor did he give her money to make contributions to any charitable institutions. The defendant belongs to the Pleasant Valley Church which occupies about 2 acres of his farm land. At the time of trial there was no minister for this church so there were no services. For the past 4 years or more, the defendant had not given the plaintiff money to purchase furniture or other household necessities. Three years ago he did purchase an electric, wood-and-cob combination stove which was installed in the kitchen, also linoleum floor covering for the kitchen. The plaintiff further testified that the house is not equipped with a bathroom, bathing facilities, or inside toilet. The kitchen is not modern. She does not have a kitchen sink. Hard and soft water is obtained from a well and cistern. She has a mechanical Servel refrigerator, and the house is equipped with electricity. There is a pipeless furnace which she testified had not been in good working order for 5 or 6 years, and she testified she was tired of scooping coal and ashes. She had requested a new furnace but the defendant believed the one they had to be satisfactory. She related that the furniture was old and she would like to replenish it, at least to be comparable with some of her neighbors; that her silverware and dishes were old and were primarily gifts, outside of what she purchased; that one of her daughters was good about furnishing her clothing, at least a dress a year, or sometimes two; that the defendant owns a 1929 Ford coupé equipped with a heater which

is not efficient, and on the average of every 2 weeks he drives the plaintiff to Wayne to visit her mother; and that he also owns a 1927 Chevrolet pickup which is used for different purposes on the farm. The plaintiff was privileged to use all of the rent money she wanted to from the 80-acre farm, and when she goes to see her daughters, which is not frequent, she uses part of the rent money for that purpose, the defendant providing no funds for such use. The defendant ordinarily raised hogs on his farm, but the last 4 or 5 years has leased his farm land to tenants, and he generally keeps up the fences and the buildings. At the present time the plaintiff is not able to raise chickens and sell eggs. She has about 25 chickens. The plaintiff has had three abdominal operations for which the defendant has paid. She selected her own doctor, and there were no restrictions placed in that respect. When she has requested various things for the home or personal effects, defendant has informed her on many occasions that he did not have the money to pay for the same. She would like to have a new car. She visited one daughter in Spokane, Washington, in March 1951 for 3 or 4 weeks, and visited the other daughter living in Fort Worth, Texas, on three occasions for 2 to 4 weeks at a time. She had visited one of her daughters when she was living in Sioux City some weekends. The plaintiff further testified that she had very little funds, possibly $1,500 in the bank which was chicken money and money which her father furnished her, he having departed this life a few years ago; and that use of the telephone was restricted, indicating that defendant did not desire that she make long distance calls, otherwise she had free access to the telephone.

It appears that the defendant owns 398 acres of land with 2 acres deeded to a church, the land being of the value of $83,960; that he has bank deposits in the sum of $12,786.81 and government bonds in the amount of $104,500; and that his income, including interest on the bonds and rental for his real estate, is $8,000 or $9,000 a year. There are apparently some Series E United States Savings Bonds listed and registered in the names of Charles W. McGuire or Lydia M. McGuire purchased in 1943, 1944, and 1945, in the amount of $2,500. Other bonds seem to be in the name of Charles W. McGuire, without a beneficiary or co-owner designated. The plaintiff has a bank account of $5,960.22. This account includes deposits of some $200 and $100 which the court required the defendant to pay his wife as temporary allowance during the pendency of these proceedings. One hundred dollars was withdrawn on the date of each deposit.

The facts are not in dispute. . . .

In the instant case the marital relation has continued for more than 33 years, and the wife has been supported in the same manner during this time without complaint on her part. The parties have not been separated or living apart from each other at any time. In the light of the . . . cases it is clear, especially so in this jurisdiction, that to maintain an action such as the one at bar, the parties must be separated or living apart from each other.

The living standards of a family are a matter of concern to the household, and not for the courts to determine, even though the husband's attitude toward his wife, according to his wealth and circumstances, leaves little to be said in his behalf. As long as the home is maintained and the parties are living as husband and wife it may be said that the husband is legally supporting his wife and the purpose of the marriage relation is being carried out. Public policy requires such a holding. It appears that the plaintiff is not devoid of money in her own right. She

has a fair-sized bank account and is entitled to use the rent from the 80 acres of land left by her first husband, if she so chooses. . . .

For the reasons given in this opinion, the judgment rendered by the district court is reversed and the cause remanded with directions to dismiss the cause.

Reversed and remanded with directions to dismiss.

STUDY QUESTIONS

1. According to the court, what is the purpose of the marriage relation? When is it being carried out? Do you agree? Why? Why not?
2. What is the basis for the court's refusal to grant relief? Do you suppose Charles McGuire would have obtained any relief had he complained that his wife was not attending to her household duties? Would a court be likely to consider housekeeping and cooking part of a family's "living standards" that are "of concern to the household and not for courts to determine"?
3. Why are courts unwilling to intervene when married couples are still living together? Should they be? Would your answer be affected in any way by knowing that, after the court case, the McGuires continued living together until Charles McGuire's death?

The *McGuire* case illustrates two important features of family law: the judicial reluctance to intervene in intact families and the traditional allocation of family roles. Even today, *McGuire* is routinely cited for the proposition that courts will not intervene in ongoing marriages to enforce spousal obligations. Although this rule is neutral in form, its impact has been far from neutral. Historically, the control that husbands were given over their wives' persons and property allowed them sufficient leverage to coerce their wives into complying with their obligations. Wives, on the other hand, were dependent on their husbands economically and thus lacked the means to enforce the obligations due them. Although the law no longer enables men to control their wives' property, women's obligations combined with the difficulties they face in the workplace may often have the same effect.

The *McGuire* case also illustrates the traditional allocation of roles in operation. By virtue of his support duty, the husband was obliged to be the breadwinner, and by virtue of her duty to provide services, the wife was obliged to be the homemaker. The services provided by Lydia McGuire clearly contributed to the economic worth of the household and are easily recognizable as work. As the next two cases demonstrate, wives owe their husbands other services as well. These involve social and sexual activities and are far less likely to be seen as work.

The first case, *Glover v. Glover,* concerns a wife's petition for support in the context of divorce. Under New York statutes applicable until the 1970s, the trial court could refuse to award support where it considered the petitioner's conduct highly improper, even if the conduct did not endanger the physical or mental well-being of the other spouse. In finding that the wife's conduct was so reprehensible as to justify a denial of support, the court revealed its view of proper wifely conduct.

Glover v. Glover

New York Family Court, 1970.
64 Misc.2d 374, 314 N.Y.S.2d 873.

ISIDORE LEVINE, Judge.

Petitioner, a most attractive, articulate and youthful looking woman, apparently in her forties, but fiery, volatile, ruthless, self-centered, cunning and uncompromising, sues the respondent herein contending that since November, 1969 he has refused and neglected to provide fair and reasonable support for her. Petitioner also contends that respondent was physically abusive to her and in particular on June 6, 1970 when without provocation he allegedly kicked her in the lower part of her spine, requiring X-Rays and medical treatment, when all she did, she claims, was to ask him for her weekly allowance.

Respondent, a practicing attorney for 30 years, vehemently denies these allegations and claims that petitioner has been guilty of such gross misconduct that she is not entitled to support from him on a means basis.

Petitioner and respondent were married on May 20, 1962, approximately eight years ago. There are no children of the marriage.

While much of the testimony was in sharp contradiction between the parties, some critical issues were admitted by petitioner. The court, however, has had the special advantage of seeing, hearing and observing the manner of the witnesses on the stand, and evaluating their credibility.

From the credible evidence adduced at the trial, the court credits the testimony of respon-

dent, and his witnesses, including respondent's version of the alleged assault on petitioner on June 6, 1970, and finds that the petitioner did indeed grossly misconduct herself toward her husband.

The court finds that petitioner, who was obsessed with the desire to be in business for herself despite the respondent's repeated requests to her to give up her business ventures and take care of the home, and despite the fact that he had already yielded to petitioner and given her no less than $2,000, for her business ventures which he opposed, went behind respondent's back and approached several of his legal clients and friends to loan her money or co-sign loans for her. (Petitioner admitted approaching at least five whose names are in the record.)

In addition and most reprehensibly the court finds that petitioner told a number of respondent's clients that he was not a good lawyer and that they should not do business with him. (Petitioner admitted that she may have made deprecating remarks about her husband as a lawyer.)

Two witnesses, both in the real estate business, professionally engaged with respondent, testified to specific instances of professional deprecation of respondent by petitioner.

Petitioner further provoked and exacerbated deteriorating relationships with her husband by failing to keep several appointments with her husband which were vital to his business relationships with clients. On several occasions respondent was compelled to entertain clients alone at his home and cook the dinner for them, since petitioner, who was aware of the social engagements, came home several hours late, and on two occasions, corroborated by a witness for respondent who was present as a guest, came home at about midnight. The testimony evidences further social and business relationships outside the home when petitioner failed to show up on time and respondent was required to entertain his clients and their wives alone.

Further exacerbations of the marital strain between the parties were the result of petitioner's pre-occupation with animals which resulted in dispossess proceedings against her and respondent because of charges of barking emanating from the apartment at all hours of the day and night, because of the urination and defecation by the dogs on the terrace of this apartment (one of the respondent's witnesses testified that petitioner's home was a mess and that the dogs vomited in the living room when he was present in the apartment on August 14, 1970, corroborating in part testimony by respondent that the apartment was constantly in a mess).

Adding up all of this testimony, together with other testimony in the record, the court concludes that the petitioner's misconduct has been so gross as to warrant a denial of her support by respondent on a means basis. One who would destroy her husband professionally and hence financially ought not to be permitted to look to him for support and share in his income on a means basis. . . .

Having denied petitioner support on a means basis, the court now turns to consideration of support of petitioner on a public charge basis, should this eventuate, despite the court's finding that the petitioner is fully able to support herself. It will be noted that the petitioner has had excellent background as a sales representative, interior decorator, and real estate saleswoman, and is attractive, articulate and youthful. However, since at the moment petitioner claims not to have any income, the court directs her support by respondent on a public charge basis for a period not to exceed four weeks from the date hereof for which purpose the attorneys for both sides are directed to confer with the Department of Social Services to agree upon a sum. Should the attorneys fail to come to agreement within one week after receipt of the decision and order herein, either attorney may petition the court for fixing of this sum. Should petitioner not be gainfully employed after four weeks from date, she may petition the court for the continuance of this order of support on a public charge basis.

Notify attorneys for parties.

STUDY QUESTIONS

1. In what way did the court consider that Karen Glover had "grossly misconduct[ed] herself toward her husband?" By failing to be a good housekeeper? By being obsessed with the desire to be in business? By attempting to obtain loans or loan guarantees from her husband's clients and friends? By deprecating her husband?

2. How do you suppose the judge would have reacted to testimony to the effect that George Glover constantly left his clothes and other belongings strewn about their home? That the dogs had been his?

3. Are you likely to hear the same criticisms of a wife's conduct today?

The court in this divorce case seems to have seen Karen Glover's misconduct as putting her own interests and tastes ahead of her husband's, thereby neglecting her duties to him. These duties apparently included supporting her husband's professional life by entertaining his clients and their wives and refraining from making deprecating remarks about his professional capabilities. Although courts are probably less likely to cite reasons of this sort today when they withhold support or alimony, similar expectations may well continue to influence the way they exercise their discretion in such matters.

The next case involves a man's right to recover damages from another man who has had sexual relations with his wife. Such actions, although actually civil in nature, are called actions "for criminal conversation." Derived from the common law, they have historically been available only to men. In confronting such a sex-based cause of action, the Maryland Court of Appeals was inevitably required to reflect on the nature of the marital relation today.

Kline v. Ansell

Maryland Court of Appeals, 1980.
287 Md. 585, 414 A.2d 929.

DAVIDSON, Judge.

We shall here consider the question whether the common law cause of action for criminal conversation is viable in Maryland. . . .

At common law, the cause of action for criminal conversation was available only to a man. III Blackstone, *Commentaries on the Laws of England,* 139 40 (Lewis's ed. 1898). The gravamen of this action was adultery. Its elements consisted of a valid marriage and an act of sexual intercourse between a married woman and a man other than her husband. The fact that the wife consented, that she was the aggressor, that she represented herself as single, that she was mistreated or neglected by her husband, that she and her husband were separated through no fault of her own, or that her husband was impotent, were not valid defenses. *See* Prosser, *The Law of Torts,* § 124 (4th ed. 1971). The only valid defense to this action was the consent of the husband.

The cause of action for criminal conversation evolved from the action for enticing away a servant and depriving a master of his proprietary interest in the servant's services. Because at common law the status of a wife was that of a servant, that action was extended to include the deprivation of the wife's services. Prosser, § 124 at 873. The husband was regarded as having a property right in the body of his wife and an exclusive right to the personal enjoyment of her. The wife's adultery was therefore considered to be an invasion of the husband's property rights. A husband could maintain an action for criminal conversation even if his wife was a willing participant, because, under the common

law, she was considered incapable of giving her consent to what was regarded as an injury to her husband.

While the action for criminal conversation was founded on the services which the wife owed to her husband, the underlying basis of recovery was the injury to the husband's feelings and particularly to his sense of his own and his family's honor. Many of the early cases held "that the essential injury to the husband consists in the defilement of the marriage bed, in the invasion of his exclusive right to marital intercourse with his wife and to beget his own children." This right was recognized as "a right of the highest kind, upon the thorough maintenance of which the whole social order rests, and . . . [for the purpose of] the maintenance of the action it may properly be described as a property right." Thus, while these cases recognized that the essence of the action was an injury to the husband's personal feelings arising from an interference with the marital relationship, they nonetheless continued to describe the basis of the action as an interference with a property right.

Over the years, there has been a gradual shift of emphasis away from the concepts of services and property rights toward a recognition of the more intangible elements of the marital relationship, such as companionship and affection. Prosser, § 124 at 873. Greater emphasis is now placed upon the concept that the wife's act of adultery is an injury to the feelings and the marital rights of the husband, and is therefore an invasion of his personal rights. Thus, an interference with the continuance of the personal rights associated with the marital relationship is becoming recognized as the basis for this action.

In more recent years, the action for criminal conversation has come under attack. In some jurisdictions, it has been abolished by the Legislature. In others, it has been abolished by the courts. A variety of rationales have been relied upon to justify this result. The action for criminal conversation is notorious for affording a fertile field for blackmail and extortion because it involves an accusation of sexual misbehavior. Criminal conversation actions may frequently be brought, not for the purpose of preserving the marital relationship, but rather for purely mercenary or vindictive motives. An award of damages does not constitute an effective deterrent to the act of adultery, and it does not effectively help to preserve or restore a marital relationship in which adultery has already occurred. Indeed, a contested trial may destroy a chance to restore a meaningful relationship. In addition, this action, which eliminates all defenses except the husband's consent and which imposes liability without any regard to the quality of the marital relationship, is incompatible with today's sense of fairness. Most important, today's sense of the increasing personal and sexual freedom of women is incompatible with the rationale underlying this action. For all of these reasons, this harsh cause of action has been considered to be unreasonable and anachronistic.

In 1972, Art. 46 of the Maryland Declaration of Rights, Maryland's Equal Rights Amendment (ERA), was adopted. It provides:

> "Equality of rights under the law shall not be abridged or denied because of sex." . . .

At common law, the action for criminal conversation provided different benefits to and imposed different burdens upon men and women. Only a man could sue or be sued for criminal conversation. These facts remain unchanged under the common law as it exists in Maryland today. A man has a cause of action for criminal conversation, but a woman does not. Moreover, a man who engages in an act of sexual intercourse with another man's wife is civilly liable for damages, but a woman who engages in a similar activity with another woman's husband is not. Thus, Maryland's law provides different benefits for and imposes different burdens upon its citizens based solely upon their sex. Such a result violates the ERA. Any previous implicit approval by this Court of the action for criminal conversation is eradicated by the existence of the ERA. The common law cause of action for criminal conversation is a vestige of the past. It cannot be reconciled with our commitment to equality of the sexes.

We now hold that in Maryland the cause of action for criminal conversation is unconstitutional and is no longer viable. Accordingly, we shall reverse that portion of the judgment relating to criminal conversation.

STUDY QUESTIONS

1. At common law, who could bring an action for criminal conversation against whom? What was the original basis for the action? What did it become? How could the person being sued defend against the action?

2. What expectations concerning sexual fidelity in marriage are reflected in this cause of action? Do these expectations apply only to the wife or to both the wife and the husband? Do you think people generally have similar expectations today?

3. Was abolition of the cause of action the only remedy available to the court? Like suits for criminal conversation, suits for loss of consortium (loss of a spouse's services or support, companionship and sexual attentions resulting from negligent injury to the spouse) were historically only available to husbands. Yet as courts recognize this gender classification is unconstitutional or otherwise improper, they generally make the cause of action available to wives as well as husbands. Why do you suppose the Maryland court declined to extend the right to sue wives in this case?

The decision in *Kline v. Ansell* to eliminate the cause of action for criminal conversation reflects some changes in attitude toward wives' duties of fidelity in marriage. The decision should not necessarily be read as a sign that extramarital sexual conduct is totally acceptable, however, since adultery is still a ground for divorce in many jurisdictions. It may, instead, indicate an unwillingness to see women as responsible for the seduction of adulterous husbands in the same way that men have been seen as responsible for the seduction of adulterous wives.

In discussing the shift of emphasis in marriage away from services and property rights toward companionship and affection, the courts have allowed us to see how new rationales evolve to justify the continuation of sex-based doctrines rooted in coverture. Like *Kline v. Ansell,* the next case involves the durability of a traditional attribute associated with coverture. At issue here is the continued vitality of a Louisiana provision awarding husbands the power to control property held jointly by a married couple. The case also introduces one of the forms of marital property arrangements treated at greater length in the next subsection. For now, it is enough to understand that under community property, the arrangement at issue here, all income and property acquired during the marriage generally belongs to both spouses, though the man might have control over it. By contrast, under the common law system, income or property generally goes to the spouse who has title to it.

Kirchberg v. Feenstra

United States Supreme Court, 1981.
450 U.S. 455, 101 S.Ct. 1195,
67 L. Ed.2d 428.

Justice MARSHALL delivered the opinion of the Court.

In this appeal we consider the constitutionality of a now superseded Louisiana statute that gave a husband, as "head and master" of property jointly owned with his wife, the unilateral right to dispose of such property without his spouse's consent. Concluding that the provision violates the Equal Protection Clause of the Fourteenth Amendment, we affirm the judgment of the Court of Appeals for the Fifth Circuit invalidating the statute.

I

In 1974, appellee Joan Feenstra filed a criminal complaint against her husband, Harold Feenstra, charging him with molesting their minor daughter. While incarcerated on that charge, Mr. Feenstra retained appellant Karl Kirchberg, an attorney, to represent him. Mr. Feenstra signed a $3,000 promissory note in prepayment for legal services to be performed by appellant Kirchberg. As security on this note, Mr. Feenstra executed a mortgage in favor of appellant on the home he jointly owned with his wife. Mrs. Feenstra was not informed of the mortgage, and her consent was not required because a state statute . . . gave her husband exclusive control over the disposition of community property.

Mrs. Feenstra eventually dropped the charge against her husband . . . [who] obtained a legal separation from his wife and moved out of the State. Mrs. Feenstra first learned of the existence of the mortgage in 1976, when appellant Kirchberg threatened to foreclose on her home unless she paid him the amount outstanding on the promissory note executed by her husband. After Mrs. Feenstra refused to pay the obligation, Kirchberg obtained an order of executory process directing the local sheriff to seize and sell the Feenstra home.

. . . Kirchberg in March 1976 filed this action . . . seeking a declaratory judgment against Mrs. Feenstra that he was not liable under the Truth in Lending Act, 15 U.S.C. § 1601 *et seq.,* for any nondisclosures concerning the mortgage he held on the Feenstra home. In her answer to Kirchberg's complaint, Mrs. Feenstra . . . included a . . . counterclaim challenging the constitutionality of the statutory scheme that empowered her husband unilaterally to execute a mortgage on their jointly owned home. . . .

While Mrs. Feenstra's appeal from the District Court's order was pending before the Court of Appeals for the Fifth Circuit, the Louisiana Legislature completely revised its code provisions relating to community property. In so doing, the State abandoned the "head and master" concept embodied in Art. 2404, and instead granted spouses equal control over the disposition of community property. . . . These provisions, however, did not take effect until January 1, 1980, and the Court of Appeals was therefore required to consider whether Art. 2404, the Civil Code provision which had authorized Mr. Feenstra to mortgage his home in 1974 without his wife's knowledge or consent, violated the Equal Protection Clause of the Fourteenth Amendment. . . .

[The appellate court] concluded that Art. 2404 violated the Equal Protection Clause. . . .

II

By granting the husband exclusive control over the disposition of community property, Art. 2404 clearly embodies the type of express gender-based discrimination that we have found unconstitutional absent a showing that the classification is tailored to further an important governmental interest. In defending the constitutionality of Art. 2404, appellant Kirchberg does not claim that the provision serves any such interest. Instead, appellant attempts to distinguish this Court's decisions in cases such as *Craig v. Boren* and *Orr v. Orr,* which struck down similar gender-based statutory classifications, by arguing that appellee Feenstra, as opposed to the disadvantaged individuals in those cases, could have taken steps to avoid the discriminatory impact of Art. 2404. Appellant notes that under Art. 2334 of the Louisiana Civil Code, in effect at the time Mr. Feenstra executed the mortgage, Mrs. Feenstra could have made a "declaration by authentic act" prohibiting her husband from executing a mortgage on her home without her consent. By failing to

take advantage of this procedure, Mrs. Feenstra, in appellant's view, became the "architect of her own predicament" and therefore should not be heard to complain of the discriminatory impact of Art. 2404.

By focusing on steps that Mrs. Feenstra could have taken to preclude her husband from mortgaging their home without her consent, however, appellant overlooks the critical question: Whether Art. 2404 substantially furthers an important government interest. As we have previously noted, the "absence of an insurmountable barrier" will not redeem an otherwise unconstitutionally discriminatory law. Instead the burden remains on the party seeking to uphold a statute that expressly discriminates on the basis of sex to advance an "exceedingly persuasive justification" for the challenged classification. Because appellant has failed to offer such a justification, and because the State, by declining to appeal from the decision below, has apparently abandoned any claim that an important government objective was served by the statute, we affirm the judgment of the Court of Appeals invalidating Art. 2404.

Accordingly, the judgment of the Court of Appeals is affirmed.

So ordered.

STUDY QUESTIONS

1. Is Joan Feenstra's experience unusual in your view? Are women often damaged by the type of law challenged here? In what ways?
2. Why don't the procedures that allow wives to stop their husbands from disposing of property without their consent take care of the problem posed by the statute?
3. Can you see any reason why the power to manage and control property should reside only in one spouse?

Joan Feenstra had won at the appellate level, and Louisiana had amended the law while the case was pending. In taking the *Feenstra* case, the Supreme Court went out of its way to make clear that legally imposed inequalities in the marital relation cannot persist in the absence of an "exceedingly persuasive justification." In so holding, the Court followed its earlier decision in *Orr v. Orr* (see Chapter 2), which invalidated Alabama's statute making husbands, but not wives, liable for alimony. There, as in *Feenstra,* the Court found no compelling reason for continuing unequal marital obligations. Indeed, the *Orr* Court explicitly rejected a state preference for traditional allocation of roles as an acceptable justification for such inequalities.

Male management of property was an important aspect of the civil death or loss of identity women experienced under coverture. Perhaps the most conspicuous symbol of that loss of identity that endures today is a woman's assumption of her husband's name. Refusing to comply with this practice has been a form of feminist protest at least since suffragist Lucy Stone married Henry Blackwell in 1855. With the second wave of feminism, women have, on occasion, retained or reverted to their own names or have even chosen, at times with their husbands, a new name on marrying. Initially, these women encountered unofficial resistance from commercial enterprises and other private entities and official resistance from voter registrars, motor vehicle departments, and the like. As a result, a number of legal challenges were instituted in the early 1970s. Asserting violations of the First and Fourteenth Amendments, women argued that use of their own names was an important expression of their independent identity and that requiring women, but not men, to change their names on marriage was an obvious gender classification. Courts generally rejected these claims. They did, however, recognize that name changes on marriage were simply examples of the general common law principle that individuals may change their names by usage. Thus, they have held that as long as there is no criminal purpose or intent to defraud creditors, a married woman, like anyone else, may use any name she chooses.

Although it is now clear that women may retain their names on marriage, they may still lack the power to give their children their name. Some states have explicit provisions allowing parents to give children their mothers' surname, but problems arise when parents do not agree. At times, courts have acknowledged that legal rules for awarding and changing names may be premised on theories of inequality. In *Marriage of Shiffman,* 620 P.2d 579 (1980), for example, the California Supreme Court recognized the father's common law right to name his child as "part of that system, wherein he was sole legal representative of the marriage, its property, and its children." Courts that now allow mothers and fathers equal rights to determine which name their children bear are likely to look to extenuating circumstances and the children's best interests in determining which name the children will take.

Legal domicile rules are even clearer remnants of women's loss of legal identity on marriage. A legal domicile is one's official residence for such purposes as voting and being taxed. In most states, women are automatically assigned their husband's domicile when they marry. As a result, they may be required to pay higher taxes or tuition or to vote in a new place. Apart from their symbolic impact, such rules can have a considerable practical effect today on couples who spend substantial periods of time apart. Consider, for example, the problems of students attending different state universities or employees of different states or localities that maintain residency requirements. In a few circumstances involving state university residency requirements, the courts have held that rigid rules attributing husbands' domiciles to women violate equal protection guarantees. In other cases, courts have carved out exceptions to permit women living apart from their husbands to acquire separate domiciles. As a general matter, however, courts have yet to recognize the right of married women to choose their own domicile.

Thus, remnants of common law notions of marriage have lasted well into the twentieth century. In exchange for the obligation to support their spouses, men have been entitled to their wives' personal and sexual services. The law has recognized husbands as the heads of households empowered to determine family names and domiciles and to control marital property. Courts and legislatures are now engaged in a process of revising the laws to reflect more modern views of the marital relation. Much of this process is taking place in the context of determining the economic rights of marital partners.

Contemporary Marriage Models

Although cases like *Orr v. Orr* and *Kirchberg v. Feenstra* rule out legal forms that impose a sex-based hierarchy on the marital relation, they leave open the question of what new legal models will replace the old. It is possible to envision many different types of relationships that satisfy the requirements of equal protection. Two basic models are often considered. One pictures marriage as a bonding of two parties into a new unit, a unit in which the parties' interests and identities truly merge. This is often referred to as the partnership model. The other picture of marriage is a more flexible alliance between two independent individuals who have many common interests. We will call this the alliance model.

In this subsection, we explore these models of the marital relation in the context of economic relations between the spouses. We first consider property arrangements within marriage and then turn to the models of marriage embodied in the social security and tax systems.

Economic Arrangements. A little background will be helpful in understanding the different views of marriage that are inherent in legal rules that relate to property arrangements within marriage. In the United States, two basic systems have determined the property rights of married couples: the "community property" system and the "common law" system. Rooted in the civil law systems of the European continent, the community property system generally provides that income or assets (other than gifts or inheritance) acquired by either spouse during the marriage belong to both spouses. Historically, as we saw in Louisiana, male spouses were often given the right to manage and control the property. The common law system derives from English law and came into use with the enactment of the Married Women's Property Acts giving wives the right to own and control their own income and assets. Under the common law system, property belongs to the spouse who holds the title to it. There are, however, several forms of ownership that permit couples to own property together. The two systems differ in their theoretical emphasis: in merging the couple's assets, the community property system emphasizes the couple's unity or partnership, while the common law system underscores the independence of the two spouses by allowing them to hold their property individually. At present, only eight states—Arizona, California, Idaho, Louisiana, Nevada, New Mexico, Texas, and Washington—have some variation of the community property system.

Both systems have been criticized in operation. The community property system has been faulted for its inconsistencies, complexities, and failure to produce equality of result. The common law system, on the other hand, has been criticized for its highly individualized nature and its failure to recognize the economic value of women's homemaking services. A newly proposed law, however, would articulate new legal rules for marital property rights in the forty-two common law states. As of 1993 the proposed law, called the "Uniform Marital Property Act" (UMPA), has been enacted only in Wisconsin. UMPA implements a community view of marriage by declaring that anything obtained during the marriage belongs equally to both partners. Under UMPA, spousal consent would be required to sell or mortgage marital property and homemakers would be able to point to their right to control half the couple's income in seeking credit from stores and institutions. Although the proposed law does permit couples to agree that different ownership arrangements will govern particular items acquired during marriage, its basic approach is similar to that in the community property states.

The legal rules governing marital property are even more evident at the time of divorce. When a marriage is dissolved in a community property state, marital assets are supposed to be divided equally between the parties. This reflects the system's assumption that the spouses contributed equally to the marriage. In a pure common law state, in keeping with that model's emphasis on separate identities, each piece of property would go to the spouse who technically owns it. However, common law states have come to adopt the "equitable distribution" method of allocating property on divorce. With that method, they have taken a major step toward the sharing or partnership view of marriage inherent in the community property model. Under equitable distribution provisions, it is irrelevant which partner formally owns the property. Assets are allocated on divorce according to the parties' present needs and circumstances and their past contributions to the marriage.

Some of the unresolved questions facing courts concerning equitable distribution turn on differing conceptions of marriage. One important difference among states is in the type of assets recognized as subject to equitable distribution. Real estate, savings, and personal property acquired during marriage are all obvious candidates for redistribution. Assets such as professional degrees (which the husband has usually earned while being supported by his wife) are more controversial. Similarly, states vary in whether or not they subject increases in the worth of one spouse's business that occur during the marriage to equitable distribution.

Although courts may discuss the nature of such property in technical legal terms, decisions regarding reallocations of this type raise questions of fundamental fairness, particularly when the wife has given up her own education or business to further her husband's career. These decisions inevitably raise questions about the nature of the marital relation. Should marriage be viewed as an economic partnership in which the spouses decide and work jointly to achieve certain ends? Is it better understood as a more flexible alliance of individuals who go about their separate activities? Is it something in between? Under the partnership model, professional degrees and business appreciation would probably be considered marital assets subject to equitable distribution. Under the alliance model, they would probably not be subject to redistribution.

Differing views about the nature of the marital relation are also apparent when courts attempt to evaluate a homemaker's contribution. One approach seeks to determine what the services were worth in terms of their replacement cost, i.e., how much it would cost to hire workers to do all the tasks performed by that spouse. A second method looks to the homemaking spouse's opportunity costs, i.e., how much she would have earned had she followed the occupation that she sacrificed in favor of homemaking. A third approach assumes that the spouses are entitled to equal shares and makes whatever adjustments are appropriate in light of other relevant factors. The first approach suggests the wife's homemaking services are simply in exchange for the support she receives during marriage. The second suggests that marriage is an alliance of two individuals entitled to compensation for particular services rendered the other. The third suggests that spouses are partners in a single enterprise whose earnings are to be shared equally.

Legal rules regarding alimony or spousal support also reveal different concepts of marriage. Historically, alimony has been awarded for a variety of purposes: to ensure the wife's support until she died or remarried and became the responsibility of another man; to reward virtue and punish wrongdoing; to maintain the status or standard of living the wife attained by marriage; and, some say, to compensate the wife for her labor during the marriage. Alimony also came to be a means of adjusting equities, especially after property was distributed, to ensure that wives shared in the fruits of the marriage.

Almost all states still retain provisions for alimony or spousal support in their divorce statutes. The principles for awarding alimony have changed somewhat in recent years, however. Though provisions vary somewhat from state to state, there is generally a much greater emphasis on demonstrated need and the spouse's potential for becoming self-supporting. In other words, alimony awards—certainly permanent awards—are now disfavored, and the burden is on the spouse seeking support to show need. Although some states still take fault into consideration, alimony awarded now is generally thought of as temporary, transitional support to allow a period of adjustment and retraining.

While some states acknowledge the contributions and the services of the party seeking support as a spouse, parent, wage earner, and homemaker and their contributions to the career potential of the other party, in practice most states seem to emphasize future needs and ability to pay. There is some recognition that a divorced woman's earning capacity has often been impaired by her time out of the job market and that after long marriages, some women will be permanently incapable of supporting themselves. However, it may be more appropriate to regard alimony as severance pay when it is not awarded to permit a divorced wife to provide custodial care for the couple's children. This approach to alimony reflects the view that marriage is based on an exchange of services and obligations, i.e., homemaking for support, and that the obligations end essentially with the services.

Many advocates for divorced wives argue that they are entitled to more alimony, particularly, when they have put their husbands through professional school or enhanced the value of their businesses through entertaining or other efforts. Here, too, the different ways of valuing these past contributions reflect different views of the marital relation. The husband's degree or business may be valued and split by the marital partners the same way business partners would divide their assets if their partnership dissolved. A second approach would simply reimburse the wife for her actual contributions (such as her husband's support and educational or business expenses) as though the two spouses were separate individuals who in essence made a deal. Courts are beginning to follow both approaches.

In evaluating the pluses and minuses of these different views of marriage, it is well to think about how they might affect people in traditional, nontraditional, and transitional roles. Women in traditional homemaker roles have the most to gain from the partnership view of marriage since they usually do not have an independent source of income and have foregone opportunities to develop their earning potential, often with permanent effect. The situation is less clear for women who work outside the home. Often their earnings are limited by their family obligations, and they benefit from a view of marriage that involves pooling finances. On the other hand, such a view means that they are no more able to exercise independent control over their resources than are their husbands. Such control may be an important consideration for women who are in the process of establishing identities for themselves other than as wives and mothers, just as it is for the unusual women who earn more than their husbands. Thus, no one view may be appropriate for all marriages. In sum, while it is clear that the heritage of coverture with its notion of marital unity and male dominance has not faded, it is not yet clear what model of the marital relation should or will replace it in the context of economic arrangements.

Later in this chapter, we examine the serious economic consequences for women following divorce as a result of the current judicial approaches to property and support arrangements. For the moment, we shift our focus from the law that governs intrafamily disputes to issues of government policy and ask once again what views of marriage are reflected in the operative legal provisions.

Government Policies. Family law is traditionally viewed as private law—that is, as involving arrangements and disputes between private parties. Thus, like UMPA, many laws dealing with family matters merely set out the framework by which family members and third parties can make arrangements and resolve disputes among themselves. On the other hand, there are many laws that enforce public policies regarding who may enter into "private" relationships, such as marriage. Families are also affected by government policies embodied in a variety of statutes and regulations reflecting particular views of the marital relation. Prominent among these are the Social Security Act and federal tax legislation.

Like some of the approaches to marital property discussed above, the Social Security system seeks to afford some measure of protection to women who fill the traditional homemaker role. However, the Social Security system's main focus is on the breadwinner. Most of the blatant discriminatory provisions that established sex-based rules for determining eligibility and calculating benefits resulting from this focus have now been eliminated; yet, as the next selection shows, problems persist. In reading the selection, consider the view of marriage the Social Security system presupposes. To what extent do the problems identified result from that view? To what extent do the conditions for receiving government benefits appear to reinforce women's traditional obligations in marriage?

Heading for Hardship

Older Women's League.
Mother's Day Report 1990.
Pp. 4–8.

SOCIAL INSECURITY FOR WOMEN

The Social Security Act was enacted in 1935 as the cornerstone of the New Deal. The Act was designed to provide Americans with protection against the loss of wages due to retirement, disability, or death. Although the language of the Act is gender-neutral, the program was designed to meet the needs of a "typical" American family that is no longer typical.

Drafted more than 50 years ago, the Social Security program best protects a family that consists of a lifelong paid worker (usually the husband), a lifelong unpaid homemaker (usually the wife), and the dependent children—a family that is quickly becoming a thing of the past. However, 70% of older, nonmarried women depend on Social Security as their primary source of income.

As long as the underlying premises of the program remain outdated, future generations of women will continue to receive Social

Security benefits that are significantly lower than men's.

Social Security is a system of "worker" and "dependent" benefits. A woman receives Social Security benefits by either working the requisite number of years in covered employment or by being married to a worker who qualifies for a worker benefit, in which case she receives 50% of his benefit. A woman who qualifies for benefits both on her own work record and as a spouse is dually entitled but receives only the higher of the two benefits.

A lifetime homemaker has no Social Security protection in her own right. Even though she has worked for decades in the home and has contributed substantially to her family's economic well-being, she receives only a spouse benefit equal to half of the benefit her husband receives.

For the homemaker who is divorced, half a benefit can be far too little to live on. A divorced woman is eligible to receive a spouse benefit if she had been married at least 10 years. However, half of her former husband's benefit is just one third of what they would receive as a couple. Together, they were receiving 150% of his Social Security—100% for him and 50% for her. As an individual, she receives only the 50%. This provides many divorced, lifetime homemakers with benefits that leave them living in poverty. The average spouse benefit for a woman in 1989 was $294 a month.

A divorced spouse becomes financially better off after her former spouse dies, because a widow receives 100% of her deceased husband's benefit. However, a widow may not draw any benefits until age 60, unless she has a child under 16 or an older disabled child. A widow's gap is created for widows with children over age 16 who are not 60 and who, therefore, cannot draw benefits yet. Once a widow has reached age 60, should she draw her benefits early rather than wait until age 65, her benefits will be actuarially reduced to around 70% of her normal widow's benefit.

Lower wages prompt single and divorced women to draw their benefits early, and thereby have their benefits actuarially reduced. Benefits are reduced to 80% of their normal amount for workers who retire early at age 62. For the first 15 years, the worker is ahead in total retirement benefits by drawing early, but after that, the worker is behind where she would have been had she waited until age 65 and drawn full benefits. Women who live to age 62 have an average life span of 83 years. Therefore, unless a woman has a reason to believe she will die younger than the average, choosing early retirement leaves her financially disadvantaged under Social Security. Yet, 72% of retired women workers draw their benefits early. . . .

DUALLY ENTITLED, BUT SINGULARLY BENEFITED

Women who are both homemakers and wage earners are particularly disadvantaged. A woman dually entitled to both a worker benefit on her earnings and a spouse benefit on her husband's earnings can receive only the greater of the two, usually the spouse benefit. If the spouse benefit is higher—and the zeroes averaged in for her years out of the work force make it likely that it will be—those years a woman worked and paid into the system through payroll taxes do not give her an increased benefit. She will receive exactly the same spouse benefit that she would have received had she never worked outside the home.

Since 1960, the percentage of women drawing a benefit based on their own work record has remained constant, despite more women working. Thirty-eight percent of women beneficiaries drew benefits on their work record in 1960 as well as in 1988. The number of women dually entitled on both their record and that of their husband increased over this period from five to 22%, but for these women, their dependent benefit on their husband's record was greater.

Two earner married couples also are penalized under the current system. Because a spouse receives only the higher of benefits based on her work record or spouse benefits based on her husband's record, dual income couples with similar incomes can receive Social Security benefits lower than a couple with only one earner. . . .

Given that so few women will qualify for benefits on their own work record even by the year 2030, . . . increased taxes will not

lead to proportionate increases in benefits.
In 1970, women's total average benefits were
70% of men's benefits; in 1990, this figure had
increased to only 73%.

STUDY QUESTIONS

1. How does the Social Security system fail to reflect the circumstances of women in the new
"typical" family? Does the Social Security system adequately meet the needs of women in
the traditional "typical" family as we now see
them? Does the Social Security system appear
to regard the traditional wife as a dependent
or a contributor to the family's economy?

2. Should a married homemaker receive benefits in her own name? Why? In what ways
would it improve her situation? How would a
homemaker's share be measured? Is it fair to
give married homemakers benefits for their
contributions in the home, without also giving unmarried workers who do their own
housework benefits for the work they do at
home?

3. How does the Social Security system penalize women who alter their work schedules
or temporarily drop out of the paid work
force for family reasons? Does the system for
computing benefits seem to be based on the
experience of males as breadwinners?

The Social Security system has been built on a view of the marital relation that
assumes husbands and wives play fixed roles as breadwinner and dependent,
respectively. Moreover, it has reinforced these roles by awarding certain benefits on
the basis of sex. As we have seen, those same assumptions about the wife's
dependent role in the marital relation also permeate the sex-neutral provisions that
continue to guide the Social Security system. Similar assumptions permeate this
country's tax systems. This is particularly evident in the federal income tax
provisions that determine the rate different types of families pay and the exemptions
available to them. A standard law school text explains the general operation and
effect of these provisions prior to the enactment of the 1986 Tax Reform Act.

Federal Income Taxation, 8th edition

William Klein, Joseph Bankman, Boris
Bittker, and Lawrence Stone.
Boston: Little Brown and Company,
1988. Pp. 41–43, 755–756.

The relationship between the rate schedules
for married people, heads of households, single
people, and married people filing separately,
and the rules relating to their availability,
produce two important effects. First, single-
earner couples are better off than they would
be under a system with one schedule for all,
since they have the advantage of the most
favorable rate. On the other hand, two-earner
married couples may be worse off than if they
had remained single because of the requirement
that they file jointly (or use the unfavorable
schedule for separate returns of married
people). This is true because if they were single
each would use a less-favorable rate schedule,
but since they would be filing two returns they
would get two separate starts at the bottom of
the rate schedule. Married couples filing jointly
have only one start at the bottom of their rate
schedule, albeit that is a more favorable schedule. The result is the infamous "marriage
penalty"—that is, the added tax paid by two
people who have roughly the same earnings and
who marry one another. . . .

[Another] point worth noting about the rate-
structure rules is that the secondary worker in a
married couple is subject to tax rates deter-

mined by the income of the primary worker. The "secondary worker" is the person whose income is lower and whose commitment to working is generally less than that of the primary worker. In our society, the secondary worker is most often the wife rather than the husband. The secondary worker's income will be thought of as the marginal income, since it is more likely that the couple would consider sacrificing this income than the income of the primary worker. Thus, the marginal rates that must be taken into account by married secondary workers, mostly women, are the relatively high rates resulting from the fact that the primary worker's (husband's) income uses up the lower rates. This effect is magnified by the fact that the wife's alternative of providing services in the home, rather than working outside the home, results in "imputed" income, which is not taxed at all. Also, one must bear in mind that for secondary workers the social security tax is a significant burden. . . .

Both the marriage penalty and the disincentive for secondary workers would be eliminated by a system with only one rate schedule and a rule making each individual taxable on his or her own income. . . .

. . . To illustrate the marriage penalty and its sources, imagine four households. In household *A* is a single person with a taxable income of $100,000. Her tax is $28,522. . . . Household *B* consists of a married couple. The wife earns a taxable income of $100,000 and the husband earns nothing. Their tax is $25,538. In household *C* we find another married couple, with a total taxable income of $100,000, of which $50,000 is earned by the husband and $50,000 by the wife. Household *D* consists of a man and a woman who are not married to each other but are living together in an intimate, sharing, long-term relationship. Each has a taxable income of $50,000 and pays a tax of $12,022. . . .

If the two individuals in household *D* marry each other, their tax increases by $1,494. Suppose Congress decides to eliminate this marriage penalty by raising the tax for each of them so that their total tax is $25,538, the same as that of couple *C*. This means raising the single-person rate. If that is done, it would be necessary to raise the rate for single person *A* as well. But then *A* would compare herself with wife *B*; this is the kind of complaint that led to the adoption in 1969 of the single-person rate schedule. Let's return, then, to couple *D* and couple *C*. Suppose Congress allows husband *C* and wife *C* to file separately and pay a tax of $24,044. This eliminates the marriage penalty, but now couple *B* cries "foul," on the theory that married couples with the same total income should pay the same tax, a theory that seems to be popular in Congress and consistent with community property law (see Poe v. Seaborn) and with modern notions of the role of the stay-at-home spouse in generating family income. In short, if you want a progressive rate structure and at the same time (a) you want to impose equal amounts of tax on married couples with the same total income, regardless of which spouse performs the services that directly produce the income, and (b) you want to mitigate the disparity between single person *A* and couple *B*, then you cannot avoid a system that produces a marriage penalty. . . .

STUDY QUESTIONS

1. How many different tax schedules are there for the federal income tax? What two important effects result from the operation of the different tax schedules? Who benefits from the most favorable rate? How have two-earner couples been affected?
2. What impact do you suppose the tax system actually has on people's behavior? For example, does the continuing preference for single-earner couples promote traditional family roles? Does the lingering marriage penalty deter marriage?

Two aspects of the Tax Reform Act of 1986 have an impact on the marriage penalty. The law repeals Section 221, which had given two-earner couples a special deduction, thereby mitigating the impact of the marriage penalty. On the other hand, the law may make the penalty less significant by substituting only two tax rates (and three in 1990) for the many-stepped scale. Under the current law, a marriage penalty is also created by the operation of the standard deduction and the phaseout of personal exemptions for upper-income taxpayers. Nevertheless, the combined effect of the marriage penalty and the decision not to tax household services while allowing only limited deductions for work expenses incurred by two-earner households is to give more favorable tax treatment to one-earner married couples than to either single workers or to two-earner couples. As the authors note, there are substantial questions about the fairness of these provisions, whether or not they actually deter married women from working. These provisions reflect a complex history of amendments to the tax code. Moreover, the impact of the marriage penalty appears somewhat diminished by the 1986 tax reform. It is apparent, however, that these provisions reflect a view that the one-earner couple is the preferred form of the marital relation.

Taken together, modern approaches to marital economic arrangements and contemporary government programs show both common themes and important differences. One common theme is a concern for couples in traditional relationships. In the context of equitable distribution and UMPA, this concern is manifested in legal principles that rely primarily on the partnership model of marriage to provide financial protection to women playing the homemaker role and to afford them recognition for the value of their services. In the context of Social Security, however, this concern is manifested through benefit rules that ensure limited support for women who have served as homemakers, without recognizing the value of their services. Similarly, federal income tax provisions manifest their concern for traditional relationships by the favorable treatment afforded one-earner couples and by the failure to recognize household services as taxable income. A greater awareness of less traditional relationships might well produce differences in all four legal contexts.

Personalized Marriages

A common thread in the materials presented thus far is that marriage is shaped by legal rules that embody or presuppose a particular view of the marriage relation. Couples are able to make certain types of prenupital agreements, but legal rules could permit spouses much more leeway in determining the nature of their own relationships. Prior to the adoption of the Married Women's Property Acts in the nineteenth century, contracts between spouses were regarded as a legal impossibility since husband and wife were considered one person. Since that time, contractual agreements between wives and husbands, particularly concerning with property, have become widely accepted. For a time, two important restrictions endured. Couples could not alter the essentials of the marital relation by, for example, contracting away the husband's duty to support or the wife's duty to provide domestic services. Nor could they "encourage" divorce by negotiating agreements that would go into effect on divorce unless they had actually decided to separate. A much broader range of contracts is becoming enforceable as the courts come to see contracts that anticipate the possibility of divorce as realistic and helpful in resolving disputes. Courts will, however, review the agreements to ensure that they satisfy the general requirements of contract law and that they are sufficiently fair and not the result of fraud, duress, nondisclosure, or misrepresentation. Moreover, contracts concerning property arrangements during marriage are also generally recognized.

Although the courts are still reluctant to intervene in ongoing marriages, given the law's traditional role in recognizing and enforcing private agreements, it may be appropriate for the law to assist people in ordering their own affairs in this area, too. In exploring the use of contract law in intimate relationships, law professor Marjorie Shultz has considered a number of situations. She asks whether spouses should be able to negotiate enforceable agreements regarding income production and support. For example, a wife could agree to support the pair and put her husband through law school in return for the husband's commitment to support the couple and pay her tuition when he graduates and she goes back to graduate school. Another example concerns domestic services. Should a couple be able to enforce an agreement that the wife will be paid a salary for running their home that reflects the going wage and includes Social Security tax payments? Other marital examples include property agreements and agreements on procedures for determining where the couple will live or for resolving conflicts. Less conventional examples involve arrangements for the couple to place time limits on their "marital" commitment and marriage agreements between homosexuals.

Court-enforced contracts of this sort seem desirable to some for a number of reasons. Allowing people to tailor their relationships to their circumstances and desires may enhance the chances for a successful outcome. Making such agreements provides an occasion to think through and discuss the specific goals for the arrangement and assumes the parties are adults capable of shaping their relationship. Such agreements embody a commitment to comply and, if enforceable, provide a mechanism for ensuring they will be fulfilled. Others are concerned that allowing such tailoring of relationships will take away the special significance of marriage, including the ongoing commitment to give and adjust to communal needs. There is also a concern that the weaker party may be exploited in such negotiations and needs the support of state-defined obligations.

However desirable such agreements may be, courts to date have been generally unwilling to intervene in ongoing relationships and to help shape variations on marriage. Thus, of the examples explored by Shultz, only her hypothetical agreement dealing with marital property is likely to be enforced.

A number of considerations may explain this judicial reluctance to lift all limits on private ordering. For example, judges may wish to assure that collective societal decisions govern some areas, as in the societal determination that homosexuals not be permitted to marry. They may also doubt that the parties are ever sufficiently capable of bargaining on equal footing to enable them to come to fair agreements concerning income production and support. They may also fear that the courts are incapable of interpreting and enforcing provisions such as a spouse's obligation to provide "respect, fidelity and support" to the other.

Making contracts in personal relationships may be a good idea whether or not they are ultimately found enforceable by courts. There are a number of questions to consider. Does the process of negotiating and formalizing agreements enhance communication between the parties? Does it inhibit it? Does it help people think about what matters most in their relationship? Does it inject rigidities into matters that are best left fluid? As individuals work through their answers to these questions for themselves, their insights may lead to guidelines and practices that courts will eventually adopt.

Intimate Violence

"Domestic chastisement" was among the complaints of nineteenth-century feminists, but the problem of intimate violence much predated their complaint. Wife beating has been sanctioned by law at least since the days of the Roman Empire.

Blackstone reported that just as the common law gave husbands the right to discipline their children, it gave husbands the right to discipline their wives as long as they used "moderation." Although states did not adhere consistently to the common law in this respect, and wife beating was illegal in most states by the 1870s, references to the right of husbands to chastise their wives physically appeared well into the nineteenth century.

Nor did spousal abuse cease when it became illegal. As the Majority Staff of the U.S. Senate Judiciary Committee found, domestic abuse is widespread. In their words,

> In 1991, at least 21,000 domestic crimes against women were reported to the police *every week;*
>
> Almost ⅕ of all aggravated assaults (20%) reported to the police are aggravated assaults in the home;
>
> These figures reveal a total of at least *1.1 million* assaults, aggravated assaults, murders, and rapes against women committed in the home and reported to the police in 1991; unreported crimes may be more than three times this total.
>
> *Majority Staff of the Senate Judiciary Committee.* Violence against Women: A Week in the Life of America. *October 1992. P. ii.*

Nineteenth-century feminists saw liberalized divorce as crucial to improving the situation of abused women. Now that the right to divorce is firmly established, battered women's advocates are seeking additional legal remedies.

When a Woman's Home Is Not Her Castle . . . Intimate Violence against Women

Pamela Goldberg and Phyllis Eckhaus, National Lawyers Guild. *Take Action, Take Heat.* March 1993. Pp. 20–26.

Since intimate violence was first recognized as a serious social problem in this country over two decades ago, it continues in both the severity and frequency of attacks on women. In 1990 alone, more than 1.8 million women reported being battered by their partners. As many as 40% of female homicide victims in the U.S. each year are women killed by their male partners. Battering occurs across racial, ethnic,

Reprinted by permission of Pamela Goldberg and Phyllis Eckhaus.

cultural and economic lines. Rape and other sexual assault often accompany or are the sole acts of abuse committed against women by their male partners. And as the incidence and degree of battering persists, the frequency with which women who resort to violence themselves as a means of protection—often their only means of protection—from their abuser and then identify themselves as battered women and claim self-defense in criminal proceedings, has risen.

Yet despite this grim reality, much has improved over these 25 years. There now exist a variety of organizations and shelters that assist battered women. Battered women's advocates, who spear-headed the battered women's movement in its nascent stages and continue to play a leading role, along with the many lawyers who have collaborated with them, have pushed for legislative reforms, brought challenges to police and judicial conduct toward battered women, sought to develop not only protective but also compensatory measures for women who have been abused by their partners. And some have even worked toward developing counseling programs for men who commit assault and rape against their partners, albeit with very mixed results.

As a result of these efforts, there are legal remedies, however limited, available for women seeking redress through the judicial system. Almost every state in the nation has some type of anti-domestic violence legislation. At least some states, New York among them, recognize marital rape as a crime. And currently there is a bill pending in Congress, the Violence Against Women Act. If enacted, it will be the first federal statute providing redress for a wide range of acts of violence against women, including intimate violence. Perhaps most significantly the efforts of battered women's advocates and lawyers have brought with them a greater public awareness of the scope and breadth of the problem of intimate violence. . . .

During the late sixties and seventies, much of the effort made by battered women's advocates was directed at providing emergency services for battered women, increasing public awareness of intimate violence, exposing the frequency and severity of its occurrence and gaining recognition of it as a grave social problem—not merely a sign of an aberrant relationship between two individuals—warranting serious public attention. It wasn't until the late 1970s and the early 80s that feminist lawyers and legal workers, building on the foundation laid by the battered women's movement, initiated litigation seeking to define intimate violence as unlawful conduct that should be redressed through the legal system and to hold state and municipal officials accountable for their treatment and handling of cases of battering.

In New York, as recently as 1970, some police officers held the view that "there is nothing wrong with a husband hitting his wife as long as he does not use a weapon." (*Bruno v. Codd*). . . .

. . . The *Bruno* case found state liability for police failure to act to protect battered women when called to the scene of a "domestic dispute." This case spawned many other lawsuits throughout the country challenging police and other state and municipal officers' responses to intimate violence. Unfortunately, this important precedent has been undermined by a 1989 Supreme Court decision, *DeShaney v. Winnebago Department of Social Services,* limiting state liability for so-called "private" acts.

The availability of orders of protection for women against their batterers was an early and important step. Orders of protection provide a legal means of prohibiting continued violence by an abusive partner. The terms of such orders can include barring the abuser from the home, from the woman's workplace, a child's school, or even simply barring further acts of violence against her while remaining in the home. Once issued, an order of protection, if violated, serves as a vehicle for bringing the abuser into court for possible civil and/or criminal sanctions. A major advance in the issuance of orders of protection occurred when courts began to allow them to be issued on an emergency basis in *ex parte* proceedings so that a woman could seek protection without fear of interference or reprisals by the batterer before she could get to the courthouse. All fifty states now have legislation providing for civil and/or criminal orders of protection for battered women, and, in some cases, criminal penalties if these orders are violated. Still, serious obstacles remain. Many state courts require filing fees; court clerks are hostile; judges minimize battering. Despite simplified petitioning procedures, battered women are seriously disadvantaged by lack of access to counsel.

The problem of intimate violence is not limited to heterosexual couples. Lesbians and gay men also suffer at the hands of abusive partners. The nature and dynamics of intimate violence in these communities are very complex, and are not identical to those of heterosexual couples. Little research and study have been done on intimate violence in these communities. Intimate violence among these couples remains hidden in this society much as it was for heterosexual women before the battered women's movement. The women and men in this situation have even more limited recourse to gain protection from their abusers than do heterosexual women.

In the face of limited legislative remedies for battered women, lawyers and advocates have been developing innovative strategies to create alternative measures for battered women. As a result, many creative theories have been put forward in areas such as tort liability and criminal sanctions for batterers. Many law schools have clinical programs dedicated to addressing the problems confronted by battered women. And many community organizations are conducting educational programs about the legal and other needs of battered women. These efforts are helping to increase the recourse available for women who have been battered. But the number of feminists working on these issues is small, and the problem is much bigger than the limited resources that state and federal governments are willing to put into addressing it.

Much remains to be done to ensure not only that women are protected from abusive partners but, even more importantly, to begin to decrease the likelihood that abuse will occur at all. One way to bring this about is by making the social stigma attached to the behavior great and the price to be paid for such conduct high. Gradually, states are beginning to recognize acts of intimate violence as criminal. Although [it is] still difficult to obtain convictions, and even then usually only in the most extreme cases and often only after repeated abuse, at least the courts, the district attorneys and even defense counsel are beginning to recognize intimate violence against women as criminally punishable conduct. Some district attorneys offices, including some in New York City, have a special unit to address cases involving intimate violence.

While the law has been reluctant to impose criminal sanctions on an abusive partner, it has been quick to impose them on women who defend themselves against the abuser. Women who kill their batterer to protect themselves from violent attacks do so as a desperate measure, seeing no alternative and fearing their own death. In 1977 the Washington State Supreme Court took a bold step forward when it found that the "reasonable man" standard—what a "reasonable man" would have done in the same circumstance—violated a woman's right to equal protection of the law in the context of a 5'4'' woman with a cast on her leg and a crutch fending off a 6'2'' intoxicated man [*State v. Wanrow*, 88 Wash. 2d 221, 559 P.2d 548 (Sup. Ct. Wash. 1977)]. In that case, Yvonne Wanrow fatally shot William Wesler, a mentally ill child molester who had entered her home and made suggestive comments about her young son while standing over her at close range.

While Wanrow repelled a stranger's attack, the case had tremendous significance for battered women. Judicial recognition that the point of view from which to assess a woman's belief that she is in danger and must resort to self-defensive acts must be from the woman's point of view and not some abstract "man on the street" was a major breakthrough for women who act in self-defense against their abusers—and a milestone for feminist jurisprudence. From that auspicious beginning evolved the theory of self-defense most frequently used in defending women who have killed or harmed their abusers—a theory of self-defense which is supported by expert testimony explaining and validating the story and perspective of the battered woman.

Most women act in self-defense while in the midst of an attack by an abusive partner. Some women who have suffered chronic abuse act after an attack has subsided in an effort to catch the abuser unaware—and as a means to help ensure their safety. Generally these acts are committed with a weapon, the victim believing herself to be in a constant state of life-threatening danger. Through the development and use of the concept of battered women's syndrome, in conjunction with definitions of self-defense stemming from the *Wanrow* case, advocates, psychologists and lawyers have explained the context and circumstances in a chronically abused woman's life that could lead her to take such extreme measures to protect herself, and perhaps her children as well. This theory has also been used to explain why battered women, such as Hedda Nussbaum, may not defend their children or themselves from continuous abuse as well as how they may perceive a constant threat of imminent danger even though the last attack occurred hours or even days earlier.

The last decade has brought positive changes in the legal climate of the defense of battered women who kill. Expert testimony is admissible in the overwhelming majority of states. Defense lawyers across the country are better able to understand the applicability of self-defense law and to convince judges and juries that women who use deadly force should be acquitted on grounds of justification. Legal teams and advocates are increasingly sophisticated in their approaches to negotiations with prosecutors and to sentencing arguments to judges on behalf of women who elect to plead guilty or who are convicted after trial. The need for clemency for incarcerated battered women has received national attention. These gains are due in large part to the efforts of the National Clearinghouse for the Defense of Battered Women, which has provided essential leadership and assistance to many lawyers . . .

Still, many women are convicted despite their perception of being in life-imperiling jeopardy. According to the National Coalition Against Domestic Violence, abusive men convicted of crimes after having killed their partners serve an average of two-to-six years in prison. Women who have killed their partner, usually in self-defense, serve an average of fifteen years. Another study done by the prominent battered women's social researcher, theorist and advocate Lenore Walker found that a black woman who kills her partner in self-defense is twice as likely to be convicted and serve a longer prison sentence than her white anglo counter-part. This fact illustrates that race as well as gender strongly influence attitudes toward battered women. And the number of women receiving pardons or clemency after those convictions are few—Jean Harris is a prominent and rare case. Many women spend years in prison, separated from their children and loved ones, isolated and stigmatized for protecting themselves the only way they could from acts of violence that society has yet to fully recognize and address.

The battered women's movement has pressed for widespread public education and training; for more funding for shelters and hotlines, social services, lay advocates and lawyers, all of which are tremendously outstripped by the demand. Though much has been accomplished in the last 25 years, we have only begun to meet the urgent needs of battered women. . . .

STUDY QUESTIONS

1. What different forms have legal efforts to combat intimate violence taken?
2. What do you see as the remaining problems? What do you think are the best ways to attack them?

As Goldberg and Eckhaus make clear, there have been a number of significant legal developments in the area of women abuse. But these developments have not been without controversy. Feminists have split, for example, on the desirability of invoking the law altogether. Some, particularly in Great Britain, think it is preferable for women to put their energies into extricating themselves from the situation and trying to begin new lives. See R. Emerson Dobash and Russell Dobash, *Women, Violence and Social Change* (New York: Routledge, 1992). Others are fearful that by using the criminal law or relying on government-run shelters, the needs and directions of various state authorities would predominate over women's concerns. See Susan Schecker, *Women and Male Violence* (Boston: South End Press, 1982).

The desirability of mandatory arrest provisions is also disputed. One key study initially suggested that mandatory arrest was effective in stamping out violence, and by 1991, fifteen states and the District of Columbia had passed statutes mandating arrests where there was probable cause to believe that domestic violence misdemeanors had taken place. Studies conducted in six cities across the country, however, indicate that although mandatory arrest may, at times, deter violence, at other times, it tends to exacerbate it. Efforts are still underway to identify the effects different policies will have in different situations. See "Symposium on Domestic Violence," 83 *Journal of Law and Criminology* 1 (1992).

The battered women's syndrome, mentioned by Goldberg and Eckhaus in the context of defending women who kill, is illustrated by the next case.

State of North Carolina v. Norman

Supreme Court of North Carolina, 1989.
378 S.E.2d 8.

MITCHELL, Justice.

. . . The defendant presented evidence tending to show a long history of physical and mental abuse by her husband due to his alcoholism. At the time of the killing, the thirty-nine-year-old defendant and her husband had been married almost twenty-five years and had several children. The defendant testified that her husband had started drinking and abusing her about five years after they were married. His physical abuse of her consisted of frequent assaults that included slapping, punching and kicking her, striking her with various objects, and throwing glasses, beer bottles and other objects at her. The defendant described other specific incidents of abuse, such as her husband putting her cigarettes out on her, throwing hot coffee on her, breaking glass against her face and crushing food on her face. . . .

. . . Her evidence tended to show that her husband did not work and forced her to make money by prostitution, and that he made humor of that fact to family and friends. He would beat her if she resisted going out to prostitute herself or if he was unsatisfied with the amounts of money she made. He routinely called the defendant "dog," "bitch" and "whore," and on a few occasions made her eat pet food out of the pets' bowls and bark like a dog. He often made her sleep on the floor. At times, he deprived her of food and refused to let her get food for the family. During those years of abuse, the defendant's husband threatened numerous times to kill her and to maim her in various ways.

The defendant said her husband's abuse occurred only when he was intoxicated, but that he would not give up drinking. She said she and her husband "got along very well when he was sober," and that he was "a good guy"

when he was not drunk. She had accompanied her husband to the local mental health center for sporadic counseling sessions for his problem, but he continued to drink.

In the early morning hours on the day before his death, the defendant's husband, who was intoxicated, went to a rest area off I-85 near Kings Mountain where the defendant was engaging in prostitution and assaulted her. While driving home, he was stopped by a patrolman and jailed on a charge of driving while impaired. After the defendant's mother got him out of jail at the defendant's request later that morning, he resumed his drinking and abuse of the defendant.

The defendant's evidence also tended to show that her husband seemed angrier than ever after he was released from jail and that his abuse of the defendant was more frequent. That evening, sheriff's deputies were called to the Norman residence, and the defendant complained that her husband had been beating her all day and she could not take it anymore. The defendant was advised to file a complaint, but she said she was afraid her husband would kill her if she had him arrested. The deputies told her they needed a warrant before they could arrest her husband, and they left the scene.

The deputies were called back less than an hour later after the defendant had taken a bottle of pills. The defendant's husband cursed her and called her names as she was attended by paramedics, and he told them to let her die. A sheriff's deputy finally chased him back into his house as the defendant was put into an ambulance. The defendant's stomach was pumped at the local hospital, and she was sent home with her mother.

While in the hospital, the defendant was visited by a therapist with whom she discussed filing charges against her husband and having him committed for treatment. Before the therapist left, the defendant agreed to go to the mental health center the next day to discuss those possibilities. The therapist testified at trial that the defendant seemed depressed in the hospital, and that she expressed considerable anger toward her husband. He testified that the defendant threatened a number of times that night to kill her husband and that she said she should kill him "because of the things he had done to her."

The next day, the day she shot her husband, the defendant went to the mental health center to talk about charges and possible commitment, and she confronted her husband with that possibility. She testified that she told her husband later that day: "J.T., straighten up. Quit drinking. I'm going to have you committed to help you." She said her husband then told her he would "see them coming" and would cut her throat before they got to him.

The defendant also went to the social services office that day to seek welfare benefits, but her husband followed her there, interrupted her interview and made her go home with him. He continued his abuse of her, threatening to kill and to maim her, slapping her, kicking her, and throwing objects at her. At one point, he took her cigarette and put it out on her, causing a small burn on her upper torso. He would not let her eat or bring food into the house for their children.

That evening, the defendant and her husband went into their bedroom to lie down, and he called her a "dog" and made her lie on the floor when he lay down on the bed. Their daughter brought in her baby to leave with the defendant, and the defendant's husband agreed to let her baby-sit. After the defendant's husband fell asleep, the baby started crying and the defendant took it to her mother's house so it would not wake up her husband. She returned shortly with the pistol and killed her husband.

The defendant testified at trial that she was too afraid of her husband to press charges against him or to leave him. She said that she had temporarily left their home on several previous occasions, but he had always found her, brought her home and beaten her. Asked why she killed her husband, the defendant replied: "Because I was scared of him and I knowed when he woke up, it was going to be the same thing, and I was scared when he took me to the truck stop that night it was going to be worse than he had ever been. I just couldn't take it no more. There ain't no way, even if it means going to prison. It's better than living in that. That's worse hell than anything."

The defendant and other witnesses testified that for years her husband had frequently threatened to kill her and to maim her. When asked if she believed those threats, the defendant replied: "Yes. I believed him; he would, he would kill me if he got a chance. If he thought he wouldn't a had to went to jail, he would a done it."

Two expert witnesses in forensic psychology and psychiatry who examined the defendant after the shooting, Dr. William Tyson and Dr. Robert Rollins, testified that the defendant fit the profile of battered wife syndrome. This condition, they testified, is characterized by such abuse and degradation that the battered wife comes to believe she is unable to help herself and cannot expect help from anyone else. She believes that she cannot escape the complete control of her husband and that he is invulnerable to law enforcement and other sources of help.

Dr. Tyson, a psychologist, was asked his opinion as to whether, on 12 June 1985, "it appeared reasonably necessary for Judy Norman to shoot J. T. Norman?" He replied: "I believe that . . . Mrs. Norman believed herself to be doomed . . . to a life of the worst kind of torture and abuse, degradation that she had experienced over the years in a progressive way; that it would only get worse, and that death was inevitable. . . ." Dr. Tyson later added: "I think Judy Norman felt that she had no choice, both in the protection of herself and her family, but to engage, exhibit deadly force against Mr. Norman, and that in so doing, she was sacrificing herself, both for herself and for her family."

Dr. Rollins, who was the defendant's attending physician at Dorothea Dix Hospital when she was sent there for evaluation, testified that in his opinion the defendant was a typical abused spouse and that "[s]he saw herself as powerless to deal with the situation, that there was no alternative, no way she could escape it." Dr. Rollins was asked his opinion as to whether "on June 12th, 1985, it appeared reasonably necessary that Judy Norman would take the life of J. T. Norman?" Dr. Rollins replied that in his opinion, "that course of action did appear necessary to Mrs. Norman.". . .

Based on the evidence that the defendant exhibited battered wife syndrome, that she believed she could not escape her husband nor expect help from others, that her husband had threatened her, and that her husband's abuse of her had worsened in the two days preceding his death, the Court of Appeals concluded that a jury reasonably could have found that her killing of her husband was justified as an act of perfect self-defense. The Court of Appeals reasoned that the nature of battered wife syndrome is such that a jury could not be precluded from finding the defendant killed her husband lawfully in perfect self-defense, even though he was asleep when she killed him. We disagree.

The right to kill in self-defense is based on the necessity, real or reasonably apparent, of killing an unlawful aggressor to save oneself from imminent death or great bodily harm at his hands. . . .

In North Carolina, a defendant is entitled to have the jury consider acquittal by reason of perfect self-defense when the evidence, viewed in the light most favorable to the defendant, tends to show that at the time of the killing it appeared to the defendant and she believed it to be necessary to kill the decedent to save herself from imminent death or great bodily harm. That belief must be reasonable, however, in that the circumstances as they appeared to the defendant would create such a belief in the mind of a person of ordinary firmness. . . .

. . . Only if defendants are required to show that they killed due to a reasonable belief that death or great bodily harm was imminent can the justification for homicide remain clearly and firmly rooted in necessity. The imminence requirement ensures that deadly force will be used only where it is necessary as a last resort in the exercise of the inherent right of self-preservation. It also ensures that before a homicide is justified and, as a result, not a legal wrong, it will be reliably determined that the defendant reasonably believed that absent the use of deadly force, not only would an unlawful attack have occurred, but also that the attack would have caused death or great bodily harm. The law does not sanction the use of deadly force to repel simple assaults. . . .

The evidence in this case did not tend to show that the defendant reasonably believed that she was confronted by a threat of imminent death or great bodily harm. The evidence tended to show that no harm was "imminent" or about to happen to the defendant when she shot her husband. The uncontroverted evidence was that her husband had been asleep for some time when she walked to her mother's house, returned with the pistol, fixed the pistol after it jammed and then shot her husband three times in the back of the head. The defendant was not faced with an instantaneous choice between killing her husband or being killed or seriously injured. Instead, all of the evidence tended to show that the defendant had ample time and opportunity to resort to other means of preventing further abuse by her husband. There was no action underway by the decedent from which the jury could have found that the defendant had reasonable grounds to believe either that a felonious assault was imminent or that it might result in her death or great bodily injury. Additionally, no such action by the decedent had been underway immediately prior to his falling asleep. . . .

The defendant testified that, "I knowed when he woke up, it was going to be the same thing, and I was scared when he took me to the truck stop that night it was going to be worse than he had ever been." She also testified, when asked if she believed her husband's threats: "Yes. . . . [H]e would kill me if he got a chance. If he thought he wouldn't a had to went to jail, he would a done it." Testimony about such indefinite fears concerning what her sleeping husband might do at some time in the future did not tend to establish a fear—reasonable or otherwise—of imminent death or great bodily harm at the time of the killing.

We are not persuaded by the reasoning of our Court of Appeals in this case that when there is evidence of battered wife syndrome, neither an actual attack nor threat of attack by the husband at the moment the wife uses deadly force is required to justify the wife's killing of him in perfect self-defense. The Court of Appeals concluded that to impose such requirements would ignore the "learned helplessness," meekness and other realities of battered wife syndrome and would effectively preclude such women from exercising their right of self-defense. . . .

. . . [S]tretching the law of self-defense to fit the facts of this case would require changing the "imminent death or great bodily harm" requirement to something substantially more indefinite than previously required and would weaken our assurances that justification for the taking of human life remains firmly rooted in real or apparent necessity. That result in principle could not be limited to a few cases decided on evidence as poignant as this. The relaxed requirements for perfect self-defense proposed by our Court of Appeals would tend to categorically legalize the opportune killing of abusive husbands by their wives solely on the basis of the wives' testimony concerning their subjective speculation as to the probability of future felonious assaults by their husbands.

Homicidal self-help would then become a lawful solution, and perhaps the easiest and most effective solution, to this problem. . . .

For the foregoing reasons, we conclude that the defendant's conviction for voluntary manslaughter and the trial court's judgment sentencing her to a six-year term of imprisonment were without error. Therefore, we must reverse the decision of the Court of Appeals which awarded the defendant a new trial.

Reversed.

STUDY QUESTIONS

1. What must be shown, under North Carolina law, to establish a "perfect self-defense"?
2. In what way did the court say the case presented by Norman fell short? Do you agree?

As noted by the North Carolina court, jurisdictions are split on whether they will accept the battered woman's syndrome as a defense to killing. Battered women's advocates also have mixed feelings about the defense. Some see it as an effective way to get acquittals by helping a jury to see the cumulative impact of the battering that a woman is forced to undergo. Others are concerned that the defense reinforces stereotypes by focusing once again on women's psychological problems rather than the economic and social realities they face.

> [T]he initial focus of battered woman's syndrome was a psychological analysis of battered women's victimization, their sense of paralysis or "learned helplessness." Although the term is purely descriptive, its psychological content and the language and import of the term carry a different message. Regardless of its more complex meaning, the term "battered woman's syndrome" has been heard to communicate an implicit but powerful view that battered women are all the same, that they are suffering from a pyschological disability and that this disability prevents them from acting "normally."
>
> *Elizabeth Schneider. "Describing and Changing: Women's Self-Defense Work and the Problem of Expert Testimony on Battering." 9* Women's Rights Law Reporter *195, 207 (1986).*

Divorce Today

As we have seen, courts have historically been unwilling to enforce agreements between marital partners or to otherwise interfere in ongoing marriages. Nevertheless, in setting and applying the rules governing divorce, courts have made clear their expectations of the two partners during marriage. The rules governing divorce have changed in recent years—generally as a result of legislative action. The next selection describes these changes and helps us understand their impact both before and after the divorce.

Beyond No-Fault

Herma Hill Kay.
Divorce Reform at the Crossroads,
edited by Stephen D. Sugarman and
Herma Hill Kay. New Haven: Yale
University Press, 1990. Pp. 6–11.

During the past twenty years, the United States has experienced a period of rapid change in the laws governing divorce. Touched off in 1969 by California's adoption of the nation's first divorce code that dispensed entirely with traditional fault-based divorce grounds and completed in 1985 when South Dakota added a no-fault provision to its list of fault-based grounds, the concept that marriage failure is itself an adequate reason for marital dissolution has been accepted by every state. Viewed from a broader historical perspective, however, the shift from fault to no-fault as a statutory basis for divorce did not begin in 1969, nor was it fully completed in 1985. The history of divorce in Anglo-American law shows a movement from the total unavailability of permanent divorce under the jurisdiction of the ecclesiastical courts in England prior to the reign of King Henry VIII, through a limited traffic in parliamentary divorces during the latter part of the seventeenth and eighteenth centuries, to the conferral of divorce jurisdiction upon the civil courts in 1857 in England and even earlier in some American states. From this perspective, the recognition of divorce for marital fault was itself a liberalizing repudiation of the earlier doctrine that marriage was indissoluble. By the early twentieth century, all American states (except South Carolina, which did not permit permanent divorce until 1948) had enacted laws authorizing courts to dissolve marriages for cause. The most widely recognized statutory grounds were adultery, cruelty, and desertion. A few states unwittingly anticipated the subsequent no-fault ground of marriage breakdown by granting courts discretion to terminate a marriage for a cause deemed "sufficient," so long as the judge was "satisfied" that the parties could "no longer

live together," while others recognized grounds for divorce that did not involve fault, such as incurable insanity or voluntary separation for a specified period of time. Max Rheinstein characterized these early no-fault grounds as providing an "opening wedge" for the more modern recognition that marriage breakdown is itself a sufficient basis for dissolution.

Formidable religious, social, political, and economic barriers had to be overcome before these modest wedges successfully pried open the door that led to no-fault divorce. Between 1966 and 1970, however, four influential groups concluded, after respectively studying the contemporary divorce laws in England, California, and the United States, that divorce based on fault no longer represented wise social or legal policy. . . . Despite the respect these reports commanded, however, none of them enjoyed full legislative acceptance. Opposition to such a complete shift in the basis for divorce led in each case to uneasy compromise. The final product to emerge from each of these studies— the English Divorce Reform Act 1969, the California Family Law Act of 1969, and the 1973 version of the Uniform Marriage and Divorce Act (UMDA)—all differed from the original proposals, chiefly by retaining marital fault as a factor that could be considered in determining whether the marriage had broken down. The controversy and compromise are reflected in the reception of the recommendations for change in the grounds for divorce among the American states. Although the no-fault principle is firmly established in all states as a statutory basis for divorce, its formulation varies across the states, and it forms the exclusive basis for divorce only in a minority of states. Nevertheless, the impasse that had for so many years prevented meaningful reform of the grounds for divorce in both countries had been broken, and the new approach continues to spread among the American states.

. . . The no-fault principle is most intuitively appealing when it is invoked to permit the legal termination of a marriage that both spouses agree has ended in fact. In that context, the recognition of marriage breakdown is tantamount to legalization of divorce by mutual consent, and the elimination of fault as a basis for resolving the related issues of property, support, and child custody appears appropriate. Family dissolution has been analogized in such cases to the winding up of a partnership; much of the emotional work of terminating the marriage relationship may have been accomplished before the case goes to court.

As Lawrence Friedman has pointed out, however, "No-fault goes beyond consensual divorce. Either partner can end a marriage simply by asserting that the marriage has broken down." Divorce by unilateral fiat is closer to desertion than to mutual separation. Unlike divorce based on mutual consent, unilateral divorce is apt to produce unexpected emotional stress and financial dislocation that exacerbates the upheaval accompanying family breakdown. The fault doctrine may have served to lend emotional vindication to the rejected spouse, as well as a measure of financial protection and status as the preferred custodian of children. If so, greater justification may be required in those cases for eliminating that doctrine from the related core areas of support, property distribution, and child custody.

Adequate justification may be found in the ideal of marriage as a relationship characterized by the continuing existence of a mutual loving commitment between the spouses. It follows that once the marriage is no longer viable, neither its legal existence nor its related legal incidents should become weapons used to obtain revenge for the breakdown or to extort a favorable settlement. But if fault is withdrawn, the party formerly able to invoke that doctrine may be left in a vulnerable position both when negotiating a dissolution agreement and when litigating the matter in court. This vulnerability may be lessened or avoided if the elimination of fault is accompanied by a clear specification of appropriate substantive standards capable of ensuring fair treatment to both parties to replace the punitive philosophy inherent in the former approach. . . .

Instead, as Mary Ann Glendon has pointed out, the prevailing approach in the United States has been to rely on judicial discretion to decide contested cases under general standards without requiring any meticulous judicial scrutiny of the private agreements negotiated by the parties in noncontested cases. And as Lenore Weitzman has demonstrated in her award-winning study of prac-

tice under the California no-fault law, many judges exercised their discretion in ways that failed to protect the vulnerable party, thus impoverishing many dependent women and the children in their custody. Drawing on Weitzman's study and those of others, Glendon concludes that "more than any other country among those examined here, the United States has accepted the idea of no-fault, no-responsibility divorce.". . .

I have suggested elsewhere that, although the law should not penalize women at divorce whose earlier marital choices left them financially dependent upon their husbands, neither should we perpetuate a legal framework for marriage and divorce that encourages couples to choose gender roles that are financially disabling for women in the event of divorce. Yet, even if we imagine that many or most future marital unions will be composed of economically self-sufficient individuals, the presence of children normally entails periods of dependency for caretaking parents that may impair their financial security if divorce ensues. It seems necessary, therefore, that divorce law must provide what Jeremy Waldron has termed the "fallback" rights that marital partners can rely on for protection if their mutual affection fades.

The fall-back rights we create during this next phase of contemporary divorce reform should be designed for a society in which the context of family life is changing rapidly. Today, it is normal for family life to occur outside of marriage, and marriage itself may be expected to continue its present trend toward norms of greater equality between husband and wife. Some observers expect that marriage may eventually be redefined to become available to homosexual as well as heterosexual couples. We need to create a legal framework sufficiently flexible to permit the flourishing of a human intimacy that is the basis of loving commitment in all its variety and that, in turn, fosters the nurturance and guidance of children. . . .

STUDY QUESTIONS

1. How did the modern concept of no-fault divorce come about? Does the no-fault principle change the meaning of marriage? How so?
2. As compared to prior law, what problems does the no-fault approach make for divorcing partners?

The divorce reform Kay describes reflects a view that ideally, marriage should continue only so long as the partners have a loving commitment to each other and that the partners should not be blamed for their failure to feel this commitment. As she points out, however, this view and the laws that embody it have consequences for the formerly "innocent" party. The consequences—both in terms of child custody and financial outcomes—are discussed below.

II. CARE OF CHILDREN

Just as courts are historically unwilling to intervene in ongoing marriages to enforce spousal obligations or to attempt to control violence between spouses, they are reluctant to intervene in ongoing families to designate caretakers for children. Nevertheless, the law reflects and reinforces societal views regarding gender-appropriate behavior in caring for children in the same way it reinforces societal views of the marital relation. Views about the proper allocation of child care duties and the proper behavior for caretakers are often expressed when the law resolves custody conflicts between former spouses and between the state or third parties, and in government programs affecting the family.

Custody Disputes Between Parents

The rules for awarding custody have evolved from sex-based doctrines favoring fathers to sex-based doctrines favoring mothers to nominally sex-neutral standards. In considering these more modern doctrines, think about whether they in fact operate in a neutral way. Are they likely to be applied in a biased fashion? Are they based on traditional breadwinner and caretaker roles? Do their delineations of proper caretaker behavior reflect sex stereotypes? Think finally about whether the Seneca Falls complaint—that divorce laws pertaining to guardianship of children are "wholly regardless of the happiness of women"—is still valid.

The Tender Years Presumption. In the case that follows, the Alabama Supreme Court considered the mother-oriented tender years presumption that began to replace the rigid father-oriented custody rule in the mid-nineteenth century. That presumption required either that the mother be given custody of young children unless she was found unfit or that she be given a preference where all other factors were equal. By the mid-twentieth century, that presumption was found throughout the country.

Devine v. Devine

Supreme Court of Alabama, 1981.
398 So.2d 686.

MADDOX, Justice.

We granted certiorari to review the question of whether the "tender years presumption," as applied in child custody proceedings, violates the Fourteenth Amendment to the United States Constitution. In the present case, the Court of Civil Appeals affirmed the trial court's usage of that presumption in awarding custody of the parties' two minor children to the respondent, Alice Beth Clark Devine. For the reasons hereinafter set forth, we reverse and remand. . . .

At common law, it was the father rather than the mother who held a virtual absolute right to the custody of their minor children. This rule of law was fostered, in part, by feudalistic notions concerning the "natural" responsibilities of the husband at common law. The husband was considered the head or master of his family, and, as such, responsible for the care, maintenance, education and religious training of his children. By virtue of these responsibilities, the husband was given a corresponding entitlement to the benefits of his children, i.e., their services and association. It is interesting to note that in many instances these rights and privileges were considered dependent upon the recognized laws of nature and in accordance with the *presumption* that the father could best provide for the necessities of his children. . . .

By contrast, the wife was without any rights to the care and custody of her minor children. By marriage, husband and wife became one person with the legal identity of the woman being totally merged with that of her husband. As a result, her rights were often subordinated to those of her husband and she was laden with numerous marital disabilities. As far as any custodial rights were concerned, Blackstone stated the law to be that the mother was "entitled to no power [over her children], but only to reverence and respect." 1 W. Blackstone, *Commentaries on the Law of England* 453 (Tucker ed.1803).

By the middle of the 19th century, the courts of England began to question and qualify the paternal preference rule. This was due, in part, to the "hardships, not to say cruelty, inflicted upon unoffending mothers by a state of law which took little account of their claims or feelings." W. Forsyth, *A Treatise on the Law Relating to the Custody of Infants in Cases of Difference Between Parents or Guardians* 66 (1850). Courts reacted by taking a more moderate stance concerning child custody, a stance which conditioned a father's absolute custodial rights upon his fitness as a parent. Ultimately, by a series of statutes culminating with Justice Talfourd's Act, 2 and 3 Vict. c. 54 (1839), Parliament affirmatively extended the rights of mothers, especially as concerned the custody of young children. Justice Talfourd's Act expressly provided that the chancery courts, in cases of divorce and separation, could award the cus-

tody of minor children to the mother *if the children were less than seven years old.* This statute marks the origin of the tender years presumption in England.

In the United States the origin of the tender years presumption is attributed to the 1830 Maryland decision of *Helms v. Franciscus.* In *Helms,* the court, while recognizing the general rights of the father, stated that it would violate the laws of nature to "snatch" an infant from the care of its mother:

> The father is the rightful and legal guardian of all his infant children; and in general, no court can take from him the custody and control of them, thrown upon him by the law, not for his gratification, but on account of his duties, and place them against his will in the hands even of his wife. . . . Yet even a court of common law will not go so far as to hold nature in contempt, and snatch helpless, puling infancy from the bosom of an affectionate mother, and place it in the coarse hands of the father. The mother is the softest and safest nurse of infancy, and with her it will be left in opposition to this general right of the father.

Thus began a "process of evolution, perhaps reflecting a change in social attitudes, [whereby] the mother came to be the preferred custodian of young children and daughters. . . ." Foster, *Life with Father, 1978,* 11 Fam.L.Q. 327 (1978).

In Alabama, the first noticeable discussion of the tender years presumption appears in the case of *Cornelius v. Cornelius* [in 1858]. In that case the court awarded custody of a young male child to the mother because the father was found to be guilty of certain "fixed intemperate habits"; however, the court qualified its decision by stating that the father could later recover the custody of his child by presenting credible evidence that he had reformed. . . .

The attitude expressed in *Cornelius* was not readily accepted. Alabama courts continued to award custody to the father, even in cases involving very young children. . . .

As late as 1946, this Court continued to recognize the paternal preference rule; however, by that time the rule was no longer a formidable factor in resolving child custody disputes. The influence of the paternal preference rule had been gradually replaced by a growing adherence to the tender years presumption.

At the present time, the tender years presumption is recognized in Alabama as a rebuttable factual presumption based upon the inherent suitability of the mother to care for and nurture young children. All things being equal, the mother is presumed to be best fitted to guide and care for children of tender years. To rebut this presumption the father must present clear and convincing evidence of the mother's positive unfitness. Thus, the tender years presumption affects the resolution of child custody disputes on both a substantive and procedural level. Substantively, it requires the court to award custody of young children to the mother when the parties, as in the present case, are equally fit parents. Procedurally, it imposes an evidentiary burden on the father to prove the positive unfitness of the mother.

In recent years, the tender years doctrine has been severely criticized by legal commentators as an outmoded means of resolving child custody disputes. Several state courts have chosen to abandon or abolish the doctrine, noting that the presumption "facilitates error in an arena in which there is little room for error." . . .

The appellate courts of this state have held that the tender years presumption is "not a classification based upon gender, but merely a factual presumption based upon the historic role of the mother." These statements indicate that the courts in the forties had not developed the sensitivity to gender-based classifications which the courts by the seventies had developed. . . .

Having reviewed the historical development of the presumption as well as its modern status, and having examined the presumption in view of the holdings in *Reed, Frontiero, Orr* and *Caban,* we conclude that the tender years presumption represents an unconstitutional gender-based classification which discriminates between fathers and mothers in child custody proceedings solely on the basis of sex. Like the statutory presumption in *Reed,* the tender years doctrine creates a presumption of fitness and suitability of one parent without any consideration of the actual capabilities of the parties. The tender years presumption, like the statutory schemes in *Frontiero* and *Orr,* imposes

legal burdens upon individuals according to the "immutable characteristic" of sex. By requiring fathers to carry the difficult burden of affirmatively proving the unfitness of the mother, the presumption may have the effect of depriving some loving fathers of the custody of their children, while enabling some alienated mothers to arbitrarily obtain temporary custody. *Cf., Caban.* Even so, a gender-based classification, although suspect, may be justified if it is substantially related to a significant state interest. *See, Reed, Frontiero* and *Caban,* supra.

Admittedly, the State has a significant interest in overseeing the care and custody of infants. In fulfilling this responsibility in child custody proceedings, the courts of this state, in custody determinations, have applied the "best interests of the child" rule. We are convinced that the tender years presumption rejects the fundamental proposition asserted in *Caban* that "maternal and paternal roles are not invariably different in importance." Even if mothers as a class were closer than fathers to young children, this presumption concerning parent-child relations becomes less acceptable as a basis for judicial distinctions as the age of the child increases. Courts have come to rely upon the presumption as a substitute for a searching factual analysis of the relative parental capabilities of the parties, and the psychological and physical necessities of the children. . . .

The trial court's custody decree conclusively shows that the tender years presumption was a significant factor underlying the court's decision. The cause is due to be remanded to the trial court with directions that the court consider the individual facts of the case. The sex and age of the children are indeed very important considerations; however, the court must go beyond these to consider the characteristics and needs of each child, including their emotional, social, moral, material and educational needs; the respective home environments offered by the parties; the characteristics of those seeking custody, including age, character, stability, mental and physical health; the capacity and interest of each parent to provide for the emotional, social, moral, material and educational needs of the children; the interpersonal relationship between each child and each parent;

the interpersonal relationship between the children; the effect on the child of disrupting or continuing an existing custodial status; the preference of each child, if the child is of sufficient age and maturity; the report and recommendation of any expert witnesses or other independent investigator; available alternatives; and any other relevant matter the evidence may disclose.

Reversed and remanded with directions.

STUDY QUESTIONS

1. At common law, which parent had the "virtually absolute" right to custody of the children of a marriage? What was the rationale for this doctrine?

2. What does the tender years doctrine provide? Does it always result in the mother being awarded custody? What do you suppose accounts for the change in doctrine? Do you think that there is any truth to the notion that the doctrine changed to give women an edge in custody cases only after children ceased making an economic contribution to the household and became an economic liability instead?

3. Who benefits from the tender years presumption? Who is harmed by it? Do you think the presumption has any effect on a woman who is considering whether to relinquish custody of her children to their father? Does it affect a man considering relinquishing custody of his children to their mother? Do you think it has any effect on how women's and men's roles are perceived generally?

Despite its clear gender classification, not all courts considering the issue in recent years have agreed with the Alabama court that the tender years presumption violates equal protection guarantees. For example, in 1978, the Oklahoma Supreme Court applied the *Craig v. Boren* test and rejected a father's equal protection challenge on the ground that

> [C]ultural, psychological and emotional characteristics that are gender related make this custodial preference one of "those instances where the sex-centered generalization actually [comports] to fact."
>
> Gordon v. Gordon, *577 P.2d 1271, 1277 (Okla. 1978).*

Most states have, however, abandoned the tender years presumption in favor of the best interests of the child standard. By 1991, all the states had rejected the presumption as an automatic rule for awarding custody, and only three—Utah, Oklahoma, and South Dakota—have retained it as the tie-breaker when the parents are otherwise equally fit.

The Best Interests Test and the Primary Caretaker Standard. There is considerable controversy today as to the benefits of the best interests standard as a replacement for the tender years presumption. On the one hand, from a woman's perspective, it is very important for legal standards to make clear that men as well as women can take good care of children. On the other hand, the vague, open-ended best interests test often operates to women's detriment, given the realities of women's circumstances and the persistence of traditional views about what constitutes good parenting. Judges and other court personnel charged with evaluating parents competing for custody may be swayed by the economic advantages, including high quality child care, that better-paid fathers can offer their children. They may also look askance at women—but not men—who work outside the home and give the edge to remarried fathers whose new wives will serve as at-home mothers.

The best interests standard also leaves room for a double standard regarding sexual conduct to operate in custody matters. Traditionally, women who had extramarital relations were considered unfit mothers and ineligible for custody despite the tender years presumption. Fathers, however, were rarely disqualified for similar behavior. The potential for gender-based expectations regarding proper sexual behavior to influence decision making under the best interests standard is even greater since the doctrine affords judges great discretion in making custody awards. In recent years, however, courts have shown some unwillingness to distinguish between morality and good parenting. Thus, judges will indicate at times that they disapprove of a woman's sexual behavior but that behavior does not seem to have harmed her relationship with her children. Nevertheless, as a recent case shows, views of proper sexual conduct continue to play a role in custody decisions.

In *Jarrett v. Jarrett,* 400 N.E.2d 421, *cert. denied,* 449 U.S. 927 (1980), a mother was initially awarded custody of her children under the best interests test but lost it when it was learned that she was living with a man to whom she was not married. The Illinois Supreme Court's ruling was based on its finding that her conduct endangered the children's moral well-being. The court found the state's moral standards expressed in the criminal code provision outlawing open and notorious cohabitation and in case law declining to enforce contracts between cohabitants. The court also questioned the impact of the relationship on the children's emotional health in view of the possibility that they would be subjected to taunts and jibes. The court gave short shrift to Jacqueline Jarrett's argument that, in 1978, 1.1 million households were composed of unmarried heterosexual couples. It also ignored her explanations that she thought it was too soon after her divorce to get married again; that she didn't think a marriage license made a relationship; and that the divorce decree required her to sell the house within six months of remarriage.

Neither the Illinois Supreme Court nor the U.S. Supreme Court, which denied *certiorari,* explicitly addressed the potential for sex bias in decisions of this sort. Historically, however, mothers have been far more likely than fathers to be found unfit as parents for their extramarital sexual activities, and it is worth asking whether the role expectations that account for that disparity would have a similar impact today. Would a custodial father be as likely to lose custody of his children simply because he is living with a woman who is not his wife?

There is little information on the results of custody battles using the best interests standard. One frequently cited statistic indicates that 90 percent of children of divorced parents are in their mother's custody. In most instances, however, fathers do not seek custody. Studies limited to particular localities in the 1970s suggest that fathers who do seek custody in court are able to prevail about half the time. Even when fathers might not succeed in winning custody, announcing their intention to seek it may lead women to give up needed financial support in divorce negotiations and to agree to settlements under which they receive less financial support than they might have received at trial to ensure they retain custody. In this way, they avoid the possibility of losing custody at a trial conducted under a standard as vague as the best interests test.

Seeking to meet this concern, some people favor the adoption of the primary caretaker standard, a sex-neutral test that recognizes the role most women have played in raising their children. A standard of this sort was enunciated by the West Virginia Supreme Court in *Garska v. McCoy,* 278 S.E.2d 357, a 1981 decision that interpreted the state's statute requiring courts to use the best interests test in custody disputes.

In finding that the best interests standard is met by awarding custody to the parent who has been the child's primary caretaker, the West Virginia court was in large part motivated by the conviction that courts are poorly equipped to make precise judgments about the parents' relative fitness. The court was also concerned about the role uncertainty plays in settling custody disputes short of trial. The court believed an undefined best interests standard would lead women to accept inadequate levels of child support to avoid a custody fight they could not afford. In substituting the primary caretaker standard for the more open-ended best interests test, the court sought to prevent the issue of custody from being used in a coercive way. To identify the primary caretaker, the court advised judges to determine which parent had taken primary responsibility for the care and nurturing of the children.

Interestingly, the West Virginia court did not attempt to justify the primary caretaker standard in terms of the child's psychological well-being. Other advocates of the primary caretaker standard often cite the psychological parenting theory put forward by Joseph Goldstein, Anna Freud, and Albert Solnit in their 1973 book, *Beyond the Best Interests of the Child* (New York: Free Press). They argue that children's psychological well-being depends on their maintaining bonds with their psychological parent, that is, their primary caretaker and nurturer. This theory, however, may pose difficulties for nontraditional women insofar as women who work or are otherwise active outside the home may lose their status as the preeminent psychological parent. The theory poses particularly difficult problems for women whose economic or family circumstances require them to seek state-run foster care services. If it is determined that the children have formed bonds with new caretakers that must be maintained to prevent their psychological harm, the state may seek to terminate parental rights.

The primary caretaker standard is controversial for other reasons, too. Although it is sex-neutral in the sense that fathers, as well as mothers, may be primary caretakers, the primary caretaker standard may reinforce the notion that there is *one* primary caretaker. As a result, it may be harder for women to relinquish any of their tasks and for men to become involved as an equal partner in caring for their children. Additionally, as a standard that looks to the past, it has a tendency to freeze the *status quo,* leaving parental roles where they were. As such, it may serve as a barrier to fathers who now wish to become involved with their children.

Joint Custody. Until recently, rules for deciding disputes have assumed that custody could be awarded to one parent only. More recently, courts have begun to consider shared or joint custody arrangements, which give both parents the opportunity to participate in raising their children. The term "joint custody" refers to joint legal custody, i.e., arrangements giving both parents equal legal rights to make important decisions affecting the child's life, and to joint physical custody, i.e., arrangements for parents alternately living with and taking physical care of that child.

The New Jersey Supreme Court considered when such arrangements are appropriate in the following case.

Beck v. Beck

Supreme Court of New Jersey, 1981.
432 A.2d 63.

CLIFFORD, J.

The parties to this matrimonial action have been granted joint legal and physical custody of their two adopted female children. Although neither party requested joint custody, the trial court nevertheless found such an arrangement to be in the best interests of the children. On appeal by defendant-wife, the Appellate Division found in her favor, reversing and remanding the joint custody decree with directions to award sole custody to her as the children's mother and liberal visitation rights to their father, and to make an appropriate upward adjustment of child support. . . .

The initial issue is whether courts are authorized to decree the joint custody of children. The pertinent statute . . . evinces a legislative intent to grant courts wide latitude to fashion creative remedies in matrimonial custody cases. . . .

Moreover, parents involved in custody controversies have by statute been granted both equal rights and equal responsibilities regarding the care, nurture, education and welfare of their children. Although not an explicit authorization of joint custody, this clearly related statute indicates a legislative preference for custody decrees that allow both parents full and genuine involvement in the lives of their children following a divorce. This approach is consonant with the common law policy that "in promoting the child's welfare, the court should strain every effort to attain for the child the affection of both parents rather than one.". . .

In recent years the concept of joint custody has become topical, due largely to the perceived inadequacies of sole custody awards and in recognition of the modern trend toward shared parenting in marriage. Sole custody tends both to isolate children from the noncustodial parent and to place heavy financial and emotional burdens on the sole caretaker, usually the mother, although awards of custody to the father, especially in households where both parents are employed outside the home, are more common now than in years past. Moreover, because of the absolute nature of sole custody determinations, in which one parent "wins" and the other "loses," the children are likely to become the subject of bitter custody contests and post-decree tension. The upshot is that the best interests of the child are disserved by many aspects of sole custody.

Joint custody attempts to solve some of the problems of sole custody by providing the child with access to both parents and granting parents equal rights and responsibilities regarding their children. Properly analyzed, joint custody is comprised of two elements legal custody and physical custody. Under a joint custody arrangement legal custody the legal authority and responsibility for making "major" decisions regarding the child's welfare is shared at all times by both parents. Physical custody, the logistical arrangement whereby the parents share the companionship of the child and are responsible for "minor" day-to-day decisions, may be alternated in accordance with the needs of the parties and the children.

At the root of the joint custody arrangement is the assumption that children in a unified family setting develop attachments to both parents and the severance of either of these attachments is contrary to the child's best interest. . . . Through its legal custody component joint custody seeks to maintain these attachments by permitting both parents to remain decision-makers in the lives of their children. Alternating physical custody enables the children to share with both parents the intimate day-to-day contact necessary to strengthen a true parent-child relationship.

Joint custody, however, is not without its critics. The objections most frequently voiced include contentions that such an arrangement creates instability for children, causes loyalty conflicts, makes maintaining parental authority difficult, and aggravates the already stressful divorce situation by requiring interaction between hostile ex-spouses. . . .

Because we are persuaded that joint custody is likely to foster the best interests of the child in the proper case, we endorse its use as an alternative to sole custody in matrimonial actions. We recognize, however, that such an arrangement will prove acceptable in only a limited class of cases, as set forth more particularly [later in] this opinion. But . . . despite our belief that joint custody will be the preferred disposition in some matrimonial actions, we decline to establish a presumption in its favor or in favor of any particular custody determination. Our concern is that a presumption of this sort might serve as a disincentive for the meticulous fact-finding required in custody cases.

[That] is particularly important in these cases because the very interplay of parents and children that gives joint custody its potential value also creates complications different from those found in sole custody arrangements. Some of those complications are dramatized by the instant case.

The parties were married in July 1963. Their two daughters, Lauren, now age twelve, and Kirsten, now age ten, were adopted in infancy. Plaintiff-husband is a successful commercial photographer. Defendant-wife works as a part-time student teacher supervisor at a local college. Since February 14, 1976, when Mr. Beck left the marital residence, the girls have resided with their mother subject to periodic visitation by their father.

In September 1977 plaintiff-husband filed a complaint for divorce based on eighteen months separation. He sought liberal visitation rights but not custody of the children. Defendant answered and counterclaimed for divorce on grounds of desertion. The initial proceeding was concerned solely with financial matters pertaining to alimony, child support and equitable distribution. The issue of custody appeared to be settled by the pleadings until April 12, 1979 when in the course of its decision the trial court decreed sua sponte that both legal and physical custody would be shared by the parties.

The court supported the decree with reference to the "uniqueness" of this case. It found the parties to be "sophisticated," with a generally "positive attitude between themselves with regard to the girls;" that plaintiff's income is sufficient to support two households; that the children's ages presented no obstacle; that the proximity of the residences would enable continuity of schooling despite changes in physical custody; that the prior visitation arrangement had been maintained "with no difficulty whatever" between the parties; and, finally, that because the girls were adopted, they needed "the benefit, contact, and security of both parents."

Shortly thereafter, defendant moved for an order amending the findings and judgment of the trial court on the issue of joint custody. Plaintiff opposed the motion and both parties filed lengthy certifications. After reviewing the certifications and hearing argument, the trial court ordered a plenary hearing on the issue of custody. At the hearing defendant testified and also produced a child psychiatrist to testify on her behalf. Plaintiff chose not to testify himself, although he had done so extensively during the first proceeding, but offered three experts in support of his lately-adopted position favoring joint custody: a school psychologist, a clinical psychologist, and a psychiatric social worker. Also, in the course of the hearing the court for the first time met privately with the girls. . . .

At the conclusion of the plenary hearing the trial court reiterated its prior findings and modified its original decision. Viewing the issue in terms of the importance of fatherhood in the lives of the two girls, it concluded that the lack of real contact with the father would have negative developmental effects, particularly because the girls are adopted. . . .

The trial court stressed that although defendant's care of the girls was more than adequate, she is limited by an inability to be both a mother and a father. It found Mrs. Beck to be a "sensible" person, but also somewhat bitter and "stiff lipped" and more partisan than plaintiff, whom he described as "a rather . . . relaxed type of man." Noting that Mrs. Beck "honestly objects to the plan because she contends she cannot cooperate with her former husband," the court concluded, based on the testimony of Dr. Greif, that an amicable relationship between the parties is "comparatively unimportant and not essential" as long as the parties "are looking out for the best interests of the children."

The Appellate Division reversed. . . .

The question of whether a trial court may make a sua sponte custody determination need not long detain us. The paramount consideration in child custody cases is to foster the best interests of the child. This standard has been described as one that protects the "safety, happiness, physical, mental and moral welfare of the child.". . . It would be incongruous and counterproductive to restrict application of this standard to the relief requested by the parties to a custody dispute. Accordingly, a sua sponte custody determination is properly within the discretion of the trial court provided it is supported by the record. . . .

The factors to be considered by a trial court contemplating an award of joint custody require some elaboration. As indicated heretofore, we perceive that the necessary elements will coalesce only infrequently.

First, . . . the court must determine whether the children have established such relationships with both parents that they would benefit from joint custody. For such bonds to exist the parents need not have been equally involved in the child rearing process. Rather, from the child's point of view it is necessary only that the child recognize both parents as sources of security and love and wish to continue both relationships.

Having established the joint custody arrangement's potential benefit to the children, the court must focus on the parents in order to determine whether they qualify for such an arrangement. . . . In addition [to being "fit" physically and psychologically], they must each be willing to accept custody, although their opposition to joint custody does not preclude the court from ordering that arrangement. Rather, even if neither party seeks joint custody, as long as both are willing to care for the children, joint custody is a possibility.

The most troublesome aspect of a joint custody decree is the additional requirement that the parent exhibit a potential for cooperation in matters of child rearing. This feature does not translate into a requirement that the parents have an amicable relationship. . . .

. . . [T]he judge need only determine if the parents can separate and put aside any conflicts between them to cooperate for the benefit of their child. The judge must look for the parents' ability to cooperate and if the potential exists, encourage its activation by instructing the parents on what is expected of them.

The necessity for at least minimal parental cooperation in a joint custody arrangement presents a thorny problem of judicial enforcement in a case such as the present one, wherein despite the trial court's determination that joint custody is in the best interests of the child, one parent (here, the mother) nevertheless contends that cooperation is impossible and refuses to abide by the decree. Traditional enforcement techniques are singularly inappropriate in a child custody proceeding for which the best interests of the child is our polestar. Despite the obvious unfairness of allowing an uncooperative

parent to flout a court decree, we are unwilling to sanction punishment of a recalcitrant parent if the welfare of the child will also suffer. However, when the actions of such a parent deprive the child of the kind of relationship with the other parent that is deemed to be in the child's best interests, removing the child from the custody of the uncooperative parent may well be appropriate as a remedy of last resort. . . .

In addition to the factors set forth above, the physical custody element of a joint custody award requires examination of practical considerations such as the financial status of the parents, the proximity of their respective homes, the demands of parental employment, and the age and number of the children. Joint physical custody necessarily places an additional financial burden on the family. Although exact duplication of facilities and furnishings is not necessary, the trial court should insure that the children can be adequately cared for in two homes. The geographical proximity of the two homes is an important factor to the extent that it impinges on school arrangements, the children's access to relatives and friends (including visitation by the noncustodial parent), and the ease of travel between the two homes. Parental employment is significant for its effect on a parent's ability properly to care for the children and maintain a relationship with them. The significance of the ages and number of the children is somewhat unclear at present, and will probably vary from case to case, requiring expert testimony as to their impact on the custody arrangement.

If joint custody is feasible except for one or more of these practical considerations, the court should consider awarding legal custody to both parents with physical custody to only one and liberal visitation rights to the other. Such an award will preserve the decision making role of both parents and should approximate, to the extent practicable, the shared companionship of the child and non-custodial parent that is provided in joint physical custody.

Finally, as in all custody determinations, the preference of the children of "sufficient age and capacity" must be accorded "due weight." N.J.S.A. 9:2–4. . . .

The judgment of the Appellate Division is reversed and the case remanded to the trial court [for a speedy but thorough determination of the current appropriateness of joint custody]. . . .

STUDY QUESTIONS

1. How do you think the joint custody order will work in this case? How will it affect the relations between all the parties?

2. What enforcement orders did the New Jersey Supreme Court envision? What do you think will be the effects of such orders? How will the parent most concerned about keeping custody be likely to respond to the other parent's misconduct?

3. What effect do you think the decision in this case will have on other divorcing couples and their negotiations over financial matters, child custody, and visitation?

Like other approaches to resolving custody disputes, joint custody is currently the subject of a great deal of controversy. Although there is general agreement that joint custody should be available as a legal option for parents who are able to cooperate, many question whether judges should have the power to impose such arrangements on parents who do not agree. In such cases, men may avoid some of their responsibilities for support without actually performing their share of parenting, and some women may be coerced into "agreeing" to joint custody for fear that their failure to agree will be held against them at a subsequent trial to determine sole custody. Presumptions in favor of joint custody also undercut the type of case-by-case determination that is necessary to identify cases truly suited to joint custody. Joint custody poses particular dangers to battered spouses and children since, by definition, they are designed to ensure continued contact with the batterer.

Few dispute the problems joint custody and "friendly parent" provisions pose for victims of abuse. Some do suggest, however, that women may benefit from having someone share the responsibility of child care. They also question the basis for some women's resistance to joint custody. They ask whether some women are simply too angry, too hurt, or too bound up in their roles as full-time mothers to let fathers share their parenting. They suggest that much is to be gained by encouraging male involvement. In their view, exploring joint custody arrangements should be encouraged. Differences regarding the value of joint custody legislation may reflect different perceptions regarding parental cooperation, the legal system's ability to identify appropriate candidates, the importance of promoting male participation in child rearing, and the necessity of preserving women's option to control their children's upbringing.

Empirical data on the impact of joint custody arrangements are just being gathered. Initial studies that primarily involved white families in which the parents developed their custody arrangements without judicial or other professional assistance and were highly motivated to make them succeed suggested that children's postdivorce adjustment may not differ by type of custody and that both joint legal and joint physical custody may offer advantages for parents and children. Among the advantages one study reported are the freedom mothers experience to pursue their work and adult social life, the close relationship fathers are able to maintain with their children, and the clear message to children that they are loved and wanted by both parents. The children studied seemed able to relate well to two parents who did not relate positively to one another, despite the contrary prediction of Goldstein, Freud, and Solnit. Most of these children were able to deal well with switching homes, though the process made a sizable number insecure. Moreover, as the children grew older, some found it more convenient to live in one home.

However, later studies have highlighted some problems. To ensure that schooling is not interrupted, joint physical custody generally necessitates two adequate sleeping places that are near one another. However, not all families who have joint custody arrangements appear to have the resources necessary to maintain adequate sleeping spaces. See, e.g., Janet Johnston, Marsha Kline, and Jerome T. Schann, "Ongoing Postdivorce Conflicts and Their Effects on Children of Joint Custody and Frequent Access," 59 *American Journal of Orthopsychiatry* 576 (1989). Studies also indicate that to succeed, joint custody requires a high level of cooperation. When children move frequently between parental homes (or have extensive visitation), they may well be clinically disturbed when conflict is high. *Id.* Further, the imposition of joint custody may lead to parental resentment and thus poor outcomes for the children. See, e.g., Rosemary McKinnon and Judith Wallerstein, "Joint Custody and the Preschool Child," 4 *Behavioral Sciences and the Law* 169 (1986); J. Rainer Twilford, "Joint Custody: A Blind Leap of Faith," 4 *Behavioral Sciences and the Law* 157 (1986). However, when parents are able to agree without pressure, joint custody does appear to work for all concerned. *Id.*

Just as some of today's feminists have come to criticize sex-neutral approaches in other areas, so too some feminists working on custody matters have questioned the best interests and primary caretaker standards, as well as joint custody presumptions. Mary Becker, for example, points out that the best interests test is both indeterminate and open to bias against women whose resources are often limited and whose behavior may not conform to judges' expectations of women. Likewise, she argues that joint custody determinations, whether imposed or accepted as a result of external pressure, are harmful to mothers and children.

Though initially hopeful that the primary caretaker standard would narrow property, credit past work, and predict future caretaking ability without at the same time reinforcing stereotypes, Becker ultimately rejected the approach. She was concerned that it does not recognize the special contribution women make through their reproductive labor and emotional caretaking. She also finds that, as a practical matter, it has proven insufficient to overcome pro-male bias at the trial level. Becker describes her alternative proposal in the following excerpt.

Maternal Feelings, Myth, Taboo, and Child Custody

Mary Becker.
1 *Southern California Review of Law and Women Studies*
133, 203–215 (1992).

I propose that we consider a maternal deference standard. When the parents cannot agree on a custody outcome, the judge should defer to the mother's decision on custody provided that she is fit, using the "fitness" standard applicable when the state is arguing for temporary or permanent separation of parents and children in intact families. This standard would operate much like the traditional maternal preference for children of tender years. It would not, however, be limited to young children. And it would be formally expressed in terms of a *deference*, rather than a *preference*. . .

1. ARGUMENTS FOR MATERNAL DEFERENCE

I begin with the arguments for maternal deference. These arguments are organized into four headings. A maternal deference standard

(a) recognizes women's reproductive labor, competence, and authority, (b) has the potential to yield the proper result in custody disputes more often than current standards to the benefit of caretaking women and their children, (c) could improve the economic situation of divorced women and children in many families in which actual custody remains unaffected, and (d) would give fathers an incentive to change their behavior within marriage.

a. *Maternal deference would recognize women's reproductive labor, competence and authority.* A maternal deference standard would recognize that mothers, as a group, have greater competence and standing to decide what is best for their children after a divorce than judges, fathers, or adversarial experts. To paraphrase Sara Ruddick, the authority of the judge, like the authority of the father, "is not earned by care and indeed undermines the maternal authority that is so earned." In contrast, mothers *earn* their authority by the physical and emotional caretaking that qualifies them as better decisionmakers—because of their greater ability to empathize with children—than fathers, judges, or experts. I do not mean to suggest that mothers can be expected to make perfect decisions. Mothers are not perfect. But neither are judges, fathers or adversarial experts. Mothers will sometimes make wrong decisions, but in the aggregate they are likely to make better decisions than the other possible decisionmakers. . . .

Although a deference standard would recognize and legitimate maternal authority and women's caretaking, it would also suggest that there are many reasons why a mother might not want custody or consider it inappropriate. A mother might think that in her family, the husband is the better caregiver, or that joint custody would be better for all concerned. She might think that joint custody would offer her a better opportunity to combine wage work and caretaking with an ex-spouse she trusts and with whom she can comfortably coordinate care. . . .

b. *Maternal deference has the potential to yield the proper result in custody disputes more often than current standards to the benefit of caretaking women and their children.* . . .

i. *Children would be better off under a standard which protects their relationship with the primary caretaking parent.* Although fathers may be capable of being adequate caretakers, it is unlikely that a father who has not been the primary caretaker during marriage will be one after divorce. Most fathers who obtain custody are not like Dustin Hoffman's character in *Kramer v. Kramer.* Most fathers have a wife, or a mother, who becomes the primary caretaker either at the time of the divorce, or within the next few years. Thus, from the perspective of children, it is unlikely that paternal custody is a good idea because of the care the father will give the child. The father who was emotionally distant, relative to the mother, during marriage is likely to remain distant after divorce. . . .

ii. *Mothers who have been primary caretakers and who desire custody would also be better off with maternal custody.* Social engineering designed to lessen women's commitment to caretaking activities should occur earlier than at divorce. By the time of divorce, the mother has, in most families, already made the emotional investment in her children that makes the possibility of separation terrifying. At this point, we should assume that she is right when she considers custody to be desirable. To do otherwise under the pretense that it is *for her own good* would be extremely paternalistic, as well as inappropriate in terms of timing. . . .

iii. *The maternal deference standard has the potential to protect caretakers, particularly battered women and their children, better than the alternatives.* Prior to the abrogation of the maternal preference, women received custody at very high rates. A maternal deference rule has the potential to recreate that favorable climate. Indeed, women should even do better under a maternal deference standard since this standard would not be limited to children of tender years. . . .

The available data suggests that mothers who desire sole physical custody obtain it less often than they should, i.e. less often than they are primary caretakers and prefer sole physical custody. Although great data is not available on how many women in heterosexual couples are primary physical and emotional caretakers, it is likely that *at least* 92% of mothers fill this role when there are children in such families. Do these women get sole physical custody when they want it? I have not been able to find data precisely on point, but the Mnookin [California] data, as well as the outcome in the West Virginia cases, suggest no. Although 82.2% of women wanted sole maternal custody in Mnookin's sample, only 68.6% received it. If I am correct in assuming that at least 92% of women are primary caretakers, women are receiving sole physical custody much less often than they should. Under a maternal deference standard, women who have been the primary caretakers *should* receive sole physical custody whenever they desire it.

Strong legal protection of the relationships between caretaking mothers and children is particularly important for battered women. . . . Batterers routinely use threats of seeking custody of children to coerce women to stay in abusive relationships. A maternal deference standard should make such threats less powerful. Given the high rates of abuse in marriage, adequate protection of battered women must be a primary goal in choosing a sound custody standard.

c. *Maternal deference could improve the economic situation of divorced women and children in many families in which actual custody remains unaffected.* A maternal deference standard has the potential to improve the economic status of all custodial mothers and their children because it would strengthen their ability to obtain custody. Under this standard, mothers would feel less pressure to trade economic security for custody. . . .

d. *Maternal deference would give fathers an incentive to change their behavior within marriage.* It is unlikely that custody rules affect pri-

mary behavior during marriage for several reasons. Most people underestimate the chances that they will divorce. Therefore, they are unlikely to think of divorce standards as relevant to their lives. In addition, as discussed earlier, caretaking of children is an activity with deep roots in the unconscious. It is unlikely that even parents who have reasonable expectations of divorce will parent during marriage on the basis of a custody rule at divorce. For example, there is no evidence that the change in the probability of receiving custody at divorce has affected women's willingness to assume primary emotional and physical responsibility for child care during marriage or to work the second shift when necessary. Similarly, it is unlikely that custody standards affect father's willingness to care for their children.

Assuming for purposes of argument that custody standards at divorce do affect parenting behavior *during* marriage, a maternal deference standard will give fathers a greater incentive to change their behavior than do current standards. . . .

STUDY QUESTIONS

1. How does the maternal deference Becker suggests differ from a preference for mothers in custody disputes? Why does Becker advocate it? Are the reasons she cites biological or social?
2. Do you think her approach is fair? Is it necessary to ensure recognition for the work most women do today? What do you see as its long-run consequences?

Termination of Parental Rights and Adoption

The next group of cases involves state efforts to limit parental rights, usually to permit a third party to adopt. In such cases, parents may be seeking custody or simply the right to see their children. The legal issues in such cases may turn on common law, statutes, or constitutional provisions. Our focus is primarily on constitutional questions and, in particular, due process and equal protection. In terms of due process, the courts have two concerns in this context: (1) what procedures must be followed before a parent may be deprived of such rights as custody and contact with a child; and (2) what must be shown as a matter of substance before such rights are terminated.

Like the intrafamily custody cases, these materials illustrate the ways that judicial and societal expectations of parents vary according to their gender. As compared to intrafamily custody cases, however, adoption and termination cases continue to rely on sex-based classifications to a much greater extent. In studying these materials, consider whether there is a biological basis for the role expectations these classifications embody. Consider also how the roles ascribed to parents differ from the roles ascribed to other figures in a child's life. Consider, finally, the ways in which altering our conceptions of parenting might transform the lives of women whose options have been so sharply defined by their roles as mothers.

The first case to deal with the relations between unwed fathers and their children, *Stanley v. Illinois,* 405 U.S. 645 (1972), was decided only months after *Reed v. Reed.* There, the Court did reject a presumption that parents are unfit for custody of their own children if they are unwed fathers but not if they are unwed mothers. However, despite the fact that the issues in *Stanley* were in many respects the same as those addressed in *Reed,* the Court elected to decide the case under the Due Process rather than the Equal Protection Clause. There is little chance that we will ever know precisely why the Supreme Court relied on due process arguments and avoided the equal protection issue in *Stanley* at a time when it was obviously willing to hold some sex-based classifications unconstitutional. The justices' due process approach suggests, however, that they were less clear about the acceptability of sex-based generalizations in the area of parenting. Nevertheless, they did face the equal protection issue seven years later in *Caban v. Mohammed,* 441 U.S. 380 (1979), a case involving a New York statute that required the consent of an unwed mother, but not an unwed father, for adoption. By a narrow 5–4 vote, they rejected the statute as "another example of overbroad generalizations in gender-based classifications."

> Contrary to appellees' argument and to the apparent presumption underlying § 111, maternal and paternal roles are not invariably different in importance. Even if unwed mothers as a class were closer than unwed fathers to their newborn infants, this generalization concerning parent-child relations would become less acceptable as a basis for legislative distinctions as the age of the child increased. The present case demonstrates that an unwed father may have a relationship with his children fully comparable to that of the mother. Appellant Caban, appellee Maria Mohammed, and their two children lived together as a natural family for several years. As members of this family, both mother and father participated in the care and support of their children. There is no reason to believe that the Caban children—aged 4 and 6 at the time of the adoption proceedings—had a relationship with their mother unrivaled by the affection and concern of their father. We reject, therefore, the claim that the broad, gender-based distinction of § 111 is required by any universal difference between maternal and paternal relations at every phase of a child's development.
>
> Id. *at 389.*

The state had sought to justify the sex-based distinction by arguing that requiring unmarried fathers' consent to adoption impedes adoptions because it is often impossible to locate the fathers, whereas mothers are likely to remain with the children. In rejecting this argument, the Court again pointed to Caban's specific circumstances:

> Even if the special difficulties attendant upon locating and identifying unwed fathers at birth would justify a legislative distinction between mothers and fathers of newborns, these difficulties need not persist past infancy. When the adoption of an older child is sought, the State's interest in proceeding with adoption cases can be protected by means that do not draw such an inflexible gender-based distinction as that made in § 111. In those

cases where the father never has come forward to participate in the rearing of his child, nothing in the Equal Protection Clause precludes the State from withholding from him the privilege of vetoing the adoption of that child. Indeed, under the statute as it now stands the surrogate may proceed in the absence of consent when the parent whose consent otherwise would be required never has come forward or has abandoned the child. But in cases such as this, where the father has established a substantial relationship with the child and has admitted his paternity, a State should have no difficulty in identifying the father even of children born out of wedlock. Thus, no showing has been made that the different treatment afforded unmarried fathers and unmarried mothers under § 111 bears a substantial relationship to the proclaimed interest of the State in promoting the adoption of illegitimate children.

Id. *at 392.*

The Court thus rested its decision on equal protection grounds. Yet, by focusing so pointedly on Caban's particular relationship with his children, it suggested its discomfort with a broad equal protection analysis in the unwed parent situation. Indeed, the Court hinted that some distinctions may be made between unwed mothers and fathers. The narrow nature of the Court's approach is apparent when we contrast this case, for example, with *Reed v. Reed* (see Chapter 2), in which the Court was totally unconcerned with Sally Reed's ability to administer an estate. The Court simply found the statute's gender-based classification impermissible. Nothing in the opinion suggested that a statute that gave certain rights to all men and to those women who could show competence in estate administration would be constitutional. In *Caban,* however, the Court intimated that just such a distinction may be permissible with regard to unwed mothers and fathers.

Subsequent developments have borne out the intimations from *Caban.* In *Lehr v. Robertson,* the Court upheld a New York adoption that was granted without notice to or consent of the unwed father. The adoption at issue took place under the same New York law as was before the Court in *Caban.*

Lehr v. Robertson

United States Supreme Court, 1983. 463 U.S. 248, 103 S.Ct. 2985, 77 L.Ed.2d 614.

Justice STEVENS delivered the opinion of the Court.

The question presented is whether New York has sufficiently protected an unmarried father's inchoate relationship with a child whom he has never supported and rarely seen in the two years since her birth. The appellant, Jonathan Lehr, claims that the Due Process and Equal Protection Clauses of the Fourteenth Amendment, as interpreted in *Stanley v. Illinois* and *Caban v. Mohammed* give him an absolute right to notice and an opportunity to be heard before the child may be adopted. We disagree.

Jessica M. was born out of wedlock on November 9, 1976. Her mother, Lorraine Robertson, married Richard Robertson eight months after Jessica's birth. On December 21, 1978, when Jessica was over two years old, the Robertsons filed an adoption petition in the Family Court of Ulster County, New York. The court heard their testimony and received a favorable report from the Ulster County Department of Social Services. On March 7, 1979, the court entered an order of adoption. In this proceeding, appellant contends that the adoption order is invalid because he, Jessica's putative father, was not given advance notice of the adoption proceeding.

The State of New York maintains a "putative father registry." A man who files with that registry demonstrates his intent to claim paternity of a child born out of wedlock and is therefore entitled to receive notice of any proceeding to adopt that child. Before entering Jessica's adoption order, the Ulster County Family Court had the putative father registry examined. Although appellant claims to be Jessica's natural father, he had not entered his name in the registry.

In addition to the persons whose names are listed on the putative father registry, New York law requires that notice of an adoption proceeding be given to several other classes of possible fathers of children born out of wedlock—those who have been adjudicated to be the father, those who have been identified as the father on the child's birth certificate, those who live openly with the child and the child's mother and who hold themselves out to be the father, those who have been identified as the father by the mother in a sworn written statement, and those who were married to the child's mother before the child was six months old. Appellant admittedly was not a member of any of those classes. He had lived with appellee prior to Jessica's birth and visited her in the hospital when Jessica was born, but his name does not appear on Jessica's birth certificate. He did not live with appellee or Jessica after Jessica's birth, he has never provided them with any financial support, and he has never offered to marry appellee. Nevertheless, he contends that [his initiation of a separate proceeding to determine paternal support and visitation] gave him a constitutional right to notice and a hearing before Jessica was adopted. . . .

Appellant has now invoked our appellate jurisdiction. He offers two alternative grounds for holding the New York statutory scheme unconstitutional. First, he contends that a putative father's actual or potential relationship with a child born out of wedlock is an interest in liberty which may not be destroyed without due process of law; he argues therefore that he had a constitutional right to prior notice and an opportunity to be heard before he was deprived of that interest. Second, he contends that the gender-based classification in the statute, which both denied him the right to consent to Jessica's adoption and accorded him fewer procedural rights than her mother, violated the Equal Protection Clause. . . .

When an unwed father demonstrates a full commitment to the responsibilities of parenthood by "com[ing] forward to participate in the rearing of his child," *Caban,* 441 U.S. at 392, his interest in personal contact with his child acquires substantial protection under the due process clause. At that point it may be said that he "act[s] as a father toward his children." *Id.,* at 389, n. 7. But the mere existence of a biological link does not merit equivalent constitutional protection. . . .

The legislation at issue in this case, sections 111 and 111a of the New York Domestic Relations Law, is intended to establish procedures for adoptions. Those procedures are designed to promote the best interests of the child, protect the rights of interested third parties, and ensure promptness and finality. To serve those ends, the legislation guarantees to certain people the right to veto an adoption and the right to prior notice of any adoption proceeding. The mother of an illegitimate child is always within that favored class, but only certain putative fathers are included. Appellant contends that the gender-based distinction is invidious.

As we noted above, the existence or nonexistence of a substantial relationship between parent and child is a relevant criterion in evaluating both the rights of the parent and the best interests of the child. In *Quilloin v. Walcott* [434 U.S. 246, 256 (1978)] we noted that the putative father, like appellant, "ha[d] never shouldered any significant responsibility with respect to the daily supervision, education, protection, or care of the child. Appellant does not complain of his exemption from these responsibilities. . . ." We therefore found that a Georgia statute that always required a mother's consent to the adoption of a child born out of wedlock, but required the father's consent only if he had legitimated the child, did not violate the Equal Protection Clause. Because, like the father in *Quilloin,* appellant has never established a substantial relationship with his daughter, the New York statutes at issue in this case did not operate to deny appellant equal protection.

We have held that these statutes may not constitutionally be applied in that class of cases where the mother and father are in fact similarly situated with regard to their relationship with the child. In *Caban v. Mohammed,* the Court held that it violated the Equal Protection Clause to grant the mother a veto over the adoption of a four-year-old girl and a six-year-old boy, but not to grant a veto to their father, who had admitted paternity and had participated in the rearing of the children. The Court made it clear, however, that if the father had not "come forward to participate in the rearing of his child, nothing in the Equal Protection Clause [would] preclude the State from withholding from him the privilege of vetoing the adoption of that child."

Jessica's parents are not like the parents involved in *Caban.* Whereas appellee had a continuous custodial responsibility for Jessica, appellant never established any custodial, personal, or financial relationship with her. If one parent has an established custodial relationship with the child and the other parent has either abandoned or never established a relationship, the Equal Protection Clause does not prevent a state from according the two parents different legal rights.

The judgment of the New York Court of Appeals is

Affirmed.

STUDY QUESTIONS

1. If Jonathan Lehr had married and petitioned to adopt his child, would Lorraine Robertson have been given notice? Why the difference?
2. As a factual matter, how did Lehr's relationship to his child differ from Caban's relationship to his children?
3. Do New York and the Court presume that an unwed mother automatically establishes a substantial relationship with her child? Is that true? Is it true that an unwed father invariably, or even typically, does not? To the extent that the generalization is valid, does it reflect biological necessities or social realities?

More recently, in the case of *Michael H. v. Gerald D.,* 491 U.S. 110 (1989), the Supreme Court upheld a law that permitted only a husband or a wife to rebut a state statute's presumption that a child born during the marriage was legitimate. In finding that this statute did not violate the due process rights of another man seeking to establish paternity, the Court used a sex-neutral analysis. Nevertheless, it is apparent that most decisions involving unwed parents assume women and men play very different roles as parents. Women are viewed as automatically responsible for the care of their out-of-wedlock children, while men must affirmatively establish a custodial, legal, or financial relationship before the law will recognize their parental role. Although judges at times suggest sex-based legal rules reflect physical differences between the sexes, it is simply not true that all unwed mothers (and no unwed fathers) assume responsibility for their children. Most differences in parenting behavior are thus better understood as a product of social expectations rather than biological fact. However, as we have seen, even among feminists, such sex-based classifications are controversial. Some feminists support them on the ground that it is not fair to give an uninvolved father custody of a woman's child when, in reality, she most often bears the day-to-day responsibility for a child borne out-of-wedlock. Others believe that men must be encouraged to become involved in child care and that it is harmful to reinforce the stereotype of women as always being responsible for their children. Thus, the debates over adoption statutes mirror the debates over custody standards.

Like doctrines governing custody awards on divorce, legal provisions determining the rights of unwed parents to their children reinforce as well as reflect societal perceptions of appropriate parenting behavior for women and men. As the next subsection demonstrates, sex roles in regard to child care have also been influenced by a variety of governmental programs.

Governmental Programs

Just as Social Security and other governmental programs have influenced the allocation of roles between spouses, they have also influenced sex roles with respect to child care. Recall in this context the Social Security provision, struck down in *Wiesenfeld v. Weinberger, 420 U.S. 636 (1975),* which allocated special benefits to widows, but not widowers, who devoted themselves to child care. In investigating influences of this type, we first consider tax policies regarding child care expenses, which apply to the population as a whole, and then look at Aid to Families with Dependent Children (AFDC), a program geared exclusively to the poor. Finally, we consider the extent of governmental support for child care and parental leave programs.

Tax systems affect behavioral choices by making certain activities more or less expensive. The decision to work outside the home, for example, is generally influenced by the economic benefit that the work yields. Child care expenses cut into the income produced by work outside the home and diminish the attractiveness of paid employment to those who would otherwise take care of their children themselves. The deterrent effect of such expenses is even greater when they are included in taxable income. In this way, tax provisions governing the deductibility of child care expenses have had a significant impact on married women who have traditionally borne the responsibility for child care.

Income taxes are paid on net income, that is, all one's income minus the costs incurred in earning it. It is not always obvious, however, whether a particular kind of expenditure reflects a cost of earning income or a decision as to how to spend the income earned. There are, therefore, a series of rules, regulations, and court decisions determining which expenses are properly deductible.

Like expenditures for business lunches and work clothes, child care expenses may be viewed as costs of earning income or personal consumption on expenditures. Prior to 1954, no one was allowed a deduction for child care expenses. In 1937, a couple claimed the cost of a nursemaid for their child while the wife was at work as a business expense, but the claim was rejected by the Internal Revenue Service and the courts. See *Smith v. Commissioner,* 40 B.T.A. 1038 (1939), *aff'd,* 113 F.2d 114 (2d Cir. 1940). Beginning in 1954, Congress enacted a series of provisions permitting limited deductions for child care. Available initially only to single parents, the deduction was expanded over the years, so that by the 1970s, it had become a benefit to two-parent, middle-income families. In 1976, the deduction was changed to a credit, increasing its value for many taxpayers in the lower income brackets, and in 1981, it was increased and targeted even more toward the lower brackets. While not as generous as deductions for most other earning-related expenses, the child care credit survived the Tax Reform Act of 1986.

Interestingly, in 1988, when taxpayers claiming the credit were required to supply the Social Security number of the person paid to provide child care, the number of claims dropped significantly.

The search for the ideal tax treatment for child care raises complex questions about national family policies. Should the tax system and other government programs encourage one parent to stay home to care for children? Does it matter which parent? Should they encourage both parents to work outside the home and give others the major responsibility for care of their children? Should care of a certain kind or quality be encouraged? Are there kinds of child care that should be prohibited? Is there a way to encourage both parents to perform child care duties at home? Would that be desirable? The debate over tax provisions hardly allows for a thorough resolution of all these questions; yet the tax code does embody choices as to family policy. By initially disallowing child care expenses entirely and subsequently declining to make them fully deductible, the federal tax system has made it more difficult for married mothers to work outside the home, thereby reinforcing traditional roles within family.

Traditional sex roles have also been a prominent feature of the AFDC program that provides public assistance to needy children. Some, but not all, of these sex-based provisions have been challenged in court. The next case is one such challenge. In it, the Supreme Court considered an AFDC eligibility provision embodying the presumption that in two-parent families, fathers, but not mothers, were breadwinners responsible for the support of their families.

Califano v. Westcott

United States Supreme Court, 1979.
443 U.S. 76, 99 S.Ct. 2655, 61 L.Ed.2d 382.

Mr. Justice BLACKMUN delivered the opinion of the Court.

The Aid to Families with Dependent Children (AFDC) program, provides financial assistance to families with needy dependent children. The program is administered by participating States, in conformity with federal standards, and is financed by the Federal Government and the States on a matching-funds basis.

As originally enacted in 1935, the AFDC program provided benefits to families whose dependent children were needy because of the death, absence, or incapacity of a parent. This provision, which forms the core of the AFDC program today, is gender neutral: benefits are available to any family so long as one parent of either sex is dead, absent from the home, or incapacitated, and the family otherwise meets the financial requirements of eligibility. 42 U.S.C. § 606.

In 1961, and again in 1962, Congress temporarily extended the AFDC program to provide assistance to families whose dependent children were deprived of support because of a parent's unemployment. . . .

In 1968, as part of a general revision of the Social Security Act, Congress made this extension permanent. In so doing, however, it added a gender qualification to the statute. The definition of "dependent child" in § 407 was amended to include a "needy child . . . who has been deprived of parental support or care by reason of the unemployment . . . of his *father*." 42 U.S.C. § 607(a) (emphasis added). This portion of the AFDC program is known as Aid to Families with Dependent Children, Unemployed Father (AFDC–UF). Although all 50 States have chosen to participate in the basic AFDC program, only 26 States (plus Guam and the District of Columbia) take part in the AFDC–UF program. One of these is the Commonwealth of Massachusetts.

Appellees are two couples who, it is stipulated, satisfy all the requirements for AFDC–UF benefits except for the requirement that the unemployed parent be the father. Cindy and William Westcott are married and have an infant son. They applied to the Massachusetts DPW for public assistance, but were informed that they did not qualify because William, who was unable to find work, had not previously been employed for a sufficient period to qualify as an "unemployed" father under the Act and applicable regulations. Cindy, until her recent unemployment, was the family breadwinner, and would have satisfied the "unemployment" criteria had she been male.

Susan and John Westwood are also married and have an infant son. They applied for

Medicaid benefits as a family eligible for, but not receiving, AFDC–UF benefits. They, too, were turned down on the ground that John's prior work history was insufficient. Susan, like Cindy Westcott, had been the family breadwinner before losing her job, and would have qualified the family for benefits had she been male.

Appellees instituted this class action in the United States District Court for the District of Massachusetts, naming as defendants the Secretary of HEW and the Commissioner of the DPW. Appellees alleged that § 407 and its implementing regulations discriminate on the basis of gender in violation of the Fifth and Fourteenth Amendments. . . .

The Secretary [of Health, Education, and Welfare] advances two arguments in support of the constitutionality of § 407. First, he contends that although § 407 incorporates a gender distinction, it does not discriminate against women as a class. Second, he urges that the distinction is substantially related to the achievement of an important governmental objective: the need to deter real or pretended desertion by the father in order to make his family eligible for AFDC benefits.

The Secretary readily concedes that § 407 entails a gender distinction. He submits, however, that the Act does not award AFDC benefits to a father where it denies them to a mother. Rather, the grant or denial of aid based on the father's unemployment necessarily affects, to an equal degree, one man, one woman, and one or more children. As the Secretary puts it, even if the statute is "gender-based," it is not "gender-biased."

We are not persuaded by this analysis. For mothers who are the primary providers for their families, and who are unemployed, § 407 is obviously gender biased, for it deprives them and their families of benefits solely on the basis of their sex. The Secretary's argument, at bottom, turns on the fact that the impact of the gender qualification is felt by family units rather than individuals. But this Court has not hesitated to strike down gender classifications that result in benefits being granted or denied to family units on the basis of the sex of the qualifying parent. See *Frontiero v. Richardson* (military quarters allowances and medical and dental benefits);

Weinberger v. Wiesenfeld (survivor's benefits); *Califano v. Goldfarb* (survivor's benefits); *Califano v. Jablon* (spousal benefits). Here, as in those cases, the statute "discriminates against one particular category of family—that in which the female spouse is a wage earner." *Goldfarb* . . . . [However] the Secretary argues, the gender qualification of § 407 is distinguishable from those contained in the earlier cases, for it does not denigrate "the efforts of women who do work and whose earnings contribute significantly to their families' support." *Wiesenfeld*. . . .

Putting labels aside, the exclusion here is if anything more pernicious than those in *Frontiero,* *Wiesenfeld,* and *Goldfarb*. AFDC–UF benefits are not "fringe benefits," nor are they a type of social assistance paid without regard to need. Rather, they are subsistence payments made available as a last resort to families that would otherwise lack basic necessities. The deprivation imposed by § 407, moreover, is not a mere procedural barrier, like the proof-of-dependency requirement in *Frontiero* and *Goldfarb,* but is an absolute bar to qualification for aid. We therefore reject the contention that the classification imposed by § 407 does not discriminate on the basis of gender.

The Secretary next argues that the gender distinction imposed by § 407 survives constitutional scrutiny because it is substantially related to achievement of an important governmental objective. . . .

The Secretary identifies two important objectives served by § 407.

First and most obviously, the statute was intended to provide aid for children deprived of basic sustenance because of a parent's unemployment . . . . The appellant Secretary does not contend, however, that the gender qualification of § 407 serves to achieve this goal. Nor could he, since families where the mother is the principal wage earner and is unemployed are often in as much need of AFDC–UF benefits and Medicaid as families where the father is unemployed.

Second, the statute was designed to remedy a structural fault in the original AFDC program. Under that program, a family was eligible for benefits if deprived of parental support because of the "continued absence from the home . . . of a parent." 42 U.S.C. § 606(a). In times of economic adversity, this provision was thought to create an incentive for the father to desert, or to pretend to desert, in order to make the family eligible for assistance. Section 407, by providing AFDC benefits to families rendered needy by parental unemployment, was intended to reduce this incentive and thereby promote the goal of family stability. The Secretary submits that reducing the incentive for the father to desert was an important objective of the AFDC–UF program, and he argues that the gender qualification is substantially related to its achievement.

We perceive, however, at least two flaws in this argument. Although it is relatively clear that Congress was concerned about the problem of parental desertion, there is no evidence that the gender distinction was designed to address this problem. [The legislative history] suggests that the gender qualification was part of the general objective of the 1968 amendments to tighten standards for eligibility and reduce program costs. Congress was concerned that certain States were making AFDC–UF assistance available to families where the mother was out of work, but the father remained fully employed and able to support the family. Apparently, Congress was not similarly concerned about States making benefits available where the father was out of work, but the mother remained fully employed. From all that appears, Congress, with an image of the "traditional family" in mind, simply assumed that the father would be the family breadwinner, and that the mother's employment role, if any, would be secondary. In short, the available evidence indicates that the gender distinction was inserted to reduce costs and eliminate what was perceived to be a type of superfluous eligibility for AFDC–UF benefits. There is little to suggest that the gender qualification had anything to do with reducing the father's incentive to desert.

Even if the actual purpose of the gender qualification was to deal with the problem of paternal desertion, it does not appear that the classification is substantially related to the achievement of that goal. The Secretary argues there is "[s]olid statistical evidence" that fathers are more susceptible to pressure to desert than mothers, and thus that Congress was justified in excluding families

headed by unemployed mothers from the AFDC–UF program. We may assume, for purposes of discussion, that Congress could legitimately view paternal desertion as a problem separate and distinct from maternal desertion. Even so, the gender qualification of § 407 is not substantially related to the stated purpose. There is no evidence, in the legislative history or elsewhere, that a father has less incentive to desert in a family where the mother is the breadwinner and becomes unemployed, than in a family where the father is the breadwinner and becomes unemployed. In either case, the family's need will be equally great, and the father will be equally subject to pressure to leave the home to make the family eligible for benefits. . . .

We conclude that the gender classification of § 407 is not substantially related to the attainment of any important and valid statutory goals. It is, rather, part of the "baggage of sexual stereotypes," *Orr v. Orr* that presumes the father has the "primary responsibility to provide a home and its essentials," *Stanton v. Stanton,* while the mother is the " 'center of home and family life.' " *Taylor v. Louisiana.* Legislation that rests on such presumptions, without more, cannot survive scrutiny under the Due Process Clause of the Fifth Amendment.

The judgment of the District Court accordingly is affirmed.

It is so ordered.

STUDY QUESTIONS

1. Who is eligible for benefits under the AFDC-UF program? Are the eligibility criteria sex-based?

2. How does the government attempt to justify the gender classification contained in the AFDC-UF legislation? Why does the Court find the government's proffered justification insufficient?

3. Do you think that the AFDC program encourages one parent to leave the home? One parent more than the other? What might account for the fact that fathers are more susceptible to deserting than mothers? How might the AFDC-UF program prevent family breakup?

In an omitted portion of the *Westcott* decision, the Supreme Court considered whether to remedy the constitutional violation by extending AFDC-UF benefits to all families containing an unemployed parent or only to families in which the principal wage earner is unemployed. Recognizing that the principal earner test would result in terminating many families' AFDC-UF benefits and would entail a restructuring of the program that Congress may not have intended, the Court chose the broader option. Had the Court adopted the principal earner standard, the Westcotts and Westwoods would be eligible for benefits. However, families in which the parents shared the breadwinning would have suffered. Thus, even though the primary earner standard is neutral, it reflects the same traditional assumption as the AFDC-UF statute—that all households contain one principal earner and one primary caretaker.

Limiting AFDC eligibility under the unemployed parent program to cases where the father was unemployed served to reinforce traditional roles in two ways: First, the limitation underscores the assumption that men, not women, support families, while women, not men, take care of children. Second, it underscores the assumption that one parent, and only one parent, is primarily responsible for supporting the family. In invalidating the provision, the Supreme Court recognized that women may be breadwinners as well as child rearers, just as men may be child rearers as well as breadwinners. The Court's decision not to limit eligibility to needy families in which only the primary earner is unemployed was likewise important in recognizing changed sex roles. In many families today, both parents are employed, and both parents take part in child rearing. Yet, because women usually earn less than men, they are unlikely to be seen as principal wage earners under a standard that insists on designating one primary earner. Unfortunately, following the *Westcott* decision, Congress adopted the principal earner standard through an amendment to the Social Security Act.

Assumptions about traditional roles have shaped the AFDC program since its origin in 1935 as a program for mothers who lost their male breadwinners. Between 1935 and 1968, official federal policy was to permit poor mothers to choose between seeking wagework and remaining at home with their children. Reflecting the view that most children needed a mother at home to care for them, work and training opportunities and the AFDC-UF benefit discussed in *Westcott* were aimed primarily at men. At the same time, the federal government tolerated state policies that pressured women, often on a racial basis, to accept jobs deemed suitable for them. The federal government also tolerated serious incursions into the private lives of women receiving AFDC. Thus, states were permitted to disqualify mothers found to be "cohabiting" (that is, having only occasional sexual relations) with men who were deemed to be assuming the role of the absent male breadwinner. Moreover, home visits and anonymous informants became accepted means of enforcing these rules. Some welfare recipients observed that it was as if by giving benefits, the state had come to expect chastity, just as husbands did, in exchange for providing support.

Two important developments occurred in 1968. The Supreme Court decided the case of *King v. Smith*, 392 U.S. 309 (1968), which limited a state's ability to define "parent" and to add its own eligibility requirements generally. That year also saw the introduction of the "WIN" (Work Incentive) program establishing work requirements for "appropriate" recipients. In 1971, the WIN program was amended to require all able-bodied adult men to work, to require single mothers to work when their youngest child reached the age of six, and to exempt women who had men in their households irrespective of their children's ages. The WIN program's system of referrals for work and training was also sex-based. Federally mandated priorities for unemployed fathers effectively denied women work openings; and although these provisions have been successfully challenged in court by women recipients on equal protection grounds, they continued to be implemented. Those referrals actually made under the WIN program placed women disproportionately in low-paying, traditionally female jobs. In short, the WIN program encouraged families to replicate the traditional male breadwinner-female homemaker model where there were men in the home.

Since then, under the federal Family Support Act of 1988, states must implement the new JOBS program as a condition of participating in AFDC. Although the new program does not guarantee jobs, it does require all able-bodied recipients over the age of nineteen (or sixteen if not in school) to work or participate in training if they are not personally providing care for a child below age three (or as young as age one at the state's option). The state must provide supportive services, such as assessment of their needs for increased capability, and child support services. While it is easy to see how stereotypic thinking can result in biased employability plans, it is important to recognize that the exemption for child care may have a similar effect. Because jobs are first assigned to those required to work, placements, particularly in "good jobs," may not be available for women who seek work voluntarily. See, e.g., *Ford v. Griffin,* No. 91-CH-4215 (Ill. Cir. Ct. Cook County). Whether or not this potential gender bias becomes a reality will be clearer as the program becomes established.

Welfare regulations that require fathers, but not mothers, to work and give men priority in job training programs have an obvious impact on the allocation of child care responsibilities within families receiving public assistance. Another reason for the persistence of women's role as child rearer and housekeeper is the absence of alternative satisfactory arrangements for child care. A national study commissioned by the federal government reported that in 1978, for example, almost 52 percent of the country's 24.4 million families with children had a work-related need for some form of day care. As it becomes increasingly acceptable for mothers to work and as economic pressures on the family grow, the unmet need is likely to increase.

In contrast to most industrialized countries that have family policies supporting either day care facilities or parents (often mothers) who care for children in the home, alternatives available in the United States are private for the most part. Federal support for child care in the United States has been limited to five major sources. The largest is the tax credit for child care discussed above. A second source of federal support is the Head Start program, initiated in 1965 as an intensive child development program for economically disadvantaged preschool children. A portion of JOBS funds are allocated for social services including day care. AFDC recipients also receive support through provisions that permit the exclusion of some earned income spent on day care when their benefits are calculated. And finally federal block grants are available to states for social services including day care for the poor and near poor.

Recent history makes plain that the failure to make significant support available for child care services was a deliberate choice about family policy. In 1971, Congress passed a bill that would have greatly expanded the resources available to working mothers by providing $2 billion a year for day care and child development services. President Richard Nixon vetoed the bill, citing "the respectable school of opinion that this legislation would lead toward altering the family relationship." Meanwhile, whether for similar reasons or funding concerns, a comprehensive federal child care program has not yet been established, despite some relatively substantial increases in federal support to optional state programs.

Leave programs that allow parents to retain their work affiliation during the period that they are at home caring for their children are an important complement to collective or institutional day care facilities. Unlike many other countries, the United States does not provide paid leaves for such purposes. The country did take a big step forward when, at the beginning of the Clinton administration in 1993, Congress enacted the Family Medical Leave Act. Its key points are summarized below.

The Family Medical Leave Act of 1993: Highlights of the Act

New York Times, February 5, 1993. P. A14.

EMPLOYEE'S PROVISIONS:

☐ Allows a worker to take up to 12 weeks of unpaid leave in any 12-month period for the birth of a child or an adoption, to care for a child, spouse or parent with a serious health condition or for the worker's own serious health condition that makes it impossible to perform a job.

☐ Provides that an employee must be returned to his or her old job or an equivalent position upon returning to work.

☐ Requires an employer to keep providing health care benefits during the leave, as though the worker were still employed, but does not require the employer to pay for worker on leave.

☐ Prohibits a worker on leave from collecting unemployment or other government compensation.

☐ Covers only a worker who has been employed at least one year and for at least 1,250 hours (25 hours a week).

EMPLOYER'S PROVISIONS:

☐ Exempts any company with fewer than 50 workers.

☐ Allows a company to deny leave to salaried employee within the highest-paid 10 percent of its work force, if letting the worker take the leave would create "substantial and grievous injury" to the business operations.

☐ Permits an employer to obtain medical opinions and certifications on the need for the leave.

☐ Allows an employer to ask the employee to repay the health-care premiums paid by the employer during the leave if the employee does not return to work.

STUDY QUESTIONS

1. Are all workers now covered? What needs to be done to make coverage complete?

2. What effect do you imagine legislation of this sort will have on the division of labor within the family? Who is likely to use the proposed child care leave? The leave to care for a spouse or a parent? Would making the leave a paid leave affect the mix of users? How? To what extent does the answer depend on the rate of pay?

3. How can men be encouraged to take parental leaves? Do you think it would be fair to allow them more time or higher pay? Would such programs be constitutional?

The lack of a national family policy providing for paid leaves and other mechanisms for integrating work and family responsibilities still reflects the assumption that children will be—and should be—raised in a two-parent home composed of a breadwinning father and a child-rearing, though perhaps employed, mother. As we have seen, the same assumption has permeated custody, adoption, and parental rights decisions just as it has helped to shape the work and training provisions of the public assistance program. The overall effect of the law as it appears to operate in these various contexts is to make it more difficult for men to become involved in nurturing activities, thereby helping to ensure that women will continue to bear the major responsibility for child care.

III. THE FEMINIZATION OF POVERTY AND FAMILY POLICY

The alarming rate of poverty among women and children is now widely acknowledged. The Census Bureau reports that in 1990, families maintained by women accounted for approximately 13 percent of families above the poverty line and 53 percent of families below the poverty line. The National Advisory Council on Economic Opportunity has estimated that "[a]ll other things being equal, if the proportion of the poor who are in female-headed families were to increase at the same rate as it did from 1967 to 1977, the poverty population would be composed solely of women and children by about the year 2000." Two groups—older women and single parents—experience particular difficulties. The Council also found poverty among racial and ethnic minorities especially pronounced and predicted that by the year 2000, households headed by minority women will dominate the poverty population. Among women of all races, poverty is closely related to single status (never-married, divorced, or widowed).

This poverty is a consequence of the interplay of gender-related inequities in the domestic sphere and gender-related inequities in the labor market. That interplay and some of its consequences were briefly explored in Chapter 5. Earlier in this chapter, we touched on problems some women have with the Social Security system.

Here, we explore the problem from the perspective of family law, asking what it is in the operation of "private" family law that contributes to women's economic plight and what the government can do to improve the situation. In the first selection, sociologist Lenore Weitzman discusses the relation between divorce and changes in the economic circumstances of men, women, and children.

The Divorce Revolution

Lenore J. Weitzman.
New York: The Free Press, MacMillan, 1985. Pp. 337–343.

POSTDIVORCE STANDARDS OF LIVING: IMPOVERISHMENT OF WOMEN AND CHILDREN

. . .The model for our analysis was constructed by Michigan researchers who followed a sample of 5,000 American families, weighted to be representative of the U.S. population. Economists Saul Hoffman and John Holmes compared the incomes of men and women who stayed in intact families with the incomes of divorced men and divorced women over a seven-year period.

A comparison of the married and divorced couples yielded two major findings. First, as might be expected, the dollar income of both divorced men and divorced women declined, while the income of married couples rose. Divorced men lost 19 percent in income while divorced women lost 29 percent. In contrast, married men and women experienced a 22 percent rise in income. These data confirm our commonsense belief that both parties suffer after a divorce. They also confirm that women experience a greater loss than their former husbands.

The second finding of the Michigan research is surprising. To see what the income loss meant in terms of family purchasing power, Hoffman and Holmes constructed an index of family income in relation to family needs. Since this income/need comparison is adjusted for family size, as well as for the each member's age and sex, it provides an individually tailored measure of a family's economic well-being in the context of marital status changes.

The Michigan researchers found that the experiences of divorced men and women were strikingly different when this measure was used. Over the seven-year period, the economic position of divorced men actually improved by 17 percent. In contrast, over the same period divorced women experienced a 29 percent decline in terms of what their income could provide in relation to their needs.

To compare the experiences of divorced men and women in California to those in Michigan, we devised a similar procedure to calculate the basic needs of each of the families in our interview sample. This procedure used the living standards for urban families constructed by the Bureau of Labor Statistics of the U.S. Department of Labor. First, the standard budget level for each family in the interview sample was calculated in three different ways: once for the predivorce family, once for the wife's postdivorce family, and once for the husband's postdivorce family. Then the income in relation to needs was computed for each family. (Membership in postdivorce families of husbands and wives included any new spouse or cohabitor and any children whose custody was assigned to that spouse.) These data are presented in Figure 3.

Figure 3 reveals the radical change in the standards of living to which we alluded earlier. Just one year after legal divorce, *men experi-*

ence a 42 percent improvement in their postdivorce standard of living, while women experience a 73 percent decline.

These data indicate that *divorce is a financial catastrophe for most women:* in just one year they experience a dramatic decline in income and a calamitous drop in their standard of living. . . .

It is difficult to absorb the full implications of these statistics. What does it mean to have a 73 percent decline in one's standard of living? When asked how they coped with this drastic decline in income, many of the divorced women said that they themselves were not sure. It meant "living on the edge" and "living without." As some of them described it:

> We ate macaroni and cheese five nights a week. There was a Safeway special for 39 cents a box. We could eat seven dinners for $3.00 a week. . . . I think that's all we ate for months.
>
> I applied for welfare. . . . It was the worst experience of my life. . . . I never dreamed that I, a middle class housewife, would ever be in a position like that. It was humiliating . . . they make you feel it. . . . But we were desperate, and I *had* to feed my kids.
>
> You name it, I tried it—food stamps, soup kitchens, shelters. It just about killed me to have the kids live like that. . . . I finally called my parents and said we were coming . . . we couldn't have survived without them.

Even those who had relatively affluent life-styles before the divorce experienced a sharp reduction in their standard of living and faced hardships they had not anticipated. For example, the wife of a dentist sold her car "because I had no cash at all, and we lived on that money—barely—for close to a year." And an engineer's wife:

> I didn't buy my daughter any clothes for a year— even when she graduated from high school we sewed together two old dresses to make an outfit. . . .

Still, some of the women were not able to "make it." Fourteen percent of them moved onto the welfare rolls during the first year after the divorce, and a number of others moved back into their parents' homes when they had "no money left and nowhere to go and three children to feed."

FIGURE 3. Change in Standards of Living* of Divorced Men and Women (Approximately one year after divorce)

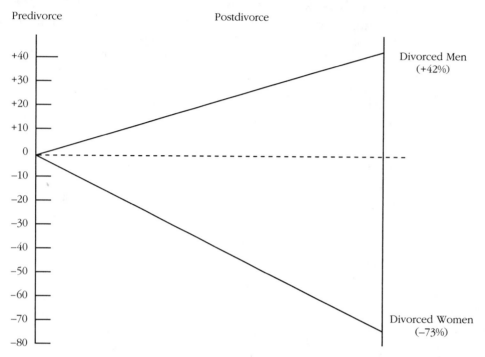

Income in relation to needs with needs based on U.S. Department of Agriculture's low standard budget. Based on weighted sample of interviews with divorced persons. Los Angeles County, California, 1978

EXPLAINING THE DISPARITY BETWEEN HUSBANDS' AND WIVES' STANDARDS OF LIVING

How can we explain the strikingly different economic consequences of divorce for men and women? How could a law aimed at fairness create such disparities between divorced men and their former wives and children?

The explanation lies first in the inadequacy of the court's awards, second in the expanded demands on the wife's resources after divorce, and third in the husband's greater earning capacity and ability to supplement his income.

Consider first the court awards for child support (and in rarer cases, alimony). Since judges do not require men to support either their children or their former wives as they did during marriage, they allow the husband to keep most of his income for himself. Since only a few wives are awarded alimony, the only supplementary income they are awarded is child support and the average child support award covers less than half of the cost of raising a child. Thus, the average support award is simply inadequate: even if the husband pays it, it often leaves the wife and children in relative poverty. The custodial mother is expected to somehow make up the deficit alone even though she typically earns much less than her former husband.

In this regard, it is also important to note the role that property awards play in contributing to—rather than alleviating—the financial disparities between divorced women and men. Under the old law, when the wife with minor children was typically awarded the family home, she started her postdivorce life on more equal footing because the home provided some stability and security and reduced the impact of the income loss suffered at divorce. Today, when the family home is more commonly sold to allow an "equal" division of property [under

California's community property system], there is no cushion to soften the financial devastations that low support awards create for women and children. Rather, the disruptive costs of moving and establishing a new household further strain their limited income—often to the breaking point.

The second explanation for the disparity between former husbands and wives lies in the greater demands on the wife's household after divorce, and the diminished demands on the husband's. Since the wife typically assumes the responsibility for raising the couple's children, her need for help and services increases as a direct result of her becoming a single parent. Yet at the very time that her need for more income and more financial support is greatest, the courts have drastically reduced her income. Thus the gap between her income and her needs is wider after divorce.

In contrast, the gap between the husband's income and needs narrows. Although he now has fewer absolute dollars, the demands on his income have diminished: he often lives alone and he is no longer financially responsible for the needs of his ex-wife and children. While he loses the benefits of economies of scale, and while he may have to purchase some services (such as laundry and cooking) that he did not have to buy during marriage, he is nevertheless much better off because he has so much more money to spend on himself. Since he has been allowed to retain most of his income for himself, he can afford these extra expenses and still have more surplus income than he enjoyed during marriage.

The final explanation for the large income discrepancy between former husbands and wives lies in the different earning capacities and starting points of the two adults at the time of the divorce. Not only do men in our society command higher salaries to begin with, they also benefit from the common marital pattern that gives priority to their careers. Marriage gives men the opportunity, support, and time to invest in their own careers. Thus marriage itself builds and enhances the husband's earning capacity. For women, in contrast, marriage is more likely to act as a career liability. Even though family roles are changing, and even though married women are increasingly working for pay during marriage, most of them nevertheless subordinate their careers to their husbands' and to their family responsibilities. This is especially true if they have children. Thus women are often doubly disadvantaged at the point of divorce. No[t] only do they face the "normal" 60 percent male/female income gap that affects all working women, they also suffer from the toll the marital years have taken on their earning capacity.

Thus marriage—and then divorce—impose a differential disadvantage on women's employment prospects, and this is especially severe for women who have custody of minor children. The responsibility for children inevitably restricts the mother's job opportunities by limiting her work schedule and location, her availability for overtime, and her freedom to take advantage of special training, travel assignments, and other opportunities for career advancement.

Although the combined income of the former spouses typically increases after divorce, most of the rise is a result of the husband's increased income. . . .

During the same period, the obligations that these men have for alimony and child support typically remain fixed or diminish: some support obligations have been reduced or terminated by terms of the divorce settlement (and others have been reduced or stopped without the courts' permission). The result, once again, is that divorced men have more "surplus income" for themselves.

STUDY QUESTIONS

1. How did the researchers measure the impact of the divorce on the parties' economic well-being?
2. What were their findings from the national sample? From the California sample?
3. What factors does Weitzman identify to explain the relative impoverishment women and children experience after a divorce?

One possible conclusion to draw from Weitzman's study is that divorces should be more difficult to obtain. In evaluating this proposition, it is helpful to take a step back in history. As the Seneca Falls Declaration suggests, women's inability to extricate themselves from unhappy marriages was an important concern of nineteenth-century feminists. Due in part to limitations on women's ability to be economically independent, this inability had legal causes as well. Initially obtainable only by the enactment of a private statute, divorce was extremely rare from the colonial period until well into the nineteenth century. As the demand for divorce grew, judicial divorces replaced legislative divorces, first in the Northern states and then in the Southern states. Controversy over the morality of divorce kept divorce laws strict in the nineteenth century: divorce was available only if adultery, abandonment, cruelty, or similar grounds were shown. Despite widespread collusion between divorcing parties that began to undercut the practical effect of strict divorce laws as early as the 1870s, such laws remained on the books for another century. In the 1970s, however, divorce law reform swept the country. Motivated by a desire to do away with the hypocrisy and perjury necessitated by the nineteenth-century divorce laws, all the states adopted "no-fault" laws that permitted marriages to be terminated without showing that one of the parties was guilty of a marital fault, such as adultery or cruelty. As Professor Kay suggests, the new laws reflect the widely felt need for divorce and the desire to eliminate its bitterness and stigma.

Restricting the availability of divorce, then, does not appear to be a realistic or desirable approach to the impoverishment of women and children. A more promising approach may be through more realistic alimony and support awards. As Weitzman indicates, one important factor contributing to poverty among divorced women and their children is the inadequacy of the alimony (spousal support) and child support courts award them. Despite myths to the contrary, the number of women receiving alimony has always been low. Census figures show, for example, that during the period from 1890 to 1920, no more than 16 percent of the women eligible to receive alimony were ever awarded it. More recent census figures show, that of the women divorced or separated in the years 1960 to 1969, less than 19 percent were entitled to alimony. Since then, however, the situation has grown worse as judges' interpretation of divorce laws has led to fewer women being awarded alimony and those who are awarded it, receiving it for shorter periods of time.

The low level of alimony awards is another problem. Many judges appear to have unrealistic notions of the earning capacity of divorced women, particularly those who have been out of the labor market for some time and those who have child care responsibilities. As a result, when it is awarded, alimony today is frequently too low to meet actual needs. Moreover, because it is usually seen now as a temporary measure to provide transitional support while women retrain themselves, locate a new job, or remarry, alimony often lasts only a few years. Similarly, judges who fail to understand the realities of life for divorced women are unlikely to be fully sympathetic to their efforts to enforce their alimony awards. Thus, judicial attitudes as much as the divorce law reforms themselves are probably responsible for the difficulties women now experience with alimony. Yet for people of moderate means, there may be a limit on what greater judicial willingness to afford women more adequate levels of support can achieve.

Like alimony, child support poses serious problems for divorced women. However, child support issues extend beyond the needs of divorced women, for inadequate awards and noncompliance with court orders also pose a major problem for unwed mothers. U.S. Census Bureau figures show that in 1989, for example, of the 3.2 million women below the poverty line living with children from an absent father, no more than 47 percent were awarded child support. For both divorced and unwed mothers in need, AFDC is supposed to provide a "safety net." The Center on Social Welfare Policy and Law gave some indication of the extent of that "net" when it reported that in 1992, there was no state in which AFDC and food stamp benefits combined equaled 100 percent of the poverty level.

Weitzman's conclusions have been criticized from a number of perspectives. See, e.g., *"Review Symposium on Weitzman's Divorce Revolution," American Bar Foundation Research* 757 (1986). Although a number of studies confirm that women are often in difficult economic straits following divorce, her statistical techniques have been questioned. More important, however, critics point out that it is not at all clear that these difficulties are due to the introduction of no-fault divorce inasmuch as women always received an inadequate amount of postdivorce support. Others point out that marriage often masks the poverty women in this country experience due to other inequities. Nevertheless, any effort to improve women's economic condition must confront the postdivorce situation Weitzman has highlighted.

The variety of approaches proposed to deal with the postdivorce difficulties Weitzman and others have identified inevitably meld financial and custody matters. In her "Beyond No-Fault" piece, for example, Herma Hill Kay speaks of the need to remedy the defects of marriage and its traditional sex-role expectations before the point of divorce. Thus, she advocates a "nonpunitive, nonsexist and nonpaternalistic" legal framework for divorce that will "safeguard those who do not maximize their separate interests, but instead engage in unselfish, sharing behavior." To this end, she advocates a system for marital property that, like modified community property systems, treats all property (and income) acquired after marriage as community property. This recognition of equal ownership, in her view, promotes shared management during marriage and also justifies equal division of the property on dissolution.

On the much discussed question of whether ex-spouses, usually wives, should share in the value of the professional license (e.g., doctor, lawyer) that their former partner acquired with their help during marriage, Kay would agree with the approach courts have taken almost universally to date. She, like the courts, would consider the degree or license as a factor to consider in setting alimony or spousal support, not property to be divided. By building on New Jersey's concept of "reimbursement alimony," Kay seeks to combine the flexibility of spousal support with the permanence and enforceability of property awards. On divorce, the contributing spouse would get both the value of her contributions and the cost of her choice to do the caretaking work. A woman who took care of the children instead of pursuing her own degree, for example, or a woman who remained in a dead-end job should, if necessary, be able to recover for her "investments" in the spouse.

In terms of custody decisions, Kay agrees that joint custody presumptions contribute to women's economic problems by encouraging them to give up financial support to obtain custody. However, she rejects the primary caretaker standard as a hidden maternal preference and instead advocates a system that will encourage divorcing spouses to reflect on their continuing roles as parents with the help of a family court system.

By contrast, Professor Martha Fineman, in the *Illusion of Equality* (Chicago: University of Chicago Press, 1991), argues for the "abdication of equality as an abstract goal." Seeking to "value and reward nurturing children, sacrifices made for others, and the future that is represented by the children who have been lost to equality," Fineman proposes rules for property division that focus on the children—and thus, their likely female caretakers. At a minimum, she would have the family home follow custody of the children and urges generally that property division rules affirmatively favor custodial parents. In her view, a focus on the children—and the liabilities they entail—will help recognize and meet women's needs, thereby obviating the need for battles such as have been waged to include professional degrees in the definition of property.

Others have focused more directly on deficiencies in child support. The increasing recognition of the need to ensure adequate support for children underscores the continuing relevance of the next selection. The child support system in this country has two aspects. As a private or individual matter, parents are responsible for the support of their children, and legal provisions permit courts to require noncustodial parents to support their children. As a public or collective matter, the government has undertaken a program of financial assistance to needy children.

Child Support and Policy: The Systematic Imposition of Costs on Women

Nan D. Hunter.
6 *Harvard Women's Law Journal* 1, 2–27 (1983).

The threshold question of whether a divorced father had any legal duty to provide support for his children was not settled until after the turn of the century. The traditional rule was that the father had a propriety right to his child's labor and services and a reciprocal duty to support the child during the marriage. Some jurists believed that he should be relieved of both if the mother gained custody upon divorce. While Blackstone described the father's duty to provide maintenance for his children, irrespective of custody, as "a principle of natural law," . . . family law commentators have observed:

> If it was such a principle, it was a moral duty without adequate legal remedy, although ecclesiastical courts perhaps lent their authority as a matter of conscience to force fathers to discharge

their natural duty, and in chancery a quasi-contractual duty of support eventually became equitable doctrine.

By the 1920's, courts had ceased to treat the child as an item of property, and the father's obligation to continue providing support after divorce was established as a matter of law. Once it was resolved that the father had a duty to provide for his children after divorce, the law often required that the duty be solely his, generally because of the mother's presumed inability to earn a sufficient income.

In practice, however, then as now, much of the support was not paid. . . .

Nonetheless, the misperception arose that divorced fathers actually did provide the full support for their children, while mothers enjoyed a windfall. Today, virtually all child support statutes provide that both parents have the same duty to provide support.

The role of the legal system since the turn of the century has been to adopt policies that purport to establish and enforce child support but succeed only in hiding the widespread reality of paternal nonsupport. Thus it functions in an unarticulated but systematic way to force women to assume the financial responsibility for childrearing—responsibility that belongs to both women and men. Though child support law is facially neutral, in practice its profound economic effects are directly tied to gender. It is women who pay the bulk of the costs that result when one household becomes two. . . .

I. THE SYSTEMS OF CHILD SUPPORT

The care and support of children is treated by the American legal system as an almost entirely private concern. For so long as a marriage continues, unless the situation degenerates into one of neglect, child support decisions are left within the realm of each nuclear family. It is only when one parent leaves or never joins the household unit that an amount of support, and thus a standard of care, may be determined for a given child. It is in the course of divorce and paternity proceedings that courts ascertain whether a duty of support exists, and if so, how much is owed.

The support obligation is established through the public mechanism of the courts, but the amount is generally determined on an individualized basis, according to how the judge hearing the case evaluates each family's situation. The law recognizes no benchmark figure for what constitutes an adequate amount to raise a child. The statutes which govern child support typically provide for an amount that is "reasonable and just" or that is based on a list of amorphous criteria, such as the financial resources of each parent, the needs of the child, and the child's previous standard of living. A few jurisdictions have adopted uniform tables of suggested amounts or formulae for setting amounts, but most parties obtaining a divorce do not know how much child support will be ordered until the court rules. Although a court hearing a divorce action has the power to divide property and award spousal support in addition to ordering child support, such relief is atypical. Only forty-five percent of divorced women receive a property award of any size, and only fourteen percent are awarded spousal support. Thus for the majority of women, child support is the only financial adjustment made at the time of divorce.

There is one partial exception to the privatized nature of the child support system. The program of Aid to Families with Dependent Children (AFDC) is the social backup system for parents who are unable to provide even subsistence-level support for their children.

A. The Private Family System

It is hard to overstate the extent of the post-divorce child support crisis in the United States. Judith Cassetty reported that, in 1974, families composed of women and children received child support payments which totaled far less than one-half of the amount designated as the poverty level that year for those families. By contrast, ninety-three percent of the fathers making the payments earned incomes that were at least twice the poverty level for their current families. Lenore Weitzman and Ruth Dixon found that the amount of child support awarded in Los Angeles in 1972 was only half the amount needed to raise children in low-income families at 1960 to 1961 prices and that it amounted to no more than twenty-five percent of the father's net income. A study of child support practice in Denver found that two-thirds of the fathers were ordered to pay less for child support than they reported spending on monthly car payments.

Because women are the custodial parents in the overwhelming majority of cases, it is almost always women who petition a court for child support. They confront all the difficulties accruing to the plaintiff in a civil action, while seeking funds to provide for their children's basic necessities. But unlike many other plaintiffs, they cannot easily eliminate expenses to minimize financial losses during the pendency of litigation. Even a request for support *pendente lite* may face a lengthy court backlog, and the smart attorney for the father may try to delay the hearing date so as to pressure the financially strained mother to accept an immediate, but relatively low, support offer. . . .

Domestic relations courts in different jurisdictions have varied widely in the methods they employ to determine support amounts. A few state appellate courts have acknowledged the confusion and unpredictability that result from the vagueness of the present criteria, and have adopted formulae. Irrespective of whether a formula or a conclusory standard is in use, however, almost all courts begin their determination of how much support is due by computing the costs of rearing the particular children before the court. After establishing these costs, the court normally proceeds to allocate between the parents responsibility for these expenses.

Most court systems now use a simple cost-division system, basing awards on information supplied by parents about the children's expenses and the net earnings of each parent. The judge will usually use this information to calculate a figure said to represent a reasonable share of child support expenses for the particular father to pay, considering the father's salary. Unofficially, many judges have adopted a "cap" on child support amounts, above which they almost never go.

In jurisdictions in which tables have been adopted setting specific support amounts according to the father's income, the rationale for the suggested amounts is presumably that a certain percentage of the father's income should go to child support. Although unstated, such a system necessarily assumes an underlying fixed cost for care of the child or children. Under this system, neither the amount of costs actually needed to raise the particular children nor the extent of the burden placed on the mother is considered. The advantage is that the amounts are predictable, and this predictability decreases litigation and its attendant expenses.

The use of these cost-sharing principles disadvantages custodial mothers by using as the starting point the minimal amount on which she and the children can subsist. An alternative is an income-sharing or equalization principle, which would seek to equalize the financial burden of one household becoming two, so that each family member would experience roughly the same proportional reduction in lifestyle as a result of the readjustment.

Whether the central principle used to set child support amounts should be based on cost-sharing or on income-sharing is one of the major debates now engaging economists and social workers active in the child support field. Critics of income-sharing argue that those formulae provide an incentive for custodial mothers to avoid paid employment, and oppose income-sharing as an improper extension of marital financial commitments beyond the point of divorce. Income-sharing advocates respond by pointing out that there is no universal standard for the "cost" of a child; cost cannot be determined except by reference to the economic status of the parents.

Although the cost-sharing method may satisfy a general reasonableness standard, it is quite possible for a child support award to be "reasonable" as an amount which the father can afford and the mother and child can subsist on, and also to be an inequitable reallocation of limited resources. A division of costs will almost always result in the mother-children household unit living on a lower post-transfer income than the single father household; most child support awards produce for the mother and children a minimal amount to defray expenses, and for the father, a relative increase in disposable income.

The cost-sharing approach raises other questions: whether a cost figure should be based on the expenses actually incurred for the child or on the amount which would have been spent had the marriage not dissolved; whether the value of personal services rendered by the custodial parent should be included in costs; how a costs approach can anticipate expenses for emergencies; and how to account for children needing more expensive items as they grow older. An income-sharing model would accommodate these concerns and be more likely to produce child support awards which equalize the relative well-being of each household.

The criteria utilized by most courts typify a simple cost-sharing principle; insofar as the emphasis is on the child's needs and the parents' ability to pay.... [most approaches] are based on variants of a cost-sharing approach. The results demonstrate the enormous disparities in the amounts that would be awarded by different courts for the same family in which the father earns a net monthly income of $1400; the mother earns a net monthly income of $815; and there are two children, ages five and ten, both in the custody of the mother. [A chart shows monthly support amounts ranging from $1364.53 to $602.95.] ...

A second aspect of the child support crisis is the issue of enforcement of awards. The Census Bureau found that, of all women who had court orders entitling them to receive child support in 1978, only forty-nine percent received the full amount, and on the average, thirty-five cents out of every dollar owed for child support was never paid. An examination of the standard procedures for payment reveals why noncompliance is so commonplace.

When a father is ordered to pay child support, he is usually told to send the mother a check every pay period. Keeping track of the payments, or lack of them, is the mother's responsibility. Most courts have a system for computerized record-keeping, but judges frequently do not order that records actually be kept, especially for middle and upper-middle class fathers, for whom it may be considered embarrassing. And even when computerized records are kept, often the failure to pay triggers no official response. Thus, it is up to the mother to institute enforcement proceedings. It will not be worthwhile for the mother to sue, however, until the support owed exceeds the fee she will probably have to pay a lawyer to bring suit. By the time it becomes worth it to proceed, her financial plans and budgeting may be in turmoil. If the amount due builds up and the case does get to court, judges in some states are permitted to adjust the amount of arrearage retroactively if they believe the father cannot afford the entire sum. The system thus provides virtually every incentive for fathers not to pay.

The literature on child support is replete with ideas for improving enforcement mechanisms. An increasing number of courts are using automated record-keeping systems. Some of these systems include automatic notice procedures, so that a father is at least contacted, and perhaps summoned when a payment becomes delinquent. A number of states have substituted administrative procedures for full-scale court hearings for both the award-setting and enforcement phases. One commentator has studied the impact of using imprisonment for nonsupport as a deterrent [and found its use was significantly related to the payment of support].

The greatest attention has been paid to developing procedures for garnishments and automatic wage withholding systems which would have the employer deduct support payments from fathers' wages like a tax deduction, and then send the support amount to the court. One proposal suggests that a federal income withholding system be instituted to allow support orders to follow the parent from job to job until the obligation ends. Another author has suggested a "federal floating wage assignment," which would essentially be a nationwide garnishment system, creating a uniform national remedy for violation of a support order.

Any proposal which succeeded in increasing child support enforcement would benefit the majority of custodial mothers. All of these ideas are refinements of judicial procedures, however, and none goes beyond the legal system in the search for a better model. Each seeks to improve incrementally the existing private family support system rather than to build a cohesive social child-care policy. Even the proposals for equalizing the costs of child raising between a woman and a man in a given family fail to address the support problems of parents who lack enough resources to divide.

B. The AFDC System

The program of Aid to Families with Dependent Children is the second component of the American child support system. Initiated in the 1930's primarily to provide for widows, AFDC became the only alternative to the purely private family support system. Since that time, the number of recipients has mushroomed, increasing by 225 percent during the 1960's and peaking in 1976. However narrow were the program's original goals, AFDC currently functions to maintain some 10.5 million children and their mothers. The role of AFDC as a government-funded backup system must thus be a major part of any discussion of child support reform.

Indeed it was a reaction to the increasing costs of AFDC and the desire to cut back expenses, rather than social alarm over the plight of mothers raising children with insufficient support amounts, that led to most of the current attention to issues of child support enforcement. . . .

On the federal level, Congress responded by amending the AFDC entitlement provisions to require that mothers cooperate with the state in establishing paternity and obtaining support payments from fathers as a condition of eligibility. Concern over the dangers to women posed by the requirement of filing suits against physically abusive fathers resulted in a compromise "good cause" exception which waives the requirement to cooperate when the recipient can prove that there is a reasonable likelihood of physical or emotional harm to her or the child.

The exception is rarely invoked successfully, probably because the "good cause" showing is difficult to make. The great majority of women who receive AFDC have no choice but to name the fathers and "cooperate" in locating and suing them. Loss of privacy is the price of receiving benefits. Thus, in contrast to women not on AFDC, who are often unable to enforce child support orders because of the difficulty and expense involved [in] initiating collection suits, women who do receive AFDC are forced into intrusive prosecutions over which they have no choice or control. The rights of both groups of women are effectively ignored.

From the traditional viewpoint of the best interests of the child, many AFDC mothers may be the worst group to coerce into pursuing child support. Studies have found that many low-income Black families rely on tight kinship bonds and unstructured mutual aid systems to cope with the conditions of poverty[;] a requirement that mothers cooperate with the state in securing paternal payments jeopardizes these bonds and secondary support systems. Some poor children receive material, psychological, and social support from their fathers or, most likely, from their father's kinship network, despite his absence from the home. If the father refuses to acknowledge the child for fear of incurring legal obligations, the child may lose a form of support which is arguably more significant than the amount of public funds saved by decreasing the welfare budget. More recently it has been suggested that the loss of a kinship network may occur among low-income communities of a variety of racial and ethnic identities. Presumably, the risk varies with each specific family, depending on the nature of the interpersonal relationships, the proximity of family members, and numerous other factors. The judgment as to whether more will be gained or lost by seeking coerced support should be left to the mother, and her decision should be respected by the state. . . .

II. THE CHILD SUPPORT SYSTEM AS A MEANS FOR THE SOCIAL CONTROL OF WOMEN

The concept of the privatized, closed family system underlies all American family law principles, including those governing intrafamily support. Until the point of destitution, when AFDC intervenes, the individual family is expected to make its own internal decisions about who in the family will receive which resources. The "hands off" principle increases the control of the more powerful party in marriage—the husband—by failing to counterbalance the various forms of social control that men in general have over women. . . .

The family support system, with its absence of legal remedies during marriage and the privatization of child support after marriage ends, exemplifies this public/private dichotomy. The system harms women both because it systematically burdens mothers and relieves fathers of the child support obligation, and because it forces individual women to bear the brunt of a major social problem.

Income data on divorced men and women illustrates the extent to which the current child support system maintains male economic supremacy by failing to equalize the impact of divorce between the two parents. Just as the child support system penalizes women, it directly benefits men. Custodial mothers experience a sharp drop in their living standard and their disposable income after divorce, but divorced fathers realize a financial gain. A father who is ordered to pay one-third of his income for child support, for example, and thus retains sixty-seven percent of his net earnings for discretionary expenses, fares better financially than when he was married.

An examination of child support orders in Cleveland from 1965 to 1978 found that divorced fathers retained about eighty percent of their pre-divorce income; the higher the man's earnings, the greater the proportion of income he retained; in fact, the proportion of the average father's income which was ordered for child support declined between 1965 and 1978, especially for the more affluent men. Weitzman's surveys of divorced men and women in Los Angeles found that the households of divorced husbands had a per capita income from one-and-a-half to three-and-a-half times greater than the per capita income of the divorced wives' households; again the disparity between husband and wife increased as the husband's income increased. Data from the University of Michigan's nationwide sample indicated that eighty-six percent of divorced fathers were economically better off than their former wives and children, and more than sixty-four percent had income-poverty ratios which were two or more times greater than those of their former wives and children. In the Cleveland study, for example, divorced fathers living alone were found to have from ten to twenty percent more after-transfer income than the mother-children unit, and if only the two parents were compared to each other, fathers had three times as much (or three-hundred percent more) after-transfer income. Thus men as a class are the winners in the universe of child support awards.

Increasing rates of divorce will, over time, lead to a major transfer from men to women of the bulk of family care expenses (in addition to family care labor). The child support system thus contributes to the "feminization of poverty," or the massive shift of women-headed households into the official zone of poverty. This process operates in tandem with broader economic discrimination against women, reflected in women's earnings averaging fifty-nine percent of men's earnings.

Among the most serious effects of the impoverishment of women brought about by divorce is the reinforcement of women's economic dependence on men. The primary route open in this society for women to raise their standard of living is to marry, remain married, or remarry. Indeed, married women are aware of the financial perils accompanying divorce. One recent study of Michigan women, with children, about to receive a divorce, found that twenty-nine percent of those either unemployed or on welfare indicated that they wanted to reconsider or to attempt reconciliation; only eight percent of full-time working women expressed this desire. Possessing a full-time job, even given the discounted "woman's wage," may operate as a functional threshold requirement for women to consider divorce to be a viable option. Research has demonstrated an inverse relationship between a wife's income and the duration of the marriage, as on the average each thousand-dollar increase in a wife's earnings produces a one percent increase in the rate of separation. This linkage appears less significant for Black women than for white women, probably because Black women have been eco-nomically forced into higher rates of labor force participation, at lower wages, than white women. Thus their earnings are less likely to produce either the perception or the reality of greater independence.

For the divorced woman with children, remarriage is the surest method to achieve financial security. A survey of women from one county in Michigan in the mid-1970's and a survey of Detroit women in the 1940's both found that remarriage significantly increased women's income. . . .

The trend in some jurisdictions toward holding stepfathers liable for the support of their wives' children also increases the pressure on women to remarry, in order to acquire a provider for their children more reliable than the typical absent father. This pressure is even stronger if the divorced father has, by his own remarriage, acquired new support obligations for stepchildren or children born in the new marriage. Under basic cost-sharing principles, the expenses of his "second family" will be seen to justify a reduction in the amount of support he is ordered to pay for his original family. The only way for the divorced mother to keep up in this cycle is to remarry. Policy choices that minimize the child support to be provided by the divorced father strengthen the bonds that tie women to men and to marriage as an institution. . . .

III. BUILDING THE BASIS FOR REFORM

There are a variety of improvements to the current system that could be achieved by state legislative enactment, amendment of court rules, or new decisional law. The most fundamental change would be to adopt income-sharing formulae which seek to equalize between the parents the relative burden of the increased costs of a split household. Other possible changes that would alleviate problems of delay and nonenforcement include: imposing continuing wage garnishments for the amount which is ordered, or wage assignments which take effect whenever a payment is more than twenty days overdue, requiring that the father post security or bond to guarantee payment; authorizing hearing officers to order payment of retroactive support for any time period prior to the hearing during which support was not paid; creating referees or administrative agencies whose only responsibility would be to establish child support amounts; providing for attorneys' fees for contested phases of a support determination; and making promptly available to non-AFDC recipients such programs as the parent locator service.

States have adopted many of these and other mechanisms for enforcing support orders, primarily as a means of trimming welfare costs. At the federal level, the Internal Revenue Service has broadened the scope of its collection program—which makes seizure of assets permissible—to encompass delinquent child support debts owed to both AFDC recipients and nonrecipients.

The aforementioned reforms would improve the daily lives of custodial mothers. None, however, addresses the problems raised by the current AFDC system, nor alters the privatized structure of family law which precludes government involvement in the sphere where it is often most needed.

The most far-reaching and thorough change in the American child support system would be the adoption of supplemental family income programs, such as those which operate in Sweden and France, where the government pays a fixed allowance to all parents with children. Yet, a family allowance alone could function as a strong incentive for the woman in an ongoing marriage to remain at home, since it could be used as a substitute for her earnings. Upon divorce, the wife would be faced with an abrupt need to enter the workforce despite a lack of job skills and experience. The French have, however, attempted to lessen this effect by developing the most extensive system of public childcare services in any Western European country. Widespread public childcare services allow divorced women to share the burdens of childrearing with the state. In Sweden, the government advances payments of private child support which are due. The amount of private child support in Sweden is determined, as in the United States, in a judicial proceeding or by private agreement, but is subject to a statutory minimum. When the amount owed by the father is set by a court at less than the

minimum, the government makes up the difference from its general revenue funds. Once the amount is set, the state will pay that sum each month to the mother and assume responsibility for collecting from the father.

Although neither country's legal system appears to accept the principle of equalizing the financial burden of divorce between mother and father, the state itself absorbs much of the impact of divorce, thus lessening the burden on women.

An American version of this kind of mixed public-private model for child support at the state level has been proposed by Irwin Garfinkel of the Institute for Research on Poverty at the University of Wisconsin. Garfinkel's plan combines a credit income tax with a public child support payment program. Its child support component would be financed by a tax imposed on the absent parent, in an amount determined by that parent's income and the number of children for whom support is owed. It would be collected through the same withholding method used for other taxes. Children whose fathers are indigent would be protected by a statutory minimum amount, which would be financed by general state revenues but distributed in the same manner—probably through a social services agency—as support amounts collected from individual fathers.

If adopted at the federal level, this method would effectively nationalize the private family system by bringing child support payments under central control. By combining the private system with AFDC, it would at least make less visible the "welfare" status of many indigent families. But despite its potential to reduce this stigma, the reform value of such a program would be limited if it did not provide for reasonable minimum support amounts and eliminate coercive methods of insuring the mother's "cooperation" in locating fathers.

The overall economic impact of such a system on women would depend largely on how the formula used set the support obligations of each parent. If the formula were structured to demand that both parents contribute the identical *proportion* of their income to child support, it would ultimately benefit women. But under Garfinkel's plan, the only variables considered would be the noncustodial parent's income and the number of children. Without giving consideration to the mother's income, it would be impossible to equalize the standard of living in the two households. Thus, while Garfinkel's plan would benefit women by providing an absolute guarantee that support would be paid, the inequity of how the burden is divided would continue.

The Garfinkel proposal could serve as the basis for an intermediate stage of reform. Like most partial improvements, however, its biggest danger is perhaps that it would be frozen into place as the last effort to overhaul the system. A more thoroughgoing reform would supplement Garfinkel's concepts with not only equalization of the burden between the parents, but also an extensive public childcare system, including a floor for support amounts, so that children with-

out support from a male wage earner would be guaranteed a humane upbringing. These components are essential to any system which would decrease women's economic dependence on men. . . .

STUDY QUESTIONS

1. What does Hunter identify as the major obstacles to women receiving adequate child support?
2. Why does she view the current child support system as a "means for the social control of women"? Do you find her argument sound?
3. What is her proposal for improving the child support system in the United States? Is her proposal a good idea?

After publication of Hunter's article, federal involvement in both the public and private aspects of child support increased significantly. The following piece outlines the history and nature of that involvement.

Child Support Manual for Legal Services

Nancy Erickson.
New York: National Center on Women and Family Law, 1992. Pp. 6–13.

Increased federal government involvement has been the latest in a series of steps leading toward uniformity among state laws, more adequate child support orders, and enforcement of those orders. The first steps toward uniformity were taken by the states themselves, via interstate compacts and enactment of "uniform" state laws. By 1957, for example, the Uniform Reciprocal Enforcement of Support Act (URESA), or its equivalent, had been enacted in all states.

The second step toward uniformity was taken by advocates of equality. Non-marital children had been discriminated against in virtually all states, and Supreme Court cases established the right of non-marital children to receive child support on an equal basis with marital children. Sex discrimination, which went to the very core of state family law, was challenged, with the result that the Supreme Court held that female children had to be supported to the same age as male children.

The third, and perhaps greatest, step (actually, a series of steps) toward uniformity and adequacy of child support laws was taken by the federal government. Alarmed by skyrocketing welfare costs, Congress addressed three major problems regarding child support that have contributed to those costs: the low numbers of non-marital children for whom paternity has been adjudicated; inadequate levels of child support; and ineffective enforcement of existing support orders. . . .

The three problems outlined above were addressed in three major pieces of federal legislation

Reprinted by permission of National Center on Women and Family Law.

and several smaller ones, all of which are based upon Congress' power to mandate state law changes as a condition of federal funding for AFDC and other purposes. Advocacy groups for children of mothers who were struggling to stay off public assistance or to attain a reasonable standard of living for their families also supported and helped to mold these laws, which are: (1) the 1975 legislation enacting Title IV-D of the Social Security Act, which established the federal child support enforcement program, (2) the Child Support Enforcement Amendments of 1984 (CSEA), and (3) the Family Support Act of 1988 (FSA).

Each state must have a "IV-D Agency," which is usually located within the state department of social services (. . . [also known as] human services or welfare) or the attorney general's office, and the state IV-D agency must have a system to locate absent parents, establish paternity, obtain support orders, and enforce those orders. These services must be offered both to AFDC and non-AFDC families. Any custodial parent, no matter what her income level, is entitled to services from the IV-D agency, although non-AFDC families may be charged small fees. The Office of Child Support Enforcement (OCSE) in the Administration for Children and Families of the Department of Health and Human Services (HHS) is the federal agency with responsibility for monitoring and assisting the state IV-D agencies, which are sometimes known as state OCSEs.

With regard to establishment of paternity, federal laws now require the following:

1. state statutes of limitations must permit paternity claims to be brought at least until the child's eighteenth birthday;
2. persons receiving AFDC and Medicaid must cooperate with the state in establishing paternity, unless "good cause" for noncooperation is shown;
3. all parties to a civil contested paternity action must, unless there is good cause, submit to genetic tests (formerly called "blood tests") if a party so requests, and the federal government will reimburse the states for 90% of the costs of such tests;
4. states must meet certain goals for paternity establishment; and

5. states are encouraged to decriminalize their paternity procedures and to provide simple procedures for voluntary acknowledgement of paternity in uncontested cases.

Adequacy of child support orders was addressed both in the CSEA and the FSA, but the FSA was the impetus for the greatest changes in state law. The CSEA required that the states develop "guidelines" for setting child support orders, and the guidelines had to be made available to the court or administrative tribunals that heard child support cases. Those decision-makers were not bound to use them, however, and, if they chose to use them, they did not have to treat the guidelines amount as presumptively correct.

The FSA put "bite" into this requirement by specifying that the guidelines would have to be presumptive. As of October 13, 1989, all states were required to have in place guidelines (formulas) setting amounts that must be ordered by a court unless the court finds that the amount is "unjust or inappropriate" and gives reasons therefor in writing or on the record. Each state's guidelines must be reviewed and revised at least once every four years after the guidelines are set. Effective October 13, 1990, any order in a IV-D case must be reviewed and, if appropriate, adjusted (modified) to comply with the guidelines if either parent or the IV-D agency so requests. As of 1993, the states must have procedures to review and adjust all IV-D orders under the guidelines at least once every three years unless neither party wants a review or, in an AFDC case, review would not be in the best interests of the child.

. . . [I]t appears that the guidelines have indeed, resulted in orders for child support that are higher than they would have been under prior laws.

Enforcement of support orders has been addressed in all three major pieces of federal legislation and several other congressional statutes. Together, those laws and related statutes contain the following requirements, among others:

1. families receiving AFDC and foster care services must assign their support rights to the

state, and the IV-D agency must pursue enforcement of these support rights; families receiving Medicaid must assign their medical support rights to the state and either the IV-D agency or the Medicaid agency will pursue these rights;

2. there must be automatic (without the necessity of going back to court) wage withholding for any IV-D order currently in effect when a non-custodial parent fails to make one month's worth of payments, and for non-IV-D cases when arrears (as specified by the state) are owed.

3. by November 1, 1990, all new or modified IV-D child support orders must provide for enforcement through immediate, automatic income withholding unless the parties agree to an alternative arrangement or the court finds good cause for not ordering immediate income withholding; as of January 1, 1994, immediate income withholding will be required in all non-IV-D cases as well, with the same exceptions noted above;

4. as an incentive for the custodial parent to assist the state IV-D agency in establishing and enforcing child support, an AFDC family is entitled to the first $50 of any child sup-

port payment made by the absent parent in the month when it was due, and this $50 "pass-through" will not affect the family's AFDC grant and will not be used to determine their AFDC eligibility;

5. all parents must furnish their Social Security numbers to the state agency that issues birth certificates (the numbers will not be put on the birth certificate but will be retained by the agency for identification purposes);

6. states must have in place procedures for certain kinds of child support enforcement mechanisms, such as liens, bonds, tax refund offsets, and credit bureau reporting; and

7. states must have laws providing that support installments cannot be cancelled or modified retroactively and are vested judgments as they fall due, making them subject to the Full Faith and Credit Clause of the Constitution.

STUDY QUESTIONS

1. What is a state IV-D agency? What services does it provide? Why do all the states have these agencies?

2. Who may use the services provided by a state's IV-D agency? Who must use them?

———————— ❧ ————————

As Hunter points out, the far-reaching reforms encompassed in a family allowance system, as well as the child support mechanisms already enacted, might have the effect of reinforcing traditional marital arrangements in which women are financially dependent on men. Other measures would then be required to counteract the incentives such a system offers to women to forego employment outside the home.

The nature of mechanisms for alleviating the feminization of poverty, may thus be one of many ways that the law shows its tendency to promote traditional family groupings. In the next section, we explore another side of the law's relation to family groupings. To what extent does the law tolerate choices to live in nontraditional relationships?

IV. BEYOND THE NUCLEAR FAMILY

As the preceding sections have suggested, governmental policies and judicial decisions frequently assume that people do and should live in stable units composed of one breadwinner (the husband), one homemaker (the wife), and their children. These units are generally referred to as nuclear families.

Assumptions regarding the nuclear family have become increasingly difficult to justify in the light of major changes that have occurred in families during the past several decades. Available statistics show that the traditional nuclear family no longer dominates the American scene, if it ever did. In 1991, households headed by married couples represented only 55 percent of all households. Marriage and remarriage rates are both falling, and, although the divorce rate is now declining, it doubled between 1965 and 1985. As marriage and remarriage rates decline, the number of nonmarital living arrangements has grown. Not surprisingly, growing up in a home with two parents is far from a universal experience for children today. In 1991, only 72 percent of American children lived with both parents; 25 percent lived with one parent; and the remainder lived in other situations. In short, a substantial segment of the population is no longer living in stable, two-parent nuclear families.

In the postindustrial United States, the heterosexual nuclear family has been closely linked with rigid gender roles and women's dependent status. The husband has been expected historically to provide for the family economically, and the wife has been expected to take care of her husband and children in the home. As we have seen repeatedly, woman's role in the traditional nuclear family has interfered with her equal participation in political and economic life and has reinforced her dependence on men. In order to break out of these rigid gender-role patterns, individuals need to have the option of forming different emotional groupings. Similarly, women's more equal participation in society may well require that the nurturing, caretaking, and homemaking services that women now generally provide in the home be made available through a greater variety of arrangements. For this reason, we now explore the law's tolerance for different forms of emotional bonds and living situations.

Two countervailing forces are at work shaping the law in this area. One is a conservative force that would deny legal recognition to nontraditional living arrangements that are seen as jeopardizing prevailing moral values. The other is a liberalizing force that calls for legal recognition of different forms of living arrangements so that the affairs of people actually living in those arrangements can be handled in an orderly fashion. The composite effect of these two forces is that legislators and judges have often been unwilling to recognize nonnuclear living arrangements until they perceive that they are widespread and that society has come to view them as morally acceptable. When they do accord legal recognition to nonnuclear arrangements, they emphasize the similarities between the new arrangements and more conventional ones and affirm traditional values.

A case striking down a restriction on marriage illustrates this process. The decision, *Zablocki v. Redhail,* 434 U.S. 374 (1978), invalidated a state prohibition on marriages by noncustodial parents whose children had received or were likely to receive public assistance. One effect of the decision was to ease the way for divorced fathers to remarry, thereby allowing them to start second families and/or legitimize new families they may already have started. In this sense, the decision responded to a societal perception that having a series of families is morally acceptable and to a practical need to regularize the legal status of family members in subsequent relationships. In recognizing these relationships, however, the Court reaffirmed the importance of marriage as an institution, as well as the close relationship between marriage and procreation. At the same time, it made clear that the state retained the power to impose "reasonable" regulations on marriage.

Issues involving legal recognition of different family forms arise in numerous contexts. Many laws govern family relationships directly, specifying, for example, who may marry and when they may divorce. Other statutes and judge-made legal rules establish principles for resolving disputes between individuals who have lived or had children together. Still other legal conflicts involving family forms arise when public bodies attempt to govern living arrangements through restrictions on employment or zoning laws. The resolution of these conflicts often involves the interpretation of a particular statute or legal doctrine. Many times, however, the question is a constitutional one: to what extent does the constitution afford protection to the individual's or family's choice of living arrangements.

The materials in this section look at three types of relationships that the law has traditionally failed to recognize: heterosexual cohabitation; same-sex relationships; and extended families. To understand these materials, it is necessary to look beyond the legal doctrines the courts discuss to the actual impact of the decisions on the parties; the practical pressures on the courts to recognize the particular arrangement; and the extent to which the courts perceive the arrangement to be widespread and acceptable.

Heterosexual Cohabitation

Courts often require people who divorce to pay child support and/or alimony and to make property settlements with their former spouses. Until recently, courts have not imposed similar requirements on unmarried cohabitants at the termination of their relationships. The following case is one of the first decisions authorizing redistribution of property at the time a nonmarital relationship is dissolved.

Marvin v. Marvin

Supreme Court of California, 1976.
18 Cal.3d 660, 134 Cal. Rptr. 815,
557 P.2d 106.

TOBRINER, Justice.

During the past 15 years, there has been a substantial increase in the number of couples living together without marrying. Such nonmarital relationships lead to legal controversy when one partner dies or the couple separates. . . .

Plaintiff avers that in October of 1964 she and defendant "entered into an oral agreement" that while "the parties lived together they would combine their efforts and earnings and would share equally any and all property accumulated as a result of their efforts whether individual or combined." Furthermore, they agreed to "hold themselves out to the general public as husband and wife" and that "plaintiff would further render her services as a compan-

ion, homemaker, housekeeper and cook to . . . defendant."

Shortly thereafter plaintiff agreed to "give up her lucrative career as an entertainer [and] singer" in order to "devote her full time to defendant . . . as a companion, homemaker, housekeeper and cook;" in return defendant agreed to "provide for all of plaintiff's financial support and needs for the rest of her life."

Plaintiff alleges that she lived with defendant from October of 1964 through May of 1970 and fulfilled her obligations under the agreement. During this period the parties as a result of their efforts and earnings acquired in defendant's name substantial real and personal property, including motion picture rights worth over $1 million. In May of 1970, however, defendant compelled plaintiff to leave his household. He continued to support plaintiff until November of 1971, but thereafter refused to provide further support. . . .

Although the past decisions hover over the issue in the somewhat wispy form of the figures of a Chagall painting, we can abstract from those decisions a clear and simple rule. The fact that a man and woman live together without marriage, and engage in a sexual relationship, does not in itself invalidate agreements between them relating to their earnings, property, or expenses. Neither is such an agreement invalid merely because the parties may have contemplated the creation or continuation of a nonmarital relationship when they entered into it. Agreements between nonmarital partners fail only to the extent that they rest upon a consideration of meretricious sexual services. Thus the rule asserted by defendant, that a contract fails if it is "involved in" or made "in contemplation" of a nonmarital relationship, cannot be reconciled with the decisions. . . .

[W]e base our opinion on the principle that adults who voluntarily live together and engage in sexual relations are nonetheless as competent as any other persons to contract respecting their earnings and property rights. Of course, they cannot lawfully contract to pay for the performance of sexual services, for such a contract is, in essence, an agreement for prostitution and unlawful for that reason. But . . . so long as the agreement does not rest upon illicit meretricious consideration, the parties may order their economic affairs as they choose, and no policy precludes the courts from enforcing such agreements.

In the present instance, plaintiff alleges that the parties agreed to pool their earnings, that they contracted to share equally in all property acquired, and that defendant agreed to support plaintiff. The terms of the contract as alleged do not rest upon any unlawful consideration. We therefore conclude that the complaint furnishes a suitable basis upon which the trial court can render declaratory relief. . . .

As we have noted, both causes of action in plaintiff's complaint allege an express contract; neither assert any basis for relief independent from the contract. In *In re Marriage of Cary*, however, the Court of Appeals held that, in view of the policy of the Family Law Act, property accumulated by nonmarital partners in an actual family relationship should be divided equally. . . . Although our conclusion that plaintiff's complaint states a cause of action based on an express contract alone compels us to reverse the judgment for

defendant, resolution of the *Cary* issue will serve both to guide the parties upon retrial and to resolve a conflict presently manifest in published Court of Appeals decisions. . . .

If *Cary* is interpreted as holding that the Family Law Act requires an equal division of property accumulated in nonmarital "actual family relationships," then . . . *Cary* distends the act. No language in the Family Law Act addresses the property rights of nonmarital partners, and nothing in the legislative history of the act suggests that the Legislature considered that subject. The delineation of the rights of nonmarital partners before 1970 had been fixed entirely by judicial decision; we see no reason to believe that the Legislature, by enacting the Family Law Act, intended to change that state of affairs. . . .

But, although parties to a nonmarital relationship obviously cannot have based any expectations upon the belief that they were married, other expectations and equitable considerations remain. The parties may well expect that property will be divided in accord with the parties' own tacit understanding and that in the absence of such understanding the courts will fairly apportion property accumulated through mutual effort. We need not treat nonmarital partners as putatively married persons in order to apply principles of implied contract, or extend equitable remedies; we need to treat them only as we do any other unmarried persons. . . .

Although we recognize the well-established public policy to foster and promote the institution of marriage, perpetuation of judicial rules which result in an inequitable distribution of property accumulated during a nonmarital relationship is neither a just nor an effective way of carrying out that policy.

In summary, we believe that the prevalence of nonmarital relationships in modern society and the social acceptance of them, marks this as a time when our courts should by no means apply the doctrine of the unlawfulness of the so-called meretricious relationship to the instant case. As we have explained, the nonenforceability of agreements expressly providing for meretricious conduct rested upon the fact that such conduct, as the word suggests, pertained to and encompassed prostitution. To equate the nonmarital relationship of today to such a subject matter is to do violence to an accepted and wholly different practice. . . .

The mores of the society have indeed changed so radically in regard to cohabitation that we cannot impose a standard based on alleged moral considerations that have apparently been so widely abandoned by so many. Lest we be misunderstood, however, we take this occasion to point out that the structure of society itself largely depends upon the institution of marriage, and nothing we have said in this opinion should be taken to derogate from that institution. The joining of the man and woman in marriage is at once the most socially productive and individually fulfilling relationship that one can enjoy in the course of a lifetime.

The judgment is reversed and the cause remanded for further proceedings consistent with the views expressed herein.

STUDY QUESTIONS

1. According to Michelle Marvin's complaint, why was she entitled to property held by Lee Marvin?
2. When will the California courts enforce agreements between cohabitants? Are all services subject to contract? Does a sexual or emotional component to a relationship preclude a valid contract? Should it?
3. Why did the court decline to interpret the Family Law Act to authorize an equal division of property in "actual family relationships"? Had it done so, would cohabitation have been tantamount to marriage? If so, would individuals be unduly restricted in their ability to order their own affairs? Is it feasible for courts to identify "actual family relationships"?

Not all states have followed California's lead in regard to the property rights of couples cohabiting without marriage. Those states that are willing to allocate the property of separating couples vary in the approach they adopt. Some, like California, use doctrines from a variety of areas to enforce both express and tacit understandings between the parties and to ensure fair results. Others will make property awards only when they find the parties made an express contract. Still others refuse altogether to intervene in such disputes, at least in part because they are unwilling to give such relationships any legal standing.

Scholars as well as judges and other lawmakers continue to debate the most appropriate way for the law to treat cohabitation. Some see contract law as the best way to settle legitimate claims against nonmarital partners while at the same time allowing individuals freedom in shaping their relationships. Others question whether women are sufficiently able to strike fair bargains in light of unequal social and economic conditions. Thus, they would impose a legal status on stable relationships that is akin to marriage and that permits support awards and property divisions on separation.

Another context in which courts determine legal and financial consequences of cohabitation involves the right to continued alimony from a previous marriage. The obligation to pay alimony usually ceases when the spouse receiving support remarries. Often ex-husbands also stop making payments when their former spouses begin cohabiting with a paramour, and the courts are then required to decide whether the new relationship suffices to terminate the alimony obligation. Decisions that terminate the alimony obligation, even though the former wife's need for alimony has not ended, have the effect of punishing the woman simply for her choice of living arrangements. Such decisions may also reflect and reinforce the view that having entered into a sexual relationship, the new man has assumed responsibility for her financial support. In any event, most states now permit alimony payments to be reduced or terminated only when the new relationship has changed the supported spouse's financial circumstances.

The courts' approach to these cases, like their approach to *Marvin v. Marvin*-type disputes, suggests that even though courts are not eager to recognize the sexual component of nonmarital relationships, they are increasingly willing to resolve the financial disputes that arise as households form, dissolve, and reform. Legal changes making it possible to resolve such financial disputes in the courts may be coming about for the same reason that divorce became available: Both may reflect a commercial need to make clear who owns particular property. Despite the modicum of legal recognition they thus gain, nonmarital relationships may nevertheless be the subject of societal opprobrium. Indeed, that is the impact of a case in which the court declined to afford constitutional protection to such relationships.

Hollenbaugh v. Carnegie Free Library, 439 U.S. 1052 (1978), involved the relationship between Rebecca Hollenbaugh, a librarian, and Fred Philburn, a custodian at a state library in Connellsville, Pennsylvania. Although Philburn was married, the two began seeing each other, and when Hollenbaugh discovered she was pregnant, they began living openly together. Responding to complaints from some members of the community, the library board of trustees fired both of them when they refused to alter their living arrangement. The federal district court upheld the firings despite the absence of any evidence that the couple's living arrangement interfered with their performance on the job. The decision was affirmed by the federal appellate court, and the United States Supreme Court denied *certiorari*. Justice Marshall wrote a vigorous dissent, arguing that the couple's right to "pursue an open rather than a clandestine relationship and rear their child together" was protected by a constitutional right to personal privacy.

Same-Sex Relationships

As we have seen, the expectation that individuals should be grouped in family units consisting of a man, a woman, and their children has been an important factor in shaping the opportunities open to women and men. In precluding alternative outlets for fulfilling emotional, sexual, and economic needs, this expectation has contributed to the pressure on both sexes to accept marriage on whatever terms were available. It has also had an especially harsh impact on those who wish to establish same-sex relationships. The legal system has been a key mechanism in reinforcing that expectation by denying opportunities to formalize those relationships and by failing to recognize their legitimacy in other contexts.

Homosexual couples have sought to marry for practical as well as emotional reasons. Constitutional challenges to statutes and governmental decisions limiting marriage to heterosexual relationships have been based on both privacy and equality guarantees. As we shall see in the next chapters, the right to privacy protects a wide range of decisions about procreation, child rearing, and family relationships. However, in declining to invalidate criminal prohibitions on nonmarital sex as applied to consensual relations between two homosexuals in a private home, the Supreme Court has made clear that the right to privacy does not protect same-sex relationships. *Bowers v. Hardwick,* 478 U.S. 186 (1986).

Equality challenges may be based on the Equal Protection Clause or on state equal rights provisions. In either case, the analysis is reminiscent of that used in Chapter 4 to deny Title VII claims based on sexual orientation. Differential treatment based on failure to conform to societal norms and social customs regarding sexual affinities are not sex-based. The Washington Court of Appeals put it this way in rejecting a claim that the denial of the right to marry violated the state ERA:

> In the instant case, it is apparent that the state's refusal to grant a license allowing the appellants to marry one another is not based upon appellants' status as males, but rather it is based upon the state's recognition that our society as a whole views marriage as the appropriate and desirable forum for procreation and the rearing of children. This is true even though married couples are not required to become parents and even though some couples are incapable of becoming parents and even though not all couples who produce children are married. These, however, are exceptional situations.
>
> Singer v. Hara, *522 P.2d 1187, 1195 (Wash. Ct. of Appeals, 1974).*

Many women and men establish same-sex relationships only after they have married and had children. Particularly for women in these circumstances, the ability to retain custody of their children is an important consideration in determining their living arrangements. Courts have varied widely in their treatment of such custody cases. Some courts deem lesbians and gays eligible for custody on the same terms as other parents. For others, custody awards to homosexuals are out of the question. Still others impose special conditions on custody awards to parents involved in same-sex relationships, limiting the extent to which they can cohabit with their partners. The three approaches are illustrated by the majority, concurring, and dissenting positions in the next case. At issue there was a lesbian couple's decision to consolidate their households several years after they had each gained custody of their children.

Schuster v. Schuster

Supreme Court of Washington, 1978.
90 Wash. 2d 626, 585 P.2d 130.

BRACHTENBACH, Justice.

These consolidated cases involve factually related divorces. The respondent women separated from their husbands and lived together in a lesbian relationship with their children of their marriages. The appellant fathers filed for divorces from their respective spouses. Each mother was given custody of her children. However, the mothers were ordered to live separate and apart and were prohibited from removing the children from the state. *Those decrees were not appealed.*

Later, each of the fathers filed modification petitions seeking custody of their children. Subsequently, motions for contempt were filed charging violations of the original decrees. The alleged violations by the mothers were: (1) renting separate apartments in the same building but in fact living together along with all the children; and

(2) taking the children out of state. The mothers filed counter petitions seeking modification of the original decrees by deleting the prohibition against their living together.

The two modification proceedings were joined for hearing. An attorney was appointed to represent the children's interests. . . .

At the outset we emphasize that these cases do not involve the question of whether it was proper to award custody of the children to lesbian mothers. That question was litigated in the original divorce actions. No appeal was taken by any party. There being no appeal, the original award of custody with all limitations contained therein is binding on all parties and upon this court. The issue is simply not before us.

The only question presented by this appeal is whether any modification of the original decrees was proper. When is a modification of the custody provisions of an original divorce decree justified? We have long held that a modification will not be granted unless there has been a subsequent substantial change in circumstances which requires a modification of custody in the best interests of the children.

The policy is obvious. Children and their parents should not be subjected to repeated relitigation of the custody issues determined in the original action. Stability of the child's environment is of utmost concern. . . .

Under these guidelines, the fathers must lose their modification petitions. Their circumstances have changed; each has remarried. They were found by the trial court to be good and capable fathers, vitally interested in their children. But the statute requires a change in the circumstances of either the child or the custodian, the mothers in this case.

Has there been any change in the circumstances of the mothers to warrant a modification of the custody decree to allow them to live together?

In their modification petitions, the respondent mothers did not allege any change of circumstances and the findings and conclusions evidence absolutely none. At best the respondents established that it was preferable for their own personal circumstances, both financially and in pursuit of their relationship, to live together. That issue had been tried, they lost and did not appeal. They did not meet the judicial or statutory standards to change it. Therefore it was error to modify that aspect of the decrees.

Respondents make a belated effort to raise constitutional questions of freedom of association, equal protection and due process from the requirement that they live separate and apart. First, there is more involved than the rights of these two women. The lives of six children are at stake. Second, neither side has briefed nor argued the constitutional issues as they relate to this requirement. . . .

Finally, we turn to the fathers' argument that the trial court erred in failing to find the mothers in contempt for alleged violations of the original divorce decrees. As we noted in *State v. Caffrey,* 70 Wash.2d 120, 122–23 (1966):

> Punishment for contempt of court is within the sound discretion of the judge so ruling. Unless there is abuse of a trial court's exercise of discretion, it will not be disturbed on appeal. . . .

The trial court is affirmed except for its deletion of the requirement that the respondent mothers live separate and apart. As to that, it is reversed. The matter is remanded for entry of decrees in accordance with this opinion.

DOLLIVER, Justice (concurring in part; dissenting in part).

I concur with the reasoning of the majority in its affirmance of the award of custody to the defendants. I dissent on the modification of the decree relating to the defendants' living arrangements. . . .

In the findings at the time of the dissolutions, the trial court specifically found Sandra Schuster and Madeleine Isaacson were cohabiting and that "such living arrangements are not in the best interest of the children." However, the court in the modification proceedings which are now before us found:

> That since the time of the Divorce Decree the respondents at first lived separate and apart and then moved into adjoining apartments where they in fact lived together as one household and that the living arrangement did not prove to be against the best interests of the children, except it added a financial burden.

Thus, contrary to the assertion of the majority, a change of circumstances is contained in the findings. This change went far beyond the personal convenience of the defendants and was not to be found against the best interests of the children. The crucial question, then, is not whether the trial court made a finding of changed circumstances but whether there is evidence in the record to support the findings.

During the trial, voluminous testimony was taken on the living environment in which the children of the parties were being raised. According to expert testimony, since the divorce decrees the Isaacsons and Schusters had come to regard themselves as a family of eight; the Isaacson and Schuster children would refer to one another as brother or sister. Testimony established that there was a "cross-over of the parent roles" between Ms. Isaacson and Ms. Schuster for the nurturing and assistance of the children. This development of a family unit and the strengthening of the relationships among the eight family members presents a significant change of circumstances which may appropriately be recognized and was recognized by the trial court in its findings.

Furthermore, in its oral opinion, the trial court stated that living apart for the sake of appearances was imposing a financial burden on the parties and their children. This circumstance was also recognized in the findings. Where the funds of the parties are limited, the children would naturally be affected adversely by an unnecessary expenditure of household resources.

The trial court should be given broad discretion in matters dealing with the welfare of the children. A finding was made of changed circumstances. Substantial evidence is in the record to support this finding. The disposition of this case should not be disturbed except for a manifest abuse of discretion.

ROSELLINI, Justice (dissenting).

. . . Granting that a change of circumstances needs to be found to modify a custody decree, such change of circumstances exists. In the finding at the time of the dissolution, the trial court specifically found that Sandra Schuster and Madeleine Isaacson were cohabiting and that such living arrangements were not in the best interest of the children.

This finding was made to insulate the children from the harmful atmosphere of living together in the same household where evidence of cohabitation would be apparent.

Since that time . . . the respondents have been engaged in publicizing the homosexual cause in general and their lesbian relationship. . . .

From such publicizing it can be readily seen that they are not content to pursue their lifestyle but are also using their children for the purpose of advocating and proselytizing that style. . . .

The State does have an interest in the matter of heterosexual acts versus homosexual acts. . . .

This state concern, in our view, should not be minimized. The nuclear, heterosexual family is charged with several of society's most essential functions. It has served as an important means of educating the young; it has often provided economic support and psychological comfort to family members; and it has operated as the unit upon which basic governmental policies in such matters as taxation, conscription, and inheritance have been based. Family life has been a central unifying experience throughout American society. Preserving the strength of this basic, organic unit is a central and legitimate end of the police power. The state ought to be concerned that if allegiance to traditional family arrangements declines, society as a whole may well suffer. . . .

In seeking to regulate homosexuality, the state takes as a basic premise that social and legal attitudes play an important and interdependent role in the individual's formation of his or her sexual destiny. A shift on the part of the law from opposition to neutrality arguably makes homosexuality appear a more acceptable sexual lifestyle, particularly to younger persons whose sexual preferences are as yet unformed. Young people form their sexual identity partly on the basis of models they see in society. If homosexual behavior is legalized, and thus partly legitimized, an adolescent may question whether he or she should "choose" heterosexuality. At the time their sexual feelings begin to develop, many young people have more interests in common with members of their own sex; sexual attraction rather than genuine interest often first draws adolescents to members of the opposite sex. If society accorded more legitimacy to expressions of homosexual attraction, attachment to the opposite sex might be postponed or diverted for some time, perhaps until after the establishment of sexual patterns that would hamper development of traditional heterosexual family relationships. For those persons who eventually choose the heterosexual model, the existence of conflicting models might provide further sexual tension destructive to the traditional marital unit. . . .

In this case the trial court found, in the original trial, that both parents were fit and proper persons to have the custody of the children. The fathers have since remarried and have established good homes. Where should the scale of justice be tipped? In favor of the mothers who are living in a lesbian relationship?

Or on the side of the fathers whose lifestyles and relationships are considered normal and moral?

On the state of this record, the primary and paramount consideration in awarding the children to a parent is the welfare of the children. I would hold that the mothers are not morally fit to have the custody of the children, and I would award the children to the fathers.

STUDY QUESTIONS

1. Who was awarded custody originally? Why do you suppose neither father appealed those orders? What relief was requested in this action? Why do you suppose neither mother appealed the original orders requiring them to live separate and apart?

2. Is the requirement that Sandra Schuster and Madeleine Isaacson "live separate and apart" in their children's best interests? Why? Why not? Why do you think the majority refused to allow the women to consolidate households in light of its refusal to disturb the custody award?

3. In denying lesbians and gays custody of their children, courts at times express the concern that children identified as the offspring of homosexual parents will suffer from societal disapproval. Does this view seem consistent with the following opinion written by Justice Burger for a unanimous court in *Palmore v. Sidoti*, 466 U.S. 429, 433 (1984), reversing an order removing custody from a white woman on the ground that her new husband was African-American?

It would ignore reality to suggest that racial and ethnic prejudices do not exist or that all manifestations of those prejudices have been eliminated. There is a risk that a child living with a stepparent of a different race may be subject to a variety of pressures and stresses not present if the child were living with parents of the same racial or ethnic origin. The question, however, is whether the reality of private biases and the possible injury they might inflict are permissible considerations for removal of an infant child from the custody of its natural mother. We have little difficulty concluding that they are not. The Constitution cannot control such prejudices but neither can it tolerate them. Private biases may be outside the reach of the law, but the law cannot directly or indirectly, give them effect. . . .

Whatever problems racially-mixed households may pose for children in 1984 can no more support a denial of constitutional rights than could the stresses that residential integration was thought to entail in 1917. The effects of racial prejudice, however real, cannot justify a racial classification removing an infant child from the custody of its natural mother found to be an appropriate person to have such custody.

—— ❧ ——

Judge Dolliver's concurring opinion in *Schuster* hints at the potential family units built around same-sex relationships offer for developing parental relationships that diverge from those based on rigid gender roles. Judge Rossillini's dissent makes clear, however, that he is unwilling to encourage exploration of this sort and is adverse to choice in matters of sexual expression. Although the majority's legalistic opinion does not address these issues directly, the nature of its compromise position suggests a willingness to tolerate nontraditional relationships so long as their sexual nature is not explicit. In this respect, the majority's approach to the problem of custody is not unlike the approach other courts have taken to problems presented by cohabitation: disputes will be resolved in a way that does not recognize or condone nonmarital forms of sexual expression.

As the next three cases show, there has been some recognition of same-sex relationships in recent times. However, this recognition is far from universal, and it seems clear that the heterosexual nuclear relationship is still much preferred.

Braschi v. Stahl Associates Co.

New York Court of Appeals, 1989.
543 N.E.2d 49.

TITONE, Judge.

In this dispute over occupancy rights to a rent-controlled apartment, the central question to be resolved . . . is whether appellant has demonstrated [that] . . . he is entitled to seek protection from eviction under New York City Rent and Eviction Regulations. That regulation provides that upon the death of a rent-control tenant, the landlord may not dispossess "either the surviving spouse of the deceased tenant or some other member of the deceased tenant's family who has been living with the tenant". Resolution of this question requires this court to determine the meaning of the term "family" as it is used in this context.

Appellant, Miguel Braschi, was living with Leslie Blanchard in a rent-controlled apartment located at 405 East 54th Street from the summer of 1975 until Blanchard's death in September of 1986. In November of 1986, respondent, Stahl Associates Company, the owner of the apartment building, served a notice to quit on appellant contending that he was a mere licensee with no right to occupy the apartment since only Blanchard was the tenant of record. In December of 1986 respondent served appellant with a notice to terminate informing appellant that he had one month to vacate the apartment and that, if the apartment was not vacated, respondent would commence summary proceedings to evict him. . . .

As a threshold matter, although the determination of an application for a provisional remedy such as a preliminary injunction ordinarily involves the exercise of discretion, the denial of such relief presents a question of law reviewable by this court on an appeal brought pursuant to CPLR 5713 when "the Appellate Division denies [the] relief on an issue of law alone, and makes clear that no question of fact or discretion entered into its decision." Here, the Appellate Division's determination rested solely on its conclusion that as a matter of law appellant could not seek noneviction protection because of the absence of a "legally recognized" relationship with Blanchard. Consequently, appellant's appeal may be entertained, and we may review the central question presented: whether, on his motion for a preliminary injunction, appellant failed to establish, as a matter of law, the requisite clear likelihood of success on the merits of his claim to the protection from eviction provided by section 2204.6(d).

It is fundamental that in construing the words of a statute "[t]he legislative intent is the great and controlling principle." Indeed, "the general purpose is a more important aid to the meaning than any rule which grammar or formal logic may lay down". Statutes are ordinarily interpreted so as to avoid objectionable consequences and to prevent hardship or injustice. . . .

. . . [W]e conclude that the term family, as used in 9 NYCRR 2204.6(d), should not be rigidly restricted to those people who have formalized their relationship by obtaining, for instance, a marriage certificate or an adoption order. The intended protection against sudden eviction should not rest on fictitious legal distinctions or genetic history, but instead should find its foundation in the reality of family life. In the context of eviction, a more realistic, and certainly equally valid, view of a family includes two adult lifetime partners whose relationship is long term and characterized by an emotional and financial commitment and interdependence. This view comports both with our society's traditional concept of "family" and with the expectations of individuals who live in such nuclear units. . . . In fact, Webster's Dictionary defines "family" first as "a group of people united by certain convictions or common affiliation" (Webster's Ninth New Collegiate Dictionary 448 [1984]) . . . . Hence, it is reasonable to conclude that, in using the term "family," the Legislature intended to extend protection to those who reside in households having all of the normal familial characteristics. Appellant Braschi should therefore be afforded the opportunity to prove that he and Blanchard had such a household. . . .

Appellant and Blanchard lived together as permanent life partners for more than 10 years. They regarded one another, and were regarded by friends and family, as spouses. The two men's families were aware of the nature of the relationship, and they regularly visited each other's families and attended family functions together, as a couple. Even today, appellant continues to maintain a relationship with Blanchard's niece, who considers him an uncle.

In addition to their interwoven social lives, appellant clearly considered the apartment his home. He lists the apartment as his address on his driver's license and passport, and receives all his mail at the apartment address. Moreover, appellant's tenancy was known to the building's superintendent and doormen, who viewed the two men as a couple.

Financially, the two men shared all obligations including a household budget. The two were authorized signatories of three safe-deposit boxes, they maintained joint checking and savings accounts, and joint credit cards. In fact, rent was often paid with a check from their joint checking account. Additionally, Blanchard executed a power of attorney in appellant's favor so that appellant could make necessary decisions—financial, medical and personal—for him during his illness. Finally, appellant was the named beneficiary of Blanchard's life insurance policy, as well as the primary legatee and coexecutor of Blanchard's estate. Hence, a court examining these facts could reasonably conclude that these men were much more than mere roommates. . . .

Reversed.

Alison D. v. Virginia M.

Court of Appeals of New York. 1991. 572 N.E.2d 27.

Per Curiam.

At issue in this case is whether petitioner, a biological stranger to a child who is properly in the custody of his biological mother, has standing to seek visitation with the child under Domestic Relations Law § 70. Petitioner relies on both her established relationship with the child and her alleged agreement with the biological mother to support her claim that she has standing. . . .

Petitioner Alison D. and respondent Virginia M. established a relationship in September 1977 and began living together in March 1978. In March 1980, they decided to have a child and agreed that respondent would be artificially inseminated. Together, they planned for the conception and birth of the child and agreed to share jointly all rights and responsibilities of child-rearing. In July 1981, respondent gave birth to a baby boy, A. D. M., who was given petitioner's last name as his middle name and respondent's last name became his last name.

Petitioner shared in all birthing expenses and, after A. D. M.'s birth, continued to provide for his support. During A. D. M.'s first two years, petitioner and respondent jointly cared for and made decisions regarding the child.

In November 1983, when the child was 2 years and 4 months old, petitioner and respondent terminated their relationship and petitioner moved out of the home they jointly owned. Petitioner and respondent agreed to a visitation schedule whereby petitioner continued to see the child a few times a week. Petitioner also agreed to continue to pay one half of the mortgage and major household expenses. By this time, the child had referred to both respondent and petitioner as "mommy." Petitioner's visitation with the child continued until 1986, at which time respondent bought out petitioner's interest in the house and then began to restrict petitioner's visitation with the child. In 1987 petitioner moved to Ireland to pursue career opportunities, but continued her attempts to communicate with the child. Thereafter, respondent terminated all contact between petitioner and the child, returning all of petitioner's gifts and letters. No dispute exists that respondent is a fit parent. Petitioner commenced this proceeding seeking visitation rights pursuant to Domestic Relations Laws § 70.

Pursuant to Domestic Relations Law § 70 "either parent may apply to the supreme court for a writ of habeas corpus to have such minor child brought before such court; and [the court] may award the natural guardianship, charge and custody of such child to either parent as the case may require." Although the Court is mindful of petitioner's understandable concern for and interest in the child and of her expectation and desire that her contact with the child would continue, she has no right under Domestic Relations Law § 70 to seek visitation and, thereby, limit or diminish the right of the concededly fit biological parent to choose with whom her child associates. She is not a "parent" within the meaning of section 70.

. . . While one may dispute in an individual case whether it would be beneficial to a child to have continued contact with a nonparent, the Legislature did not in section 70 give such nonparent the opportunity to compel a fit parent to allow them to do so. . . .

Accordingly, the order of the Appellate Division [denying visitation] should be affirmed, with costs.

STUDY QUESTIONS

1. Are the decisions in *Braschi* and *Alison D.* consistent? Is there a difference between the rights at stake?
2. Is Justice (now New York Chief Justice) Kaye right in her dissenting opinion in *Alison D.* that the majority there imposed an old-fashioned and unnecessarily narrow view of families and parenting? Do you agree that such a view ignores reality?

Baehr v. Lewin

Supreme Court of Hawaii, 1993.
852 P.2d 44

. . . [T]he plaintiffs' complaint alleges the following facts:

1. on or about December 17, 1990, Baehr/Dancel, Rodrigues/Pregil, and Lagon/Melilio (collectively "the applicant couples") filed applications for marriage licenses with the [Department of Health] DOH pursuant to HRS § 572-6 (Supp. 1992);
2. the DOH denied the applicant couples' marriage license applications solely on the ground that the applicant couples were of the same sex;
3. the applicant couples have complied with all marriage contract requirements and provisions under HRS ch. 572, except that each applicant couple is of the same sex;
4. the applicant couples are otherwise eligible to secure marriage licenses from the DOH, absent the statutory prohibition or construction

of HRS § 572-1 excluding couples of the same sex from securing marriage licenses; and
5. in denying the applicant couples' marriage license applications, the DOH was acting in its official capacity and under color of state law.

Based on the foregoing factual allegations, the plaintiffs' complaint avers that:

1. the DOH's interpretation and application of HRS § 572-1 to deny same-sex couples access to marriage licenses violates the plaintiffs' right to privacy, as guaranteed by article I, section 6 of the Hawaii Constitution, as well as to the equal protection of the laws and due process of law, as guaranteed by article I, section 5 of the Hawaii Constitution;
2. the plaintiffs have no plain, adequate, or complete remedy at law to redress their alleged injuries. . . .

. . . The Right to Privacy Does Not Include a Fundamental Right to Same-Sex Marriage. . . .

. . . [T]he United States Supreme Court has declared that "the right to marry is part of the fundamental 'right of privacy' implicit in the

Fourteenth Amendment's Due Process Clause." *Zablocki v. Redhail,* 434 U.S. 374, 384 . . . (1978). The issue in the present case is, therefore, whether the "right to marry" protected by article I, section 6 of the Hawaii Constitution extends to same-sex couples. Because article I, section 6 was expressly derived from the general right to privacy under the United States Constitution and because there are no Hawaii cases that have delineated the fundamental right to marry, this court, as we did in *Mueller,* looks to federal cases for guidance. . . .

The United States Supreme Court has set forth its most detailed discussion of the fundamental right to marry in *Zablocki, supra,* which involved a Wisconsin statute that prohibited any resident of the state with minor children "not in his custody and which he is under obligation to support" from obtaining a marriage license until the resident demonstrated to a court that he was in compliance with his child support obligations. . . .

Implicit in the *Zablocki* court's link between the right to marry, on the one hand, and the fundamental rights of procreation, childbirth, abortion, and child rearing, on the other, is the assumption that the one is simply the logical predicate of the others.

The . . . case . . . demonstrates that the federal construct of the fundamental right to marry—subsumed within the right to privacy implicitly protected by the United States Constitution—presently contemplates unions between men and women. . . .

Therefore, the precise question facing this court is whether we will extend the *present* boundaries of the fundamental right of marriage to include same-sex couples, or, put another way, whether we will hold that same-sex couples possess a fundamental right to marry. . . .

[However,] we do not believe that a right to same-sex marriage is so rooted in the traditions and collective conscience of our people that failure to recognize it would violate the fundamental principles of liberty and justice that lie at the base of all our civil and political institutions. Neither do we believe that a right to same-sex marriage is implicit in the concept of ordered liberty, such that neither liberty nor justice would exist if it were sacrificed. Accordingly, we hold that the applicant couples do not have a fundamental constitutional right to same-sex marriage arising out of the right to privacy or otherwise. . . .

. . . . Inasmuch as the Applicant Couples Claim That the Express Terms of HRS § 572-1, which Discriminates against Same-Sex Marriages, Violate Their Rights under the Equal Protection Clause of the Hawaii Constitution, the Applicant Couples Are Entitled to an Evidentiary Hearing to Determine Whether [The Defendant] Can Demonstrate that HRS § 572-1 Furthers Compelling State Interests and Is Narrowly Drawn to Avoid Unnecessary Abridgments of Constitutional Rights.

In addition to the alleged violation of their constitutional rights to privacy and due process of law, the applicant couples contend that they have been denied the equal protection of the laws as guaranteed by article I, section 5 of the Hawaii Constitution. . . .

Marriage is a state-conferred legal partnership status, the existence of which gives rise to a multiplicity of rights and benefits reserved exclusively to that particular relation. . . .

The applicant couples correctly contend that the DOH's refusal to allow them to marry on the basis that they are members of the same sex deprives them of access to a multiplicity of rights and benefits that are contingent upon that status. . . . They include:

1. a variety of state income tax advantages, including deductions, credits, rates, exemptions, and estimates . . .;
2. public assistance from and exemptions relating to the Department of Human Services . . .;
3. control, division, acquisition, and disposition of community property . . .;
4. rights relating to dower, curtesy, and inheritance . . .;
5. rights to notice, protection, benefits, and inheritance . . .;
6. award of child custody and support payments in divorce proceedings . . .;

7. the right to spousal support . . .;
8. the right to enter into premarital agreements . . .;
9. the right to change of name pursuant . . .;
10. the right to file a nonsupport action . . .;
11. post-divorce rights relating to support and property division . . .
12. the benefit of the spousal privilege and confidential marital communications . . .;
13. the benefit of the exemption of real property from attachment or execution . . .; and
14. the right to bring a wrongful death action . . .

2. HRS § 572-1, on its face, discriminates based on sex against the applicant couples in the exercise of the civil right of marriage, thereby implicating the equal protection clause of article I, section 5 of the Hawaii Constitution. . . .

The equal protection clauses of the United States and Hawaii Constitutions are not mirror images of one another. . . . Thus, by its plain language, the Hawaii Constitution prohibits state-sanctioned discrimination against any person in the exercise of his or her civil rights on the basis of sex. . . .[O]n its face and . . . as applied, HRS § 572-1 denies same-sex couples access to the marital status and its concomitant rights and benefits. . . .

Relying primarily on four decisions construing the law [the defendant] . . . proposes that "the right of persons of the same sex to marry one another does not exist because marriage, by definition and usage, means a special relationship between a man and a woman." . . . We believe [the] argument to be circular and unpersuasive.

. . . [In a prior case] we clearly and unequivocally established, for purposes of equal protection analysis under the Hawaii Constitution, that sex-based classifications are subject, as a *per se* matter, to some form of "heightened" scrutiny, be it "strict" or "intermediate," rather than mere "rational basis" analysis.[31] Second, we assumed, *arguendo*, that such sex-based classifications were subject to "strict scrutiny." Third, we reaffirmed the longstanding principle that this court is free to accord greater protec-

tions to Hawaii's citizens under the state constitution than are recognized under the United States Constitution. And fourth, we looked to the *then current* case law of the United States Supreme Court for guidance. . . .

In light of the [implication in *Frontiero* that at least seven members (and probably eight) of the *Frontiero* Court would have subjected statutory sex-based classifications to "strict" judicial scrutiny] on the one hand, and the presence of article I, section 3—the Equal Rights Amendment—in the Hawaii Constitution, on the other, it is time to resolve once and for all the question left dangling in [our earlier case]. Accordingly, we hold that sex is a "suspect category" for purposes of equal protection analysis under article I, section 5 of the Hawaii Constitution[31] and that HRS § 572-1 is subject to the "strict scrutiny" test. It therefore follows, and we so hold, that

1. HRS § 572-1 is presumed to be unconstitutional
2. unless [the defendant], as an agent of the State of Hawaii, can show that (a) the statute's sex-based classification is justified by compelling state interests and (b) the statute is narrowly drawn to avoid unnecessary abridgments of the applicant couples' constitutional rights. . . .

STUDY QUESTIONS

1. In what ways are the plaintiffs disadvantaged by the State's failure to permit same-sex marriages?
2. Who won? On what grounds? What do you think will happen when the trial court acts on the case again?
3. Do you agree that prohibitions on same-sex marriages are sex based?

---

[31] *In subsequent decisions, we have reaffirmed that sex-based classifications are subject, at the very least, to "intermedite scrutiny" under the equal protection clause of the Hawaii Constitution* State v. Tookes, *67 Haw. 608, 614, 699 p.2d 983, 988 (1985);* State v. Rivera, *62 Haw. 120, 123, 612 P.2d 526, 529 (1980).*

Extended Families

Legal constraints on family units that extend beyond a single man, a single woman, and their joint children appear in a number of contexts. Prohibitions on polygamy are one obvious example. Laws setting conditions on marriages by noncustodial parents, are another example. Zoning laws that limit the numbers and types of persons who may live together legally are yet a third example. During the 1970s, laws of this sort were frequently challenged on constitutional grounds. The judicial response to these challenges reflects the tendency to protect variations in living arrangements in terms that affirm traditional values.

Moore v. City of East Cleveland

United States Supreme Court, 1977.
431 U.S. 494, 97 S.Ct. 1932,
52 L.Ed.2d 531.

Mr. Justice POWELL announced the judgment of the Court, and delivered an opinion in which Mr. Justice BRENNAN, Mr. Justice MARSHALL, and Mr. Justice BLACKMUN joined.

East Cleveland's housing ordinance, like many throughout the country, limits occupancy of a dwelling unit to members of a single family. . . . But the ordinance contains an unusual and complicated definitional section that recognizes as a "family" only a few categories of related individuals. Because her family, living together in her home, fits none of those categories, appellant stands convicted of a criminal offense. The question in this case is whether the ordinance violates the Due Process Clause of the Fourteenth Amendment.

I

Appellant, Mrs. Inez Moore, lives in her East Cleveland home together with her son, Dale Moore, Sr., and her two grandsons, Dale, Jr., and John Moore, Jr. The two boys are first cousins rather than brothers; we are told that John came to live with his grandmother and with the elder and younger Dale Moores after his mother's death. . . .

II

The city argues that our decision in *Village of Belle Terre v. Boraas* requires us to sustain the or-

dinance attacked here. Belle Terre, like East Cleveland, imposed limits on the types of groups that could occupy a single dwelling unit. Applying the constitutional standard announced in this Court's leading land-use case, *Euclid v. Ambler Realty Co.,* we sustained the Belle Terre ordinance on the ground that it bore a rational relationship to permissible state objectives.

But one overriding factor sets this case apart from *Belle Terre.* The ordinance there affected only *unrelated* individuals. It expressly allowed all who were related by "blood, adoption, or marriage" to live together, and in sustaining the ordinance we were careful to note that it promoted "family needs" and "family values." . . . East Cleveland, in contrast, has chosen to regulate the occupancy of its housing by slicing deeply into the family itself. This is no mere incidental result of the ordinance. On its face it selects certain categories of relatives who may live together and declares that others may not. In particular, it makes a crime of a grandmother's choice to live with her grandson in circumstances like those presented here.

When a city undertakes such intrusive regulation of the family, neither *Belle Terre* nor *Euclid* governs; the usual judicial deference to the legislature is inappropriate. "This Court has long recognized that freedom of personal choice in matters of marriage and family life is one of the liberties protected by the Due Process Clause of the Fourteenth Amendment." *Cleveland Board of Education v. LaFleur.* A host of cases, tracing their lineage to *Meyer v. Nebraska,* and *Pierce v. Society of Sisters,* have consistently acknowledged a "private realm of family life which the state cannot enter." *Prince v. Massachusetts.*

Of course, the family is not beyond regulation. . . . But when the government intrudes on choices concerning family living arrangements, this Court must examine carefully the importance of the governmental interests advanced and the extent to which they are served by the challenged regulation. . . .

When thus examined, this ordinance cannot survive. The city seeks to justify it as a means of preventing overcrowding, minimizing traffic and parking congestion, and avoiding an undue financial burden on East Cleveland's school system. Although these are legitimate goals, the ordinance before us serves them marginally, at best. For example, the ordinance permits any family consisting only of husband, wife, and unmarried children to live together, even if the family contains a half dozen licensed drivers, each with his or her own car. At the same time it forbids an adult brother and sister to share a household, even if both faithfully use public transportation. The ordinance would permit a grandmother to live with a single dependent son and children, even if his school-age children number a dozen, yet it forces Mrs. Moore to find another dwelling for her grandson John, simply because of the presence of his uncle and cousin in the same household. We need not labor the point. Section 1341.08 has but a tenuous relation to alleviation of the conditions mentioned by the city.

III

The city would distinguish the cases based on *Meyer* and *Pierce*. It points out that none of them "gives grandmothers any fundamental rights with respect to grandsons," Brief for Appellee 18, and suggests that any constitutional right to live together as a family extends only to the nuclear family—essentially a couple and their dependent children.

To be sure, these cases did not expressly consider the family relationship presented here. They were immediately concerned with freedom of choice with respect to childbearing, . . . with the rights of parents to the custody and companionship of their own children, [or] with traditional parental authority in matters of child rearing and education. . . . But unless we close our eyes to the basic reasons why certain rights associated with the family have been accorded shelter under the Fourteenth Amendment's Due Process Clause, we cannot avoid applying the force and rationale of these precedents to the family choice involved in this case. . . .

Our decisions establish that the Constitution protects the sanctity of the family precisely because the institution of the family is deeply rooted in this Nation's history and tradition. It is through the family that we inculcate and pass down many of our most cherished values, moral and cultural.

Ours is by no means a tradition limited to respect for the bonds uniting the members of the nuclear family. The tradition of uncles, aunts, cousins, and especially grandparents sharing a household along with parents and children has roots equally venerable and equally deserving of constitutional recognition. Over the years millions of our citizens have grown up in just such an environment, and most, surely, have profited from it. Even if conditions of modern society have brought about a decline in extended family households, they have not erased the accumulated wisdom of civilization, gained over the centuries and honored throughout our history, that supports a larger conception of the family. Out of choice, necessity, or a sense of family responsibility, it has been common for close relatives to draw together and participate in the duties and the satisfactions of a common home. Decisions concerning child rearing, which *Yoder, Meyer, Pierce* and other cases have recognized as entitled to constitutional protection, long have been shared with grandparents or other relatives who occupy the same household—indeed who may take on major responsibility for the rearing of the children. Especially in times of adversity, such as the death of a spouse or economic need, the broader family has tended to come together for mutual sustenance and to maintain or rebuild a secure home life. This is apparently what happened here.

Whether or not such a household is established because of personal tragedy, the choice of relatives in this degree of kinship to live together may not lightly be denied by the State. *Pierce* struck down an Oregon law requiring all children to attend the State's public schools, holding that the Constitution "excludes any general power of the State to standardize its children by forcing them to accept instruction from public teachers only." . . . By the same token the Constitution prevents East Cleveland from standardizing its children—and its adults—by forcing all to live in certain narrowly defined family patterns.

Reversed.

STUDY QUESTIONS

1. Why do the family and family living arrangements merit special protection against state interference? How do you suppose Justice Powell would define "family" for purposes of this special protection?

2. In a concurring opinion, Justice Brennan emphasized the "cultural myopia of the arbitrary boundary drawn by the East Cleveland ordinance," pointing to "the prominence of other than nuclear families among ethnic and racial minority groups, including our black citizens." Would an East Cleveland-type ordinance restricting the definition of family to legal and blood ties, however extended, be equally culturally myopic in view of social science data indicating that socially recognized kinships based on emotional bonds and actual behavior rather than law or blood are common in certain racial communities? Would it be culturally myopic in view of its impact on homosexual households?

3. Justice Powell's opinion suggests that at least one purpose of the family is to permit us to "inculcate and pass down many of our most cherished values, moral and cultural." Do you agree that this is a reason for affording the family special recognition and protection? What other purposes do you see the family serving? What other groupings serve those same purposes? Do they deserve special recognition and protection too?

The *Moore* decision, taken with *Belle Terre*, strongly suggests that constitutional protection will only be afforded households organized around blood and legal ties. If so, people who prefer to live in same-sex relationships are not the only ones to be adversely affected by the legal preference for the traditional nuclear family. Certain racial and ethnic groups that tend to rely on nonfamily ties will also be adversely affected. Similarly, legal preferences for traditional nuclear families will penalize the very poor for pooling their resources and sharing child care with unrelated, "honorary kin." Groups who consciously seek to experiment with different emotional groupings are similarly hindered in their efforts to establish communal households.

Moore and *Belle Terre* are, of course, federal decisions dealing with the reach of the United States Constitution. A number of state courts have been somewhat more liberal in affording unrelated households protection under state constitutional provisions. In *State v. Baker,* 405 A.2d 368 (1979), for example, the New Jersey Supreme Court invalidated a local ordinance prohibiting more than four persons not related by blood, marriage, or adoption from occupying a single dwelling unit. Expressly declining to follow *Belle Terre* in interpreting the state constitution, it found the ordinance insufficiently related to the community's legitimate interest in preserving a "family style" of living. The court did, however, make clear that it would uphold ordinances that were better designed to preserve a "family style" of life by proscribing, among other things, boarding homes and nonfamilial institutions. In so ruling, the court may well have been influenced by the fact that the *Baker* case involved a religiously-motivated extended family.

The New Jersey Supreme Court's approach to unrelated households is plainly more protective than that of the United States Supreme Court. Yet it too implied there are limits to its tolerance of nontraditional living arrangements. By analogizing the Baker household to an extended family and by reaffirming the legitimacy of community efforts to preserve a family style of living, the New Jersey Court seemed to rule out protection for more daring attempts at restructuring eating and living arrangements. For example, if a community's legitimate interest in preserving a "family style" of living could justify its prohibition of kitchenless apartment units sharing a common dining facility, an option advocated by many feminists for lightening women's domestic burdens would be ruled out. However, experimentation with restructuring of this kind may be essential to finding ways of meeting personal needs that do not rely on rigid gender roles. Without such experimentation and without a legal system that accepts such diversity, the set gender-based allocation of family responsibilities we have observed throughout this chapter may well persist.

8 Reproduction

This chapter is concerned with decisions relating to whether, when, and how people have children. While these matters have a great impact on people of both sexes, the nature of that impact is very different for the two sexes. With present technology, the biological consequences of conception are very different for women and men. Pregnancy has a very real and intrusive impact on women physically. Under present social arrangements, the responsibility for caring for the children that are produced falls overwhelmingly on women. As we have seen throughout the preceeding chapters, women's childbearing and child-rearing responsibilities have been the basis for limiting their opportunities to participate in society. Finally, the conditions under which people make their reproductive choices have been shaped by gender. Notions of appropriate social behavior, ability to control one's sexual partner, access to information and services, and influence in shaping the legal rules governing birth control are different for women and men.

In considering these questions from a legal perspective, it may be helpful to think of the law as establishing a framework that allocates the power to make reproductive choices, rather than determining the actual choices. For example, as we shall see, although the Supreme Court has made clear that the Constitution sets some limits on government's ability to interfere with the ability of women to choose abortions, it did not hold that particular women should or should not get abortions. Courts have often resolved fertility control cases in "privacy" terms; that is, by saying that decisions involving procreation should be made by the individual without state interference. Thus, courts look to see whether governmental action interferes with private decision making and if so, whether there is adequate justification for that interference. As you consider this approach, think about whether courts seem to appreciate the connection between reproduction and gender sufficiently.

I. DEVELOPING THE RIGHT TO REPRODUCTIVE CHOICES

The Historical Context

The major Supreme Court decisions protecting reproductive choice are quite recent. Constitutional protection for procreation dates from the Court's 1942 decision, *Skinner v. Oklahoma,* 316 U.S. 535, invalidating a state statute authorizing sterilization of persons convicted two or more times of felonies "involving moral turpitude."

The *Skinner* Court used heightened scrutiny to invalidate the statute, which only authorized sterilization of embezzlers and certain other criminals, under the Equal Protection Clause on the ground that it "forever deprived [these criminals] of a basic liberty." The *Skinner* holding and the protection it accorded procreation as "fundamental to the very existence and survival of the race" reflect a rather sharp break with the view held of sterilization and reproductive rights earlier in our history. *Griswold v. Connecticut,* 318 U.S. 479, the landmark case striking down Connecticut's ban on the use of contraceptives by married couples, was decided in 1965. *Roe v. Wade,* 410 U.S. 113, the historic decision recognizing a constitutional right to abortion, came in 1973.

Birth control attitudes and practices in the United States have varied considerably over the years. As James C. Mohr explains in his book, *Abortion in America* (Oxford: Oxford University Press, 1978), like contraception, abortion prior to quickening (when the first fetal movement can be perceived) was considered perfectly legal and acceptable prior to 1800. In the early nineteenth century, urbanization and industrialization began to undercut the economic reasons for large families, and the birth rate among whites began to fall, even in rural areas. A rise in abortion, particularly among "respectable" married women, played an important role in this change. By the 1840s, abortion had become a common commercialized practice in most states. Newspapers, for example, routinely advertised pills and midwives' services to help women with "irregular periods." Similarly, a typical circular publicized the availability of "novel inventions" to assist women who did not want children for health or financial reasons.

Although the use of abortion and contraception remained widespread throughout most of the nineteenth century, the legal framework changed significantly during that period. During the first half of the nineteenth century, most jurisdictions followed the English common law rule that held that abortion with a woman's consent was not a crime prior to quickening. Between 1840 and 1860, a number of antiabortion laws were enacted, but these generally preserved the woman's right to end her pregnancy prior to quickening. However, a doctors' crusade initiated in the 1850s by "regular physicians" led to the enactment of restrictive abortion legislation in the next several decades.

As contrasted with the more experientially oriented populist healers, the "regulars" were predominantly male doctors committed to scientific research and education and organized into medical societies. Their campaign, carried out under the auspices of the American Medical Association, focused on moral and safety concerns about abortions, as well as on white, native-born Protestants' fear of being outbred by Catholic immigrants. Although the Catholic Church had banned abortion for the first time in the mid-nineteenth century, the physicians did not succeed in enlisting the aid of the American religious community. They did, however, find valuable allies in the antiobscenity movement. Meaningful prohibitions on abortion were widely enacted between 1860 and 1880; but the courts did not enforce them stringently for another twenty years.

As Mohr points out, one important indication of the physicians' effectiveness following the Civil War was the ability to have all abortion-related matters included in the definition of obscenity. The prime mover in the antiobscenity crusade was Anthony Comstock, head of the New York Society for the Suppression of Vice. In 1873, at Comstock's urging, Congress passed "an Act for the Suppression of Trade in, and Circulation of, Obscene Literature and Articles of Immoral Use." Aimed at the distribution of contraceptive and abortifacient articles and information, as well as more conventionally defined pornography, the law permitted Comstock and his associates to prosecute numerous abortionists for obscenity throughout the decade. Remaining on the books intact until challenged judicially in 1938, the statute also led to birth control advocate Margaret Sanger's prosecution and exile for distributing birth control information in the second decade of the twentieth century. In short, although legal options were ultimately restricted for many people, reproductive decisions during most of the nineteenth century were made in a permissive legal climate.

The legal and economic nature of slavery meant, however, that a special set of constraints governed the reproductive lives of many black women. As historian Herbert Gutman explains in his classic book, *The Black Family in Slavery and Freedom 1750– 1925* (New York: Vintage Books, 1979), the system of slavery was plain. It required slave women, especially after the abolition of the overseas slave trade, to reproduce the slave labor force. From the slaveowner's perspective, the birth of a child meant more profits. From the slave woman's perspective, giving birth might demonstrate her fertility, thereby reducing her chances of being sold and separated from her family. Sexual advances from owners were not always welcome, however, and slave women exercised considerable ingenuity in resisting them. Reports in Southern medical journals and elsewhere suggest that slave women also resorted to home remedies to avoid reproducing. Often they relied on herbal brews rather than mechanical means. Infusions of tansy, rue, and cottonroot served as abortifacients, and camphor was used as a contraceptive.

Significant changes for reproductive choice also occurred in the twentieth century. These developments reflect the influences of the three important reproductive control movements of the nineteenth century: a neo-Malthusian movement for population control; a eugenics movement aimed at improving the human race; and a feminist movement for Voluntary Motherhood. Historian Linda Gordon traces these influences and their connection with twentieth-century birth control movements in her article, "Feminism, Reproduction, and the Family" in *Rethinking the Family* (Barrie Thorne and Marilyn Yalom, eds., New York: Longman, 1982).

The neo-Malthusian movement supported contraception as a means to ameliorate social problems by reducing population size on a large scale. Now a recognizable strain in global population control efforts, the movement came later to the United States than to Europe because this country was more preoccupied with underpopulation than overpopulation until World War II.

The eugenics movement initially sought to improve the human stock by eliminating idiocy, criminality, and drunkenness, all mistakenly thought to be hereditary. As the upperclass WASP (white Anglo-Saxon Protestant) elite of the Northeast became increasingly aware of their small-family pattern as opposed to the large-family pattern of immigrants and the rural poor, eugenicists advocated selective use of contraception and sterilization to ensure the survival of the superior stock.

Widespread sterilization became possible in this country at the end of the nineteenth century with the perfection of safe and simple operations for both sexes. The eugenics movement stimulated compulsory sterilization. That movement, which held force during the first three decades of the twentieth century and which was supported by a number of liberals and progressives at the time, attempted to prevent those considered biologically unfit from propagating and to encourage those considered worthy of procreating. By the 1930s, more than thirty states had adopted laws authorizing sterilization of convicted rapists and other criminals, such as those judged "insane," "idiotic," "imbicilic," or "moronic."

Eugenicists made no bones about those they deemed worthy of reproducing, and their movement reflected definite race and class biases. As implemented, the compulsory sterilization laws they inspired also had a definite gender bias. Laws authorizing the sterilization of criminals were directed at men, and there is some evidence that courts were reluctant to order men sterilized under these statutes. Due process and cruel and unusual punishment arguments frequently sufficed to block sterilization in the lower courts, and when the United States Supreme Court faced the issue in the 1942 *Skinner v. Oklahoma* decision, it invalidated compulsory sterilization of certain felons on equal protection grounds.

Sterilization of women, on the other hand, was thought crucial to ending feeblemindedness, and of those sterilized for that reason two-thirds were women. In 1927, the United States Supreme Court upheld the compulsory sterilization of the feebleminded in *Buck v. Bell,* 274 U.S. 200, the famous decision in which Justice Oliver Wendell Holmes declared, "Three generations of imbeciles are enough." As biologist Stephen Jay Gould showed in his article, "Carrie Buck's Daughter," appearing in *Natural History* (July 1984), that case illustrates a subtler aspect of the gender bias in sterilization abuse. As Gould convincingly demonstrated, there was no evidence that Carrie Buck, her mother, or her daughter were deficient mentally. Rather, Carrie Buck, one of several illegitimate children, was institutionalized to hide the pregnancy that had resulted from her rape by one of her foster relatives. Not only was Carrie Buck blamed for her pregnancy, but, as Gould's article suggests, her improper sexual behavior was considered a key indicator of feeblemindedness.

Unlike the neo-Malthusian and the eugenics movements, the Voluntary Motherhood movement, which dated from the 1840s, advocated birth control through abstinence rather than contraception. Voluntary Motherhood proponents saw birth control as crucial to achieving feminist goals of the day. Abstinence, rather than contraception, however, was best suited to winning the freedom women required from excessive childbearing, marital rape, and other forms of male sexual tyranny without devaluing motherhood. Self-respect and respect for motherhood were, as they saw it, essential to equal rights.

Feminists in the following century took a distinctly different view. The feminists who sparked the twentieth-century birth control movement were radicals—feminist socialists such as Emma Goldman and Margaret Sanger, who argued that free sexual expression and reproductive self-determination were essential to women's liberation. Subsequently, under Margaret Sanger's leadership, the movement sought and gained respectability through professionalization. Activities focused increasingly on opening clinics and lobbying for legislation. Male physicians assumed more visible leadership roles and women generally assumed staff and organizer positions. Eugenics, with its overtones of racial superiority, also became an important theme in the early twentieth-century struggle to legalize contraception and abortion, resulting in the loss of black support.

With the coming of the Depression in the 1930s, social workers also became involved in the birth control movement. Emphasizing contraception as a tool against poverty, and in some locations as a means of limiting the growth of the black population, some state, local, and federal agencies developed small-scale birth control programs. Nevertheless, laws prohibiting contraception and abortion persisted in a number of states. In 1939, the American Birth Control League and the Birth Control Clinical Research Bureau merged to form the Birth Control Federation of America, which in 1942 adopted the name Planned Parenthood Federation of America (PPFA).

During the 1940s, PPFA stressed the importance of family planning in achieving healthier marriages and parenthood. In the 1950s and 1960s, population control on a national and global level assumed greater importance for the birth control movement (including PPFA). Programs and policies advanced by the United States, at times through the United Nations, urged reduction in the birth rate as a way of combating poverty at home and promoting economic development abroad. Family planning thus gained a political acceptability that led ultimately to a transformation of the legal climate surrounding reproduction.

Contraception

From the 1920s on, the birth control movement sought the enactment of measures legalizing contraceptives. When religious and other birth control opponents repeatedly succeeded in blocking legislative reforms, Planned Parenthood sought to challenge bans on contraception in court. *Skinner v. Oklahoma,* the 1942 decision invalidating the compulsory sterilization of certain criminals, prepared the way for these challenges. As noted, the Court there asserted for the first time that the right to reproduce was "one of the basic civil rights of man." It took almost a quarter of a century more for the Court to recognize the right *not* to reproduce.

The Supreme Court twice rejected challenges to Connecticut's prohibitions on birth control on procedural grounds related to the statute not having been enforced against a user or prescribing physician. Finally, in 1965, the Supreme Court reached the statute's merits after the Planned Parenthood affiliate actually provoked arrests by opening a clinic.

Griswold v. Connecticut

United States Supreme Court, 1965.
381 U.S. 479, 85 S.Ct. 1678,
14 L.Ed.2d 510.

Mr. Justice DOUGLAS delivered the opinion of the Court.

Appellant Griswold is Executive Director of the Planned Parenthood League of Connecticut. Appellant Buxton is a licensed physician and a professor at the Yale Medical School who served as Medical Director for the League at its Center in New Haven—a center open and operating from November 1 to November 10, 1961, when appellants were arrested.

They gave information, instruction, and medical advice to *married persons* as to the means of preventing conception. They examined the wife and prescribed the best contraceptive device or material for her use. Fees were usually charged, although some couples were serviced free.

The statutes whose constitutionality is involved in this appeal are §§ 53–32 and 54–196 of the General Statutes of Connecticut (1958 rev.). The former provides:

"Any person who uses any drug, medicinal article or instrument for the purpose of preventing conception shall be fined not less than fifty dollars or imprisoned not less than sixty days nor more than one year or be both fined and imprisoned."

Section 54–196 provides:

"Any person who assists, abets, counsels, causes, hires or commands another to commit any offense may be prosecuted and punished as if he were the principal offender."

The appellants were found guilty as accessories and fined $100 each, against the claim that the accessory statute as so applied violated the Fourteenth Amendment. The Appellate Division of the Circuit Court affirmed. The Supreme Court of Errors affirmed that judgment. . . .

Coming to the merits, we are met with a wide range of questions that implicate the Due Process Clause of the Fourteenth Amendment. . . . We do not sit as a super-legislature to determine the wisdom, need, and propriety of laws that touch economic problems, business affairs, or social conditions. This law, however, operates directly on an intimate relation of husband and wife and their physician's role in one aspect of that relation.

The association of people is not mentioned in the Constitution nor in the Bill of Rights. The right to educate a child in a school of the parents' choice—whether public or private or parochial—is also not mentioned. Nor is the right to study any particular subject or any foreign language. Yet the First Amendment has been construed to include certain of those rights. . . .

The right of "association," like the right of belief, is more than the right to attend a meeting; it includes the right to express one's attitudes or philosophies by membership in a group or by affiliation with it or by other lawful means. Association in that context is a form of expression of opinion; and while it is not expressly included in the First Amendment its existence is necessary in making the express guarantees fully meaningful.

The foregoing cases suggest that specific guarantees in the Bill of Rights have penumbras, formed by emanations from those guarantees that help give them life and substance. Various guarantees create zones of privacy. The right of association contained in the penumbra of the First Amendment is one, as we have seen. The Third Amendment in its prohibition against the quartering of soldiers "in any house" in time of peace without the consent of the owner is another facet of that privacy. The Fourth Amendment explicitly affirms the "right of the people to be secure in their persons, houses, papers, and effects, against unreasonable searches and seizures." The Fifth Amendment in its Self-Incrimination Clause enables the citizen to create a zone of privacy which government may not force him to surrender to his detriment. The Ninth Amendment provides: "The enumeration in the Constitution, of certain rights, shall not be construed to deny or disparage others retained by the people."

The Fourth and Fifth Amendments were described in *Boyd v. United States,* as protection against all governmental invasions "of the sanctity of a man's home and the privacies of life." We recently referred in Mapp v. Ohio to the Fourth Amendment as creating a "right to privacy, no less important than any other right carefully and particularly reserved to the people." . . .

We have had many controversies over these penumbral rights of "privacy and repose." These cases bear witness that the right of privacy which presses for recognition here is a legitimate one.

The present case, then, concerns a relationship lying within the zone of privacy created by several fundamental constitutional guarantees. And it concerns a law which, in forbidding the *use* of contraceptives rather than regulating their manufacture or sale, seeks to achieve its goals by means having a maximum destructive impact upon that relationship. Such a law cannot stand in light of the familiar principle, so often applied by this Court, that a "governmental purpose to control or prevent activities constitutionally subject to state regulation may not be achieved by means which sweep unnecessarily broadly and thereby invade the area of protected freedoms." Would we allow the police to search the sacred precincts of marital bedrooms for telltale signs of the use of contraceptives? The very idea is repulsive to the notions of privacy surrounding the marriage relationship.

We deal with a right of privacy older than the Bill of Rights—older than our political parties, older than our school system. Marriage is a coming together for better or for worse, hopefully enduring, and intimate to the degree of being sacred. It is an association that promotes a way of life, not causes; a harmony in living, not political faiths; a bilateral loyalty, not commercial or social projects. Yet it is an association for as noble a purpose as any involved in our prior decisions.

Reversed.

Mr. Justice BLACK, with whom Mr. Justice STEWART joins, dissenting. . . .

One of the most effective ways of diluting or expanding a constitutionally guaranteed right is to substitute for the crucial word or words of a constitutional guarantee another word or words more or less flexible and more or less restricted in meaning. This fact is well illustrated by the use of the term "right of privacy" as a comprehensive substitute for the Fourth Amendment's guarantee against "unreasonable searches and seizures." "Privacy" is a broad, abstract and ambiguous concept which can easily be shrunken in meaning but which can also, on the other hand, easily be interpreted as a constitutional ban against many things other than searches and seizures. . . .

I agree with my Brother Stewart's dissenting opinion. And like him I do not to any extent whatever base my view that this Connecticut law is constitutional on a belief that the law is wise or that its policy is a good one. . . .

There is no single one of the graphic and eloquent strictures and criticisms fired at the policy of this Connecticut law either by the Court's opinion or by those of my concurring Brethren to which I cannot subscribe—except their conclusion that the evil qualities they see in the law make it unconstitutional. . . .

The Court talks about a constitutional "right of privacy" as though there is some constitutional provision or provisions forbidding any law ever to be passed which might abridge the "privacy" of individuals. But there is not. There are, of course, guarantees in certain specific constitutional provisions which are designed in part to protect privacy at certain times and places with respect to certain activities. . . .

I like my privacy as well as the next one, but I am nevertheless compelled to admit that government has a right to invade it unless prohibited by some specific constitutional provision. For these reasons I cannot agree with the Court's judgment and the reasons it gives for holding this Connecticut law unconstitutional.

. . . I think that if properly construed neither the Due Process Clause nor the Ninth Amendment, nor both together, could under any circumstances be a proper basis for invalidating the Connecticut law. I discuss the due process and Ninth Amendment arguments together because on analysis they turn out to be the same thing—merely using different words to claim for this Court and the federal judiciary power to invalidate any legislative act which the judges find irrational, unreasonable or offensive.

The due process argument . . . is based . . . on the premise that this Court is vested with

power to invalidate all state laws that it considers to be arbitrary, capricious, unreasonable, or oppressive, or on this Court's belief that a particular state law under scrutiny has no "rational or justifying" purpose, or is offensive to a "sense of fairness and justice." If these formulas based on "natural justice," or others which mean the same thing, are to prevail, they require judges to determine what is or is not constitutional on the basis of their own appraisal of what laws are unwise or unnecessary. The power to make such decisions is of course that of a legislative body. . . .

I do not believe that we are granted power by the Due Process Clause or any other constitutional provision or provisions to measure constitutionality by our belief that legislation is arbitrary, capricious or unreasonable, or accomplishes no justifiable purpose, or is offensive to our own notions of "civilized standards of conduct." . . .

STUDY QUESTIONS

1. Did Justice Douglas and the majority of the Court find that the statute violated any specific provision of the Constitution? What is the source of the "right to privacy" that was violated by the statute, according to Justice Douglas' opinion?

2. What is the scope of the right of privacy recognized in *Griswold*? May states punish single persons for using contraceptives? May states proscribe the distribution of contraceptives? May states make adultery and fornication crimes?

3. In a concurring opinion, Justice Goldberg made the point that if the Constitution does not protect the right not to become a parent, it does not protect the right to become a parent, so that a state could subject an individual to compulsory sterilization. Do you agree?

4. What was the basis of Justice Black's dissent? Is he correct that when judges recognize constitutional rights that are not guaranteed by explicit provisions of the Constitution, they inevitably impose their own views of what are wise or necessary laws?

In *Griswold,* the Court struck down a state restriction on the use of contraceptive by married couples. The decision's effect was to reinforce the fundamental right to procreative choice first recognized in *Skinner,* but its reasoning emphasized the privacy rights of married couples. *Griswold* thus left open the question of whether a state may restrict the distribution of contraceptives to *unmarried* persons. In answering that question, the Supreme Court by a plurality of four justices endorsed the view that the right of privacy inheres in individuals as well as married couples.

As Justice Brennan put it for the plurality in *Eisenstadt v. Baird,* 405 U.S. 438, 453 (1972):

> It is true that in *Griswold* the right of privacy in question inhered in the marital relationship. Yet the marital couple is not an independent entity with a heart and mind of its own, but an association of two individuals each with a separate intellectual and emotional makeup. If the right of privacy means anything, it is the right of an *individual,* married or single, to be free from unwanted governmental intrusion into matters so fundamentally affecting a person as the decision whether to bear or beget a child.

As we shall see in the next section, this individual right of privacy right first articulated in the contraception context was later developed in the abortion context. *Eisenstadt* is also noteworthy because it extended *Griswold*'s prohibition on laws barring the use of contraceptives to laws barring the distribution of contraceptives. Other restrictions on access fell as a result of the *Carey* decision, which we examine next.

Carey v. Population Services International

United States Supreme Court, 1977.
431 U.S. 678, 97 S.Ct. 2010,
52 L.Ed.2d 675.

Mr. Justice BRENNAN delivered the opinion of the Court [with respect to the issues presented here].

Under New York Ed. Law § 6811(8) (McKinney 1972) it is a crime (1) for any person to sell or distribute any contraceptive of any kind to a minor under the age of 16 years; (2) for anyone other than a licensed pharmacist to distribute contraceptives to persons 16 or over; and (3) for anyone, including licensed pharmacists, to advertise or display contraceptives. . . .

Although "[t]he Constitution does not explicitly mention any right of privacy," the Court has recognized that one aspect of the "liberty" protected by the Due Process Clause of the Fourteenth Amendment is "a right of personal privacy, or a guarantee of certain areas or zones of privacy." *Roe v. Wade.* . . .

The decision whether or not to beget or bear a child is at the very heart of this cluster of constitutionally protected choices. . . .

That the constitutionally protected right of privacy extends to an individual's liberty to make choices regarding contraception does not, however, automatically invalidate every state regulation in this area. The business of manufacturing and selling contraceptives may be regulated in ways that do not infringe protected individual choices. And even a burdensome regulation may be validated by a sufficiently compelling state interest. . . .

"Compelling" is of course the key word; where a decision as fundamental as that whether to bear or beget a child is involved, regulations imposing a burden on it may be justified only by compelling state interests, and must be narrowly drawn to express only those interests. . . .

We consider first the wider restriction on access to contraceptives created by § 6811(8)'s prohibition of the distribution of nonmedical contraceptives to adults except through licensed pharmacists. . . .

Restrictions on the distribution of contraceptives clearly burden the freedom to make such decisions. A total prohibition against sale of contraceptives, for example, would intrude upon individual decisions in matters of procreation and contraception as harshly as a direct ban on their use. Indeed, in practice, a prohibition against all sales, since more easily and less offensively enforced, might have an even more devastating effect upon the freedom to choose contraception. . . .

Limiting the distribution of nonprescription contraceptives to licensed pharmacists clearly imposes a significant burden on the right of the individuals to use contraceptives if they choose to do so.

The burden is, of course, not as great as that under a total ban on distribution. Nevertheless, the restriction of distribution channels to a small fraction of the total number of possible retail outlets renders contraceptive devices considerably less accessible to the public, reduces the opportunity for privacy of selection and purchase, and lessens the possibility of price competition. . . .

There remains the inquiry whether the provision serves a compelling state interest.

. . . Insofar as § 6811(8) applies to nonhazardous contraceptives, it bears no relation to the State's interest in protecting health.

Appellants therefore suggest that § 6811(8) furthers other state interests. But none of them is comparable to those the Court has heretofore recognized as compelling. Appellants argue that the limitation of retail sales of nonmedical contraceptives to pharmacists (1) expresses "a proper concern that young people not sell contraceptives"; (2) "allows purchasers to inquire as to the relative qualities of the varying products and prevents anyone from tampering with them"; and (3) facilitates enforcement of the other provisions of the statute. The first hardly can justify the statute's incursion into constitutionally protected rights, and in any event the statute is obviously not substantially related to any goal of preventing young people from selling contraceptives. Nor is the statute designed to serve as a quality control device. Nothing in the record suggests that pharmacists are particularly qualified to give advice on the merits of different nonmedical contraceptives, or that such advice is more necessary to the purchaser of contraceptive products than to consumers of other nonprescription items. Why pharmacists are better able or more inclined than other retailers to prevent tampering with prepackaged products, or, if they are, why contraceptives are singled out for this special protection, is also unexplained. As to ease of enforcement, the prospect of additional administrative inconvenience has not been thought to justify invasion of fundamental constitutional rights. . . .

The District Court also held unconstitutional, as applied to nonprescription contraceptives, the provision of § 6811(8) prohibiting the distribution of contraceptives to those under 16 years of age. Appellants contend that this provision of the statute is constitutionally permissible as a regulation of the morality of minors, in furtherance of the State's policy against promiscuous sexual intercourse among the young.

The question of the extent of state power to regulate conduct of minors not constitutionally regulable when committed by adults is a vexing one, perhaps not susceptible of precise answer. . . .

Certain principles, however, have been recognized. "Minors, as well as adults, are protected by the Constitution and possess constitutional rights." *Planned Parenthood of Central Missouri v. Danforth*. . . .

On the other hand, we have held in a variety of contexts that "the power of the state to control the conduct of children reaches beyond the scope of its authority over adults." *Prince v. Massachusetts*. . . .

Of particular significance to the decision of this case, the right to privacy in connection with decisions affecting procreation extends to minors as well as to adults. . . .

Appellants argue . . . that significant state interests are served by restricting minors' access to contraceptives, because free availability to minors of contraceptives would lead to increased sexual activity among the young, in violation of the policy of New York to discourage such behavior. The argument is that minors' sexual activity may be deterred by increasing the hazards attendant on it. . . .

[As] was stated in *Eisenstadt v. Baird*: "It would be plainly unreasonable to assume that [the State] has prescribed pregnancy and the birth of an unwanted child [or the physical and psychological dangers of an abortion] as punishment for fornication." . . .

Moreover, there is substantial reason for doubt whether limiting access to contraceptives will in fact substantially discourage early sexual behavior. . . .

. . . [W]hen a State, as here, burdens the exercise of a fundamental right, its attempt to justify that burden as a rational means for the accomplishment of some significant state policy requires more than a bare assertion, based on a conceded complete absence of supporting evidence, that the burden is connected to such a policy. . . .

The District Court's holding that the prohibition of any "advertisement or display" of contraceptives is unconstitutional was clearly correct. Only last Term *Virginia State Board of Pharmacy v. Virginia Citizens Consumer Council* held that a State may not "completely suppress the dissemination of concededly truthful information about entirely lawful activity," even when that information could be categorized as "commercial speech."

Appellants contend that advertisements of contraceptive products would be offensive and embarrassing to those exposed to them, and that permitting them would legitimize sexual activity of young people. But these are classically not justifications validating the suppression of expression protected by the First Amendment. At least where obscenity is not involved, we have consistently held that the fact that protected speech may be offensive to some does not justify its suppression. . . .

As for the possible "legitimation" of illicit sexual behavior, whatever might be the case if the advertisements directly incited illicit sexual activity among the young, none of the advertisements in this record can even remotely be characterized as "directed to inciting or producing imminent lawless action and . . . likely to incite or produce such action." *Brandenburg v. Ohio*. . . .

These arguments therefore do not justify the total suppression of advertising concerning contraceptives.

Affirmed.

Mr. Justice POWELL, concurring in part and concurring in the judgment. . . .

Although I concur in the judgment of the Court, I am not persuaded that the Constitution requires the severe constraints that the Court's opinion places upon legislative efforts to regulate the distribution of contraceptives, particularly to the young. . . .

There is . . . no justification for subjecting restrictions on the sexual activity of the young to heightened judicial review. . . .

New York has made it a crime for anyone other than a physician to sell or distribute contraceptives to minors under the age of 16 years. Ed. Law § 6811(8) (McKinney 1972). . . .

. . . [T]his provision prohibits parents from distributing contraceptives to their children, a restriction that unjustifiably interferes with parental interests in rearing their children. . . .

The State points to no interest of sufficient magnitude to justify this direct interference with the parental guidance that is especially appropriate in this sensitive area of child development. But in my view there is considerably more room for state regulation in this area than would be permissible under the plurality's opinion. It seems clear to me, for example, that the State would further a constitutionally permissible end if it encouraged adolescents to seek the advice and guidance of their parents before deciding whether to engage in sexual intercourse. . . .

STUDY QUESTIONS

1. What test does the Court say it will apply in reproductive cases? Is the test the same where minors are involved? Should it be?
2. Does provision (2) of the statute relating to the distribution of contraceptives to adults satisfy that test? Why not?
3. Was the same test applied to provision (1) of the statute? Why was that provision invalidated?
4. What was the constitutional basis of the challenge to provision (3)? What arguments were offered in support of that provision? Why were these arguments dismissed as inadequate? Do you think that this is a sound result?

In *Carey,* the Court clearly indicated that the government must justify a restriction on reproductive choice—whether total or not—by a compelling state interest. The Court in *Carey* also seems to have recognized and accepted the idea that adults engage in sexual activity divorced from reproduction. However, the several concurring opinions in *Carey* (not all reproduced here) regarding minors' access to contraception make clear that the justices have much more difficulty accepting the idea of "children" engaging in sexual activity and demonstrate their reluctance to encourage it.

Adolescent sexuality poses difficult questions for many people, and there has been much debate in recent years over the appropriate role for government in this troublesome area. Justice Powell's concurring opinion in *Carey* points to "parental" interests in rearing their children as a possible basis for limiting minors' access to contraception. He suggests a requirement of prior parental consultation would be a permissible regulation in this area. Subsequently, the U.S. Department of Health and Human Services (formerly Health, Education and Welfare) pursued this suggestion by adopting the so-called "squeal rule."

The squeal rule required all recipients of federal funding for family planning services under Title X of the Public Health Services Act to notify parents or guardians within ten days of prescribing contraceptives to unemancipated minors and to comply with all state laws requiring parental notification or consent for such services. Although the agency attempted to justify the regulations as required by amendments to Title X that reflected a congressional desire to encourage family participation in preventing unwanted teen pregnancies, the courts rejected these arguments and invalidated the regulations. Rather, the courts found that Congress did not intend to *mandate* family involvement in large part because Congress had found that it was essential to maintain adolescents' confidentiality in order to attract them to family planning clinics. See *Planned Parenthood Federation of America, Inc. v. Heckler,* 712 F.2d 650 (D.C. Cir. 1983) and *New York v. Heckler,* 719 F.2d 1191 (2d Cir. 1983).

Unlike similar state laws, the squeal rule received widespread denunciation by the public, and the episode seems to have ended attempts to enforce notification at the federal level. However, because the decisions were based on statutory grounds, the question of constitutionality of such requirements is still open.

Abortion

During the years between *Griswold* (1965) and *Roe v. Wade* (1973), state legislatures considered and adopted a variety of changes in abortion statutes. By 1973, nineteen states had changed their abortion laws. The Supreme Court preempted this process of piecemeal reform when it handed down its decision in *Roe v. Wade.* Drawing on the legal foundation it laid in *Griswold* and *Eisenstadt,* the Supreme Court explicitly extended the right of reproductive choice to abortion in 1973. As political theorist Rosalind Petchesky argued in her book, *Abortion and Women's Choice* (New York: Longman, 1985), the *Roe v. Wade* decision and the liberalization of abortion laws that preceded it must be seen as the product of social and political forces as well as legal developments. Petchesky identifies the efforts of the women's liberation movement, which stressed the need for women to be able to control their bodies, and the more established population control and medical organizations, which stressed public health concerns and medical control, as the immediate factors. However, Petchesky saw the large demand for abortions—legal or illegal—as crucial to stimulating the efforts of both groups. This demand for abortion services was part of the overall drop in fertility that began among women in the United States in the early 1960s. This decline reflected their greater labor force participation and college attendance, increasing divorce rates, and their continued responsibility for child care in the absence of adequate government funding for social services.

Although the demand for abortion services persisted through the 1980s and early 1990s, as we shall see, this did not mean that *Roe v. Wade* would remain the law of the land. We look first at the *Roe v. Wade* decision and some of the theory behind it, then at its application, and finally, at the limitations imposed on it.

The Decision. Although abortion law reform was underway as early as the 1960s, the Court's ruling in *Roe v. Wade* has proved extremely controversial, both legally and politically. We now consider the decisions and the controversies it engendered.

Roe v. Wade

United States Supreme Court, 1973.
410 U.S. 113, 93 S.Ct. 705,
35 L.Ed.2d 147.

Mr. Justice BLACKMUN delivered the opinion of the Court.

This Texas federal appeal and its Georgia companion, *Doe v. Bolton,* present constitutional challenges to state criminal abortion legislation. The Texas statutes under attack here are typical of those that have been in effect in many States for approximately a century. The Georgia statutes, in contrast, have a modern cast and are a legislative product that, to an extent at least, obviously reflects the influences of recent attitudinal change, of advancing medical knowledge and techniques, and of new thinking about an old issue.

We forthwith acknowledge our awareness of the sensitive and emotional nature of the abortion controversy, of the vigorous opposing views, even among physicians, and of the deep and seemingly absolute convictions that the subject inspires. One's philosophy, one's experiences, one's exposure to the raw edges of human existence, one's religious training, one's attitudes toward life and family and their values, and the moral standards one establishes and seeks to observe, are all likely to influence and to color one's thinking and conclusions about abortion.

In addition, population growth, pollution, poverty, and racial overtones tend to complicate and not to simplify the problem.

Our task, of course, is to resolve the issue by constitutional measurement free of emotion and of predilection. We seek earnestly to do this, and, because we do, we have inquired into, and in this opinion place some emphasis upon, medical and medical-legal history and what that history reveals about man's attitudes toward the abortive procedure over the centuries. We bear in mind, too, Mr. Justice Holmes' admonition in his now vindicated dissent in *Lochner v. New York,* 198 U.S. 45, 76 (1905): . . .

> [The Constitution] is made for people of fundamentally differing views, and the accident of our finding certain opinions natural and familiar or novel and even shocking ought not to conclude our judgment upon the question whether statutes embodying them conflict with the Constitution of the United States.

The Texas statutes . . . make it a crime to "procure an abortion," as therein defined, or to attempt one, except with respect to "an abortion procured or attempted by medical advice for the purpose of saving the life of the mother." Similar statutes are in existence in a majority of the States. . . .

Jane Roe, a single woman who was residing in Dallas County, Texas, instituted this federal action in March 1970 against the District Attorney of the county. . . .

Roe alleged that she was unmarried and pregnant; that she wished to terminate her pregnancy by an abortion "performed by a competent, licensed physician, under safe, clinical conditions"; that she was unable to get a "legal" abortion in Texas because her life did not appear to be threatened by the continuation of her pregnancy; and that she could not afford to travel to another jurisdiction in order to secure a legal abortion under safe conditions. . . .

The principal thrust of appellant's attack on the Texas statutes is that they improperly invade a right, said to be possessed by the pregnant woman, to choose to terminate her pregnancy. Appellant would discover this right in the concept of personal "liberty" embodied in the Fourteenth Amendment's Due Process Clause; or in personal, marital, familial, and sexual privacy said to be protected by the Bill of Rights or its penumbras, see *Griswold v. Connecticut; Eisenstadt v. Baird* (White, J., concurring); or among those rights reserved to the people by the Ninth Amendment, *Griswold v. Connecticut* (Goldberg, J., concurring). Before addressing this claim, we feel it desirable briefly to survey, in several aspects, the history of abortion, for such insight as that history may afford us, and then to examine the state purposes and interests behind the criminal abortion laws.

It perhaps is not generally appreciated that the restrictive criminal abortion laws in effect in a majority of States today are of relatively recent vintage. Those laws, generally proscribing abortion or its attempt at any time during pregnancy except when necessary to preserve the pregnant woman's life, are not of ancient or even of common law origin. Instead, they derive from statutory changes effected, for the most part, in the latter half of the 19th century. . . .

Gradually, in the middle and late 19th century the quickening distinction disappeared from the statutory law of most States and the degree of the offense and the penalties were increased. By the end of the 1950's, a large majority of the States banned abortion, however and whenever performed, unless done to save or preserve the life of the mother. The exceptions, Alabama and the District of Columbia, permitted abortion to preserve the mother's health. Three other States permitted abortions that were not "unlawfully" performed or that were not "without lawful justification," leaving interpretation of those standards to the courts. In the past several years, however, a trend toward liberalization of abortion statutes has resulted in adoption, by about one-third of the States, of less stringent laws, most of them patterned after the ALI Model Penal Code. . . .

It is thus apparent that at common law, at the time of the adoption of our Constitution, and throughout the major portion of the 19th century, abortion was viewed with less disfavor than under most American statutes currently in effect. Phrasing it another way, a woman enjoyed a substantially broader right to terminate a pregnancy than she does in most States today. At least with respect to the early stage of pregnancy, and very possibly without such a limitation, the opportunity to make this choice was present in this country well into the 19th century. Even later, the law continued for some time to treat less punitively an abortion procured in early pregnancy. . . .

Three reasons have been advanced to explain historically the enactment of criminal abortion laws in the 19th century and to justify their continued existence.

It has been argued occasionally that these laws were the product of a Victorian social concern to discourage illicit sexual conduct. Texas, however, does not advance this justification in the present case, and it appears that no court or commentator has taken the argument seriously. . . .

A second reason is concerned with abortion as a medical procedure. When most criminal abortion laws were first enacted, the procedure was a hazardous one for the woman. This was particularly true prior to the development of antisepsis. Antiseptic techniques, of course, were based on discoveries by Lister, Pasteur, and others first announced in 1867, but were not generally accepted and employed until about the turn of the century. Abortion mortality was high. Even after 1900, and perhaps until as late as the development of antibiotics in the 1940's, standard modern techniques such as dilation and curettage were not nearly so safe as they are today. Thus it has been argued that a State's real concern in enacting a criminal abortion law was to protect the pregnant woman, that is, to restrain her from submitting to a procedure that placed her life in serious jeopardy.

Modern medical techniques have altered this situation. Appellants and various amici refer to medical data indicating that abortion in early pregnancy, that is, prior to the end of first trimester, although not without its risk, is now relatively safe. Mortality rates for women undergoing early abortions, where the procedure is legal, appear to be as low as or lower than the rates for normal childbirth. Consequently, any interest of the State in protecting the woman from an inherently hazardous procedure, except when it would be equally dangerous for her to forgo it, has largely disappeared. Of course, important state interests in the area of health and medical standards do remain. The State has a legitimate interest in seeing to it that abortion, like any other medical procedure, is performed under circumstances that insure maximum safety for the patient. This interest obviously extends at least to the performing physician and his staff, to the facilities involved, to the availability of after-care, and to adequate provision for any complication or emergency that might arise. The prevalence of high mortality rates at illegal "abortion mills" strengthens, rather than weakens, the State's interest in regulating the conditions under which abortions are performed. Moreover, the risk to the woman increases as her pregnancy continues. Thus the State retains a definite interest in protecting the woman's own health and safety when an abortion is proposed at a late stage of pregnancy.

The third reason is the State's interest—some phrase it in terms of duty—in protecting prenatal life. Some of the argument for this justification rests on the theory that a new human life is present from the moment of conception. The State's interest and general obligation to protect life then extends, it is argued, to prenatal life. Only when the life of the pregnant mother herself is at stake, balanced against the life she carries within her, should the interest of the embryo or fetus not prevail. Logically, of course, a legitimate state interest in this area need not stand or fall on acceptance of the belief that life begins at conception or at some other point prior to live birth. In assessing the State's interest, recognition may be given to the less rigid claim that as long as at least *potential* life is involved, the State may assert interests beyond

the protection of the pregnant woman alone. . . .

It is with these interests, and the weight to be attached to them, that this case is concerned. . . .

The Constitution does not explicitly mention any right of privacy. In a line of decisions, however, going back perhaps as far as *Union Pacific R. Co. v. Botsford,* 141 U.S. 250, 251 (1891), the Court has recognized that a right of personal privacy, or a guarantee of certain areas or zones of privacy, does exist under the Constitution. In varying contexts the Court or individual justices have indeed found at least the roots of that right in the First Amendment, in the Fourth and Fifth Amendments, in the penumbras of the Bill of Rights, in the Ninth Amendment, or in the concept of liberty guaranteed by the first section of the Fourteenth Amendment.

This right of privacy, whether it be founded in the Fourteenth Amendment's concept of personal liberty and restrictions upon state action, as we feel it is, or, as the District Court determined, in the Ninth Amendment's reservation of rights to the people, is broad enough to encompass a woman's decision whether or not to terminate her pregnancy. The detriment that the State would impose upon the pregnant woman by denying this choice altogether is apparent. Specific and direct harm medically diagnosable even in early pregnancy may be involved. Maternity, or additional off-spring, may force upon the woman a distressful life and future. Psychological harm may be imminent. Mental and physical health may be taxed by child care. There is also the distress, for all concerned, associated with the unwanted child, and there is the problem of bringing a child into a family already unable, psychologically and otherwise, to care for it. In other cases, as in this one, the additional difficulties and continuing stigma of unwed motherhood may be involved. All these are factors the woman and her responsible physician necessarily will consider in consultation.

On the basis of elements such as these, appellants and some amici argue that the woman's right is absolute and that she is entitled to terminate her pregnancy at whatever time, in whatever way, and for whatever reason she alone chooses. With this we do not agree.

Appellants' arguments that Texas either has no valid interest at all in regulating the abortion decision, or no interest strong enough to support any limitation upon the woman's sole determination, [are] unpersuasive. The Court's decisions recognizing a right of privacy also acknowledge that some state regulation in areas protected by that right is appropriate. As noted above, a state may properly assert important interests in safeguarding health, in maintaining medical standards, and in protecting potential life. At some point in pregnancy, these respective interests become sufficiently compelling to sustain regulation of the factors that govern the abortion decision. The privacy right involved, therefore, cannot be said to be absolute . . .

Where certain "fundamental rights" are involved, the Court has held that regulation limiting these rights may be justified only by a "compelling state interest," and that legislative enactments must be narrowly drawn to express only the legitimate state interests at stake. . . .

The District Court held that the appellee failed to meet his burden of demonstrating that the Texas statute's infringement upon Roe's rights was necessary to support a compelling state interest, and that, although the [appellee] presented "several compelling justifications for state presence in the area of abortions," the statutes outstripped these justifications and swept "far beyond any areas of compelling state interest." Appellant and appellee both contest that holding. . . .

The appellee and certain amici argue that the fetus is a "person" within the language and meaning of the Fourteenth Amendment. In support of this they outline at length and in detail the well-known facts of fetal development. If this suggestion of personhood is established, the appellant's case, of course, collapses, for the fetus' right to life [would] then [be] guaranteed specifically by the Amendment. The appellant conceded as much on reargument. On the other hand, the appellee conceded on reargument that no case could be cited that holds that a fetus is a person within the meaning of the Fourteenth Amendment.

The Constitution does not define "person" . . . in so many words. Section 1 of the Fourteenth Amendment contains three references to "person."

But in nearly all . . . instances, the use of the word is such that it has application only postnatally. None indicates, with any assurance, that it has any possible pre-natal application.

All this, together with our observation, supra, that throughout the major portion of the 19th century prevailing legal abortion practices were far freer than they are today, persuades us that the word "person," as used in the Fourteenth Amendment, does not include the unborn. This is in accord with the results reached in those few cases where the issue has been squarely presented. . . .

The pregnant woman cannot be isolated in her privacy. She carries an embryo and, later, a fetus, if one accepts the medical definitions of the developing young in the human uterus. See Dorland's Illustrated Medical Dictionary, 478-479, 547 (24th ed. 1965). The situation therefore is inherently different from marital intimacy, or bedroom possession of obscene material, or marriage, or procreation, or education, with which *Eisenstadt* and *Griswold, Stanley, Loving, Skinner, Pierce,* and *Meyer* were respectively concerned. As we have intimated above, it is reasonable and appropriate for a State to decide that at some point in time another interest, that of health of the mother or that of potential human life, becomes significantly involved. The woman's privacy is no longer sole and any right of privacy she possesses must be measured accordingly.

Texas urges that, apart from the Fourteenth Amendment, life begins at conception and is present throughout pregnancy, and that, therefore, the State has a compelling interest in protecting that life from and after conception. We need not resolve the difficult question of when life begins. When those trained in the respective disciplines of medicine, philosophy, and theology are unable to arrive at any consensus, the judiciary, at this point in the development of man's knowledge, is not in a position to speculate as to the answer.

It should be sufficient to note briefly the wide divergence of thinking on this most sensitive and difficult question. There has always been strong support for the view that life does not begin until live birth. This was the belief of the Stoics. It appears to be the predominant, though not the unanimous, attitude of the Jewish faith. It may be taken to represent also the position of a large segment of the Protestant community, insofar as that can be ascertained; organized groups that have taken a formal position on the abortion issue have generally regarded abortion as a matter for the conscience of the individual and her family. As we have noted, the common law found greater significance in quickening. Physicians and their scientific colleagues have regarded that event with less interest and have tended to focus either upon conception, upon live birth, or upon the interim point at which the fetus becomes "viable," that is, potentially able to live outside the mother's womb, albeit with artificial aid. Viability is usually placed at about seven months (28 weeks) but may occur earlier, even at 24 weeks. The Aristotelian theory of "mediate animation," that held sway throughout the Middle Ages and the Renaissance in Europe, continued to be official Roman Catholic dogma until the 19th century, despite opposition to this "ensoulment" theory from those in the Church who would recognize the existence of life from the moment of conception. The latter is now, of course, the official belief of the Catholic Church. As one of the briefs amicus discloses, this is a view strongly held by many non-Catholics as well, and by many physicians. Substantial problems for precise definition of this view are posed, however, by new embryological data that purport to indicate that conception is a "process" over time, rather than an event, and by new medical techniques such as menstrual extraction, the "morning-after" pill, implantation of embryos, artificial insemination, and even artificial wombs.

In areas other than criminal abortion, the law has been reluctant to endorse any theory that life, as we recognize it, begins before live birth or to accord legal rights to the unborn except in narrowly defined situations and except when the rights are contingent upon live birth. For example, the traditional rule of tort law had denied recovery for prenatal injuries even though the child was born alive. That rule has been changed in almost every jurisdiction. In most States, recovery is said to be permitted only if the fetus was viable, or at least quick, when the injuries were sustained, though few courts have squarely so held. . . .

In view of all this, we do not agree that, by adopting one theory of life, Texas may override the rights of the pregnant woman that are at stake. We repeat, however, that the State does have an important and legitimate interest in preserving and protecting the health of the pregnant woman, whether she be a resident of the State or a nonresident who seeks medical consultation and treatment there, and that it has still *another* important and legitimate interest in protecting the potentiality of human life. These interests are separate and distinct. Each grows in substantiality as the woman approaches term and, at a point during pregnancy, each becomes "compelling."

With respect to the State's important and legitimate interest in the health of the mother, the "compelling" point, in the light of present medical knowledge, is at approximately the end of the first trimester. This is so because of the now established medical fact that until the end of the first trimester mortality in abortion may be less than mortality in normal childbirth. It follows that, from and after this point, a State may regulate the abortion procedure to the extent that the regulation reasonably relates to the preservation and protection of maternal health. Examples of permissible state regulation in this area are requirements as to the qualifications of the person who is to perform the abortion; as to the licensure of that person; as to the facility in which the procedure is to be performed, that is, whether it must be a hospital or may be a clinic or some other place of less-than-hospital status; as to the licensing of the facility; and the like.

This means, on the other hand, that, for the period of pregnancy prior to this "compelling" point, the attending physician, in consultation with his patient, is free to determine, without regulation by the State, that, in his medical judgment the patient's pregnancy should be terminated. If that decision is reached, the judgment may be effectuated by an abortion free of interference by the State.

With respect to the State's important and legitimate interest in potential life, the "compelling" point is at viability. This is so because the fetus then presumably has the capability of meaningful life outside the mother's womb. State regulation protective of fetal life after viability thus has both logical and biological justifications. If the State is interested in protecting fetal life after viability, it may go so far as to proscribe abortion during that period, except when it is necessary to preserve the life or health of the mother.

Measured against these standards, Art. 1196 of the Texas Penal Code, in restricting legal abortions to those "procured or attempted by medical advice for the purpose of saving the life of the mother," sweeps too broadly. The statute makes no distinction between abortions performed early in pregnancy and those performed later, and it limits to a single reason, "saving" the mother's life, the legal justification for the procedure. The statute, therefore, cannot survive the constitutional attack made upon it here. . . .

To summarize and to repeat:

1. A state criminal abortion statute of the current Texas type, that excepts from criminality only a *life-saving* procedure on behalf of the mother, without regard to pregnancy stage and without recognition of the other interests involved, is violative of the Due Process Clause of the Fourteenth Amendment.

   (a) For the stage prior to approximately the end of the first trimester, the abortion decision and its effectuation must be left to the medical judgment of the pregnant woman's attending physician.

   (b) For the stage subsequent to approximately the end of the first trimester, the State, in promoting its interest in the health of the mother, may, if it chooses, regulate the abortion procedure in ways that are reasonably related to maternal health.

   (c) For the stage subsequent to viability, the State, in promoting its interest in the potentiality of human life may, if it chooses, regulate, and even proscribe, abortion except where it is necessary, in appropriate medical judgment, for the preservation of the life or health of the mother.

2. The State may define the term "physician," as it has been employed in the preceding numbered paragraphs . . . of this opinion, to mean only a physician currently licensed by the State, and may proscribe any abortion by a person who is not a physician as so defined.

In *Doe v. Bolton,* procedural requirements contained in one of the modern abortion statutes are considered. That opinion and this one, of course, are to be read together.

This holding, we feel, is consistent with the relative weights of the respective interests involved, with the lessons and example of medical and legal history, with the lenity of the common law, and with the demands of the profound problems of the present day. The decision leaves the State free to place increasing restrictions on abortion as the period of pregnancy lengthens, so long as those restrictions are tailored to the recognized state interests. The decision vindicates the right of the physician to administer medical treatment according to his professional judgment up to the points where important state interests provide compelling justifications for intervention. Up to those points, the abortion decision in all its aspects is inherently, and primarily, a medical decision, and basic responsibility for it must rest with the physician. If an individual practitioner abuses the privilege of exercising proper medical judgment, the usual remedies, judicial and intraprofessional, are available. . . .

STUDY QUESTIONS

1. What provision of the Constitution did the Court apply to evaluate the Texas statute? Why? Would another provision be stronger?
2. What reasons did the Court give for asserting that, at least initially, the decision is that of the woman and her physician? To what extent does the Court's decision reflect the fact that women bear the burdens of pregnancy and child rearing?
3. At what points in pregnancy may a state restrict access to abortions, according to the *Roe* Court? What reasons did the Court give for permitting that intervention? Must a state intervene at those points?
4. How did the Court deal with Texas's claims that a fetus is a person protected by the Fourteenth Amendment? Do you find this resolution satisfactory?

After a detailed review of historical and current attitudes towards abortion (much of which is omitted from the version of the case reprinted here), the Court in *Roe* determined that carrying a pregnancy to term so fundamentally affects a woman that her decision, made in consultation with her physician, to terminate her pregnancy is protected by the right of privacy recognized in *Griswold*. For this reason, her decision must be free from governmental intrusion except where a compelling state interest is at stake. The Court went on to identify two such interests and to specify the points at which they become compelling. The Court, however, rejected the state's claim that the fetus is a person within the meaning of the Fourteenth Amendment and that the state has a compelling interest in protecting it by forbidding all abortions.

The decision in *Roe* established that, at least during the first twelve weeks of pregnancy, the state may not prohibit or otherwise regulate abortions so long as they are performed by licensed physicians. *Roe* does, however, permit a state to regulate abortions during the next twelve weeks, but only for the purpose of protecting the health of the woman. After the point when the fetus becomes viable, which the Court defined as the point at which the fetus is capable of meaningful life outside the womb, the state has greater leeway in imposing restrictions. After this point, which the Court placed at the beginning of the third trimester, a state may restrict abortions either to promote the woman's health or to protect the potential life that the fetus represents. Nevertheless, even in this third trimester, the state must permit abortions that are necessary to protect the woman's life or health.

Heated controversy greeted the Court's decision in *Roe*. A number of critics claimed that, rather than applying a previously recognized right, the Court drafted the equivalent of a new constitutional provision. Like Justice Rehnquist dissenting in *Roe* and Justice Black dissenting in *Griswold*, some critics argued that it is wrong for courts to overrule legislative decisions when they can identify no specific provision in the Constitution that guides them in doing so. In the words of John Hart Ely:

> What is so frightening about *Roe* is that this super-protected right [abortion] is not inferable from the language of the Constitution, the Framers' thinking respecting the specific problem in issue, any general value derivable from the provisions they included, or the nation's governmental structure. Nor is it explainable in terms of the usual political importance of the group judicially protected vis-a-vis the interest that legislatively prevailed over it. And that . . . is a charge that can responsibly be leveled at no other decision of the [previous] twenty years.
>
> *"The Wages of Crying Wolf: A Comment on* Roe v. Wade.*" 82* Yale Law Journal *920, 935-36 (1973).*

A number of responses have been made to this criticism. Constitutional scholars have argued that courts, like legislatures, inevitably make value judgments and that it is proper for them to do so. Others, contrary to Ely, have suggested that the Court needed to act in order to correct defects in the political process. For example, in an article published shortly after the decision, Laurence Tribe took the position that judgments concerning abortion are inherently religious and that they therefore should not be made by legislatures. He thus viewed the Court's action as a way of eliminating excessive government entanglement with religion. Kenneth Karst, echoing feminist concerns expressed in the litigation campaign against abortion laws, saw the Court's action as necessary to ensure that women are treated as full and equal citizens.

Several feminist legal scholars have sought to ground the abortion right in the equality principle. Arguing that *Roe v. Wade*'s approach obscures the connection between reproductive autonomy and gender equality, Sylvia Law, for example, has written:

The rhetoric of privacy, as opposed to equality, blunts our ability to focus on the fact that it is *women* who are oppressed when abortion is denied. A privacy right that demands that "the abortion decision . . . be left to the medical judgment of the pregnant woman's attending physician," gives doctors undue power by falsely casting the abortion decision as primarily a medical question.

"Rethinking Sex and the Constitution." 132 University of Pennsylvania Law Review *995, 1020 (1984).*

Feminist legal scholars and advocates have also attempted to show that the right to choose abortion is rooted in values well respected in our legal tradition. Focusing on the physical intrusiveness and sheer work of pregnancy, they have argued that the abortion right is essential to the right to bodily integrity safeguarded by the common law and the right to be free of involuntary servitude guaranteed by the Thirteenth Amendment. They have also argued that denying a woman the right to terminate her pregnancy violates equal protection guarantees. Proponents of these equality arguments point both to pregnancy's effect on women's bodily integrity and the limitations childbearing imposes on women's ability to choose their place in society. Thus, they point to both sex-based physical factors that will not change (at least in the foreseeable future) and the theoretically changeable social role that women play as mothers.

Although many people agree that procreative choice and gender equality are closely linked, the argument that denying women reproductive control violates their rights to equal protection is not one that the United States Supreme Court is likely to accept in the near future. As we saw in Chapter 2, the Court held in its 1974 decision in *Geduldig v. Aiello* that when women are treated differently because of their unique reproductive functions, they are not being discriminated against on the basis of sex. Like the pregnancy classification at issue in *Geduldig,* the laws that restrict access to abortion are classifications having to do with women's unique reproductive functions and are not, under the *Geduldig* reasoning, denials of equal protection. Moreover, as we shall see, in 1992, three key Supreme Court justices declined to reverse *Roe v. Wade* in large part because they believed so strongly in sustaining earlier decisions and principles. In all probability, then, to the extent that the Court continues to protect the right to choose, it will do so using the liberty and privacy analysis announced in *Griswold, Carey,* and *Roe.*

Although opinion polls continued to show that a sizable majority of people in the United States supported legalized abortion, the *Roe* decision prompted considerable political opposition. Initially expressed through restrictive legislation at the state level, this opposition ultimately led to several federal attempts to overrule *Roe v. Wade* through statutes and constitutional amendments. Following its 1973 action, the Supreme Court applied the *Roe* decision to strike down a number of state provisions that impinged on the abortion choice. Among the key decisions were *Planned Parenthood of Central Missouri v. Danforth,* 428 U.S. 52 (1976); *Akron v. Akron Center for Reproductive Rights,* 462 U.S. 416 (1983); and *Thornburgh v. American College of Obstetricians & Gynecologists,* 476 U.S. 747 (1986), which invalidated, among other things, so-called informed consent requirements, mandatory counseling and waiting periods, and spousal consent requirements. Thus, in the *Danforth* case, for example, the Supreme Court struck down state provisions requiring special efforts to save the fetus at any age, notification of parents and spouses, and limitations on the use of saline abortions. Similarly, its 1983 *Akron I* decision invalidated "informed consent" and waiting period requirements, parental consent requirements, and limitations on second- and third-trimester procedures. So, too, in its 1986 *Thornburgh* decision, the Court struck down "informed consent" and reporting requirements, as well as second physician requirements in certain cases.

The first real blow to the abortion right came in the funding context when the Supreme Court declined to invalidate a state provision allowing Medicaid payments for medical procedures related to pregnancy and childbirth but not for abortion. Thus, in its 1977 decision in *Maher v. Roe,* 432 U.S. 526, the Supreme Court upheld Connecticut's refusal to provide elective abortions through Medicaid. In so ruling, the Court stated:

> The Connecticut regulation before us is different in kind from the laws invalidated in our previous abortion decisions. The Connecticut regulation places no obstacles—absolute or otherwise—in the pregnant woman's path to an abortion. An indigent woman who desires an abortion suffers no disadvantage as a consequence of Connecticut's decision to fund childbirth; she continues as before to be dependent on private sources for the service she desires. The State may have made childbirth a more attractive alternative, thereby influencing the woman's decision, but it has imposed no restriction on access to abortions that was not already there. The indigency that may make it difficult—and in some cases, perhaps, impossible—for some women to have abortions is neither created nor in any way affected by the Connecticut regulation. We conclude that the Connecticut regulation does not impinge upon the fundamental right recognized in *Roe.*
>
> Our conclusion signals no retreat from *Roe* or the cases applying it. There is a basic difference between direct state interference with a protected activity and state encouragement of an alternative activity consonant with legislative policy. Constitutional concerns are greatest when the State attempts to impose its will by force of law; the State's power to encourage actions deemed to be in the public interest is necessarily far broader. . . .
>
> Id. *at 527–28.*

All hopes that *Maher* could be limited to refusals to pay for elective abortions were dashed in 1980 as opposition to abortion became increasingly vocal and, in the case of *Harris v. McRae* 448 U.S. 297, the Supreme Court upheld the Hyde Amendment, a federal statute barring Medicaid funding for almost all abortions. Nevertheless, the Supreme Court declined in the subsequent *Akron I* and *Thornburgh* decisions to overrule *Roe.*

Starting in 1989, however, the Court did begin to signal that *Roe* was in trouble. In that year, the Court upheld a number of provisions that seemed vulnerable, and a plurality of the Court suggested an interest in reversing *Roe.* Thus, *Webster v. Reproductive Health Services,* 492 U.S. 490 (1989), let stand Missouri's statutory preamble containing its value judgment favoring childbirth over abortion, a bar on public employees and facilities participating in abortion procedures, and a requirement that specified viability tests be performed starting at twenty weeks. Although it found that the case did not afford it the occasion to revisit the precise holding in *Roe,* the Court did modify and narrow *Roe* in succeeding cases.

A year later, in *Hodgson v. Minnesota,* 497 U.S. 417 (1990), and *Ohio v. Akron Center for Reproductive Health,* 497 U.S. 502 (1990), the Court upheld two-parent notification provisions that allowed a minor to avoid the notification requirements by showing a court that she is mature or that an abortion is in her best interest. In finding that such a parental notification requirement "does not impose an undue, or otherwise unconstitutional, burden on a minor seeking an abortion," the Court indicated it was "both rational and fair for the State to conclude that, in most instances, the family will strive to give a lonely or even terrified minor advice that is both compassionate and mature." The Court thus disregarded both situations where this is not so and the difficulty such legislation would pose for many teenagers seeking abortions.

Finally, in *Rust v. Sullivan,* 500 U.S. 173, 111 S. Ct. 1759 (1991), the Supreme Court upheld regulations prohibiting doctors employed by recipients of Title X family planning funds from even mentioning abortion in the context of assisting pregnant (or non-pregnant) teenagers against both due process and First Amendment challenges. The Court demonstrated its hostility to abortion by applying its earlier decisions denying funding to the speech context. The regulations upheld make this clear:

> The regulations attach three principal conditions on the grant of federal funds for Title X projects. First, the regulations specify that a "Title X project may not provide counseling concerning the use of abortion as a method of family planning or provide referral for abortion as a method of family planning." . . .
>
> Second, the regulations broadly prohibit a Title X project from engaging in activities that "encourage, promote or advocate abortion as a method of family planning." . . .
>
> Third, the regulations require that Title X projects be organized so that they are "physically and financially separate" from prohibited abortion activities. . . .
> Id. *at 1765–66.*

Shortly after his inauguration, President Bill Clinton took action to rescind the "gag rule" challenged in *Rust v. Sullivan.* Finding it violative of underlying statute, he instructed the new Secretary of the Department of Health and Human Services to issue new regulations governing the discussion and performance of abortions by providers receiving Title X monies, which were later enacted into law.

Particularly, given the extreme nature of the *Rust* holding, many doubted that *Roe* would survive when a Court containing a majority of Reagan and Bush appointees was asked once again to consider the abortion question. Nevertheless, it did survive challenge the following year—although in a more limited form. The decision in *Planned Parenthood of Southeastern Pennsylvania v. Casey* declined both to overrule the basic holding of *Roe* and to strike abortion restrictions previously stricken. In an unusual anonymous opinion, Justices O'Connor, Kennedy, and Souter explained their reasons for upholding *Roe* as well as all the restrictions except those requiring spousal notification. Chief Justice Rehnquist and Justices White, Scalia, and Thomas concurred in the judgment in part and dissented in part. Justices Blackmun and Stevens also filed separate opinions, indicating that they would uphold *Roe* but not the statute. The three-judge plurality is excerpted here. In reading it, consider what right is given constitutional protection, when it is protected by the Constitution, what justification the state must give for interfering with the right, and whose right it is. Consider also the ways the answers to these questions may have changed since the *Roe* decision was first issued.

Planned Parenthood of Southeastern Pennsylvania v. Casey

United States Supreme Court, 1992.
___U.S. ___ , 113 S.Ct. 2791,
120 L.Ed.2d 674.

Justice O'CONNOR, Justice KENNEDY, and Justice SOUTER announced the judgment of the Court. . . .

I

Liberty finds no refuge in a jurisprudence of doubt. Yet 19 years after our holding that the Constitution protects a woman's right to terminate her pregnancy in its early stages, *Roe v. Wade,* that definition of liberty is still questioned. Joining the respondents as amicus curiae, the United States, as it has done in five other cases in the last decade, again asks us to overrule *Roe.*

At issue in these cases are five provisions of the Pennsylvania Abortion Control Act of 1982 as amended in 1988 and 1989. . . . The Act requires that a woman seeking an abortion give her informed consent prior to the abortion procedure, and specifies that she be provided with certain information at least 24 hours before the abortion is performed. For a minor to obtain an abortion, the Act requires the informed consent of one of her parents, but provides for a judicial bypass option if the minor does not wish to or cannot obtain a parent's consent. Another provision of the Act requires that, unless certain exceptions apply, a married woman seeking an abortion must sign a statement indicating that she has notified her husband of her intended abortion. The Act exempts compliance with these three requirements in the event of a "medical emergency" . . . . In addition to the above provisions regulating the performance of abortions, the Act imposes certain reporting requirements on facilities that provide abortion services.

Before any of these provisions took effect, the petitioners, who are five abortion clinics and one physician representing himself as well as a class of physicians who provide abortion services, brought this suit seeking declaratory and injunctive relief. . . . The District Court . . . held all the provisions at issue here unconstitutional, entering a permanent injunction against Pennsylvania's enforcement of them. The Court of Appeals for the Third Circuit affirmed in part and reversed in part, upholding all of the regulations except for the husband notification requirement. . . .

After considering the fundamental constitutional questions resolved by *Roe,* principles of institutional integrity, and the rule of stare decisis, we are led to conclude this: the essential holding of *Roe v. Wade* should be retained and once again reaffirmed.

It must be stated at the outset and with clarity that *Roe*'s essential holding, the holding we reaffirm, has three parts. First is a recognition of the right of the woman to choose to have an abortion before viability and to obtain it without undue interference from the State. Before viability, the State's interests are not strong enough to support a prohibition of abortion or the imposition of a substantial obstacle to the woman's effective right to elect the procedure. Second is a confirmation of the State's power to restrict abortions after fetal viability, if the law contains exceptions for pregnancies which endanger a woman's life or health. And third is the principle that the State has legitimate interests from the outset of the pregnancy in protecting the health of the woman and the life of the fetus that may become a child. These principles do not contradict one another; and we adhere to each.

II

. . . Men and women of good conscience can disagree, and we suppose some always shall disagree, about the profound moral and spiritual implications of terminating a pregnancy, even in its earliest stage. Some of us as individuals find abortion offensive to our most basic principles of morality, but that cannot control our decision. Our obligation is to define the liberty of all, not to mandate our own moral code. The underlying constitutional issue is whether the State can resolve these philosophic questions in such a definitive way that a woman lacks all choice in the matter, except perhaps in those rare circumstances in which the pregnancy is itself a danger to her own life or health, or is the result of rape or incest.

It is conventional constitutional doctrine that where reasonable people disagree the government can adopt one position or the other. That theorem, however, assumes a state of affairs in which the choice does not intrude upon a protected liberty. Thus, while some people might disagree about whether or not the flag should be saluted, or disagree about the proposition that it may not be defiled, we have ruled that a State may not compel or enforce one view or the other.

Our law affords constitutional protection to personal decisions relating to marriage, procreation, contraception, family relationships, child rearing, and education. Our cases recognize "the right of the individual, married or single, to be free from unwarranted governmental intrusion into matters so fundamentally affecting a person as the decision whether to bear or beget a child." Our precedents "have respected the private realm of family life which the state cannot enter." These matters, involving the most intimate and personal choices a person may make in a lifetime, choices central to personal dignity and autonomy, are central to the liberty protected by the Fourteenth Amendment. At the heart of liberty is the right to define one's own concept of existence, of meaning, of the universe, and of the mystery of human life. Beliefs about these matters could not define the attributes of personhood were they formed under compulsion of the State.

These considerations begin our analysis of the woman's interest in terminating her pregnancy but cannot end it, for this reason: though the abortion decision may originate within the zone of conscience and belief, it is more than a philosophic exercise. Abortion is a unique act. It is an act fraught with consequences for others: for the woman who must live with the implications of her decision; for the persons who perform and assist in the procedure; for the spouse, family, and society which must confront the knowledge that these procedures exist, procedures some deem nothing short of an act of violence against innocent human life; and, depending on one's beliefs, for the life or potential life that is aborted. Though abortion is conduct, it does not follow that the State is entitled to proscribe it in all instances. That is because the liberty of the woman is at stake in a sense unique to the human condition and so unique to the law. The mother who carries a child to full term is subject to anxieties, to physical constraints, to pain that only she must bear. That these sacrifices have from the beginning of the human race been endured by woman with a pride that ennobles her in the eyes of others and gives to the infant a bond of love cannot alone be grounds for the State to insist she make the sacrifice. Her suffering is too intimate and personal for the State to insist, without more, upon its own vision of the woman's role, however dominant that vision has been in the course of our history and our culture. The destiny of the woman must be shaped to a large extent on her own conception of her spiritual imperatives and her place in society.

It should be recognized, moreover, that in some critical respects the abortion decision is of the same character as the decision to use contraception, to which *Griswold, Eisenstadt* and *Carey* afford constitutional protection. We have no doubt as to the correctness of those decisions. . . . *Roe* was, of course, an extension of those cases and, as the decision itself indicated, the separate States could act in some degree to further their own legitimate interests in protecting pre-natal life. . . .

III

. . . We have seen how time has overtaken some of *Roe's* factual assumptions: advances in maternal health care allow for abortions safe to the mother later in pregnancy than was true in 1973 and advances in neonatal care have advanced viability to a point somewhat earlier. But these facts go only to the scheme of time limits on the realization of competing interests, and the divergences from the factual premises of 1973 have no bearing on the validity of *Roe's* central holding, that viability marks the earliest point at which the State's interest in fetal life is constitutionally adequate to justify a legislative ban on nontherapeutic abortions. The soundness or unsoundness of that constitutional judgment in no sense turns on whether viability occurs at approximately 28 weeks, as was usual at the time of *Roe,* at 23 to 24 weeks, as it sometimes does today, or at some moment even slightly earlier in pregnancy, as it may if fetal respiratory capacity can somehow be enhanced in the future. Whenever it may occur, the attainment of viability may continue to serve as the critical fact, just as it has done since *Roe* was decided; which is to say that no change in *Roe's* factual underpinning has left its central holding obsolete, and none supports an argument for overruling it.

The sum of the precedential inquiry to this point shows *Roe's* underpinnings unweakened in any way affecting its central holding. While it has engendered disapproval, it has not been unworkable. An entire generation has come of age free to assume *Roe's* concept of liberty in defining the capacity of women to act in society, and to make reproductive decisions; no erosion of principle going to liberty or personal autonomy has left *Roe*'s central holding a doctrinal remnant; *Roe* portends no developments at odds with other precedent for the analysis of personal liberty; and no changes of fact have rendered viability more or less appropriate as the point at which the balance of interests tips. Within the bounds of normal stare decisis analysis, then, and subject to the considerations on which it customarily turns, the stronger argument is for affirming *Roe*'s central holding, with whatever degree of personal reluctance any of us may have, not for overruling it. . . .

IV

From what we have said so far it follows that it is a constitutional liberty of the woman to have some freedom to terminate her pregnancy. We conclude that the basic decision in *Roe* was based on a constitutional analysis which we cannot now repudiate. The woman's liberty is not so unlimited, however, that from the outset the State cannot show its concern for the life of the unborn, and at a later point in fetal development the State's interest in life has sufficient force so that the right of the woman to terminate the pregnancy can be restricted. . . .

Some guiding principles should emerge. What is at stake is the woman's right to make the ultimate decision, not a right to be insulated from all others in doing so. Regulations which do no more than create a structural mechanism by which the State, or the parent or guardian of a minor, may express profound respect for the life of the unborn are permitted, if they are not a substantial obstacle to the woman's exercise of the right to choose. Unless it has that effect on her right of choice, a state measure designed to persuade her to choose childbirth over abortion will be upheld if reasonably related to that goal. Regulations designed to foster the health of a woman seeking an abortion are valid if they do not constitute an undue burden.

. . . We give this summary:

a. To protect the central right recognized by *Roe v. Wade* while at the same time accommodating the State's profound interest in potential life, we will employ the undue burden analysis as explained in this opinion. An undue burden exists, and therefore a provision of law is invalid, if its purpose or effect is to place a substantial obstacle in the path of a woman seeking an abortion before the fetus attains viability.

b. We reject the rigid trimester framework of *Roe v. Wade.* To promote the State's profound interest in potential life, throughout pregnancy the State may take measures to ensure that the woman's choice is informed, and measures designed to advance this interest will not be invalidated as long as their purpose is to persuade the woman to choose childbirth over abortion. These measures must not be an undue burden on the right.

c. As with any medical procedure, the State may enact regulations to further the health or safety of a woman seeking an abortion. Unnecessary health regulations that have the purpose or effect of presenting a substantial obstacle to a woman seeking an abortion impose an undue burden on the right.

d. Our adoption of the undue burden analysis does not disturb the central holding of *Roe v. Wade,* and we reaffirm that holding. Regardless of whether exceptions are made for particular circumstances, a State may not prohibit any woman from making the ultimate decision to terminate her pregnancy before viability.

e. We also reaffirm *Roe*'s holding that "subsequent to viability, the State in promoting its interest in the potentiality of human life may, if it chooses, regulate, and even proscribe, abortion except where it is necessary, in appropriate medical judgment, for the preservation of the life or health of the mother."

These principles control our assessment of the Pennsylvania statute, and we now turn to the issue of the validity of its challenged provisions.

V

. . . We now consider the separate statutory sections at issue.

[The three justices first determined that] the statute's definition of medical emergency [complied with *Roe*'s bar on] interfering with a woman's choice to undergo an abortion procedure if continuing her pregnancy would constitute a threat to her health. . . .

We next consider the informed consent requirement. . . . [There, they concluded that] requiring that the woman be informed of the availability of information relating to fetal development and the assistance available should she decide to carry the pregnancy to full term is a reasonable measure to insure an informed choice, one which might cause the woman to choose childbirth over abortion. This requirement cannot be considered a substantial obstacle to obtaining an abortion, and, it follows, there is no undue burden. . . .

. . . The idea that important decisions will be more informed and deliberate if they follow some period of reflection does not strike us as unreasonable, particularly where the statute directs that important information become part of the background of the decision. . . . [A]s the District Court held, the waiting period has the effect of "increasing the cost and risk of delay of abortions," but the District Court did not conclude that the increased costs and potential delays amount to substantial obstacles. . . . Yet, as we have stated, under the undue burden standard a State is permitted to enact persuasive measures which favor childbirth over abortion, even if those measures do not further a health interest. And while the waiting period does limit a physician's discretion, that is not, standing alone, a reason to invalidate it. In light of the construction given the statute's definition of medical emergency by the Court of Appeals, and the District Court's findings, we cannot say that the waiting period imposes a real health risk. . . .

[Addressing the spousal notification provision, the Court observed that social science studies] and the District Court's findings reinforce what common sense would suggest. In well-functioning marriages, spouses discuss important intimate decisions such as whether to bear a child. But there are millions of women in this country who are the victims of regular physical and psychological abuse at the hands of their husbands. Should these women become pregnant, they may have very good reasons for not wishing to inform their husbands of their decision to obtain an abortion. Many

may have justifiable fears of physical abuse, but may be no less fearful of the consequences of reporting prior abuse to the Commonwealth of Pennsylvania. Many may have a reasonable fear that notifying their husbands will provoke further instances of . . . abuse; these women are not exempt from [the] notification requirement. Many may fear devastating forms of psychological abuse from their husbands, including verbal harassment, threats of future violence, the destruction of possessions, physical confinement to the home, the withdrawal of financial support, or the disclosure of the abortion to family and friends. These methods of psychological abuse may act as even more of a deterrent to notification than the possibility of physical violence, but women who are the victims of the abuse are not exempt from [the] notification requirement. And many women who are pregnant as a result of sexual assaults by their husbands will be unable to avail themselves of the exception for spousal sexual assault, because the exception requires that the woman have notified law enforcement authorities within 90 days of the assault, and her husband will be notified of her report once an investigation begins. If anything in this field is certain, it is that victims of spousal sexual assault are extremely reluctant to report the abuse to the government; hence, a great many spousal rape victims will not be exempt. . . .

. . . The unfortunate yet persisting conditions we document above will mean that in a large fraction of the cases in which [this provision] is relevant, it will operate as a substantial obstacle to a woman's choice to undergo an abortion. It is an undue burden, and therefore invalid. . . .

We next consider the parental consent provision. . . . Our cases establish, and we reaffirm today, that a State may require a minor seeking an abortion to obtain the consent of a parent or guardian, provided that there is an adequate judicial bypass procedure. Under these precedents, in our view, the one-parent consent requirement and judicial bypass procedure are constitutional. . . .

[Finally, the Court turned to] the recordkeeping and reporting requirements of the statute. . . . In *Danforth,* we held that recordkeeping and reporting provisions "that are reasonably directed to the preservation of maternal health and that properly respect a patient's confidentiality and privacy are permissible." We think that under this standard, all the provisions at issue here except that relating to spousal notice are constitutional. . . .

VI

Our Constitution is a covenant running from the first generation of Americans to us and then to future generations. It is a coherent succession. Each generation must learn anew that the Constitution's written terms embody ideas and aspirations that must survive more ages than one. We accept our responsibility not to retreat from interpreting the full meaning of the covenant in light of all of our precedents. We invoke it once again to define the freedom guaranteed by the Constitution's own promise, the promise of liberty.

The judgment is affirmed.

STUDY QUESTIONS

1. What interests did the plurality see at play in abortion cases? Whose rights are involved? To what extent do they reflect equality as well as liberty concerns? To what extent does the Constitution protect them?
2. What is "the central holding of *Roe*"? What aspects of the *Roe* decision are rejected here? In what ways is the standard announced here different from the one announced in *Roe?*
3. At what point does a regulatory measure become an "undue burden"?

In upholding *Roe v. Wade,* the joint opinion recognizes a right grounded in the liberty aspect of the Due Process Clause, which includes bodily integrity and privacy interests, to choose whether to continue her pregnancy. Requirements designed to further the woman's health, such as informed consent provisions, are not necessarily inconsistent with this right. Moreover, the decision as to what value to give the fetus must be an individual one. The state cannot preclude all abortions in the name of protecting "unborn persons." The authors of the joint opinion do make clear, however, that in their view, the state has an interest in potential life from the moment of conception. At the point of viability, this interest becomes strong enough to bar abortions that are not needed to protect the life and health of the woman. But even before this point, the state may act to further its interest in potential life. Thus, for example, a state may adopt provisions that seek to make sure the woman considers the value of the potential life she is carrying.

Only when the stated regulations or restrictions place an "undue burden" on or pose "substantial obstacles" for the woman would the three justices hold them unconstitutional. Furthermore, as is evident from their opinion, findings as to impermissible burdens and obstacles must be very specific and fact-based. In the course of discussing the provisions of the Pennsylvania law in Section V of the decision, the three justices gave some indication of what the Court means by "undue burden" and "substantial obstacles." Thus, the "informed consent" provision that required giving particular information to the women was upheld because it was seen as enhancing, not interfering with, her decision. The spousal notification provision, however, was invalidated because it was seen as interfering with the rights of women who feared physical or psychological abuse.

Although *Casey* says it is reaffirming *Roe,* it also allows much more leeway for state bodies to act. Moreover, in declining to review an intermediate-level decision rejecting a challenge to a recent Mississippi statute that also required "informed consent" after a twenty-four-hour waiting period, the Court failed even to consider whether the lower courts must afford complainants a chance to demonstrate the burdens that restrictions impose (*Barnes v. Moore,* 970 F.2d 12 (5th Cir. 1992), *cert. den.,* 113 S. Ct. 656 (1992)). As a result, the coming days may see considerable political activity, at both the federal and the state levels. Choice advocates, for example, wish to enact a federal Freedom of Choice bill that seeks to enact the protections announced in *Roe v. Wade* and subsequent decisions into law. Two key exceptions would allow states to deny funding for abortions and to adopt parental notification requirements. They also wish to restore Medicaid funding and other federal health care services, either by repeal of the "Hyde Amemdment," which was unsuccessfully challenged in *Harris v. McRae,* or by passage of the federal Reproductive Health Equity Act. Activity at the state level will vary from state to state. State court litigation drawing on state constitutional protections, begun in earnest after the *Maher* decision, is also likely to expand greatly.

As noted, following the *Casey* decision, the Supreme Court declined to review lower court rulings on challenges to local statutes. It did, however, issue one abortion-related ruling. In the case of *Bray v. Alexandria Women's Health Clinic,* ___U.S. , 113 S. Ct. 753 (1993), the Court held, in an opinion by Justice Scalia, that the federal civil rights laws do not provide the basis for enjoining persons obstructing access to an abortion clinic. In so holding, the Court ruled that opposition to abortion is not like racial hostility and does not qualify as an "otherwise class-based invidiously discriminatory animus," which the law says must underlie an impermissible joint action. The Court thus rejected the plaintiffs' claim that the obstructors' actions were directed at women as a class. However, an antiabortionist's killing in early 1993 of a doctor who performed procedures in an abortion clinic may prompt protective federal legislation. Until then, efforts to contain clinic obstructors will have to proceed in state courts, just as many challenges to restrictive abortion laws have been brought in the state courts under state law.

II. APPLYING THE RIGHT TO REPRODUCTIVE CHOICE

Deciding on Sterilization

As we have seen, the issue of compulsory sterilization played an important role in developing constitutional protection for reproductive choice. Restrictions on voluntary sterilization have also presented a serious problem. The tension between the need to ensure access to sterilization and prevent sterilization abuse highlights issues of race and class bias as well as the general problem of informed consent.

Generally, consensual sterilization is legally permitted throughout the United States. However, because the available techniques are medical procedures, access to voluntary sterilization requires cooperation from providers. Men have rarely been denied vasectomies. On the other hand, women seeking tubal ligations or other sterilization procedures have encountered resistance from both doctors and medical facilities. Perhaps reflecting the eugenicist notion that certain women should propagate as well as a general reluctance to afford women reproductive autonomy, restrictions on women's sterilization procedures have taken several forms: outright prohibitions, minimum age and pregnancy requirements, and spousal consent requirements.

Legal attacks brought in the early 1970s were helpful in eliminating hospital policies embodying restrictions of this sort. Clearly influenced by *Roe,* courts tended to focus on the refusal to accommodate one reproductive choice. In the words of the

First Circuit Court of Appeals in *Hathaway v. Worcester City Hospital,* 475 F.2d 701, 706 (1st Cir. 1973),

> . . . [W]e are not mandating the city or state to maintain the hospital, or to retain its present size, staff, or facilities. The hospital is not required to perform all kinds of non-therapeutic or even all therapeutic surgical procedures. We are merely saying . . . that once the state has undertaken to provide general short-term care, as here, it may not constitutionally draw the line at medically indistinguishable surgical procedures that impinge on fundamental rights.

It is not clear that such reasoning will suffice under *Casey* and the cases that preceded it upholding Medicaid and other government programs that provided childbirth services but denied abortion services. Under *Casey,* a court may certainly question whether a hospital's failure to permit certain voluntary sterilizations unduly burdens reproductive choice. Moreover, it may find such restrictions further the state's interest in potential life. Challenges brought under state constitutions, on the other hand, are likely to be more successful. Indeed, this type of equal protection analysis has generally been the basis for invalidating Medicaid restrictions on abortion funding under various state constitutions.

Hospitals that are willing to permit the use of their facilities for sterilization have routinely conditioned that use on consent by the spouse. Although many women seem to object to it, this requirement has rarely been challenged. A spousal consent requirement was found unconstitutional by a New Jersey trial court in *Ponter v. Ponter,* 342 A.2d 574 (Ch. Div. 1975). That case, however, involved a woman who had been separated from her husband for a number of years. There has yet to be a ruling that explicitly addresses the question of whether a husband's interest in his wife's fertility is sufficient to require his consent in an ongoing marriage. The analysis of the spousal notification requirement in *Casey* may well resolve the question in this context. Arguably, a husband has a greater interest in his wife's long-run fertility than in a particular pregnancy. It would seem, however, that her bodily integrity and reasons to fear telling him are the same in both cases.

Because the courts' findings of unconstitutionality in *Hathaway* and *Ponter* depended on their finding state action, the decisions regarding sterilization restrictions do not apply directly to private hospitals and physicians. Nevertheless, cases like *Hathaway* and *Ponter,* combined with changing attitudes on reproductive rights in the 1970s, appear to have had some effect in overcoming policies and practices restricting access to voluntary sterilization procedures. During this same period, however, it became apparent that some women were being subjected to sterilization without their consent.

The problem of compulsory sterilization reemerged in the 1970s with revelations of abuse involving both health care providers and government officials. Southern doctors required poor black patients to submit to sterilization as a condition of receiving medical assistance with pregnancy and childbirth. Public hospitals in California obtained consent forms for sterilization from Mexican-American patients while they were in labor. In one particularly notorious incident, Alabama welfare workers tricked an illiterate public assistance recipient into signing for the sterilization of her young daughters by threatening to cut off benefits unless she signed. Indeed, in the decade after Medicaid began funding sterilization in 1966, there was a tenfold increase in the number of tubal ligations performed on poor women.

The litigation resulting from these revelations of abuse was often unsuccessful. For example, women in Los Angeles were unable to establish that the consent procedures were inadequate, even though their English was poor and they were asked to sign while in extreme discomfort. See *Madrigal v. Quilligan,* United States District Court, Central District of California, No. CV 75–2057–JNC (June 30, 1978). Women sterilized as a condition for receiving medical assistance for pregnancy and childbirth were unable to establish state action sufficient to render the doctor's conduct unconstitutional. See *Walker v. Pierce,* 560 F.2d 609 (4th Cir. 1977).

Litigation directed against federal welfare officials challenging the sufficiency of national regulations intended to protect public assistance recipients against coerced sterilization was more successful. As a result of that litigation and the publicity of the abuses, the federal government adopted regulations that conditioned reimbursement on a seventy-two-hour waiting period, set the minimum age at twenty-one, and imposed a moratorium on the sterilization of all incompetents. See *Relf v. Weinberger,* 372 F. Supp. 1196 (D.D.C. 1974). During the same period, a coalition of women's and health organizations and community groups succeeded in having the New York City Health and Hospitals Corporation adopt stringent protections to ensure informed consent. These provisions, later enacted into law by the New York City Council, required, among other things, a thirty-day waiting period, a minimum age of twenty-one, and that the patient not be hospitalized at the time consent is given. The federal government subsequently issued revised reimbursement regulations based on the New York provisions.

The constitutionality of the informed consent provisions of these sterilization regulations has yet to be decided by any court. Nor does the most recent abortion decision resolve the matter. Although the Supreme Court made clear in *Casey* that certain waiting periods and informational requirements regarding abortions will be upheld against challenges under the federal constitution, such provisions may still fall under state constitutional guarantees. Moreover, a number of differences exist between abortion and sterilization decisions. First, the two procedures have a very different impact on one's ability to reproduce at a later time. Tubal ligation (as opposed to vasectomy) is rarely reversible. Second, abortions must be performed within a very short period of time. Third, the history of state policy toward the two procedures has differed greatly. Since the late nineteenth century, access to abortion has been limited by the state, while sterilization of certain segments of the population has been compelled. The medical profession, in contrast to the state, has supported abortion as an option in recent years while its conduct in regard to sterilization has been much more equivocal. As a result, some women have been deprived of their right to choose sterilization while others have been deprived of their right not to choose it.

The proponents of the regulations argued that abortion and sterilization should not be equated and that sterilization, unlike abortion, has become accessible. They contended that a thirty-day waiting period, minimum-age provisions, and specific informed consent requirements detailing the nature of the sterilization procedure were necessary to ensure that all the women obtaining the procedure really intend their choice, even at the cost of making it more difficult for some women to exercise their choice. These provisions—with an exception for emergencies—were ultimately adopted for both New York City and federal subsidized procedures.

Perhaps the most difficult problems in the use of sterilization are posed by its application to the mentally incompetent. Historically, incompetents have been subjected to terrible abuses; but recognizing this has not made clear the best way to avoid abuses in the future. At least three issues must be addressed: What justifications should suffice to permit their sterilization? What procedural guarantees should attend the procedure? Who should be permitted to initiate the process? Consider the New Jersey Supreme Court's approach to these questions in the case of *In re Grady,*

85 N.J. 235, 426 A.2d 467 (1981). There, the New Jersey court held that (1) a temporary guardian should be appointed as soon as possible when an application to sterilize an incompetent is made; (2) medical and psychological evaluations must be obtained by the court; and (3) although the procedures may be authorized whether or not they are necessary, the court must be satisfied that sterilization is in the best interest of the incompetent.

Other states have attempted to devise substantive and procedural guarantees regarding the sterilization of incompetents. For example, North Carolina will permit retarded persons to be sterilized when the court finds it is in the state's, as opposed to the individual's, best interest. The state's interest is defined as preventing the birth of "defective" children or of children whose parents would be mentally incapable of caring for them. The North Carolina scheme provides fairly extensive procedural safeguards to ensure that the proper findings are made. However, as is the case with other regulations seeking to resolve the tension between voluntary and involuntary sterilization, there have been no definitive Supreme Court rulings adjudicating the rights of incompetents with regard to sterilization.

Preventing Birth

Constraints on freedom of choice in preventing pregnancy appear in many forms and many contexts today. Decisions may be coerced or pressured in a number of ways. Information necessary to make a knowledgeable choice may be distorted or withheld. Restrictions on distributors of birth control devices and drugs may preclude access by users.

A concern underlying many of the efforts to solve these problems is the tension familiar from the sterilization controversy of the 1970s—the tension between guaranteeing access and preventing coercion. The emerging debate over the contraceptive drug Norplant, recently approved for use in the United States, illustrates this tension. Although Norplant is used for contraception, not sterilization, its use requires physical invasion of a woman's body and its long-run effect on fertility is not known. Nevertheless, because it automatically releases the appropriate dose for up to five years once it is implanted in a woman's upper arm, it is a preferred means of contraception for some women. On the other hand, for other women, particularly the young and the poor, there may be a problem of pressure or even compulsion to use it. A recent report from the Alan Guttmacher Institute explores problems Norplant poses, particularly for poor women.

Norplant: Opportunities and Perils for Low-Income Women

Alan Guttmacher Institute.
December 1992.

In December 1990, the federal Food and Drug Administration (FDA) approved Norplant for contraceptive use in the United States. Norplant has been available in many other countries for several years, with an estimated 1.1 million users worldwide. The Norplant system consists of six thin capsules surgically implanted into a woman's upper arm that slowly release a low dosage of progestin to prevent conception over a five-year period. Research and extensive studies of women using Norplant have shown that it becomes effective within 24 hours when inserted during the first seven days of the menstrual cycle, and that it has an annual pregnancy rate over five years of less than one percent. The most common side effect is irregular bleeding; other less common side effects include headaches, mood swings, weight gain and acne. Norplant was developed by the Population Council; Wyeth-Ayerst Laboratories is the exclusive distributor of Norplant in the United States.

According to a spokesperson at Wyeth-Ayerst, an estimated 300,000–350,000 Norplant kits have been sold in the United States since it was first made available in February 1991; and, 30,000 health care clinicians have been trained by Wyeth-Ayerst on insertion and removal procedures. A small-scale study of 100 physicians who provide Norplant, commissioned by Wyeth-Ayerst one year after FDA approval, indicated that 71% of their Norplant clients were under age 30, that there was an even split between married and single users and that 71% had one or two children. . . .

. . . Each Norplant kit costs $365 (a $15 increase over the initial price was instituted October 1), with additional charges for counseling and insertion, bringing the total cost to $500–$750 per client. Norplant cannot be left in the woman's arm after discontinuation of use, so removal is necessary, at a cost between $50–$150. . . .

Approximately 20 bills, amendments and welfare reform proposals in 13 legislatures . . . [were introduced during the 1991–1992 term] regarding Norplant. . . . Of the measures that did not offer incentives or mandate use, most sought to provide information and outreach to low-income women and substance abusers to help them gain access to Norplant.

Attracting the greatest amount of attention nationwide were two bills in Tennessee that were hotly debated, but not approved, before the legislative session ended. As initially introduced in each house, they would have established a special program administered by the Department of Human Services to offer $500 to women receiving AFDC (cash public assistance) to use Norplant and $50 annually while using the method. This "pilot project" would be limited to the first 5% who signed up and would provide follow-up examinations for every year of use. Although the bill was approved in the House with amendments, it died when the legislature adjourned for the year. . . .

Opponents of the bill charged both sexism and racism saying it perpetuated the "brood-sow myth" that characterizes the common, but unfounded, belief that mothers receiving welfare become pregnant again to increase their cash assistance benefits. Others charge it was a backdoor attempt at badly conceived welfare reform and amounted to nothing more than a bribe to poor women to use a long-lasting contraceptive. Since the bill's counterpart in the Senate was rejected, it did not go into effect. . . .

Anger and fear muted the approval of Norplant in the United States when state judges in California and Texas sought to require the use of Norplant as a condition of probation. . . . Although required use of contraception in sentencing arrangements and in determining conditions of probation has cropped up in several cases in the recent past Norplant has only been specifically targeted in two cases, both in 1991.

In the California case, a superior court judge sentenced a woman convicted of child abuse to one year in jail and four years on probation; one of the conditions of her probation was that she use Norplant. The defendant was a 27-year-old black woman receiving welfare benefits. The woman originally agreed to use Norplant, but later changed her mind saying her lawyer was not present at the sentencing hearing and she did not understand what Norplant was or how it worked.

An appeal was filed contending that her acceptance of Norplant was not a free decision and not an informed one, and that she had medical problems that contraindicated Norplant use. Prior to a hearing on the appeal motion, the judge was shot at, but not harmed, by an antiabortion activist. In April 1992, the appeal was dismissed as moot after the woman violated another condition of her probation and was sent to prison.

The other case involved a state judge in Texas who ordered a woman guilty of child abuse to use Norplant as a condition of her probation. The woman did not appeal her conviction or her sentence and Norplant was inserted. However, she experienced adverse side effects and had it removed; she later had a tubal ligation.

STUDY QUESTIONS

1. Do criminal sentences that condition probation on the acceptance of Norplant insertion violate the woman's right to refuse medical treatment? Do state proposals offering money for using Norplant violate this right?

2. Do most low-income women have the option of using Norplant? At what point should a drug like Norplant be available through Medicaid? As soon as it is generally available? When it is generally covered by insurance programs?

───────────────────── ❧ ─────────────────────

As the Alan Guttmacher Institute memorandum indicates, poor women have been pressured to take Norplant both directly by threats of incarceration and indirectly through potential loss of welfare benefits. A number of states have considered placing similar indirect pressures on general reproductive choices. One example is the key provision of New Jersey's Family Development Act, signed into law on January 21, 1992, which denies families receiving benefits under the Aid to Families with Dependent Children (AFDC) program any additional benefits for children born to the head of the household after the family begins to receive welfare benefits. According to the bill's sponsor, the provision's purpose is "to discourage AFDC recipients from having additional children while enrolled on public assistance and to encourage recipients to be self-sufficient and earn the funds necessary to sustain the family through gainful employment."

A central claim in challenges to this "additional child provision" is that the law deliberately interferes with reproductive choice despite both the state and federal constitutional protections. This argument focuses on the pressure to terminate their pregnancies that New Jersey's special kind of maximum grant places on AFDC recipients. While this argument seems closely analogous to the New Jersey Constitutional argument against the denial of Medicaid funding for abortions that succeeded earlier, no definitive judicial ruling is yet available.

Like Norplant, other contraceptive drugs pose a tension between the need for protection against damaging health consequences and the need for access. Problems with the drug RU-486 have highlighted these twin concerns. Discovered in France, the drug permits early, but not physically invasive, abortions that are believed by many to be safe and effective. Nevertheless, an import ban imposed in 1988 by the Bush Administration made the drug inaccessible to women in the United States. In late 1992, a woman who unsuccessfully attempted to enter the country with RU-486 to terminate her pregnancy during the seventh week and several other plaintiffs brought a class action challenging the import ban. (See Complaint, *Benton v. Kessler*, United States District Court for the Eastern District of New York, 92 Civ. 3161.) The complaint alleges that the ban was improperly issued and violates her privacy and other constitutional rights. However, on January 22, 1993, newly sworn-in President Clinton called for a review of the import ban, leaving the need for the lawsuit unclear.

While many feminists are among its proponents, RU-486 opponents include feminists as well as the antichoice community. The debate within the prochoice community involves different perspectives on the desirability of having the drug available. Both camps agree on the need to avoid past abuses, such as the inadequate testing of oral contraceptives before marketing, the nondisclosure of evidence likely to have prevented the marketing of defective interuterine devices, and the widespread use of damaging drugs during pregnancy, but their views differ as to how safe or burdensome RU-486 is.

Thus, Janet Callum and Rebecca Chalker sum up the thoughts of feminist proponents:

> We feel that it is essential to keep RU 486 in perspective. RU 486 is not a magic potion that will end all unwanted pregnancies and eliminate the need for surgical abortions. Nor will it, as the antiabortion zealots fear, bring the capability of abortion to every bedroom. Furthermore, it is essential that careful tracking of RU 486 be undertaken, particularly as it is introduced in the "developing" world to populations of women who are, on the whole, poorer and less healthy than are the women who have used this method thus far. RU 486 could prove to be less successful among women with fewer resources and poorer health. But given the information that we have, RU 486 appears to provide a safe and effective abortion alternative for many women at a time when we need more, not fewer, abortion options. "RU-486—YES." Ms., *March/April 1993. P. 36.*

Janice Raymond, Renate Klein, and Lynette Dumble sum up the contrary view:

> We disagree with the statement that "RU 486 appears to provide a safe and effective abortion alternative." We do agree, however, that it "could prove to be less successful among women with fewer resources and poorer health." Abortion is one of the simplest of presently medicalized gynecological procedures, requiring less expertise, training, and skill than attending births. Trained paramedics in "Third World" countries perform abortions safely and competently. Why then cannot trained laywomen do abortions safely and competently in Western contexts? Rather than advocating for one more dubious reproductive technology such as RU 486, feminists should be fighting for demedicalizing conventional abortion methods, and doctors and family planning groups should be joining suit." RU-486—NO." Ms., *March/April 1993. P. 37.*

The consequences of these differences in terms of the applicable legal rules, as opposed to women's own decisions, are not entirely clear, however. Opponents' concerns about the safety of RU-486 would seem to argue against permitting it to be marketed, while proponents want access and testing.

With the growing awareness of teenage sexuality and increasing concern about the spread of AIDS, problems of access to means of reproductive control have taken another new twist. As government bodies seek to make condoms and other contraceptives available to teenagers, various parent groups are challenging their efforts. One common argument the parents make focuses on their constitutional rights to raise their children as they see fit. A recent decision concerning a New York City school board condom distribution program indicates how these arguments are likely to fare in court.

> The voluntary aspect of the Board of Education's program does not infringe upon the parents' rights to raise their children or teach them the doctrines of their religious beliefs. There is no coercive effect to the program, no forfeitures exist for choosing not to participate, and the existence of the program in the schools is a mere exposure to other ideas.
> Alfonso v. Fernandez, *584 N.Y.S.2d 406, 412 (Sup. 1992).*

As we have seen, the way to promote reproductive choice seems relatively simple in some situations. For example, conditions on probation and conditions on the receipt of public benefits need only to removed. However, determining the affirmative role that is appropriate for government to play seems more difficult. For example, if the government is obligated to make RU-486 freely available, can it, at the same time, ensure adequate testing and restrict the distribution of other drugs and devices? Similarly, if school officials have a right to make condoms available without parental interference, do they also have the right to make Norplant available? Guaranteeing freedom of choice will require finding the right way to protect users and to promote access at the same time.

Assisting Parenthood

Insemination by Donor. Artificial insemination was initially developed using the husband's sperm in an effort to address the fertility problems of married couples; eventually, the sperm of donors also came to be used. In the 1980s, as many as twenty thousand women per year were reported artificially inseminated in the United States. Of these, fifteen hundred were unmarried. To ensure that the husband (in the case of a married couple) was officially regarded as the father in cases of donor insemination, laws originally designed for adultery situations were held to apply to artificial insemination. Thus, laws declaring the husband to be the father of any children born to the wife during marriage were interpreted to include children resulting from artificial insemination.

Recently, unmarried women—both lesbian and heterosexual—have sought insemination by donor as a way of procreating without being married or otherwise having the biological father involved. They have, at times, been denied access to service facilities or providers. The case of *Smedes v. Wayne State University,* No. 80–72583, United States District Court for the Eastern District of Michigan, is an example of one successful challenge to such restraints. As a result of the American Civil Liberties Union suit, the only public facility providing artificial insemination in Michigan agreed to lift its ban on single women having access to its sperm bank.

Access is often restricted indirectly. Even though there appears to be no medical need for such requirements, state laws require doctors to perform the inseminations. By outlawing this action by others, such laws allow physicians to determine who may become parents via insemination. While the selection of "appropriate" parents has varied with the doctor, some physicians have insisted on a certain IQ level, "good moral character," or financial ability to provide for the child. Particularly prevalent have been refusals to assist single women.

Insemination by donor continues to raise questions about whether the sperm-donor/biological father or the husband/social father should be officially recognized as the parent. However, as the following case illustrates, today's questions may take a sightly different form.

Jhordan C. v. Mary K.

California Appellate Division, 1986.
179 Cal.App.3d. 386, 224 Cal.Rptr. 530.

KING, Associate Justice.

. . . In late 1978 Mary decided to bear a child by artificial insemination and to raise the child jointly with Victoria, a close friend who lived in a nearby town. Mary sought a semen donor by talking to friends and acquaintances. This led to three or four potential donors with whom Mary spoke directly. She and Victoria ultimately chose Jhordan after he had one personal interview with Mary and one dinner at Mary's home.

The parties' testimony was in conflict as to what agreement they had concerning the role, if any, Jhordan would play in the child's life. According to Mary, she told Jhordan she did not want a donor who desired ongoing involvement with the child, but she did agree to let him see the child to satisfy his curiosity as to how the child would look. Jhordan, in contrast, asserts they agreed he and Mary would have an ongoing friendship, he would have ongoing contact with the child, and he would care for the child as much as two or three times per week.

None of the parties sought legal advice until long after the child's birth. They were completely unaware of the existence of Civil Code section 7005. They did not attempt to draft a written agreement concerning Jhordan's status.

Jhordan provided semen to Mary on a number of occasions during a six month period commencing in late January 1979. On each occasion he came to her home, spoke briefly with her, produced the semen, and then left. The record is unclear, but Mary, who is a nurse, apparently performed the insemination by herself or with Victoria.

. . . Mary gave birth to Devin on March 30, 1980. Victoria assisted in the delivery. Jhordan was listed as the father on Devin's birth certificate. Mary's roommate telephoned Jhordan that day to inform him of the birth. Jhordan visited Mary and Devin the next day and took photographs of the baby.

Five days later Jhordan telephoned Mary and said he wanted to visit Devin again. Mary initially resisted, but then allowed Jhordan to visit, although she told him she was angry. During the visit Jhordan claimed a right to see Devin, and Mary agreed to monthly visits.

Through August 1980 Jhordan visited Devin approximately five times. Mary then terminated the monthly visits. Jhordan said he would consult an attorney if Mary did not let him see Devin. Mary asked Jhordan to sign a contract indicating he would not seek to be Devin's father, but Jhordan refused.

In December 1980 Jhordan filed an action against Mary to establish paternity and visitation rights. In June 1982, by stipulated judgment in a separate action by the County of Sonoma, he was ordered to reimburse the county for public assistance paid for Devin's support. . . . In November 1982 the court granted Jhordan weekly visitation with Devin at Victoria's home. . . .

After trial the court rendered judgment declaring Jhordan to be Devin's legal father. However,

the court awarded sole legal and physical custody to Mary, and denied Jhordan any input into decisions regarding Devin's schooling, medical and dental care, and day-to-day maintenance. Jhordan received substantial visitation rights as recommended by a court-appointed psychologist. . . .

. . . Civil Code section 7005 . . . provides in pertinent part: "(a) If, under the supervision of a licensed physician and with the consent of her husband, a wife is inseminated artificially with semen donated by a man not her husband, the husband is treated in law as if he were the natural father of a child thereby conceived. . . . (b) The donor of semen provided to a licensed physician for use in artificial insemination of a woman other than the donor's wife is treated in law as if he were not the natural father of a child thereby conceived." . . .

[T]he California Legislature has afforded unmarried as well as married women a statutory vehicle for obtaining semen for artificial insemination without fear that the donor may claim paternity, and has likewise provided men with a statutory vehicle for donating semen to married and unmarried women alike without fear of liability for child support. Subdivision (b) states only one limitation on its application: the semen must be "provided to a licensed physician." Otherwise, whether impregnation occurs through artificial insemination or sexual intercourse, there can be a determination of paternity with the rights, duties and obligations such a determination entails. . . .

. . . [T]here are at least two sound justifications upon which the statutory requirement of physician involvement might have been based. One relates to health: a physician can obtain a complete medical history of the donor (which may be of crucial importance to the child during his or her lifetime) and screen the donor for any hereditary or communicable diseases. . . .

Another justification for physician involvement is that the presence of a professional third party such as a physician can serve to create a formal, documented structure for the donor-recipient relationship, without which, as this case illustrates, misunderstandings between the parties regarding the nature of their relationship and the donor's relationship to the child would be more likely to occur.

It is true that nothing inherent in artificial insemination requires the involvement of a physician. Artificial insemination is, as demonstrated here, a simple procedure easily performed by a woman in her own home. Also, despite the reasons outlined above in favor of physician involvement, there are countervailing considerations against requiring it. A requirement of physician involvement, as Mary argues, might offend a woman's sense of privacy and reproductive autonomy, might result in burdensome costs to some women, and might interfere with a woman's desire to conduct the procedure in a comfortable environment such as her own home or to choose the donor herself. . . .

However, because of the way section 7005 is phrased, a woman (married or unmarried) can perform home artificial insemination or choose her donor and still obtain the benefits of the statute. . . . [A] woman who prefers home artificial insemination or who wishes to choose her donor can still obtain statutory protection from a donor's paternity claim through the relatively simple expedient of obtaining the semen, whether for home insemination or from a chosen donor (or both), through a licensed physician. . . .

Mary and Victoria next contend that even if section 7005, subdivision (b), by its terms does not apply where semen for artificial insemination has not been provided to a licensed physician, application of the statute to the present case is required by constitutional principles of equal protection and privacy. . . .

[T]he statutory provision at issue here—Civil Code section 7005, subdivision (b)—treats married and unmarried women equally. Both are denied application of the statute where semen has not been provided to a licensed physician. The true question presented is whether a completely different set of paternity statutes—affording protection to husband and wife from any claim of paternity by an outsider denies equal protection by failing to provide similar protection to an unmarried woman. The simple answer is that, within the context of this question, a married woman and an unmarried woman are not similarly situated for purposes of equal protection analysis. In the case of a married woman, the marital relationship invokes a long-recognized social policy of preserving the integrity of the marriage. No such concerns arise where there is no marriage at all. Equal protection is not violated by providing that certain benefits or legal rights arise only out of the marital relationship. . . .

Mary and Victoria argue that the physician requirement . . . infringes a fundamental right to procreative choice, also encompassed by the constitutional right of privacy.

But the statute imposes no restriction on the right to bear a child. Unlike statutes in other jurisdictions proscribing artificial insemination other than by a physician, subdivision (b) of section 7005 does not forbid self-inseminations nor does the statute preclude personal selection of a donor or in any other way prevent women from artificially conceiving children under circumstances of their own choice. The statute simply addresses the perplexing question of the legal status of the semen donor, and provides a method of avoiding the legal consequences that might otherwise be dictated by traditional notions of paternity. . . .

We wish to stress that our opinion in this case is not intended to express any judicial preference toward traditional notions of family structure or toward providing a father where a single woman has chosen to bear a child. Public policy in these areas is best determined by the legislative branch of government, not the judicial. Our Legislature has already spoken and has afforded to unmarried women a statutory right to bear children by artificial insemination (as well as a right of men to donate semen) without fear of a paternity claim, through provision of the semen to a licensed physician. We simply hold that because Mary omitted to invoke Civil Code section 7005, subdivision (b), by obtaining Jhordan's semen through a licensed physician, and because the parties by all other conduct preserved Jhordan's status as a member of Devin's family, the trial court properly declared Jhordan to be Devin's legal father.

The judgment is affirmed.

STUDY QUESTIONS

1. On what basis did the court determine that Jhordan C. should have rights as the child's father? Was that outcome inevitable?

2. Do you agree with the court's decision? Does such a decision have the effect of encouraging male responsibility for child rearing? Of discouraging women-determined family structures?

3. In light of *Jhordan C.,* how would you counsel an unmarried woman who wished to bear a child through donor insemination and preclude the biological father's obtaining parental rights?

Some women seeking to establish nontraditional family forms excluding male parents have used anonymous donors in order to prevent biological fathers from trying to "join the family." Another route such women may take is to make a very clear contractual agreement regarding the donor's rights and responsibilities before the insemination begins. If such arrangements involve payment, their enforceability is not at all clear. On the one hand, such contracts seem closely akin to contracts by biological parents to waive their parental rights. On the other hand, the donation process is quick and easy, and our society has had a long history of not considering sperm donors to be parents. Nor is it at all clear what the consequences of honoring such contracts would be for the relatively new practice of egg donation. On the one hand, given the greater intrusiveness of the donation process, the egg donor's involvement in the reproductive process is generally more extensive. On the other hand, unlike a sperm donor, the egg donor has only contributed part of what her sex contributes to the birth of a child. In sum, the egg donor is both more and less involved.

In Vitro *Fertilization.* *In vitro* fertilization (IVF) and related techniques involve the insertion of eggs obtained from a woman (or a donor) into the woman's body once they have been fertilized. First used successfully in the 1960s, such techniques are both expensive and invasive. Although success rates have improved considerably in recent years, they are still low. For example, when 19,095 women were treated by 180 reporting clinics using IVF and related reproductive technologies in 1990, only 3,951 live births resulted. Nevertheless, such services seem to be sought out increasingly to address female fertility problems often attributed to postponement of childbearing.

Here, too, questions may arise concerning the rights of the biological mother and the biological father.

Davis v. Davis

Supreme Court of Tennessee, 1992.
842 S.W.2d 588, *cert. den. sub. nom.*
State v. Davis, ___U.S. ___ ,
113 S.Ct. 1042 (1993).

DAUGHTREY, Justice.

This appeal presents a question of first impression, involving the disposition of the cryo-genically-preserved product of in vitro fertilization (IVF), commonly referred to in the popular press and the legal journals as "frozen embryos." The case began as a divorce action, filed by the appellee, Junior Lewis Davis, against his then wife, appellant Mary Sue Davis. The parties were able to agree upon all terms of dissolution, except one: who was to have "custody" of the seven "frozen embryos" stored in a Knoxville fertility clinic that had attempted to assist the Davises in achieving a much-wanted pregnancy during a happier period in their relationship.

I. INTRODUCTION

Mary Sue Davis originally asked for control of the "frozen embryos" with the intent to have the transferred to her own uterus, in a post-divorce effort to become pregnant. Junior Davis objected, saying that he preferred to leave the embryos in their frozen state until he decided whether or not he wanted to become a parent outside the bounds of marriage.

Based on its determination that the embryos were "human beings" from the moment of fertilization, the trial court awarded "custody" to Mary Sue Davis and directed that she "be permitted the opportunity to bring these children to term through implantation." The Court of Appeals reversed, finding that Junior Davis has a "constitutionally protected right not to beget a child where no pregnancy has taken place" and holding that "there is no compelling state interest to justify . . . ordering implantation against the will of either party." The Court of Appeals further held that "the parties share an interest in the seven fertilized ova" and remanded the case to the trial court for entry of an order vesting them with "joint control . . . and equal voice over their disposition."

Mary Sue Davis then sought review in this Court, contesting the validity of the constitutional basis for the Court of Appeals decision. . . .

[The parties] both have remarried and Mary Sue Davis (now Mary Sue Stowe) has moved out of state. She no longer wishes to utilize the "frozen embryos" herself, but wants authority to donate them to a childless couple. Junior Davis is adamantly opposed to such donation and would prefer to see the "frozen embryos" discarded. The result is, once again, an impasse, but the parties' current legal position does have an effect on the probable outcome of the case, as discussed below.

At the outset, it is important to note the absence of two critical factors that might otherwise influence or control the result of this litigation. When the Davises signed up for the IVF program at the Knoxville clinic, they did not execute a written agreement specifying what disposition should be made of any unused embryos that might result from the cryopreservation process. Moreover, there was at that time no Tennessee statute governing such disposition, nor has one been enacted in the meantime. . . .

II. THE FACTS

Mary Sue Davis and Junior Lewis Davis met while they were both in the Army and stationed in Germany in the spring of 1979. After a period of courtship, they came home to the United States and were married on April 26, 1980. When their leave was up, they then returned to their posts in Germany as a married couple.

Within six months of returning to Germany, Mary Sue became pregnant but unfortunately suffered an extremely painful tubal pregnancy, as a result of which she had surgery to remove her right fallopian tube. This tubal pregnancy was followed by four others during the course of the marriage. After her fifth tubal pregnancy, Mary Sue chose to have her left fallopian tube ligated, thus leaving her without functional fallopian tubes by which to conceive naturally. The Davises attempted to adopt a child but, at the last minute, the child's birth-mother changed her mind about putting the child up for adoption. Other paths to adoption turned out to be prohibitively expensive. In vitro fertilization became essentially the only option for the Davises to pursue in their attempt to become parents.

As explained at trial, IVF involves the aspiration of ova from the follicles of a woman's ovaries, fertilization of these ova in a petri dish using the sperm provided by a man, and the transfer of the product of this procedure into the uterus of the woman from whom the ova were taken. Implantation may then occur, resulting in a pregnancy and, it is hoped, the birth of a child. . . .

IV. THE "PERSON" VS. "PROPERTY" DICHOTOMY

One of the fundamental issues the inquiry poses is whether the preembryos in this case should be considered "persons" or "property" in the contemplation of the law. The Court of Appeals held, correctly, that they cannot be considered "persons" under Tennessee law. The policy of the state on the subject matter before us may be gleaned from the state's treatment of fetuses in the womb. . . . The state's Wrongful Death Statute does not allow a wrongful death for a viable fetus that is not first born alive. Without live birth, the Supreme Court has said, a fetus is not a "person" within the meaning of the statute. Other enactments by the legislature demonstrate even more explicitly that viable fetuses in the womb are not entitled to the same protection as "persons." Tenn.Code Ann. § 39–15–201 incorporates the trimester approach to abortion outlined in *Roe v. Wade*. . . . This statutory scheme indicates that as embryos develop, they are accorded more respect than mere human cells because of their burgeoning potential for life. But, even after viability, they are not given legal status equivalent to that of a person already born. . . .

V. THE ENFORCEABILITY OF CONTRACT

. . . We believe, as a starting point, that an agreement regarding disposition of any untransferred preembryos in the event of contingencies (such as the death of one or more of the parties, divorce, financial reversals, or abandonment of the program) should be presumed valid and should be enforced as between the progenitors. This conclusion is in keeping with the proposition that the progenitors, having provided the gametic material giving rise to the preembryos, retain decision-making authority as to their disposition.

At the same time, we recognize that life is not static, and that human emotions run particularly high when a married couple is attempting to overcome infertility problems. It follows that the parties' initial "informed consent" to IVF procedures will often not be truly informed because of the near impossibility of anticipating, emotionally and psychologically, all the turns that events may take as the IVF process unfolds. Providing that the initial agreements may later be modified by agreement will, we think, protect the parties against some of the risks they face in this regard. But, in the absence of such agreed modification, we conclude that their prior agreements should be considered binding. . . .

VI. THE RIGHT OF PROCREATIONAL AUTONOMY

. . . For the purposes of this litigation it is sufficient to note that, whatever its ultimate constitutional boundaries, the right of procre-ational autonomy is composed of two rights of equal significance—the right to procreate and the right to avoid procreation. . . .

The equivalence of and inherent tension between these two interests are nowhere more evident than in the context of in vitro fertilization. None of the concerns about a woman's bodily integrity that have previously precluded men from controlling abortion decisions is applicable here. We are not unmindful of the fact that the trauma (including both emotional stress and physical discomfort) to which women are subjected in the IVF process is more severe than is the impact of the procedure on men. In this sense, it is fair to say that women contribute more to the IVF process than men. Their experience, however, must be viewed in light of the joys of parenthood that is desired or the relative anguish of a lifetime of unwanted parenthood. As they stand on the brink of potential parenthood, Mary Sue Davis and Junior Lewis Davis must be seen as entirely equivalent gamete-providers. . . .

. . . When weighed against the interests of the individuals and the burdens inherent in parenthood, the state's interest in the potential life of these preembryos is not sufficient to justify any infringement upon the freedom of these individuals to make their own decisions as to whether to allow a process to continue that may result in such a dramatic change in their lives as becoming parents.

. . . We conclude, moreover, that an interest in avoiding genetic parenthood can be significant enough to trigger the protections afforded to all other aspects of parenthood. The technological fact that someone unknown to these parties could gestate these preembryos does not alter the fact that these parties, the gamete-providers, would become parents in that event, at least in the genetic sense. The profound impact this would have on them supports their right to sole decisional authority as to whether the process of attempting to gestate these preembryos should continue. This brings us directly to the question of how to resolve the dispute that arises when one party wishes to continue the IVF process and the other does not. . . .

VII. BALANCING THE PARTIES' INTERESTS

Resolving disputes over conflicting interests of constitutional import is a task familiar to the courts. One way of resolving these disputes is to consider the positions of the parties, the significance of their interests, and the relative burdens that will be imposed by differing resolutions. In this case, the issue centers on the two aspects of procreational autonomy—the right to procreate and the right to avoid procreation. . . .

Junior Davis testified that he was the fifth youngest of six children. When he was five years old, his parents divorced, his mother had a nervous break-down, and he and three of his brothers went to live at a home for boys run by the Lutheran Church. . . .

In light of his boyhood experiences, Junior Davis is vehemently opposed to fathering a child that would not live with both parents. Regardless of whether he or Mary Sue had custody, he feels that the child's bond with the non-custodial parent would not be satisfactory. He testified very clearly that his concern was for the psychological obstacles a child in such a situation would face, as well as the burdens it would impose on him. Likewise, he is opposed to donation because the recipient couple might divorce, leaving the child (which he definitely would consider his own) in a single-parent setting.

Balanced against Junior Davis's interest in avoiding parenthood is Mary Sue Davis's interest in donating the preembryos to another couple for implantation. Refusal to permit donation of the preembryos would impose on her the burden of knowing that the lengthy IVF procedures she underwent were futile, and that the preembryos to which she contributed genetic material would never become children. While this is not an insubstantial emotional burden, we can only conclude that Mary Sue Davis's interest in donation is not as significant as the interest Junior Davis has in avoiding parenthood. If she were allowed to donate these preembryos, he would face a lifetime of either wondering about his parental status or knowing about his parental status but having no control over it. He testified quite clearly that if these preembryos were brought to term he would fight for custody of his child or children. Donation, if a child came of it, would rob him twice—his procreational autonomy would be defeated and his relationship with his offspring would be prohibited.

The case would be closer if Mary Sue Davis were seeking to use the preembryos herself, but only if she could not achieve parenthood by any other reasonable means. We recognize the trauma that Mary Sue has already experienced and the additional discomfort to which she would be subjected if she opts to attempt IVF again. Still, she would have a reasonable opportunity, through IVF, to try once again to achieve parenthood in all its aspects—genetic, gestational, bearing, and rearing.

Further, we note that if Mary Sue Davis were unable to undergo another round of IVF, or opted not to try, she could still achieve the child-rearing aspects of parenthood through adoption. The fact that she and Junior Davis pursued adoption indicates that, at least at one time, she was willing to forego genetic parenthood and would have been satisfied by the child-rearing aspects of parenthood alone.

VIII. CONCLUSION

In summary, we hold that disputes involving the disposition of preembryos produced by in vitro fertilization should be resolved, first, by looking to the preferences of the progenitors. If their wishes cannot be ascertained, or if there is dispute, then their prior agreement concerning disposition should be carried out. If no prior agreement exists, then the relative interests of the parties in using or not using the preembryos must be weighed. Ordinarily, the party wishing to avoid procreation should prevail, assuming that the other party has a reasonable possibility of achieving parenthood by means other than use of the preembryos in question. If no other reasonable alternatives exist, then the argument in favor of using the preembryos to achieve pregnancy should be considered. However, if the party seeking control of the preembryos intends merely to donate them to another couple, the objecting party obviously has the greater interest and should prevail. . . .

For the reasons set out above, the judgment of the Court of Appeals is affirmed. . . .

STUDY QUESTIONS

1. What did the court hold in this case? Would the result have been different if Mary Sue had sought to implant the embryo in her own body? What guidance did it give for future cases?

2. Do you agree that the desires of the woman and the man should be given equal weight? Why? Why not?

Contract Parenthood

Not all assisted parenthood involves biological ties for both parents. Some couples, who are unwilling or unable to employ these techniques, have turned to contract parenthood, whereby through artificial insemination with the husband's sperm, another woman bears a child whom she then relinquishes to the couple. The well-publicized case, *In re Matter of Baby M,* highlighted the problems that can occur when such a "surrogate" changes her mind.

In the Matter of Baby M

New Jersey Supreme Court, 1988.
573 A.2d. 1127.

WILENTZ, C.J.

In this matter the Court is asked to determine the validity of a contract that purports to provide a new way of bringing children into a family. For a fee of $10,000, a woman agrees to be artificially inseminated with the semen of another woman's husband; she is to conceive a child, carry it to term, and after its birth surrender it to the natural father and his wife. The intent of the contract is that the child's natural mother will thereafter be forever separated from her child. The wife is to adopt the child, and she and the natural father are to be regarded as its parents for all purposes. The contract providing for this is called a "surrogacy contract," the natural mother inappropriately called the "surrogate mother." . . .

I. FACTS

In February 1985, William Stern and Mary Beth Whitehead entered into a surrogacy contract. It recited that Stern's wife, Elizabeth, was infertile, that they wanted a child, and that Mrs. Whitehead was willing to provide that child as the mother with Mr. Stern as the father.

The contract provided that through artificial insemination using Mr. Stern's sperm, Mrs. Whitehead would become pregnant, carry the child to term, bear it, deliver it to the Sterns, and thereafter do whatever was necessary to terminate her maternal rights so that Mrs. Stern could thereafter adopt the child. Mrs. Whitehead's husband, Richard, was also a party to the contract; Mrs. Stern was not. Mr. Whitehead promised to do all acts necessary to rebut the presumption of paternity under the Parentage Act. N.J.S.A. 9:17-43a(1), -44a. Although Mrs. Stern was not a party to the surrogacy agreement, the contract gave her sole custody of the child in the event of Mr. Stern's death. Mrs. Stern's status as a nonparty to the surrogate parenting agreement presumably was to avoid the application of the baby-selling statute to this arrangement. N.J.S.A. 9:3-54.

Mr. Stern, on his part, agreed to attempt the artificial insemination and to pay Mrs. Whitehead $10,000 after the child's birth, on its delivery to him. In a separate contract, Mr. Stern agreed to pay $7,500 to the Infertility Center of New York ("ICNY"). The Center's advertising campaigns solicit surrogate mothers and encourage infertile couples to consider surrogacy. ICNY arranged for the surrogacy contract by bringing the parties together, explaining the process to them, furnishing the contractual form, and providing legal counsel.

The history of the parties' involvement in this arrangement suggests their good faith. William and Elizabeth Stern were married in July 1974, having met at the University of Michigan, where both were Ph.D. candidates. Due to financial considerations and Mrs. Stern's pursuit of a medical degree and residency, they decided to defer starting a family until 1981. Before then, however, Mrs. Stern learned that she might have multiple sclerosis and that the disease in some cases renders pregnancy a serious health risk. Her anxiety appears to have exceeded the actual risk, which current medical authorities assess as minimal. Nonetheless that anxiety was evidently quite real, Mrs. Stern fearing that pregnancy might precipitate blindness, paraplegia, or other forms of debilitation. Based on the perceived risk, the Sterns decided to forego having their own children. The decision had a special significance for Mr. Stern. Most of his family had been destroyed in the Holocaust. As the family's only survivor, he very much wanted to continue his bloodline.

Initially the Sterns considered adoption, but were discouraged by the substantial delay apparently involved and by the potential problem they saw arising from their age and their differing religious backgrounds. They were most eager for some other means to start a family.

The paths of Mrs. Whitehead and the Sterns to surrogacy were similar. Both responded to advertising by ICNY. The Sterns' response, following their inquiries into adoption, was the result of their long-standing decision to have a child. Mrs. Whitehead's response apparently resulted from her sympathy with family members and others who could have no children (she stated that she wanted to give another couple the "gift of life"); she also wanted the $10,000 to help her family. . . .

The two couples met to discuss the surrogacy arrangement and decided to go forward. On February 6, 1985, Mr. Stern and Mr. and Mrs. Whitehead executed the surrogate parenting agreement. After several artificial inseminations over a period of months, Mrs. Whitehead became pregnant. The pregnancy was uneventful and on March 27, 1986, Baby M was born. . . .

Mrs. Whitehead realized, almost from the moment of birth, that she could not part with this child. She had felt a bond with it even during pregnancy. . . .

Nonetheless, Mrs. Whitehead was, for the moment, true to her word. Despite powerful inclinations to the contrary, she turned her child over to the Sterns on March 30 at the Whiteheads' home. . . . The next day she went to the Sterns' home and told them how much she was suffering. . . .

The Sterns, concerned that Mrs. Whitehead might indeed commit suicide, not wanting under any circumstances to risk that, and in any event believing that Mrs. Whitehead would keep her word [and return the child], turned the child over to her. It was not until four months later, after a series of attempts to regain possession of the child, that Melissa was returned to the Sterns, having been forcibly removed from the home where she was then living with Mr. and Mrs. Whitehead, the home in Florida owned by Mary Beth Whitehead's parents. . . .

The Sterns' complaint, in addition to seeking possession and ultimately custody of the child, [seeks] enforcement of the surrogacy contract. Pursuant to the contract, it ask[s] that the child be permanently placed in their custody, that Mrs. Whitehead's parental rights be terminated, and that Mrs. Stern be allowed to adopt the child, *i.e.,* that, for all purposes, Melissa become the Sterns' child. . . .

II. INVALIDITY AND UNENFORCEABILITY OF SURROGACY CONTRACT

We have concluded that this surrogacy contract is invalid. Our conclusion has two bases: direct conflict with existing statutes and conflict with the public policies of this State, as expressed in its statutory and decisional law. . . .

A. Conflict with Statutory Provisions The surrogacy contract conflicts with: (1) laws prohibiting the use of money in connection with adoptions; (2) laws requiring proof of parental unfitness or abandonment before termination of parental rights is ordered or an adoption is granted; and (3) laws that make surrender of custody and consent to adoption revocable in private placement adoptions.

(1) Our law prohibits paying or accepting money in connection with any placement of a

child for adoption. *N.J.S.A.* 9:3-54a. Violation is a high misdemeanor. *N.J.S.A.* 9:3-54c. Excepted are fees of an approved agency (which must be a non-profit entity, *N.J.S.A.* 9:3-38a) and certain expenses in connection with childbirth. *N.J.S.A.* 9:3-54b. . . .

The payment of the $10,000 occurs only on surrender of custody of the child and "completion of the duties and obligations" of Mrs. Whitehead, including termination of her parental rights to facilitate adoption by Mrs. Stern. As for the contention that the Sterns are paying only for services and not for an adoption, we need note only that they would pay nothing in the event the child died before the fourth month of pregnancy, and only $1,000 if the child were stillborn, even though the "services" had been fully rendered. Additionally, one of Mrs. Whitehead's estimated costs, to be assumed by Mr. Stern, was an "Adoption Fee," presumably for Mrs. Whitehead's incidental costs in connection with the adoption. . . .

The evils inherent in baby bartering are loathsome for a myriad of reasons. The child is sold without regard for whether the purchasers will be suitable parents. . . . The natural mother does not receive the benefit of counseling and guidance to assist her in making a decision that may affect her for a lifetime. In fact, the monetary incentive to sell her child may, depending on her financial circumstances, make her decision less voluntary. Furthermore, the adoptive parents may not be fully informed of the natural parents' medical history. . . . The negative consequences of baby buying are potentially present in the surrogacy context, especially the potential for placing and adopting a child without regard to the interest of the child or the natural mother.

(2) The termination of Mrs. Whitehead's parental rights . . . fails to comply with the stringent requirements of New Jersey law. Our law, recognizing the finality of any termination of parental rights, provides for such termination only where there has been a voluntary surrender of a child to an approved agency or to the Division of Youth and Family Services ("DYFS"), accompanied by a formal document acknowledging termination of parental rights . . . or where there has been a showing of parental abandonment or unfitness.

A termination may ordinarily take one of three forms: an action by an approved agency, an action by DYFS, or an action in connection with a private placement adoption. The three are governed by separate statutes, but the standards for termination are substantially the same, except that whereas a written surrender is effective when made to an approved agency or to DYFS, there is no provision for it in the private placement context. . . .

Our statutes, and the cases interpreting them, leave no doubt that where there has been no written surrender to an approved agency or to DYFS, termination of parental rights will not be granted in this state absent a very strong showing of abandonment or neglect. That showing is required in every context in which termination of parental rights is sought, be it an action by an approved agency, an action by DYFS, or a private placement adoption proceeding, even where the petitioning adoptive parent is, as here, a stepparent. . . .

It is clear that a "best interests" determination is never sufficient to terminate parental rights; the statutory criteria must be proved.

In this case a termination of parental rights was obtained not by proving the statutory prerequisites but by claiming the benefit of contractual provisions. From all that has been stated above, it is clear that a contractual agreement to abandon one's parental rights, or not to contest a termination action, will not be enforced in our courts. The Legislature would not have so carefully, so consistently, and so substantially restricted termination of parental rights if it had intended to allow termination to be achieved by one short sentence in a contract.

Since the termination was invalid, it follows, as noted above, that adoption of Melissa by Mrs. Stern could not properly be granted. . . .

(3) Mrs. Whitehead, shortly after the child's birth, had attempted to revoke her consent and surrender by refusing, after the Sterns had allowed her to have the child "just for one week," to return Baby M to them. The trial court's award of specific performance therefore reflects its view that the consent to surrender the child was irrevocable. We accept the trial court's construction of the contract; indeed it appears quite clear that this was the parties' intent. Such

a provision, however, making irrevocable the natural mother's consent to surrender custody of her child in a private placement adoption, clearly conflicts with New Jersey law. . . .

There is only one irrevocable consent, and that is the one explicitly provided for by statute: a consent to surrender of custody and a placement with an approved agency or with DYFS. The provision in the surrogacy contract, agreed to before conception, requiring the natural mother to surrender custody of the child without any right of revocation is one more indication of the essential nature of this transaction: the creation of a contractual system of termination and adoption designed to circumvent our statutes.

B. Public Policy Considerations   The surrogacy contract's invalidity, resulting from its direct conflict with the above statutory provisions, is further underlined when its goals and means are measured against New Jersey's public policy. The contract's basic premise, that the natural parents can decide in advance of birth which one is to have custody of the child, bears no relationship to the settled law that the child's best interests shall determine custody. . . .

The surrogacy contract guarantees permanent separation of the child from one of its natural parents. Our policy, however, has long been that to the extent possible, children should remain with and be brought up by both of their natural parents. . . .

The surrogacy contract violates the policy of this State that the rights of natural parents are equal concerning their child, the father's right no greater than the mother's. . . .

The policies expressed in our comprehensive laws governing consent to the surrender of a child . . . stand in stark contrast to the surrogacy contract and what it implies. Here there is no counseling, independent or otherwise, of the natural mother, no evaluation, no warning.

. . . Under the contract, the natural mother is irrevocably committed before she knows the strength of her bond with her child. She never makes a totally voluntary, informed decision, for quite clearly any decision prior to the baby's birth is, in the most important sense, uninformed, and any decision after that, compelled by a pre-existing contractual commitment, the

threat of a lawsuit, and the inducement of a $10,000 payment, is less than totally voluntary. Her interests are of little concern to those who controlled this transaction.

Although the interest of the natural father and adoptive mother is certainly the predominant interest, realistically the *only* interest served, even they are left with less than what public policy requires. They know little about the natural mother, her genetic makeup, and her psychological and medical history. Moreover, not even a superficial attempt is made to determine their awareness of their responsibilities as parents.

Worst of all, however, is the contract's total disregard of the best interests of the child. There is not the slightest suggestion that any inquiry will be made at any time to determine the fitness of the Sterns as custodial parents, of Mrs. Stern as an adoptive parent, their superiority to Mrs. Whitehead, or the effect on the child of not living with her natural mother.

This is the sale of a child, or, at the very least, the sale of a mother's right to her child, the only mitigating factor being that one of the purchasers is the father. Almost every evil that prompted the prohibition of the payment of money in connection with adoptions exists here. . . .

The point is made that Mrs. Whitehead *agreed* to the surrogacy arrangement, supposedly fully understanding the consequences. Putting aside the issue of how compelling her need for money may have been, and how significant her understanding of the consequences, we suggest that her consent is irrelevant. There are, in a civilized society, some things that money cannot buy. In America, we decided long ago that merely because conduct purchased by money was "voluntary" did not mean that it was good or beyond regulation and prohibition. . . .

Employers can no longer buy labor at the lowest price they can bargain for, even though that labor is "voluntary," or buy women's labor for less money than paid to men for the same job, or purchase the agreement of children to perform oppressive labor, or purchase the agreement of workers to subject themselves to unsafe or unhealthful working conditions. There are, in short, values that society deems more important than granting to wealth whatever it can buy, be it labor, love, or life. Whether this principle recommends prohibition of surrogacy, which presumably sometimes results in great satisfaction to all of the parties, is not for us to say. We note here only that, under existing law, the fact that Mrs. Whitehead "agreed" to the arrangement is not dispositive.

The long-term effects of surrogacy contracts are not known, but feared—the impact on the child who learns her life was bought, that she is the offspring of someone who gave birth to her only to obtain money; the impact on the natural mother as the full weight of her isolation is felt along with the full reality of the sale of her body and her child; the impact on the natural father and adoptive mother once they realize the consequences of their conduct. . . .

Beyond that is the potential degradation of some women that may result from this arrangement. In many cases, of course, surrogacy may bring satisfaction, not only to the infertile couple, but to the surrogate mother herself. The fact, however, that many women may not perceive surrogacy negatively but rather see it as an opportunity does not diminish its potential for devastation to other women.

In sum, the harmful consequences of this surrogacy arrangement appear to us all too palpable. In New Jersey the surrogate mother's agreement to sell her child is void. Its irrevocability infects the entire contract, as does the money that purports to buy it.

III. TERMINATION

. . . Nothing in this record justifies a finding that would allow a court to terminate Mary Beth Whitehead's parental rights under the statutory standard. . . .

IV. CONSTITUTIONAL ISSUES

. . . The right to procreate very simply is the right to have natural children, whether through sexual intercourse or artificial insemination. It is no more than that. Mr. Stern has not been deprived of that right. Through artificial insemination of Mrs. Whitehead, Baby M is his child. The custody, care, companionship, and nurturing that follow birth are not parts of the right to procreation; they are rights that may also be constitutionally protected,

but that involve many considerations other than the right of procreation. To assert that Mr. Stern's right of procreation gives him the right to the custody of Baby M would be to assert that Mrs. Whitehead's right of procreation does *not* give her the right to the custody of Baby M; it would be to assert that the constitutional right of procreation includes within it a constitutionally protected contractual right to destroy someone else's right of procreation. . . .

Mrs. Whitehead, on the other hand, asserts a claim that falls within the scope of a recognized fundamental interest protected by the Constitution. As a mother, she claims the right to the companionship of her child. This is a fundamental interest, constitutionally protected. Furthermore, it was taken away from her by the action of the court below. Whether that action under these circumstances would constitute a constitutional deprivation, however, we need not and do not decide. By virtue of our decision Mrs. Whitehead's constitutional complaint—that her parental rights have been unconstitutionally terminated—is moot. . . .

V. CUSTODY

Having decided that the surrogacy contract is illegal and unenforceable, we now must decide the custody question without regard to the provisions of the surrogacy contract that would give Mr. Stern sole and permanent custody. . . . The applicable rule given these circumstances is clear: the child's best interests determine custody. . . . The issue here is which life would be *better* for Baby M, one with primary custody in the Whiteheads or one with primary custody in the Sterns. . . .

There were eleven experts who testified concerning the child's best interests, either directly or in connection with matters related to that issue. Our reading of the record persuades us that the trial court's decision awarding custody to the Sterns (technically to Mr. Stern) should be affirmed. . . .

VI. VISITATION

The trial court's decision to terminate Mrs. Whitehead's parental rights precluded it from making any determination on visitation. 217 *N.J. Super.* at 399, 408. Our reversal of the trial court's order, however, requires delineation of Mrs. Whitehead's rights to visitation. It is apparent to us that this factually sensitive issue, which was never addressed below, should not be determined *de novo* by this Court. We therefore remand the visitation issue to the trial court for an abbreviated hearing and determination as set forth below. . . .

STUDY QUESTIONS

1. Why did the court reverse the trial court's order terminating parental rights? Do you agree that surrogacy contracts present the same dangers as payments for adoptions? Do you think the New Jersey Supreme Court would have refused to enforce the contract even in the absence of a state law prohibiting payments for adoptions?

2. Do you agree with the New Jersey Supreme Court that a woman agreeing to bear and relinquish a child under a surrogacy agreement "never makes a totally voluntary, informed decision, for quite clearly any decision prior to the baby's birth is, in the most important sense, uninformed, and any decision after that, compelled by a pre-existing contractual commitment, the threat of a lawsuit, and the inducement of a [substantial] payment, is less than totally voluntary?" How does such a decision differ from the decision to enter into an agreement to perform difficult or dangerous work that a person may never have performed before?

3. In an omitted portion of the opinion, the court stated that "when father and mother are separated and disagree, at birth, on custody, only in an extreme, truly rare, case should the child be taken from its mother . . . before the dispute is finally determined by the court on its merits." Do you agree? Does it make a difference whether the child is a product of a surrogacy arrangement or a more conventional relationship between the biological parents?

4. Mary Beth Whitehead was Baby M's mother in two senses: She both gave the egg and carried the pregnancy that produced Baby M. Is a woman who gestates a fetus produced by the egg and sperm of another couple also the mother of the resulting child in your view? What rights do you believe such a woman should have with respect to the child?

The *Baby M* case and the surrogacy issue generally caused a big controversy. State legislatures considered bills to permit, bills to regulate, and bills to ban parenthood contracts. A number of considerations shape the varying views. There is disagreement over whether a woman's "consent" to relinquish her child can ever be voluntary if it is given prior to birth. There is disagreement over whether commitments concerning children yet to be born are different than commitments concerning other future events. There is disagreement over the inevitability of exploitation resulting from class differences between the birth mother and the contracting couple. Finally, there is disagreement over whether it is possibile to protect the birth mother, the child, and society in general from harmful aspects of the practice—and if so, how to do it. Lori Andrews summarizes these developments in a 1992 update.

Surrogacy Wars: A Scoreboard

Lori Andrews.
California Lawyer, October 1992. P. 50.

Reprinted with permission.

Since the *Baby M* case, nearly every state legislature has considered laws to ban or regulate surrogate motherhood. In addition to California, 15 states have adopted laws regarding surrogacy, but none of the others has addressed the full range of issues raised by surrogacy. Few address the key issue of who should be given custody of the child when the surrogate changes her mind. Nor have the legislatures caught up with the new wave of surrogacy arrangements. Only eight of the 15 statutes (In Arizona, Florida, Indiana, Michigan, New Hampshire, New York, Virginia and Washington) explicitly apply to gestational surrogacy. Restrictions in other states apparently apply only to situations in which the surrogate is inseminated with the intended father's sperm.

Despite the controversies surrounding surrogacy, only four states have outright bans: Arizona bans surrogacy contracts, and Kentucky, Michigan and Utah ban payment to a surrogate. Five more states (Florida, New Hampshire, New York, Virginia and Washington) ostensibly ban payment to surrogates, but these laws contain wide exceptions that allow surrogates' expenses to be paid.

Eight states (Florida, Kentucky, Michigan, New Hampshire, New York, Utah, Virginia and Washington) focus on the role of the intermediary—prohibiting compensation for bringing together couples and surrogates or otherwise facilitating arrangements. The Florida and Virginia laws provide that lawyers may receive compensation for regular professional services such as advising on the contract.

The most common regulations, applicable in 11 states (Arizona, Florida, Indiana, Kentucky, Louisiana, Michigan, Nebraska, North Dakota, Utah, Virginia and Washington), are statutes voiding paid-surrogacy contracts. The Arizona, Indiana, Michigan, New York, North Dakota and Utah statutes void unpaid-surrogacy contracts as well.

Arkansas clearly provides that the intended parents are the legal parents. Florida, New Hampshire and Virginia make a similar assumption but give the surrogate a certain time period in which to change her mind. In Arizona, North Dakota and Utah, the surrogate and her husband are the legal parents of the child.

Virginia and New Hampshire provide an extensive regulatory structure for unpaid-surrogacy contracts, which includes medical and psychological screening and a requirement that the contract be submitted to a judge for approval in advance of the pregnancy. In addition, under both laws there must be a home study of the intended parents, as well as of the surrogate and her husband, to determine all parties' suitability for parenthood.

The recent development of gestational surrogacy makes us ask to what extent is the situation different where there are two biological mothers—the genetic and the gestational. In gestational surrogacy, an egg taken from one woman is fertilized and placed in another woman who ultimately gives birth. Should the decision of such a woman not to relinquish the child she bears to its genetic parents be considered differently than Mary Beth Whitehead's decision not to relinquish Baby M. to Bill Stern?

A recent California Supreme Court decision, *Johnson v. Calvert* 851, P.2d 776 (1993), concerned the unsuccessful claim of a gestational surrogate to parental rights. By contract, Anna Johnson was implanted with an embryo created by the egg and sperm of a wife and husband, Crispina Calvert and Mark Calvert. Johnson ultimately bore their genetic child.

The California Supreme Court made plain its view that a gestational surrogate does not have the rights of a biological mother. Thus the Court held that a woman who, by agreement, has a zygote implanted in her and carries the resulting fetus to term, provides a necessary and important service, but has no privacy, liberty or other constitutional rights requiring recognition or protection of her status as "birth mother." The Court also refused to invalidate gestational surrogacy agreements on the grounds that they inevitably run afoul of constitutional prohibitions on involuntary servitude or tend to degrade and dehumanize women. This holding is particularly noteworthy in view of the fact that the gestational mother in *Johnson v. Calvert* was an Afro-American, the genetic mother was Filipino and the genetic father was Caucasian.

Concerns raised by the *Johnson* case, as well as the phenomenon of gestational surrogacy generally, involve its potential for class and race exploitation of surrogates by better-off contracting couples. Competing with these concerns, however, is the interest in allowing women to make contracts and the perceived need to designate both male and female "blood" parents as the parent.

Are donor insemination fertilization, *in vitro* and other complex reproductive technologies, or surrogacy arrangements the best way to combat fertility problems? One commentator suggests it would be better to address the causes of infertility, such as pelvic inflammatory disease, medically prescribed drugs, devices, and operations and environmental and workplace hazards directly. She also argues for basic assistance to help infants survive their first year of life, as well as ways to integrate work and family so that childbearing will not be postponed beyond the point of fertlity. Finally, she contends that it is important to address the social pain of infertility by expanding the ways adults may relate to children to include informal arrangements as well as adoption, step-parenthood, and foster care. See Nadine Taub, "Surrogacy: A Preferred Treatment for Infertility?" 16 *Law, Medicine and Health Care* 89 (1988).

Are there race and class overtones to emphasizing individual, high-tech approaches rather than aiming resources collectively at societal inequalities? Consider the words of Barbara Omolade in "The 1987 James McCormick Mitchell Lecture—Looking Toward the Future: Feminism and Reproductive Technologies," 37 *Buffalo Law Review* 217, 220 (Winter 1988/89):

> The racial patriarch has placed biological reproduction at the top of the list and, of course, that biological reproduction is of healthy white children. At the same time, social reproduction of black and other children of color is placed at the very bottom of the list. This is a source of tremendous conflict. Resources are here, but children are starving over there, literally malnourished. . . . Poverty and unemployment among men and women of color are directly related to social and political policies which undermine the development of the black working class. However, the underdevelopment of the black working class is tied directly to the reproduction and development of the white middle class through reproductive technologies.

Birthing Arrangements

Our discussions of contraception, abortion, and sterilization have all centered on the question of procreative choice: the ability of individuals—particularly women—to determine if and when to have children. We now consider the conditions and arrangements under which their children will be born. As before, a key concern is the law's role in determining who may make such decisions, particularly in light of technological advances bearing on these conditions. Initially, we will consider decisions involving the choice of caregivers and the nature of the care given during pregnancy and childbirth.

Medical control of pregnancy and childbirth has historically been closely linked to the view that health care services for mothers and children, like other aspects of health care, are a private matter. In 1921, shortly after women received the vote, Congress enacted a program to reduce maternal and infant mortality, the country's first federally funded health care program. The Sheppard-Towner Act, which created a network of prenatal and well-baby centers, was an important victory for women reformers. They had fought to establish the principle that preventive health care was a public, not merely private, responsibility and to give women a primary role in community health and welfare. The centers were generally staffed by female physicians and public health nurses, leaving to male physicians in private practice the care of those who were already sick. Though very successful in providing the services mandated by the law, the program was dismantled by the end of the decade as a result of a highly effective campaign mounted by the medical profession under the leadership of the American Medical Association. With Sheppard-Towner's downfall, women lost their special role in the field of maternal and child health, and preventive health care shifted back to the male-dominated private sector.

Since that time, as of mid 1993, there has been no similar comprehensive program to combat infant and maternal mortality despite some initiatives by the Clinton Administration. At present, some maternal and infant care services are available to the poor through Medicaid and other government programs. Although the United States has made great strides in reducing infant mortality, its infant mortality rates far exceed those of other industrialized nations. Moreover, black babies continue to die at nearly twice the rate of white babies. When race and class effects are combined, infant death rates are even higher. Among the problems low-income women face in seeking maternity care are the lack of community-based programs offering prenatal care, physicians' refusal to accept Medicaid patients, and hospital policies requiring large cash deposits as a condition for admitting uninsured patients.

The trend toward viewing childbirth as a medical rather than a natural event has had an important impact on the allocation of decision-making power as both a practical and a legal matter. This trend dates back at least to the nineteenth century, when the more "scientific" and predominately male medical profession sought to drive out "irregular," often female, health practitioners. By 1900, most middle- and upper-class women had accepted the idea that childbirth required a physician's intervention and supervision. However, 50 percent of babies—those of the rural poor and immigrant working classes in the cities—were still being delivered by midwives. In the early twentieth century, despite evidence that midwives were actually safer than doctors, physicians succeeded in having the practice of midwifery narrowly restricted by a series of licensing requirements and other laws and regulations adopted at the state level.

Medical control has meant a change in the nature of care as well as a change in personnel. Doctors' care has been characterized by greater intervention, initially with forceps and later with hospitalization, anesthesia, and surgery. Increasing caesarean section rates, prenatal testing, and use of fetal monitors are modern manifestations of the treatment of pregnancy as a medical event. The women's health movement and other consumer drives of the late 1960s and 1970s have led women and men to question the benefits of this medical focus and prompted potential parents to seek greater control over childbearing. Some have sought to change their relations with physicians so as to participate more actively in the care. Others have expressed renewed interest in natural childbirth methods, midwifery, birthing centers, and home births.

Legal challenges to medical hegemony over pregnancy and childbirth have come about in a variety of ways. As middle- and upper-class consumers increasingly began to seek alternative forms of care, licensing boards and prosecutors cracked down on professional and lay midwives. In a well-publicized California case, for example, three unlicensed California midwives associated with the Santa Cruz Birth Center were prosecuted for practicing medicine without a license. In a unanimous opinion, the California Supreme Court held in *Bowland v. Municipal Court*, 556 P.2d 1081

(1976), that attending normal childbirth did constitute practicing medicine and that only those midwives licensed before 1949, when the licensing provisions were abolished, could legally assist at births. This ruling was followed by new state legislation authorizing nurse-midwives to provide prenatal, intrapartum, and post-partum care, including family planning care, for the mother and immediate care for the infant, so long as they practiced under the general supervision of a physician. Midwives and consumers have fought similar battles in other jurisdictions to protect and extend the midwives' right to practice.

Other legal challenges to medical hegemony in the birthing context have involved providers' efforts to compel pregnant women to undergo caesarean sections rather than natural childbirth. A question clearly at stake in such cases is the weight to be accorded the interests of the fetus compared to those of the women. In thinking about this area, consider whether you believe the woman or the medical profession is best able to determine the interests of the fetus.

In re A.C.

D.C. Court of Appeals, 1990.
573 A.2d 1234.

On hearing en banc TERRY, Associate Judge:

This case comes before the court for the second time. [In 1987, a three-judge court] denied a motion to stay an order of the trial court which had authorized a hospital to perform a caesarean section on a dying woman in an effort to save the life of her unborn child. The operation was performed, but both the mother and the child died. A few months later, the court ordered the case heard en banc and vacated the [earlier] opinion. . . .

We are confronted here with [a] profoundly difficult and complex [issue]. . . .[W]e must determine who has the right to decide the course of medical treatment for a patient who, although near death, is pregnant with a viable fetus. [The discussion of how that decision should be made if the patient cannot make it for herself is omitted.] We hold that in virtually all cases the question of what is to be done is to be decided by the patient—the pregnant woman—on behalf of herself and the fetus. . . .

A.C. was first diagnosed as suffering from cancer at the age of thirteen. In the ensuing years she underwent major surgery several times, together with multiple radiation treatments and chemotherapy. A.C. married when she was twenty-seven, during a period of remission, and soon thereafter she became pregnant. She was excited about her pregnancy and very much wanted the child. Because of her medical history, she was referred in her fifteenth week of pregnancy to the high-risk pregnancy clinic at George Washington University Hospital.

On Tuesday, June 9, 1987, when A.C. was approximately twenty-five weeks pregnant, she went to the hospital for a scheduled check-up. Because she was experiencing pain in her back and shortness of breath, an x-ray was taken, revealing an apparently inoperable tumor which nearly filled her right lung. On Thursday, June 11, A.C. was admitted to the hospital as a patient. By Friday her condition had temporarily improved, and when asked if she really wanted to have her baby, she replied that she did.

Over the weekend A.C.'s condition worsened considerably. Accordingly, on Monday, June 15, members of the medical staff treating A.C. assembled, along with her family, in A.C.'s room. The doctors then informed her that her illness was terminal, and A.C. agreed to palliative treatment designed to extend her life until at least her twenty-eighth week of pregnancy. The "potential outcome [for] the fetus," according to the doctors, would be much better at twenty-eight weeks than at twenty-six weeks if it were necessary to "intervene." A.C. knew that the palliative treatment she had chosen presented some increased risk to the fetus, but she opted for this course both to prolong her life for at least another two weeks and to maintain her own comfort. When asked if she still wanted to have the baby, A.C. was somewhat equivocal, saying "something to the effect of 'I don't know, I think so.' " As the day moved toward evening, A.C.'s condition grew still worse, and at about 7:00 or 8:00 P.M. she consented to intubation to facilitate her breathing.

The next morning, June 16, the trial court convened a hearing at the hospital in response to the hospital's request for a declaratory judgment. The court appointed counsel for both A.C. and the fetus, and the District of Columbia was permitted to intervene for the fetus as parens patriae. The court heard testimony on the facts as we have summarized them, and further testimony that at twenty-six and a half weeks the fetus was viable, i.e., capable of sustained life outside of the mother, given artificial aid. A neonatologist, Dr. Maureen Edwards, testified that the chances of survival for a twenty-six week fetus delivered at the hospital might be as high as eighty percent, but that this particular fetus, because of the mother's medical history, had only a fifty to sixty percent chance of survival. Dr. Edwards estimated that the risk of substantial impairment for the fetus, if it were delivered promptly, would be less than twenty percent. However, she noted that the fetus' condition was worsening appreciably at a rapid rate, and another doctor—Dr. Alan Weingold, an obstetrician who was one of A.C.'s treating physicians—stated that any delay in delivering the child by caesarean section lessened its chances of survival. . . .

There was no evidence before the court showing that A.C. consented to, or even contemplated, a caesarean section before her twenty-eighth week of pregnancy. There was, in fact, considerable dispute as to whether she would have consented to an immediate caesarean delivery at the time the hearing was held. . . .

. . . The operation took place, but the baby lived for only a few hours, and A.C. succumbed to cancer two days later.

. . . [O]ur analysis of this case begins with the tenet common to all medical treatment cases:

that any person has the right to make an informed choice, if competent to do so, to accept or forego medical treatment. The doctrine of informed consent, based on this principle and rooted in the concept of bodily integrity, is ingrained in our common law. . . .

In the same vein, courts do not compel one person to permit a significant intrusion upon his or her bodily integrity for the benefit of another person's health. See, *McFall v. Shimp,* 10 Pa.D. & C.3d 90 (Allegheny County Ct. 1978) [refusing to order Shimp to donate bone marrow which was necessary to save the life of his cousin, McFall].

. . . It has been suggested that fetal cases are different because a woman who "has chosen to lend her body to bring [a] child into the world" has an enhanced duty to assure the welfare of the fetus, sufficient even to require her to undergo caesarean surgery. Robertson, Procreative Liberty, supra, 69 VA.L.REV. at 456. Surely, however, a fetus cannot have rights in this respect superior to those of a person who has already been born. . . .

In those rare cases in which a patient's right to decide her own course of treatment has been judicially overridden, courts have usually acted to vindicate the state's interest in protecting third parties, even if in fetal state. See *Jefferson v. Griffin Spalding County Hospital Authority,* 274 S.E.2d 457 (1981) (ordering that caesarean section be performed on a woman in her thirty-ninth week of pregnancy to save both the mother and the fetus); *Raleigh Fitkin-Paul Morgan Memorial Hospital v. Anderson,* 201 A.2d 537 (ordering blood transfusions over the objection of a Jehovah's Witness, in her thirty-second week of pregnancy, to save her life and that of the fetus), cert. denied, 377 U.S. 985 (1964). . . .

What we distill from the cases discussed in this section is that every person has the right, under the common law and the Constitution, to accept or refuse medical treatment. . . . Further, it matters not what the quality of a patient's life may be; the right of bodily integrity is not extinguished simply because someone is ill, or even at death's door. To protect that right against intrusion by others—family members, doctors, hospitals, or anyone else, however well-intentioned—we hold that a court must determine the patient's wishes by any means available, and must abide by those wishes unless there are truly extraordinary or compelling reasons to override them. . . .

. . . We hold . . . that without a competent refusal from A.C. to go forward with the surgery, and without a finding through substituted judgment that A.C. would not have consented to the surgery, it was error for the trial court to proceed to a balancing analysis, weighing the rights of A.C. against the interests of the state.

There are two additional arguments against overriding A.C.'s objections to caesarean surgery. First, as the American Public Health Association cogently states in its amicus curiae brief:

> Rather than protecting the health of women and children, court-ordered caesareans erode the element of trust that permits a pregnant woman to communicate to her physician—without fear of reprisal—all information relevant to her proper diagnosis and treatment. An even more serious consequence of court-ordered intervention is that it drives women at high risk of complications during pregnancy and childbirth out of the health care system to avoid coerced treatment.

Second, and even more compellingly, any judicial proceeding in a case such as this will ordinarily take place—like the one before us here—under time constraints so pressing that it is difficult or impossible for the mother to communicate adequately with counsel, or for counsel to organize an effective factual and legal presentation in defense of her liberty and privacy interests and bodily integrity. Any intrusion implicating such basic values ought not to be lightly undertaken when the mother not only is precluded from conducting pre-trial discovery (to which she would be entitled as a matter of course in any controversy over even a

modest amount of money) but also is in no position to prepare meaningfully for trial. . . .

. . . [I]n virtually all cases the decision of the patient, albeit discerned through the mechanism of substituted judgment, will control. We do not quite foreclose the possibility that a conflicting state interest may be so compelling that the patient's wishes must yield, but we anticipate that such cases will be extremely rare and truly exceptional. This is not such a case. . . .

STUDY QUESTIONS

1. Would the majority of the appellate court have required A.C. to submit to the cesarean section? Why not? Would it ever order such operations over the woman's wishes? Under what circumstances? Do you agree?

2. Are cases such as *Jefferson v. Griffin Spaulding Cty. Hosp. Auth.*, 274 S.E.2d 457 (Ga. 1981), distinguishable from *In re A.C.* in that the medical procedure used in the former was in the medical interests of both the woman and the fetus? Should the medical interest in attempting to preserve both their lives suffice to overcome religious objections on the part of the woman?

3. Was A.C. expressing her interests only or both her interests and her view of any future child's best interests? To what extent do you think the medical profession's views of the fetus's interests should replace the woman's? Does an American College of Obstetrics and Gynecology Ethics Committee finding that "[t]he welfare of the fetus is of the utmost importance to the majority of women: thus only rarely will a conflict arise" influence your views?

As the *A.C.* Court suggests, actual court decisions dealing with this situation are rare. Providers have, however, acted to supersede women's choices more often than the reported cases might suggest. Moreover, as in other areas, a race and class pattern is discernible in these actions. For example, as Janet Gallagher points out in "Fetus as Patient," in *Reproductive Laws for the 1990s* (S. Cohen and N. Taub, eds., Totowa N.J.: Humana Press, 1989, p. 203), "[a] 1986 survey of doctors revealed that 81 percent of the pregnant women subjected to court-ordered interventions were black, Asian, or Hispanic; 44 percent were unmarried; 24 percent did not speak English as their primary language; and one [percent] were private patients." Do these facts influence your views or suggest other alternatives to you?

Behavior during Pregnancy

Finally, reproductive questions have recently arisen in the context of efforts to control woman's behavior during pregnancy. Focusing largely on pregnant users of illegal drugs, such efforts have included prosecutions under various criminal statutes and quasi-criminal actions under various child abuse and termination of parental rights provisions. The following case illustrates the criminal approach.

Johnson v. State of Florida

Supreme Court of Florida, 1992.
602 So.2d 1288.

HARDING, Justice. [The Supreme Court adopts the view and opinion of the dissenting judge below.]

. . . The issue before the court is whether section 893.13(1)(c)(1), Florida Statutes (1989), permits the criminal prosecution of a mother, who ingested a controlled substance prior to giving birth, for delivery of a controlled substance to the infant during the thirty to ninety seconds following the infant's birth, but before the umbilical cord is severed. . . .

The record in this case establishes the following facts. On October 3, 1987, Johnson delivered a son. The birth was normal with no complications. There was no evidence of fetal distress either within the womb or during the delivery. About one and one-half minutes elapsed from the time the son's head emerged from his mother's birth canal to the time he was placed on her stomach and the cord was clamped.

The obstetrician who delivered Johnson's son testified he presumed that the umbilical cord was functioning normally and that it was delivering blood to the baby after he emerged from the birth canal and before the cord was clamped. Johnson admitted to the baby's pediatrician that she used cocaine the night before she delivered. A basic toxicology test performed

on Johnson and her son was positive for benzoylecgonine, a metabolite or "breakdown" product of cocaine. In December 1988, Johnson, while pregnant with a daughter, suffered a crack overdose. Johnson told paramedics that she had taken $200 of crack cocaine earlier that evening and that she was concerned about the effects of the drug on her unborn child. Johnson was then taken to the hospital for observation. Johnson was hospitalized again on January 23, 1989, when she was in labor. Johnson told Dr. Tompkins, an obstetrician, that she had used rock cocaine that morning while she was in labor. With the exception of finding meconium stain fluid in the amniotic sac, there were no other complications with the birth of Johnson's baby daughter. Approximately sixty-to-ninety seconds elapsed from the time the child's head emerged from her mother's birth canal until her umbilical cord was clamped.

The following day, the Department of Health and Rehabilitative Services investigated an abuse report of a cocaine baby concerning Johnson's daughter. Johnson told the investigator that she had smoked pot and crack cocaine three to four times every-other-day throughout the duration of her pregnancy with her daughter. Johnson's mother acknowledged that Johnson had been using cocaine for at least three years during the time her daughter and son were born.

At Johnson's trial, Dr. Tompkins testified that a mother's blood passes nutrients, oxygen and chemicals to an unborn child by a diffusion exchange at the capillary level from the womb to the placenta. The umbilical cord then circulates the baby's blood (including the exchange from its mother) between the placenta and the child. Metabolized cocaine derivatives in the mother's blood thus diffuse from the womb to the placenta, and then reach the baby through its umbilical cord. Although the blood flow is somewhat restricted during the birthing process, a measurable amount of blood is transferred from the placenta to the baby through the umbilical cord during delivery and after birth. . . .

However, in my view, the primary question in this case is whether section 893.13(1)(c)(1). was intended by the Legislature to apply to the birthing process. Before Johnson can be prosecuted under this statute, it must be clear that the Legislature intended for it to apply to the delivery of cocaine derivatives to a newborn during a sixty-to-ninety second interval before severance of the umbilical cord. I can find no case where "delivery" of a drug was based on an involuntary act such as diffusion and blood flow. . . .

[The court examined the legislative history of the child abuse and neglect statute and found] that the Legislature considered and rejected a specific statutory provision authorizing criminal penalties against mothers for delivering drug-affected children who received transfer of an illegal drug derivative metabolized by the mother's body, in utero. In light of this express legislative statement, I conclude that the Legislature never intended for the general drug delivery statute to authorize prosecutions of those mothers who take illegal drugs close enough in time to childbirth that a doctor could testify that a tiny amount passed from mother to child in the few seconds before the umbilical cord was cut. . . .

There can be no doubt that drug abuse is one of the most serious problems confronting our society today. Of particular concern is the alarming rise in the number of babies born with cocaine in their systems as a result of cocaine use by pregnant women. Some experts estimate that as many as eleven percent of pregnant women have used an illegal drug during pregnancy, and of those women, seventy-five percent have used cocaine. Report of the American Medical Association Board of Trustees, Legal Interventions During Pregnancy, 264 *J[ournal]*

of the A[merican] M[edical] A[ssociation] 2663 (Nov. 28, 1990). Others estimate that 375,000 newborns per year are born to women who are users of illicit drugs. *American Public Health Association 1990 Policy Statement.*

It is well-established that the effects of cocaine use by a pregnant woman on her fetus and later on her newborn can be severe. On average, cocaine-exposed babies have lower birth weights, shorter body lengths at birth, and smaller head circumferences than normal infants. Cocaine use may also result in sudden infant death syndrome, neural-behavioral deficiencies as well as other medical problems and long-term developmental abnormalities. The basic problem of damaging the fetus by drug use during pregnancy should not be addressed piecemeal, however, by prosecuting users who deliver their babies close in time to use of drugs and ignoring those who simply use drugs during their pregnancy.

Florida could possibly have elected to make in utero transfers criminal. But it chose to deal with this problem in other ways. One way is to allow evidence of drug use by women as a ground for removal of the child to the custody of protective services, as was done in this case. Some states have responded to this crisis by charging women with child abuse and neglect. See *In re Baby X,* 293 N.W.2d 736 (1980) (newborn suffering from narcotics withdrawal symptoms due to prenatal maternal drug addiction is neglected and within jurisdiction of the probate court); *In re Smith,* 492 N.Y.S.2d 331 (N.Y. Fam.Ct.1985) (person under Family Court Act includes unborn child who was neglected as the result of mother's conduct); [and] *In re Ruiz,* 500 N.E.2d 935 (Com.Pl.1986) (mother's use of heroin close to baby's birth created substantial risk to the health of the child and constituted child abuse).

However, prosecuting women for using drugs and "delivering" them to their newborns appears to be the least effective response to this crisis. Rather than face the possibility of prosecution, pregnant women who are substance abusers may simply avoid prenatal or medical care for fear of being detected. Yet the newborns of these women are, as a group, the most fragile and sick, and most in need of hospital neonatal care. A decision to deliver these babies "at home" will have tragic and serious consequences. . . .

. . . Prosecution of pregnant women for engaging in activities harmful to their fetuses or newborns may also unwittingly increase the incidence of abortion.

Such considerations have led the American Medical Association Board of Trustees to oppose criminal sanctions for harmful behavior by a pregnant woman toward her fetus and to advocate that pregnant substance abusers be provided with rehabilitative treatment appropriate to their specific psychological and physiological needs. Likewise, the American Public Health Association has adopted the view that the use of illegal drugs by pregnant women is a public health problem. It also recommends that no punitive measures be taken against pregnant women who are users of illicit drugs when no other illegal acts, including drug-related offenses, have been committed.

In summary, I would hold that section 893.13(1)(c)(1) does not encompass "delivery" of an illegal drug derivative from womb to placenta to umbilical cord to newborn after a child's birth. If that is the intent of the Legisla-

ture, then this statute should be redrafted to clearly address the basic problem of passing illegal substances from mother to child in utero, not just in the birthing process. . . .

It is so ordered.

STUDY QUESTIONS

1. What harm do you suppose is meant to be addressed by prosecutions of mothers for abusing illegal drugs during their pregnancies? Do you believe such prosecutions achieve their purposes? Are there alternative approaches? Which approach do you see as most desirable? Why?
2. Why did this court reverse Johnson's conviction for delivering of drugs to another? Might the legislature make a separate criminal offense of drug taking during pregnancy?
3. Do you see any dangers in specially punishing abuse of illegal substances during pregnancy? Should a woman who abuses legal substances, such as prescription drugs and alcohol, during pregnancy also be punished? Why? Why not?

Many see the criminal focus on pregnant substance abusers as troublesome for a number of reasons. As various health care organizations have pointed out, the criminal approach is likely to be counterproductive, inasmuch as fear of punishment drives many pregnant abusers from the health care system. Health care providers also worry that an obligation to cooperate with authorities will prevent them from having the sort of confidential relationship they need with their patients. Pregnant abusers who seek treatment are often excluded from treatment programs, both because they are pregnant and because there is no provision for taking care of their existing children.

Another concern is the disproportionate impact a focus on users of illegal drugs has on poor women, often women of color. While formulating a broader definition of substance abuse for criminal purposes would seem quite difficult, the narrow focus has a number of drawbacks. Not only does such a focus seem class- and race-biased, but it also runs the risk of diverting attention from deeper economic and social problems.

As we have seen, constitutional protection for procreative choice was first announced in the male sterilization context and then developed considerably in the context of contraception and abortion. Today, much of the discussion focuses on abortion. But, as we have also seen, that right applies in many different contexts.

Appreciating the full range of people who must be protected by it and the full range of their experiences is crucial to determining the contours of the right. In the words of Dorothy Roberts:

> [An] emphasis on abortion fails to incorporate the needs of poor women of color. The primary concern of white, middle-class women are laws that restrict choices otherwise available to them. The main concerns of poor women of color, however, are the material conditions of poverty and oppression that restrict their choices. The reproductive freedom of poor women of color, for example, is limited significantly not only by the denial of access to safe abortions, but also by the lack of resources necessary for a healthy pregnancy and parenting relationship. Their choices are limited not only by direct government interference with their decisions, but also by government's failure to facilitate them. The focus of reproductive rights discourse on abortion neglects this broader range of reproductive health issues that affect poor women of color. Addressing the concerns of women of color will expand our vision of reproductive freedom to include the full scope of what it means to have control over one's reproductive life.
>
> *Dorothy Roberts. "Punishing Pregnant Drug Addicts Who Have Babies: Women of Color, Equality and The Right of Privacy." 104* Harvard Law Review *1419, 1461–62 (1991).*

9 Sexuality and Sexual Violence

The last chapter dealt in large measure with laws that make it difficult to be sexually active without reproducing. By contrast, this chapter is concerned with law in relation to nonreproductive aspects of sexuality, including sexual violence. The chapter first explores the law's past and potential role in controlling women's sexual behavior and then turns to two problem areas: rape and pornography.

Earlier chapters have shown the close connection between notions of appropriate sexual behavior and limitations on women's opportunities. Historically, women who worked outside the home were often considered loose and immoral, and, as the *Dothard v. Rawlinson* case (see Chapter 4) shows, women have been foreclosed at times from employment to prevent sexual assaults. Expectations regarding sexual conduct have also had consequences in the family realm. For example, when women engage in sexual activity outside marriage, they risk losing custody of their children and their right to determine their household composition. Middle-class women receiving alimony and poor women receiving public assistance may also jeopardize their financial support by being sexually active.

Often embodied in religious or moral ideas, some of these constraints are gender-neutral; others are plainly gender-based. Rethinking these constraints is a complex and controversial task. While there is general agreement that nonconsensual sexual violence is bad, there is little consensus otherwise about the desirability of different kinds of sexual activity or the possibilities for real consent in sexual matters. One reason it is so hard to agree on such matters is that we know so little about the origins and effects of sexual tastes and behavior. Evidence is increasing that sexual attraction is a natural, biological phenomenon while we generally assume that it is a product of cultural factors that vary from time to time and place to place. Is it both? Does sexual activity—of particular kinds or in general—enhance or interfere with societal well-being?

Confusion about the spectre of sexual exploitation also makes it hard to agree about limits on sexual activity. Sexuality presents opportunities for gratification and fulfillment, and at the same time makes people vulnerable to exploitation and abuse. Male sexual aggression has posed special problems for women. Some regard it as the most fundamental element in women's subordination, the one that drives women into dependence on other men for protection. Others see it as one of the many ways men dominate women. Given women's historic vulnerability, some protection seems in order. It is not clear, however, whether protections should explicitly recognize women's special vulnerability or take a gender-neutral form. As we have seen in the discussion of statutory rape laws in the *Michael M.* case (Chapter 2), protections against sexual aggression may also interfere with consensual gratification. Further-more, it is difficult to determine in certain areas, such as prostitution, whether women are in fact victims of male oppression or autonomous agents who benefit from their activity. Thus, we are hard put to know whether or not to restrain the activity, let alone whether to pose the restraint in sex-based terms. These, then, are problems to ponder as we consider codes of sexual conduct.

I. CODES OF SEXUAL CONDUCT

Society has narrowly circumscribed the ways in which individuals may express themselves sexually. Both men and women are expected to express themselves sexually through heterosexual relationships. Other constraints are directed only at women. For women, sexual expression must be through relationships that are initiated by men and lead to marriage. Unchaste women who take the sexual initiative are "bad girls" who are generally thought to deserve what they get. Our society does not entertain similar expectations about the behavior of men. This sexual double standard has been embodied in a wide variety of legal provisions ranging from common law doctrines governing the right to recover damages to statutes directly addressing sexual conduct.

Feminist writings, appearing in a variety of contexts, have sought to expose the law's role in imposing these sex-based codes. One such passage appeared in a brief written by a feminist group formed to challenge a pornography ordinance discussed later in this chapter.

The Sexual Double Standard in the Law

Brief Amici Curiae of the Feminist Anti-Censorship Task Force, et al.
American Booksellers Assn., Inc. v. Hudnut
U.S. Court of Appeals, 7th Cir. No. 84–3147. Pp. 4–8.

... The legal system has used many vehicles to enforce the sexual double standard which pro-tected "good" women from both sexual activity and explicit speech about sex. For example, the common law of libel held that "an oral imputation of unchastity to a woman is actionable without

Reprinted by permission of Nan D. Hunter, Esq., and Sylvia A. Law, Esq.

proof of damage ... Such a rule never has been applied to a man, since the damage to his repu-tation is assumed not to be as great." W. Prosser. *Law of Torts.* pp. 759–60 (West, 1971).

The common law also reinforced the image of "good" women as asexual and vulnerable by providing husbands, but not wives, remedies for "interference" with his right to sole posses-sion of his wife's body and services. The early writ of "ravishment" listed the wife with the husband's chattels. To this day, the action for criminal conversation allows the husband to maintain an action for trespass, not only when his wife is raped

> "but also even though the wife had consented to it, or was herself the seducer and had invited and procured it, since it was considered that she was no more capable of giving a consent which would prejudice the husband's interests than was his horse ..."

W. Prosser, pp. 874–77.

While denying the possibility that "good" women could be sexual, the common dealt harshly with the "bad" women who were. Prostitution laws often penalized only the woman, and not the man, and even facially neutral laws were and are enforced primarily against women.

Prostitution is defined as "the practice of a female offering her body to indiscriminate sexual intercourse with men," 63 AM.JUR. 2d *Prostitution,* Sec. 1 (1972), or submitting "to indiscriminate sexual intercourse which she invites or solicits." *Id.* A woman who has sexual relations with many men is a "common prostitute" and a criminal while a sexually active man is considered normal.

The sexual double standard is applied with particular force to young people. Statutory rape laws often punished men for consensual intercourse with a female under a certain age. Such laws reinforce the stereotype that in sex the man is the offender and the woman the victim, and that young men may legitimately engage in sex, at least with older people, while a young woman may not legally have sex with anyone.

The suppression of sexually explicit material most devastating to women was the restriction on dissemination of birth control information, common until 1971. In that year, the Supreme Court held that the constitutional right to privacy protects an unmarried person's right to access to birth control information. *Eisenstadt v. Baird,* 405 U.S. 438 (1971). To deny women access to contraception "prescribes pregnancy and the birth of an unwanted child as punishment for fornication." 405 U.S. at 448. For the previous century the federal Comstock law, passed in 1873, had prohibited mailing, transporting or importing of "obscene, lewd, or lascivious" items, specifically including all devices and information pertaining to "preventing contraception and producing abortion." Women were jailed for distributing educational materials regarding birth control to other women because the materials were deemed sexually explicit in that they "contain[ed] pictures of certain organs of women" and because the materials were found to be "detrimental to public morals and welfare." *People v. Byrne,* 99 Misc. 1, 6 (N.Y. 1917).

The Mann Act also was premised on the notion that women require special protection from sexual activity. It forbids interstate transportation of women for purposes of "prostitution, debauchery, or any other immoral purposes," and was enacted to protect women from reportedly widespread abduction by bands of white slavers, coercing them into prostitution. As the legislative history reveals, the Act reflects the assumption that women have no will of their own and must be protected against themselves. Like the premises underlying this ordinance, the Mann Act assumed

> that women were naturally chaste and virtuous, and that no woman became a whore unless she had first been raped, drugged or deserted. [Its] image of the prostitute . . . was of a lonely and confused female . . . [Its proponents] maintained that prostitutes were the passive victims of social disequilibrium and the brutality of men . . . [Its] conception of female weakness and male domination left no room for the possibility that prostitutes might consciously choose their activities.
> Note, "The White Slave Traffic Act: The Historical Impact of a Criminal Law Policy of Women," 72 *Georgetown* L.J. 1111 (1984).

The Mann Act initially defined a 'white slave' to include "only those women or girls who are literally slaves—those women who are owned and held as property and chattels . . . those women and girls who, if given a fair chance, would, in all human probability, have been good wives and mothers . . .", H.R. Rep. No.47, 61st Cong., 2d Sess. (1910) at 9–10. Over the years, the interpretation and use of the Act changed drastically to punish voluntary 'immoral' acts even when no commercial intention or business profit was involved. *See Caminetti v. U.S.,* 242 U.S. 470 (1917); and *Cleveland v. U.S.,* 329 U.S. 14 (1946).

> The term 'other immoral acts' was held to apply to a variety of activities: the interstate transportation of a woman to work as a chorus girl in a theatre where the woman was exposed to smoking, drinking, and cursing; a dentist who met his young lover in a neighboring state and shared a

hotel room to discuss her pregnancy, two students at the University of Puerto Rico who had sexual intercouse on the way home from a date; and a man and woman who had lived together for four years and traveled around the country as man and wife while the man sold securities.
72 *Georgetown L.J.* at 1119.

Society's attempts to "protect" women's chastity through criminal and civil laws have resulted in restrictions on women's freedom to engage in sexual activity, to discuss it publicly and to protect themselves from the risk of pregnancy. These disabling restrictions reinforced the gender roles which have oppressed women for centuries. . . .

STUDY QUESTIONS

1. What is the sexual double standard to which the brief refers? How, according to the brief's authors, has the double standard limited the options open to women? Do you agree? Do you think the double standard has also limited the options open to men? In what ways?
2. What illustrations does the brief provide of ways in which the legal system has enforced the sexual double standard? What other examples have you encountered in this book? Have these legal vehicles always incorporated sex-based classifications? What are some examples that do not include sex-based classifications?
3. What stereotypes do the authors claim are reinforced by statutory rape laws? Are these similar to the assumptions the authors claim are reflected in the Mann Act? In your view, do such stereotypes and assumptions accurately depict the nature of social and sexual relations between women and men?

———————————— 🙦 ————————————

The Feminist Anti-Censorship Task Force brief points out that the legal system has, in the guise of protecting women, reflected and reinforced a double sexual standard that restricts women's freedom to engage in sexual activity. As we have seen in earlier chapters, sex-based classifications often depend on this double standard for their justification. Recall the Supreme Court decision in *Michael M.* (see Chapter 2), upholding a statutory rape law that punishes males but not females for engaging in sexual intercourse with a minor. Remember also the earlier case of *Goessart* (see Chapter 1), indicating that women could constitutionally be denied jobs as bartenders in order to protect them from the tavern environment. Notions about proper sexual behavior for females have also led to the unequal application of facially neutral laws. Statutes defining juvenile delinquency in general terms, such as "incorrigibility" or "waywardness," have often been applied to punish girls, but not boys, for engaging in sexual acts.

Another way that the legal system embodies this sexual code relates to public nudity. In some jurisdictions, women, but not men, are subject to criminal prosecution if they appear unclothed to the waist in public. A recent decision by New York's highest court represents a successful challenge to this double standard.

———————————————————————————

People v. Santorelli
New York Court of Appeals, 1992.
600 N.E.2d 232.

———————————————

The order of Monroe County Court should be reversed and the informations dismissed. . . .

Defendants were arrested for violating Penal Law § 245.01 (exposure of a person) when they bared "that portion of the breast which is below the top of the areola" in a Rochester public park. The statute, they urge, is discriminatory on its face since it defines "private or intimate parts" of a woman's but not a man's body as including a specific part of the breast. That assertion being made, it is settled that the People then have the burden of proving that there is an important government interest at stake and that the gender classification is substantially related to that interest (see, *Mississippi University for Women v. Hogan*). In this case, however, the People have made no attempt below and make none before us to demonstrate that the statute's discriminatory effect serves an important governmental interest or that the classification is based on a reasoned predicate. Moreover, the People do not dispute that New York is one of only two states which criminalizes the mere exposure by a woman in a public place of a specific part of her breast.

Despite the People's virtual default on the constitutional issue, we must construe a statute, which enjoys a presumption of constitutionality, to uphold its constitutionality if a rational basis can be found to do so. Penal Law § 245.01, when originally enacted, "was aimed at discouraging 'topless' waitresses and their promoters." Considering the statute's provenance, we held in [*People v.*] *Price* that a woman walking along a street wearing a fishnet, see-through pull-over blouse did not transgress the statute and that it "should not be applied to the noncommercial, perhaps accidental, and certainly not lewd, exposure alleged." Though the statute and the rationale for that decision are different, we believe that underlying principle of *People v. Price* should be followed. We, therefore, conclude that Penal Law § 245.01 is not applicable to the conduct presented in these circumstances and that the City Court was correct in dismissing the informations.

TITONE, J. (concurring):

[After examining the legislative history of § 245.01, Justice Titone concluded that the] . . . Court's reliance on the "presumption of constitutionality" in these circumstances is thus nothing more than an artful means of avoiding a confrontation with an important constitutional problem. . . .

The equal protection analysis that the majority has attempted to avoid is certainly not a complex or difficult one. When a statute explicitly establishes a classification based on gender, as Penal Law § 245.01 unquestionably does, the State has the burden of showing that the classification is substantially related to the achievement of an important governmental objective (e.g., *Caban v. Mohammed; Craig v. Boren; People v. Liberta*). . . .

It is clear from the statute's legislative history, as well as our own case law and common sense, that the governmental objective to be served by Penal Law § 245.01 is to protect the sensibilities of those who wish to use the public beaches and parks in this State. And, since the statute prohibits the public exposure of female—but not male—breasts, it betrays an underlying legislative assumption that the sight of a female's uncovered breast in a public place is offensive to the average person in a way that the sight of a male's uncovered breast is not. It is this assumption that lies at the root of the statute's constitutional problem.

Although protecting public sensibilities is a generally legitimate goal for legislation, it is a tenuous basis for justifying a legislative classification that is based on gender, race or any other grouping that is associated with a history of social prejudice (see, *Hogan* ["[c]are must be taken in ascertaining whether the statutory objective itself reflects archaic and stereotypic notions"]). Indeed, the concept of "public sensibility" itself, when used in these contexts, may be nothing more than a reflection of commonly-held preconceptions and biases. One of the most important purposes to be served by the equal protection clause is to ensure that "public sensibilities" grounded in prejudice and unexamined stereotypes do not become enshrined as part of the official policy of government. Thus, where "public sensibilities" constitute the justification for a gender-based classification, the fundamental question is whether the particular "sensibility" to be protected is, in fact, a reflection of archaic prejudice or a manifestation of a legitimate government objective.

Viewed against these principles, the gender-based provisions of Penal Law § 245.01 cannot, on this record, withstand scrutiny. Defendants contend that apart from entrenched cultural expectations, there is really no objective reason why the exposure of female breasts should be considered any more offensive than the exposure of the male counterparts. They offered proof that, from an anatomical standpoint, the female breast is no more or less a sexual organ than is the male equivalent. They further contend that to the extent that many in our society may regard the uncovered female breast with a prurient interest that is not similarly aroused by the male equivalent, that perception cannot serve as a justification for differential treatment because it is itself a suspect cultural artifact rooted in centuries of prejudice and bias toward women. Indeed, there are many societies in other parts of the world—and even many locales within the United States—where the exposure of female breasts on beaches and in other recreational areas is commonplace and is generally regarded as unremarkable. It is notable that other jurisdictions have taken the position that breasts are not "private parts" and that breast exposure is not indecent behavior, and twenty-two states specifically confine their statutory public exposure prohibitions to uncovered genitalia.

The People in this case have not refuted this evidence or attempted to show the existence of evidence of their own to indicate that the non-lewd exposure of the female breast is in any way harmful to the public's health or well being. Nor have they offered any explanation as to why, the fundamental goal that Penal Law § 245.01 was enacted to advance—avoiding offense to citizens who use public beaches and parks—cannot be equally well served by other alternatives.

In summary, the People have offered nothing to justify a law that discriminates against women by prohibiting them from removing their tops and exposing their bare chests in public as men are routinely permitted to do. The mere fact that the statute's aim is the protection of "public sensibilities" is not sufficient to satisfy the state's burden of showing an "exceedingly persuasive justification" for a classification that expressly discriminates on the basis of sex. Accordingly, the gender-based classification established by Penal Law § 245.01 violates appellants' equal protection rights and, for that reason, I concur in the majority's result and vote to reverse the order below.

Order reversed and informations dismissed in a memorandum.

STUDY QUESTIONS

1. Does the majority apply the Equal Protection Clause correctly in your opinion? According to the majority opinion, are there times when it is lawful to punish women for being stripped to the waist? Could the statute ever be applied to men?
2. What would the concurring justice do? Why?

Sexual conduct is also governed directly by a variety of laws concerning consensual sexual behavior. These laws generally proscribe sexual activity outside marriage and often limit the types of activity permitted within marriage. Rooted in ecclesiastical law, these statutes prohibit such conduct as fornication, adultery, and "crimes against nature," including oral and anal sex. As such, they have the effect of making heterosexuality the mandatory form of sexual expression and of reinforcing the importance of marriage and family. Laws of this type restrict the sexual freedom of both sexes by limiting the range of available opportunities for obtaining sexual gratification and fulfillment; but to the extent that marital and family obligations have been a source of difficulty for women, they harm women disproportionately.

Griswold and other Supreme Court decisions concerned with reproductive rights suggested to a number of observers that the Supreme Court was ready to invalidate laws of this sort by expanding the right of privacy to protect a wide range of sexual activity. Following these decisions, however, the Supreme Court sustained a number of sex laws. Law professor Thomas Grey offered a hypothesis to explain why the Court is reluctant to expand the privacy right in this way in his article, "Eros, Civilization and the Burger Court," 43 *Law & Contemporary Problems* 83 (1980).

Grey argues that the members of the Supreme Court in 1980 shared the Freudian belief that it is necessary to repress sex drives and channel sexuality into family settings in order to deflect energy into work and creative achievement and to contain human aggression. This belief still provides a strong incentive for denying constitutional protection to diverse forms of sexual expression. In Grey's view, restrictive sex laws will only be struck down when social practices (such as cohabitation outside marriage and homosexuality) are sufficiently widespread and/or public that their recognition becomes necessary to maintaining an orderly society. United States Supreme Court decisions since the appearance of Grey's article have generally borne out his assessment of the Court's reluctance to recognize a right to sexual freedom. In *Bowers v. Hardwick,* 478 U.S. 186 (1986), the Court explicitly refused to afford federal constitutional protection to homosexual conduct so as to invalidate a Georgia sodomy statute. In so doing, the Court ignored the willingness of some courts, including the highest courts of several states, to afford protection to a variety of homosexual and heterosexual activities. *People v. Onofre,* 415 N.E.2d 936 (1980), *cert. denied* 451 U.S. 987 (1981), for example, invalidated a criminal statute prohibiting consensual sodomy as violative of the federal right to privacy (as long as the decisions are made voluntarily by adults and the activity takes place in noncommercial settings).

Hardwick clearly rules out, at least temporarily, using the federal constitution to challenge provisions prohibiting certain sexual conduct and seems to have encouraged criminal charges of consensual oral sex between heterosexual couples, both married and unmarried. See, e.g., *Schochet v. Md.,* 541 A.2d 183 (Spec. App. 1988), rev'd. 580 A.2d 176, 184 (1990). Legislative and administrative efforts may, of course, alter existing constraints. However, as the extensive controversy that greeted President Clinton's efforts to lift the prohibitions on homosexuals' participation in the armed forces demonstrates, such changes will not come easily. Indeed, as in the armed forces case, they may require compromises that entail general restrictions on sexual activity. Nevertheless, state constitutions may provide some guarantees. See, e.g., *State v. Saunders,* 381 A.2d 333 (1971) (J. Shreiber, concurring). In so doing, they provide the basis for a "right to be sexual" that could also provide a powerful tool for eliminating legal constraints that reinforce the notion that only one sort of sexual behavior is proper for females, a notion that has been used to justify significant constraints on women's opportunities and promote their dependence on men.

Even though the "right to be sexual" is unlikely to extend to coercive conduct, such as rape, the elimination of restraints on nominally consensual conduct might easily permit extremely destructive behavior that exploits and abuses the vulnerable, particularly women. In her article "Toward Recognition of a Right to Be Sexual," 7 *Women's Rights Law Reporter* 245 (1982), attorney Mary Dunlap captured this dilemma. As she pointed out:

> Once we have *rejected* the idea that "proper" sexual behavior in the female consists of nothing more, less or different than sexual intercourse within the bounds of legal marriage—aimed at pregnancy and resulting in childbirth and the fulfillment of the "noble and benign offices of wife and mother"—and once we have rejected all related notions of "impropriety" based on gender, we face a vast array of difficult questions.

Among these are: What should be the legal basis for a "right to be sexual"? Should it be privacy only? What about freedom of speech and association related to sex? Is there a way to encourage tolerance for a diversity of behaviors? Will such tolerance lead to more abuse? Will it reinforce images of men as violent predators and of women as victims? And, as we must ask today, how should the rapid spread of AIDS affect our thinking about sexuality?

There are no easy answers to these questions. The materials on rape, and pornography that follow may assist you in formulating your own response. These materials explore the relation of law to what Dunlap calls "the realities of sexual violence, exploitation and repressiveness of our society." Rape represents the epitome of sexual violence and the total negation of sexual autonomy for women. Pornography presents more complex situations, containing at once the potential for exploitation and repression. As you ponder the role of the law in these contexts, consider whether it is possible to formulate a right to be sexual that enhances the sexual freedom of both sexes and combats special behavior rules for women without at the same time making women vulnerable to further sexual abuse. Is it possible to experience sexual freedom, or is modern sexuality, however free, inevitably a socially constructed reflection of patriarchal values?

II. RAPE

The Law and Its Impact on Women

The forcible rape of women is now recognized as a crime against the person of the woman. This is a very recent development. Susan Brownmiller, one of the feminist writers who sensitized the public to the full dimensions of this crime, traced the historical origins of traditional rape law.

The Origins of the Law of Rape

Susan Brownmiller.
Against Our Will: Men, Women and Rape.
New York: Simon and Schuster, 1975.
Pp. 8–22.

A female definition of rape can be contained in a single sentence. If a woman chooses not to have intercourse with a specific man and the man chooses to proceed against her will, that is a criminal act of rape. Through no fault of woman, this is not and never has been the legal definition. . . . Rape entered the law through the back door, as it were, as a property crime of

man against man. Woman, of course, was viewed as the property.

Ancient Babylonian and Mosaic law was codified on tablets centuries after the rise of formal tribal hierarchies and the permanent settlements known as city-states. Slavery, private property and the subjugation of women were facts of life, and the earliest written law that has come down to us reflects this stratified life. Written law in its origin was a solemn compact among men of property, designed to protect their own male interests by a civilized exchange of goods or silver *in place of force* wherever possible. The capture of females by force remained perfectly acceptable *outside* the tribe or city as one of the ready fruits of warfare, but clearly *within* the social order such a happenstance would lead to chaos. A payment of money to the father of the house was a much more civilized and less dangerous way of acquiring a wife. And so the bride price was codified, at fifty pieces of silver. By this circuitous route the first concept of criminal rape sneaked its tortuous way into man's definition of law. Criminal rape, as a patriarchal father saw it, was a violation of the new way of doing business. It was, in a phrase, the theft of virginity, an embezzlement of his daughter's fair price on the market. . . .

Concepts of rape and punishment in early English law are a wondrous maze of contradictory approaches reflecting a gradual humanization of jurisprudence in general, and in particular, man's eternal confusion, never quite resolved, as to whether the crime was a crime against a woman's body or a crime against his own estate. . . .

The comprehensive Statutes of Westminster put forward by Edward I at the close of the thirteenth century showed a gigantic advance in legal thinking as the Crown, and by "Crown" Americans should read "state," began to take an active interest in all kinds of rape prosecutions, not just those concerning violated virgins. Our modern principle of *statutory* rape—felonious carnal knowledge of a child in which her "consent" is altogether immaterial—dates from this time and these statutes.

Of critical significance, Westminster extended the king's jurisdiction to cover the forcible rape of married women as well as virgins, with no difference in punishment to offending males. To further erase the distinction between the rape of a virgin and the rape of a wife, the old, ignoble custom of redemption through marriage was permanently banned under suits by the king. In concession to the proprietary rights of husbands—for the Crown had ventured into an area it had never ventured into before—Westminster also saw fit to legislate a definition of lesser ravishment, a sort of misdemeanor, applicable in cases where it could be argued that a wife did not object strenuously enough to her own "defilement." The aggrieved party in these cases was the husband, and the wife was preemptorily stripped of her dower. *Within* a marriage, the theory went—and still goes—that there could be no such crime as rape by a husband since a wife's "consent" to her husband was a permanent part of the marriage vows and could not be withdrawn.

To give the new law teeth, Edward I decreed that if a raped woman or her kin failed to institute a private suit within forty days, the right to prosecute automatically passed to the Crown. This bold concept, applicable only to virgins in previous reigns, was a giant step for the law and for women. It meant that rape was no longer just a family misfortune and a threat to land and property, but an issue of public safety and state concern.

The First Statute of Westminster, enacted in 1275, set the Crown's penalty for rape at a paltry two years' imprisonment plus a fine at the king's pleasure, no doubt to ease the effect of a major transition, for what had occurred at the Parliament of Westminster was only tangentially and in retrospect a recognition of women's rights; its inexorable, historic purpose had been to consolidate political power in the hands of the king. But within a decade an emboldened Second Statute of Westminster amended the timorous First. By a new act of Parliament, any man who ravished "a married woman, dame or damsel" without her consent was guilty of a full-blown felony under the law of the Crown, and the penalty was death.

It read better on parchment than it worked in real life, but the concept of rape as a public wrong had been firmly established.

From the thirteenth to the twentieth century, little changed. The later giants of jurisprudence, Hale, Blackstone, Wigmore and the rest, continued to point a suspicious finger at the female victim and worry about her motivations and "good fame."

"If she be of evil fame and stand unsupported by others," Blackstone commented, "if she concealed the injury for any considerable time after she had the opportunity to complain, if the place where the act was alleged to be committed was where it was possible she might have been heard and she made no outcry, these and the like circumstances carry a strong but not conclusive presumption that her testimony is false or feigned."

STUDY QUESTIONS

1. Explain how rape was considered a crime against property. Does it retain any of this meaning in our society?

2. Why was the distinction between a virginal and nonvirginal victim given any significance in the Westminister statutes? Is a woman any less violated by forced intercourse after her first voluntary sexual relationship than before it?

3. Do you think that the death penalty is excessive for the crime of forcible rape?

————————————— ❧ —————————————

As Brownmiller suggests, special features of traditional rape law distinguish it from other types of criminal law. We consider those features next.

Man's Trial and Woman's Tribulation: Rape Cases in the Courtroom

Vivian Berger.
77 *Columbia Law Review* 1, 7–10 (1977).

THE PECULIAR LAW OF RAPE

How exactly is rape "different"? For one thing, . . . rape is a sex-specific crime: "unlawful sexual intercourse with a female person without her consent." The ancient definition, which used the phrase "against her will," made it clear that non-consent by the female partner constitutes the essence of rape. At what point, and to what extent, an element of "force" came to be added to the notion of lack of consent is unclear. Nowadays, a representative American statute provides "Whoever ravishes and carnally knows any female who has attained her 14th birthday, by force and against her will . . . shall be punished by imprisonment for any term of years." Unfortunately, the injection of a concept of "force," over and above the coercion implicit in denying freedom of sexual choice, led to the rather illogical idea that the victim had to "resist to the utmost." Some jurisdictions even in-

cluded a form of resistance among the statutory elements of rape. Thus, an offense whose gravamen was non-consent acquired a gloss that shifted the focus from the woman's subjective state of mind, as affected by the man's actions, to her behavior in response. By contrast, in a crime like robbery, also "a nonconsensual and forcible version of an ordinary human interaction," the law imposes no special burden of opposition: It simply inquires whether the accused took something from another person by violence or intimidation.

A second distinctive feature of rape is its penalty structure: always harsh, often draconian. Before the case of *Furman v. Georgia* [408 U.S. 238 (1972)] invalidated arbitrary capital punishment laws, sixteen states permitted imposition of death for rape. . . . Now, some thirty-odd states permit imposition of life imprisonment; many others provide for maximum prison terms of thirty, forty or fifty years. Finally, several jurisdictions call for stated minimum sentences. . . .

A third anomaly is the fact that a man cannot "rape" his wife by forcing her to submit to intercourse. This norm derives not from the presumed common law unity of husband and wife but rather from an equally fictional notion that marriage implies continuing consent to sexual relations. Although it has less practical impact than the laws on sentencing or resistance, this exception to the rule of criminal liability for harm inflicted upon a spouse only serves to underline the unique nature of this offense.

Requirements of corroboration, which occupy a borderland between substantive law and evidence, comprise yet another oddity. Where these exist, the prosecution cannot rest on the mere word of the rape victim; it must produce some other evidence tending to support its case. Depending on the common law rule or statute in question, the state may have to corroborate each material element of the crime [i.e. force, penetration, and the perpetrator's identity] or only some particular aspect of the prosecutrix's story. Such requirements—like so much else in the law of rape—run counter to the usual criminal law norms. In the very jurisdictions demanding proof to bolster that of the rape complainant, "the word of the victim of a robbery, assault, or any other crime may alone . . . sustain a conviction."

To complete this survey of features peculiar to the offense of rape and its prosecution two widespread phenomena bear mention. One is the critical role at trial of evidence respecting the complainant's chastity. . . . The other is the prevalence of special kinds of cautionary jury charges. The most common of these, derived almost verbatim from the words of Sir Matthew Hale, warns the triers of fact that a rape accusation "is one which is easily made and, once made, difficult to defend against, even if the person accused is innocent." The instruction concludes: "[T]he law requires that you examine the testimony of the [complainant] with caution." Though courts may warn the jury in other situations to scrutinize certain proof very closely, such instructions—on accomplice witnesses, for example—cut across disparate kinds of cases and do not, as here, depend on the nature of the crime charged. Once again, where rape is involved the rules of the game are simply different. . . .

STUDY QUESTIONS

1. What are the six features of forcible rape that Berger claims make it different from other types of crimes? Which relate to the definition of the crime and which relate to the manner in which it is proven in court?
2. Why do you suppose the definition of rape has traditionally focused on sexual intercourse in the sense of penetration of the vagina by the penis? Why has society regarded performing this act without consent as different from penetrating the vagina with fingers or other objects or penetrating other orifices without consent? What reasons can you see for forcible rape and forcible sodomy being treated as separate crimes? Why is it considered different from other types of sexual touching?

Reforming the Law of Rape

Recognizing the tremendous psychological and physical toll taken by sexual violence, women organized in the 1970s to combat unwanted intercourse. Their initial efforts were directed at exposing the myth that women invite and enjoy rape and at providing support to victims through rape crisis centers and similar groups. They underscored the violent rather than the sexual aspect of rape and the restraints it has imposed on women's freedom of movement. They pointed out that the threat of violence has forced women to depend on men for protection and that the blame cast on rape victims has served to reinforce gender-based behavior codes.

Later efforts were addressed more directly to legal institutions. In particular, women sought to eliminate legal provisions that excused sexual violence, reinforced sex-based stereotypes, and allowed rape victims to be treated differently from victims of other crimes. Those efforts form the core of this section.

One of the special features of rape laws identified by Berger was their excessive penalty structure. As late as 1972, rape was a capital offense in sixteen states. Such provisions were declared unconstitutional in a 1977 case, *Coker v. Georgia,* 433 U.S. 584. The Supreme Court there reversed Georgia's imposition of the death penalty in a rape case on the ground that the death sentence for the rape of an adult woman was excessive in its severity and disproportionate to the gravity of the offense. This violated the Eighth Amendment's prohibition of cruel and unusual punishment. Women's rights groups supported this decision because such excessive penalties inhibited prosecutions of rape cases, reduced conviction rates, and reinforced sexist and racist attitudes.

Berger also pointed to three special rules that render rape charges more difficult to prosecute than other criminal cases: (1) the requirement that the victim's testimony be substantiated or corroborated by independent evidence; (2) the rule allowing evidence regarding the victim's reputation for chastity and/or prior sexual conduct; and (3) the rule authorizing cautionary jury instructions impugning the victim's credibility. Rules like these not only make convictions less likely in cases going to trial, but they also discourage victims from complaining and prosecutors from bringing rape charges to trial. The harsh operation of these rules, highlighted in the following cases, has led increasingly to their rejection by courts and legislatures.

The first case, *People v. Watson,* illustrates the difficulties posed by corroboration requirements. *Watson* involves the prosecution of a rape occurring in the early 1970s. Under the law applicable at the time of the crime, to obtain a valid conviction, the prosecutor was required to present independent evidence substantiating each aspect of the crime, including the use of force. The defendant, convicted at trial, argued on appeal that the corroboration requirement had not been met.

People v. Watson

Court of Appeals of New York, 1978.
45 N.Y.2d 867, 382 N.E.2d 1352,
410 N.Y.S.2d 577.

Opinion of the Court.

The order of the Appellate Division should be reversed, the convictions vacated and the indictment dismissed.

To sustain the conviction of rape in the first degree under the ... applicable provisions of the Penal Law, there must have been corroborative evidence, *inter alia,* of the element of "forcible compulsion". The People urge three items of proof as meeting this requirement—evidence of prompt complaint, evidence of the complainant's distraught emotional state immediately after the alleged assault, and evidence of bruises on the complainant's body. We conclude that the proof in this record is insufficient as a matter of law. The proof of prompt complaint and distraught emotional state on the part of this complainant might go to an issue of consent, but would not tend to establish "forcible compulsion" as that term is

defined. There was proof by the complainant's mother that she was shown "a bruise on her back"—not otherwise located or described. The only further evidence that might in any way suggest that this bruise was referable to the alleged rape came from the complainant herself and accordingly cannot be accepted as satisfying the requirement of corroboration independent of the testimony of the alleged victim. . . .

STUDY QUESTIONS

1. What evidence did the prosecution offer to substantiate the victim's testimony? Why did the appellate court find it insufficient?
2. How might difficulties in finding independent evidence affect a prosecutor's willingness to bring rape cases to trial? How might such difficulties affect the chances of obtaining convictions in cases that do go to trial?
3. Why should independent evidence be required to substantiate a rape victim's testimony? Why isn't independent evidence equally necessary in assault or robbery cases? Are there special reasons to believe women will fabricate rape charges?

Corroboration and evidentiary rules used in rape cases have traditionally allowed defendants to present testimony and question witnesses about the victim's sexual behavior and reputation. As a result, victims have often been subjected to extraordinarily intrusive and humiliating interrogations. The practical effect of such rules has been to put the victim on trial to determine whether, sexually speaking, she has been a "good girl." If she has not, the clear implication is her word is not worth accepting.

In the 1970s, a number of courts and legislatures reviewed and rejected rules of this type. For example, New York's corroboration requirement was repealed in 1974. Another example is the *McClean v. United States* case, set forth below. In reading it, you may find it helpful to know the meaning of some of the legal terminology appearing in the case: "Admissible" evidence is evidence that the judge should allow the jury to hear or see. Evidence that tends to prove a point in either side's case is regarded as "probative." "Prejudicial" evidence is evidence that is detrimental to a party's case, whether or not it bears on the issues before the court. "Credibility" refers to the believability of a witness. "Impeaching" the credibility of a witness refers to undercutting his or her testimony by showing the witness is untrustworthy or has a faulty memory.

McLean v. United States

Court of Appeals of the District
of Columbia, 1977.
377 F.2d 74.

KERN, Associate Judge.

Appellant was tried by a jury and convicted of rape and sentenced to a term of fifteen years under the Federal Youth Corrections Act. On appeal, he urges that it was reversible error for the trial judge to exclude (a) testimony that the complaining witness had engaged in sexual relations *with others* on prior occasions, and (b) testimony that she had a reputation in the community for unchastity. Appellant offered this evidence to support his defense that the complaining witness consented to have intercourse with him.

The government's evidence disclosed that appellant and the complaining witness, who was seventeen at the time of the incident, were neighbors and had known each other for nine or ten years. On June 25, 1975 at about 9:30 p.m., complainant was at home with her friend, Diane Tyler, when appellant called and made arrangements with her to go to the movies. They left shortly thereafter in appellant's sister's car and drove to the vicinity of 14th and Sheridan Streets, N.W., where appellant told her that he had to speak to someone. Appellant went into an apartment house while complainant waited in the car. Several minutes later he returned and said that the stop-over would take longer than expected and invited her to accompany him inside. Moments after she entered the apartment three young men came into a room where she was sitting and with the assistance of appellant, forced her into an unlit bedroom. Complainant testified that she pleaded with appellant to make them stop, but instead he was helping them. The four men disrobed her, held her down, and according to her testimony, made comments while appellant had intercourse with her. The other three in turn had intercourse with her and then left the room. . . .

Defense counsel requested a ruling at the beginning of trial whether he could offer witnesses who would testify that complainant had engaged in sexual intercourse with others in the past. The trial judge ruled that such evidence was not relevant to the issues at trial and therefore inadmissible. During trial appellant proffered two witnesses who testified in a hearing out of the presence of the jury that they had heard other members of the community comment on complainant's reputation for unchastity. The trial court refused to allow these witnesses to testify because they had not convinced the trial judge that there was an adequate basis for their knowledge of the prosecutrix's reputation.

Central to appellant's position in the instant case is his assertion that the probative value of proof of complainant's prior acts of sexual intercourse with others outweighs the prejudice to the complainant. The prejudice of such evidence is readily seen: it diverts the jury's attention to collateral matters and probes into the private life of the victim of a rape. . . . On the other hand, the probative value of the evidence is less easily recognized. Apparently, appellant views evidence of past sexual intercourse by a woman with others as admissible because it tends to establish her sexually promiscuous character which in turn tends to prove that on the particular occasion she consented to sexual intercourse with the accused rather than submitted against her will out of fear. We agree with the Supreme Court of Arizona in *Pope v. Superior Court,* 545 P.2d 946, 952 (1976), that "[t]he fact that a woman consented to sexual intercourse on one occasion is not substantial evidence that she consented on another, but in fact may indicate the contrary."

Generally, the law disfavors the admission of evidence of a person's character in order to prove conduct in conformity with that character. . . . There are exceptions to this general proposition, however, but none appear[s] to encompass the proffer here. . . .

We note that the recent trend in other jurisdictions is that specific acts of sexual intercourse on the part of the complaining witness are *not* admissible to prove that she consented to sexual intercourse with the accused.

We endorse the approach taken by these courts, *viz.,* the exclusion from evidence of prior acts of sexual intercourse with others besides the defendant because such evidence is not probative to the issue of the prosecutrix's consent.[5] . . .

We therefore conclude the trial court properly excluded evidence of the complainant's sexual relations with others than the accused.[6] . . .

. . . [T]he rationale for excluding evidence of specific acts of sexual intercourse applies *with equal force* to the exclusion of reputation testimony. The reputation of a woman for unchastity raises unnecessary collateral issues which are nearly impossible to rebut, it diverts the jury's attention from the principal issues at trial and it results in prejudice to the complaining witness which greatly outweighs its extremely limited probative value. Reputation testimony should not be admitted except in the most unusual cases where the probative value is precisely demonstrated and outweighs the prejudicial effect of the testimony.[9] . . .

Affirmed.

STUDY QUESTIONS

1. What is the difference between evidence regarding reputation for unchastity and evidence regarding prior sexual acts? What did the court identify as the possible relevance of each type of evidence? What assumptions about women's behavior underlie such reasoning?

2. Do you think that the fact that the victim had previously engaged in sexual intercourse with the defendant makes it more likely that she consented to intercourse on the occasion in question? Do you agree with the *McLean* court that the jury should be allowed to hear such evidence? Are there any circumstances in which the court would permit evidence regarding other prior sexual conduct and reputation to be introduced?

---

[5]*We note that evidence of specific acts of sexual intercourse with the* defendant *himself should be admitted where either there may be an issue of identity at trial or to rebut the government's evidence that the prosecutrix did not consent to sexual intercourse on the particular occasion. . . .*

[6]*There can be* unusual circumstances *where the defense may inquire into specific sexual acts by the prosecutrix when the probative value of the evidence is clearly demonstrated and is shown to outweigh its prejudicial effect. As an example of such a situation, the Arizona Supreme Court in* Pope v. Superior Court, *noted that evidence would be admissible "which directly refutes physical or scientific evidence, such as the victim's alleged loss of virginity, the origin of semen, disease or pregnancy". . . .*

[9]*The court in* Pope v. Superior Court, *supra at 953, would admit reputation testimony "[where] the defendant alleges the prosecutrix actually consented to an act of prostitution," or when the prosecution offered evidence of the complainant's chastity.*

Under what circumstances should courts permit such evidence to be introduced?

3. What might be the effect of the court's ruling in this case on rape victims' willingness to make criminal complaints? On prosecutors' willingness to bring charges? On the conviction rate in rape cases?

State courts considering statutes that limit evidence concerning the alleged rape victim's past sexual conduct have generally strained to uphold their constitutionality. The constitutionality of certain provisions became somewhat clearer when, with two dissents, the U.S. Supreme Court upheld one provision of the Michigan rape shield law.

Michigan v. Lucas

United States Supreme Court, 1991.
___U.S. ___ , 111 S.Ct. 1743,
114 L.Ed.2d 205.

Justice O'CONNOR delivered the opinion of the Court.

Because Nolan Lucas failed to give statutorily required notice of his intention to present evidence of an alleged rape victim's past sexual conduct, a Michigan trial court refused to let him present the evidence at trial. The Michigan Court of Appeals reversed, adopting a per se rule that preclusion of evidence of a rape victim's prior sexual relationship with a criminal defendant violates the Sixth Amendment. We consider the propriety of this per se rule.

I

Like most States, Michigan has a "rape-shield" statute designed to protect victims of rape from being exposed at trial to harassing or irrelevant questions concerning their past sexual behavior. This statute prohibits a criminal defendant from introducing at trial evidence of an alleged rape victim's past sexual conduct, subject to two exceptions. One of the exceptions is relevant here. It permits a defendant to introduce evidence of his own past sexual conduct with the victim, provided that he follows certain procedures. Specifically, a defendant who plans to present such evidence must file a written motion and an offer

of proof "within 10 days" after he is arraigned. The trial court may hold "an in camera hearing to determine whether the proposed evidence is admissible"—i.e., whether the evidence is material and not more prejudicial than probative.

Lucas was charged with two counts of criminal sexual conduct. The State maintained that Lucas had used a knife to force Wanda Brown, his ex-girlfriend, into his apartment, where he beat her and forced her to engage in several nonconsensual sex acts. At no time did Lucas file a written motion and offer of proof, as required by the statute. At the start of trial, however, Lucas' counsel asked the trial court to permit the defense to present evidence of a prior sexual relationship between Brown and Lucas, "even though I know it goes against the statute."

The trial court reviewed the statute then denied the motion, stating that "[n]one of the requirements set forth in [the statute] have been complied with." The court explained that Lucas' request was not made within the time required by Michigan law and that, as a result, no in camera hearing had been held to determine whether the past sexual conduct evidence was admissible. A bench trial then began, in which Lucas' defense was consent. The trial court did not credit his testimony. The court found Lucas guilty on two counts of criminal sexual assault and sentenced him to a prison term of 44 to 180 months. . . .

II

Michigan's rape-shield statute is silent as to the consequences of a defendant's failure to comply with the notice-and-hearing requirement. The trial court assumed, without explanation, that preclusion of the evidence was an authorized remedy. Assuming, arguendo, that the trial court was correct, the statute unquestionably implicates the Sixth Amendment. To the extent that it operates to prevent a criminal defendant from presenting relevant evidence, the defendant's ability to confront adverse witnesses and present a defense is diminished. This does not necessarily render the statute unconstitutional. "[T]he right to present relevant testimony is not without limitation. The right 'may, in appropriate cases, bow to accommodate other legitimate interests in the criminal trial process.' " We have explained, for example, that "trial judges retain wide latitude" to limit reasonably a criminal defendant's right to cross-examine a witness "based on concerns about, among other things, harassment, prejudice, confusion of the issues, the witness' safety, or interrogation that is repetitive or only marginally relevant." Lucas does not deny that legitimate state interests support the notice-and-hearing requirement. The Michigan statute represents a valid legislative determination that rape victims deserve heightened protection against surprise, harassment, and unnecessary invasions of privacy. The statute also protects against surprise to the prosecution. . . .

The sole question presented for our review is whether the legitimate interests served by a notice requirement can ever justify precluding evidence of a prior sexual relationship between a rape victim and a criminal defendant. . . .

We have indicated that probative evidence may, in certain circumstances, be precluded when a criminal defendant fails to comply with a valid discovery rule. . . . [That precedent does not hold] that preclusion is permissible every time a discovery rule is violated. Rather, we acknowledged that alternative sanctions would be "adequate and appropriate in most cases." We stated explicitly, however, that there could be circumstances in which preclusion was justified because a less severe penalty "would perpetuate rather than limit the prejudice to the State and the harm to the adversary process.". . .

. . . [T]he Michigan Court of Appeals erred in adopting a per se rule that Michigan's notice-and-hearing requirement violates the Sixth Amendment in all cases where it is used to preclude evidence of past sexual conduct between a rape victim and a defendant. The Sixth Amendment is not so rigid. The notice-and-hearing requirement serves legitimate state interests in protecting against surprise, harassment, and undue delay. Failure to comply with this requirement may in some cases justify even the severe sanction of preclusion. . . .

We express no opinion as to whether or not preclusion was justified in this case. The Michigan Court of Appeals, whose decision we review here, did not address whether the trial court abused its discretion on the facts before it. Rather, the Court of Appeals adopted a per se rule that preclusion is unconstitutional in all cases where the victim had a prior sexual relationship with the defendant. That judgment was error. We leave it to the Michigan courts to address in the first instance whether Michigan's rape-shield statute authorizes preclusion and whether, on the facts of this case, preclusion violated Lucas' rights under the Sixth Amendment.

The judgment of the Michigan Court of Appeals is vacated and remanded for further proceedings not inconsistent with this opinion.

It is so ordered.

STUDY QUESTIONS

1. Under the Michigan statute, what procedure is a rape defendant who seeks to introduce evidence as to the complainant's past sexual conduct with him required to follow? What consequences may flow from his failure to follow this procedure?
2. Would a trial court's ruling enforcing the statute's notice-and-hearing procedure always violate the Sixth Amendment's guarantee of the right to confront adverse witnesses? Why not?

The enactment of rape shield laws has met many feminist concerns. However, as Tamar Lewin explains, the process is not yet complete.

Rape and the Accuser: The Debate Still Rages on Citing Sexual Past

Tamar Lewin.
New York Times, February 12, 1993.
P. B16.

The passage of laws by dozens of states largely prohibiting the use of an accuser's sexual history or reputation as evidence in rape cases was an early achievement of the women's movement.

From the mid-1970's to the mid-1980's, one state after another adopted a version of this kind of legislation. According to the NOW Legal Defense and Education Fund, Utah is the only state today that does not have some kind of rape shield law or a court ruling that protects rape victims. . . .

DISPUTE LINGERS ON

Despite the proliferation of the state laws—and despite the fact that both defense lawyers and women's advocates say such laws generally work well—a debate is still simmering over when a man charged with rape should be able to tell the jury about the sexual past of the woman accusing him.

Some lawyers say that even with the shield laws, judges in many states have a good deal of discretion in deciding what evidence should be allowed, and that sometimes they make these decisions based more on their attitudes toward women's sexuality than the intent of the law. Some women's advocates are thus concerned that the courts still do not provide enough protection to the accuser. To underline their concerns they point to these three current cases:

☐ In Glen Ridge, N.J., in the trial of four young men charged with sexually assaulting a mildly retarded 17-year-old, the judge has allowed evidence of the young woman's sexual history, on the ground that the defendants needed to use such evidence if they were to have a fair trial. The men contend that their accuser willingly performed the sex acts. But some women's advocates say the evidence is being used to smear the young woman: defense lawyers are portraying her as a seductress.

☐ In New York, in a case to be argued before the state's highest court in March, defense lawyers for three black men convicted of raping a white woman are seeking to overturn the convictions on the ground that they were not allowed to introduce evidence that the woman had previously had consensual group sex with other black men.

☐ In Massachusetts, rape crisis centers in Worcester and Lowell were recently found to be in contempt of court and fined for refusing to turn over the counseling records of two girls under age 16 to the defense lawyers for the men charged with raping them. The state's highest court ruled last year that defense lawyers, but not necessarily juries, are entitled to see a woman's psychotherapy records. Lawyers for the rape crisis centers are appealing. . . .

HUMILIATION FOR VICTIM

While laws vary by state, their goal is the same: to spare rape victims the humiliation of having the most intimate part of their lives discussed in public—and to encourage women to report rapes without fear that a judge and jury will focus more on their sexual histories than on whether the defendants assaulted them. . . .

Some state laws say that as a rule, evidence of an accuser's past sexual conduct cannot be admitted in court. But that is not an absolute; judges and lawyers acknowledge that sometimes defendants cannot get a fair trial if such evidence is excluded. So some laws provide a list of exceptions for situations in which the woman has previously been convicted of prostitution, has had a consensual sexual relationship with the defendant or has a particular motive to lie.

Several states, including New York and Connecticut, have a catchall provision saying that in addition to any specified exceptions, the judge can allow evidence of sexual history when it is in the best interests of justice. Other states, including New Jersey, give judges wide discretion to decide whether, in a particular case, the evidence is more inflammatory than useful to the jury.

"The not-so-secret defense in a lot of rape cases is not that the woman consented, but that she's a slut," said Abbe Smith, deputy director of the Criminal Justice Institute at Harvard Law School. "Even in the William Kennedy Smith case in Palm Beach, where the rape shield was firmly in place, there was sure a lot of suggestion of that, all around the edges. It's not just a legal question. It's one of social dynamics, and our values about women's sexuality."

The New York case going to the state's highest court illustrates those dynamics well. The case involves three black men, Otis Fearon, Martin Williams and Bruce Richardson, who were convicted in 1990 of raping a white woman. In court testimony, they were said to have forced her into their car as she came out of a Manhattan nightclub and drove her to the home of one of the men in Brooklyn, where they raped and sodomized her.

At the trial, defense lawyers argued that the woman had agreed to go home with the defendants and had been a willing participant in the sexual acts. They also tried to present evidence that the woman had previously had consensual group sex with black men. But the judge refused to hear the evidence, ruling that it was precluded by the rape shield law.

WHAT CONDUCT IS NORMAL

"I believe that the jury found my client guilty because it was just too repugnant to them to imagine that a person of one race could jump into a car with three strangers of another race and go off for an evening of fun and games," said Mark Baker, a defense lawyer. "I don't think you have to be a racist to think that's not normal conduct. We need the evidence of her sexual history to level the playing field, to get the jury to see that what is abhorrent to them might not have been abhorrent to her."

As a legal matter, Mr. Baker argues, the judge should not have rejected the proffered evidence without first hearing it to determine its relevance. "The reason the New York statute has the catchall provision is that it would be unconstitutional without it, since it might deprive someone of a fair trial," he said.

Mr. Baker's views are backed by the state association of criminal defense lawyers, which is filing a "friend of the court" brief.

Prosecutors and women's groups, however, see the case differently.

"Any evidence of what she may have done in the past is irrelevant to what happened in this case," said Anthea Bruffee, an appeals lawyer in the Kings County District Attorney's office. "And I find it offensive to assume that the jurors are so racist that they cannot manage the idea of a sexual relationship between people of different races."

Last month, 14 women's organizations and rape crisis centers filed a "friend of the court" brief arguing that overturning the lower court's ruling on the evidence could set a precedent nationwide and discourage the reporting and prosecution of rape.

"What they're really trying to do, even if it's not what they say, is smear the woman by saying she had group sex with black men, that if she consented once she probably consented again," said Danielle Ben Jehuda, the NOW Legal Defense and Education Fund lawyer who wrote the brief. "But the whole point of rape shield laws is that consent in a previous situation is irrelevant. Right now, in most of the cases, the problem isn't the rape shield laws but the judges who still have old attitudes about women's sexuality."

The special doubts about the trustworthiness of women who complain of rape that are reflected in corroboration requirements and special evidentiary rules received direct expression in the special cautionary instruction traditionally given juries in rape cases. Like the evidentiary rules reviewed and rejected in *McLean,* the special cautionary instruction also was subjected to judicial scrutiny in the 1970s. In *People v. Rincon-Pineda,* the California Supreme Court was called upon to review a rape conviction in a case where the instruction had not been given.

People v. Rincon-Pineda

Supreme Court of California, 1975.
14 Cal.3d 864, 538 P.2d 247,
123 Cal. Rptr. 119.

WRIGHT, Chief Justice.

. . . By reason of the issue presented on appeal we have decided that the time is ripe for review of the cautionary instruction which should have been given at defendant's trial, to the end of determining whether it should continue to be mandated in the trial of every case involving a charge of a sex offense. . . .

[The instruction reads as follows:] "A charge such as that made against the defendant in this case is one which is easily made and, once made, difficult to defend against, even if the person accused is innocent.

"Therefore, the law requires that you examine the testimony of the female person named in the information with caution."

The instruction has its origin in the writings of Sir Matthew Hale, Lord Chief Justice of the Court of King's Bench from 1671 to 1676, which were published posthumously in 1736. . . .

. . . [It] became the rule in California that upon request [these] cautionary instructions . . . were to be given in rape cases "either when the prosecutrix is a child of tender years, or when her testimony is uncorroborated." . . .

In light of our . . . examination of the evolution of the cautionary instruction, and with the benefit of contemporary empirical and theoretical analyses of the prosecution of sex offenses in general and rape in particular, we are of the opinion that the instruction omitted below has outworn its usefulness and in modern circumstances is no longer to be given mandatory application.

As we observed, Sir Matthew Hale himself was convinced that the best test of the credibility of a prosecutrix was the surrounding circumstances, including any corroborating evidence, of a particular case. . . .

The credibility of a witness, by Hale's lights as by ours, is to be determined by the circumstances of the alleged crime and the narration of it by the witness, and these circumstances vary markedly from case to case.

Even if the mandatory instruction here in issue did square with Hale's analysis, the changes in criminal procedure wrought in the intervening 300 years would suffice of themselves to sap the instruction of contemporary validity. . . . But the spectre of wrongful conviction, whether for rape or for any other crime, has led our society to arm modern defendants with the potent accouterments of due process which render the additional constraint of Hale's caution superfluous and capricious. . . .

We next examine whether such a charge is so difficult to defend against as to warrant a mandatory cautionary instruction in the light of available empirical data. Of the FBI's four "violent crime" offenses of murder, forcible rape, robbery, and aggravated assault, forcible rape has the highest rate of acquittal or dismissal. . . . A similar situation is indicated by California crime [reports]. . . .

These findings are consistent with the leading study of jury behavior, which found that "the jury chooses to redefine the crime of rape in terms of its notions of assumption of risk," such that juries will frequently acquit a rapist or convict him of a lesser offense, notwithstanding clear evidence of guilt. (Kalven & Zeisel, The American Jury (1966) p. 254.) This tendency is especially dramatic in the situation supposedly most conducive to fabricated accusations: where the prosecutrix and the accused are acquainted, and there is no "evidence of extrinsic violence" to the prosecutrix. The jury "closely, and often harshly, scrutinizes the female complainant and is moved to be lenient with the defendant whenever there are suggestions of contributory behavior on her part." . . .

The low rate of conviction of those accused of rape and other sexual offenses does not appear to be attributable to a high incidence of unwarranted accusations. . . .

The initial emotional trauma of submitting to official investigatory processes, the fear of subsequent humiliation through attendant publicity and embarrassment at trial through defense tactics which are often demeaning, and a disinclination to encounter the discretion of the police in deciding whether to pursue charges of rape, especially with regard to what may appear to the police to be "victim-precipitated" rapes, are among the powerful yet common disincentives to the reporting of rape. . . .

Those victims with the pluck to disregard such disincentives discover the utter fallaciousness of the conventional wisdom that rape is a charge easily made. A large number of reports of rape are deemed "unfounded" by the police and are pursued no further. . . . Even when an arrest is made, the charge may well proceed no further. . . .

Since it does not in fact appear that the accused perpetrators of sex offenses in general and rape in particular are subject to capricious conviction by inflamed tribunals of justice, we conclude that the requirement of a cautionary instruction in all such cases is a rule without a reason. . . .

STUDY QUESTIONS

1. What did the cautionary instruction ask the jury to do? Why do you suppose juries are considered able to evaluate their doubts about witnesses' truthfulness without special instructions in other types of criminal cases? What reasons did the court give for abandoning the cautionary instruction? Are those reasons sound?
2. An underlying theme in the *Rincon-Pineda* decision is that rape victims—who are usually women—have no greater motivation to lie than the victims of other crimes. Do you agree? What does your answer suggest about our society's attitude toward sexual matters? Toward women?
3. Are the social and practical consequences of being accused of rape in fact different from those of being accused of other sorts of wrongdoing? Are there other areas of the law in which accusations of wrongdoing generate particular concern for the defendant? Sexual harassment, for example, or other types of discrimination?

❧

As a result of decisions like *Rincon-Pineda,* special rules governing the trial of rape cases have been abolished. Other decisions have concerned the definition of the crime itself. Who can be raped? Who can be a rapist? As Berger indicates, rape has been defined traditionally as forcible sexual intercourse in the sense of vaginal penetration by the penis, as long as the woman is not married to the man. Reformers have questioned marital exemption as well as the specific nature of the definition, and their legislative and litigation efforts have resulted in the definition of rape being expanded in both respects. A New York Court of Appeals decision reflects these developments.

People v. Liberta

Court of Appeals of New York, 1984.
64 N.Y.2d 152, 474 N.E.2d 567,
485 N.Y.S.2d 207.

WACHTLER, Judge.

The defendant, while living apart from his wife pursuant to a Family Court order, forcibly raped and sodomized her in the presence of their 2 ½ year old son. Under the New York Penal Law a married man ordinarily cannot be prosecuted for raping or sodomizing his wife. The defendant, however, though married at the time of the incident, is treated as an unmarried man under the Penal Law because of the Family Court order. On this appeal, he contends that because of the exemption for married men, the statutes for rape in the first degree (Penal Law, § 130.35) and sodomy in the first degree (Penal

Law, § 130.50), violate the equal protection clause of the Federal Constitution (U.S. Const., 14th Amdt.). The defendant also contends that the rape statute violates equal protection because only men, and not women, can be prosecuted under it. . . .

A. The Marital Exemption

As noted above, under the Penal Law a married man ordinarily cannot be convicted of forcibly raping or sodomizing his wife. This is the so-called marital exemption for rape. . . . The assumption, even before the marital exemption was codified, that a man could not be guilty of raping his wife, is traceable to a statement made by the 17th century English jurist Lord Hale, who wrote: "[T]he husband cannot be guilty of a rape committed by himself upon his lawful wife, for by their mutual matrimonial consent and contract the wife hath given up herself in this kind unto her husband, which she cannot retract" (1 Hale, History of Pleas of the Crown, p. 629). Although Hale cited no authority for his statement it was relied on by State Legislatures which enacted rape statutes with a marital exemption and by courts which established a common-law exemption for husbands. . . .

We find that there is no rational basis for distinguishing between marital rape and nonmarital rape. The various rationales which have been asserted in defense of the exemption are either based upon archaic notions about the consent and property rights incident to marriage or are simply unable to withstand even the slightest scrutiny. We therefore declare the marital exemption for rape in the New York statute to be unconstitutional.

Lord Hale's notion of an irrevocable implied consent by a married woman to sexual intercourse has been cited most frequently in support of the marital exemption. . . . Any argument based on a supposed consent, however, is untenable. Rape is not simply a sexual act to which one party does not consent. Rather, it is a degrading, violent act which violates the bodily integrity of the victim and frequently causes severe, long-lasting physical and psychic harm. . . . To ever imply consent to such an act is irrational and absurd. Other than in the context of rape statutes, marriage has never been viewed as giving a husband the right to coerced intercourse on demand. . . . Certainly, then, a marriage license should not be viewed as a license for a husband to forcibly rape his wife with impunity. A married woman has the same right to control her own body as does an unmarried woman. . . . If a husband feels "aggrieved" by his wife's refusal to engage in sexual intercourse, he should seek relief in the courts governing domestic relations, not in "violent or forceful self-help." . . .

The other traditional justifications for the marital exemption were the common-law doctrines that a woman was the property of her husband and that the legal existence of the woman was "incorporated and consolidated into that of the husband" (Blackstone's Commentaries) . . . [The marital right of privacy is sometimes cited to justify the exemption.].

The marital exemption simply does not further marital privacy because this right of privacy protects consensual acts, not violent sexual assaults. . . . Just as a husband cannot invoke a right of marital privacy to escape liability for beating his wife, he cannot justifiably rape his wife under the guise of a right to privacy. . . .

Another rationale sometimes advanced in support of the marital exemption is that marital rape would be a difficult crime to prove. A related argument is that allowing such prosecutions could lead to fabricated complaints by "vindictive" wives. The difficulty of proof argument is based on the problem of showing lack of consent. Proving lack of consent, however, is often the most difficult part of any rape prosecution, particularly where the rapist and the victim had a prior relationship. . . . Similarly, the possibility that married women will fabricate complaints would seem to be no greater than the possibility of unmarried women doing so. . . . The criminal justice system, with all of its built-in safeguards, is presumed to be capable of handling any false complaints. Indeed, if the possibility of fabricated complaints were a basis for not criminalizing behavior which would otherwise be sanctioned, virtually all crimes other than homicides would go unpunished.

The final argument in defense of the marital exemption is that marital rape is not as serious an offense as other rape and is thus adequately dealt with by the possibility of prosecution under criminal statutes, such as assault statutes, which provide for less severe punishment. The fact that rape statutes exist, however, is a recognition that the harm caused by a forcible rape is different, and more severe, than the harm caused by an ordinary assault. . . .

Moreover, there is no evidence to support the argument that marital rape has less severe consequences than other rape. On the contrary, numerous studies have shown that marital rape is frequently quite violent and generally has *more* severe, traumatic effects on the victim than other rape. . . .

Among the recent decisions in this country addressing the marital exemption, only one court has concluded that there is a rational basis for it. We agree with the other courts which have analyzed the exemption, which have been unable to find any present justification for it. . . .

B. The Exemption for Females

Under the Penal Law only males can be convicted of rape in the first degree. Insofar as the rape statute applies to acts of "sexual intercourse", which as defined in the Penal Law can only occur between a male and a female, it is true that a female cannot physically rape a female and that therefore there is no denial of equal protection when punishing only males for forcibly engaging in sexual intercourse with females. The equal protection issue, however, stems from the fact that the statute applies to males who forcibly rape females but does not apply to females who forcibly rape males.

Rape statutes historically applied only to conduct by males against females, largely because the purpose behind the proscriptions was to protect the chastity of women and thus their property value to their fathers or husbands. . . . New York's rape statute has always protected only females, and has thus applied only to males. . . . Presently New York is one of only 10 jurisdictions that does not have a gender-neutral statute for forcible rape. . . .

The People bear the burden of showing both the existence of an important objective and the substantial relationship between the discrimination in the statute and that objective. This burden is not met in the present case, and therefore the

gender exemption also renders the statute unconstitutional.

The first argument advanced by the People in support of the exemption for females is that because only females can become pregnant the State may constitutionally differentiate between forcible rapes of females and forcible rapes of males. This court and the United States Supreme Court have upheld statutes which subject males to criminal liability for engaging in sexual intercourse with underage females without the converse being true (*People v. Whidden, Michael M. v. Sonoma County Superior Ct.*). The rationale behind these decisions was that the primary purpose of such "statutory rape" laws is to protect against the harm caused by teenage pregnancies, there being no need to provide the same protection to young males.

There is no evidence, however, that preventing pregnancies is a primary purpose of the statute prohibiting forcible rape, nor does such a purpose seem likely. Rather, the very fact that the statute proscribes "forcible compulsion" shows that its overriding purpose is to protect a woman from an unwanted, forcible, and often violent sexual intrusion into her body. Thus, due to the different purposes behind forcible rape laws and "statutory" (consensual) rape laws, the cases upholding the gender discrimination in the latter are not decisive with respect to the former, and the People cannot meet their burden here by simply stating that only females can become pregnant.

The People also claim that the discrimination is justified because a female rape victim "faces the probability of medical, sociological, and psychological problems unique to her gender". This same argument, when advanced in support of the discrimination in the statutory rape laws, was rejected by this court in *People v. Whidden* (51 N.Y.2d at p. 461), and it is no more convincing in the present case. "[A]n ' "archaic and overbroad" generalization' . . . which is evidently grounded in long-standing stereotypical notions of the differences between the sexes, simply cannot serve as a legitimate rationale for a penal provision that is addressed only to adult males".

Finally, the People suggest that a gender-neutral law for forcible rape is unnecessary, and that therefore the present law is constitutional, because a woman either cannot actually rape a man or such attacks, if possible, are extremely rare. Although the "physiologically impossible" argument has been accepted by several courts, it is simply wrong. The argument is premised on the notion that a man cannot engage in sexual intercourse unless he is sexually aroused, and if he is aroused then he is consenting to intercourse. "Sexual intercourse" however, "occurs upon any penetration, however slight"; this degree of contact can be achieved without a male being aroused and thus without his consent.

As to the "infrequency" argument, while forcible sexual assaults by females upon males are undoubtedly less common than those by males upon females, this numerical disparity cannot by itself make the gender discrimination constitutional. Women may well be responsible for a far lower number of all serious crimes than are men, but such a disparity would not make it permissible for the State to punish only men who commit, for example, robbery. . . . A gender-neutral law would indisputably better serve, even if only marginally, the objective of deterring and punishing forcible sexual assaults. The only persons "benefitted" by the gender exemption are females who forcibly rape males. As the Supreme Court has stated, "[a] gender-based classification which, as compared to a gender-neutral one, generates additional benefits only for those it has no reason to prefer cannot survive equal protection scrutiny" (*Orr v. Orr*).

Accordingly, we find that section 130.35 of the Penal Law violates equal protection.

Having found that the statutes for rape in the first degree and sodomy in the first degree are unconstitutionally underinclusive, the remaining issue is the appropriate remedy for these equal protection violations. . . .

The question then is whether the Legislature would prefer to have statutes which cover forcible rape and sodomy, with no exemption for married men who rape or sodomize their wives and no exception made for females who rape males, or instead to have no statutes proscribing forcible rape and sodomy. In any case where a court must decide whether to sever an exemption or instead declare an entire statute a nullity it must look at the importance of the statute, the significance of the exemption within the over-all statutory scheme, and the effects of striking down the statute. . . . Statutes prohibiting such behavior are of the utmost importance, and to declare such statutes a nullity would have a disastrous effect on the public interest and safety. The inevitable conclusion is that the Legislature would prefer to eliminate the exemptions and thereby preserve the statutes. . . .

Though our decision does not "create a crime", it does, of course, enlarge the scope of two criminal statutes. We recognize that a court should be reluctant to expand criminal statutes, due to the danger of usurping the role of the Legislature, but in this case overriding policy concerns dictate our following such a course in light of the catastrophic effect that striking down the statutes and thus creating a hiatus would have. . . .

STUDY QUESTIONS

1. What possible justifications for the marital rape exemption did the court identify? Why did the court find these justifications inadequate?
2. Did the court consider the question of whether men can be rape victims? Do you believe men can be raped? By women or only by other men? Do men who are victims of homosexual rape suffer the same sort of harm women rape victims suffer? Why? Why not? Do men who are raped by women? Why? Why not?
3. How did the court distinguish the *Michael M.* case? Do you find the distinction convincing?
4. Some feminists see the traditional treatment of rape as distorting and overemphasizing women's sexuality. They advocate that rape be treated as a form of assault, rather than a separate crime. What arguments do you see for and against such a course?

In invalidating New York's marital rape exemption, the *Liberta* court rejected the notion that a woman expresses her consent to sexual relations with her husband whenever he wishes simply by marrying him. Imposing criminal liability on someone who justifies his unwanted sexual acts by such "consent" does not seem unfair since consent of this sort is obviously a fiction. Determining more generally when it is fair to impose a criminal liability for nonconsensual sexual relations, however, is not such an easy matter. Should a perpetrator be held criminally responsible for his sexual acts whenever the other party fails to express consent clearly? When the other party's words or conduct should have led the perpetrator to understand that there was no consent? Should liability be imposed only when the perpetrator actually knew that the acts were unwanted?

Traditional rape laws have avoided this problem by defining rape as sexual intercourse without consent but then equating "without consent" with the use or threat of physical force. Many jurisdictions have continued this approach, though they have expanded the definition of force to include mental and economic coercion. A few jurisdictions have actually redefined lack of consent to mean the absence of words or conduct expressing freely given agreement. One effect of such provisions is to shift the focus at trial from the extent of the victim's resistance to the meaning to be accorded her conduct. Another may be to permit convictions where the other party made no verbal or physical response—whether positive or negative.

One possible challenge to a statute that redefines consent in this way is that it impermissibly criminalizes consensual sexual relations since consenting parties do not always show their consent through words or acts. The following case reveals one court's response to this argument.

State v. Lederer

Court of Appeals of Wisconsin, 1980.
99 Wis.2d 430, 299 N.W.2d 457.

CANNON, Judge.

Defendant was convicted of third degree sexual assault contrary to sec. 940.225(3), Stats. Defendant challenges: the constitutionality of the consent definition as well as the sufficiency of evidence presented to establish that the victim had not consented. . . We find no error and affirm.

On July 11, 1978, defendant telephoned the prosecutrix at her residence. At the suggestion of the defendant, the prosecutrix agreed to inspect a residence for rental purposes. The prosecutrix met the defendant at a service station where she was dropped off by her roommate. Before leaving with the defendant, the prosecutrix took down the license number of defendant's van and gave it to her roommate. The prosecutrix got into defendant's van, and they drove to an unfurnished home in River Hills.

At the home, defendant began to disrobe the prosecutrix. The prosecutrix objected and pushed defendant's hand away. The defendant allegedly told her that it would be worse if she fought. She permitted the defendant to disrobe her. Defendant performed an act of sexual intercourse, despite the verbal protestations of the prosecutrix. Defendant fell asleep on top of the prosecutrix. When defendant awoke in the early hours of July 12, 1978, defendant performed a second act of sexual intercourse. Defendant again fell asleep with his arm and part of his body across the prosecutrix. A third act of intercourse was performed when defendant awoke, as well as an act of fellatio. Defendant then took several photographs of the prosecutrix in the nude. Acts of sexual intercourse and fellatio were again performed. Defendant then drove the prosecutrix home.

At trial, testimony was produced regarding the photographs of the prosecutrix in the nude found at the residence. Testimony was produced regarding the bedding found at the residence and the tests performed for saliva, blood and semen on the bedding. Testimony was also presented about a medical report prepared at Family Hospital. The trial court denied defendant's motion to dismiss at the close of the state's case. The defense rested without calling any witnesses. Judgment on the guilty verdict was entered October 12, 1979. . . .

. . . Defendant contends that application of the definition of consent contained in sec. 940.225(4) could subject an individual to punishment for engaging in consensual sexual activities where no testimony was produced regarding acts or words which evidenced freely given consent. We do not agree. . . .

The plain terms of sec. 940.225(3), Stats. define third degree sexual assault as sexual intercourse *without consent*. Consent is defined by sec. 940.225(4), as "words or overt actions by a person who is competent to give informed consent indicating a freely given agreement to have sexual intercourse or sexual contact." . . .

We reject defendant's contention that a defendant could be convicted under sec. 940.225(3), Stats., for engaging in consensual sexual relations. The plain terms of the statute require that the state must prove that the act of sexual intercourse must be without consent. In *Gates v. State* this court stated that for conviction for second degree sexual assault "[t]he State must introduce evidence that there was no consent, and this evidence must be sufficient to convince the jury beyond a reasonable doubt." Our supreme court has also determined that "[t]he plain wording of the statutory definition of consent demonstrates that failure to resist is not consent . . ." *State v. Clark.* We hold that these definitions of consent apply equally well to third degree sexual assault. In so defining consent the legislature has relieved the state of the burden of proving that the victim resisted in order to establish that the act was nonconsensual.

Defendant contends that two parties may enter into consensual sexual relations without

manifesting freely given consent through words or acts. We reject this contention as we know of no other means of communicating consent. . . .

. . . In reviewing a challenge to the sufficiency of the evidence "the question is whether the evidence, considered most favorably to the state, is 'so insufficient in probative value and force that it can be said as a matter of law that no trier of facts acting reasonably could be convinced to that degree of certitude which the law defines as beyond a reasonable doubt.' " *State v. Clark.*

The record discloses that the prosecutrix objected when the defendant initially disrobed her and continued to object throughout the night when defendant performed the various acts of sexual intercourse. The record further discloses that the prosecutrix testified that when asked to open her mouth prior to the performance of the act of fellatio she did not, but instead turned her head away and only complied when the defendant took her head in his hands. These actions on the part of the prosecutrix can hardly be said to be manifestations of consent, particularly when viewed together with the threat of the defendant that things would be worse if she did not comply. "No" means no, and precludes any finding that the prosecutrix consented to any of the sexual acts performed during the night. . . .

Affirmed

STUDY QUESTIONS

1. Under the applicable Wisconsin statute, what must the prosecution prove to obtain a valid conviction for sexual assault? Must it show resistance by the victim? Must it show that the victim expressed her lack of consent by words or conduct?

2. Do you think the defendant in this case actually understood that the prosecutrix had not consented to sexual intercourse and fellatio with him? Did the defendants in the other cases in this section?

3. Is there a risk under this law that men will be convicted of rape when they simply have not realized that the woman did not wish to have sexual intercourse? Does that strike you

as unfair? As a practical matter, are prosecutors likely to proceed in such cases? Are women likely to complain about rape in these circumstances?

&

A recent New Jersey Supreme Court decision, *State of New Jersey In the Interest of M.T.S.*, 609 A.2d 1266 (1992), makes even clearer that sexual intercourse without affirmative consent is rape. The case involved two teenagers who were kissing and petting. When the young woman fell asleep, the young man penetrated her. She woke and asked him to stop, which he did. In ruling that no force is required, the Court spelled out the prosecutor's burden of proof.

> . . . In short, in order to convict under the sexual assault statute in cases such as these, the State must prove beyond a reasonable doubt that there was sexual penetration and that it was accomplished without the affirmative and freely-given permission of the alleged victim. . . . [S]uch proof can be based on evidence of conduct or words in light of surrounding circumstances and must demonstrate beyond a reasonable double that a reasonable person would not have believed that there was affirmative and freely-given permission. If there is evidence to suggest that the defendant reasonably believed that such permission had been given, the State must demonstrate either that defendant did not actually believe that affirmative permission had been freely-given or that such a belief was unreasonable under all of the circumstances. Thus, the State bears the burden of proof throughout the case.
> Id. *at 1278*

While the *M.T.S.* case is part of an important new trend, its consequences may be mixed. On the one hand, the court's "no means no" approach seems to place a key limit on males' historical prerogatives. On the other hand, since the approach puts both the defendant's actual belief that the necessary affirmative permission was given under the circumstances and the reasonableness of any such belief in issue, the approach may once again make relevant evidence regarding the complainant's past sexual conduct.

In reaching the landmark *M.T.S.* decision, the court made plain it was well aware of today's concern over forced sexual intercourse between acquaintances. Although the concern is recent, the prevalence of nonstranger rapes has been known for some time. In the early 1980s, for example, more than half of all rapes were committed by male relatives, current or former husbands, boyfriends, or lovers. Moreover, as Table 9.1 shows, nonstranger rapes are accounting for a greater and greater share of the overall rates of sexual assault.

Whether the figures reflect a greater incidence or a greater sensitivity to the problem, as some contend, the concern about "date rape" or "acquaintance rape" has prompted a variety of responses. For example, the Higher Education Reauthorization Act of 1992 requires universities receiving federal support to develop programs aimed at the prevention of sexual offenses and procedures to be followed once such offenses have occurred.

Determining whether or not there was consent may be a serious problem when the man and the woman are acquainted. Under the *M.T.S.* standard, the consent need not always be in words. Thus, a key challenge for decision makers will be to determine when a reasonable person would in fact have believed that there was affirmative and freely-given permission. Just what should be considered a reasonable mistake as to the giving of permission is the subject of the next selection.

TABLE 9.1. Rape rates per 1,000 population

Year	Stranger	Nonstranger	Total
1973	.7	.3	.9
1974	.7	.3	1.0
1975	.6	.3	.9
1976	.6	.3	.8
1977	.6	.3	.9
1978	.6	.3	1.0
1979	.7	.4	1.1
1980	.7	.3	.9
1981	.6	.4	1.0
1982	.5	.3	.8
1983	.5	.3	.8
1984	.5	.4	.9
1985	.4	.3	.7
1986	.3	.3	.7
1987	.4	.3	.8
1988	.3	.3	.6
1989	.4	.2	.7
1990	.3	.4	.6
1991	.4	.4	.8

SOURCE: *George C. Thomas, III. "A Critique of the Anti-Pornography Syllogism." 52 Maryland Law Review 701, 706 (1993).*

Date Rape, Social Convention, and Reasonable Mistakes

Douglas N. Husak and George Thomas.
11 *Law and Philosophy* 95 (1992).
Pp. 102–26.

. . . Suppose that a man is challenged to explain how he came to believe that a woman consented to sex who in fact did consent. Not just any kind of explanation would indicate that his belief is reasonable. What kind of explanation will suffice?

Perhaps progress in answering this question can be made by thinking about situations other than those involving sex in which people formulate beliefs about the presence or absence of consent. A cab driver believes that someone who enters his

Reprinted by permission of Kluwer Academic Publishers.

taxi agrees to pay for a ride after the passenger says simply, "Take me to the airport". A waiter believes that someone who sits in his restaurant agrees to pay for food after the customer says simply, "I'll have the chicken sandwich". How do the cab driver and waiter come to have these beliefs, and what answers to this question indicate that their beliefs are reasonable? . . .

The empirical data on which the answers to these questions depend are data about social conventions. A social convention is a societal "norm which there is some presumption that one ought to conform to". It is clear that the taxi driver would appeal to a convention in explaining why he believes that a passenger expresses his consent to pay for a ride simply by entering a taxi and being taken to the destination he requests. If the driver is pressed about why he has this belief, he will probably say something like: "That's just the way things are. That's how passengers express their agreement to pay. I've been driving for years, and I know how these things are done around here". In other words, his answer cites a social convention. This social convention helps to establish the reasonableness of his belief. . . .

If reasonableness is partly dependent on convention in the way we have suggested, it is crucial to understand the convention by which women express their agreements to sexual relations. Since we will refer to this particular social convention often, it will be convenient to give it a name. We will call it convention "wcs", to stand for "women's consent to have sex". . . .

We begin with more general questions about the social conventions involving courtship. Do women give nonexplicit encouragement to men in courtship settings not involving sexual intercourse? If so, how is this encouragement communicated, and what is the risk that a man will make a mistake of fact about whether he has been encouraged? Later we will proceed to the more narrow question of whether women give nonexplicit consent to sex and the attendant risks of mistake. By "nonexplicit", we mean both nonverbal and verbally indirect conduct.

No one should be surprised that the empirical evidence confirms that women give nonexplicit consent to such courtship rituals as whether they want to be approached by a particular man. Monica Moore and Diana Butler documented fifty-two "nonverbal solicitation behaviors" that women use in "social contexts such as singles' bars and the university snack bar". These behaviors included "glancing, primping, smiling, laughing, nodding, kissing, requesting aid, touching, and caressing". . . .

Whether women engage in nonexplicit courtship behaviors with the conscious purpose of getting men to approach them is not relevant for our purposes. What matters is that women in fact engage in these behaviors, and that men typically respond in a way women find appropriate. When the male response is appropriate, no mistake has been made, and the social interaction is wholly consensual. But the possibility of mistake is always present. The women judged "approachable" in the Moore and Butler study did not accept all male invitations. Sometimes a man correctly perceived that the woman was interested in an invitation, but incorrectly perceived that she was interested in an invitation from him.

If women engage in nonverbal solicitation behaviors to induce men to invite them to dance in singles bars, they might use similar tactics to signal their interest in having sex. Reasonable misreadings of these behaviors could occur. Timothy Perper and David Weis concluded that women frequently exhibit what they call "proceptive" behaviors, that is, active behaviors designed to elicit an offer to have sex from a particular man. In the Perper and Weis study, 87.2% of the women described proceptive behaviors when asked how they would "influence" a man to have sex with them for the first time. The remaining subjects in the study did not describe proceptive behaviors, but said, in one way or another, that they would wait for a man to initiate sex "naturally". . . .

Again, it is useful to compare the situation in which the man mistakes the meaning of the woman's behavior with the situation in which he correctly perceives that she is indirectly signalling her consent to have sex. Assume that M observes several of the nonexplicit proceptive strategies from his date, F, which culminate in an invitation to her apartment. If M initiates a physical advance, as by putting his arm around F, she may respond in a nonexplicit manner; for example, she may "snuggle up to the man". M may escalate his physical advance, and F may meet each successive escalation with further encouraging, proceptive behaviors. In this way, M and F can engage in consensual sex without either explicitly signifying consent. We will call this Outcome 1.

On the other hand, if M is mistaken, and F does not want to engage in sex, she is likely to engage in what Perper and Weis call a "rejection strategy". One option, of course, is for the woman to engage in explicit, blunt rejection behaviors that will escalate if the man does not desist. However, most of the women in the Perper and Weis study described what the researchers called an "incomplete rejection" strategy. In this strategy, the woman "wishes not to terminate the relationship with the man but wants to avoid further sexual involvement with the man at this time". If F wishes the relationship to continue, she may engage in behaviors that look somewhat similar to proceptive behaviors—for example, permitting the man to hug and kiss her but not responding "in a really warm way". Perper and Weis tentatively suggest that "not all men could distinguish seduction and incomplete rejection strategies".

If the man misunderstands the significance of the incomplete rejection strategy, he may continue to make advances. But surely (common sense suggests that) under normal circumstances a woman who is faced with imminent sexual intercourse against her will should have no difficulty delivering an explicit, unambiguous "no". If so, virtually all incomplete rejection strategies would eventually escalate into blunt, explicit rejections (Outcome 2). Again, however, reality is more complex than ideology. Assuming that M does not desist in his efforts to have sex with F, two other categories of possible outcomes remain. F may escalate her incomplete rejection strategy but stop short of saying "no" or physically resisting (Outcome 3). Or F may decide to have sex with M as a way of maintaining the relationship (Outcome 4).

Outcome 4 raises the issue of the significance of consent in the context of a rape prosecution. As we have indicated, the law regards nonconsent as a necessary condition for the commission of rape. Some recent literature, however, does not regard the presence or absence of consent as the crucial variable to distinguish rape from noncriminal sex. According to this view, rape should be understood as unwanted sex. Interpreting rape as unwanted rather than as nonconsensual sex will (perhaps self-consciously) result in an exponential increase in the incidence of rape. One commentator has concluded that the so-called "epidemic" of rape is "phantom" partly because female respondents to surveys were counted as victims of rape if they indicated that they had engaged in sex when they did not want to do so.

The following example illustrates the difference between nonconsensual and unwanted sex. Suppose that M and F are alone after their third date. M attempts to initiate sex; F declines; M stops. M explains to F that he hopes to continue to date her, but he regards sexual intimacy as an essential part of a satisfactory relationship. He indicates that he is unwilling to go on future dates unless she acquiesces to his sexual demands. Prior to M's ultimatum, F believed that the following three alternatives were viable:

1. They would continue to date, without having sex.
2. They would continue to date, while having sex.

3. They would not continue to date.

Suppose that F prefers (1) to (2) or (3) but believes that M has foreclosed option (1). She must now choose between (2) and (3). She may choose (3) and tell M that she is unwilling to date him on his terms. But if she chooses (2), there is a sense in which she has consented to unwanted sex. Since (2) represents her volition, she has consented to sex. But there is a sense in which she does not really want sex, because (1) continues to be her first choice.

It is likely that many sex acts fall in the "consensual but unwanted" category. For one reason or another, many women (as well as men) agree to unwanted sex. . . .

Even if some competing account of volition is correct, and F does not act volitionally in the above scenario, it would seem that M's belief to the contrary is reasonable. A long tradition holds that choices made in the absence of a threat of harm are voluntary. So, in Outcome 4, either F consented, or M made a reasonable mistake about her consent. In either case, M would not be liable for rape.

The issue is more complex in Outcome 3 (F escalates her incomplete rejection strategy but never to the point of objecting or physically resisting). To differentiate this Outcome from Outcomes 2 and 4, it is necessary to assume that F does not decide to have sex with M, but never physically resists or objects. She becomes, in effect, a passive participant in an activity to which (we have presupposed) she has not consented. . . .

As we have indicated, the empirical evidence suggests that the prevailing convention wcs is that women do not explicitly ask for sex when they want it. Indeed, part of convention wcs may still manifest residues of the Victorian ideology that viewed women as passionless, passive participants in the sex act. If this convention describes a sufficiently large number of women, M's mistake in a particular case might be reasonable. Given the lack of empirical research in this area, we believe that Outcome 3 presents a series of problems that are too complex to permit a generalized judgment. . . . Contrast Outcome 3 with Outcome 1—the scenario in which M and F engage in consensual sex without expressing explicit consent. In Outcome

1, F signalled her interest in sex by responding to M's advances. But to distinguish an affirmative response from passive participation involves a subtle matter of degree about which mistakes are possible.

Of course, Outcome 2—when F follows an incomplete rejection strategy by physically resisting or by saying no in an unambiguous manner—is the most unlikely Outcome in which a mistake could be reasonable. Before examining the empirical evidence, it seemed to us that there could be little question about the legal consequences here. How can it be possible for M to make a reasonable mistake about F's consent when she says "no" or actively resists? The answer, of course, is that it is not impossible for the social convention wcs to interpret no as yes when it comes on the heels of an incomplete rejection strategy. The empirical evidence offers some support for this reading of wcs. In a 1988 study, 39% of Texas female college undergraduates reported that had said "no" when they wanted to have sex. And 60.8% of the sexually experienced women in this study stated that they had said "no" when they intended to have sex. From these data, Abbey concluded: "It is easy to see how a man who has previously turned a 'no' into a 'yes' might force sexual intercourse on a date who says 'no' and means it".

Why would so many women say no when they wanted to have sex? Ninety percent of the women in the Texas study who fit this category said that the fear of appearing promiscuous was at least somewhat important in explaining their behavior. Indeed, compared to other factors such as fear of sexually transmitted diseases and pregnancy, fear of appearing promiscuous explained far more of the variance between women who had used this strategy and those who had not.

The discussion to this point has paid insufficient attention to the almost infinite complexity of the factual settings that produce an Outcome 2. A single physical rejection (for example, F moves M's hand from her leg) following hours of intense foreplay obviously presents a very different picture of nonconsent than repeated physical and verbal rejections, delivered in an emotional and frightened manner. At some point along this spectrum, it is no longer reasonable for M to think that F has consented.

The reason that M's mistake-of-fact defense fails at this point is not that the word no has a magic, transcendental quality. Rather, M's defense becomes unreasonable because the social convention is that a certain pattern of linguistic and nonlinguistic behavior could not reasonably be understood to mean anything other than no. The social convention wcs provides the vehicle through which M interprets the words or actions of F. Until we more fully understand the social convention about consent to have sex, any judgment about the reasonableness of a mistake about consent is fragile.

STUDY QUESTIONS

1. Why would the authors—and the New Jersey court—acquit a defendant of rape when the alleged victim at times tried to indicate she did not want to have intercourse? How does this standard for rape cases compare to that in hostile environment sexual harassment cases (see Chapter 5)?

2. Do you believe that social conventions would change if the law did not acquit men for reasonable misunderstandings? Would it be fair to find them guilty in such circumstances?

A number of feminists disagree with Husak and Thomas's position, arguing that the law should hold men responsible for their failure to ascertain the woman's desires.

Explicit protest to the contrary aside, the conventions of dating confer on it its social meaning, and this social meaning implies a relationship which is more like friendship than the cutthroat competition of opposing teams. As such, it requires that we do more than stand on our rights with regard to each other. As long as we are operating under the auspices of a dating relationship, it requires that we behave in the mode of friendship and trust. But if a date is more like a friendship than a business contract, then clearly respect for the dialectics of desire is incompatible with the sort of sexual pressure that is inclined to end in date rape. And clearly, also, a conquest mentality which exploits a situation of trust and respect for purely selfish ends is morally pernicious. Failure to respect the dialectics of desire when operating under the auspices of friendship and trust is to act in flagrant disregard of the moral requirement to avoid manipulative, coercive, and exploitive behaviour. Respect for the dialectics of desire is *prima facie* inconsistent with the satisfaction of one person at the expense of the other. The proper end of friendship means that we must take a communicative approach to discovering the ends of the other, and this entails that we respect the dialectics of desire.

But now that we know what communicative sexuality is, and that it is morally required, and that it is the only feasible means to mutual sexual enjoyment, why not take this model as the norm of what is reasonable in sexual interaction. The evidence of sexologists strongly indicates that women whose partners are aggressively uncommunicative have little chance of experiencing sexual pleasure. But it is not reasonable for women to consent to what they have little chance of enjoying. Hence it is not reasonable for women to consent to aggressive noncommunicative sex. Nor can we reasonably suppose that women have consented to sexual encounters which we know and they know they do not find enjoyable. With the communicative model as the norm, aggressive contractual model should strike us as a model of deviant sexuality, and sexual encounters patterned on that model should strike us as encounters to which *prima facie* no one would reasonably agree. But if acquiescence to an encounter counts as consent only if the acquiescence is reasonable, something to which a reasonable person, in full possession of knowledge relevant to the encounter, would agree, then acquiescence to aggressive noncommunicative sex is not reasonable. Hence, acquiescence under such conditions should not count as a consent.

Lois Pineau. "Date Rape: A Feminist Analysis." 8 Law and Philosophy *217, 238–239 (1989).*

In short, feminists like Pineau submit that men are obligated to attempt "communicative" sex and that if they are not sure what the signals they get mean, they simply should not go ahead. Moreover, because these feminists believe that legal rules can be important in changing social conventions, they want to hold men accountable legally.

As a result of the antirape movement of the 1970s, we have come to recognize the impact rape has had throughout the centuries. Rape has traumatized and confined women, depriving them of their physical integrity and their ability to interact with men without being subject to sexual coercion. Particularly when women have deviated from the behavior expected of "good girls," they have been blamed for their own victimization, and their attackers have been forgiven. The legal system's treatment of rape has compounded this effect. The process of reforming the law and legal institutions to eliminate this secondary, reinforcing effect is well underway. As the *McLean, Rincon-Pineda,* and *Liberta* decisions demonstrate, significant reforms of the traditional rape laws have come from the judicial branch. The legislative branch, however, has been equally, if not more, instrumental in achieving rape law reform. By 1980, all states had considered, and most had passed, some form of rape reform legislation.

Current resources suggest the law has changed considerably since the movement for rape reform began. As noted, forty nine states plus the federal system have adopted some form of rape shield provision that rejects the automatic admissibility of proof of unchastity. By 1981, every state except Nebraska had abandoned the requirement of specific corroboration in rape prosecutions. Approximately half of the states have eliminated the special cautionary instruction. As of 1990, marital rape was a crime without exceptions in sixteen states and with exceptions in twenty-six, leaving eight states where husbands could not be prosecuted for the rape of their wives. Four states have adopted the *Lederer-M.T.S.* standard defining rape as the absence of freely given affirmative permission.

The Need for Different Approaches

What has been the effect of these reforms? It is always difficult to measure the effect of legal changes and especially difficult when the changes themselves change. However, the preliminary study of Jeanne Marsh, Alison Geist, and Nathan Caplan, in *Rape and the Limits of Law Reform* (Boston: Auburn House, 1982, pp. 49–56), that looked at Michigan's comprehensive rape reform bill enacted in 1974 is of some interest. A model for reform efforts of other states, the Michigan law substitutes for the traditional crime of rape four degrees of sexual misconduct, ranging from sexual penetration, broadly defined, to sexual contact. It prohibits spousal rape where the couple lives apart and one partner has filed for separate maintenance. It also prohibits the use of any evidence relating to the victim's prior sexual conduct with anyone other than the defendant. The impact of this law was studied using time series analysis of crime statistics for the period 1972 to 1978 and interviews with criminal justice officials and rape crisis counselors. The research had surprising results. Law reformers had expected that there would be resistance to implementing the statute and that it would, therefore, have little effect on reporting, arrest, and conviction rates. They also expected that the visibility of the law reform effort and the redefinition of the statute would change the attitudes of those in the criminal justice system regarding the crime and the role of women in society. Researchers found instead that conviction rates have gone up for forcible rape but that attitudes have not changed. Thus, they report that although victims are more frequently able to pursue their cases without derisive and discourteous treatment within the criminal justice system, criminal justice officials continue to be skeptical of women reporting sexual assaults and to pursue more readily the cases of "worthy" victims.

As Table 9.1 suggests, despite the decrease in reported rapes by strangers, legal reforms appear to have done little to bring down the high incidence of acquaintance rape. For example, a survey described by Mary Koss and several colleagues in "The Scope of Rape: Incidence and Prevalence of Sexual Aggression and Victimization in a National Sample of Higher Education Students," 55 *Journal of Consulting and Clinical Psychology* 162 (1987), found that a shocking 27.5 percent of college women reported experiencing rape and 7.7 percent of college men reported perpetrating at least one rape or attempted rape since the age of fourteen. While such figures are substantially higher than official estimates, the official figures are believed to underestimate the incidence of rape in the population as a whole.

More recent critiques have noted problems with the police, prosecutors, judges, and juries. For example, Susan Estrich in her book, *Real Rape* (Cambridge: Harvard University Press, 1987), tells numerous stories of women mistreated when they dared to complain about rape even under the new laws. She is particularly concerned about the pre-*M.T.S.* standard for consent, arguing once again that women are blamed for leading men on. Whether the "new trend" in interpreting the consent standard will lead to real changes or simply a replication of existing problems is too early to tell. Critics also point to the inequities of the criminal system and stress the need to change societal attitudes about rape. The call is to recognize the harm that is being done to women and to find ways of empowering them.

To avoid the frustrations and humiliations of criminal law system and to achieve these ends generally, rape victims have been encouraged to bring civil damage suits against their assailants. One way that victims may recover for the injuries their assailants cause them is by suing for common law torts, such as assault.

The Violence Against Women Act, pending in Congress, may provide another route. Under Title III of the act, victims of rape and other sexual assaults will be able to recover for federal civil rights violations by showing they were harmed because of their sex. The act will provide remedies for all sorts of violence against women—be it rape, domestic violence, or other assaults—and a way to make clear it happens because they are women. Just one of the statistics gathered by the Senate Judiciary Committee indicates the magnitude of the violence and the interconnections between the problems. In the words of Committee Chair Senator Joseph Biden, figures gathered by the committee reveal "a total of at least *1.1 million* assaults, aggravated assaults, murders, and rapes against women committed in the home and reported to the police in 1991." Moreover, as he noted, "unreported crimes may be more than three times this total." Majority Staff of the Senate Judiciary Committee, *Violence against Women: A Week in the Life of America*, October 1992, p. ii.

The bill's supporters have several goals. They seek to make clear that society will simply not tolerate the violence that women suffer. They seek recognition of the role gender plays in triggering the violence. Finally, they seek to give women control over the legal proceedings. The Senate Judiciary Committee Majority Staff explains the approach further.

Questions and Answers on the Civil Rights Remedy

Majority Staff of the Senate Judiciary Committee. February 1993.

. . . Crime and Civil Rights: How can a crime be a "civil rights" violation?

☐ The two categories—"crime" and "civil rights"—are not mutually exclusive. A race-based attack is an attack and also a civil rights violation. Similarly, a gender-based attack is an attack and also a civil rights violation.

. . . What kind of cases would fall under Title III?

The short answer is: cases about equality. In practice, however, the circumstances will determine whether the case qualifies as a "gender-motivated" crime. Here are some cases the bill may cover:

☐ A woman, Jane Doe, is promoted at work. Joe, who also applied for the job, tells his coworkers that he thinks Jane got the job "only because she is a woman." Joe starts to make harassing phone calls to Jane at home, telling her he intends to expose the company's biased policies. Two weeks later, as Jane is walking down the street, Joe assaults her, screaming that she is getting what she "deserves" for seeking a promotion.

☐ The popular head of a major business organization, Susan Leader, receives threatening letters and phone calls from a man claiming that he intends to end the women's movement by violence. Two weeks later, as Susan is leaving a political function for women in business, the man approaches her and stabs her.

☐ A man, Harry Criminal, enters a department store carrying a gun. He picks out the women in the store, and demands that they perform sexual acts. The ten men are left standing unharmed. Harry shouts anti-woman epithets as these acts take place.

. . . Mechanics: Who can sue under this remedy? And who do they sue?

☐ A victim of gender-based crime may sue. The statute is gender neutral, so that it applies to both men and women. The conduct cannot be a minor dispute, however. It must be a crime of violence, typically a felony.

. . . Proving Gender Bias: How do you prove that an attack is "gender-motivated"?

☐ The same way the victim of a race-based attack proves the attack was racially-motivated. Often, the key is the circumstances surrounding the attack. For example, judges and juries can tell the difference between an everyday assault and a case where a gang of white kids beat up a black kid [while] shouting racial slurs. Courts can do the same for gender-motivated crimes.

. . . Why do we need a civil rights remedy?
There are 3 reasons:

A. *State law remedies have not proven adequate to protect women:*

☐ For example, our criminal laws on rape often discriminate—some states still do not criminalize rape if the rapist is married to the victim and over half the states still impose limits on marital or date rape prosecutions that do not apply to other crimes. . . .

☐ Similarly, criminal justice systems often treat "domestic violence" as a second-class crime—police do not arrest, prosecutors do not prosecute, and courts do not sentence spouse abusers as they would if the crime happened on the street corner.

B. *This civil rights remedy protects against discrimination, not assault.*

☐ The purpose of this remedy is not to prevent all crimes against women; the purpose is to identify that class of crimes that are based on gender and to target those crimes.

☐ Existing state law does not protect against discrimination; it protects against physical invasion.

C. *This civil rights remedy, unlike state criminal laws, puts the judicial system in the hands of the victim.*

☐ State criminal laws do not provide the victim with compensation, nor do they allow the victim to call her assailant to the stand to account for his behavior (in a criminal case, the defendant may remain silent). A civil rights remedy does.

. . . How would a civil rights remedy solve this problem, if it only covers "gender-motivated" crime?

Title III does not attempt to solve all the problems in the state criminal justice systems. However, existing problems show why federal courts are a better place for this new remedy to be enforced. If States have a poor track record in protecting women, there is little reason to believe that should be the "front line" of attack against violently expressed prejudice against women. . . .

. . . Compensatory Purpose: What is the purpose of allowing such a remedy against assailants who are unlikely to have any money to compensate the victim?

☐ It is a myth that those who commit this kind of crime are never going to be able to pay a judgment. Sex offenders, for example, come from a variety of economic backgrounds and include doctors, lawyers, and dentists.

☐ But even if we now knew that no person violating this statute could ever compensate a victim, the civil rights remedy would still be useful. Victims have told us that they want more legal tools in their power to call assailants to account.

☐ As one survivor explained to the Committee, even though she will never see any part of a 70 million dollar judgment, she felt that the system *validated her* by that award in a civil case.

. . . Constitutional Legitimacy: Does Congress have the constitutional power to create such a

"civil rights" remedy for one person against another private person?

☐ Yes. Congress's power is firmly based in the commerce clause and section 5 of the Fourteenth Amendment. The Judiciary Committee held a hearing on this question affirming Title III's constitutionality.

Other critics suggest there may be limitations to current legal approaches, including the Violence Against Women Act's civil rights approach. The conviction of world champion prizefighter Mike Tyson and the acquittal of William Kennedy Smith have brought to mind the history of discriminatory prosecutions and the continuing potential for racial discrimination. Focusing on the criminal context, attorney Jennifer Wriggins has pointed out that, "given existing disparities in punishments between Whites and Blacks an across-the-board increase would simply reproduce these inequalities." Such disparities, she suggests, implicitly indicate that men are being punished on racial grounds, not for committing rape. To press for use of the criminal law would both suggest that women accept a too male-oriented definition of sexual abuse and validate a criminal law system that has radical shortcomings in terms of treatments. See Jennifer Wriggins, "Rape, Racism and the Law," 6 *Harvard Women's Law Journal* 103 (1983). Law professor Kimberlé Crenshaw expresses related concerns.

Violence Against Women: Forging a Legal Response

Kimberlè Crenshaw.
Address to the National Organization for Women
Legal Defense and Education Fund Conference,
New York, October 23, 1992.

Reprinted by permission of Kimberlè Crenshaw.

Within the Black community, the relationship between sexual violence and racism is usually represented through images of Black men being falsely accused of the rape of white women. For example, the Scottsboro Boys, Emmett Till or other men in our community who have been unfairly and unjustly lynched serve to symbolize the subordinating interaction of racism and sexual violence. Yet the names and the experiences of Black women whose bodies also bore the signs of sexualized racial subordination are essentially lost to history. This marginalization of Black women's experiences of sexual violence has consequences even today. Consider the Clarence Thomas hearings; while Thomas was able to mobilize the Black community by throwing down the lynching card, Anita Hill—had she wanted to play that game—could only draw on some hazy, vague images of Black women's sexual victimization.

The same tendency to center the Black male/white female dyad is apparent in the way sexual violence and race is currently read, not only within the Black community but with the society-at-large. For example, it is still the case, as studies have told us, that the disposition of defendants in rape trials is largely determined by the race of the defendant and the race of the victim. Black men who rape white women tend to receive longer sentences than any other racial dyad. This tends to be articulated in terms of discrimination against Black men, which, in fact, it is. Yet, the fact that Black men are punished disproportionately depending on the race of the victim—when the victim is white they're punished more, when the victim is Black they're punished less—is as much discrimination against Black female victims as it is discrimination against Black men. In a recent study in Dallas it was shown that the average sentence given to rapists of African American women was 2 years, while the average sentence given to rapists of white women was 10 years.

The reason that this disproportionality is seldom understood as racial discrimination against Black women is that racism is usually seen as relationships between different groups of men with respect to something else—property, resources or, in the case of sexual assault—women. It is racist, then, that Black men are punished more readily than white men when victims are white. Yet the fact that white women are more likely to see their rapists punished than Black women is not understood as racist, especially when the assailant is Black. So as long as racism is primarily seen as a male-male phenomenon, the racial stratification of women and the consequences for Black rape victims will not be understood as another moment of racism, either within society at large or within the Black community.

Some of these dynamics are apparent in the polarization over the Tyson/Washington rape trial. Many white feminists could not quite understand why there was so much support for Mike Tyson and so little support for Desiree Washington. One of the reasons why there was so little support for Desiree Washington was that the historical experience of lynching has created a ready response that is skeptical toward rape allegations and protective of Black defendants, particularly accomplished ones. The basic problem again is that as long as there are these statistics that suggest that race does play a role in rape adjudication, the reaction is going to be one that is going to be largely protective of those who are most readily recognized as racism's victims. In the case of sexual violence, it's Black men.

Now what kind of feminist reaction to this problem is appropriate? One factor that contributed to the polarization surrounding the Tyson case was the fact that many feminists rejoiced to a certain extent when Mike Tyson was convicted. There were op-ed pieces, for example, that characterized the conviction of Mike Tyson as vindication for what had happened to Patri-

cia Bowman. This kind of uncritical celebration of something that was very painful for the Black community reinforces the tendency to see rape primarily as a white women's issue rather than an issue women across the board have to deal with. Of course I think that the use of race to deny the reality of rape in communities of color is an unfortunate, inaccurate, and emotionally damaging kind of political rhetoric. But I do believe that feminists need to take the concerns that fuel this rhetoric seriously in attempts to find ways to mobilize women of all races around this problem and to create a more cohesive movement.

The close connection between rape and lynching in this country reveals then that race exists just under the surface of rape. Historian Jacqueline Dowd Hall has written about how the history of lynching and the repression of Black male sexuality is closely linked to the repression of white female sexuality. Because contemporary events suggest that those links still exist, it behooves us to acknowledge and try to counter them.

Let me offer two recent examples; the cases of the Central Park jogger and Charles Stewart. We all know that what happened to the investment banker was a heinous crime, one that rightfully was condemned throughout society. Yet, I think many of us also have a hunch that part of the reaction to it, as exemplified by the full page ad taken out by Donald Trump calling for the death penalty for rapists, was as much a reaction to the particular race of the parties as to the actual rape itself. I think it would strain our imagination to think that Trump, or for that matter other men in his class, would have reacted in the same way had that investment banker been, let's say, a Black social service worker. We know this also for a fact: At least 28 other women were raped that week, and most of them women of color. One Black woman was gang raped and thrown down an elevator shaft and left to die in Brooklyn. Yet she received no outpouring of public concern. I urge you to also think about the Charles Stewart case. Consider how easy it was for Charles Stewart to divert attention from his own savagery by displacing the act onto those from whom savagery is expected, Black men.

Both of these events tell us how race still shapes the way violence in perceived in our society. It tells us first that certain victims count more than others and that certain assailants are feared more than others.

To the extent that prosecutors' choices are influenced by these very factors, not only Black women and Black men, but also the majority of white women, will be discriminated against in the distribution of resources in the criminal justice system. Prosecutors are political animals, and being rational actors that they are, they will no doubt make choices based on crimes that are easier to prosecute and which, depending on the likelihood of success, will reap most benefits. If attitudes remain that certain victims are truer victims because they've been abused by those who fit the stereotype of the threat, then the rest of us will be marginalized. An effective mobilization against violence, one that then does not reproduce racial cleavages and that empowers women across the board, cannot be silent on the question of racism, but must directly acknowledge and grapple with it. And by grappling with it, I don't mean simply repeating ad naseum that rape happens to all women, regardless of color. . .

Let me give you an example of how our failure to actively name racism and address it can reproduce the marginalization of certain women. Many of you are familiar with the Violence Against Women Act. Much of the testimony supporting the VAW Act was based on the idea that violence is experienced across all races and across all classes, which is of course true. This testimony was meant to displace the stereotyped victim of domestic violence, which is usually imagined to be a poor woman or a woman of color. But the problem with stating that women of all races and classes confront domestic violence is that the reasons why domestic violence was not seen as an important problem as long as it was imagined to be a problem of the "other" never gets addressed. As a consequence then, the message heard by our white male senators is that we've got to do something about this problem now—it isn't just a "them" problem, it is an "us" problem. In fact, in the introductory comments to the VAW Act, many of the sponsors seemed to imply as

much. In order to ensure that feminism reaches and incorporates the "other," that it reaches into communities where feminism is not yet taken seriously, we have to be willing to grapple with these questions of race.

Some feminists were also concerned about why, for example, many young African American women did not support Desiree Washington. There was an interesting newspaper article in the Washington Post. A woman was interviewing several Black women about their support or lack of support of Desiree Washington and they all repeated that Washington knew what she was getting into, that she shouldn't have gone up to his room. But as the reporter was interviewing these teenagers, they repeatedly told stories about the ways they had to confront threat of their own sexual abuse and the ways in which they were forced to look out for themselves. In fact, while the interview was going on, a couple of incidents actually happened where they had to negotiate their way around unwanted sexual aggression. One might ask how this contradiction can be. How can women, themselves threatened by sexual violence, fail to support a woman who was struggling to survive that very problem?

Unless women are given a way to step outside of the sexual system in which they are in, unless they are empowered to criticize and reject the gendered rules of conduct dictated by that system, they are going to be stuck trying to protect themselves by playing the game—no matter how subordinating—the best way they can. Indeed, the pressure to conform—and indeed, the threat of harm from not conforming—is so overwhelming that many women have yet to confront how their sexuality and freedom are forcefully constrained by the rules of the game. I believe that this is why many times women jurors are harder on rape victims than the men are. For some women, identifying too closely with a rape victim raises questions of their own vulnerability. Any way that that responsibility for what happened can be projected onto the rape victim is a way that they can protect themselves from the threat of sexual assault. You know this routine—if she hadn't been there, worn this or said that, the rape wouldn't have happened. Unless we can find ways of reaching out to women and showing them that it is the gender system that should be changed, not their behavior, then the only way in which women can imagine protecting themselves—both physically and emotionally—is to buy into the system, validating themselves as the good woman or the smart woman who is safe as opposed to the stupid woman or the sexually promiscuous woman who is raped.

As a last item, I think it's also important to recognize that when we try to reach across race and class issues to mobilize on questions of violence, it is important to recognize that gender bias is not the only violence that many women have to fear. There are any number of other kinds of violence that women have to deal with in their lives, and the singling out of gender as opposed to other sources of vulnerability strikes people who have to deal with other kinds of violence as once again the imposition of white middle-class concerns. We need a broader women's agenda, one that seeks to uncover the way violence shapes our lives across the board.

In conclusion, let me suggest a few approaches to develop boundary crossing strategies to address race. First, I think it's important to do more than to say all women experience violence. We have to be able to articulate the way different women experience violence in race and class terms. Second, I think it's important to propose and lobby for the equivalent of the Racial Justice Act. Some of you know that there was a proposal that was introduced in Congress to provide defendants who had been sentenced to death the ability to show that the penalty was distributed in a racially biased way. Where there were statistics to show that the penalty was distributed in a racially biased way, that sentence would be commuted to a life sentence. I think that if we are to politicize and to create a VAW Act, we should also try to find a way to make sure that the prosecutions will not be pursued in a racially biased way. Not only will it ensure that Black women and other women of color are equally protected, it will also make sure that white women who are not interracially raped will have the same access to resources as those rapes that fit the stereotype that the society seems to be most concerned about.

Thirdly, whenever a highly publicized interracial rape occurs, we should be sure to talk about the millions of interracial rapes that occur regularly. Moreover, we should show how women across the board are harmed by focusing on a particular kind of violent act rather than on all of the violent acts that occur on a day to day basis. Fourth, I think it's important to make sure that antiviolence resources are earmarked for communities of color, acknowledging that effective interventions will probably raise unique issues in different communities. And finally, we should remember that differences almost always matter, at some level, and consequently, we should always try to question and figure out how the differences are playing themselves out. I think that racial differences can strengthen a movement, but we have to be willing to accept and work with them. . .

STUDY QUESTIONS

1. How does this country's racist history complicate discussions of today's sexual violence, according to Crenshaw?
2. What steps does Crenshaw suggest to take race into account and mobilize more effectively on questions of violence against women?

For some feminists, it is not at all clear that legal reforms—civil or criminal—will suffice to stop rape and other forms of sexual victimization. Many believe that more fundamental changes are necessary to eliminate sexual coercion. Andrea Dworkin, for example, argues in "The Rape Atrocity and the Boy Next Door," in *Our Blood: Prophecies and Discourses on Sexual Politics* (New York: Harper and Row, 1976, p. 22), that rape is a direct consequence of the polar definitions of men and women.

She sees that men in our society are defined as aggressive, dominant, and powerful, while women are defined as passive, submissive, and powerless. Rape, then, is committed by exemplars of our social norms, not psychopaths or deviants. It occurs "when a man who is dominant by definition, takes a woman, who according to men and all organs of their culture was put on this earth for his use and gratification." *Id.* at 45. Thus, she argues, that "in order to stop rape, and all of the other systematic abuses against us, we must destroy those very definitions of masculinity and feminity, of men and women." *Id.* at 48. Change, in her view, can only result from a thoroughgoing societal transformation "excising these definitions from our social fabric."

Such views raise difficult questions regarding all sexual relations between women and men today. Do you agree that women are not able to function actively in sexual relations with men? Do you think similar concerns apply to sexual relations between women? Do you see any role for the law in achieving the types of societal changes you consider necessary to eliminate rape?

III. PORNOGRAPHY

Historically, efforts to combat pornography have been associated with campaigns against prostitution and rape. As Judith Walkowitz has pointed out in her book, *Prostitution and Victorian Society, Women Class and the State* (Cambridge: Cambridge University Press, 1982), the late nineteenth-century feminist campaign against regulation of prostitution evolved into a broader social purity movement directed against prostitution, pornography, white slavery, and homosexuality. A key consequence of this movement in the United States was the Comstock law enacted by Congress in 1873 (mentioned in Chapter 8). Like its twenty-two state counterparts, this law prohibited publication, possession, and dissemination of writings as well as drugs and articles associated with contraception and abortion.

In this century, the antipornography drive of the 1980s evolved from the antirape movement of the 1970s. Susan Brownmiller, for example, drew the connection this way in her book, *Against Our Will* (New York: Simon and Schuster, p. 394):

> The gut distaste that a majority of women feel when we look at pornography, a distaste that . . . comes, I think, from the gut knowledge that we and our bodies are being stripped, exposed and contorted for the purpose of ridicule to bolster that "masculine esteem" which gets its kick and sense of power from viewing females as anonymous, panting playthings, adult toys, dehumanized objects to be used, abused, broken and discarded.
>
> This, of course, is also the philosophy of rape. It is no accident (for, what else could be its purpose?) that females in the pornographic genre are depicted in two clearly delineated roles: as virgins who are caught and "banged" or as nymphomaniacs who are never sated. The most popular and prevalent pornographic fantasy combines the two: an innocent, untutored female is raped and "subjected to unnatural practices" that turn her into a raving, slobbering nymphomaniac, a dependent sexual slave who can never get enough of the big, male cock.
>
> There can be no "equality" in porn, no female equivalent, no turning of the tables in the name of bawdy fun. Pornography, like rape, is a male invention, designed to dehumanize women, to reduce the female to an object of sexual access, not to free sensuality from moralistic or parental inhibition. The staple of porn will always be the naked female body, breasts and genitals exposed, because as man devised it, her naked body is the female's

"shame," her private parts the private property of man, while his are the ancient, holy, universal, patriarchal instrument of his power, his rule by force over her.

Pornography is the undiluted essence of anti-female propaganda.

Copyright © 1975 by Susan Brownmiller. Reprinted by permission of SIMON & SCHUSTER, Inc.

There is, however, substantial controversy among today's feminists about the desirability of enacting antipornography legislation. Many, like Brownmiller, view such legislation as essential to combating sexual oppression. Others fear a repetition of repression associated with the social purity movements and subsequent censorship efforts. This section explores these twin concerns, first by reviewing traditional obscenity legislation and then by examining a new form of legislation that seeks to incorporate antipornography measures into existing civil rights laws.

The Traditional Approach

Sexual anatomy and sexual activities have long been the subjects of art. All major cultures have their collections of ancient erotic art and writings. Although this genre of expression has probably always had its opponents, organized resistance became apparent only around the time of the Reformation. Since that time, religious bodies have repeatedly objected to the explicit representation of sexual subjects on moral grounds. Central to their objections was the view that sexual activity and interests are permissible only in the context of procreation within marriage. Sexually explicit expression is thus objectionable for several reasons. It suggests that sexual activity is enjoyable and fulfilling in itself; it prompts impure thoughts, improper desires, and/or sinful motives in those who see it; and, at times, it represents activities that are intrinsically wrong because they occur outside the approved procreative context. These include masturbation, nonvaginal intercourse, and any sexual activity that occurs outside of marriage.

Censorship in the form of licensing was prevalent in England as early as the first half of the sixteenth century; however, pornographic publications were readily licensed while political works were more closely scrutinized. Obscenity legislation and prosecutions became more common in the second half of the nineteenth century with the advent of social purity movements in the United States and England. As we noted in Chapter 8, obscenity laws were used to prosecute birth control advocates for their speeches and publications prior to World War I.

In a series of decisions that came after World War I, the Supreme Court began to accord speech protection under the First Amendment. That protection does not extend to obscene speech, however. Thus, in considering speech that contains sexually explicit material, the Court has been forced to define obscenity. The Supreme Court has struggled repeatedly to articulate that definition. In its 1973 decision in *Miller v. California,* 413 U.S. 15, the Court set forth the definition that currently applies. The Court there held that a state may regulate a work of art that explicitly expresses sexual activity if: (a) the average person, applying contemporary community standards, would find that the work, taken as a whole, appeals to the prurient interest in sex; (b) the work depicts or describes, in a patently offensive way, sexual conduct specifically defined by the applicable state law; and (c) the work, taken as a whole, lacks serious literary, artistic, political, or scientific value. If any of these tests are not met, the material is protected by the First Amendment. Although it had been argued that the "community standards" aspect of the *Miller* holding would increase the likelihood of conviction, surveys published during the late 1970s and early 1980s indicate that *Miller* did not lead to an increase in general prosecutions for obscenity.

In *Miller,* the Court held that unless the sexually expressive material can be shown to be obscene, it may not be regulated by the state. However, the Court permitted some departure from that principle in its 1976 decision in *Young v. American Mini Theatres,* 427 U.S. 50, which upheld several zoning ordinances that required the dispersal of "adult" movie theatres. Under the plurality opinion in *American Mini Theatres,* governments are permitted to restrict access to sexually explicit materials without reaching the question of whether the material is obscene. To reach this result, the Court endorsed the view that some types of expression are less deserving of First Amendment protection and may be regulated (although not completely suppressed) where they interfere with more important government interests, such as the improvement of the quality of life in an inner city. Where a certain type of expression is found to be of lesser importance, the burden of justification on the government is correspondingly lighter.

Several years after *American Mini Theatres,* the Court opened another avenue for government regulation of explicit sexual speech. In so doing, the Court focused on additional grounds for concern about such materials, i.e., the harm to children employed in the production of child pornography. A unanimous Court thus approved, in *New York v. Ferber,* 458 U.S. 747 (1982), an overt ban on one form of sexually explicit expression not because of its supposed corrupting influence on viewers but because of a legislative finding of tangible harm to the subject/model. Here, as in *American Mini Theatres,* the Court found it unnecessary to hold the materials obscene under *Miller* and again imposed only a minimal burden of justification on the government.

Two factors seem particularly important to the *Ferber* Court's decision to uphold a law imposing criminal sanctions on the production and distribution of nonobscene pornography: (1) the consensus on the dangers of child pornography manifested in the near universality of state efforts to outlaw it; and (2) the strength of the social science data appearing to confirm the justices' intuitive sense that children who participate in the production of pornography suffer enduring psychological damage.

For many, the *Ferber* decision was evidence of an awakening on the part of the Supreme Court to the fact that the production of pornography often involves abuse and exploitation. Even though *Ferber* dealt only with child pornography, the decision encouraged some pornography opponents to believe that the Court might uphold state regulations directed at protecting women as a class from the psychological, emotional, and physical harm they saw caused by pornography. A new legal approach to the regulation of pornography was thus developed with the interests of women in mind.

The Civil Rights Approach

As we have seen, pornography foes have traditionally based their attacks on obscenity laws. Under current constitutional doctrine, the reach of these laws is limited by the *Miller* test. As opposition to pornography has hardened among a segment of the feminist community, some feminist strategists and legal theorists have devised a different approach. This approach seeks to restrict pornography because it subordinates women, thereby interfering with their civil rights. This civil rights approach has been the subject of considerable controversy.

The effort first surfaced in 1983 when proponents of the civil rights approach, Law professor Catharine MacKinnon and author Andrea Dworkin, succeeded in convincing the Minneapolis City Council to consider their approach. Specifically, they persuaded the council to add pornography-based claims to the city's civil rights ordinance instead of enacting zoning legislation to curb the distribution of pornography in certain neighborhoods. More specifically, the proposed law allowed victims to file sex discrimination claims for damages on the ground that pornography promotes violence against women, keeps women subordinate, and inhibits access to equal employment, education, and other opportunities. The ordinance was approved by the council but immediately vetoed by the mayor, who believed it violated the First Amendment.

Next, in 1984, a revised version of that ordinance, introduced by a stop-ERA, anti-abortion, Eagle Forum city councilwoman, was enacted in Indianapolis. The revised law narrowed the definition to focus on violent pornography and created an exception for "soft-core" porn. Under the Indianapolis ordinance, pornography was defined as

> the graphic sexually explicit subordination of women, through pictures and/or words [and] one or more of the following:
>
> (i) women are presented dehumanized as sexual objects, things, or commodities; or
>
> (ii) women are presented as sexual objects who enjoy pain or humilation; or
>
> (iii) women are presented as sexual objects who experience sexual pleasure in being raped; or
>
> (iv) women are presented as sexual objects tied up or cut up or mutilated or bruised or physically hurt; or
>
> (v) women are presented in postures or positions of sexual submission, servility, or display; or
>
> (vi) women's body parts—including but not limited to vaginas, breasts, or buttocks—are exhibited such that women are reduced to those parts; or
>
> (vii) women are presented as whores by nature; or
>
> (viii) women are presented being penetrated by objects or animals; or
>
> (ix) women are presented in scenarios of degradation, injury, torture, shown as filthy or inferior, bleeding, bruised, or hurt in a context that makes these conditions sexual.

Of the four causes of action in the ordinance, the most controversial was the trafficking clause, which covered the sale, distribution, or exhibition of pornography.

Although both experts and victims went on record in support of the approach, critics questioned the connection between pornography and harm. Members of the Feminist Anti-Censorship Taskforce, for example, pointed out that the ordinance did not mention nonviolent sexist images, such as those pervading advertisements. They also pointed out that the ordinance did nothing about violent images that were not sexist. Critics were particularly concerned that conservative judges would consider depictions of "loose women" or women who did not fit traditional role expectations to be pornographic.

Proponents of the ordinance, on the other hand, took the view that pornography is inevitably harmful to women; that it operates in a subliminal way; that it is extremely difficult, if not impossible, to correct with additional speech; and that pornography, together with the sexual violence that it engenders, keeps women from countering pornography with more speech. Thus, they argued that even pornography that does not fall within the definition of obscenity does not deserve constitutional protection and, in any event, the ordinance's restraints are justified by the compelling state interest in eliminating sex discrimination.

To date, few legislative bodies in this country have considered the civil rights approach to adult pornography, and only Indianapolis has enacted it into law. This is in part due to the strong disagreement within and without the feminist community regarding the benefits of the approach. As indicated, that disagreement turns in part on different evaluations of the available social science data on the consequences of exposure to adult pornography. Proponents of the civil rights approach claim experimental research demonstrates that pornography covered by the ordinance causes measurable harm to women. Their position gained some support from a 1986 report of the federal Attorney General's (Meese) Commission, which concluded that "available evidence strongly supports the hypothesis that substantial exposure to sexually violent materials . . . bears a crucial relationship to antisocial . . . and for some subgroups possibly unlawful acts of sexual violence." In her 1984 lecture, "Francis Biddle's Sister: Pornography, Civil Rights, and Speech" appearing in *Feminism Unmodified* (Cambridge: Harvard University Press, 1987, pp. 187–89), Catharine MacKinnon pointed to a number of studies showing a connection between pornography and violence. Some studies do show that under laboratory conditions, men exposed to expressly violent pornography are more willing to take aggressive action against women. Other studies show that exposure to certain pornography affects men's attitudes toward women, increasing their scores on such measures as hostility toward women, propensity to rape, condoning rape, and predicting that a person would rape or force sex on a woman if he knew that he would not get caught. MacKinnon also cited studies showing that long-term exposure to all pornography covered by the ordinance—whether or not it is expressly violent—makes men perceive a rape victim as more worthless and leaves them less able to see she was harmed. These studies, taken together with testimony by individual women, establish a causal connection between pornography and sexual aggression and sexual subordination in the view of those advocating the civil rights approach.

Opponents of antipornography legislation questioned the conclusions drawn from such studies on a number of grounds. As Barry Lynn, then an American Civil Liberties Union lawyer, pointed out in his article, " 'Civil Rights' Ordinances and the Attorney General's Commission: New Developments in Pornography Regulations," 21 *Harvard Civil Rights—Civil Liberties Law Review* 27 (1986), much of the research involved small numbers of college students exposed to violent pornography in a highly artificial laboratory setting without taking account of differences in past development and experience. Such studies, he argued, are of little value in predicting real-world behavior based on repeated exposure to all types of pornography. Lynn and others questioned the relevance of rape-attitude studies for failing to distinguish between pornographic and nonpornographic stimuli and for failing to establish an adequate link between attitude and behavior. More generally, they questioned the claim made by ordinance proponents that pornography is central to the subordinate place of women in our society. How, they asked, can the effects of pornography be separated from the negative opinions about women and the subordination and dominance by violence that are promoted throughout the media?

The Indianapolis ordinance was challenged in federal court immediately after its enactment. Ordinance opponents pressed two traditional claims. First, they argued that the ordinance violated free speech guarantees inasmuch as its restraints were not limited to obscene materials and the city had demonstrated no compelling state interest to justify them. Second, they argued that the ordinance was unduly vague in its definition of pornography. Ruling in their favor on both grounds, the district court enjoined the ordinance.

On appeal, feminists who opposed the ordinance on less traditional grounds also made their views known. They did not dispute that pornography is extremely offensive; rather, they argued that the ordinance would be used to suppress sexually explicit material that responds to women's erotic tastes and needs and affirms their sexuality. They also saw the ordinance as constituting the type of protective legislation that reinforces sex-based stereotypes without effectively improving women's circumstances. The appellate court agreed with the district court that ordinance was unconstitutional, but for other reasons.

American Booksellers Association, Inc. v. Hudnut

United States Court of Appeals, Seventh Circuit, 1985.
771 F.2d 323, *aff'd,* 475 U.S. 1001 (1986).

EASTERBROOK, Circuit Judge.

Indianapolis enacted an ordinance defining "pornography" as a practice that discriminates against women. "Pornography" is to be redressed through the administrative and judicial methods used for other discrimination. The City's definition of "pornography" is considerably different from "obscenity," which the Supreme Court has held is not protected by the First Amendment.

To be "obscene" under Miller v. California, "a publication must, taken as a whole, appeal to the prurient interest, must contain patently offensive depictions or descriptions of specified sexual conduct, and on the whole have no serious literary, artistic, political, or scientific value." Offensiveness must be assessed under the standards of the community. Both offensiveness and an appeal to something other than "normal, healthy sexual desires" are essential elements of "obscenity." . . .

The Indianapolis ordinance does not refer to the prurient interest, to offensiveness, or to the standards of the community. It demands attention to particular depictions, not to the work judged as a whole. It is irrelevant under the

ordinance whether the work has literary, artistic, political, or scientific value. . . .

Civil rights groups and feminists have entered this case as amici on both sides. Those supporting the ordinance say that it will play an important role in reducing the tendency of men to view women as sexual objects, a tendency that leads to both unacceptable attitudes and discrimination in the workplace and violence away from it. Those opposing the ordinance point out that much radical feminist literature is explicit and depicts women in ways forbidden by the ordinance and that the ordinance would reopen old battles. It is unclear how Indianapolis would treat works from James Joyce's Ulysses to Homer's Iliad; both depict women as submissive objects for conquest and domination.

We do not try to balance the argument for and against an ordinance such as this. The ordinance discriminates on the ground of the content of the speech. Speech treating women in the approved way—in sexual encounters "premised on equality"—is lawful no matter how sexually explicit. Speech treating women in the disapproved way—as submissive in matters sexual or as enjoying humiliation—is unlawful no matter how significant the literary, artistic, or political qualities of the work taken as a whole. The state may not ordain preferred viewpoints in this way. The Constitution forbids the state to declare one perspective right and silence opponents. . . .

. . . Under the First Amendment the government must leave to the people the evaluation of ideas. Bald or subtle, an idea is as powerful as the audience allows it to be. A belief may be pernicious—the beliefs of Nazis led to the death of millions, those of the Klan to the repression of millions. A pernicious belief may prevail. Totalitarian governments today rule much of the planet, practicing suppression of billions and spreading dogma that may enslave others. One of the things that separates our society from theirs is our absolute right to propagate opinions that the government finds wrong or even hateful. . . .

Indianapolis justifies the ordinance on the ground that pornography affects thoughts. Men who see women depicted as subordinate are more likely to treat them so. Pornography is an aspect of dominance. It does not persuade people so much as change them. It works by socializing, by establishing the expected and the permissible. In this view pornography is not an idea; pornography is the injury.

There is much to this perspective. Beliefs are also facts. People often act in accordance with the images and patterns they find around them. People raised in a religion tend to accept the tenets of that religion, often without independent examination. People taught from birth that black people are fit only for slavery rarely rebelled against that creed; beliefs coupled with the self-interest of the masters established a social structure that inflicted great harm while enduring for centuries. Words and images act at the level of the subconscious before they persuade at the level of the conscious. Even the truth has little chance unless a statement fits within the framework of beliefs that may never have been subjected to rational study.

Therefore we accept the premises of this legislation. Depictions of subordination tend to perpetuate subordination. The subordinate status of women in turn leads to affront and lower pay at work, insult and injury at home, battery and rape on the streets. . . .

Yet this simply demonstrates the power of pornography as speech. . . .

Racial bigotry, anti-semitism, violence on television, reporters' biases—these and many more influence the culture and shape our socialization. None is directly answerable by more speech, unless that speech too finds its place in the popular culture. Yet all is protected as speech, however insidious. Any other answer leaves the government in control of all of the institutions of culture, the great censor and director of which thoughts are good for us. . . .

Much of Indianapolis's argument rests on the belief that when speech is "unanswerable," and the metaphor that there is a "marketplace of ideas" does not apply, the First Amendment does not apply either. . . .

The Supreme Court has rejected the position that speech must be "effectively answerable" to be protected by the Constitution. . . .

We come, finally, to the argument that pornography is "low value" speech, that it is enough like obscenity that Indianapolis may prohibit it. . . . True, pornography and obscenity have sex in common. But Indianapolis left out of its definition any reference to literary, artistic, political, or scientific value. The ordinance applies to graphic sexually explicit subordination in works great and small. . . .

. . . Free speech has been on balance an ally of those seeking change. Governments that want stasis start by restricting speech. Culture is a powerful force of continuity; Indianapolis paints pornography as part of the culture of power. Change in any complex system ultimately depends on the ability of outsiders to challenge accepted views and the reigning institutions. Without a strong guarantee of freedom of speech, there is no effective right to challenge what is. . . .

Affirmed.

STUDY QUESTIONS

1. Some pornography opponents distinguish pornography from other types of speech by pointing to its direct impact on women's situation. As the court put it, "In this view, pornography is not an idea; pornography is the injury." To what extent did the court accept this view? Did it offer any remedy for the harm that pornography inflicts? Do you see any? Can you remedy the harm the same way you would remedy a vicious lie told about someone you care about?

2. The court made clear that the First Amendment protects hate messages of the Klan and the Nazi Party and concluded that pornography should be treated no differently. Do you think violent pornography is equivalent to such hate messages? If so, is there any reason to treat it differently?

3. Does the court accurately depict the views of feminists who support the ordinance? Of feminists who oppose it? Do you agree with the result? The reasoning? Why? Why not?

ᴥ

Following the court of appeals decision in *American Booksellers Association v. Hudnut,* the Supreme Court affirmed the decision without a hearing. However, this summary action is unlikely to resolve the controversy within the feminist community regarding the desirability of legal restrictions on pornography.

Despite their defeat in the *American Booksellers* case, antipornography forces continued their efforts, ultimately achieving success in Canada. There, the top court upheld a ban on the possession and sale of obscene material even though it acknowledged that the law violated the country's free speech guarantees. Thus, in *R. v. Butler and McCord,* 134 N.R. 81 (1992), the Canadian Supreme Court unanimously found the threat to equality resulting from the dissemination of obscene materials exploiting women and children sufficient to justify their criminalization.

Efforts of antipornography forces in this country have focused once again on legislation, pressing on the federal level for passage of the Pornography Victims Compensation Act. That law would punish distributors of pornography for the sexual assaults of others if the sexual assaults were "caused" by pornography distributed by the defendant. On the state level, they have pressed for legislation much like the Indianapolis ordinance at issue in the *American Booksellers* case.

Feminist controversy continues over these matters. The next two selections highlight the competing concerns.

Six Questions about Pornography

Women Against Pornography.
New York, 1993.

Pornography has existed in other times and other cultures, but never has it been so readily available and so pernicious in content and effect. We are feminists who have fought for equal rights, civil liberties and social change.

The time has come for us to face the challenge of pornography and fight for its abolition.

Here are our replies to some common questions about pornography.

We ask you to think about them.

Reprinted by permission of Women Against Pornography, New York City.

Isn't pornography a safety valve? Doesn't it provide a harmless outlet for those men who might otherwise commit crimes of violence?

On the contrary, pornography contributes to the climate of violence around us. There is no evidence to support the claim that pornography reduces male violence and aggressive sexual behavior. We believe that there is a strong connection between the spread of pornography and the increase in rape, battering of women, and molesting of children. Violence on television and violence in society have been shown to imitate each other. Why should violence disguised as sexuality be an exception?

If you don't like pornography, who's forcing you to look at it?

We would like to look away, but we can't avoid seeing it. Images of brutality confront us everywhere, even in our own communities. Pictures of women in humiliating poses assault us from newsstands, billboards, movie marquees, record album covers, and even in the window displays of fashionable department stores.

Don't some women enjoy pornography?

Some women say so, but for centuries women have struggled to conform to male definitions of their sexuality. But those definitions change. Today pornography is said to be chic. The current dictate is "Enjoy pornography; it's good for both of us. If you don't, you're a prude." Name-calling is a powerful weapon. Pornography is protected in part by women's reluctance to speak out against it for fear of ridicule and rejection by men.

Okay, pornography is offensive, but don't we have to protect freedom of expression?

We affirm the First Amendment principle of free speech—however, we also believe that pornography constitutes a threat to our physical safety and emotional well-being. One concern must be balanced against another. Even the First Amendment "absolutists" among us agree that we must create a moral climate in which women's bodies cannot be exploited for profit. Others in our association, who also uphold the principle of free speech and the right of political dissent, maintain that the First Amendment was never intended to protect pornographic images: the rape, humiliation, torture and murder of women for erotic entertainment.

Where do you draw the line and who draws it?

We would draw the line wherever violence or hostility toward women is equated with sexual pleasure. We would draw the line wherever children are sexually exploited. We do not oppose sex education, erotic literature or erotic art. But the essence of pornography is the defamation of womanhood. That is why women must draw the line.

Isn't pornography really a trivial issue?

No, not when our most intimate relationships are affected by the way pornography teaches women and men to view themselves and each other. Not when pornography is a multi-million-dollar industry linked to organized crime, illicit drugs and prostitution. Nothing that has so powerful an impact on the mental and physical well-being of all of us can be dismissed as trivial.

Feminists against the First Amendment

Wendy Kaminer. *Atlantic Monthly,* November 1992. Pp. 114–15 and 117.

With [their] exclusive focus on prohibiting material that reflects incorrect attitudes toward women, anti-porn feminists don't deny the chilling effect of censorship; they embrace it. . . . [A]ll men are deemed potential abusers whose violent impulses are bound to be sparked by pornography. It needs to be said by feminists, that efforts to censor pornography reflect a profound disdain for men. Catharine

MacKinnon has written that "pornography works as a behavioral conditioner, reinforcer and stimulus, not as idea or advocacy. It is more like saying 'kill' to a trained guard dog—and also the training process itself." That's more a theory of sexuality than of speech: pornography is action because all men are dogs on short leashes.

This bleak view of male sexuality condemns heterosexuality for women as an exercise in wish fulfillment (if only men weren't all dogs) or false consciousness (such as male-identified thinking). True feminism, according to MacKinnon, unlike liberal feminism, "sees sexuality as a social sphere of male power of which forced sex is paradigmatic." . . . MacKinnon and [Andrea] Dworkin suggest that in a context of pervasive institutionalized inequality, there can be no consensual sex between men and women: we can never honestly distinguish rape from intercourse. . . .

A modified version of this message may well have particular appeal to some college women today, who make up a important constituency for the anti-porn movement. . . .

Feminism on campus tends to focus on issues of sexuality, not of economic equity. . . .

Off campus the anti-porn feminist critique of male sexuality and heterosexuality for women has little appeal. . . .

If censoring pornography is the central feminist issue for Catharine MacKinnon, it is a peripheral issue for activists. . . .

The likelihood that feminists would not be the ones to police Forty-second Street should anti-porn legislation pass is one reason that many feminists oppose the anti-porn campaign. If society is as sexist as Andrea Dworkin and Catharine MacKinnon claim, it is not about to adopt a feminist agenda when it sets out to censor pornography. The history of anti-porn campaigns in this country is partly a history of campaigns against reproductive choice and changing roles for men and women. The first federal obscenity legislation, known as the Comstock Law, passed in 1873, prohibited the mailing of not only dirty pictures but also contraceptives and information about abortion. Early in this century Margaret Sanger and the sex educator Mary Ware Dennett were prosecuted for obscenity violations. Recently the New Right campaign against socially undesirable literature has focused on sex education in public schools. Anti-porn activists on the right consider feminism and homosexuality (which they link) to be threats to traditional family life (which, in fact, they are). In Canada a landmark Supreme Court ruling this year which adopted a feminist argument against pornography was first used to prohibit distribution of a small lesbian magazine, which a politically correct feminist would be careful to label erotica.

Gay and lesbian groups, as well as advocates of sex education and the usual array of feminist and nonfeminist civil libertarians, actively oppose anti-pornography legislation. Some state chapters of the National Organization for Women—New York, California, and Vermont—have taken strong anti-censorship stands, but at the national level NOW has not taken a position in the pornography debate. Its president, Patricia Ireland, would like to see pornography become socially unacceptable, "like smoking," but is wary of taking legal action against it, partly because she's wary of "giving people like Jesse Helms the power to decide what we read and see." But for major, national feminist organizations, like NOW and the NOW Legal Defense and Education Fund, the pornography debate is a minefield to be carefully avoided. Pornography is probably the most divisive issue feminists have faced since the first advocates of the ERA, in the 1920s, squared off against advocates of protective labor legislation for women. Feminists for and against anti-porn legislation are almost as bitterly divided as pro-choice activists and members of Operation Rescue. . . .

Still, censorship campaigns will always have considerable appeal. . . .

. . . But it may be wishful thinking to believe that penalizing the production and distribution of hard-core pornography would have much effect on sexual violence. . . . It would, however, complicate campaigns to distribute information about AIDS, let alone condoms, in the public schools. It would distract us from the harder, less popular work of reforming sexual stereotypes and roles, and addressing actual instead of metaphorical instruments of violence. The promise of the anti-porn movement is the promise of a world in which almost no one can buy pornography and almost anyone can buy a gun.

STUDY QUESTIONS

1. Why do the Women Against Pornography believe it is important to work on its issue? Do you agree?
2. What risks do those who oppose the anti-pornography civil rights approach see? Do you share their fears?
3. What other means do you see to combat pornography? What do you see as their strengths and weaknesses?

Without question, most women find much of the sexually explicit material available today extremely offensive. On the other hand, as the definitions contained in the Indianapolis ordinance demonstrate, it is extremely difficult to distinguish between pornography that degrades women and inoffensive erotica. Nor is there agreement regarding the relative importance of degrading depictions of women that are not sexually explicit. Moreover, the data concerning the effect of pornography are far from clear. To what extent does pornography promote violence, and to what extent does it provide a legitimate source of pleasure and a helpful outlet for aggression?

What is the likelihood that feminists will retain control of these legislative initiatives? If controlled by others, are antipornography initiatives likely to result in obscenity laws that reinforce gender-based expectations regarding sexual behavior?

These questions have arisen and been debated in the context of pornography, but as Kaminer suggests, they clearly reflect more basic tensions in the feminist community. These tensions flow from very different views of the role sexuality does and can play in today's society and how that role relates to women's current subordination. The concluding selection's exploration of these concerns still pertains today.

Sex War: The Debate between Radical and Libertarian Feminists

Ann Ferguson.
10 *SIGNS* 106–12, 1984.

... In the last four years, there has been an increasing polarization of American feminists into two camps on issues of feminist sexual morality. The first camp, the radical feminists, holds that sexuality in a male-dominant society involves danger—that is, that sexual practices perpetuate violence against women. The opposing camp, self-styled "anti-prudes," I term "libertarian feminists," for whom the key feature of sexuality is the potentially liberating aspects of the exchange of pleasure between consenting partners. As thus constituted these are not exclusive positions: obviously it is quite consistent to hold that contemporary sexual practices involve both danger and pleasure. . . .

1. It is important to note that feminists in the first phase of the women's movement during the

late 1960s did not make this distinction in thinking about sexuality; they emphasized both a defense of women's right to pleasure (female orgasms) and legal protection from one of the dangers of heterosexual intercourse: unwanted pregnancies (i.e., the right to abortion). During the second phase in the early 1970s, feminists emphasized women's right to sexual pleasure with women (lesbian feminism). It is only in the third phase of the movement, when the goals of sexual pleasure have become culturally legitimated to a greater extent, that many feminists have begun to emphasize the violence and danger of heterosexual institutions like pornography.

TWO PARADIGMS CONTRASTED

Radical feminists' views on sexuality include the following:

1. Heterosexual sexual relations generally are characterized by an ideology of sexual objectification (men as subjects/masters; women as objects/slaves) that supports male sexual violence against women.

2. Feminists should repudiate any sexual practice that supports or "normalizes" male sexual violence.

3. As feminists we should reclaim control over female sexuality by developing a concern

with our own sexual priorities, which differ from men's—that is, more concern with intimacy and less with performance.

4. The ideal sexual relationship is between fully consenting, equal partners who are emotionally involved and do not participate in polarized roles.

From these four aspects of the radical-feminist sexual ideology, one can abstract the following theoretical assumptions about sexuality, social power, and sexual freedom:

5. Human sexuality is a form of expression between people that creates bonds and communicates emotion (the primacy of intimacy theory).

6. Theory of Social Power: In patriarchal societies sexuality becomes a tool of male domination through sexual objectification. This is a social mechanism that operates through the institution of masculine and feminine roles in the patriarchal nuclear family. The attendant ideology of sexual objectification is sadomasochism, that is, masculinity as sadistic control over women and femininity as submission to the male will.

7. Sexual freedom requires the sexual equality of partners and their equal respect for one another both as subject and as body. It also requires the elimination of all patriarchal institutions (e.g., the pornography industry, the patriarchal family, prostitution, and compulsory heterosexuality) and sexual practices (sadomasochism, cruising, and adult/child and butch/femme relationships) in which sexual objectification occurs.

The libertarian-feminist paradigm can be summarized in a manner that brings out in sharp contrast its emphasis and that of the radical-feminist paradigm:

1. Heterosexual as well as other sexual practices are characterized by repression. The norms of patriarchal bourgeois sexuality repress the sexual desires and pleasures of everyone by stigmatizing sexual minorities, thereby keeping the majority "pure" and under control.

2. Feminists should repudiate any theoretical analyses, legal restrictions, or moral judg-

ments that stigmatize sexual minorities and thus restrict the freedom of all.

3. As feminists we should reclaim control over female sexuality by demanding the right to practice whatever gives us pleasure and satisfaction.

4. The ideal sexual relationship is between fully consenting, equal partners who negotiate to maximize one another's sexual pleasure and satisfaction by any means they choose.

The general paradigms of sexuality, social power, and sexual freedom one can draw from this sexual ideology are:

5. Human sexuality is the exchange of physical erotic and genital sexual pleasures (the primacy of pleasure theory).

6. Theory of Social Power: Social institutions, interactions, and discourses distinguish the normal/legitimate/healthy from the abnormal/illegitimate/unhealthy and privilege certain sexual expressions over others, thereby institutionalizing sexual repression and creating a hierarchy of social power and sexual identities.

7. Sexual freedom requires oppositional practices, that is, transgressing socially respectable categories of sexuality and refusing to draw the line on what counts as politically correct sexuality.

CRITIQUE OF RADICAL AND LIBERTARIAN FEMINISMS

The problem with both radical and libertarian theories is that they describe social power in too simple a fashion. There may be, in fact, no universal strategy for taking back sexual power. Although the radical feminists are right that sexual objectification characterizes patriarchally constructed heterosexuality, their account is overdrawn. We need a more careful study of sexual fantasies and their effects. Even when fantasies involve images of dominance and submission, they may empower some women to enjoy sex more fully, a phenomenon that, by enhancing connections to one's body, develops self-affirmation. Nonetheless, in order to test the possibility of a different type of sexual practice that would provide mental affirmation as well, we do need to develop an alternative feminist sexual fantasy therapy for women, and for men, that does not involve such images.

Libertarian feminists are ingenuous in their insistence that any consensual sexual activity should be acceptable to feminists. This begs the question, for any feminist position has to examine the concept of *consent* itself in order to explore hidden power structures that place women in unequal (hence coercive) positions. That some avowed feminists think they consent to sadomasochism and to the consumption of pornography does not indicate that the true conditions for consent are present. Libertarians must show why these cases differ from the battered wife and "happy housewife" syndromes—something they have not yet convincingly done.

Pornography is an especially difficult topic, in part because the distinction between erotica and pornography is dependent on the context, that is, on the gender, class, and culture of the audience. Pornographic practices, discourses, and images primarily directed at men reduce women to sex objects. But there are other contradictory popular discourses directed primarily at women or mixed audiences—for example, the literature of romance, "PG" movies, and television soap operas.

If we look at the whole entire system of such ideological sexual communications, we find a set of conflicting assumptions. These assumptions constitute a distinctive blend of liberal individualist and patriarchal ideals peculiar to advanced capitalist patriarchal societies. On the one hand, the ideology of romantic love permeates much erotica, assuming that sexual liaisons should be between peers who each have a right to equal sexual pleasure. On the other hand, it is also true that in much sexually explicit material the message is what Andrea Dworkin and Kathleen Barry call "cultural sadism"—that is, that men should initiate and control sex and women should submit to it (men are consumers, women providers, of sex).

Libertarian and radical feminists each choose to emphasize opposing sides of these contradictions. I argue, instead, that we should develop feminist erotica and sex education that aims to make people conscious of these contradictions in order to encourage new forms of feminist fantasy production. This erotica and education must emerge in a variety of contexts (high school courses, soap operas, and Harlequin novels as well as avant-garde art) and be geared to all types of audiences. This means avoiding the sexual vanguardism of either radicals or libertarians, who interact primarily within closed countercultural communities (lesbian feminists, middle-class radicals, and other sexual minorities).

To further resolve this dilemma I think we must adopt a transitional feminist sexual morality that distinguishes between basic, risky, and forbidden sexual practices. Forbidden sexual practices are those in which relations of dominance and submission are so explicit that feminists hold they should be illegal. Such practices include incest, rape, domestic violence, and sexual relations between very young children and adults. The difference between a forbidden and a risky practice is an epistemological one: that is, a practice is termed "risky" if it is suspected of leading to dominant/subordinate relationships, although there is no conclusive proof of this, while forbidden practices are those for which there is such evidence. Sadomasochism, capitalist-produced pornography, prostitution, and nuclear family relations between male breadwinners and female housewives are all risky practices from a feminist point of view. This does not mean that feminists do not have a right to engage in these practices. But since there is conflicting evidence concerning their role in structures of male dominance, they cannot be listed as basic feminist practices, that is, those we would advise our children to engage in. Basic feminist practices can include both casual and more committed sexual love, co-parenting, and communal relationships. They are distinguished by self-conscious negotiation and equalization of the partners in terms of the different relations of power (economic, social [e.g., age, gender], etc.) that hold between them. A feminist morality should be pluralist with respect to basic and risky practices. That is, feminists should be free to choose between basic and risky practices without fear of moral condemnation from other feminists.

STUDY QUESTIONS

1. What views on sexuality did Ferguson attribute to "radical feminists"? To "libertarian feminists"? Are these diverse views recognizable in this chapter's materials? Have you encountered them elsewhere? Do you identify more with one set of views than the other? Why?

2. What weaknesses did Ferguson find in the two positions? Does her approach deal adequately with these problems?

3. What consequences would flow from a particular sexual practice being considered "basic," "risky," or "forbidden"? Would the different categories carry with them different legal consequences? Who would assign various sexual practices to the different categories? How would that be done? What is to be gained by using these categories?

Like Kaminer, Ferguson identifies camps in the feminist debates about sexuality. One, which Ferguson terms "radical," stresses the dangers posed by unrestrained sexuality in a male-dominated society. The other, which she terms "libertarian," emphasizes the repressive aspects of today's sexual norms. The first, as she points out, may well lead to intolerance of certain sexual practices that are truly pleasurable for some. The second may well underestimate the barriers to real consent and thus ignore continued sexual coercion. Finding each position overdrawn, she advocates a strategy by which women can regain their sexual autonomy, taking into account both the dangers and the pleasures sexuality offers.

Ferguson's discussion explicitly concerns moral judgments that feminists make about sexual practices, and her specific proposals go more to developing types of erotica and sex education programs than to specific laws. Nevertheless, her notion of distinguishing between basic, risky, and forbidden practices has continuing relevance for the development of legal approaches to sexuality. Embodying these distinctions in the law would presumably entail criminalizing forbidden practices while permitting the others. Individual and collective educational efforts might then still be aimed at encouraging basic practices considered beneficial and at discouraging practices whose impact was less understood, but considered risky.

Such an approach acknowledges both the limits of our current understanding of the nature of sexuality and the limits of law in determining behavior. It also seeks to provide a way to resolve the tension between freedom and abuse we have observed throughout this chapter. Whether it does so in a manner society can successfully implement remains to be seen.

Supplementary Readings

GENERAL:

Bartlett, Katharine T. *Gender and the Law: Theory, Doctrine, Commentary.* Boston: Little, Brown, 1993.

Caldwell, Paulette. "Hair Pieces: Perspectives on the Intersection of Race and Gender," *Duke Law Journal* 365 (1991).

Crenshaw, Kimberle. "Demarginalizing the Intersection of Race and Sex: A Black Feminist Critique of Antidiscrimination Doctrine, Feminist Theory and Anti-Racist Politics," *University of Chicago Legal Forum* 139 (1989).

DeCoste, F.C., K. M. Munro, and Lillian MacPherson. *Feminist Legal Literature: A Selected Annotated Bibliography.* New York: Garland, 1991.

Hartmann, Susan M. *From Margin to Mainstream: American Women and Politics Since 1960.* Philadelphia: Temple University Press, 1989.

Kay, Herma H. *Sex-Based Discrimination.* 3d ed. St. Paul: West, 1988.

Mezey, Susan Gluck. *In Pursuit of Equality: Women, Public Policy, and the Federal Courts.* New York: St. Martin's Press, 1992.

Rhode, Deborah L. *Justice and Gender: Sex Discrimination and the Law.* Cambridge: Harvard University Press, 1989.

Thomas, Clair Sherman. *Sex Discrimination in a Nutshell.* St. Paul: West, 1991.

Wing, Adrienne Katherine. "Brief Reflections toward a Multiplicative Theory and Praxis of Being," 6 *Berkeley Women's Law Journal* 181 (1990–91).

HISTORICAL:

Abraymovitz, Mimi. *Regulating the Lives of Women: Social Welfare Policy from Colonial Times to the Present.* Boston: South End Press, 1988.

Baer, Judith. *Women in American Law: The Struggle toward Equality from the New Deal to the Present.* Vol. 2. New York: Holmes & Meier, 1991.

Berry, Mary Frances, and John W. Blassingame. *Long Memory: The Black Experience in America.* New York: Oxford University Press, 1982.

Chafe, William H. *The American Woman.* New York: Oxford University Press, 1972.

Davis, Angela Y. *Women, Race & Class.* New York: Random House, 1983.

Davis, Flora. *Moving the Mountain: The Women's Movement in America Since 1960.* New York: Simon & Schuster, 1991.

Flexner, Eleanor. *Century of Struggle.* Rev. ed. Cambridge: Harvard University Press, 1975.

Giddings, Paula. *When and Where I Enter: The Impact of Black Women on Race and Sex in America.* New York: William Morrow, 1984.

Hoff, Joan. *Law, Gender, and Injustice: A Legal History of U.S. Women.* New York: New York University Press, 1991.

Lerner, Gerda. *The Creation of Patriarchy.* New York: Oxford University Press, 1986.

Wortman, Marlene Stein. *Women in American Law. Vol. 1: From Colonial Times to the New Deal.* New York: Holmes & Meier, 1985.

CONSTITUTIONAL:

Freedman, Ann. "Sex Equality, Sex Differences, and the Supreme Court," 92 *Yale Law* Journal 913 (1984).

Law, Sylvia A. "Rethinking Sex and the Constitution," 132 *University of Pennsylvania Law Review* 955 (1984).

Mansbridge, Jane J. *Why We Lost the ERA.* Chicago: University of Chicago Press, 1986.

Mathews, Donald G., and Jane Sharron DeHart. *Sex, Gender and the Politics of ERA.* New York: Oxford University Press, 1990.

Matsuda, Lawrence, Delgado, and Crenshaw. *Words that Wound: Critical Race Theory, Assaultive Speech, and The First Amendment.* Boulder, CO, 1993.

Minow, Martha. "Justice Engendered," 101 *Harvard Law Review* 10 (1986).

Scales-Trent, Judith. "Black Women and the Constitution: Finding Our Place, Asserting Our Rights," 24 *Harvard Civil Rights-Civil Liberties Law Review* 9 (1989).

FEMINIST JURISPRUDENCE:

Bartlett, Katharine T., and Rosanne Kennedy, eds. *Feminist Legal Theory: A Reader in Law and Gender.* Boulder, Colo.: Westview Press, 1991.

Bock, Gisela, and Susan James, eds. *Beyond Equality and Difference: Citizenship, Feminist Politics and Female Subjectivity,* New York: Routledge, 1992.

Finley, Lucinda M. "Transcending Equality Theory: A Way out of the Maternity and the Workplace Debate," 86 *Columbia Law Review* 1118 (1986).

Frug, Mary Joe. *Postmodern Legal Feminism.* New York: Routledge, 1992.

Harris, Angela. "Essentialism and Feminist Theory," 42 *Stanford Law Review* 581 (1990).

Kay, Herma Hill. "Models of Equality," *University of Illinois Law Review* 39 (1985).

———. "Equality and Difference: The Case of Pregnancy," 1 *Berkeley Women's Law Journal* 1 (1985).

Kline, Marlee. "Race, Racism, and Feminist Theory," 12 *Harvard Women's Law Journal* 115 (1989).

Littleton, Christine A. "Reconstructing Sexual Equality," 75 *California Law Review* 1279 (1987).

———. "Does It Still Make Sense to Talk about 'Women'?" 1 *UCLA Women's Law Journal* 15 (1991).

MacKinnon, Catherine A. *Toward a Feminist Theory of the State.* Cambridge: Harvard University Press, 1989.

Minow, Martha. *Making All the Difference: Inclusion, Exclusion, and American Law.* Ithaca, N.Y.: Cornell University Press, 1990.

Rhode, Deborah L., ed. *Theoretical Perspectives on Sexual Difference.* New Haven: Yale University Press, 1990.

Scott, Joan. "Deconstructing Equality versus Difference," 14 *Feminist Studies* 33 (1988).

Smith, Patricia, ed. *Feminist Jurisprudence.* New York: Oxford University Press, 1993.

Taub, Nadine, and Wendy Williams. "Will Equality Require More Than Assimilation, Accommodation, or Separation from the Existing Social Structure?" 37 *Rutgers Law Review/Civil Rights Developments* 825 (1985).

Williams, Joan. "Deconstructing Gender," 87 *Michigan Law Review* 797 (1989).

———. "Dissolving the Sameness/Difference Debate: A Post-Modern Path beyond Essentialism in Feminist and Critical Race Theory," 1991 *Duke Law Journal* 296 (1991).

Williams, Wendy. "The Equality Crisis: Some Reflections on Culture, Courts, and Feminism," 7 *Women's Rights Law Reporter* 175 (1982).

EMPLOYMENT:

Acker, Joan. *Doing Comparable Worth: Gender, Class and Pay Equity.* Philadelphia: Temple University Press, 1991.

Bergmann, Barbara R. *The Economic Emergence of Women.* New York: Basic Books, 1986.

Fullinwider, Robert K. *The Reverse Discrimination Controversy: A Legal and Moral Analysis.* Totowa, N.J.: Rowman and Littlefield, 1980.

Goldin, Claudia. *Understanding the Gender Gap: An Economic History of American Women.* New York: Oxford University Press, 1990.

Gunderson, Morley, and W. Craig Riddel. "Comparable Worth: Canada's Experience," 10 *Contemporary Policy Issues* (July 1992).

Jacobs, Jerry A. *Revolving Doors: Sex Segregation and Women's Careers.* Stanford, Calif.: Stanford University Press, 1989.

Kessler-Harris, Alice. *A Woman's Wage: Historical Meanings and Social Consequences.* Lexington: University of Kentucky Press, 1990.

MacKinnon, Catherine A. *Sexual Harassment of Working Women.* New Haven: Yale University Press, 1979.

Morrison, Toni, ed. *Race-ing Justice, En-gendering Power: Essays on Anita Hill, Clarence Thomas, and the Construction of Social Reality.* New York: Pantheon Books, 1992.

Rosenfeld, Michele. *Justice and Affirmative Action.* New Haven: Yale University Press, 1991.

Scarborough, Cathy. "Conceptualizing Black Women's Employment Experiences," 98 *Yale Law Journal* 1457 (1989).

Siegal, Deborah. *Sexual Harassment: Research and Resources.* New York: National Council for Research on Women, 1992.

The World's Women— 1970– 1990: Trends and Statistics. Social Statistics and Indicators: Series K, No. 8. New York: United Nations, 1991.

EDUCATION:

American Association of University Women. *How Schools Change Girls.* Washington, D.C.: AAUW, 1992.

Dziech, Billie W., and Linda Weiner. *The Lecherous Professor*. Boston: Beacon Press, 1984.

Guttmann, Allen. *Women's Sports: A History*. New York: Columbia University Press, 1991.

Nelson, Mariah Burton. *Are We Winning Yet: How Women Are Changing Sports and Sports Are Changing Women*. New York: Random House, 1991.

Rothenberg, Paula. *Race, Class and Gender in the United States*. 2d ed. New York: St. Martin's Press, 1992.

Schwager, Sally. "Educating Women in America," 12 *Signs* 333 (1987).

FAMILY:

Areen, Judith. *Cases and Materials on Family Law*. 3d ed. Westbury, N.Y.: Foundation Press, 1992.

Erickson, Nancy. *Child Support Manual for Attorneys and Advocates*. New York: National Center on Women and Family Law, 1992.

Fineman, Martha. *The Illusion of Equality: The Rhetoric and Reality of Divorce Reform*. Chicago: University of Chicago Press, 1991.

Grossberg, Michael. *Governing the Hearth: Law and the Family*. Chapel Hill, N.C.: University of North Carolina Press, 1986.

Polikoff, N. "The Child Does Have Two Mothers: Redefining Parenthood to Meet the Needs of Children in Lesbian Mother and Other Nontraditional Families," 78 *Georgetown Law Journal* 459 (1990).

Riley, Glenda. *Divorce: An American Tradition*. New York: Oxford University Press, 1991.

Schecter, Susan. *Women and Male Violence: The Visions and Struggles of the Battered Women's Movement*. Boston: South End Press, 1982.

Sugarman, Stephen D., and Herma H. Kay. *Divorce Reform at the Crossroads*. New Haven: Yale University Press, 1990.

Wallanstein, Judith, and Sandra Blakeslee. *Second Chance: Men, Women and Children a Decade after Divorce*. New York: Tichnor & Fields, 1989.

REPRODUCTION:

Austin, Regina. "Sapphire Bound!" *Wisconsin Law Review* 539 (1989).

Banks, Taunya Lovell. "Women and AIDS—Racism, Sexism and Classism," 17 *New York University Review of Law and Social Change* 351 (1989–90).

Center for Constitutional Rights. *Reflections after Casey*. New York, 1993.

Cohen, Sherril, and Nadine Taub. *Reproductive Laws for the 1990s*. Totowa, N.J.: Humana Press, 1989.

Field, Martha A. *Surrogate Motherhood*. Exp. ed. Cambridge: Harvard University Press, 1990.

Fried, Marlene. *From Abortion to Reproductive Freedom: Transforming a Movement*. Boston: South End Press, 1990.

Roberts, Dorothy. "The Future of Reproductive Choice for Poor Women and Women of Color," 12 *Women's Rights Law Reporter* 59 (1990).

Stearns, Nancy. "*Roe v. Wade:* Our Struggle Continues," 4 *Berkeley Women's Law Journal* 1 (1989).

Tribe, Laurence. *Abortion: The Clash of Absolutes*. New York: Norton. 1990.

SEXUALITY AND SEXUAL VIOLENCE:

Austin, Regina. "Black Women, Sisterhood, and the Difference/Deviance Divide," 26 *New England Law Review* 877 (1992).

Donat, Patricia L.N., and John D'Emilio. "A Feminist Redefinition of Rape and Sexual Assault: Historical Foundations and Change," 48 *Journal of Social Issues* (1992).

Estrich, Susan. *Real Rape*. Cambridge: Harvard University Press, 1987.

Hunter, Nan, and Sylvia Law. "Brief Amici Curiae of Feminist Anti-Censorship Taskforce et al. in *American Booksellers Association v. Hudnut*," 21 *Journal of Law Reform* 69 (1987–88).

Lederer, Laura, ed. *Take Back the Night*. New York: Morrow & Co., 1980.

MacKinnon, Catherine A. *Feminism Unmodified: Discourses on Life and Law*. Cambridge: Harvard University Press, 1987.

Pateman, Carole. *The Sexual Contract*. Stanford, Calif.: Stanford University Press, 1988.

Russell, Diana. *Rape in Marriage*. Bloomington: Indiana University Press, 1990.

———. *The Secret Trauma: Incest in the Lives of Girls and Women*. New York: Harper Collins, 1986.

Snitow, Ann, Christine Sinansett, and Sharon Thompson. *Powers of Desire*. New York: Monthly Review Press, 1983.

Strossen, Nadine. "A Feminist Critique of 'the' Feminist Critique of Pornography," 79 *University of Virginia Law Review* (1993).

Tong, Rosemarie. *Women, Sex and the Law*. Totowa, N.J.: Rowman and Allanheld, 1984.

Table of Abbreviations

For additional assistance with legal abbreviations, see the latest edition of *A Uniform System of Citations* issued by the Harvard Law Review Association.

A.B.A.	American Bar Association
A.2d	Atlantic Reporter, 2d Series
ACLU	American Civil Liberties Union
AFDC	Aid to Families with Dependent Children
AFLA	Adolescent Family Life Act
Am.Jur.2d	American Jurisprudence, 2d Edition
ALI	American Law Institute
Bl.Comm.	Blackstone's Commentaries
BFOQ	Bona Fide Occupational Qualification
Cal.Rptr.	California Reporter
C.F.R.	Code of Federal Regulations
C.J.S.	Corpus Juris Secundum
Cert.denied	Certiorari denied
Cir.	Circuit, Circuit Court of Appeals
EEOC	Equal Employment Opportunity Commission
E.P.D.	Employment Practices Decisions
ERA	Equal Rights Amendment
Et al.	And others
Ex.Ord.	Executive Order
F.2d.	Federal Reporter, 2d Series
Fed.Reg.	Federal Register
FEP	Fair Employment Practices
F.R.D.	Federal Rules Decisions
F.Supp.	Federal Supplement
Ibid.	In the same place
Idem.	The same

i.e.	That is
Infra	Following
L.Ed.2d	U.S. Supreme Court Reports, Lawyers' Edition, 2d Series
Misc.2d	Miscellaneous Reports [of the New York courts], 2d Series
n.	Footnote number
N.E.2d	North Eastern Reporter, 2d Series
NOW	National Organization for Women
N.W.2d	North Western Reporter, 2d Series
OFCCP	Office of Federal Contract Compliance Programs
P.2d	Pacific Reporter, Second Series
PDA	Pregnancy Discrimination Act
PPFA	Planned Parenthood Federation of America
Rev'd	Reversed
§, §§	Section, sections
S.Ct.	Supreme Court Reporter
So.2d	Southern Reporter, 2d Series
Sup.Ct.	Supreme Court
Supp.	Supplement
Stat.	Statute, U.S. Statutes at Large
Supra	Above
UMPA	Uniform Marital Property Act
U.S.	United States Reports
U.S.C.	United States Code

Selected Amendments to the Constitution of the United States (with year of ratification)

ARTICLE XIII (1865)

Section 1. Neither slavery nor involuntary servitude, except as a punishment for crime whereof the party shall have been duly convicted, shall exist within the United States, or any place subject to their jurisdiction.

ARTICLE XIV (1868)

Section 1. All persons born or naturalized in the United States, and subject to the jurisdiction thereof, are citizens of the United States and of the State wherein they reside. No State shall make or enforce any law which shall abridge the privileges or immunities of citizens of the United States; nor shall any State deprive any person of life, liberty, or property, without due process of law; nor deny to any person within its jurisdiction the equal protection of the laws.

ARTICLE XV (1870)

Section 1. The right of citizens of the United States to vote shall not be denied or abridged by the United States or by any State on account of race, color, or previous condition of servitude.

ARTICLE XIX (1920)

The right of citizens of the United States to vote shall not be denied or abridged by the United States or by any State on account of sex.

APPENDIX B

Court Systems

TRIAL AND APPELLATE COURTS

There are two parallel court systems in the United States: the federal courts and the state courts. Both systems have two principal types of courts: trial courts and appellate courts. Cases are usually initiated at the trial level: evidence is taken, and initial decisions are made. A trial court's decision becomes final if there is no attempt to have it reviewed by an appellate court within a specified time period. In reviewing a trial-level decision, an appellate court usually does not take additional evidence; it considers only whether the trial court properly disposed of the case as it was presented. An appellate court may affirm the decision below, or it may reverse and remand (send back) the case to the trial court with instructions on how to proceed. Less often, the appellate court reverses a decision and actually substitutes its own decision on the content of the case. Appellate courts in both the federal and state systems also review decisions made by administrative agencies, such as human services departments or civil rights divisions. Appellate decisions are usually made by several judges hearing the case together, while a single judge or a judge and a jury decide disputes at the trial level, and agency heads make decisions at the administrative level.

THE FEDERAL COURT SYSTEM

The structure of the federal court system is determined in part by provisions of the United States Constitution and in part by statutes passed by Congress under the power given to it by the Constitution. Federal courts are limited to hearing certain kinds of cases: cases involving federal law including federal constitutional questions; cases involving parties from different states where the amount in controversy exceeds ten thousand dollars; and cases involving actions by or against the federal government and its

agencies. The principal trial courts in the federal system are organized along geographical lines and are called district courts. A district may consist of a state, as in the District of New Jersey, or of a portion of a state, as in the Southern District of New York.

Prior to 1976, there was an exception known as the "three-judge district court." Under the past law, a special court consisting of one circuit judge and two district judges was convened to hear cases seeking to enjoin federal and state statutes on federal constitutional grounds. Appeals from injunctions issued by three-judge district courts went straight to the U.S. Supreme Court. As a result, some of the older cases in this book refer to three-judge districts and direct appeals rather than the tri-level, district-circuit-Supreme Court system now in effect in almost all cases.

Appeals are heard by courts of appeals, which are grouped into circuits. There are thirteen circuits. The First through the Eleventh Circuits are organized along geographical lines. The First Circuit, for example, hears appeals from the federal district courts in Maine, Massachusetts, New Hampshire, Puerto Rico, and Rhode Island. The Twelfth is the Court of Appeals for the District of Columbia Circuit, and the Thirteenth is the new Federal Circuit, which is a nationwide court hearing certain kinds of appeals, such as those involving patents, international trade, and tariffs. Federal appeals are usually heard by panels of three judges, although occasionally a case is decided by all the judges belonging to the circuit, who are then said to be sitting "en banc." This generally occurs in response to petitions for rehearing en banc filed by a losing party after a panel decision is issued.

The court of last resort in the federal system is the United States Supreme Court. Although suits brought by one state against another and a few other types of cases may begin in the Supreme Court, the overwhelming majority of cases heard by the Supreme Court begin in other courts. In theory, any case beginning in a federal district court may reach the Supreme Court. These cases, however, must first be considered at the circuit level, and they reach the Supreme Court only after the Supreme Court has given its permission (usually called "granting *certiorari*"). State court cases involving federal questions, such as the meaning of a federal statute or a constitutional provision, may also be reviewed by the United States Supreme Court once they are decided by the highest state court authorized to decide the particular case. Very few cases actually reach the Supreme Court, however.

STATE COURT SYSTEMS

State court systems vary from state to state. Usually determined by the state's constitution and state statutes, state court systems generally include intermediate appellate courts and a court of last resort. Names of the different levels also vary by state. For example, trial level courts are known as superior courts in California and New Jersey and as supreme courts in New York. The highest court is known as the supreme court in California and New Jersey and as the court of appeals in New York.

Unlike the federal system, state court systems include courts that may hear all kinds of cases without limits on subject matter or amount of money in controversy. Such courts are said to have "general jurisdiction." There are also special courts of limited jurisdiction in most states, such as municipal courts and domestic relations courts. These too vary from state to state.

COURT CITATIONS

References or citations to decisions indicate basic information about the cases and about how to find them. There are official and unofficial reports of the decisions from many court systems. They all follow a uniform format.

The citation for *Reed* v. *Reed,* the first case applying the equal protection clause to invalidate a state law discriminating on the basis of sex, is 404 U.S. 71, 92 S.Ct. 251, 30 L.Ed. 2d 225 (1971). "U.S." refers to *United States Reports,* the official reports of decisions by the United States Supreme Court; "S.Ct." refers to the *Supreme Court Reporter,* and "L.Ed. 2d" refers to the *U.S. Supreme Court Reports, Lawyers Edition, Second Series,* both unofficial reports of United States Supreme Court decisions. The first number in each case designates the volume of the particular report, and the second number designates the page. The date of the decision appears in parentheses. Thus *Reed* v. *Reed,* decided by the United States Supreme Court in 1971, can be found in volume 404 of the *United States Reports,* beginning at page 71; in volume 92 of the *Supreme Court Reporter,* beginning at page 251; and in volume 30 of the *Lawyers Edition, Second Series,* beginning at page 225.

For further information, speak to a law librarian or consult a legal research reference, such as *The Legal Research Manual* by C. G. Wren and J.R. Wren (Madison, WI: A–R Editions, 1984).

Map of the Thirteen Federal Circuits

The Thirteen Federal Judicial Circuits

APPENDIX D

An Introduction to Case Briefing

The word "brief" can refer to three different kinds of documents:

- an appellate brief,
- a trial brief, and
- a case brief.

An appellate brief is a party's formal written argument to a court of appeals on why a lower court's decision should be affirmed, modified, or reversed. A trial brief is an attorney's set of notes on how he or she proposes to conduct an upcoming trial. It is sometimes called a trial manual or trial book. A case brief, our primary concern here, is an *analytical summary of an opinion.*

To "brief a case" means to identify the essential components of an opinion. This brief serves two functions:

a. to help you clarify your thinking on what the opinion "really" means, and
b. to provide you with a set of notes on the opinion to which you can refer later without having to reread the entire opinion every time you need to use it. . . .

There are many styles of briefing, and the same person may, in fact, employ several different styles of briefing for different purposes. The process, however, is the same regardless of the format used. The task of briefing consists of carefully reading and analyzing the opinion, of breaking down the information contained in the opinion into categories, and of organizing this data into a structured outline. [The following categories are often included in case briefs.]

1. The *Citation*
   Where the opinion can be found
2. The *Parties*

   Names, relationship, litigation status
3. The *Objectives* of the Parties
   What each side is seeking
4. The *Theory of the Litigation*
   The cause of action and the defense
5. The *Prior Proceedings*
   What happened below
6. The *Facts*
   Those facts that were key to the holdings
7. The *Issue(s)*
   The questions of law
8. The *Holding(s)*
   The answers to the issues
9. The *Reasoning*
   Why the court answered the issues the way it did
10. The *Disposition*
    What order was entered by the court as a result of its holdings
11. *Commentary* on opinion
    Concurring and dissenting opinions, personal views, counter brief (narrower or broader interpretations), history of the case, the case in sequence, case notes in law reviews. . . .*

The formats of case briefs vary depending on the needs of the reader. The following are examples of a long and a short version of case briefing formats.

LONG VERSION

Citation:
Muller v. Oregon, 208 U.S. 412 (1908)

The preceding is from William P. Statsky and R. John Wernet, Jr., Case Analysis and Fundamentals of Legal Writing, 3d ed. (St. Paul: West, 1989), pp. 77–79.

530

Pages in Text:
38–40

Parties:
Muller is the plaintiff in error here and the defendant below.

The state of Oregon is the defendant in error here and the prosecution below.

Objectives:
Muller wants his conviction overturned. The state of Oregon wants its law upheld and the conviction affirmed.

Cause of Action:
Muller violated an Oregon law that says employers cannot require women to work more than ten hours a day.

Defense:
Muller: The law is unconstitutional because it violates liberty of contract guaranteed to by the Due Process Clause in the Fourteenth Amendment.

Prior Proceedings:
(1) Trial: conviction in state court. (2) Appeal: conviction upheld by the Oregon Supreme Court.

Present Proceedings:
U.S. Supreme Court review on writ of error.

Facts:
Muller employed a woman to work in his laundry for more hours than the legal limit.

Issue:
Does this statute setting maximum hours for women violate liberty of contract protected by the Due Process Clause of the Fourteenth Amendment?

Holding:
No

Reasoning:

1. This case differs from the maximum hour law for bakeries struck down in *Lochner v. New York* as an unreasonable interference with liberty of contract because the difference between the sexes justifies different rules.
2. Widely held beliefs, reflected in legislation and numerous reports and which the Court can note, indicate that women's physical structure

and maternal functions place them at a disadvantage in the struggle for existence.
3. The state may limit individuals' liberty of contract where, as here, women's health and the "vigor of the race" justify such legislation.

Disposition:
Judgment affirmed.

Comments:

1. Then attorney, later Justice, Brandeis made empirical claims about women in arguing for the state of Oregon.
2. Arguments about women's right to contract equally with men were made by a male employer.

SHORT VERSION

Citation:
Muller v. Oregon, 208 U.S. 412 (1908)

Pages in Text:
38–40

Facts:
Ore. Sup. Ct. affirmed Muller's conviction for violating an Ore. statute prohibiting employment of women > 10 hrs/day. On writ of error, he challenged the statute, arguing state interference with liberty of contract in a way not justified by the health, welfare or safety of the community in viol'n of Due Process.

Disposition:
Affirmed.

Reasons:

1. *Lochner* distinguished. Difference between sexes justifies different rules.
2. Widely believed that physical structure and maternal functions of women place them at disadvantage in struggle for existence.
3. These factual beliefs are sufficient to justify legislation to protect women from the greed and passion of men, both for their own sake and for the good of the race [*sic*].

Comment:
Then attorney Brandeis argued the case for the state using empirical claims to persuade the Court.

Glossary

For additional assistance with legal terms and expressions, see *Black's Law Dictionary*, 6th ed., by Henry C. Black (St. Paul: West, 1991) or *Law Dictionary*, 2d ed, by Steven H. Gifis (New York: Barron's, 1984).

Admissible Evidence is admissible if, under applicable rules of evidence, it may be considered by the jury or other fact-finder at trials or formal hearings.

A Priori A form of reasoning that infers the truth of a proposition from other propositions assumed to be true.

Ad Litem For the purposes of the suit.

Administratrix The person appointed to handle the affairs of someone who dies without leaving a will or without designating anyone to manage the will.

Aegis Protection or sponsorship.

Affirm To decide that the judgment of the court below is correct and should stand.

Affirmative Action Any measure taken to ensure compliance with an existing obligation, generally used in context of efforts to desegregate.

Alienage The status of having been born in a foreign country.

Alimony The allowance that a court orders one to pay for the support of one's former spouse.

Alimony Pendente Lite The allowance one pays for the support of a spouse until one's suit for divorce has finally been decided.

Allocatur It is allowed.

Amicus Curiae A friend of the court, generally used in connection with briefs submitted by non-parties expressing views on a pending case.

Animus Hostility.

Appellant The party who appeals a decision. The party who brings the proceeding to a court of review.

Appellee The party who argues before a reviewing court that the decision of the lower court should stand.

Arguendo For the sake of argument.

Arrearage The amount already due that has yet to be paid.

Availability Ratio The proportion of women to men, of African-Americans to whites, etc., in the pool of qualified persons in the relevant geographical area.

Aver Declare to be true.

Back Pay A remedy available in employment and labor law cases. Courts frequently order employers found in violation of antidiscrimination statutes to pay plaintiffs the wages that they would have received but for the employer's unlawful practice.

Bench Trial A trial in which the final decision is rendered by a judge without the participation of a jury.

Benign Classification A legislative classification adopted for the purpose of advancing the welfare of members of a protected class.

Bloc-Vote To vote as one (said of a group of persons).

Bondsman One who guarantees another's performance, i.e., who gives bond.

532

Breach   Failure by a party to perform some contracted or agreed upon act.

Brief   A written statement, generally from the attorney of a party in a suit, that sets forth the legal argument that favors the decision desired by her or his client.

Burden of Persuasion   The duty of a party to convince the judge or jury of the truth of a claim. Failure to meet this duty results in a judgment against that party.

Burden of Production   The duty of a party to produce evidence on a particular issue.

Burden of Proof   The duty of a party to substantiate a claim. Includes both the burden of production and the burden of persuasion.

Certiorari   Review of a decision by a court of review, usually initiated by a petition. The decision to grant or refuse this type of petition is discretionary.

Chattels   Any tangible or movable thing; personal as opposed to real property, such as land.

Citation   A reference to a legal authority, such as a case, a statute, or a regulation.

Class Action   A lawsuit brought by representative members of a large group of persons on behalf of all the members of the group.

Common Law   Legal rules or principles developed by the courts on a case-by-case basis, as opposed to statutory law, which is developed by the legislature, and regulatory law, which is developed by the executive branch.

Common Law Property System   A system of allocating marital property according to title.

Community Property System   A system of assigning ownership of property acquired during marriage to the spouses jointly.

Comparable Worth   A theory of pay equity that holds that wages paid to employees in various job categories should be proportionate to the value that the employer places on the tasks performed.

Compensatory Damages   A money award granted by a court to a victim for the purpose of restoring the victim to her or his condition prior to the violation.

Compensatory Remedy   Any sanction imposed by a court after finding of a violation that is aimed at restoring the injured party to the condition she or he would have enjoyed but for the violation. As distinguished from punative and prophylactic remedies.

Conciliation   Any process short of trial by which a court or public official attempts to bring disputing parties into agreement.

Consent Decree   A court order settling a lawsuit according to terms agreed by the parties.

Consolidation   The act or process of uniting several actions into one trial and judgment.

Consortium   The right of husband and wife to the company, cooperation, affection, and aid of the other. At common law, this right was vested only in the husband and referred mainly to the sexual services of his spouse.

Constructive Discharge   If an employee involuntarily resigns to avoid intolerable and illegal requirements, courts regard the termination of employment as the equivalent of a discharge initiated by the employer.

Contempt   Courts may hold those appearing before them "in contempt" and impose punishment for disruptive and disobedient conduct.

Corroboration   Evidence that tends to confirm or substantiate a witness's testimony or other evidence.

Coverture   The legal condition of a married woman under common law.

Credibility   The believability of a witness.

Cross-Appeal   A request by an appellee for review of one or more aspects of a lower court decision made after an appeal has already been initiated by the appellant.

Custody   Legal guardianship over a child granted to a parent in a divorce action may include physical and/or decision-making custody.

Damages   Money given to a prevailing party in a lawsuit because of the unlawful conduct of the other party.

De Minimus   An issue, amount, or act that is not of sufficient importance to make a difference in the outcome of the case.

Declaratory Judgment   A judgment of a court that establishes the rights of the parties or addresses a question of law without ordering that anything be done.

Defendant   In a civil suit, the party who is responding to a complaint. In a criminal suit, the party who is being prosecuted is also called the accused.

Demurrer   A claim that, even if everything stated in the complaint were true, it would not be sufficient to find the violation that is alleged.

Deposition   A statement of a party or witness, given under oath, before trial begins. A deposition often takes a question-and-answer form.

Directed Verdict   A verdict returned by a jury at the direction of the trial judge by whose instructions the jury is bound. In civil suits, either party may receive a directed verdict if the opposing party fails to present a prima facie case or a necessary defense. In criminal cases, there may be a directed verdict of acquittal but not of conviction.

Discovery   A pretrial procedure by which one party gains information that is held by the opposing party.

Discretion   The reasonable exercise of power by an official acting within the rights of her or his office.

Disparate Impact   A method for analyzing claims that a policy or practice is discriminatory that focuses on the disproportionate effect the policy or practice has upon a particular group.

Disparate Treatment   A method for analyzing claims that differences in treatment afforded individuals or groups are discriminatory.

Dower   That part of a husband's estate to which a wife is entitled upon his death.

En Banc   A hearing before all the members of a court.

Enjoin   To command or instruct someone to do or not to do something.

Equitable Distribution   Allocation of marital property by the court without regard to title to achieve equity between the divorcing spouses.

Ex parte   Refers to an application made by one party to a proceeding in the absence of the other.

Entirety   The state of being whole and undivided.

Entitlement   A right to have something or to do something.

Equitable Power   The power of a court to act as fairness between the parties may require.

Estate   All that a person owns.

Feme-covert   A married woman.

Feme-sole   An unmarried woman.

Goals and Timetables   Standards used to measure the impartiality of selection procedures.

Grand Jury   A body of persons selected from the community for the purpose of investigating crimes and accusing persons of crimes.

Gravaman   The main point or essence of a complaint or argument.

Guardian   A person charged with the responsibility of taking care of a person or of managing the property of another.

Hiring Ratio   The proportion of women to men, of African-Americans to whites, etc., hired in a job category.

Immunity   An exemption from a duty or penalty.

Impeach   Testimony is impeached if doubt is cast upon its truthfulness. A person is impeached if she or he is removed from office.

Imprimatur   Mark of official approval or authorization.

Indictment   A formal accusation by a grand jury charging one or more persons with a crime.

Indigent   Anyone who is needy and poor.

Information   A written statement of a prosecutor accusing a person of a crime. An alternative to an indictment.

Injunction   A judicial order directing a party to perform or refrain from performing an act or activity.

Inter Alia   Among other things.

Intervening Party   A party permitted to participate in a suit after the plaintiff has initiated action against the defendant or defendants.

Intestate   Died without leaving directions for the disposition of one's property.

Invidious   Impermissible. Sometimes including a tendency to arouse ill will or animosity.

Jurisdiction   The power to hear and decide a matter.

Jurisprudence   The theory behind law and legal systems.

Jury Instruction   Direction given by the judge to the jury setting forth the law that is to guide the jury in its deliberations.

Legal Fiction   Something known to be false but assumed in law to be true.

Legislative History   The record of legislative deliberations on a statute prior to its adoption.

Liquidated Damages   An amount agreed upon by parties to a contract as a reasonable estimate of the damages owed to one party in the event that the contract is breached by the other.

Litigation A lawsuit; a controversy in which legal rights are determined by a court.

Magistrate A civil official with power to administer and enforce law.

Manumit To place beyond the reach or power of an official. Most frequently used to refer to the act of liberating a slave from bondage.

Mens Rea The mental state accompanying a forbidden act.

Model Penal Code A comprehensive code of statutes dealing with crime prepared as a model by the American Law Institute upon which a number of states have drawn in drafting their own penal codes.

Moot A point is moot if it is debatable, arguable, or unresolved. A case is moot if the question to be determined does not rest on existing facts.

Moral Turpitude The state of being base, vile, or dishonest to a high degree. Indicative of depravity.

Multiple Regression Analysis A method of statistical analysis that estimates the relative contribution of a number of independent variables to variations in a dependent variable.

Municipal Pertaining to a local government unit, a city, or a town.

Negligence Failure to act in the way that a reasonable person would in the circumstances.

Overinclusive A statutory classification is overinclusive if not everyone designated as due similar treatment under the statute is similarly situated with respect to the advancement of the statutory objective.

Overrule To supersede, annul, or make void by subsequent action or decision. A judicial decision is said to be overruled if a later decision by the same court or by a superior court in the same system expresses a contrary judgment on the same question of law.

Parens Patriae The state's power to protect and control the property and custody of minors and incompetent persons.

Parish A district in Louisiana corresponding to a county.

Parity An outcome that is the same as or equivalent to a result that would be generated by a fair procedure.

Parole A conditional release of a person from serving the remainder of her or his criminal sentence in jail.

Party A litigant, a person directly interested in the subject matter of the case and entitled to participate in its resolution.

Per Curiam An opinion "by the court" expressing the decision of the court but whose author is not identified.

Petit Jury An ordinary jury as opposed to a grand jury. Its function is to determine issues of fact and return verdicts.

Petitioner One who presents a petition to a court.

Plaintiff The party who initiates a civil lawsuit.

Plurality Decision A judgment of a reviewing court that is agreed to by a majority of the judges but that is not supported by any one opinion endorsed by a majority of the judges.

Police Power The power of governments at all levels to impose restrictions reasonably related to the promotion and maintenance of the health, safety, morals, and general welfare of the public.

Poll Tax A tax levied upon all persons within a specified class who live within a certain area. State requirements making payment of such taxes a prerequisite to registration and voting have been barred by the Twenty-Fourth Amendment to the U.S. Constitution.

Preemption The doctrine that federal law takes priority over state and local legislation dealing with the same subject matter.

Preferential Treatment The award of positions to people on the basis of characteristics unrelated to qualifications for the positions. Often used in the context of debating efforts to eliminate discrimination.

Prejudicial Causing unfair or preconceived judgments to come into play.

Preponderance of the Evidence The general standard of proof in civil cases. Evidence is said to meet this standard if it is more convincing than opposing evidence.

Present Value What something is worth now.

Presumption An assumption, required by a rule of law, that certain factual claims are true. A presumption may be either "conclusive," in which case no contrary evidence will be considered, or "rebuttable," as is the presumption of innocence.

Pretermit To pass by or omit; to disregard.

Pretext An explanation that serves to disguise or obscure one's real purposes.

Prima Facie Case A case sufficient on its face, that is, supported by sufficient evidence to shift the burden of persuasion to the defendant.

Pro Forma As a matter of established routine. For the sake of form.

Probate The act or process of proving a will.

Probative Tending to prove or establish a fact.

Prophylactic Remedy Any sanction imposed by a court that is aimed at preventing a recurrence of some violation.

Prothonotary The principal clerk of some courts.

Proviso A condition or stipulation.

Proxy A substitute; one person who is authorized to act for another.

Punitive Damages A money award granted by a court to a victim for the purpose of expressing its disapproval of the defendant's behavior and for the purpose of deterring others from similar conduct.

Punitive Remedy Any sanction imposed by a court after the finding of a violation that is aimed at expressing disapproval of the defendant's behavior.

Quash To annul, make void, or overthrow a judicial decision.

Quid Pro Quo An arrangement in which parties give one valuable thing in exchange for another. Mutual consideration.

Rational Relation A standard used in equal protection cases that requires that the statutory classification be rationally related to the advancement of a legitimate government interest.

Rebuttal The opportunity to introduce evidence that undermines confidence in the arguments made in support of a claim.

Red Circle A personnel practice used in connection with making major corrections to wage rates. Rates that are already at or higher that the target are held stable or "red circled" until the others catch up.

Reductio ad Absurdum Disproof through showing that the argument leads to an absurdity.

Remand To send back for further deliberation or action.

Remedy The means by which a right is enforced or an injury redressed.

Respondent The party who answers a petition.

Respondeat Superior The doctrine that holds a principal liable for the torts of his or her agent.

Reverse To overthrow, make void, annul, or set aside the judgment of a lower court.

Sanction A coercive measure imposed for the purpose of enforcing legal rights after a finding of a violation.

Show Cause Order An order directing one party to demonstrate why certain things should not be done. Usually used to bring an issue before a court or other tribunal on short notice.

Sine Qua Non That without which a thing cannot be; a necessary condition.

Special Master A person appointed to assist a court in a particular case or type of case by hearing testimony, gathering evidence, and recommending a decision.

State Action An act performed by, caused by, or otherwise attributable to a government or to an instrumentality of a government.

Statutory Classification Those characteristics used to identify people who will be treated similarly under the statute.

Statutory Objective The result that a statute promotes or the result that courts understand a statute to be aimed at promoting.

Stipulation A term or condition in an agreement.

Strict Liability Liability that is not contingent upon a showing of mens rea or even of negligence.

Strict Scrutiny A standard used in equal protection cases that requires that a statutory classification be the least restrictive way of advancing a compelling government interest.

Sua Sponte On its own initiative.

Sub Judice Under judicial consideration.

Subpoena An order of a court compelling the appearance of a witness before a judicial proceeding.

Sub Silentio Without any notice being taken.

Sui Juris Of his own right; not under any disability; possessing full rights and powers.

Summary Judgment A means by which a judge decides a suit without a full trial; this occurs when the facts of the situation are not in dispute and one party is entitled to the decision as a matter of law.

Suspect Classification A statutory classification that the courts suspect of being used to further discriminatory purposes against certain protected groups. Such classifications are subject to review under the strict scrutiny standard.

Temporary Restraining Order A court order designed to maintain the status quo until the court has time to look fully into the matter.

Testament The statement of a person's wishes concerning the disposition of her or his property after death.

Tort Any civil wrong, independent of contract, resulting from the breach of a legal duty.

Underinclusive A statutory classification is underinclusive if not everyone similarly situated in respect to the advancement of the statutory objective is designated as due similar treatment under the statute.

Underutilization The condition of having fewer women and minorities in a particular job group than would reasonably be expected by their availability.

Vacate To set aside or render void.

Vel Non Or not.

Venire The panel of people from which a trial jury is chosen.

Ward A person placed under the guardianship of another.

Will A person's declaration of how her or his property is to be distributed after her or his death.

Work Force Ratio The proportion of women to men, of African-Americans to whites, etc., in any employment category.

Workers' Compensation A statutory system for covering employee expenses for injuries and sickness that arise out of and in the course of employment. Funded by employee contributions.

Writ One of a series of traditional court orders requiring that something be done or authorizing it to be done.

Writ of Error An early common law order that initiates an appeal of a lower court decision.

Writ of Habeas Corpus An order initiating a proceeding, whose function is to release an individual being held illegally by the state or by a private party.

Wrongful Death Action A suit brought by the beneficiaries, alleging that decedent's death was caused by defendant's wrongful act and seeking to recover economic benefits lost as a result.

Index